Contents

P9-CDH-533

Introduction to
Southwest USA

A vast expanse of stunning desert scenery, the Southwest is the most spectacular region of the United States. For splendour and sheer scale, the landscape consistently defies belief – a glorious panoply of cliffs and canyons, buttes and mesas, carved from rocks of every imaginable colour, and enriched here by shimmering aspens and cottonwoods, there by cactuses and agaves. Lured by iconic images like John Wayne riding through Monument Valley in *The Searchers*, David Bowie slithering down the other-worldly dunes of White Sands in *The Man Who Fell to Earth*, and Walter White skulking in the *arroyos* of Albuquerque in *Breaking Bad*, visitors flock to experience the Wild West for themselves. Whether you're driving or hiking, biking or backpacking, wilderness beyond measure awaits.

The area covered by this book roughly corresponds to the former Spanish colony of **New Mexico**, which has only belonged to the US since 1847, and is now divided between the modern states of New Mexico, Arizona, Utah, Colorado and Nevada. Though rainfall is scarce everywhere, it's not all **desert**; indeed, the popular image of the Southwest as scrubby hillsides studded with many-armed saguaro cactuses is true only of the Sonoran Desert of southern Arizona. Towering snow-capped **mountains** rise not only in southern Colorado and northern New Mexico, at the tail end of the Rockies, but also in scattered locations across Utah and Arizona, while dense **pine forests** cloak much of northern Arizona.

Where to go

The Southwest's most dramatic landscapes lie on the **Colorado Plateau**, an arid mile-high tableland, roughly the size of California, which extends across the **Four Corners** region of Arizona, Utah, Colorado and New Mexico. Atop the main body of the plateau, further layers of rock are piled level upon level, creating a "**Grand Staircase**" of successive cliffs and

ABOVE MOUNTAIN BIKING NEAR MOAB **OPPOSITE** ANTELOPE CANYON plateaus. During the last dozen or so million years, subterranean forces have pushed the entire complex steadily upwards. As it has risen, the earth has cracked, warped, buckled and split, and endless quantities of crumbling sandstone have been washed away by the Colorado River. The **Grand Canyon** is simply the most famous of hundreds of **canyons**, so vast that it can scarcely be grasped by the human mind. No one, however, could fail to be overwhelmed by the sheer weirdness of **southern Utah** – the red rocks of **Monument Valley**, the fiery sandstone pinnacles of **Bryce Canyon**, the endless expanses of **Canyonlands**.

Reminders of the Southwest's remarkable **history** are everywhere you look. Though century after century has brought fresh waves of intruders, none has entirely succeeded in displacing its predecessors, leaving the various groups to coexist in an intriguing blend of cultures and traditions. Ancient archeological sites abound, ranging from the free-standing pueblos of Chaco Canyon and the cliff dwellings of Mesa Verde to the hollowed-out caves of Bandelier and the haunting rock art of Horseshoe Canyon. The region now holds fifty distinct Native American reservations, ranging from tiny **pueblo** villages in New Mexico to the huge "**Navajo Nation**", which covers 27,000 square miles and extends across much of the Colorado Plateau. Unlike elsewhere in the US, where all too often Native Americans were forcibly displaced onto poorer lands with which they lack any spiritual connection, most Southwestern tribes continue to occupy their ancestral homelands.

The **Spanish** too have been in the region for almost five hundred years; exquisite eighteenth-century missions survive at San Xavier and Tumacácori in Arizona, while New Mexico holds stunning adobe churches such as San Francisco de Asis at Taos, and the humbler shrine at Chimayó. Next to arrive after the Spaniards were the **Mormons**, who through utter determination and communal effort colonized Utah in the nineteenth century. **American** settlers arrived soon after, and swiftly outnumbered everyone else.

SOUTHWEST USA

GREAT BASIN NAT. PARK

U T A H

NEVADA

CANYONLANDS NAT. PARK

Green River

ARCH NAT. P

Mo

CAPITOL REEF NAT. PARK

Torrey

Natural Bridges Nat. Mon.

Cedar Breaks Nat. Mon.

BRYCE CANYON NAT. PARK

Boulder

Blanding

Cedar City

Escalante

GLEN CANYON NAT. REC. AREA

Bluff

Tropic

ZION NAT. PARK

Grand Staircase-Escalante Nat. Mon.

Mexican Hat

St George

Springdale

Kanab

Lake Powell

Monument Valley

Page

Kayenta

GRAND CANYON NAT. PARK

North Rim

Navajo Nat. Mon.

NAVAJO INDIAN RESERVATION

Can de C Nat.

Las Vegas

Hoover Dam

Lake Mead

Colorado River

South Rim

Tuba City

Keams Canyon

GRAND CANYON WEST

HAVASUPAI RES.

HOPI INDIAN RES.

NAVAJO INDIAN RESERVATION

Laughlin

Peach Springs

Seligman

Williams

Wupatki Nat. Mon.

Sunset Crater Nat. Mon.

Kingman

Flagstaff

PETRIFIED FOREST NAT. PAR

CALIFORNIA

Lake Havasu City

Sedona

Walnut Canyon Nat. Mon.

Winslow

Holbrook

Jerome

Prescott

Montezuma Castle Nat. Mon.

Show Low

Parker

Colorado River

A R I Z O N A

Quartzsite

Wickenburg

Phoenix

Tonto Nat. Mon.

Globe

Saffo

Yuma

SAGUARO NAT. PARK

SAGUARO NAT. PARK

Tucson

Benson

Chiri Nat.

Organ Pipe Cactus Nat. Mon.

Kartchner Caverns

Tombstone

MEXICO

Gulf of California

TUMACÁCORI NAT. HISTORIC PARK

Bisbee

Nogales

0   100
miles

In the early years of US rule, the Southwest was very much the **Wild West**. A sense of that era survives in towns like **Lincoln**, New Mexico, where Billy the Kid blazed his way out of jail, and **Tombstone**, Arizona, where the Earps and the Clantons fought it out at the OK Corral. The century since Utah, Arizona and New Mexico achieved statehood has seen the landscape transformed on an unprecedented – not to say unnatural, let alone unsustainable – scale. Monumental **water** projects, including the construction of the **Hoover Dam**, the damming of Utah's Glen Canyon to form **Lake Powell**, and the creation of a network of canals across hundreds of miles of the Arizona desert, have brought the region prosperity as the **Sunbelt**.

While the wilderness remains the supreme attraction for most visitors, certain Southwestern **cities** make worthwhile destinations. **Santa Fe** is the best example, with its four-hundred-year history, top-quality museums and galleries, and superb hotels and restaurants; **Tucson** holds an enjoyable combination of desert parks, Hispanic history, restaurants and ranch resorts; and **Las Vegas**, entirely and quintessentially a product of the modern era – it was only founded in 1905 – is far too amazing to miss. **Phoenix** is less obviously appealing, though it too has its fair share of top-quality parks and museums.

Though most of the region's **smaller towns** are best treated as overnight pit stops, some have blossomed into appealing bases for a few days' stay. **Moab** and **Springdale** make welcome exceptions to the typical monotony of southern Utah farming communities; the college town of **Flagstaff** is a lively enclave within easy reach of the Grand Canyon; **Durango** and **Telluride** are vibrant mountain towns; and **Taos** still has the feel of the artists' colony that attracted Georgia O'Keeffe and D.H. Lawrence.

The only practicable way to explore the Southwest in any detail is to **drive** yourself around; public transport options are very limited (see p.29).

CLOCKWISE FROM TOP LEFT COW SKULLS, TUCSON; NAVAJO WOMAN, MONUMENT VALLEY; ADOBE FACADE, SANTA FE; *RISTRAS*, ALBUQUERQUE

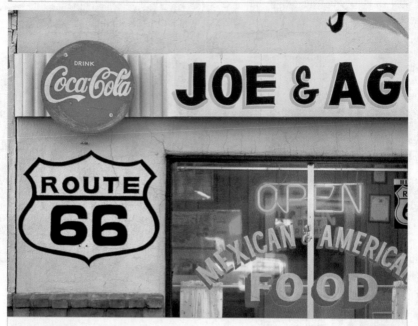

ROUTE 66

If you ever plan to motor west, there's still one definitive highway. Ninety years since it was completed, eighty since John Steinbeck called it **"the mother road, the road of flight"** in *The Grapes of Wrath*, and seventy since songwriter Bobby Troup set it all down in rhyme, what better reason to visit the Southwest could there be than to get hip to this timely tip, and get your kicks on **Route 66**?

The heyday of Route 66 as the nation's premier cross-country route – winding from Chicago to LA – lasted barely twenty years, from when it was first paved in 1937 until freeways began to supersede it in 1957. It officially became defunct in 1984, with the bypassing of the last town en route, Williams, Arizona. Nonetheless, substantial stretches of the original Route 66 survive, complete with the motels and drive-ins that became icons of vernacular American architecture. Restored 1950s roadsters and Harley-Davidsons alike flock to cruise along the neon-lit frontages of towns such as Albuquerque and Flagstaff, or through the empty desertscapes that lie between Grants and Gallup in New Mexico, and Seligman and Kingman in Arizona.

When to go

Summer is the peak tourist season for most of the Southwest, even though temperatures in excess of 100°F (38°C) make cities such as Phoenix and Tucson all but unbearable, and it's an ordeal even to get out of your car in many of the national parks. Hikers, bikers and rafters do better to come either between mid-September and late October, when the crowds are gone and dazzling fall colours brighten the canyons, or in April and May, when wildflowers bloom in the desert.

RIGHT FROM TOP HUBBELL TRADING POST; HIKERS ON MESA ARCH, CANYONLANDS; *STRATER HOTEL*, DURANGO

Author picks

Ranging through the Four Corners, and plenty of other corners besides, our author has been exploring the highways, byways, nooks and crannies of the Southwest for more than 25 years. Here are some of his personal highlights:

Hiking it easy You don't always have to tackle the longest and hardest trails; sometimes the shortest and most obvious ones are the best, as with the trail to Shoshone Point in the Grand Canyon (see p.308), or the Mesa Arch Trail in Canyonlands (see p.409).

Slot canyons Ethereal, almost translucent, and often downright dangerous, these delicate hidden canyons attract daredevil devotees – try to see at least one, like Antelope Canyon (see p.396) or Peek-A-Boo Gulch (see p.381).

Historic hotels Wild West relics that make memorable overnight halts include the *Strater* in Durango (see p.82), *La Fonda* in Santa Fe (see p.120), and Mary Jane Colter's extraordinary *La Posada* at Winslow (see p.263).

Best new museum Only the exhibit on local boy Alice Cooper might count as especially "Southwestern", but you could spend a whole day enjoying the toe-tapping array of world music that's celebrated in Phoenix's Musical Instrument Museum (see p.211).

New Mexico's new national monuments
A couple of new, multi-part national monuments are attracting hikers, climbers and river-runners to New Mexico. The Rio Grande del Norte monument (see p.142), located both north and south of Taos, preserves two separate segments of the mighty Rio Grande, while Organ Mountains–Desert Peaks (see p.196), both east and west of Las Cruces, gives adventurous visitors access to some superb and little-known tracts of wilderness.

Trading posts Here and there, the outposts where Yankee storekeepers traded with tribes like the Navajo during the nineteenth century have survived into the twenty-first, and make great places to buy crafts and souvenirs; prime specimens include Cameron Trading Post (see p.330) and Hubbell Trading Post (see p.64).

Our author recommendations don't end here. We've flagged up our favourite places – a perfectly sited hotel, an atmospheric café, a special restaurant – throughout the guide, highlighted with the ★ symbol.

If your timings aren't flexible, however, don't worry. It's always possible to escape the heat – the thermometer drops by around 4°F (2.2°C) for every thousand feet above sea level, so Santa Fe, for example, is always relatively cool – and the summer is also peak period for festivals (see p.33).

Winters can be seriously cold, and snowfalls close down certain areas altogether – don't reckon on seeing high-altitude destinations like Mesa Verde or the Grand Canyon's North Rim between October and April. Those parks that remain open are often at their most beautiful when frosted with snow, however – Bryce Canyon is quite magical – while ski resorts like Telluride and Taos are in full swing, and Tucson and Phoenix fill with sun-seeking "snowbirds" from colder states. The major disadvantage of visiting in winter is that with fewer hours of daylight, there's simply not enough time to drive from your overnight base into a national park, do any great amount of touring or hiking, and then drive on to your next stop.

ROCK ART

The Southwestern deserts abound in both **petroglyphs**, images scratched or chipped onto stone surfaces, and painted **pictographs**. At the single most remarkable site, Utah's **Great Gallery**, Archaic shamans daubed enigmatic ghost-like figures onto remote canyon walls. Other locations include "Newspaper Rocks" in Utah and Arizona, carvings in Monument Valley, and painted panels in Capitol Reef. The best-known motif in Ancestral Puebloan rock art, found throughout the Four Corners, is the "hunchback" flute-player **Kokopelli** (see box, p.114).

The rock art tradition continued into recent times. Thus the Navajo depicted nineteenth-century Spanish raids on the sandstone walls of the Canyon de Chelly, while the Spaniards themselves added their own carvings to the remarkable Inscription Rock at El Morro.

AVERAGE TEMPERATURES AND RAINFALL

To convert °F to °C, subtract 32 and multiply by 5/9

	Jan	Feb	Mar	Apr	May	Jun	Jul	Aug	Sep	Oct	Nov	Dec
GRAND CANYON (SOUTH RIM)												
Av high °F	41	45	51	60	70	81	84	82	76	65	52	43
Av low °F	18	21	25	32	39	47	54	53	47	36	27	20
Rainfall (in)	1.3	1.5	1.4	0.9	0.7	0.4	1.8	2.3	1.6	1.1	0.9	1.6
LAS VEGAS, NV												
Av high °F	56	67	68	77	87	98	104	101	94	81	66	57
Av low °F	33	37	42	49	59	68	75	73	65	53	41	33
Rainfall (in)	0.5	0.5	0.4	0.2	0.2	0.1	0.5	0.5	0.3	0.3	0.4	0.3
PHOENIX, AZ												
Av high °F	65	69	75	84	93	102	105	102	98	88	75	66
Av low °F	38	41	45	52	60	68	78	76	69	57	45	39
Rainfall (in)	0.8	0.8	0.8	0.5	0.3	0.3	0.7	0.9	0.6	0.6	0.6	0.8
SANTA FE, NM												
Av high °F	40	44	51	60	69	79	82	80	74	63	50	41
Av low °F	19	22	28	35	43	52	57	56	49	38	27	20
Rainfall (in)	0.6	0.8	0.8	0.9	1.2	1.1	2.4	2.3	1.7	1.1	0.7	0.7
ZION NATIONAL PARK, UT												
Av high °F	52	57	63	73	83	93	100	97	91	78	63	53
Av low °F	29	31	36	43	52	60	68	66	60	49	37	30
Rainfall (in)	1.6	1.6	1.7	1.3	0.7	0.6	0.8	1.6	0.8	1.0	1.2	1.5

ABOVE WOODPECKER ON A SAGUARO CACTUS

things not to miss

It's not possible to see everything that the Southwest has to offer in one trip – and we don't suggest you try. What follows is a selective and subjective taste of the region's highlights: spectacular national parks, unforgettable outdoor activities, Wild West towns and Las Vegas glitz. All highlights are colour-coded by chapter and have a page reference to take you straight into the Guide, where you can find out more.

1

1 CANYON DE CHELLY

Page 58

Arguably the most beautiful canyon in the entire Southwest, all the more extraordinary for its magnificent Ancestral Puebloan ruins.

2 NATIVE AMERICAN CRAFTS

Page 38

From silver and turquoise jewellery to Hopi *kachinas* or fine Pueblo ceramics, the Southwest is renowned for its craft works and souvenirs.

3 LA FONDA DE SANTA FE

Page 120

Historic Western hotels don't come any more atmospheric than this beauty at the end of the Santa Fe Trail.

4 RIDE THE DURANGO & SILVERTON RAILROAD

Page 82

Taking a steam train up to the old Colorado mining town of Silverton is the perfect way to spend a day in the Rockies.

15

TORREON

One of Lincoln's earliest structures. Built in the 1850's, its thick walls protected Spanish-Americans against the Apaches. In Lincoln Co. War Murphy's sharpshooters were here stationed. In 1937 Chaves County Historical Society undertook restoration of tower.

OLD LINCOLN COUNTY MEMORIAL COMMISSION, 1940

16

17

22

24 THE INTER-TRIBAL INDIAN CEREMONIAL

Page 95

The classic Route 66 town of Gallup, New Mexico, comes alive in August for this annual Navajo fair.

25 CIRQUE DU SOLEIL
Page 457

Staging several of the finest shows the city has to offer, the Canadian circus troupe dominates Las Vegas' entertainment scene.

26 ZION CANYON
Page 352

Carved by the Virgin River into the red-rock country of southern Utah, Zion makes the ideal escape from the mayhem of Las Vegas.

27 CALF CREEK FALLS
Page 384

Not far off the highway in the heart of southern Utah, this glorious two-part waterfall is the highlight of Grand Staircase-Escalante National Monument.

28 RAFTING IN CANYONLANDS
Page 427

Whether you choose a gentle float or a multi-day whitewater epic, Canyonlands National Park makes a fabulous destination for a raft trip.

29 HIKING IN THE GRAND CANYON
Page 310

Explore the innermost secrets of the Grand Canyon on one of its many superb hiking trails.

Itineraries

The Southwest is not really a place for quick visits. A week only gives time for a brief circuit, looping perhaps to Grand Canyon and Zion national parks from Las Vegas; through all Utah's national parks from Salt Lake City; or up to Santa Fe and Taos from Albuquerque. With two weeks, you can take in more of the Four Corners region and/or southern Utah. Only with three weeks or more is it really worth venturing into southern New Mexico and southern Arizona as well.

WESTERN WONDERS

Allow ten days or more to complete this grand route around the dramatic desertscape of the Colorado Plateau.

❶ Las Vegas Fly into Sin City to spend your first two nights – not a weekend, to avoid high room rates – savouring the sights, sounds and assorted flavours of the Strip. **See p.438**

❷ Zion Utah's most beautiful national park, a little over two hours' drive from Las Vegas, is a tranquil idyll, with superb hiking. **See p.351**

❸ Bryce Canyon Quite the weirdest array of top-heavy, multicoloured rock formations you're ever likely to see. **See p.368**

❹ Capitol Reef Driving through the remote wilderness at the heart of southern Utah, a fresh bizarre desertscape unfolds at every turn in the road. This gorgeous oasis makes the perfect overnight base. **See p.386**

❺ Moab A dynamic former mining town that's abuzz with adventurous types setting off each morning for yet more hiking and biking in Arches and Canyonlands parks. **See p.422**

❻ Monument Valley Immense, glowing buttes and mesas, silhouetted against the desert sun, and familiar from a thousand Western movies. **See p.55**

❼ South Rim, Grand Canyon Be sure to allow at least one full day on the South Rim, from sunrise to sunset, to appreciate the full majesty of this vast and varied chasm. **See p.302**

INDIAN COUNTRY

This loop through millennia of Southwest history takes a (very) good two weeks, heading beyond New Mexico into the deserts of the Four Corners, once the Ancestral Puebloan heartland and now home to the Navajo and Hopi.

❶ Albuquerque As well as its Route 66 frontage, New Mexico's largest city is home to the Pueblo Indian Cultural Center. **See p.166**

❷ Santa Fe After more than four centuries as a meeting place for different cultures, Santa Fe remains as fascinating as it is beautiful, with superb museums and galleries. **See p.104**

❸ Taos A thriving arts centre, Taos is also renowned as the home of a spectacular, thousand-year-old pueblo. **See p.147**

❹ Durango Take a day to venture into the snow-capped peaks of the Rockies, perhaps taking the steam train up to tiny, time-forgotten Silverton as well. **See p.80**

❺ Mesa Verde Tucked into clifftop recesses, the Ancestral Puebloan "palaces" of Mesa Verde provide an extraordinary glimpse of life in

ABOVE WUPATKI NATIONAL MONUMENT

North America long before the Europeans knew the continent even existed. **See p.75**

❻ Navajo National Monument Ranger-led hikes can take you up to, and into, a golden ancient community nestled into a colossal natural alcove. **See p.52**

❼ Hopi Mesas Descendants of the Ancestral Puebloans, the Hopi still live atop isolated mesas, far removed from modern Arizona. **See p.66**

❽ Canyon de Chelly Now home to a handful of Navajo sheep farmers, unsullied by paved roads, this glorious canyon holds magnificent rock formations as well as countless Ancestral Puebloan sites. **See p.58**

❾ Acoma Pueblo The people of Acoma fought off Spanish conquistadors in the sixteenth century, and remain in proud possession of "Sky City", a mesa-top settlement that also features a monumental mission church. **See p.99**

THE WILD WEST AND ROUTE 66

Take ten days to tour the cowboy-haunted frontier towns of southern Arizona and New Mexico, then motor west along Route 66 – or combine with the other itineraries here to make a three-week trip of a lifetime.

❶ Phoenix This sunbaked megalopolis of the New West is a convenient springboard for venturing into the region's past. **See p.204**

❷ Tucson With its saguaro cactuses and whitewashed mission churches, Tucson is a very likeable desert city. **See p.222**

❸ Tombstone Sawdust-floored saloons and daily gunfights at the OK Corral; what more could any Western fan want? **See p.239**

❹ Silver City Childhood home of the Kid himself, this mining town retains a nineteenth-century charm. **See p.198**

❺ White Sands Dazzling white dunes, hundreds of miles from the ocean. **See p.186**

❻ Lincoln The town where Billy the Kid blazed his way to fame has barely changed in a hundred years. **See p.181**

❼ Carlsbad Caverns Detour south to take in this eerie subterranean world – served with a side order of Fifties' kitsch. **See p.190**

❽ Fort Sumner Billy the Kid lies buried where Pat Garrett gunned him down. **See p.179**

❾ Albuquerque Follow Route 66 west into the sunset, through the heart of *Breaking Bad* territory, and you'll be rewarded with the glowing neon signs of Albuquerque's vintage motels and diners. **See p.166**

❿ Gallup Long a rendezvous for New Mexico's cowboys and Indians, Gallup oozes old-West atmosphere. **See p.95**

⓫ Winslow Stop off in this quintessential Route 66 town to stay in the splendid *La Posada* hotel – or simply stand on the corner. **See p.262**

⓬ Flagstaff As lively a Wild West town as Route 66 has to offer – and a great base for the Grand Canyon, just north. **See p.264**

VINTAGE HOTEL SIGNS, LAS VEGAS

Basics

Getting there

For US and Canadian travellers who live too far from the Southwest simply to drive there, and for international travellers, the most cost-effective way to visit Southwest USA is to fly to one of three major cities covered in this book, rent a car, drive a loop tour, and fly home from the same airport.

Las Vegas, Nevada, is probably the best bet, as it offers low air fares and rental-car rates, welcomes more direct flights from overseas than its rivals, and makes an exhilarating starting point for tours to the Grand Canyon and the national parks of southern Utah. **Phoenix**, Arizona, is equally well served by the major domestic carriers, and although Phoenix itself may not be such an appealing destination it's convenient for both the Grand Canyon and the deserts of southern Arizona. New Mexico's principal airport, in **Albuquerque**, receives fewer long-distance flights, but it's the obvious point of arrival if you want to see Santa Fe and Taos, and it's also the closest airport to the Four Corners region.

If **Utah** is your prime destination, you could also fly to Salt Lake City. Although the state capital lies in Utah's mountainous northwest corner, outside the area covered in this guide, it's little more than half a day's drive from lively Moab and national parks such as Canyonlands and Arches.

Flights from North America

Flights to the Southwest are at their most expensive in summer, which despite soaring temperatures is the peak season for travel. Prices drop from September until shortly before Christmas, and from March through May, and are cheapest from January to February. Flying on **weekends**, to Las Vegas in particular, can add a hefty premium to fares; price ranges quoted below assume midweek travel.

In general, the best bargains tend to be on flights to **Las Vegas**. It's usually possible to find round-trip fares to Las Vegas for little more than $100 from Los Angeles, $200 from Seattle, $300 from New York, and CAN$350 from Toronto. A round-trip to **Phoenix** from New York or Chicago will cost from around $250; the equivalent figure for Los Angeles would be from perhaps $100. Fares from Montréal or Vancouver to Phoenix start from CAN$450. Fares to **Albuquerque** and **Salt Lake City** are similar, with round-trips from New York costing upwards of $300. A good first call is to contact **Southwest Airlines** (ⓦsouthwest.com), which flies to Phoenix, Las Vegas, Tucson, Salt Lake City and Albuquerque from around

fifty other US cities. **JetBlue** (ⓦjetblue.com) serves Phoenix, Las Vegas, and Salt Lake City, while **Westjet** (ⓦwestjet.com) connects Albuquerque, Las Vegas, Phoenix and Tucson with various cities in Canada.

Commuter airlines like Skywest (ⓦskywest.com), Great Lakes Airlines (ⓦflygreatlakes.com), Frontier Airlines (ⓦflyfrontier.com) and Utah Airways (ⓦflyutahair.com) connect the Southwest's major airports with smaller communities in the region. Thus Phoenix has links with towns such as Durango, Farmington, Flagstaff, Page, Show Low, Tucson and Yuma; Denver with several towns in the Four Corners region and beyond; and Salt Lake City is connected with airports in southern Utah such as St George. Las Vegas also has good connections, including direct flights to – and over – the Grand Canyon (see p.318).

Few commuter flights are particularly suited to the needs of tourists, however. The cheapest fares tend to be on the scale of $75–150 for a one-way trip, and it's far easier to drive from place to place than to have to rent another car every few days. If you absolutely have to fly somewhere that only has a minor airport, your best bet is to fly to the Southwest with a specialist regional carrier that will also provide a connecting service to your ultimate destination for a small additional cost.

Flights from the UK and Ireland

Only two airlines offer direct, nonstop flights from Britain or Ireland to any of the cities covered in this book. **British Airways** (ⓦba.com) flies from both London Gatwick and London Heathrow to Las Vegas, and to Phoenix from London Heathrow only. Virgin Atlantic (ⓦvirgin-atlantic.com) flies to Las Vegas daily from London Gatwick, and once weekly from Manchester. In addition, Delta has a nonstop flight from London Heathrow to Salt Lake City, just outside the scope of this book but within easy driving range of Utah's national parks. Typical round-trip fares for all these routes range from around £600 in winter up to £900 in summer.

Most other transatlantic carriers can get you to Phoenix, Las Vegas or Albuquerque, with at least one stop en route, for lower fares. From the UK, you can either fly nonstop to the West Coast and then double back towards the Southwest, or touch down on the East Coast and then fly west; time-wise, it makes little difference. If you'd rather keep your flying time to a minimum, it's also worth considering flying nonstop to California and driving to the Southwest from there, taking advantage of the state's low rental-car rates.

From Ireland, Aer Lingus (ⓦaerlingus.com) flies from Dublin or Shannon to Boston, Chicago, New York,

A BETTER KIND OF TRAVEL

At Rough Guides we are passionately committed to travel. We believe it helps us understand the world we live in and the people we share it with – and of course tourism is vital to many developing economies. But the scale of modern tourism has also damaged some places irreparably, and climate change is accelerated by most forms of transport, especially flying. All Rough Guides' flights are carbon-offset, and every year we donate money to a variety of environmental charities.

Orlando and Washington DC, and Delta (ⓦdelta.com) from Dublin to New York. Alternatively, you can fly to London and take your pick of transatlantic routes.

Packages

Packages can work out cheaper than arranging the same trip yourself, especially for a short-term stay. **Fly-drive** deals, which include cut-rate (sometimes free) car rental when you buy a transatlantic ticket from an airline or tour operator, are likely to be cheaper than renting on the spot, and give great value if you intend to do a lot of driving.

Several operators go one stage further and book accommodation for **self-drive tours**; some travellers consider having their itineraries planned and booked by experts to be a real boon. However, schemes under which you buy prepaid hotel vouchers in advance, and then have to seek out hotels that will accept them, tend to be more bother than they're worth, and seldom save any money.

Companies such as TrekAmerica (ⓦtrekamerica .com) organize **camping tours** of the Southwest, usually starting in California or Las Vegas and circling through Utah's national parks and the Grand Canyon. Typical trips range in price – excluding flights – from £620 for a week in low season up to around £750 in midsummer. TrekAmerica also offers some trips that use hotel accommodation, like the fourteen-day version of their "Westerner" tour, which starts at £1419.

Flights from Australia, New Zealand and South Africa

There are no direct flights from Australia, New Zealand or South Africa to any of the Southwestern cities, so you'll have to fly to one of the main US gateway airports and pick up onward connections – or a rental car – from there.

The cheapest route from Australia and New Zealand, and the one with the most frequent services, is to Los Angeles, which also has plenty of onward flights to Albuquerque, Las Vegas and Phoenix. Air New Zealand (ⓦairnewzealand.com) and Qantas/ American (ⓦqantas.com.au) fly to LA at least twice daily, while United (ⓦunited.com) flies once a day.

From South Africa, by far the cheapest route is usually to fly with Virgin Atlantic (ⓦvirgin-atlantic.com) from Johannesburg to London, and then from London to Las Vegas, which costs in the region of 19,000SAR.

Packages and tours

Package deals available to travellers in Australia and New Zealand range from fly-drive options to fully escorted bus tours and camping treks, and can work out significantly cheaper than making the same arrangements yourself; no-frills flight and car rental packages, for example, can cost less than a flight alone. You can also add on whatever extra tours you choose; by way of example, Adventure World (ⓦadventure world.com.au) offers trips from LA like the two-week "Western Dream" that starts at A$2711, or the one-week "Canyons and Indian Lands" jaunt to the Grand Canyon, Zion and Monument Valley for A$2339.

Trains

Amtrak rail service to and within the Southwest is restricted to three completely separate east–west routes. Two pass through Arizona and New Mexico on the way to and from Los Angeles, while the other crosses northern Utah.

The daily **Southwest Chief** originates in Chicago and crosses from Colorado into northern New Mexico near Raton, passing close to Santa Fe (connected by a bus service from tiny Lamy) and through Albuquerque before heading west via Gallup, Flagstaff – where connecting buses run north to the Grand Canyon – and Williams, the home of the entirely distinct Grand Canyon Railway (see p.318). The thrice-weekly **Sunset Limited** from New Orleans reaches southern New Mexico via El Paso, Texas, then calls at Deming and Lordsburg, before hitting the Arizona towns of Benson, Tucson, Maricopa and Yuma. En route between Chicago and San Francisco, the daily **California Zephyr** calls at Green River in Utah, as well as Denver and Salt Lake City.

There is no rail service to **Phoenix** – the closest station is Maricopa, 35 miles south – or to **Las Vegas**, which is linked by bus with Barstow, California, on the Southwest Chief route.

For fares and schedules, visit ⓦamtrak.com.

Buses

If you're happy to sit on a bus for days on end, you can reach the Southwest using Greyhound. It's not necessarily cheaper than flying, though if you book in advance online you can find some reasonable fares. A one-way trip to Albuquerque from Los Angeles takes around nineteen hours and costs $84 if booked at least two weeks in advance, or $132 on the day of travel; the ride from Milwaukee to Phoenix takes up to 44 hours and costs $109 or $224, respectively; and the cross-country trek from New York to Las Vegas takes almost three days and costs $129 or $274.

For details of routes, fares and potential discounts, and to make reservations, visit Ⓦ greyhound.com.

AGENTS AND OPERATORS

North South Travel UK ☎ 01245 608291, Ⓦ northsouthtravel .co.uk. Friendly, competitive flight agency, offering discounted fares. Profits are used to support projects in the developing world.

STA Travel US ☎ 800 781 4040, Ⓦ statravel.com; UK ☎ 0333 321 0099, Ⓦ statravel.co.uk; Australia ☎ 134 782, Ⓦ statravel.com.au; New Zealand ☎ 0800 474 400, Ⓦ statravel.co.nz; South Africa ☎ 0861 781 781, Ⓦ www.statravel.co.za. Worldwide specialists in low-cost flights for students and under-26s; other customers also welcome.

Trailfinders UK ☎ 020 7368 1200, Ⓦ trailfinders.com; Ireland ☎ 01 677 7888, Ⓦ trailfinders.ie. Efficient and well-informed agency for independent travellers.

SOUTHWEST USA TOUR OPERATORS

Backroads ☎ 800 462 2848, Ⓦ backroads.com. Hiking and/or biking tours covering New Mexico, Arizona, and southern Utah. A five-night cycling trip to Zion and Bryce, staying in motels, costs around $2600; five nights' walking in New Mexico, staying in good hotels, from $3100.

Canyonlands Field Institute ☎ 435 259 7750 or ☎ 800 860 5262, Ⓦ cfimoab.org. NPS-authorized adult and family wilderness expeditions, not exclusively in Canyonlands; from around $1940 for the epic five-night hike to remote Rainbow Bridge, $915 for a four-night, women-only rafting trip on the Colorado River. Also one-day tours near Moab.

Grand Canyon Field Institute ☎ 928 638 2481 or ☎ 800 858 2808, Ⓦ grandcanyon.org/learn/grand-canyon-field-institute. Highly recommended, park-sponsored programme of hikes and educational expeditions in the Grand Canyon. Typical prices range from around $645 for a three-night hike down into the canyon to $920 for a four-night rim-to-rim backpacking trip.

Green Tortoise ☎ 800 867 8647, Ⓦ greentortoise.com. California-based, youth-oriented bus tours. The nine-day "Canyons of the West" tour from Los Angeles costs around $900 including food kitty.

MNA Ventures ☎ 928 774 5213, Ⓦ musnaz.org/ventures-tours. Flagstaff's prestigious Museum of Northern Arizona runs an extensive programme of tours and excursions in the Four Corners region, camping and/or staying in hotels. A four-night backpacking trip along Comb Ridge in Utah costs around $1000.

REI Adventures ☎ 800 622 2236, Ⓦ rei.com/travel. Small-group

hiking trips in Utah and Arizona; a six-night trip, with accommodation, typically starts at around $2400.

Sierra Club Outings ☎ 415 977 5522, Ⓦ sierraclub.org/outings. The environmental group offers some fabulous opportunities to come to grips with the landscapes and resources of the Southwest, such as a week in Utah's Dark Canyon or Arizona's Rainbow Plateau for $1145.

Southwest Ed-ventures ☎ 800 525 4456, Ⓦ fourcornersschool .org. Hiking, backpacking and rafting trips for all ages on the Colorado Plateau, with a strong educational element. A week hiking the side canyons off Lake Powell, based on a houseboat, costs $1770.

TrekAmerica/Grand American Adventures US ☎ 800 873 5872, UK ☎ 0333 999 7951; Ⓦ trekamerica.com or Ⓦ grandamerican adventures.com. A wide array of Southwest expeditions, costing from £1049 for ten days' camping, £1489 staying in hotels; rates exclude flights. The TrekAmerica branded tours are targeted at ages 18–38.

Getting around

Attempting to tour the Southwest by public transport is a very bad idea. While buses and planes – and, to a much lesser extent, trains – connect the major urban areas, the national parks and wide-open landscapes that are the region's greatest attractions simply cannot be explored without your own vehicle. Even public transport within the cities is minimal. Unless you're an extremely energetic cyclist, therefore, you'll need a motorbike or car.

For non-drivers, the only itinerary that makes much sense is to cross northern Arizona and northern New Mexico by bus or train, flying in or out of Albuquerque in the east or Las Vegas in the west. Obvious stops would include Flagstaff, with a side trip by bus to the Grand Canyon, and Santa Fe, the only city small enough to be seen on foot. Phoenix and Tucson are no fun at all without a car, while what little public transport exists in southern Utah is no use for seeing the parks. Hitchhiking is not recommended under any circumstances.

By car

To rent a car, you need to have held your licence for at least one year; drivers under 25 may encounter problems and have to pay higher than normal insurance premiums.

All the major rental companies have outlets at the main regional airports. Reservations are handled centrally rather than locally, so the best way to shop around for rates is online. Potential variations are endless; certain cities and states are consistently cheaper than others, while individual travellers may be eligible for corporate, frequent-flier, or AAA discounts. In low season, you might find a tiny car (a "subcompact") for as little as $125 per week, but a typical budget rate would be more like $45 per day, and $200 per week. A car rented in Las Vegas can easily cost $100 less per week than one rented in Colorado, while prices in Arizona, New Mexico and Utah range between the two.

Don't automatically go for the cheapest rate. Little-known local rental companies may offer appealing prices, but if your vehicle breaks down several hundred miles from their offices it may be hard to get assistance. Even between the major operators, there can be a big difference in the quality of cars. Always be sure to get free unlimited mileage, and remember that leaving the car in a different city from the one where you rent it can incur a drop-off charge of as much as $200.

When you rent a car, read the small print carefully for details on Collision Damage Waiver (CDW), sometimes called Liability Damage Waiver (LDW), a form of insurance that often isn't included in the initial rental charge but is well worth considering. This specifically covers the car that you are driving yourself; you are in any case insured for damage to other vehicles. At $15–25 a day extra, it can add substantially to the total cost, but without it you're liable for every scratch to the car – even those that aren't your fault. Some credit card companies offer automatic CDW coverage to anyone using their card; contact your issuing company for details. Your rental papers should include an emergency number to call in case of breakdown or accident; contact the rental company before you arrange, or pay, for any repairs.

The American Automobile Association, or AAA (❶ 800 222 4357, ⓦ aaa.com), provides free maps and assistance to its members and to members of affiliated associations overseas, such as the British AA and RAC.

Renting an RV

Recreational vehicles – RVs – can be rented at prices starting at around $800 per week (plus mileage charges) for a basic camper on the back of a pick-up truck, with sleeping room for two adults. For a huge juggernaut that comes complete with multiple bedrooms, bathrooms, and kitchens, you'll have to pay significantly more. Though good for groups or families travelling together, RVs can be unwieldy on the road, and as Americans tend to own their own, rental outlets are not as common as you might expect. On top of rental fees, you'll also have to take into account the cost of gas (some RVs do twelve miles to the gallon or less) and any drop-off charges. It's rarely legal simply to pull up in an RV and spend

> ## TOP 5 SCENIC DRIVES
> **The High Road** Northern NM. See p.143
> **Hwy-12** Southern UT. See p.378
> **Road between the Rims** Northern AZ. See p.330
> **Route 66** Northern NM and AZ. See p.10
> **San Juan Skyway** Southwest CO. See p.83

the night at the roadside; you are expected to stay in designated parks that cost $20–40 per night.

The National RV Dealers Association (ⓦ rvda.org) maintains a searchable online directory of rental firms. Large companies offering RV rentals include Cruise America (ⓦ cruiseamerica.com) and USA RV Rentals (ⓦ usarvrentals.com).

Advice for drivers from overseas

Foreign nationals from English-speaking countries can drive in the US using their full domestic **driving licences**. (International Driving Permits are not always regarded as sufficient.) Not having your licence with you while driving is an arrestable offence.

Fly-drive deals are good value if you want to rent a car, though you can save up to sixty percent simply by booking in advance with a major firm. If you choose not to pay until you arrive, be sure you take a written confirmation of the price with you. Remember that most standard rental cars have **automatic** transmissions, and that it's safer not to drive immediately after a long transatlantic flight.

It's easier and cheaper to book RVs in advance from Britain. Most travel agents who specialize in the US can arrange **RV rental**, and usually do it cheaper if you book a flight through them as well. A price of £1500 for a five-berth van for two weeks is fairly typical.

Desert driving

Whenever you drive in the **desert**, be sure to have two gallons of water per person in the car. You should also carry flares, matches, a first-aid kit and a compass, plus a shovel, air pump and extra gas. If the car's engine overheats, don't turn it off; instead, try to cool the engine quickly by turning the front end toward the wind. Carefully pour some water on the front of the radiator, and turn the air conditioning off and heating up full blast. In an emergency, never panic and leave the car; you'll be harder to find wandering around alone.

By bus

Greyhound buses link all major cities and many smaller towns in the Southwest; for fares, schedules, and reservations, visit Ⓦgreyhound.com. Routes that are particularly useful for tourists – as well as services offered by other operators – are detailed at the relevant points in this book.

While scheduled buses can get you from city to city, they're of no use when it comes to enjoying the great outdoors. Tour buses, however, do set off into the wilderness from most major towns; they, too, are detailed throughout this book.

By train

There is a very limited **Amtrak** rail service to and across the Southwest (see p.28). The region also holds a number of **historic and scenic railroads** – some steam-powered or running along narrow-gauge mining tracks – including the Cumbres & Toltec line in northern New Mexico (Ⓦcumbres toltec.com); the Grand Canyon Railway between Williams and the Grand Canyon in northern Arizona (Ⓦthetrain.com); the Verde Canyon Railroad in northern Arizona (Ⓦverdecanyonrr.com); and the Durango & Silverton Narrow Gauge Railroad in Colorado (Ⓦdurangotrain.com).

By bike

Although **cycling** in the Southwest can be absolutely exhilarating, long-distance riders face a fearsome challenge, above all in the heat of summer. Neighbouring towns can be as much as a hundred miles apart, along desert highways that offer no food, water or shade. Quite apart from the high mountains and deep canyons, most areas covered in this book are a mile or more above sea level, so the **altitude** alone can be a real problem. The only road from A to B may well turn out to be a major interstate; when there's no alternative, cyclists are generally allowed to ride on interstate shoulders, but they have to battle the slipstream of mighty trucks.

If you have a good bike and know how to maintain it, however, and you time your trip for the cooler months, it is feasible to explore the Southwest by bike. Specific regions that lend themselves to cycle touring are north-central New Mexico, where countless routes radiate from Santa Fe; the vicinity of Flagstaff and Sedona in Arizona; and southwest Utah, around Zion National Park. Areas especially popular with mountain bikers include **Moab**, Utah – home of the gruelling Slickrock Bike Trail (see p.427) – and **Durango**, Colorado.

For general information and advice, contact the New Mexico Touring Society (Ⓦnmts.org), the Arizona Bicycle Club (Ⓦazbikeclub.com), or Bike Utah (Ⓦbikeutah.org). The national, non-profit Adventure Cycling Association (formerly Bikecentennial; Ⓦadventurecycling.org) publishes maps ($15.75 each) of several 400-mile routes, including the Grand Canyon Connector, detailing campgrounds, motels, restaurants, bike shops, and sites of interest. Backroads Bicycle Tours (☎800 462 2848, Ⓦback roads.com) arranges group tours.

Greyhound, Amtrak and major airlines all carry passengers' bicycles – dismantled and packed into a box – for a small additional fee.

Accommodation

Accommodation in the Southwest is relatively inexpensive. Most travellers simply want a bed for the night before moving on the next day, so motels everywhere provide clean, no-frills places to sleep without bothering to offer additional amenities.

Basic room rates in rural areas start as low as $50 per night, while prices along the principal highways and interstates tend to cost from around $75. Only in the most popular summer destinations – cities such as Santa Fe, or "gateway" towns near the major national parks – will you find it hard to get a room for under $100. If you prefer a bit more comfort, it's almost always available; in most areas covered by this book you can get a room in a top-class hotel for under $160.

Many motel rooms hold two double beds, and will accommodate three or four guests for slightly over the normal two-person rate. On the other hand, the lone traveller has a hard time of it: a "single" room is just a double at a fractionally reduced rate.

Wherever you stay, you'll be expected to pay in advance – by credit card, though they'll also accept cash or dollar travellers' cheques – at least for the first night and perhaps for further nights too. Reservations – essential in busy areas in summer – are only held until 5pm or 6pm unless you've warned the hotel you'll be arriving late.

Hotels and motels

It's easy to find a basic **motel room** in the Southwest. Drivers approaching any significant town pass lines of motels along the highway, while the choice along major cross-country routes is phenomenal. Most of the towns mentioned in this book hold more motels than there's room to review; the very few that have none at all are clearly indicated.

Hotels and **motels** are essentially the same thing, although motels tend to be beside main roads away from city centres, and thus much more accessible to drivers. The budget ones are pretty basic, but in general there's a uniform standard of comfort – each room comes with a double bed, a TV, a phone and an attached bathroom – and you don't get a much better deal by paying, say, $120 instead of $80. Almost all hotels and motels (except in Las Vegas) offer free **wi-fi**.

While the cheapest properties tend to be family-run, independent motels, there's a lot to be said for paying a few dollars more to stay in the national **chains**. Most travellers find that a particular chain consistently suits their requirements and budget. Few budget hotels or motels offer **breakfast**, although many provide free self-service coffee and pastries.

Travellers who belong to the AAA can usually get a discount of around ten percent, as can members of similarly named foreign organizations such as Britain's AA. Look out for **discount coupons**, especially in the free brochures available at state and local visitor centres. These can offer excellent value – say, $60 for a double room in a mid-range chain – but rates are often limited to midweek.

Many towns throughout the Southwest still hold **historic hotels**, whether dating back to the arrival of the railroads or to the heyday of Route 66 in the 1940s and 1950s. Not all have up-to-date facilities to match their period charm, but they can make wonderfully characterful places to spend a night or two. Those that are exceptionally well preserved or restored may charge $200 or more per room, but a more typical rate for a not overly luxurious but atmospheric, antique-furnished room would be more like $120. Occasionally, venerable Western hotels have been refitted to serve as budget-oriented accommodation options, as with Tucson's *Hotel Congress* (p.230) and Flagstaff's *Monte Vista* and *Weatherford* (p.268).

Several **national parks** feature long-established and architecturally distinguished hotels, traditionally known as **lodges**. Thanks to their federally controlled rates, these can be real bargains, but all rooms tend to be reserved far in advance. Among the best are *El Tovar* and *Grand Canyon Lodge* on the south and north rims, respectively, of the Grand Canyon, and *Zion Lodge* in Zion Canyon.

Bed and breakfasts

Bed and breakfast has become ever more popular, often as a luxurious – if not necessarily more expensive – alternative to conventional hotels.

The price you pay for a B&B – which typically varies from around $90 to $180 – always includes a huge and wholesome breakfast. The crucial determining factor in price is whether each room has an en-suite bathroom, even though providing private bath facilities can damage the authenticity of a fine old house.

In many areas, B&Bs have grouped together to form central booking agencies, making it much easier to find a room at short notice; we've given addresses and numbers for these where appropriate. Statewide organizations include the Arizona Association of B&B Inns (Ⓦ arizona-bed-breakfast .com); B&B Inns of Utah (Ⓦ bbiu.org); B&B Innkeepers of Colorado (Ⓦ innsofcolorado.org); and the New Mexico B&B Association (Ⓦ nmbba.org).

Hostels

Around a dozen **hostels** provide accommodation for backpackers and budget travellers in the Southwest. Most work out little cheaper than motels for two people travelling together, so there's not much point staying in hostels unless you prefer their youthful ambience and sociability. Many are not accessible on public transport, or particularly convenient for sightseeing in the towns and cities, let alone in rural areas.

These days, most hostels are **independent**, with no affiliation to **HI-AYH** (Hostelling International-American Youth Hostels) network. Many are no more than converted motels, where the "dorms" consist of a couple of sets of bunk beds in a musty room that's also let out as a private unit on demand; others may be purpose-built rural properties, or at least modernized to a high standard. Most expect guests to bring sheets or sleeping bags. Rates range from $18 up to about $30 for a dorm bed, from more like $40 for a double room. Those few hostels that do belong to HI-AYH tend to impose curfews and limit daytime access hours, and segregate dormitories by sex.

Especially in high season, it's advisable to reserve ahead. The maximum stay is often restricted to three days, though this rule tends to be ignored if space is available. Few hostels provide meals, but most have cooking facilities.

Food and drink

The short-lived international craze for contemporary Southwestern cuisine did little to turn the Southwest itself into a gourmet's paradise. However, Santa Fe still holds dozens of top-class restaurants, while the upscale resorts of Phoenix, Tucson, Taos and Sedona – as well, of course, as Las Vegas – all offer opportunities for fine dining.

Out on the road, the great American **diner** still holds sway. Southern Utah, for example, is the last place to go if lingering over an exquisite meal in atmospheric surroundings ranks high on your vacation wish list. With typical prices for a diner meal starting below $12, however, travellers happy to eat the same old steak or chicken, with baked potato and salad bar, can get excellent value for money. Note that the word "entree" is invariably used to refer to the main course of a meal, while the first course is an "appetizer".

The **Hispanic** regions of New Mexico and southern Arizona have their own indigenous cuisine, broadly similar to Mexican food but influenced by the Pueblo Indians. The essential ingredient is the chile, technically the "fruit" of the pepper plant. (New Mexicans insist it should never be spelled chili or chilli, which indicates the Texas-style stew made with ground beef and tomato sauce.) Bright-red ristras – strings of dried peppers – adorn the region's doorways and restaurant entrances, celebrating the fiery delights that lie within. In principle, the red pepper is the mature version of the green, but if you're confronted with a plateful there's no guarantee which will be hotter. Both are used to make spicy salsa, which usually contains tomato and onion, cilantro (coriander) and other herbs, oil and lemon juice, plus other secret ingredients. If it's too hot for you, the best remedy is to drink milk.

A basic meal in a New Mexican café or diner is broadly similar to what you'd eat south of the border, though it may make more use of fresh meats and vegetables. The essentials are: lots of rice and pinto beans, often served refried as frijoles (ie boiled, mashed and fried), with variations on the tortilla, a very thin cornmeal or flour pancake that can be wrapped around the food and eaten by hand (a burrito); folded, fried, and filled (a taco); rolled, filled, and baked in sauce (an enchilada); or fried flat and topped with a stack of filling (a tostada). Meals are usually served with complimentary nachos (chips) and salsa dip, or with sopaipillas, deep-fried air-filled pastry "pillows", often sweetened with honey. The chile relleno is a good **vegetarian** option – a green pepper stuffed with cheese, dipped in egg batter and fried.

You'll also find **Native American** restaurants, both on and off the reservations. The most ubiquitous dish, generally known as a **Navajo taco**, consists of a piece of **fry bread** – a puffy deep-fried slab of bread – smothered with beans, lettuce and cheese. A Hopi taco, an Apache taco, and a Pueblo taco are all surprisingly similar. Corn or maize, the first crop cultivated in the Americas, comes in some amazing multicoloured varieties. Blue corn chips have spread beyond the Southwest, but you may also encounter blue cornflakes and wafer-thin piki or piiki bread made with blue cornflour.

Drinking

To buy and consume alcohol in the US, you must be **aged 21** or over; you may be asked for ID even if you look much older. In New Mexico and Arizona, most restaurants have liquor licences, and it's always easy to find a drink. In Mormon-dominated Utah things are a bit more complicated, though it's not quite the "dry" state of popular legend, and most small towns have at least one restaurant licensed to sell beer or wine to diners. Alcohol is prohibited altogether on **Indian reservations**; you can't have beer in your car, let alone in your motel room.

Festivals and events

The Southwest's major annual festivals are listed below. Specific events are described in the relevant town accounts, while the pueblos of New Mexico also stage an extensive annual programme of events (see p.141). Tourist offices for each state (see p.43) can provide full lists, but as a rule, only the Indian Market in Santa Fe and the Balloon Festival in Albuquerque attract large enough crowds to place a serious strain on accommodation and other facilities.

The great outdoors

Cut by deep canyons, coated by dense forests, and capped by great mountains, the Southwest glories in some of the most fabulous wilderness areas in the United States.

The easiest way for visitors to enjoy this natural wonderland is to plot an itinerary that samples the countless national, state and county parks. Although these are not invariably the most beautiful places of all – some are simply lands that pioneer farmers, Indian tribes and mining corporations never bothered or managed to grab – they do offer the campgrounds and hiking trails that make backcountry exploration possible even for the least experienced tourists.

National parks and monuments

The National Park Service administers both national parks and national monuments. Park rangers do a superb job of providing information and advice to visitors, maintaining trails and organizing such activities as free guided hikes and campfire talks.

In principle, a **national park** preserves an area of outstanding natural beauty, encompassing a wide range of terrain as well as sites of historic interest, while a **national monument** is smaller, focusing perhaps on a single archeological site or geological phenomenon and thus holding a narrower appeal for tourists. In practice, however, that distinction is somewhat blurred in the Southwest. Most **parks** cover desert regions that have barely known human occupation, and thus boast little historic significance, and although the **Grand Canyon** and **Zion** are huge and very varied, parks such as **Bryce Canyon** and **Carlsbad Caverns** are essentially one-trick wonders. And while many **monuments** do consist of a single native American ruin or nineteenth-century fort, several more are as diverse and spectacular as the parks – Arizona's **Canyon de Chelly**, for example, would surely be a national park were it not on the Navajo reservation. In addition, vast national monuments have been created in areas that need extra federal protection but are not intended to become major tourist destinations. **Grand Staircase-Escalante** monument in Utah, the best-known example, is larger than any of the national parks in this book.

Other public lands

National parks and monuments are often surrounded by tracts of **national forest**, also federally administered but much less protected. While these also tend to hold appealing rural campgrounds, most allow limited logging or other land-based industry – ski resorts more often than strip mines, fortunately.

Further government departments administer wildlife refuges, national scenic rivers, recreation areas and the like by basically leaving the natural landscape alone. The **Bureau of Land Management** (BLM) has the largest holdings of all, most of it open rangeland, such as in Utah, but also including some enticingly out-of-the-way reaches.

State parks and state monuments are a mirror-image of the national system, preserving sites of more limited, local significance. Many are explicitly designed for recreational use and thus hold better campgrounds than their federal equivalents.

Fees and passes

Most national parks and monuments charge an admission fee of between $5 and $30, which covers a vehicle and all its occupants for up to a week. For anyone on a touring vacation, it will almost certainly make more sense to buy one of various **passes**. The annual **National Parks Pass**, officially known as the "America the Beautiful – National Parks and Federal Recreational Lands Pass – Annual Pass", costs $80, and can be bought at all national parks and monuments, or online at Ⓦstore.usgs .gov/pass. It grants unrestricted access for a year from the date of purchase to the bearer, and any accompanying passengers, to all national parks and monuments, as well as sites managed by such agencies as the US Fish and Wildlife Service, the Forest Service, and the BLM. It does not, however, cover or reduce additional fees like camping charges or permits for backcountry hiking or rafting.

Two further passes grant **free access** for life to all national parks and monuments, again to the holder and any accompanying passengers, and also provide a fifty percent discount on camping fees. The **Senior Pass** is available to any US citizen or permanent resident aged 62 or older for a one-time fee of $10, while the **Access Pass**, obtainable at any park but not online, is issued free to blind or permanently disabled US citizens or permanent residents.

Information resources

For information on the National Park Service, access Ⓦnps.gov. Websites for individual parks appear throughout this book. For general maps and camping information, Ⓦpubliclands.org, the **Public Lands Information Center** website, has details on BLM and forest-service lands, or visit the **state parks**

TOP 5 HIKING TRAILS
Mesa Arch Trail Canyonlands; 1hr.
See p.409
Delicate Arch Trail Arches; 2hr. See p.420
White House Trail Canyon de Chelly; 2hr
30min. See p.61
Horseshoe Canyon Canyonlands; 5hr.
See p.411
West Rim Trail Zion; 1 day. See p.357

offices for **Arizona** (Ⓦazstateparks.com); Colorado (Ⓦcpw.state.co.us); **New Mexico** (Ⓦwww.emnrd .state.nm.us/spd); or **Utah** (Ⓦstateparks.utah.gov).

Camping and backpacking

The ideal way to see the Southwest – especially if you're on a low budget – is to tour the region by car and **camp** at night in state and federal campgrounds. These may lack the amenities of the many commercially run campgrounds near the larger towns, but they tend to be far more peaceful, scenic and better positioned for days of hiking and canyoneering. Typical public campgrounds range in price from free (usually when there's no water available, which may be seasonal) to around $20 per night; commercial fees are more like $25–40, for sites that can be more like open-air hotels, with shops and restaurants.

There may be plenty of campgrounds, but plenty of people want to use them: if you're camping during public holidays or the high season, reserve in advance or avoid the most popular areas. By contrast, basic campgrounds in isolated areas may well be completely empty whatever time you go.

Backcountry camping in the national parks – the word "**backpacking**" is universally used to describe overnight hiking-and-camping trips in the wilderness – is usually by permit and may be free or cost a few dollars per night. Before you set off on anything more than a half-day hike, and whenever you're headed for anywhere at all isolated, be sure to inform a ranger of your plans and ask about weather conditions and specific local tips. Carry sufficient food and drink to cover emergencies, as well as all the necessary equipment and maps. In summer, you have to carry so much **water** that you'll need to lighten your load as much as possible, perhaps by sleeping in a light-weight sack rather than a sleeping bag.

When camping rough, check whether **fires** are permitted. Even if they are, try to use a camp stove instead of local materials – in some places firewood is scarce, although you may be allowed to use deadwood. In wilderness areas, try to camp on previously used sites. Where there are no toilets, bury human waste at least six inches into the ground and a hundred feet from the nearest water supply and campground. Burn what trash you can and take the rest away.

Finally, you may have heard reports of deaths caused by a **hantavirus** that's spread by exposure to the droppings of deer mice. This first came to attention in the Southwest when around fifty people succumbed to a "mystery illness" in the Four Corners region in 1993. Such viruses are still present hereabouts, so backpackers should take care to avoid camping near rodent nests.

Flora and fauna

Though the Southwest is commonly imagined as an arid wasteland, it holds a broad spectrum of plant and animal life. Scientists divide the earth, according to climate and distance from the equator, into "**life zones**" that hold different groups of species. In the Southwest, altitude substitutes for latitude; the higher you are, the cooler it gets. Within the Grand Canyon alone, the range of habitat is equivalent to a trip from the deserts of Mexico to the forests of the Canadian mountains.

It's the lowest, hottest level, the **Lower Sonoran** zone, that's home to the rattlesnakes and cacti you're probably expecting. Southern Arizona is the obvious example, with its dramatic saguaro and organ-pipe cactuses. By the time you reach a mile above sea level – the altitude of most of Utah's national parks – you're in the **Upper Sonoran** zone. This is characterized by smaller prickly pear cactuses and sagebrush, animals such as rabbits and prairie dogs, and predators like coyotes and mountain lions (not that tourists are at all likely to encounter lions). Low rainfall results in a "pygmy forest" where gnarled, long-lived trees such as the piñon (or pinyon) pine and Utah juniper grow to a maximum height of little over twenty feet.

Around ten thousand feet up in the mountains of southern Colorado, northern New Mexico, and central-southern Utah, the **Canadian** zone is even more densely forested, with Douglas firs joining the aspen and ponderosa, and bighorn sheep making an appearance in remoter areas. The Colorado Rockies and Utah's Henry and La Sal ranges rise higher still into the **Hudsonian** zone, between eleven and twelve thousand feet. Before the tree cover gives out altogether, ultra-resilient species such as the bristlecone pine, which can live for literally thousands of years, cling to the slopes.

The highest summits in the Southwest – like the San Francisco Peaks (12,633ft) near Flagstaff,

Arizona, and Uncompahgre Peak (14,309ft) near Ouray, Colorado – belong to the **Arctic** or **Alpine** zone, where the occasional tiny mammal scuttles through the tundra-like grasses and mosses.

Wherever and whenever **water** is abundant, however, the picture changes. Southwestern riverbeds are lined with magnificent **cottonwood** and **aspen** trees, so many a canyon buried deep in the desert still manages a superb display of fall colours, while spring snowmelts help bring the mountain hillsides and the meadows of Zion alive with wildflowers.

Health

The major health and safety issues facing Southwest travellers centre on coping with desert conditions. For anyone unused to dealing with extremes of heat and cold, and the sheer inhospitality of this kind of terrain, it's essential to take precautions.

Desert survival

If you plan to **hike in the desert**, it's crucial to plan ahead. Don't expect mobile (cell) phones to provide coverage in all the remote regions described in this book; tell somebody where you are going and write down all pertinent information, including your expected time of return. Carry an extra two days' food and water, and never go anywhere without a map. Try to cover most of your ground in early morning: the midday heat is too debilitating.

Stick to official trails in the national parks and you shouldn't face any serious technical difficulties. Many trails are marked only by occasional stone cairns, however, and if your concentration starts to wander your feet may do so too. If you do get lost, try your utmost to retrace your steps; if that fails, find

> ### ADVENTURE TRAVEL
>
> The Southwest offers vast opportunities for active travelling; guides, outfitters and local tour operators are recommended throughout this book. In its major base for adventure travel of all kinds, the former mining town of **Moab**, Utah (see p.422), mountain biking is the speciality, with rafting and four-wheel-driving (4WD) as close rivals. Other towns popular with energetic visitors include **Durango**, Colorado (see p.80), and **Sedona**, Arizona (see p.274).

some shade and wait. As long as you've registered, the rangers will eventually come and fetch you.

There are two more good reasons not to try to blaze your own trail. The first is the risk of becoming **rim-rocked**; picking your way across even a shallow gully, it's much easier to climb up than down, and you may well find yourself stuck above a drop that you're unable to negotiate. The other is the **crypto-biotic crust** – what looks like a faint coating of dead moss on the sand is the building block on which all desert life depends, and merely treading on it has serious ecological consequences.

Whatever experience you may have had elsewhere, hiking in **canyons** is different. Most hikers are far more familiar with walking *up* hills and mountains, where it's the initial climb that's most demanding, and when your energy levels flag you can simply turn around and walk back to base. Canyon hiking, on the other hand, is deceptively seductive. The descent seems easy, and your progress quick. Eventually, however, you have to pay: start the climb back out when you're already tired and the midday heat has set in, and you're in for a murderously long haul. Turn back after a third of your allotted time; if you plan a six-hour hike, allow two hours hiking down and four hours to hike up.

To stay cool during the day, wear full-length sleeves and trousers. Shorts and a T-shirt will expose you to far too much sun – something you won't be aware of until it's too late. A wide-brimmed hat and good sunglasses will spare you the blinding headaches that can result from the desert light.

You may also have to contend with **flash floods**, which can appear from nowhere. One innocent-looking dark cloud can turn a dry wash into a raging river, and rain elsewhere can cause a flood even when the sky above is clear. Never camp in a dry wash, and don't attempt to cross flooded areas until the water has receded.

Much of the Southwest is more than a mile above sea level, so the **altitude** alone can impose severe demands on even the fittest of athletes. Be prepared for below-freezing temperatures at high elevations at night.

Water

It's essential to carry – and **drink** – large quantities of liquid in the desert. An eight-hour hike in typical summer temperatures of more than 100°F (38°C) would require you to drink a phenomenal **fourteen litres** of water. Early symptoms of heat exhaustion include loss of both thirst and appetite, so it's possible to become seriously dehydrated without

feeling thirsty. Watch out for dizziness or nausea; if you feel weak and stop sweating, it's time to get to the doctor. You should always know whether water will be available on your chosen trail – ask park rangers – and carry at least a litre per person even if you expect to be able to pick up more en route. Just to confuse things, there's also the risk of **hyponatremia**, or water intoxication, which in its first stages closely resembles heat exhaustion, and happens if you drink too much without eating. As hikers can burn up to a thousand calories per hour, expect to eat at least twice as much **food** as normal, both during your hike and also, ideally, before it. Salty snacks such as cookies, crackers and trail mix are recommended, as well as jerky or salami and dried ready-made meals. Finally, it's easy to forget that at the end of a long hike there may be no facilities at the trailhead. Don't forget to leave some food and water in your vehicle as well.

Backpackers should never drink from rivers and streams, however clear and inviting they may look; you never know what unspeakable acts people – or animals – have performed further upstream. **Giardia** – a water-borne bacteria that causes an intestinal disease, characterized by chronic diarrhoea, abdominal cramps, fatigue and weight loss – is a serious problem. Water that doesn't come from a tap should be boiled for at least five minutes or cleansed with an iodine-based purifier, or a giardia-rated filter, available from any outdoor store.

Insects and allergies

Mosquitoes and biting insects are rarely a problem in the Southwest, though in springtime you may encounter them near rivers in parks such as Zion. Anything containing DEET is a fairly reliable repellent.

Ticks – tiny beetles that plunge their heads into your skin and swell up with your blood – can be a hazard. If you pluck them off you can sometimes leave their heads inside, causing blood clots or infections, so get advice from a park ranger if you've been bitten. **Lyme disease**, which is transmitted by infected tick bites and rendered more likely if a biting tick remains attached, has been detected in all the Southwestern states. Seek medical advice if you're concerned about a tick bite, and especially if you experience flu-like symptoms. For more information, visit ⓦ lymedisease.org.

Beware, too, of **poison oak**, an allergenic shrub that grows all over the western states, usually among oak trees. Its leaves come in groups of three and are distinguished by prominent veins and shiny surfaces. If you come into contact, wash your skin (with soap and cold water) and clothes as soon as possible – and don't scratch. In serious cases, hospital emergency rooms can give antihistamine or adrenaline jabs.

Snakes and creepy-crawlies

Though the Southwestern deserts are home to **poisonous creatures** that include snakes, scorpions and spiders, these are rarely aggressive towards humans. By observing obvious precautions, you should be able to avoid trouble. Don't attempt to handle wildlife; keep your eyes open as you walk, and watch where you put your hands when scrambling over obstacles; shake out shoes, clothing and bedding before use; and back off if you do spot a creature, to give it room to escape.

If you are **bitten** or stung – whatever creature is responsible – apply a cold compress to the wound, constrict the area with a tourniquet to prevent the spread of venom, drink lots of water, and bring your temperature down by resting in a shady area. Stay as calm as possible and seek medical help immediately.

Medical resources for travellers

CDC ☎ 800 232 4636, ⓦ cdc.gov/travel. Official US government travel health site.
International Society for Travel Medicine ⓦ istm.org. An extensive list of travel health clinics, including many in the Southwest.

Travelling in Indian country

The Southwest holds around fifty separate Indian reservations, ranging in size from the vast "Navajo Nation", which extends across three states in the Four Corners region, to the nineteen autonomous pueblos of New Mexico, many of which consist of a single village.

Some reservations make no effort to attract or inform visitors; some do the bare minimum to sate tourists' curiosity; some eagerly encourage paying guests to stay in tribal-run motels and campgrounds. Among the most compelling attractions on Native American soil are **Monument Valley**, and **Canyon de Chelly** and **Navajo** national monuments, all on the Navajo reservation; the stupendous waterfalls of the **Havasupai reservation**, deep in the Grand Canyon; the **Skywalk** on the Hualapai reservation, in the so-called "Grand Canyon West"; and the adobe pueblos of **Taos** and **Acoma** in New Mexico.

Many outsiders – Americans and non-Americans alike – feel uncomfortable about entering Native American land, but so long as you behave with due **cultural sensitivity** you will almost always be made welcome. In particular, travellers in what's widely known as "Indian Country" should respect the laws that bar the sale, possession and consumption of **alcohol** on the reservations. Always request permission before **photographing** (or even drawing) people or personal property, and accept that you may be asked for a fee. As well as obeying explicit signs that ask you not to enter specific areas, such as shrines or *kivas*, remember that off-road driving and off-trail hiking or climbing is forbidden. If you have to drive up to someone's home or *hogan,* stay in your car and wait to be approached, rather than blundering in.

On a more general note, attempts to be friendly may run contrary to what Native Americans regard as **good manners**. In the words of a leaflet issued by the Navajo, "the general exuberance many cultures define as friendliness is not considered such by the American Indians". Most Southwestern Indians regard **eye contact** as rude and will avoid meeting your eye; they may also prefer not to shake hands. Your clothing may also be an issue; the Hopi, for example, request that visitors not wear shorts or hats, or use umbrellas. Persistent, intrusive questioning is obviously liable to offend. In Pueblo communities especially, don't ask about religious matters when children are present, as children are only initiated into religious secrets at the appropriate age.

Buying Indian crafts

For many tourists, the quest to buy **Indian crafts** becomes a major focus of their visit to the Southwest. Museums and galleries throughout the region display beautiful Pueblo pots, Navajo rugs, Apache baskets, and silver and turquoise jewellery of all kinds, stimulating a desire for affordable gifts and souvenirs with which stores can barely keep up.

Much of what's widely regarded as traditional Indian craftwork has in fact only developed recently. The collapse of traditional tribal economies coincided with the nineteenth-century arrival of the railroads, and with them the Southwest's first wave of tourists. Enterprising traders encouraged Indians to adapt or learn craft techniques to make souvenirs; as one anthropologist put it, the resultant hybrid was "the Indian's idea of the trader's idea of what the white man thought was Indian design".

To ensure good prices and good quality, you should ideally buy specific Indian crafts as near as possible to where they're made. On the Navajo reservation, head for the **Hubbell Trading Post** (see p.64); on the Hopi reservation, try the **Hopi Cultural Center** and the nearby stores; Acoma, Taos and San Ildefonso pueblos are also good bets. More accessibly, the Indian traders in front of the Palace of the Governors in **Santa Fe** are a reliable source, while that city's summer **Indian Market** is a showcase for the entire region. In addition, the Museum of Northern Arizona in Flagstaff, the Heard museum in Phoenix, and the Millicent Rogers museum in Taos all have excellent stores.

If you want to be sure that whatever you're buying was individually crafted by a Southwestern Indian, you're entitled to ask the vendor for a written certificate of authenticity. Only the phrase "Authentic Indian handmade" has any legal force. "Indian handmade" means that the object was designed and assembled by American Indians; "Indian crafted" means that American Indians had a hand in the process; and words such as "real" and "genuine" mean nothing. The website of the **Indian Arts & Crafts Association** (Ⓦiaca.com) lists recommended crafts workers and retail outlets, plus upcoming events.

Jewellery

Jewellery is perhaps the oldest Southwestern craft of all. The Ancestral Puebloans made necklaces of disks cut from seashells; a single specimen unearthed near Kayenta was 36 feet long and held over fifteen thousand beads. Such necklaces are now known as *heishi* and are the speciality of New Mexico's Santo Domingo Pueblo.

Turquoise has always been prized by Southwestern peoples; the prehistoric city at Chaco Canyon was probably founded on the turquoise trade, while the Navajo see the greenish-blue, semi-precious stone as symbolizing the state of harmony and beauty known as *hozho*. Necklaces of raw and polished turquoise beads are widely available; the stone also adds colour and character to the **silver** jewellery made by the Hopi, Zuni and Navajo in particular.

Silversmithing is a relatively recent tradition, probably introduced from Mexico in the mid-nineteenth century. For many years, acquiring chunky silver bracelets or belts studded with solid-silver conches was the standard Navajo way to accumulate wealth. Such items could be pawned for cash at trading posts and then redeemed when times got easier; now known as pawn jewellery, they count as valuable collectors' pieces. Casual buyers tend to prefer – and to be more able to afford – the more delicate **overlay** style, in which a

stencilled design is cut from a thin sheet of silver, then soldered onto a backing sheet. This technique originated in 1947, when returning Hopi servicemen were trained in the technique, and the Hopi remain its finest exponents. Overlay designs can be seen on earrings, belt buckles, rings and, especially, the clasps of *bola*, or bootlace, ties.

Weaving

The finest **weavers** in the Southwest are generally acknowledged to be the Navajo. In legend, they acquired the craft from Spider Woman, who lives atop Spider Rock in the Canyon de Chelly; in fact, they were probably taught by the Pueblo peoples after the Pueblo Revolt of 1680. That was also when they began to raise sheep, which were introduced by the Spanish a century earlier.

Originally, the Navajo wove blankets and clothing; **Navajo rugs** were the brainchild of nineteenth-century traders, who also suggested that using "earth" colours such as brown would appeal to tourists expecting a "natural" look. Many individual Navajo communities or families weave designs named for their own area, such as Teec Nos Pos, Ganado or Two Gray Hills. As a rule, the patterns have no religious significance, but most include an "escape route" or "spirit line", which runs to the edge of the rug and ensures that the weaver's spirit is not trapped within it. Traditional rugs also have a hole in the centre, as in a spider's web.

Authentic Navajo rugs take months to create and sell for thousands of dollars; anything you see cheaper is probably a mass-produced Mexican imitation. The **Navajo Rug Auction** at Crownpoint in New Mexico (Ⓦcrownpointrugauction.com) is the best opportunity to pick up a genuine bargain.

New Mexico, incidentally, is also home to a separate **Hispanic** weaving tradition, centred especially on **Chimayó** (p.143).

Pottery

Spanish explorers in 1540 spoke of Pueblo women as making "jars of extraordinary labour and workmanship, which were worth seeing". The **ceramic** tradition of northern New Mexico's pueblos remains as strong as ever, having been revitalized in the twentieth century by the San Ildefonso potter **Maria Martínez**. Although she consciously modelled her earlier work on ancient designs, the black-on-black museum pieces for which she became famous are a far cry from the popular conception of Native American crafts. Many tourists prefer either the straightforward pots and jars, painted with rectilinear "pueblo motifs", created at Acoma Pueblo, or the "storyteller" figures, showing a mother surrounded by children, that were first created at Cochiti Pueblo.

Travel essentials

Costs and money

This book contains detailed price information for lodging and eating throughout the Southwest. Accommodation rates (see p.31), exclude any local taxes that may apply, while restaurant prices include food only and not drinks or tip. For museums and similar attractions, the entrance fees quoted are for adults; unless specified otherwise, assume children get in half-price.

North American travellers find **prices** in the Southwest broadly similar to the rest of the US, with food and lodging generally cheaper than in major US cities and tourist regions, and gas and groceries, especially in out-of-the-way places, a little more expensive. Most visitors from Europe and Australasia feel that their money goes further in the US than it does at home. However, if you're used to travelling in the less expensive countries of Europe, let alone in the rest of the world, you can't expect to scrape by on the same minuscule budget in the US.

The only way to reach most places in this book is to drive. If you can't bring your own vehicle, your least avoidable major expense will be **car rental**, costing from around $150 per week (see p.29). What you spend on **accommodation** is more flexible. For most of the year, in most places, you should have no problem getting a motel room for under $80, though even the cheapest peak-season rates in or near certain national parks, or in downtown Santa Fe, are more like $120. Although **hostels** offering dorm beds – usually for $15 to $30 – are reasonably common, they're by no means everywhere, and in any case save little money for two or more travelling together. **Camping** is not only cheap, with park campgrounds ranging from free to perhaps $20 per night, but in many wilderness areas it's the only option.

As for food, $25 per day is enough to get an adequate life-support diet, consisting of perhaps one full-scale diner meal plus a stash of groceries, while for a daily total of around $40 you can eat pretty well. If you're visiting national parks and monuments, buy an annual pass (see p.35); the $80 fee covers all passengers in your vehicle. You'll probably also spend $5 to $15 a day on admissions to state parks, museums and the like.

Sales tax is added to virtually everything you buy in a shop, but isn't included in the marked price. In the states covered in this book it's currently set at around five percent – except on Indian reservations, which do not levy sales tax. Most towns also charge lodging taxes of between five and fifteen percent.

Expect to pay most of your major expenses by **credit** or **debit card**; hotels and car rental agencies usually demand a card imprint as security, even if you intend to settle the bill in cash, and you'll be at a serious disadvantage if you don't have one.

You'll also need to carry a certain amount of **cash**. If you have a Mastercard or Visa, or a cash-dispensing card linked to an international network such as Cirrus or Plus, you can withdraw cash from appropriate automated teller machines (ATMs). **Travellers' cheques** are much less widely used than they used to be, but those issued in US dollars by American Express, Visa and Thomas Cook are universally accepted as cash in shops, restaurants and gas stations, and change from your transactions will be rendered in hard currency.

Crime and personal safety

No one could pretend that America is crime-free, although away from the urban centres crime levels are often remarkably low. All the major tourist areas and the main nightlife zones in cities are invariably brightly lit and well policed. By planning carefully and taking good care of your possessions, you should, generally speaking, have few problems.

When parking in the wilderness, in national or state parks for example, leave your belongings out of sight, and carry any valuables with you.

Electricity

The US **electricity** supply is 110 volts AC. Plugs are standard two-pins – foreign visitors will need an

---

TIPPING

You shouldn't depart a bar or restaurant without leaving a **tip** of at least 15–20 percent (unless the service is utterly disgusting). About the same amount should be added to taxi fares – and round them up to the nearest 50¢ or dollar. Tip hotel porters roughly $1 per item for carrying your baggage to your room. When paying by credit or charge card, you're expected to add the tip to the total bill before filling in the amount and signing.

adapter and voltage converter for their own electrical appliances.

Entry requirements

Under the **visa waiver scheme**, passport-holders from Britain, Ireland, Australia, New Zealand and most European countries do not require visas for trips to the US, so long as they stay less than ninety days and have an onward or return ticket. However, anyone using the visa waiver scheme must apply for **travel authorization** in advance, a quick and straightforward process via ⓦesta.cbp.dhs.gov /esta/. Fail to do so, and you may well be denied entry. Once you have authorization, which costs $14, you can simply fill in the visa waiver form that's handed out on incoming planes. Immigration control takes place at your point of arrival on US soil.

In addition, your passport must be **machine-readable**, with a barcode-style number. All children need to have their own individual passports. Holders of older non-readable passports should either obtain new ones, or apply for visas prior to travel.

Prospective visitors from parts of the world not mentioned above need a valid passport and a non-immigrant visitor's visa. How to obtain a visa depends on what country you're in and your status when you apply, so contact the nearest US embassy or consulate. For full details visit ⓦtravel.state.gov.

Gay and lesbian travellers

Information resources catering to gay and lesbian visitors to, and residents of, the Southwest include ⓦgayarizona.com and ⓦgaytucson.com in Arizona; ⓦgogaynewmexico.com, ⓦnmglbt.org and Albuquerque Pride (ⓦabqpride.com) in New Mexico; and ⓦgayvegas.com and the Gay and Lesbian Community Center of Southern Nevada in Las Vegas (ⓦthecenterlv.org). Note that **same-sex marriage** has been legally recognized throughout the entire US since 2015.

Insurance

Because medical care in the US is expensive, all travellers visiting from overseas should be sure to buy some form of **travel insurance**. American and Canadian citizens should check that they're not already covered by their homeowners, renters or – in some cases – credit card policies. Most Canadians are covered for medical mishaps overseas by their provincial health plans.

Internet

Unless otherwise specified, every hostel, motel and hotel listed in this book offers free **wi-fi access**. Las Vegas, where most casinos charge high access fees, is the exception. Guests usually also have the option of using a computer in the lobby of many hotels. Most cafés also have free wi-fi, but otherwise **public internet access** is not as widely available as you might expect; local and university libraries are your best bet.

Mail

Post offices in the Southwest are usually open Monday to Friday from 9am until 5pm, and Saturday from 9am to noon, and there are blue mailboxes on many street corners. Ordinary mail within the US costs 49 cents for a letter weighing up to an ounce. Airmail between the US and Europe or Australia costs $1.20 for postcards, and generally takes about a week.

Maps

The best general-purpose **road map** for the principal areas covered in this book is the *Indian Country Guide Map*, available free to members of the AAA and sold throughout the Southwest for $4.95. It focuses on the Four Corners region, however, and does not extend into southern Arizona, southern New Mexico or Nevada, and furthermore it's not reliable for dirt roads and backcountry routes. Each individual state also

---

ROUGH GUIDES TRAVEL INSURANCE

Rough Guides has teamed up with WorldNomads.com to offer great travel insurance deals. Policies are available to residents of over 150 countries, with cover for a wide range of adventure sports, 24hr emergency assistance, high levels of medical and evacuation cover and a stream of travel safety information. Roughguides.com users can take advantage of their policies online 24/7, from anywhere in the world – even if you're already travelling. And since plans often change when you're on the road, you can extend your policy and even claim online. Roughguides.com users who buy travel insurance with WorldNomads.com can also leave a positive footprint and donate to a community development project. For more information, go to ⓦroughguides.com/travel-insurance.

issues a free **highway map**, which is fine for general route planning and can be obtained from local visitor centres, which also offer free **town maps**. In addition, Rand McNally (@randmcnally.com) produces good regional and state maps, while Benchmark Maps (@benchmarkmaps.com) publishes large-scale recreational atlases of each state.

All national parks, and most state parks, national forests and the like provide reasonable maps. Both these, and the maps throughout this book, are adequate for day-hikes on the most popular trails. Serious hikers and backpackers, however, should equip themselves with detailed **topographical maps**. Among the best are the waterproof and tearproof national park maps published by National Geographic–Trails Illustrated.

Opening hours and public holidays

On national **public holidays**, shops, banks and offices are liable to be closed all day. The traditional summer season for tourism runs from Memorial Day, in late May, to Labor Day, in early September; some tourist attractions are only open during that period. Normal **banking hours** are from 9am or 10am until 3pm or 4pm Monday to Thursday, and slightly longer on Friday.

Jan 1 New Year's Day
3rd Mon in Jan 15 Martin Luther King Day
3rd Mon in Feb Presidents' Day
Last Mon in May Memorial Day
July 4 Independence Day
1st Mon in Sept Labor Day
2nd Mon in Oct Columbus Day
Nov 11 Veterans' Day
Last Thurs in Nov Thanksgiving Day
Dec 25 Christmas Day

Phones

Foreign visitors can generally assume that their **mobile phones** (cell phones) will work in the US. Check with your phone provider that your payment scheme will cover you, and what charges you may incur. Many providers offer short-term packages that make phone usage on the road more affordable. If you plan to go online via your phone, make sure you know the relevant roaming charges, which can be hugely expensive.

Making an international call from a motel-room phone will almost certainly be very expensive. The cheapest way to communicate is to use **Skype**, or a similar app, to make free wi-fi calls from your phone or laptop. Alternatively, use a prepaid **phone card**; these are widely available from gas stations, supermarkets and other outlets.

Senior travellers

For **older travellers**, the Southwest makes a wonderful vacation destination. So long as you're driving rather than using public transport, everywhere is easily accessible, with motels and hotels of a high standard available almost everywhere. All the national parks hold overlooks and short trails suitable for older travellers.

Anyone over the age of 62 can enjoy certain discounts. Amtrak and Greyhound, for example, offer (smallish) percentage reductions on fares to older passengers. US residents aged 50 or over can join the **American Association of Retired Persons** (@aarp .org), which organizes group travel for senior citizens and can provide discounts on accommodation and vehicle rental. **Road Scholar** (@roadscholar.org) runs educational and activity programmes in the Southwest for persons aged 60 and over. Senior Passes allow free admission to national parks for US citizens or residents aged 62 or older (see p.35).

Spectator sports

The most popular spectator sports in the Southwest are baseball and football. Phoenix is home to renowned pro and college teams.

Study and work programmes

American Institute for Foreign Study @aifs.com. Language study and cultural immersion, as well as au pair and Camp America programmes.
BUNAC @bunac.org. Working holidays in a range of destinations for students, including 8- to 12-week programmes in Western national parks.
Camp America @campamerica.co.uk. Nine-week stints on summer camps in the US.
Crow Canyon Archaeological Center @crowcanyon.org. Week-long residential courses in southwest Colorado, assisting archeologists working on Ancestral Puebloan sites.

Time

New Mexico, Utah, Colorado and Arizona all operate on **Mountain Standard Time**, which is two hours behind Eastern Standard Time, and seven hours behind Greenwich Mean Time, so 2pm in Santa Fe is 4pm in New York City and 9pm in London. Nevada and California are on Pacific Standard Time, another hour behind.

Between the second Sunday in March and the first Sunday in November, New Mexico, Utah, Colorado and Nevada adopt **Daylight Savings Time** and advance their clocks by one hour. Arizona, however, does not, so in summer it joins Nevada in being an hour behind New Mexico and Utah. That said, confusingly, the Navajo Nation in northeast Arizona does shift to Daylight Savings Time, making it one hour later than the rest of Arizona in summer, while the Hopi reservation, entirely surrounded by the Navajo Nation, stays put.

Tourist information

There's no single perfect source for information on the entire Southwest; that's the point of this book, after all. Each state covered here has its own tourist office. In addition, the region includes ten national parks, as well as dozens of federally managed national monuments, national forests and the like, and fifty or so Indian reservations, each of which attempts to meet the needs of visitors in its own way.

Local information

Most towns run their own **visitor centres**, often known as the "Convention and Visitors Bureau", or CVB. In cities such as Las Vegas, Phoenix, Albuquerque and Santa Fe, **free newspapers** carry dining and entertainment listings. In addition, you're likely to come across the useful **Welcome Centers** along the interstates close to the state borders, which dispense maps and information on the entire state.

STATE TOURIST OFFICES

Arizona Office of Tourism Ⓦ visitarizona.com
Colorado Tourism Ⓦ colorado.com
New Mexico Tourism Department Ⓦ newmexico.org
Travel Nevada Ⓦ travelnevada.com
Utah Travel Industry Ⓦ utah.com

SOUTHWEST USA WEBSITES

Websites for regional and local tourism information, activity operators, hotels and accommodation options, parklands and other attractions are listed throughout this book. In addition, the following more general sites may be of interest.

The AmericanSouthwest Ⓦ americansouthwest.net. Fan site devoted to the national parks and wilderness areas of the desert Southwest, featuring great photos, masses of links, and a copious section on slot canyons.
Discover Navajo Ⓦ discovernavajo.com. The official tourism website of the Navajo Nation is packed with useful information for Four Corners travellers.
High Country News Ⓦ hcn.org. Newspaper devoted to environmental issues in the West as a whole, with special reference to national parks and public lands, and a useful online archive.

Las Vegas Review-Journal Ⓦ reviewjournal.com. The online version of Las Vegas's daily newspaper provides national and international news as well as up-to-date listings of what's happening in the city.
National Park Service Ⓦ nps.gov. This invaluable website covers every component of the national park system, with full practical details for the whole gamut of monuments and recreation areas as well as for the parks themselves. For big names, such as the Grand Canyon, the range of information is breathtaking, covering camping, hiking, wildlife and lodging, with links to accommodation options and activity operators in the vicinity.
National Scenic Byways Online Ⓦ byways.org. Sponsored by the Federal Highway Administration, this luscious site honours America's most beautiful driving routes.
Santa Fe Reporter Ⓦ sfreporter.com. This weekly local magazine is an invaluable source for news on New Mexico, as well as current listings.
Sierra Club Ⓦ sierraclub.org. The veteran environmental organization uses its website to promote awareness of issues and events throughout the US, with links to "chapters" in each state for coverage of local activities. The useful "Outdoors" section details not only fully fledged adventure-travel expeditions, but also weekly activities for local volunteers.

Travellers with disabilities

For information on specific states, contact the tourism departments listed above. Useful independent sources of information include SATH (Ⓦ sath.org), Mobility International USA (Ⓦ miusa .org), Disabled World (Ⓦ disabled-world.com) and Tourism Abroad – Disabled Accessibility (Ⓦ ta-da .org.uk). The Access Pass, issued without charge to permanently disabled US citizens, gives free lifetime admission to all national parks.

Travelling with children

The Southwest is primarily an outdoors, wilderness destination. While Las Vegas holds plenty of themed attractions aimed at older kids, and larger cities like Phoenix and Albuquerque have child-friendly museums, exploring the region inevitably entails long days on the road. Although children are likely to be enthralled by the spectacular Western-movie landscapes and the cowboys-and-Indians atmosphere of many frontier towns – and the national parks cater especially well for kids, offering "Junior Ranger" programmes to enthuse and educate younger visitors – parents planning a road trip in the region need to be realistic about quite how much time they'll have to spend in the car. If your kids don't like hours of driving, consider limiting your travels to one specific area. Unless otherwise stated, the museums and attractions listed in this book offer half-price admission for children. Car rental companies, on the other hand, typically charge around $10 per day for kids' car seats.

The Four Corners

FULL MOON OVER MONUMENT VALLEY

1

The Four Corners

The Four Corners region is the heartland of the Southwest, not because the states of Arizona, Utah, Colorado and New Mexico happen to meet here, but because it remains dominated by Native American cultures to an extent that's unique in the modern United States. The region centres on the Colorado Plateau, said to be the highest inhabited plateau in the world, bar Tibet. These dramatic and hauntingly beautiful uplands may have held a larger population a thousand years ago, when the people now known as the Ancestral Puebloans occupied settlements scattered throughout the deserts. Although they're chiefly remembered for their fabulous "cliff dwellings", which cling like eagles' nests to the walls of soaring red-rock canyons, in fact the Ancestral Puebloans lived everywhere, from the valley floors to the mesa-tops.

Around eight centuries ago, the Ancestral Puebloans left the plateau, to be replaced at some point thereafter by the nomadic Navajo. Now around 300,000 strong, the Navajo are the largest single Native American group in the United States, and their reservation occupies the bulk of the Four Corners area. Contrary to popular legend, however, the Ancestral Puebloans did not vanish completely. Some of their descendants still live nearby, in the **Hopi** villages of Arizona and the pueblos of **Zuni** and **Acoma**, across the border in New Mexico. Still more migrated further west, to the valley of the Rio Grande.

The ruins left by the Ancestral Puebloans have become the Four Corners' prime visitor destinations. Among the most significant are those at **Mesa Verde National Park** in southwest Colorado, where dozens of graceful pueblo complexes are tucked into high rocky alcoves, and the fully fledged cities of New Mexico's remote **Chaco Canyon**, where Ancestral Puebloan civilization reached its peak. For sheer beauty, however, **Canyon de Chelly National Monument** in Arizona, where Navajo farmers live alongside the ancient remains, far surpasses both. Elsewhere, the main appeal is the scenery, which ranges from the Western-movie deserts epitomized by **Monument Valley**, via lone outcrops such as **Shiprock**, to the snow-capped peaks of southwest Colorado.

Planning a Four Corners itinerary can be hard work. The major attractions tend to be widely separated, while the towns in between are nothing special. Apart from a handful of expensive motels near Canyon de Chelly and Monument Valley, **accommodation** tends to be concentrated around the fringes. "Edge-of-the-res" towns like Gallup and Farmington may no longer be the alcohol-fuelled hellholes of yesteryear, but they're basically characterless concrete conglomerations, and you'd do better to stay slightly further afield, in places like **Durango**, Colorado, or **Flagstaff**, Arizona (covered in Chapter 5).

CLIFF PALACE, MESA VERDE NATIONAL PARK

Highlights

❶ Hiking to Betatakin Beautiful ranger-led hike to one of the Southwest's most spectacular ancient ruins, in Navajo National Monument. **See p.53**

❷ Monument Valley Where the West was won, in the movies at any rate; nowhere in the world can match it. **See p.55**

❸ The Hopi Mesas These unbelievably remote and isolated desert fastnesses are home to the oldest communities in North America. **See p.56**

❹ White House Trail Everything about the Canyon de Chelly is magnificent, but the one free-access trail down into it is absolutely unmissable. **See p.61**

❺ Mesa Verde Perhaps the most photogenic of all the Southwest's ancient cliff dwellings, tucked into the hillsides of southwest Colorado. **See p.74**

❻ Durango & Silverton Railroad Ride a steam train through the majestic Colorado Rockies to the romantic old mining town of Silverton. **See p.82**

❼ Chaco Canyon North America's largest pre-Columbian city remains remarkably intact, hidden deep in the New Mexican desert. **See p.92**

❽ Acoma Pueblo With the most dramatic setting of any Pueblo community, "Sky City" has occupied a sheer-sided butte for almost a thousand years. **See p.99**

HIGHLIGHTS ARE MARKED ON THE MAP ON PP.48–49

HIGHLIGHTS

1. Hiking to Betatakin
2. Monument Valley
3. The Hopi Mesas
4. White House Trail
5. Mesa Verde
6. Durango & Silverton Railroad
7. Chaco Canyon
8. Acoma Pueblo

CAPITOL
REEF
NATIONAL
PARK

CANYONLANDS
NATIONAL PARK
(NEEDLES DISTRICT)

95

21

Hite

276

U T A H

95

Natural
Bridges
National
Monument

Cannonville

BRYCE
CANYON
NATIONAL
PARK

KODACHROME BASIN
STATE PARK

Bullfrog

95

Grand Staircase Escalante
National Monument

276

261

Valley of
the Gods

Muley
Point

San Juan

Rainbow Bridge
Nat. Mon.

Lake
Powell

163

Mexican
Hat

Kanab

89

Page

Lees Ferry

89A

MONUMENT VALLEY
NAVAJO TRIBAL PARK

2

Mexican
Water

Echo Cliffs

Colorado River

67

NAVAJO
INDIAN
RESERVATION

Navajo
National
Monument

1

564

Kayenta

160

Tsegi

98

BLACK MESA

59

19

GRAND CANYON
NORTH RIM

89

HOPI
INDIAN
RESERVATION

Chinle

Grand
Canyon
Village

Tuba
City

64

Moenkopi

GRAND CANYON
SOUTH RIM

Cameron

264

THIRD MESA

SECOND MESA

FIRST MESA

Oraibi

3

Walpi

Second
Mesa

Keams
Canyon

19

Ganado

Hubbell
Trading Post

Wupatki
National
Monument

99

A R I Z O N A

NAVAJO
INDIAN
RESERVATION

180

89

SAN
FRANCISCO
MTS

Sunset Crater
National
Monument

87

77

Williams

Flagstaff

Walnut
Canyon
National
Monument

40

Winslow

PETRIFIED
FOREST
NATIONAL PARK

89A

17

Sedona

Phoenix

Meteor
Crater

87

Holbrook

1

Northeast Arizona: the Navajo Nation

The **Navajo Indian Reservation** – or, as it prefers to style itself, the **NAVAJO NATION** – is the largest of all Native American reservations. Extending for 27,000 square miles across northeast Arizona, northwest New Mexico, and southern Utah, it's larger than ten of the fifty US states. While the total count of enrolled tribal members is over 300,000, the population of the reservation itself is more like 200,000, of whom two-thirds are under 21 and between a quarter and a half are Christians.

Although tourist facilities on the reservation are minimal – only half a dozen widely scattered towns offer even a single motel – the region holds a trio of top-class attractions. The stunning sandscape of **Monument Valley** presents the definitive image of the Southwest, and is now home to a superb Navajo-run hotel; the beautiful **Canyon de Chelly** cradles both magnificent Ancestral Puebloan remains and traditional Navajo *hogans*; and **Navajo National Monument** preserves further awe-inspiring ancient cliff dwellings.

The Navajo Nation has minimal water resources – the **San Juan River** and **Colorado River** simply skirt its borders to the north and west respectively. Monument Valley in the north and the Painted Desert region in the south technically count as desert, but most of the rest of the terrain is **steppe**, where the land is too poor to grow crops but can just about support livestock. It used to be covered with native grasses, but having evolved in tandem with the Southwest's indigenous fauna, these could not survive being gnawed to the roots by imported animals. The sagebrush that now dominates the region looks appropriately Western to most visitors, but is, like the tumbleweed or Russian thistle, just another interloper.

While a declining proportion of Navajo are now farmers or shepherds, their nomadic origins remain evident. Most Navajo choose not to live in urbanized areas, so what few towns there are on the reservation tend to be ugly modern accretions, consisting of trailer homes gathered around a few dishevelled lots.

Spend a day or two driving across the Navajo Nation, and you'll swiftly sense you're in another land. Whether in diners, stores or on the radio, you're sure to hear spoken Navajo, a language of such complexity that it was adapted during World War II as an uncrackable military code. You're also sure to get a chance to sample the ubiquitous **Navajo taco**, a piece of open-topped fry bread smothered with chile and/or refried beans. Bear in mind, though, that no **alcohol** is available anywhere on the reservation, not even in tourist-oriented restaurants.

Between early April and late October, when the Navajo Nation joins Utah and New Mexico on Daylight Savings Time, it's one hour later than the rest of Arizona, including the Hopi reservation.

For more information on the nation as a whole, check out the official websites ⓦdiscovernavajo.com, ⓦexplorenavajo.com; and ⓦnavajo-nsn.gov.

Brief history

The Navajo, who call themselves the **Diné** ("the People"), are relative newcomers to the Four Corners region. Having drifted down from the far Northwest less than a thousand

---

NAVAJO FAIRS

The ideal time to visit the Navajo Nation is to coincide with one of its various annual fairs. The week-long **Navajo Nation Fair** takes place in Window Rock in early September (ⓦnavajonationfair.com), while the **Eastern Navajo Nation Fair** is in Crownpoint in late July, the **Central Navajo Nation Fair** is held in Chinle in late August, and Tuba City welcomes the **Western Navajo Nation Fair** in mid-October. Largely secular occasions, characterized much like county or state fairs throughout the West by country music, rodeos and other livestock-related events, these also double as pow-wows, and attract Native Americans from far and wide.

years ago, they occupied their present territory within the last four or five centuries. They have always been great assimilators, quick to adapt to new environments and acquire skills from their neighbours. Navajo religion and social organization draw heavily on Pueblo examples, while many "traditional" crafts, now sold in roadside stalls and trading posts, were learned from outsiders and adapted in response to tourist demand. Above all, contemporary Navajo culture was shaped by the acquisition of the horses and sheep brought by the Spanish, which were originally seized in raids on settlements along the Rio Grande.

Tuba City

Though it's the largest community on the western side of the Navajo Nation, there's no great reason to stop at **TUBA CITY** unless you need a place to spend the night. Straddling US-160 ten miles northeast of US-89, just under eighty miles north of Flagstaff and as far east of the Grand Canyon's South Rim, it's also an important crossroads, marking the point where Hwy-164 begins its fifty-mile journey east to the Hopi Mesas (see p.66). If you're feeling weary, incidentally, spare a thought for the Hopi runner reported as having *run* to Flagstaff and back from Tuba City in under 24 hours.

The town's name is a corruption of "Tuuvi", a Hopi from nearby Moenkopi who converted to Mormonism in 1877 and invited a group of Mormon families to settle here. Soon, however, the Mormons were monopolizing the site's precious springs, fed by an aquifer that reaches to Monument Valley. They were forced to move out when the area was added to Navajo lands in 1903.

Tuba City has two unusual claims to fame. The first is a set of petrified **dinosaur tracks**, near the highway five miles southwest of town. These widely spaced 65-million-year-old sandstone imprints were left by a ten-foot creature known as a Dilophosaurus. It's hard to spot the tracks on your own – in truth, they're not all that riveting – but waiting Navajo guides can lead you to them for a small donation. Secondly, Tuba City straddles two separate **time zones**. Most businesses along the highway, such as Basha's supermarket, operate on Mountain Standard Time, while clocks in the town proper, a block or two uphill to the north, are set in summer to Daylight Savings Time, an hour later.

ACCOMMODATION AND EATING   TUBA CITY

Grey Hills Inn US-160 ☎ 928 283 6271. This bare-bones hostel, north of the highway half a mile east of the central intersection, is attached to the high school, and only open during the summer holiday period. Staffed by students training for tourism jobs, it offers utterly plain grey-brick rooms with shared bathrooms. **$50**

Hogan Restaurant 10 N Main St ☎ 928 283 5260. Adjoining the *Quality Inn*, this local family restaurant is the most conventional option in town. The lunch buffet is atrocious, but if you order from the long, inexpensive Mexican-American menu, the food is OK. There's an espresso café alongside. Daily 7am–9pm.

★**Moenkopi Legacy** US-160 ☎ 928 283 4500, ⓦ experiencehopi.com. Tuba City's fanciest hotel by far, at the crossroads that provides access to the Hopi reservation, this impressive hundred-room structure is run by the nearby Hopi community of Moenkopi (and thus operates on Hopi time, an hour earlier than the Navajo time used elsewhere in Tuba City). Beyond its attractive facade,

designed to evoke traditional Pueblo architecture, and the huge lobby adorned with historic photos, the actual rooms could be in any generic high-end motel, but they have whirlpool baths, there are some larger suites, and there's also a decent pool. **$165**

Quality Inn 10 N Main St ☎ 928 283 4545, ⓦ qualityinntubacity.com. Standing alongside the *hogan*-shaped Tuba City Trading Post, a mile north of Tuba City's central intersection, this large, well-maintained motel offers pricey but acceptable rooms, with RV spaces also available. **$123**

Tuuvi Cafe US-160 ☎ 928 283 4374, ⓦ experiencehopi .com. Part of a Hopi-run complex that also includes a gas station, this all-day diner serves all-American egg, ham and pancake breakfasts, followed by $8–10 burgers and sandwiches including Hopi tacos (much the same as Navajo tacos), and a different Hopi stew each day. Daily 6am–9pm.

1

Navajo National Monument

50 miles northeast of Tuba City, 20 miles southwest of Kayenta, reached via a ten-mile spur road that runs north from US-160 • Free • ☎ 928 672 2700, ⓦ nps.gov/nava

Despite its name, **NAVAJO NATIONAL MONUMENT** has little to do with the Navajo. Instead, it's among the most beautiful Ancestral Puebloan sites in the Southwest.

Each of the monument's three separate parcels preserves a long-lost Ancestral Puebloan **cliff dwelling**, a ravishing, centuries-old pueblo of interlocking, adobe-walled homes, plazas and *kivas*. Set in an enormous rocky alcove, **Betatakin** can be admired from an overlook near the visitor centre, or accessed via a half-day, ranger-led hike. The even larger **Keet Seel** is a seventeen-mile round-trip hike from the road, and so is only seen by a dedicated few. Finally, fragile **Inscription House** has been closed to visitors for fifty years.

Brief history

Archeologists divide the Ancestral Puebloans of the Four Corners into three subgroups. One centres on Mesa Verde (see p.74), and another on Chaco Canyon (see p.92), while **Tsegi Canyon**, the focus of Navajo National Monument, is the definitive **Kayenta** site. Though its inhabitants were still living in pithouses long after the people of Chaco and Mesa Verde were constructing sophisticated pueblos, they were fine potters, and Kayenta ceramics are now much-prized museum pieces. Tree-ring dating pinpoints their move into the alcoves of Tsegi Canyon to around 1250 AD. Within fifty years, intensive irrigation had lowered the water table and rendered farming impossible, and the canyon had been abandoned.

What became of the Kayenta people is no mystery; their descendants can clearly be found among the **Hopi**. According to the Navajo, Keet Seel was built by settlers from Navajo Mountain, and Betatakin by a group from Chaco. That dovetails with the Hopi legend that eight of their clans lived here shortly before their migrations ended at the Hopi Mesas, fifty miles south. A pictograph at Betatakin – a bird-like figure within a large white circle – depicts Masaw, the symbol of the Hopi Fire Clan, and Hopis regularly return for ceremonies.

Navajo National Monument was established in 1909, after Navajo guides led members of the Wetherill family of Mesa Verde fame (see p.78) to Keet Seel. Betatakin was "discovered" a year or two later, by chance already within the monument boundaries.

Visitor Centre

10 miles north of US-160, along Hwy-564 • Daily: summer 8am–5.30pm; winter 9am–5pm • Free • ☎ 928 672 2700, ⓦ nps.gov/nava

It takes at least half an hour to drive to the **visitor centre** and back from the main road, and even once you're there you have to hike a mile (round-trip) to see the actual ruins. The visitor centre does holds some interesting displays, including a mock-up of three rooms from Betatakin, and a reconstruction of a Navajo *hogan*. Hwy-564 continues beyond the monument, but is not paved; ordinary vehicles should not drive any further.

The Sandal Trail

If you only have time for a brief visit to Navajo National Monument, all you can do is gaze across the canyon to **Betatakin** from the end of the **Sandal Trail**, an easy, paved, one-mile round-trip hike from the visitor centre. The view from Betatakin Overlook at the end, where a sumptuous orange recess in the canyon wall arches above the 135-room cluster of dwellings, is especially amazing in late afternoon, when direct sunlight penetrates the alcove. Their straight walls rise in tiers from a ledge above the canyon floor; hence the Navajo name Betatakin, or "house on ledges". It's all in such good condition – everything you see is original, except for the ladders and a few of the roof beams – that it's hard to believe the 120 or so inhabitants left not eight years but eight centuries ago.

1

Hiking to Betatakin

Accessible on guided hikes only; late May to early Sept, daily 8.15am & 10am • Free • ☎ 928 672 2700, ⓦ nps.gov/nava

It's worth visiting Navajo National Monument for the long-distance views from the end of the Sandal Trail. However, if you plan ahead, you can enjoy an even more rewarding experience by joining one of the **free ranger-guided hikes** that go all the way to **Betatakin** itself. Numbers are limited, so call a day or two in advance to reserve a place; the 8.15am tour is along a 5-mile route and takes 4–5 hours, while the more demanding 10am tour follows a much steeper 3-mile route and takes 3–4 hours. Remember the time difference if you're hurrying here from beyond the Navajo Nation; the monument is an hour ahead of other Arizona locations, like the Grand Canyon or Flagstaff, during Daylight Savings Time.

All hikers must bring enough food and water (at least half a gallon) for the round-trip. Although you rendezvous for a briefing at the visitor centre, both trails start a mile or two's drive away, dropping steeply into spectacular **Tsegi Canyon** from the top of Skeleton Mesa. Betatakin itself only comes into sight right at the end, as you head up a steadily narrowing side canyon, filled with delicate aspens that turn a gorgeous yellow in the fall. The closer you approach, the more overwhelming the awesome dimensions of the alcove become; it's 452ft high, 370ft wide and 135ft deep. Rangers normally lead visitors right into the ruin itself; you can't enter individual dwellings, but sitting in the plaza of the ancient pueblo is an extraordinarily evocative experience. Its remarkable echo was no doubt exploited to the full in ceremonies.

Keet Seel

Getting all the way to **Keet Seel** – Arizona's largest cliff dwelling – is a major undertaking. The gruelling seventeen-mile, self-guided round-trip **hike**, which branches into Tsegi Canyon off the Betatakin trail, is generally considered too much to attempt in a single day, so most hikers spend the night at the primitive campground near the ruin. There's no drinkable water en route.

All hikers *must* make reservations through the visitor centre, anywhere from one day to five months in advance. The trail is only open in summer, when up to twenty (free) permits per day are issued, on condition that you attend a briefing session, held daily at 8.15am and 3pm. You won't have time to do it as a day-hike unless you attend the briefing the day before.

Visitors to Keet Seel can only enter the ruins with the ranger stationed nearby. The village reaches deep back into the hillside, so well sheltered that its 150-plus rooms have barely deteriorated. No more than half a dozen are *kivas* – the Kayenta were not such relentless builders of these ceremonial chambers as their neighbours at Mesa Verde. Keet Seel was a longer-lasting and more dynamic settlement than Betatakin; its cliff dwellings date from the same era, but people lived in the vicinity from around 950 AD, and migrating groups came and went for the next few hundred years. Little now survives of the large free-standing pueblo that stood on the valley floor not far away.

ACCOMMODATION AND EATING   NAVAJO NATIONAL MONUMENT

Anasazi Inn Tsegi, on US-160, 8 miles northeast of the intersection with Hwy-564 ☎ 928 697 3793. This sprawling, run-down 57-room motel offers the closest accommodation to the monument, but it's still 20 miles from the visitor centre, and is only worth considering as a fallback when everything in Kayenta, another 13 miles northeast, is booked up. Some of the accommodation is in rudimentary trailers with poor plumbing, and there's no wi-fi. Its desert setting is dramatic, though, and it does at least have a small, if unremarkable, restaurant (open noon–2.30pm & 5.30–8pm). $95

★ **Sunset View Campground** Near the visitor centre ☎ 928 672 2700, ⓦ nps.gov/nava. This lovely little campground remains open year-round, and all its first-come first-served sites are free; there are no hook-ups for RVs. In summer, visitors who arrive after the campground is full are accommodated in the more primitive *Canyon View Campground* a mile north. Free

1

Kayenta

KAYENTA, where US-160 meets US-163 twenty miles northeast of Navajo National Monument, is not in any sense an historic town. Having begun life in the 1950s as a dormitory community for workers in the uranium mines to the north, it later became the main base for the miners of Black Mesa. Just twenty miles south of **Monument Valley**, it also caters these days to large numbers of overnight visitors, while remaining little more than a conglomeration of trailer homes, with barely a two-storey building to its name.

ACCOMMODATION AND EATING   KAYENTA

As well as some unenthralling diners and fast-food places, Kayenta is home to three relatively upscale **hotels**, two of which hold restaurants. With Monument Valley so close at hand, room rates are very high; you're unlikely to find anything available if you simply turn up between May and September, so be sure to reserve in advance.

Hampton Inn Kayenta US-160 ☎928 697 3170, ⓦhamptoninn.com. Much the smartest hotel in Kayenta, just west of the central intersection, with 73 comfortable rooms plus an open-air terrace and heated outdoor pool. Rates are way above what you'd pay for the same standard off the reservation, but include a buffet breakfast, and the on-site *Reuben Heflin* restaurant is recommended. **$199**

Kayenta Monument Valley Inn US-160 ☎928 697 3221 or ☎8663063458, ⓦkayentamonumentvalleyinn .com. Large motel complex, facing drivers arriving from Monument Valley immediately south of the US-160/ US-163 intersection. Its 164 rooms are plain but perfectly adequate, and there's a small outdoor pool, heated in low season, and tiny fitness centre. The *Wagon Wheel* restaurant isn't bad. **$219**

Reuben Heflin Hampton Inn Kayenta US-160 ☎928 697 3170. The pick of the motel restaurants, named after its original owner, serving everything from $12 Navajo tacos to $29 steaks, with daily dinner specials like Wednesday's $16 lamb shank, in an appealing environment. Daily: mid-March to mid-Oct 11.30am–10pm; mid-Oct to mid-March 5–9pm.

Wetherill Inn 1000 Main St ☎928 697 3231, ⓦwetherill-inn.com. This standard chain motel, a mile north of the highway intersection towards Monument Valley, offers two storeys of dark but perfectly acceptable rooms at the lowest rates in town, plus an indoor swimming pool. There's no restaurant, but they provide free continental breakfast. **$146**

Monument Valley

1

The classic Wild West landscape of stark sandstone buttes and forbidding pinnacles of rock, poking from an endless expanse of drifting red sands, has become an archetypal image. Only when you arrive at **MONUMENT VALLEY** do you realize how much your perception of the West has in fact been shaped by this one spot. Such scenery does exist elsewhere, but nowhere is it so perfectly concentrated and distilled. While movie-makers have flocked here since the early days of Hollywood, the sheer majesty of the place still takes your breath away. Add the fact that it remains a stronghold of **Navajo** culture, and Monument Valley may well prove to be the absolute highlight of your trip to the Southwest.

Although you can see the buttes for free – whether silhouetted on the skyline from anything up to fifty miles away, or towering alongside US-163 – the four-mile detour to enter **Monument Valley Navajo Tribal Park** rewards with much closer views, while the tours beyond the end of the road are unforgettable.

Brief history

Monument Valley is not really a valley. There's no permanent stream, nor higher ground to either side, and no true valley has buttes along its floor. This whole region was once a flat plain, concealing the top of what are now the tallest "monuments". In the past ten million years, the Monument Uplift – part of the general upthrust of the Colorado Plateau – has pushed that plain up from below, bulging to create cracks that have since eroded to leave only isolated nuggets of harder rock.

On the surface, thanks to annual rainfall of under ten inches, this looks like an unpromising region in which to live. However, sand dunes are surprisingly efficient at conserving moisture, and a huge aquifer deeper down stretches all the way to Tuba City. Beneath the small **cliff dwellings** that burrow into the rocks, the slopes are littered with ancient potsherds; the Ancestral Puebloans were here until around 1300 AD. After that, the area may have remained unoccupied until a band of Navajo retreated here to avoid Kit Carson's round-up in 1864 (see p.60). Their leader, **Hoskinnini**, discovered silver nearby. Two white prospectors sneaked some of the metal away in 1880, but were killed when they returned, at the bases of **Mitchell Mesa** and **Merrick Butte** respectively.

The Navajo, who named Monument Valley *Tse Tbübndisgaün*, or "there is a treeless area amid the rocks", see the whole place as a *hogan*, with its "door" facing east from the visitor centre, and the butte behind *Goulding's Lodge* (see p.58) as its central hearth.

HARD TIMES AT BLACK MESA

Immediately opposite the Navajo National Monument turn-off, a broad but poorly surfaced road sets off south to climb **Black Mesa**. With care, you can nurse an ordinary 2WD vehicle along this route to Chinle, 90 miles east, but very few tourists do in fact venture this way. That spares them the ugly sight of the gaping and highly controversial **strip mines** where for many years the Peabody Western Coal Company extracted the prodigious coal deposits for which the mesa is named.

The notorious **Black Mesa Mine** itself, which supplied coal to the Mohave Power Plant in Laughlin, Nevada, closed down at the end of 2005. In its extraordinarily profligate heyday, the coal was crushed and slurried on its 265-mile, three-day trip around the Grand Canyon by pipeline – a process that used an extravagant 1.3 billion gallons of pure water per year. When springs and water sources, many of which were considered sacred, started to run dry across the Hopi and Navajo reservations, many tribal members called for Peabody's leases to be discontinued, or at least renegotiated. Black Mesa Mine closed not because of local activism, however, but because the Mohave Power Plant could not afford to reduce its sulfur dioxide emissions to meet air pollution standards. Peabody has been fighting in the courts ever since to be allowed to reopen the mine, potentially in conjunction with the still-operational **Kayenta Mine** nearby, but thanks largely to Hopi opposition permission has not been granted.

1

MONUMENT VALLEY TOURS

Taking a **guided tour** in and around Monument Valley is very highly recommended.

Several Navajo-run outfits offer **jeep tours** and **guided hikes** of varying lengths. All can be booked in advance, through the *View Hotel* or *Goulding's Lodge*, or via the operators listed on ⓦ discovernavajo.com; you can also get on a tour by simply asking around the kiosks at the tribal park's parking area. Shop around, as prices can vary enormously for what's essentially the same experience. Broadly speaking, though, jeep tours cost from $75 for 1hr 30min up to $175 for a full day, while hiking tours tend to start from $100.

Horseriding tours generally work out cheaper if you book in advance rather than arranging them with the outfitters waiting in the parking lot. Typical prices, through operators such as Roy Black (☎ 928 429 1959, ⓦ blacksmonumentvalleytours.com), range from $79 for 1hr 30min up to $195 for a full day. In addition, if you drive down to the stables at John Ford's Point on the valley floor, it's often possible to saddle up on the spur of the moment for a good price, and you don't have to pay for the extra riding time to and from the valley proper.

Monument Valley Navajo Tribal Park

Straddling the Arizona-Utah state line, 24 miles north of Kayenta and 25 miles southwest of Mexican Hat • **Parking lot** Daily 24hr • **Visitor centre** Daily: May–Sept 6am–8pm; Oct–April 8am–5pm • $20 per vehicle; National Park passes not accepted • ☎ 435 727 5870, ⓦ navajonationparks.org

The approach road to **MONUMENT VALLEY NAVAJO TRIBAL PARK** ends at a large parking lot, four miles east of US-163, just beyond a booth where the park admission fee is collected. Every new arrival rushes to the walled terrace that lines the parking lot's upper edge, for the first close-up view of the valley's signature buttes.

The most prominent buttes visible from here are the pair known as **The Mittens**, which consist logically enough of the Left or West Mitten and the Right or East Mitten. Rising a thousand feet from the desert floor, each has a distinct "thumb" that splinters off from its bulkier central section. Alongside them stands **Merrick Butte**, completing a trio that's illuminated a glowing red at sunset.

The complex of buildings that sprawls beside the parking lot includes the *View Hotel and Restaurant* (see p.58), and a gift store, as well as the park's **visitor centre**, which holds displays on Navajo culture and history as well as on the valley itself.

The road through the valley

Daily: summer 6am–8pm; winter 8am–4.30pm

A rough, **unpaved road** drops from the western end of the tribal park's parking area, to run through Monument Valley. While taking a guided tour is preferable, the 13-mile loop signposted as the **self-drive** route makes a hugely enjoyable, if bumpy, ride of around an hour and a half in an ordinary vehicle. You're allowed to stop en route to stroll around and take photos, but not to hike for any distance; RVs and motorbikes are not permitted.

At the main halt, **John Ford's Point**, you can swoon at the classic wide-screen valley panorama and also browse a few jewellery stalls. A Navajo man normally poses on horseback at the tip of the nearby promontory, while closer at hand, children in traditional dress invite you to photograph them for a dollar or two. The road goes on to pass near the **Totem Pole** before heading back via **Artist Point** to the visitor centre.

Guided tours follow the same route, but also take visitors "behind the scenes", beyond the main road, and offer a fascinating Navajo perspective. Likely stops on longer tours include the **Sun's Eye** – a high natural arch, with petroglyphs of bighorn sheep at its base – and the similar, even more dramatic **Ear of the Wind**, as well as an obligatory visit to a *hogan* for a weaving demonstration. The most striking **Ancestral Puebloan remains** are in adjacent **Mystery Valley**, which you'll probably only visit if you take a full-day tour.

Wildcat Trail

The one opportunity to hike without a Navajo guide in Monument Valley is along the utterly exhilarating **Wildcat Trail** (allow at least 2hr to complete the full 3.8-mile loop). Branching off from the top of the unpaved road, as it sets off down towards the valley floor from the visitor centre, this takes almost four miles to circle the Left Mitten butte. Although only the brief uphill trudge back to the trailhead at the end is at all physically demanding, the pitiless lack of shade means it's best undertaken early or late in the day, and for that matter early or late in the year as well.

MONUMENT VALLEY AND THE MYTHIC WEST

The real star of my Westerns has always been the land … My favorite location is Monument Valley. It has rivers, mountains, plains, desert, everything that land can offer … I consider this the most complete, beautiful, and peaceful place on earth.   John Ford, *Cosmopolitan*, March 1964

In 1937, Harry Goulding, of *Goulding's Lodge*, heard that Hollywood producers were planning to shoot Western-themed movies in the Southwest. Although Monument Valley had featured in a 1925 silent, *The Vanishing American*, its splendours remained largely unknown. Goulding set off for California with a portfolio of photographs. Within a year, **John Ford** brought a crew to Goulding's remote desert outpost and was filming *Stagecoach*.

From their first moment on screen, Monument Valley's emblematic buttes served as a visual shorthand for the **Wild West**. The geographical reality was irrelevant. While *Stagecoach* supposedly followed a coach through Apache territory from Tonto in southern Arizona to Lordsburg in New Mexico, it did no more than duck in and out of Monument Valley; as John Wayne put it, "there's some things a man just can't run away from." Similarly, in *The Searchers* (1956), Wayne spent five years scouring Texas for Scar's band of Comanche, although in reality both he and they remained within the same five-mile radius of the Mittens. In *My Darling Clementine* (1946), Henry Fonda as Wyatt Earp drove his cattle across Monument Valley and into Tombstone, somehow transplanted from southern Arizona complete with saguaro cactuses; the OK Corral perched on a mesa nearby. Monument Valley consistently symbolized the untamed wilderness that lay beyond the ramshackle towns, beleaguered forts, isolated cabins, or crude fences of the West's earliest white pioneers.

In total, John Ford made seven movies in Monument Valley, including his "cavalry trilogy" of *Fort Apache* (1948), *She Wore A Yellow Ribbon* (1949), and *Rio Grande* (1950). Ford worked closely with the Navajo, who featured as all-purpose Indians, camping out in wigwams in *The Searchers*, for example, at what's now known as John Ford's Point. Medicine man Hosteen Tso, kept on hand to control the weather, is credited with producing a snowstorm and a sandstorm to order for *Stagecoach*. The construction of Monument Valley's first road, in the 1950s, spoiled Ford's hitherto pristine landscape, but he carried on filming here until *Cheyenne Autumn* (1963). He died shortly after announcing plans to make *Appointment at Precedence* in the valley, in 1972.

The spectacle of Henry Fonda's son smoking marijuana in Monument Valley, in *Easy Rider* (1969), may have marked an end to the days of the classic Western, but the valley itself has remained in demand. Clint Eastwood had some perilous moments atop the Totem Pole in *The Eiger Sanction* (1975), and Michael J. Fox's souped-up DeLorean outgunned pursuing Indian warriors in *Back to the Future III* (1989). Other visitors have included Tom Hanks in *Forrest Gump* (1994), while in Mario van Peebles' hip-hop *Western Posse* (1993), Monument Valley was bursting with Sioux Indians, gold mines, railroads and buffalo soldiers.

Monument Valley's starring role as the setting for many **Roadrunner** cartoons probably stems from its appearances in the popular *Krazy Kat* comic strip of the 1920s and 1930s. Learned critics such as e.e. cummings, who referred to the strip's "strictly irrational landscape", and Umberto Eco, who spoke of "surrealistic inventions, especially in the improbable lunar landscapes", were clearly oblivious that artist **George Herriman** was a regular visitor to *Goulding's Lodge*. The adventures of Krazy Kat and Ignatz Mouse – set in Coconino County – were played out against realistic depictions of Monument Valley formations.

1

Assorted plants used by the Navajo are labelled along the way, but the real glory of the trail is the chance to be alone in this overwhelming landscape, dwarfed beneath the mighty rock formations. Stretches of broad, rutted sandy roads are interspersed with narrow, scrubby tracks; keep your eyes peeled to spot the cairns that mark the route.

ACCOMMODATION AND EATING   MONUMENT VALLEY

Goulding's Lodge Two miles west of US-163, across from the park approach road ☎435 727 3231, ⓦgouldings.com. Originally a 1920s trading post, *Goulding's Lodge* incorporates an upscale motel with dramatic, long-range valley views, plus an indoor pool, a general store, a gas station, a museum of movie memorabilia, a campground, and their own programme of valley tours. They also offer assorted newly built larger apartments and studios nearby. It's a good if pricey overnight alternative to *The View* hotel, oozing old-West atmosphere, but there's no reason to go out of your way to visit, or to dine at its *Stagecoach Dining Room*, open for all meals daily. Tents and RVs without hook-ups $29, RV hook-ups $49, doubles $215

★**The View Campground** Monument Valley Tribal Park ☎928 727 5555, ⓦmonumentvalleyview.com. The park campground, a short way down the road that leads from the visitor centre to the valley itself, is now under the same management as the *View* hotel, and has been totally revamped. The tent pitches and RV sites share use of restrooms and showers, while very comfortable stand-alone cabins now line up along the rim, each with one queen bed and two bunk beds, a full bathroom, and its own private deck with full-on valley views. Closed Jan to mid-March. Tents $21, RV spaces $42, cabins $225

★**The View Hotel** Monument Valley Tribal Park ☎928 727 3470, ⓦmonumentvalleyview.com. Each of the luxuriously and tastefully furnished rooms in this stunning Navajo-owned hotel, alongside the park visitor centre, has a private balcony commanding a magnificent panorama of Monument Valley; the best, and most expensive, are on the top, third floor. Casual visitors can enjoy the same view from the adjoining terrace. $236

The View Restaurant Monument Valley Tribal Park ☎928 727 3470, ⓦmonumentvalleyview.com. The only eating option in the tribal park enjoys prime position overlooking the valley, with some irresistible outdoor tables. The food is good but not exceptional, and they make a point of serving authentic Navajo dishes such as mutton stew or pork with red chile posole (both $14) and blue-corn fry bread ($5), alongside more conventional burgers and salads, and Western-style steaks and other meats – there's even Clint Eastwood fried chicken ($16). They also operate a little espresso stand by the main entrance. Daily 7am–2pm & 5pm until late.

From Monument Valley to Canyon de Chelly

The most direct – and most scenic – route between the Navajo Nation's two major tourist attractions, Monument Valley and Canyon de Chelly, is **Arrowhead Hwy-59**. This gorgeous drive heads south off US-160 eight miles east of Kayenta, and then spends almost fifty miles skirting the northern flanks of Black Mesa.

For most of the way, it runs across flat desert grasslands, like a slightly more fertile version of Monument Valley, with cracks in the plains to either side hinting at unfathomable canyons. Occasionally, off to the south, villages such as **Chilchinbito** and **Rough Rock** nestle against the mesa, but the road ignores them. When it finally drops down **Carson Mesa** to reach Chinle Valley, you're confronted by the unlikely waters of **Many Farms Lake**. The road meets US-191 at the community of **Many Rivers**, fourteen miles north of Chinle.

Canyon de Chelly National Monument

2 miles east of Chinle, Arizona; 87 miles southeast of Monument Valley, 85 miles north of the I-40 town of Chambers, Arizona • 24hr access, but to rim drives only, not valley floor • Free • ☎928 674 5500, ⓦnps.gov/cach

A short way east of **Chinle**, twin sandstone walls emerge abruptly from the desert floor, then climb with phenomenal speed to become the thousand-foot cliffs of **CANYON DE CHELLY NATIONAL MONUMENT**. Between these sheer sides, the cottonwood-fringed Chinle Wash meanders through an idyllic oasis of meadows and planted fields. Here and there, a *hogan* stands in a grove of fruit trees, a straggle of sheep is penned in by a crude wooden fence, or ponies drink at the water's edge. And everywhere, perched above the valley on ledges in the canyon walls and dwarfed by the towering cliffs, are the long-abandoned dwellings left by the **Ancestral Puebloans**.

The monument in fact holds two main canyons, which branch apart a few miles upstream: **Canyon de Chelly** to the south and **Canyon del Muerto** to the north. Each twists and turns in all directions, scattered with immense rock monoliths, while several smaller canyons break away. The whole labyrinth threads its way upwards for thirty miles into the Chuska Mountains.

Canyon de Chelly is a magnificent place, easily on a par with any of the Southwest's national parks. Its relative lack of fame owes much to the presence of the **Navajo**, for whom the canyon retains enormous symbolic significance. Although the Navajo did not themselves construct its cliff dwellings, and only arrived on the scene several centuries later, their claims to be descended in some unspecified way from the Ancestral Puebloans have recently been acknowledged by the park service, due more to tactful respect for traditional beliefs than any archeological evidence.

Casual visitors are restricted to peering into the canyon from above, from overlooks along the two "**rim drives**". There's no road in, and apart from one short but superb hike, the **White House Trail**, you can only enter the canyons with a Navajo guide. Incidentally, "de Chelly" is pronounced "de shay"; it's a corruption of the Navajo *tségi*, meaning "rock canyon".

ACCOMMODATION

Best Western Canyon de Chelly	1
Chinle Holiday Inn	2
Cottonwood Campground	3
Sacred Canyon Lodge	4
Spider Rock RV & Campground	5

o Ruin/cave
● Overlook

CANYON DE CHELLY NATIONAL MONUMENT

1

CANYON DE CHELLY TOURS

With the exception of the White House Trail (see opposite), the only way to get a close-up view of Canyon de Chelly's amazing Ancestral Puebloan remains, or to see the rock art that lines its walls, is to take a **guided tour** with a Navajo guide. The best-known operators are listed below, but you can find more extensive listings via the park website, or on ⓦnavajonationparks.org.

JEEP TOURS

Only sturdy 4WD vehicles can negotiate the rutted riverbed and deep sandy drifts inside the Canyon de Chelly. Recommended local tour companies include **Beauty Way Jeep Tours** (☏928 674 3772, ⓦacanyondechellytour.com) and **Canyon de Chelly Tours** (☏928 349 1600, ⓦcanyondechellytours.com). These charge around $75 per person for a 3hr trip, which is enough to get you to and from White House Ruin, and typically set off at 9am, 1pm and 4pm; longer tours, to Spider Rock for example, cost significantly more, and there's normally a surcharge for paying by credit card rather than cash. If you have your own 4WD vehicle, you can hire a Navajo guide to accompany you, for around $20 per hour.

GUIDED HIKES

National Monument Visitor Center ☏928 674 5500, ⓦnps.gov/cach. In season, the National Park Service organizes free, highly recommended Navajo-led group hikes into the canyon. To pick up current details, call in at the visitor centre as soon as you arrive, but be warned that in recent years the trips have become much less frequent, and operate to no fixed schedule.

HORSERIDING TOURS

Tso's Horse Tours Start of South Rim Drive ☏928 674 5678, ⓦtsoshorsetours.com. Evelyn Tso offers horseriding tours into the canyon that cost $15/hr for each person, including the guide – you'll need at least 4hr to get to White House Ruin and back – plus overnight expeditions from $300/person.

Brief history

Ancestral Puebloan Basketmakers first occupied Canyon de Chelly around 200 AD, digging primitive pithouses into the valley floor. Over the next thousand years, their descendants moved first into free-standing "pueblo" apartment-style blocks, and then into elegant cliff dwellings. Virtually all these canyon-wall complexes face south to catch the sun, with cooler storage chambers set in deep recesses. Many now look more inaccessible than they actually were, thanks to rock falls and the erosion of toe- and hand-holds in the soft sandstone. The valley's population peaked at roughly one thousand, shortly before drought drove the Ancestral Puebloans out around 1300 AD.

For the next few centuries, **Hopis** from the west farmed the canyon floor in summer, but no permanent inhabitants returned before the Pueblo Revolt of 1680 (see p.469). As the Spanish reasserted control over New Mexico, the first **Navajo** arrived in the region, quite possibly accompanied by Pueblo refugees. From then on, the Navajo and Spanish were locked in a bloody cycle of armed clashes and slave raids. As the "stronghold of the Navajo", Canyon de Chelly became the target of punitive Spanish expeditions. In 1805, Lieutenant Narbona's party gunned down over a hundred Navajo in the Canyon del Muerto.

After the Yankees took over in Santa Fe, the US Army in turn set about dislodging the Navajo. The process culminated in 1864, when General Carleton's men despatched all the Navajo they could round up on the **"Long Walk"** to Fort Sumner (see p.179). In Canyon de Chelly, **Kit Carson** starved the last Navajo warriors down from the natural Navajo Fortress and destroyed their homes, livestock and beloved peach orchards. Within a few years, however, Congress allowed the Navajo to return from their barbaric imprisonment. To this day, 25 Navajo families still farm the Canyon de Chelly in summer, the land having passed down from mother to daughter from the women between whom it was reapportioned in the 1870s.

Visitor centre

2 miles east of Chinle • Daily 8am–5pm • Free • ☎ 928 674 5500, ⓦ nps.gov/cach

The **visitor centre** for Canyon de Chelly National Monument, an essential first stop to pick up details of current conditions and activities, is located immediately west of the mouth of the canyon itself. Perched on the low mound where Kit Carson signed the "treaty" that ended his siege of the canyon in 1864, it holds useful displays and is the best place to arrange hiking or motorized expeditions.

The rim drives

Each of the monument's two rim drives is equally superb. The dead-end **South Rim Drive** traces the south rim of the Canyon de Chelly, while the **North Rim Drive** follows the north rim of the Canyon del Muerto and then continues off northeast. Each involves a round-trip drive of up to forty miles from the visitor centre, punctuated by overlooks where short walks across the mesa-top lead to views of natural or archeological wonders. Even if you don't stop at every overlook, each drive takes around half a day; for the best **photographs**, tour the North Rim in the morning and the South Rim in the afternoon. Thefts from cars are a major problem, so be careful.

South Rim Drive

The first stop along the South Rim Drive – **Tunnel Overlook**, two miles from the visitor centre – is a trailhead for guided hikes; unaccompanied travellers have no reason to stop. **Tsegi Overlook**, just beyond, stands high above a sweeping curve in the canyon. Though the wash itself is seldom more than a trickle, its broad sandy floor clears a wide gap between the fringe of cottonwoods. Behind the *hogan* near the stream, fields and paddocks reach to the cliffs.

Two miles further, **Junction Overlook** marks the meeting of the two main canyons. Canyon de Chelly narrows off to the right, behind a large monolith, while Canyon del Muerto to the left is much less conspicuous. Two tiny ruins indent the base of the canyon walls opposite.

By **White House Overlook**, six miles from the visitor centre, Canyon de Chelly is 550ft deep, its rim topped by strange whorls of slickrock. Pale and majestic, the cliff that drops on the far side of the wash forms a stupendous backdrop for the photogenic **White House Ruin**. Squeezed into a tiny recess, well above the fields, this cluster of rooms originally stood above a larger pueblo on the valley floor, half of which has now eroded away; it was probably reached by ladders on the roofs of the topmost towers.

From **Sliding House Overlook** – twelve miles along, and reached first by following a spur road off the main road, and then walking across a couple of hundred yards of cairned slickrock – the **Sliding House Ruin** appears to be tucked into the slenderest of crevices in the cliff face. It's now steadily slipping down toward the ploughed Navajo fields below.

South Rim Drive ends fifteen miles from the visitor centre – twenty if you take the detour to Sliding House en route – at the astonishing double monolith of **Spider Rock**, where Monument and Bat canyons split away from Canyon de Chelly. A short walk from the parking area leads to a railed, 200-yard cement path overlooking the abyss; keep going right to the end for the best views. Soaring to within two hundred feet of the canyon rim, the eight-hundred-foot twin pinnacles of rock are said by the Navajo to be home to Spider Woman. She taught them the art of weaving, but also steals misbehaving children; their bleached, gnawed bones lie strewn across the top.

White House Trail

Trailhead at White House Overlook, 6 miles from the visitor centre on South Rim Drive • 2.5-mile round-trip; it takes 30–45min to get down to the ruin, and 1hr to climb up again, so allow at least 2hr

As the sole opportunity for visitors to hike alone into the Canyon de Chelly, the **White House Trail**, which sets off to the right of the viewing area at White House Overlook, is

1

a major highlight of any Southwest itinerary. A beautiful if slightly precarious walk – anyone prone to vertigo will most likely be scared off by the brief sections along ledges chiselled into the rock – it reaches the canyon floor through a tunnel that perfectly frames a Navajo *hogan* and its glowing attendant cottonwood. Thus far the ruin has been hidden from view, but once across the wooden footbridge that spans the wash you can admire it close up, separated only by a fence. Sixty feet above you, the ancient dwelling seems in almost perfect condition, still with the dazzling coat of plaster that gave it its name. Navajo traders nearby sell sodas and trinkets and ensure hikers wander no further than the permitted hundred yards in either direction.

North Rim Drive

Hwy-64, which heads northeast beyond the monument, doubles as the **North Rim Drive**. It runs parallel to, but roughly a mile from, the canyon rim, so there no views from the road itself. Instead, successive spur roads run south to reach the various overlooks.

You'll miss little by skipping the **Ledge Ruin Overlook**, five miles along the North Rim Drive, but both the viewpoints at **Antelope House Overlook**, five miles beyond that and an utterly beautiful spot in its own right, are well worth seeing. They stand five minutes' walk apart, along an unpaved, cairned trail over the slickrock. The first faces across to **Navajo Fortress**, at the tip of the mesa that divides Canyon del Muerto from Black Rock Canyon. It took Kit Carson's besieging forces three months, from December 1863 onwards, to starve down defiant Navajo warriors who reached the summit of this solitary tower of rock using ladders that they drew up behind them.

The other viewpoint looks down on **Antelope House Ruin**, at the base of a huge white overhang in a separate twist of Canyon del Muerto. This site was first occupied in 693 AD, and grew to comprise two square towers to the rear, plus a central plaza that held half a dozen dwellings. It's named after an antelope pictograph painted by the Navajo artist Dibé Yazhi, or Little Sheep, in the 1830s. He was also responsible for the "Spanish Mural" a little further along, which shows a Spanish lieutenant, priest and troops advancing through the canyon. Across the wash, in the **Tomb of the Weaver**, the embalmed body of an old man was found wrapped in golden eagle feathers.

THE NAVAJO HOGAN

The traditional dwelling known as a *hogan* (pronounced *ho-wun*), as seen throughout Canyon de Chelly, is the focus of Navajo life. Each is built as the home for a family, but can also be transformed to become the venue for sacred ceremonies. Few Navajo now live in a *hogan* year-round, but every family owns at least one, and those who still farm and raise sheep in the backcountry often have several.

The earliest *hogans*, first described in the sixteenth century and still widely used until the 1940s, were **"male"** *hogans*. They consisted of three vertical forked sticks propped against each other, aligned to the north, south and west, covered with logs, brush and mud, and with a door that faced east to greet the rising sun.

Virtually all *hogans* today are **"female"**, larger six- or eight-sided structures made of cribbed horizontal cedar logs and once again covered with mud. These became more popular at the end of the nineteenth century, with the advent of steel saws to cut the timber and wagons to haul it; in fact many were made from salvaged railroad ties. The doorway still faces east, with a floor of hard-packed dirt to provide contact with the earth and a smoke hole in the domed roof for access to the sky. Each area of the *hogan* has a particular significance; the south side "belongs" to the women and the north to the men, while the male head of the household sits to the west. Food is prepared and stored on the northeast side; the southwest is the sleeping area.

Since the 1970s, more and more Navajo have chosen to live in trailers rather than face the labour of constantly renewing a *hogan*'s protective mud coating. However, it's also said that as many Navajo now die in hospital, the custom that a dwelling place in which a death has occurred must be abandoned has become less of a deterrent against building elaborate homes.

The next, final spur road off the North Rim Drive splits to reach two separate overlooks, well over a mile apart. To the south, **Mummy Cave Overlook** offers a clear view of the single most striking ruin in the monument – **Mummy Cave Ruin**, which the Navajo call **House Under The Rock**. Inhabited for over a thousand years, it consists of two pueblo complexes deep in the shade of adjacent alcoves, with a prominent **Central Tower** on the spur in between. The sophisticated masonry of the tower has been dated to 1284, so archeologists speculate it was built by migrants from Mesa Verde.

In the "cave" visible from **Massacre Cave Overlook**, to the north, Narbona's expeditionary forces killed more than a hundred Navajo in 1805 (see p.60). It's less of a cave than a pitifully exposed ledge, far above the canyon floor, on which the huddled group were easily picked off by the Spanish, using ricochets off the overhang above. The cement path curves onwards from here to reach another railed overlook, facing down the canyon. Continue over the rocks to the protective wall around the tip of the outcrop, lower down to your right, to see **Yucca Cave Ruin**, which is unusually close to the mesa-top. It's an amazing location, set in a hollow in the rock above a sheer drop, with no conceivable way down to the valley floor, but almost none of the buildings survive.

Hwy-64 continues for another fifteen miles to meet Arrowhead Hwy-12 in little **TSAILE**. The upper floors of Diné College here hold the stimulating **Ned Hatathli Museum** of Navajo history (Mon–Fri 8.30am–4.30pm; free; ☎928 724 6982), which also sells craft items. It's possible to hike into Canyon del Muerto from this end, with a guide hired in Chinle.

ACCOMMODATION AND EATING   CANYON DE CHELLY

Although Canyon de Chelly remains remarkably unspoiled, nearby facilities are overstretched in summer, so it's essential to book **accommodation** well in advance. No **camping** is permitted in the actual canyons. In addition to the **restaurants** in the hotels, there's a handful of fast-food places in Chinle, which is otherwise a brief nondescript straggle on the highway.

HOTELS

Best Western Canyon de Chelly 100 Main St, Chinle ☎928 674 5875 or ☎800 327 0354, ⓦcanyondechelly .com. This low-slung motel, immediately east of the US-191 intersection in Chinle, makes an adequate but somewhat characterless spot to spend the night, and has its own restaurant, the *Junction* (open daily for all meals), as well as a heated indoor pool. $116

Chinle Holiday Inn Route 7, Chinle ☎928 674 5000, ⓦholiday-inn.com/chinle-garcia. Smart, adobe-fied motel, half a mile short of the monument entrance, where the hundred comfortable, well-equipped rooms are often snapped up by tour groups. *Garcia's Restaurant*, the cosy, colourful on-site dining room, serves a breakfast buffet, full lunches (summer Mon–Fri only, winter Tues–Thurs only), and dinner. The food itself is generally unremarkable, with the exception of the $13 roast chicken, and the salad bar is poor, but it's as good as you'll find in Chinle. $133

Sacred Canyon Lodge At the start of South Rim Drive ☎928 674 5841 or ☎800 679 2473, ⓦsacredcanyon lodge.com. The closest accommodation to the canyon, reached by turning right just past the visitor centre. Conventional, clean if somewhat faded motel rooms surround a century-old trading post, which houses a large, reasonably priced self-service cafeteria (daily 6.30am–9pm, shorter hours in winter) that most visitors find interesting only because it's often busy with Navajo from surrounding communities. The consistently boring food is made no better by the prohibition of alcohol. The dining room is festooned with rugs from the giftshop next door. $112

CAMPGROUNDS

Cottonwood Campground At the start of South Rim Drive ☎928 674 2106, ⓦnavajonationparks.org. The first-come first-served *Cottonwood Campground* spreads among the trees beside *Sacred Canyon Lodge*; each of the 93 sites accommodates up to four for no additional fee. There's a five-day maximum stay, but there are no showers, and it's prone to mosquitoes in summer. When the water is cut off, as it often is between November and March, there are no restrooms. No RVs. Cash only. $14

Spider Rock RV & Campground 12 miles along South Rim Drive ☎928 781 2016, ⓦspiderrockcampground .com. This primitive Navajo-owned campground, on private land beside South Rim Drive beyond Sliding House Overlook, offers a chance to escape the crowds. As well as tent and RV sites, it also holds three forked-stick *hogans* that provide welcome shelter in winter especially, and sleep from two to four campers. Canyon tours also available. Cash only. Tents $11, RVs $16, hogans $31

1

Hubbell Trading Post

1 mile west of Ganado, 30 miles west of Window Rock • Daily: mid-May to Sept 8am–6pm; Oct to mid-May 8am–5pm • Free, home tours $2 • ☎ 928 755 3475, ⓦ nps.gov/hutr

After the Navajo returned from New Mexico following the Long Walk, white entrepreneurs set up trading posts at the edge of the reservation, supplying goods from the world beyond in return for craft items such as blankets and jewellery. One such merchant, John Hubbell (1853–1930), established more than thirty trading posts during his long career. His original base, founded in the 1870s, stands near the village of **GANADO**, halfway between Chinle and I-40 to the south, which was named after Chief Ganado Mucho ("Won a lot"), a signatory of the 1868 treaty that ended the Navajo's imprisonment at Fort Sumner.

Set beside the Pueblo Colorado Wash, at the end of a tree-lined avenue, the **Hubbell Trading Post** is now a fascinating living museum, which still operates as a traditional trading post. Beyond the main general store, where the groceries on sale are pretty historic in themselves, further rooms hold expensive and exquisite rugs, silverwork and *kachinas*, while in the separate visitor centre you can watch Navajo weavers at work and learn all about the history of the place. Regular tours explore the fascinating Hubbell family home, behind the store.

To the east, Hwy-264 climbs onto the thickly wooded Defiance Plateau and heads for Window Rock, while US-191 undulates for forty miles due south, through more forests, to Chambers on I-40.

Window Rock

The capital of the Navajo Nation, **WINDOW ROCK** sits on the Arizona–New Mexico border 25 miles northwest of Gallup. An administrative headquarters rather than a lively town, it only became the capital in the 1930s. Technically, if you simply pass through on Hwy-264 like most casual visitors, you're not in Window Rock at all; you also won't see the rock itself.

Both "town" and rock are a mile or two north on Arrowhead Hwy-12. The **Window Rock**, an impressive, almost circular hole in a golden sandstone cliff, used to surmount a spring where water was collected for the Water Way ceremony. With the spring now dry, it's the focus of a picnic area, where a statue of a crouching Navajo soldier, complete with walkie-talkie, commemorates the work of the Code Talkers during World War II. Nearby, the **Navajo Tribal Council** meets at least four times yearly in the octagonal **Council Chamber**.

Window Rock also hosts the annual week-long **Navajo Nation Fair** (ⓦ navajonationfair .com), in early September.

Navajo Nation Museum and zoo

Hwy-264 • **Museum** Summer Mon 8am–5pm, Tues–Fri 8am–6pm, Sat 9am–5pm; winter Mon–Fri 8am–5pm • Donation • ☎ 928 871 7941, ⓦ navajonationmuseum.org • **Zoo** Mon–Sat 10am–4.30pm • Free • ☎ 928 871 6574, ⓦ navajozoo.org

Located on Hwy-264, the large **Navajo Nation Museum** is a good spot to pick up tourist information and ask questions. Surprisingly, it doesn't hold permanent displays covering Navajo history and culture, but there are often interesting temporary exhibitions.

Tucked among the rocky outcrops across the parking lot, a small **zoo** holds specimens of local wildlife. All were rescued at a time when they would not otherwise have survived; they include a bald eagle and a growling cougar that endlessly eyes the neighbouring elk. The captions are in Navajo, so visits double as language lessons.

Navajoland Inn & Suites 392 W Hwy-264, St Michaels ☎ 928 871 5690, ⓦ navajolandsuites.com. Smart motel, on the brow of a hill two miles west of Window Rock, with spacious rooms, wi-fi and a good-sized indoor pool. $76
Quality Inn Navajo Nation Capital 48 W Hwy-264 ☎ 928 871 4108, ⓦ qualityinnwindowrock.com. The good-value rooms in this showpiece motel tend to be

reserved long in advance in summer. Much of the Navajo's day-to-day business is conducted in its *Diné* restaurant, open for all meals daily, where Navajo tacos or mutton stew cost around $10. Ask for details of their local tours, tailored to incorporate pretty much anything you're interested in doing. $89

The Hopi Indian Reservation

A remote desert enclave, dwarfed and entirely surrounded by the huge Navajo reservation, the **HOPI INDIAN RESERVATION** extends across 1.5 million acres in northeast Arizona. Its ten thousand inhabitants live in twelve villages, set atop the **Hopi mesas** roughly fifty miles north of I-40, fifty miles east of Tuba City, and ninety miles southwest of Canyon de Chelly. All can be accessed along a 25-mile stretch of

HOPI RELIGION: THE KACHINAS

The Hopi do not feel the urge, let alone the obligation, to divulge details of their **religious beliefs** and practices to outsiders. While anthropologists and missionaries have gleaned what they can, well-known accounts of Hopi spirituality, such as Frank Waters' *Book of the Hopi*, are based on the reports of informants not initiated into its innermost secrets. Inevitably, Hopi spirituality has been repeatedly misrepresented, whether as barbarous devil worship or New Age guff.

There is in any case no single Hopi religion; ceremonials vary from clan to clan and village to village. The basic common element is the role of the *kachina* (often spelled *katsina*, with the plural *katsinum*). These "spirit messengers", which may represent the spirits of the dead, live in the San Francisco peaks north of Flagstaff, and return to the mesas in the form of rain-bearing clouds.

There are over three hundred different *kachinas*. At one time, they visited the mesas in person; now they come in the form of masked dancers. Not every village follows the same **ceremonial calendar**, but in general the *kachinas* arrive in early February for the *Powamuya* ceremony, or **Bean Dance**. Each matriarch receives fresh bean sprouts to plant for the coming year, and the *so'so'yoktu* ogres that threaten to eat disobedient (*ka-hopi*) children are placated by gifts of food. The *kachinas* continue to visit throughout the growing season, then return home after the *Niman* ceremony or **Home Dance** in July.

The Hopi do not worship the *kachinas*; they are primarily teaching tools for children. A Hopi baby receives a *tihu* – what outsiders call a **kachina doll** – at its first *Niman* ceremony, and the girls receive further dolls at each *Powamuya* and *Niman* ceremony thereafter. Most boys and girls alike are initiated into a **kachina society** at around the age of 10.

All the Southwestern pueblos had some form of *kachina* cult, a belief system that is thought to have developed in **Mexico**, and to have spread north to the Hopi mesas and Zuni Pueblo around 1300 AD, arriving via the **Mimbres** culture to the south. It then moved east to the Rio Grande, where it was subsequently almost entirely stamped out by the Spanish colonists.

The role and iconography of specific Hopi *kachinas* strongly echo **Aztec** deities such as **Tlaloc**, the god of rain, and **Quetzalcoatl**, the plumed serpent who also brought rain and corn. For the Aztec preoccupation with death, blood and human sacrifice, however, the Hopi and other Southwestern peoples substituted an obsessive focus on **rain**.

ATTENDING HOPI CEREMONIES

The Hopi used to promote their ceremonies as tourist attractions. Even after cameras were banned in 1916, the **Snake Dance**, when members of the Snake clan dance with live snakes between their teeth, would draw as many as 2500 observers. These days, however, the Hopi **exclude** non-Indians. Second Mesa closed all its ceremonies to outsiders by 1989, and was joined by all the First Mesa villages in 1992 after a *Marvel* comic characterized the *kachinas* as violent avengers.

Hwy-264, where three distinct spurs, numbered from east to west as **First**, **Second** and **Third** mesas, poke from the southern flanks of **Black Mesa**.

The Hopi trace their ancestry back well over a thousand years, to the **Ancestral Puebloan** people who formerly dominated the entire Four Corners region. What's more, they have occupied this same spot for at least eight hundred years. To outsiders, it's not immediately obvious why, with the whole Southwest to pick from, they chose to live on these barren and unprepossessing fingers of rock. The answer lies within Black Mesa itself: although it has no perennial streams, its subterranean rocks are tilted at just the correct angle to deliver a tiny but dependable trickle of water to the Hopi settlements, while the "black" in its name comes from the coal that gives the Hopi limitless reserves of fuel. In addition, the Hopi used to farm and hunt across a much wider area, only to be restricted to their mesa-top villages by the steady encroachment of their Navajo neighbours. Although the Hopi are celebrated for their skill at **"dry farming"**, preserving enough precious liquid to grow corn, beans and squash on hand-tilled terraces laid out beneath the villages, this precarious way of life was forced upon them.

The Hopi **language**, Hopic, belongs to the Uto-Aztecan group of languages, and different dialects are spoken on each mesa. Although it bears similarities to Ute and

---

While spectators are now unlikely to be allowed at any *kachina* dances, some **social dances**, held between August and January when the *kachinas* are away from the mesas, may still be "open". Held in the village plazas, these usually take place at the weekend. Specific timings tend not to be announced until a few days in advance; for information, ask at the Cultural Center (see p.69) or call ☎ 928 734 2401. If you do get the chance to attend a ceremony, wear clothing that fully covers your body, keep your distance, and do not photograph sketch or question either dancers or audience.

KACHINA DOLLS

Kachina **masks**, as worn by ceremonial dancers, are sacred objects. The Hopi have successfully petitioned to remove them from museum displays, and raised an international outcry when masks were sold in a much-publicized auction in Paris in 2015. However, a "*kachina* doll" or *tihu* (the plural is *ti'tihu*) is simply an instructional tool, and can therefore be sold to outsiders as a collector's item.

The *ti'tihu* given to Hopi children were originally flat dolls to be hung within the home. Made from white kaolin clay, the basic shape was painted to show a head, plus a pair of arms folded over a kilt that represented rain. Trading posts stocked these simple dolls in the 1890s, and by 1900 they were being made specifically for sale.

Since then, they have become much more complex in form and colour, and acquired feet. Most are carved from cottonwood roots; the carving is seen as a prayer for water, symbolizing the roots' own search for water. Thanks to the art market's desire for signed pieces, the artists themselves are no longer anonymous. Strictly speaking, only men should carve *ti'tihu*, but some women make them now as well.

Not all *ti'tihu* represent *kachinas*. Some depict the **clowns** who also appear during ceremonies, such as the black-and-white-striped *koshares*, and the knobbed "mudheads" or *koyemsi*. Just as the clowns may devise costumes to mock tourists, for example, certain *ti'tihu* caricature figures like basketball players or anthropologists.

The Hopi do, however, draw the line at attempts by others to cash in on the commercial success of the *kachina*-doll business, though the tribal council has been unable to copyright the word "*kachina*" to stop Navajo and other non-Indian copyists using the name. Genuine hand-carved dolls are both exquisite and expensive, and a top-class carver will produce fewer than fifty per year, while fake *kachinas* are mass-produced in New Mexico. Good places to buy a *kachina* doll include the Hopi Cultural Center on Second Mesa, the Museum of Northern Arizona in Flagstaff, and Albuquerque's Indian Pueblo Cultural Center, though it's hard to find a reasonable-sized piece for under $300. Prices on the reservation itself tend to be cheaper; carvers show their work to visitors on tours of Walpi or at the entrance to Oraibi, and there are also several crafts stores, including Tsakurshovi, at milepost 381 on Hwy-284 on Second Mesa (☎ 928 734 2478) and the Monongya Gallery at Oraibi (☎ 928 734 2344).

1

Paiute, the Hopi have little in common with either tribe. Their culture and beliefs are instead closely related to those of the Pueblo peoples of New Mexico. The Hopi are a matriarchal society, with homes, land and clan affiliation passing down the female line. They are not a united people; each village is an independent entity, and only four currently recognize the Hopi Tribal Council.

By their very survival, and the persistence of their ancient beliefs and ceremonies, the Hopi have long fascinated outsiders. Visitors are welcomed, but the Hopi have no desire to turn themselves into a tourist attraction. A motel makes it possible to stay on the reservation, and stores and galleries sell prized **crafts** such as pottery, basketwork, silver overlay jewellery and hand-carved **kachina dolls**. However, tourists who arrive in the hope of extensive sightseeing – let alone spiritual revelations – are likely to leave disappointed, and quite possibly dismayed by what they perceive as conspicuous poverty.

Since 1986, when increased mining revenues finally placed the tribal economy on a relatively secure footing, non-Indians have been barred from almost all Hopi ceremonies. These days, the easiest way for visitors to get a sense of traditional life is to join a guided tour of either the magnificently situated village of **Walpi** on First Mesa, or **Sipaulovi** on Second Mesa.

Touring the Hopi mesas

Each of the mesa-top Hopi villages centres around a **plaza**, where successive generations have built new houses on top of the old ones as they crumble into sand. Often the main entrance is via the roof, itself reached by a wooden ladder. Though some buildings are now constructed of grey concrete blocks, they still blend almost imperceptibly into the ruins that trail away down the slopes. Several villages stand on open seams of coal, and large chunks of coal lie scattered around. Outhouses are dotted across the hillsides; all waste was traditionally thrown over the edge of the mesa to tumble down and fertilize the terraces, a policy that works less well now that refrigerators and old bedsteads are thrown over too.

As you tour the reservation, signs beside the highway point out shops and stalls selling Hopi handicrafts. At some point down any side road you choose to follow, as you approach a village, a large notice will forbid you to drive any further, but may allow you to walk within a specified area.

First Mesa

Walpi tours daily: summer 8am–4.30pm, last tour 3pm; winter 9am–3pm, last tour 2pm · $20 · ☎ 928 737 2670, ⊕ experiencehopi.com

First Mesa, 75 miles southwest of the Canyon de Chelly, is home to the most impressive of the two Hopi villages that offer guided tours. To reach **WALPI**, take Hwy-264 to modern **POLACCA**, at the foot of the mesa, and follow signs to the **First Mesa Consolidated Village Office**, where you register for a guided tour. You can then drive a mile up the twisting paved road until it ends in **SICHOMOVI**. Although you can't tell where one village stops and the next begins, you've just passed through **HANO**. Its inhabitants arrived during the Pueblo Revolt to offer their services as the defenders of First Mesa, and still speak the Tewa language.

Tours set off from Sichomovi at regular intervals, and consist of an hour-long walk to and around Walpi. Although this spot has been occupied since around 900 AD, Walpi as it appears today is by Hopi standards not that old; it was hastily thrown together in the aftermath of the Pueblo Revolt of 1680, as a more secure site in the face of possible Spanish or Navajo attack. Its location is absolutely stunning, standing alone at the narrow southernmost tip of the mesa, and connected to the other First Mesa villages by the merest slender neck of stone, with a drop of three hundred feet to either side.

Walpi lacks electricity or running water, and has since 2011 no longer held any permanent inhabitants. Villagers do however come up each day to sell crafts, and return to their family homes here for special events. Depending on the season, you may be in a group of twenty or so, or on your own, but either way there's plenty of opportunity to ask questions and to buy pottery, *kachina* dolls, and fresh-baked *piiki*, a flatbread made with blue cornflour.

Second Mesa
Second Mesa, most easily reached by driving sixty miles north of I-40 on Hwy-67, holds three separate villages – Shungopavi, Mishongnovi and Sipaulovi. As on First Mesa, the original Hopi settlements here stood alongside springs that seeped from the foot of the mesa, and were relocated to the mesa-top after the Pueblo Revolt. Unlike on First Mesa, however, Hwy-264 climbs onto and crosses the mesa itself here, so the villages no longer seem nearly so isolated.

Hopi Cultural Center
Hwy-264, 4 miles northwest of intersection with Hwy-67 • **Museum** Summer Mon–Fri 8am–5pm, Sat & Sun 9am–3pm; winter Mon–Fri 8am–5pm • $3 • ☎ 928 734 2401, ⓦ hopiculturalcenter.com

The roadside **Hopi Cultural Center** on Second Mesa makes an obvious first stop for visitors to the Hopi reservation. As well as holding a motel and restaurant (see p.70), it serves as a gift store and information centre. If tours of the mesa-top village of **SIPAULOVI** are currently operating, or any forthcoming events are open to tourists, the friendly staff should be able to tell you about them.

The adjoining **museum** is absolutely fascinating, incorporating wall-sized blow-ups of century-old photos of Hopi ceremonies, and displaying all sorts of historic documents and press cuttings. Visitors are not allowed to take photos or even write notes, however. Several small **galleries** in the same complex sell Hopi arts and crafts.

Third Mesa
Fifty miles southeast of Tuba City (see p.51), **Third Mesa** is remarkable as the home of the village of **ORAIBI**, which is regarded as the oldest Hopi settlement of all. No scheduled tours can guide you around, but there's usually a cluster of carvers and craftspeople waiting at the edge of the village who can give permission for you to explore on foot. You're not allowed to walk to the very edge of the mesa, where conspicuous ruins date back as much as a thousand years.

ARRIVAL AND DEPARTURE   THE HOPI INDIAN RESERVATION

By car Both roads from the I-40 interstate up to the Hopi mesas, Hwy-87 from Winslow and Hwy-77 from Holbrook, run through a superbly desolate butte-studded segment of the Navajo reservation, on the western fringes of the Painted Desert. If you're coming from the Grand Canyon, take Hwy-264 east from US-160. Once beyond the Hopi outpost of Moenkopi, just outside Tuba City (see p.51), this traverses rugged canyonlands before climbing onto Third Mesa after fifty miles.

TOURS

Guides Joining a Hopi guide for your own private tour will show you far more of the reservation than you can see alone. Guides like Gary Tso of the Left-Handed Tour Co (☎ 928 734 2567, ✉ lhhunter68@hopitelecom .net), sculptor Evelyn Fredericks (☎ 928 255 2112, ⓦ evelynfredericks.com), and Micah Loma'omvaya of Hopi Tours (☎ 928 205 1634, ⓦ hopitours.com) take visitors around Oraibi and to little-known petroglyph sites, as well as to craftspeople and galleries. Rates depend on how many of you there are; with just two, expect to pay from $75/person for a 3hr tour, up to $195/person for a full day. If you prefer to make your own way around, visit the ⓦ hopiartstrail.com website for details of galleries and craftspeople throughout the reservation.

ACCOMMODATION AND EATING

The *Hopi Cultural Center Motel* is the only accommodation option on the reservation itself, but the Hopi also run the larger, more luxurious and more accessible *Moenkopi Legacy* hotel in **Tuba City** (see p.51). **Winslow**, on I-40 sixty miles south of Second Mesa, also makes a good base, and is home to the wonderful *La Posada* hotel (see p.263).

1

Hopi Cultural Center Motel Second Mesa ☎ 928 734 2401, ⓦ hopiculturalcenter.com. Built in a faux-Pueblo architectural style, this motel offers 34 plain but acceptable rooms that are usually booked solid well in advance in summer. The cafeteria serves good, substantial meals, including local delicacy *noqkwivi*, lamb stewed with hominy ($11), and very tasty blue-corn fry bread, but be warned that there's precious little to do between the time it closes, at 9pm (8pm in winter), and 7am the next morning, when you can indulge your curiosity by having blue cornflakes for breakfast. $105

Southwest Colorado

In ancient times, of course, the straight-line boundaries that divide the states of Arizona, New Mexico, Utah and Colorado – and mark the northeastern limits of the Navajo Nation – did not exist. As a result, although Colorado might not spring to mind as a "Southwestern" state, its far southwest corner holds some fascinating archeological sites. **Mesa Verde National Park** is absolutely unmissable, while the ancient ruins in **Ute Mountain Tribal Park**, which lies well off the beaten track and can only be accessed with a Ute guide, offer adventurous travellers an even more exhilarating sense of discovery.

Once you've crossed the border into Colorado, it's hard to resist the lure of the Rockies, looming along the skyline to the north. There's no scope in this book to do more than sketch out a brief tour, looping up the **San Juan Skyway** from vibrant **Durango** to historic mining towns such as **Silverton** and **Ouray**, and back south again by way of lively **Telluride**.

Four Corners Monument Navajo Tribal Park

Daily: April to late May and early Sept to Oct 8am–7pm; late May to early Sept 8am–8pm; Nov–March 8am–5pm • $5 per person • ☎ 928 206 2540, ⓦ navajonationparks.org

The **Four Corners Monument Navajo Tribal Park**, reached by a short spur road half a mile northeast of US-160, is the only place in the United States where four states meet at a single point. Despite news reports from 2009 onwards that it may have been sited in the wrong place, it was the erection of the monument itself that fixed the legal boundary, so by definition it cannot be wrong.

In any case, however exciting you may find the concept, the reality is bleak and dull. A steady stream of visitors mooch around the pivotal brass plaque, ponderously contorting a limb into each state for demeaning photographs. Navajo stalls on all sides sell crafts, T-shirts and fry bread.

Ute Mountain Ute Reservation

For a couple of centuries after **Ute Indians** acquired horses from the Spanish, their hunting territory extended east from Utah as far as Nebraska. As miners pushed the Victorian-era frontier westwards, however, the Ute were confined to poorer land. The creation of reservations split them into three separate groups: the **Northern Utes**, who now live in the mountains near Utah's border with Wyoming; the **Southern Utes**, who occupy a strip of southern Colorado south of Durango; and the **Ute Mountain Utes**.

The two-thousand-strong band of Ute Mountain Utes take their name from a long, low mountain ridge in Colorado's far southwestern corner, known to outsiders as **Sleeping Ute Mountain** because of its uncanny resemblance, when seen from the east, to a slumbering warrior. Also known as the Weeminuche, they long ranked among the Southwest's poorest peoples, and draw their income these days from mineral leases and a large **casino** near the main settlement of **Towaoc**.

Although the road through Mesa Verde National Park passes through a tiny corner of the Ute Mountain Ute reservation, only visitors who take a guided tour of the remote, dramatic Ancestral Puebloan ruins in the entirely separate **Ute Mountain Tribal Park** are likely to have any contact with the Utes themselves.

Ute Mountain Tribal Park

Guided tours leave from the visitor centre • April–Oct only, usually 9am daily, but schedules vary with demand; in season you can usually join a tour if you turn up at 8.30am, but it's much safer to reserve in advance • Full-day tours, using your own vehicle, cost $60/person and get you back to the highway around 5pm, half-day tours cost $35 and finish by 1pm; riding in the guide's van costs an extra $12 • ☎ 970 565 9653 or ☎ 970 749 1452, ⊛ utemountainute.com, ⊛ utemountaincasino.com & ⊛ mesaverdecountry.com

The inaccessible but utterly enthralling **Ute Mountain Tribal Park**, which abuts Mesa Verde National Park, preserves an equally extraordinary but far less visited assortment of ancient **Ancestral Puebloan** – not Ute – remains, which can only be seen on Ute-guided tours.

If you don't have the time to take a full-day tour, the half-day tour makes a very poor alternative. On the half-day trip, you simply leave the group at the end of the morning, having seen a couple of potsherd-scattered mounds, concealing ancient surface-level pueblos, at the foot of the cliffs. On the full-day tour, you continue along a remote and circuitous dirt road to the top of the mesa, and then inch down ladders onto a three-mile ledge skirting **Lion Canyon**. This leads to three beautifully preserved **cliff dwellings**, built at the same time as those on Mesa Verde: Tree House Ruin, the eighty-room Lion House, and the precarious Eagle's Nest, perched in a colossal natural alcove. The whole expedition demands a fair amount of walking and something of a head for heights, but only the final ascent to Eagle's Nest is difficult for vertigo sufferers – you can admire it from below if you prefer.

Visitors are expected to drive their own sturdy vehicles on the tour and to bring food and drink. However, the tour leader's van accommodates half a dozen passengers; if there's room, you can pay extra to ride along, and thus get much more informed commentary on what you're seeing. It's also possible to arrange trips to more remote areas of the park, which involve significantly more **hiking**; groups must consist of four or more members, each of whom pays $75.

INFORMATION

Visitor centre The tribe's visitor centre-cum-museum is housed in a former gas station where US-160 meets US-491, 20 miles up from the Four Corners Monument

UTE MOUNTAIN UTE RESERVATION

(April–Oct daily 8am–3pm, but hours subject to fluctuation; ☎ 970 749 1452).

ACCOMMODATION AND EATING

Ute Mountain Casino Towaoc, on US-491 12 miles south of Cortez, 8 miles north of visitor centre ☎ 970 565 8837 or ☎ 888 565 8837, ⊛ utemountaincasino .com. While there's nothing appealing about the smoke-filled casino itself, the hotel rooms are large, clean and good value compared to Cortez; they also have a cheap restaurant, open for all meals, and, between April & Oct, camping space. Tents $̲1̲7̲, RVs $̲3̲3̲, doubles $̲5̲5̲

Ute Mountain Tribal Park Campground Near intersection of US-160 and US-491 ☎ 970 565 9653 or ☎ 800 847 5485, ⊛ utemountainute.com. This primitive campground, just off the main highway, is entirely devoid of facilities, apart from basic cabins and tent sites, but is handy for the park tours and feels deliciously remote at night. Cabins $̲1̲0̲, tents $̲1̲2̲

Hovenweep National Monument

Hidden in the fifty-mile-wide swathe of no man's land that straddles the Utah-Colorado border, the Ancestral Puebloan ruins at **HOVENWEEP NATIONAL MONUMENT** lack the scale and setting of the Mesa Verde cliff dwellings or similar Four Corners sites. Instead, sprouting from the rims of shallow desert canyons and dwarfed by the distant mountains, they offer a haunting sense of timeless isolation. They also have one unique feature: the tall **towers** that many archeologists regard as astronomical observatories.

The monument includes five abandoned villages – its name comes from a Ute word meaning "deserted valley" – a few miles apart, in four distinct parcels. Easy year-round access is restricted to one section, the **Square Tower Unit**; ask at the visitor centre which

1

if any of the remainder are accessible at the time you visit, which will depend on current road conditions, and whether you have a 4WD vehicle.

Square Tower Unit

Trail open daily sunrise–sunset • No entrance fee

A shallow, barely noticeable cleft in the desert expanse, **Little Ruin Canyon** lies immediately behind Hovenweep's smart **visitor centre**. It's no longer possible to walk among or into the structures ranged above and below its rim, which are known collectively as the **Square Tower Unit**; instead, a single trail loops around the edge, keeping visitors at a safe distance.

A complete circuit of the trail takes just under an hour. After meeting the canyon near the fortress-like **Stronghold House**, the trail heads right, past the prosaically named **Unit-type House**, where niches in the walls appear to line up with the angle of the sun at the summer and winter solstices. **Hovenweep Castle**, a four-square building five minutes' walk farther on at the head of the canyon, was constructed around 1200 AD. It may have stood guard over a much larger pueblo complex that nestled on the sandy canyon floor a mere thirty feet below, clustered around the perennial spring that was the site's only source of water. Of that whole complex, only **Square Tower Ruin** can still be discerned, while up above Hovenweep Castle has endured, a perfect illustration of the biblical admonition that only a house built on rock shall stand. It takes another ten minutes to reach the final significant ruin, the **Twin Towers**. Doubling back on yourself at that point, rather than completing the loop, will spare you the final steep dip and climb through the middle of the canyon, but saves no time overall.

ARRIVAL AND INFORMATION

HOVENWEEP NATIONAL MONUMENT

By car Whatever most tourist maps may suggest, all the roads to Hovenweep are paved, thanks largely to companies drilling for oil and gas around Aneth. The monument is best reached by driving 35 miles due west from Cortez along County Road G, which leaves US-160 near the airstrip at the south end of town; 25 miles east from US-191 via Hwy-262, which branches off halfway between Bluff and Blanding in Utah; or 25 miles southwest from Pleasant View in Colorado through Canyons of the Ancients National Monument.

Visitor centre Located at Little Ruin Canyon (daily: April & Oct 8am–5pm; May–Sept 8am–6pm; Nov–March 9am–5pm; ☎ 970 562 4282, ⓦ nps.gov/hove).

ACCOMMODATION

Hovenweep Campground Little Ruin Canyon ☎ 970 562 4282, ⓦ nps.gov/hove. While no accommodation, gas or food is available at or anywhere near Hovenweep, this first-come, first-served 31-site campground, close to the visitor centre, remains open all year. It has a few RV spaces, but no hook-ups. Running water is available in summer only. No reservations, cash only. $10

Cortez

The town of **CORTEZ**, twenty miles north of the point where US-160 meets US-491, consists of little more than a long curve of over-developed highway. Were it not so close to Mesa Verde National Park, there would be no reason to visit; as it is, Cortez offers a large, if not exactly broad, selection of roadside motels and diners.

INFORMATION

CORTEZ

Visitor centre The Colorado Welcome Center, 928 E Main St, on the edge of City Park (daily: June–Aug 8am–6pm; Sept & Oct 8am–5pm; Nov–May 9am–5pm; ☎ 970 565 3414, ⓦ cortezchamber.com), has information on the entire state as well as Cortez itself.

ACCOMMODATION

A couple of dozen **motels** line Cortez's main strip, with a few big-name chains scattered among the local operators. There's no great advantage in staying somewhere central, as the whole place is so spread out you'll almost certainly have to drive to wherever you eat.

Aneth Lodge 645 E Main St ☎970 565 3453 or ☎877 515 8454, ⓦanethlodge.com. The good-sized rooms at this *Budget 6* motel are more kitsch than fancy, but at least they're clean and cheap, and if Cortez could be said to have a heart this would be somewhere close to it. **$58**

Best Western Turquoise Inn & Suites 535 E Main St ☎970 565 3778 or ☎800 780 7234, ⓦbestwestern mesaverde.com. Central two-storey motel, with a small outdoor pool open in summer only and an indoor one for the winter. **$125**

Holiday Inn Express Mesa Verde-Cortez 2121 E Main St ☎970 565 6000, ⓦhiexpress.com/cortez. Large modern motel at the east end of town, with huge comfortable rooms, attractive landscaped gardens, and a tasteful Navajo theme. **$179**

★**Kelly Place** 14663 County Rd G ☎970 565 3125 or ☎800 745 4885, ⓦkellyplace.com. Exceptional B&B ranch, tucked amid the peach orchards of McElmo Canyon, ten miles west of Cortez towards Hovenweep. Accommodation, all en-suite, is in seven comfortable lodge rooms, three cabins, or a 2-bedroom suite; they also offer tent sites. Breakfast is served in the central dining room. Archeologist-led hikes to Ancestral Puebloan ruins cost $150 for a group of up to four for half a day, or $235 for a full day; it's also possible to ride horses. Tents **$45**, doubles **$125**, cabins **$160**, suite **$215**

Retro Inn 2040 E Main St ☎970 565 3738, ⓦretroinnmesaverde.com. Comfortable and nicely presented motel, as the main road curves east out of Cortez toward Mesa Verde, which besides its appealing 1950s theming has a pool and hot tub. **$114**

EATING

The Farm Bistro 34 W Main St ☎970 564 3834, ⓦthefarmbistrocortez.com. Drawing on fresh ingredients from an organic farm in nearby Mancos, this friendly, informal downtown bistro is open for lunch only, serving salads, sandwiches and burgers for $9–12, and a delicious $7.50 green chile stew. Mon–Fri 11am–3pm.

Main Street Brewery 21 E Main St ☎970 564 9112, ⓦmainstreetbrewerycortez.com. Colourful central brewpub with a pressed tin ceiling, a wide range of microbrews, a lengthy wine list, and a hearty menu of $10–20 burgers, pizzas, ribs and steaks. Mon–Thurs 3.30–10.30pm, Fri–Sun 11.30am–10.30pm.

Silver Bean 410 W Main St ☎970 946 4404. This eye-catching, old-fashioned silver Airstream trailer just west of downtown serves espresso coffees, chais and smoothies as well as $5 burritos and pastries; drive-through customers welcome. Mon–Fri 6.30am–3pm, Sat 7am–3pm.

Stonefish Sushi & More 16 W Main St ☎970 565 9244. Wonders will never cease – this smart, crisply modern Japanese restaurant in the centre of Cortez serves salmon or steak for $14–19, and noodles, speciality sushi rolls or a "sushi pizza" for $8–12. It may not all be exactly authentic, but it tastes as good as it looks. Tues–Thurs 11am–2pm & 4.30–9pm, Fri 11am–2pm & 4.30–10pm, Sat 4.30–10pm.

Canyons of the Ancients National Monument

While Cortez is very much the largest town in **Montezuma Valley** these days, a thousand years ago the entire valley was densely populated. In fact, it's said to contain the highest density of archeological sites in the United States, which explains why much of it was designated in 2000 as the **Canyons of the Ancients National Monument**. That said, the monument largely consists of several pre-existing small museums and lesser-known sites dotted around the valley, run under the overall aegis of the Bureau of Land Management rather than the National Park Service. Its creation attracted considerable local opposition, because the local economy depends on extracting gas, oil and minerals from the canyons all around; all leases, however, which cover 85 percent of the monument, are still being exploited.

Romantic notions that Montezuma Valley was a peaceful agricultural community have been dashed by archeological research that as well as uncovering evidence of warfare and wholesale slaughter has even provided conclusive proof of ancient **cannibalism**. Human excrement discovered alongside the butchered remains of 23 Ancestral Puebloans in Cowboy Wash contained proteins that could only have come from eating their flesh.

Anasazi Heritage Center

27501 Hwy-184, Dolores • Daily: March–Oct 9am–5pm; Nov–Feb 10am–4pm • March–Oct $3, Nov–Feb free • ☎970 882 5600, ⓦco.blm.gov/canm

The **Anasazi Heritage Center**, three miles west of **DOLORES** and six miles north of Cortez, serves as the headquarters of Canyons of the Ancients National Monument. It centres

1

on a couple of twelfth-century pueblos, excavated during the construction of nearby McPhee Dam, responsible for turning the Dolores River into a broad lake at this point. The pueblos were named after the eighteenth-century Spanish friars Domínguez and Escalante, who first noted the traces of prehistoric Indians in the area. A trail leads around the ruins themselves, and there's a well-equipped **museum** of Pueblo life.

Lowry Pueblo

23 miles northwest of Dolores • No fixed hours • Free • Drive 9 miles west along County Road CC from Pleasant View, fourteen miles northwest of Dolores on US-491

There's not a tremendous amount to see at this free-standing **Lowry Pueblo Ruins**, but in summer, it's noteworthy as one of the few sites where at least part of an **Ancestral Puebloan mural** remains in place on the walls of a "Great Kiva" (see p.90), albeit in a state of great decay. In winter, the gravel surface of the approach road's last four miles is often impassable to vehicles.

Crow Canyon Archeological Center

23390 County Rd K, 5 miles northwest of Cortez • May–Sept Wed & Thurs 8.45am • $60, week-long course $1720 • ☎ 970 564 4341 or ☎ 800 422 8975, ⊚ crowcanyon.org

Each summer, the **Crow Canyon Archeological Center** runs day programmes for amateur archeologists, and week-long residential courses for more serious students of Southwestern prehistory. Both provide the chance to assist on digs at Ancestral Puebloan sites in the valley, such as the 1800-room **Yellow Jacket** and **Sand Canyon Pueblo**.

Sand Canyon Pueblo

12 miles northwest of Cortez • Either drive straight there on county roads P and N, which leave US-491 5 miles northwest of Cortez, or follow County Road G, which leaves US-491 2 miles south of Cortez, for 10 miles, then hike to the pueblo along the rough, 6.5-mile Sand Canyon Trail

Sand Canyon Pueblo, a walled city that once covered the clifftops at Crow Canyon, is among the sites being excavated under the auspices of the **Crow Canyon Archeological Center**, and is a frequent destination on their day programmes. It's also possible to make your own free, unguided visit at any time, though it takes a very long day-hike to reach it. Signs on the spot explain how the 420-room pueblo may once have looked, but there are no facilities.

Mancos

Just off US-160 fourteen miles east of Cortez, and seven miles east of the foot of the approach road that climbs into Mesa Verde, **MANCOS** is a spruce, compact and attractive little residential community that caters almost exclusively to visitors to the national park.

ACCOMMODATION AND EATING **MANCOS**

Absolute Bakery & Cafe 110 S Main St ☎ 970 533 1200, ⊚ absolutebakery.com. This welcoming little bakery serves coffees and fresh breads plus breakfast and lunch daily, with everything priced below $10; it also doubles as a bookstore. Mon–Sat 7am–2pm, Sun 7am–noon; closed Tues in winter.
Fahrenheit Coffee Roasters 201 Grand Ave ☎ 970 533 7624. Set back behind a large patio forecourt at

Mancos's principal intersection, this local hub offers coffee, smoothies and $5 burritos. Mon–Fri 6.30am–5pm, Sat 7am–5pm, Sun 7am–2pm.
Mesa Verde Motel 191 W Railroad Ave ☎ 970 533 7741 or ☎ 800 825 6372, ⊚ mesaverdemotel.com. The pick of Mancos's small crop of motels, this low-slung single-storey place beside the through highway holds decent clean rooms with a friendly family welcome. $75

Mesa Verde National Park

15 miles up from US-160, 10 miles east of Cortez and 35 miles west of Durango • Late May to early Sept $15/vehicle, $8 for motorcyclists, cyclists and pedestrians; early Sept to late May $10 and $5 respectively; valid for 7 days • ☎ 970 529 4465, ⊚ nps.gov/meve

MESA VERDE NATIONAL PARK, the only US national park exclusively devoted to archeological remains, is set high in the plateaus of southwest Colorado, south of

US-160 halfway between Cortez and Mancos. It's an astonishing place, so far off the beaten track that its extensive **Ancestral Puebloan ruins** remained unseen by outsiders until late in the nineteenth century.

Mesa Verde itself – the "green table" – is a densely wooded sandstone plateau, cut at its southern edge by sheer canyons that divide the land into narrow fingers. Hundreds of natural alcoves, eaten high into the canyon walls by seeping water, served as homes

MESA VERDE NATIONAL PARK

Cortez

160

ACCOMMODATION
Far View Lodge 2
Morefield Campground 1

EATING
Spruce Tree Terrace 1

Visitor Center

0   1
mile

Durango

N

MESA VERDE
NATIONAL PARK BOUNDARY

CLOSED IN WINTER

FAR VIEW

Mummy Lake

Far View Ruins

M E S A   V E R D E   N A T I O N A L   P A R K

Spruce Canyon

Soda Canyon

Chapin Mesa

Step House

Long House

Weberill Mesa

Chapin Mesa
Archeological
Museum

Spruce
Tree House

Sun
Temple

RUINS ROAD

RUINS ROAD

Square Tower
House

Cliff Palace

Balcony
House

UTE MOUNTAIN TRIBAL PARK

Tram Route

UTE MOUNTAIN TRIBAL PARK

1

for over seven hundred years; by the time they were abandoned, around 1300, several held multistorey **cliff dwellings** that have remained virtually intact to this day.

By Southwestern standards, the mesa is not especially pretty, and it doesn't offer the same **hiking** opportunities as the region's other national parks. Its compelling relics, however, make Mesa Verde an essential stop on any Four Corners itinerary; readers of

MESA VERDE TOURS AND TICKETS

The major ruins in Mesa Verde National Park can only be visited on guided tours, though it is possible to see Cliff Palace and Long House from nearby overlooks. To take a tour, you must first buy **tickets**, which are available up to two days in advance, at either the visitor centre; the Colorado Welcome Center in Cortez (see p.72); or the Morefield Ranger Station (late May to Aug only). While the exact seasons and times of the tours vary according to both funding and climate – the schedules below are for general guidance only – each costs $4, with tickets valid for one specific time only. If you take tours on both Chapin and Wetherill mesas, allow several hours between the two.

On Chapin Mesa, during the busiest months, you will probably not be allowed to tour **Balcony House** and **Cliff Palace** on the same day (though many couples circumvent the regulations by queuing separately for tickets). If you're forced to choose, Note that Cliff Palace can at least be seen from a distance without joining a tour, though on the other hand, touring Balcony House is much more strenuous than Cliff Palace. On days when they let you tour both, photographers should visit Balcony House first, for the best light. For most other ruins, the best time for photography is late afternoon.

In recent summers, there has been one additional one-hour-thirty-minute evening tour of Cliff Palace each evening between late May and early Sept, starting at times varying between 6.45pm & 7.15pm. Designated as either Twilight Tours (Sun–Thurs; $12) or Photography Tours (Fri & Sat; $20), they can be reserved online at ⓦrecreation.gov from early March onwards.

	Hours	Tour frequency
Cliff Palace, Chapin Mesa		
early April to late May	9am–5pm	half-hourly
late May to mid-Sept	9am–6pm	half-hourly
mid-Sept to Oct	9am–5pm	half-hourly
Balcony House, Chapin Mesa		
second half of April	9am–4pm	7 in day
first 3 wks in May	9am–5pm	hourly + 9.30am & 3.30pm
late May to late Aug	9am–5pm	half-hourly
late Aug to mid-Oct	9am–5pm	hourly + 9.30am & 3.30pm
Second half of Oct	10am–4pm	hourly
Long House, Wetherill Mesa		
late May to early Sept	9.30am–4pm	9.30am, 10.30am, 2pm & 4pm
early Sept to late Sept	9.30am–2pm	9.30am & 2pm

BACKCOUNTRY TOURS

The park service also offers more demanding backcountry hikes to lesser-known cliff dwellings:

Oak Tree House, Chapin Mesa	
late May to early Sept	Tues, Thurs & Sat 8am; $25
Square Tower House, Chapin Mesa	
first 3 wks in May	Sat & Sun 8am; $18
mid-Sept to mid-Oct	Thurs & Sun 8am; $18
Bike & Hike, Wetherill Mesa; includes Long House	
late May to early Sept	Wed & Sun 9.30am; $18

Condé Nast Traveler even voted it the world's top tourist attraction. As things can get very crowded in summer, the **best months** to visit are May, September and October. The 8000ft elevation means that most of the sights become inaccessible in **winter**, though the park itself, its main museum and one ruin – Spruce Tree House – remain open year-round. **Concessions** such as gas, food and lodging only operate between mid-April and late October.

Mesa Verde is not a park to visit on sudden impulse. Quite apart from the time it takes to reach this remote corner of Colorado, even a cursory visit will require a detour off US-160 of at least half a day. The access road climbs south from US-160 ten miles east of Cortez and 35 miles west of Durango. Beyond the visitor centre at the foot of the mesa, it twists and turns for fifteen laborious miles to the point known as Far View, then divides to reach two separate constellations of remains: **Chapin Mesa** to the south, and **Wetherill Mesa** to the west, which is open in summer only.

Visitor centre

Daily: mid-April to late May and early Sept to Oct 8am–5pm, late May to early Sept 7.30am–7pm, Nov to mid-April 8.30am–4.30pm • ☏ 970 529 4465, ⓦ nps.gov/meve

Mesa Verde National Park's state-of-the art **visitor centre** stands beside US-160 at the entrance to the park. As well as holding informative displays on the park and its history, it sells tickets for the timed tours of the various ruins. While you can pay the park entry here, you don't have to; rangers also accept payments at the entrance station at the foot of the park access road just beyond.

Far View

The area known as **Far View**, fifteen miles up from US-160, is home to the park's only hotel and principal restaurant. The impressive structure near those that resembles an Ancestral Puebloan tower used to be the main park visitor centre, but is closed for refurbishment.

A couple of miles further on towards Chapin Mesa you'll come to the archeological site from which Far View takes its name – a mesa-top pueblo abandoned in the thirteenth century. Thanks to the coal-burning power plants that stand in the middle distance, it seldom lives up to its name. Archeologists speculate that a large open area nearby, which has been dubbed **Mummy Lake**, doubled as both an open-air plaza and a reservoir which could hold half a million gallons. Some suggest that the rhythmic shuffling feet of ceremonial dancers were deliberately choreographed to wear grooves in the rock, along which rainwater would flow to be collected.

Chapin Mesa Archeological Museum

20 miles from the park entrance, 2 miles beyond Far View • Daily: Jan to late Feb & Nov–Dec 9am–4.30pm; late Feb to early April 9am–5pm; early April to mid-Oct 8am–6.30pm; 2nd half of Oct 8am–5pm • ☏ 970 529 4631

Although the displays in the venerable **Chapin Mesa Archeological Museum** can't match those in the main park visitor centre, it's worth calling in to enjoy historical exhibits that include several 1930s dioramas depicting how archeologists then saw Ancestral Puebloan life.

Spruce Tree House

Accessible on foot from Chapin Mesa Museum • Early March to Oct, free self-guided visits; Nov to late Feb, free guided tours 10.30am, 1pm & 3pm, late Feb to early March, free guided tours 10am, 1pm and 3.30pm

The short, steep hike down to **Spruce Tree House**, the only ruin that can be seen in winter, drops from alongside Chapin Mesa Museum. Consisting of several well-preserved three-storey structures, snugly moulded into the recesses of a rocky alcove and fronted by open plazas, the neat little village was occupied from 1200 AD until 1276 AD. One *kiva* has been re-roofed, and visitors can enter the dusty, unadorned interior by way of a ladder. Allow around 40min for the complete half-mile loop.

1

Ruins Road
April to late Oct, daily 8am–sunset

Ruins Road, beyond the Chapin Museum area, has two one-way, six-mile loops. The park's two best-known attractions, Cliff Palace and Balcony House, are on the **eastern** loop, and can be explored on guided tours only. To see them properly, be sure to buy tour tickets before you come this far; once here though, it's well worth exploring the

MESA VERDE: A HUMAN HISTORY

Although Archaic sites in Montezuma Valley, below Mesa Verde, date back to 5500 BC, the earliest trace of humans found on the mesa itself is an Ancestral Puebloan pithouse from 550 AD. People first moved to the mesa, therefore, around the time they acquired the skill of pottery. Not so much farmers as gardeners, they continued to gather wild plants and hunt deer and rabbits as well as grow small fields of corn and own dogs and turkeys. For five hundred years, they lived in pithouses dug into the floors of sheltered caves; then, around 1100, they congregated in walled villages on the mesa-tops. A century later, they returned to the canyon-side alcoves to build the "palaces" for which Mesa Verde is now famous.

Archeologists believe each settlement held significantly fewer people than it did rooms; the largest, **Cliff Palace**, housed a population of around 120. Two or three people may have slept in a typical living room, measuring six feet by eight feet, while each family had its own *kiva* (see p.463), which when not in ceremonial use was used for weaving and domestic activities. No rigid social hierarchy is indicated either in the architecture, or the relatively few burials to have been found – some in sealed chambers, and some simply, if reverentially, in the trash heaps.

Mesa Verde may well have been a **peripheral community**. While its population is thought to have peaked at around 2500, in the middle of the thirteenth century, there were at least eight larger surface pueblos down in Montezuma Valley, whose inhabitants are thought to have been generally hostile to the Mesa Verdeans.

Ironically, archeologists regard the cliff dwellings that seem so elegant to modern visitors as signs of a declining culture. They say the mesa-top pueblos were more sophisticated in both design and construction, while the alcove complexes are haphazard accretions, contorted by the constraints of the rock and characterized by inferior craftsmanship. These were not ideal homes; older villagers must have found it impossible to get in or out, while children lived in peril of fatal falls. In theory, each complex got its water from the seep or spring that originally created its alcove, but many of those springs had run dry, leaving the occupants forever fetching and carrying.

All of which begs the question of **why** the cliff dwellings were built. Some experts argue that sites like Balcony House were primarily defensive, but there's little evidence they were ever attacked, and dwellings such as Spruce Tree House lie exposed to assault, while the towers are of little use as lookouts. Agricultural space may have been at a premium, with the entire mesa-top crisscrossed by dams, terraces and irrigation channels.

In any case, Mesa Verde was **abandoned** by the end of the thirteenth century; no one has lived here since then. The traditional explanation, that a **drought** between 1276 and 1299 drove the Ancestral Puebloans away, tells only part of the story; six previous droughts had been just as bad. It's likely that both firewood and game animals had become seriously depleted, the climate had turned too cold to grow crops, and survival became too much of a struggle. Most Mesa Verdeans migrated into what's now New Mexico, to establish the pueblos where their descendants still live.

THE REDISCOVERY OF MESA VERDE

Although Mesa Verde was named by the Spanish in the seventeenth century, its ruins went unrecorded for two hundred more years. Photographer William Henry Jackson snapped some lesser sites in 1874, and a passing prospector spotted Balcony House in 1884, but the outside world first took notice when **Richard Wetherill** stumbled upon Cliff Palace in a snowstorm in 1888. The Wetherills, a local ranching family, took to selling Ancestral Puebloan artefacts as a way of life, and helped the Swedish Count Gustaf Nordenskïold to ship caseloads of ancient pottery to Europe in 1891. The National Museum of Finland, to which they were donated, now holds the world's finest collection of Mesa Verde artefacts. The activities of the Wetherills prompted both the Antiquities Act of 1906, which prohibited dealing in archeological treasures, and the creation of Mesa Verde National Park in the same year.

many lesser known, and much less crowded, relics in the vicinity. In particular, try to allow enough time to tour the self-guided sites along the **western** loop as well.

Technically, Ruins Road passes out of the national park just beyond Cliff Palace and briefly enters **Ute Mountain Tribal Park**, where you can pick up information on tours (see p.71).

Cliff Palace

The first stop on the **eastern** portion of Ruins Road, **Cliff Palace**, is the largest Ancestral Puebloan cliff dwelling that survives anywhere. Tucked a hundred feet below an overhanging ledge of pale rock, it holds 217 rooms and 23 *kivas*, each thought to have belonged to a separate family or clan. It's thought this was a ceremonial or storage centre rather than simply a communal habitation, and may have been home to around 120 people.

Cliff Palace can only be seen close up on guided tours (see p.76), but if you don't have a ticket you can still get a great view from the promontory where the tour groups gather, just below the parking lot. For participants on the tours, the chance to walk through the empty plazas and peer down into the mysterious *kivas*, especially on a quieter day, provides a haunting evocation of a lost and little-known world. Fading murals can still be discerned inside some structures. As you leave, climbing an unalarming metal stairway through a narrow crevice, you may spot the original toe- and footholds used by the Ancestral Puebloans.

Note that Cliff Palace had to be closed to visitors for much of 2015 so that essential re-stabilization work could be carried out on its southern portion. Depending on the success of that project, tours may be restricted in future.

Balcony House

Balcony House is one of the few Mesa Verde complexes that was clearly geared towards defence. Built around 1240, it was remodelled during the 1270s to make it even more impregnable; access is very difficult, and it's not visible from above. Guided tours involve scrambling up three hair-raising ladders and crawling through a narrow tunnel, above a steep drop into Soda Canyon. It's a spectacular site, with two circular *kivas* standing side by side in a commanding central position, but those who don't share the fearless Ancestral Puebloan attitude to heights should give it a miss.

Distant views of Balcony House can be had from 1200 yards along the forested **Soda Canyon Overlook Trail**, which starts a short way further around Ruins Road.

The western loop

A 500-foot stroll at the first stop along the western loop of Ruins Road, **Square Tower House**, is rewarded by views of an eighty-room alcove complex, focused around the four-storey Square Tower – at 26 feet, the park's tallest tower. **Sun Point Overlook** looks across Spruce Canyon to as many as twelve distinct cliff dwellings, including Cliff Palace, making it clear just how crowded the canyon was in its heyday. Unlike the alcove sites, the mesa-top **Sun Temple**, next, was built to a premeditated design, and may have been a ceremonial centre for the whole community. It was never finished, however, and its shape and function can only really be appreciated from aerial photos.

Wetherill Mesa

Late May until Oct 31 or until winter weather precludes accesss road open daily 8am–sunset

The tortuous twelve-mile drive onto **Wetherill Mesa** from Far View is open in summer only, and even then just for ordinary-sized vehicles. Cycles and RVs are always banned.

From the parking lot at the far end of the road, where there's a ranger station (late May to early Sept, daily 9am–6.30pm) and snack kiosk, a free **miniature train** loops around the tip of the mesa. Priority is given to visitors with tickets for the timed Long House tours (see p.76). Any time spent waiting can be occupied by walking down to

1

nearby **Step House**, where a single alcove contains a restored pithouse, dating to 626 AD, as well as a pueblo from 1226.

The mini-train stops at various trailheads from which hikers can walk to early mesa-top sites or alcove overlooks, but its principal destination is the **Long House**. The park's second-largest ruin is set in its largest cave; hour-long tours descend sixty or so steps to reach its central plaza, then scramble around its 150 rooms and 21 *kivas*. These ruins are said to be especially authentic, having been "restabilized" in recent years, rather than subjected to the same extensive rebuilding as the better-known sites were earlier last century. Excavations here uncovered a number of unburied bodies, some of whom had clearly met violent deaths.

TOURS
MESA VERDE

Bus tours Half-day bus tours of the park, run by park concessionaires Aramark rather than by NPS rangers, start from the *Far View Lodge* daily between late April and late October. The 8am "700 Years Tour" costs $48 for adults and $41 for ages 5–11, while the slightly shorter 1.30pm "Classic Pueblo Tour" costs $41 and $28; both visit Chapin

Mesa only and include a tour of Cliff Palace. Reserve in advance, online at ⓦ visitmesaverde.com, if at all possible. Taking a tour can ease the laborious business of driving around Mesa Verde, and of queuing for tickets, but the sheer cost makes it hard to recommend them for family groups.

ACCOMMODATION AND EATING

Far View Lodge 15 miles up from US-160 ☎ 970 564 4300 or ☎ 800 449 2288, ⓦ visitmesaverde.com. This summer-only lodge offers the only rooms at Mesa Verde. It's a peaceful place, away from the bustle of the park itself; guestrooms, which lack phones or TVs but have wi-fi, are in two-storey units dotted around the mesa-top. The standard rooms have private balconies, while the "Kiva" rooms offer a/c and are more luxurious. Though the sweeping views reach into the Rockies to the north, no archeological sites are visible. The *Metate Room*, in the mock-adobe main lodge, is a pretty good restaurant that's open daily for dinner only; mains such as elk tenderloin are priced at up to $32. Closed late Oct to mid-April. Standard doubles $142, Kiva $169

Morefield Campground 4 miles up from US-160

☎ 970 564 4300 or ☎ 800 449 2288, ⓦ visitmesaverde .com. The park's official campground – so large that it's almost never full – is located a long way from the ruins. Reservations are available, though seldom essential. Closed early Oct to early May. One or two vehicles $31, hook-ups $42

Spruce Tree Terrace near the Chapin Mesa museum ☎ 970 564 4300, ⓦ visitmesaverde.com. The one place in the park to offer food year-round, this straightforward cafeteria serves sandwiches, salads and Navajo tacos at very affordable prices (typically well under $10), and has a pleasant shaded terrace. Daily: mid-March to mid-April 11am–4.30pm; mid-April to late May & late Aug to Oct 10am–5pm; late May to late Aug 9am–6.30pm; Nov to mid-March 11am–3.30pm.

Durango

Named after Durango, Mexico, with which it's also twinned, and stretching out along the verdant Animas Valley, **DURANGO** was founded in 1880 as a rail junction for the Gold Rush community of Silverton, fifty miles further north and almost 3000ft higher. **Steam trains** still run the same high-altitude route and thanks to their superb close-up views of the mountains are the main tourist attraction hereabouts. In addition, Durango has become a new-style Wild West boom town, attracting a large influx of computerized teleworkers. Combine them with outdoors enthusiasts, who come to ride their **mountain bikes** on the gruelling local back roads, and in the morning at least the place has a youthful, energetic buzz. By the evening, most people seem too wiped out to do anything much.

Downtown Durango, located along Main Avenue between 7th and 11th streets, remains the liveliest urban area in the Four Corners, and is worth an hour or two of anyone's time. As well as the outdoors outfitters, restaurants, brewpubs and cafés you might expect, it's packed with funky and upscale fashion and home furnishing stores. That said, in terms of any kind of formal tourist attraction, there's precious little to see. Like, say, Moab, Durango is very much a place where visitors come to do stuff, not see stuff.

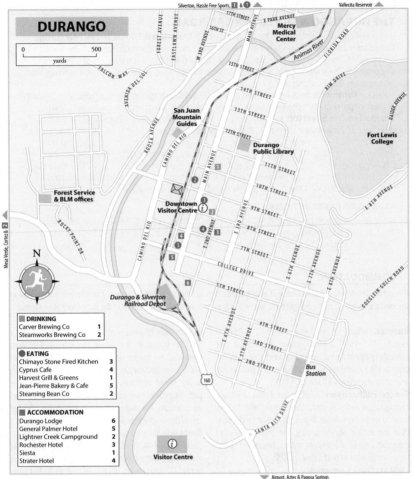

DRINKING

| Carver Brewing Co | 1 |
| Steamworks Brewing Co | 2 |

EATING

Chimayo Stone Fired Kitchen	3
Cyprus Cafe	4
Harvest Grill & Greens	1
Jean-Pierre Bakery & Cafe	5
Steaming Bean Co	2

ACCOMMODATION

Durango Lodge	6
General Palmer Hotel	5
Lightner Creek Campground	2
Rochester Hotel	3
Siesta	1
Strater Hotel	4

INFORMATION

DURANGO

Visitor centres Durango has two visitor centres, downtown at 802 Main Ave (daily 9am–6pm; ☏ 970 247 3500 or ☏ 800 525 8855, ⊛ durango.org) and near the train station in Santa Rita Park not far south, at 111 S Camino del Rio (June–Sept Mon–Fri 8am–6pm, Sat 9am–5pm, Sun 11am–4pm; Oct–May Mon–Fri 8am–5pm; same contact details).

ACTIVITIES

Bike rental Bikes of all kinds can be rented for around $50 per day from Hassle Free Sports, 2615 Main Ave (☏ 970 259 3874, ⊛ hasslefreesports.com).

Climbing and backpacking San Juan Mountain Guides, 1111 Camino del Rio (☏ 800 642 5389, ⊛ mtnguide.net), runs a wide array of guided climbing and backpacking tours.

Mountain biking Between mid-June and September, San Juan Huts offers a seven-day self-guided biking package from Durango all the way to Moab, Utah, following remote mountain back roads and spending six nights in mountain huts en route, pre-stocked with food that you cook yourself ($895; ☏ 970 626 3033, ⊛ sanjuanhuts.com).

River-rafting Several operators run river-rafting and kayaking excursions on the Animas River. Full-day expeditions with Mild to Wild Rafting (☏ 970 247 4789 or ☏ 800 567 6745, ⊛ mild2wildrafting.com), for example, cost from $89 upwards. If you just want a taster, consider a brief float trip with Flexible Flyers (☏ 970 247 4628, ⊛ flexibleflyersrafting.com), which cost from as little as $23.

1

THE DURANGO & SILVERTON RAILROAD

Between May and October, the steam trains of the **Durango & Silverton Narrow Gauge Railroad** make up to three daily return trips along a spectacular route through the mountains that parallels the gorgeous San Juan Skyway. Opened in 1882, the track took just nine months to construct. The most memorable of the train's many movie appearances came when it was blown up in *Butch Cassidy and the Sundance Kid* in 1969.

Precise **summer** schedules vary, but all trains leave **Durango** in the morning, with the first at 8am, departing from the depot at 479 Main Ave at the south end of town, and allowing time for lunch in **Silverton** at the far end. The journey takes 3 hours 30 minutes in each direction, at a maximum speed of 18mph. In **winter**, when the higher mountain reaches are closed by snow, shorter excursions operate on the most scenic section only, departing at 9.45am and running as far as Cascade Canyon. No trains run for most of November, while between late November and mid-December they operate on weekends only. There are daily departures during the last two weeks of December; then trains run Thurs–Sat from January until early March, and Mon–Sat between early March and early May.

FARES AND RESERVATIONS

Reservations should be made at least two weeks in advance, via ☎970 247 2733, ☎888 872 4607, or ⊛durangotrain.com. Summer fares are $85 for adults, $51 for ages 5–11; in winter they drop to $62 and $36 respectively. First and Deluxe Class service is also available.

ACCOMMODATION

Downtown Durango only has a handful of **accommodation** options, including a couple of fancy historic hotels. Most of the **motels**, including all the budget ones, are well to the north, on the farther reaches of the forty-block Main Avenue.

Durango Lodge 150 East Fifth St ☎970 247 0955 or ☎888 440 4489, ⊛durangolodge.com. Small, not particularly attractive but very convenient central motel, close to the railroad station. Spacious rooms plus a pool; rates drop dramatically off season. **$125**

General Palmer Hotel 567 Main Ave ☎800 523 3358, ⊛generalpalmerhotel.com. Very pleasant, old historic hotel, close to the railroad depot, that's slightly chintzier than the similar *Strater* nearby, but still provides an enjoyable taste of old-Western style. Lower-priced rooms face inwards, not out to the street. **$175**

Lightner Creek Campground 1567 Lightner Creek Rd ☎970 247 5406, ⊛camplightnercreek.com. Lovely riverside campground, in a peaceful location a couple of miles north of US-160 and a total of 5 miles west of town, and equipped with a summer-only heated pool and small store. As well as well-shaded tent sites, they also offer basic wooden cabins. Closed mid-Oct to April. Tents **$33**, cabins **$47**, RVs **$51**

★**Rochester Hotel** 721 E Second Ave ☎970 385 1920, ⊛rochesterhotel.com. Charming, intimate, romantic – and allegedly haunted – nineteenth-century B&B inn, a block up from Main Ave, where the differing Wild West themes of the fifteen very comfortable rooms, some of which have kitchenettes, are inspired in part by classic, locally filmed Westerns. The breakfasts are great, the pleasant patio bar is open Wed–Sat 4–7pm, and free bikes are available. The owners also run the similar, cheaper *Leland House* across the street. **$249**

Siesta 3475 Main Ave ☎970 247 0741 or ☎877 314 0741, ⊛durangosiestamotel.com. Very inexpensive old-style motor court, at the curve in the highway well north of the centre; all rooms have phone, TV and wi-fi, but little more. **$85**

★**Strater Hotel** 699 Main Ave ☎970 247 4431 or ☎800 247 4431, ⊛strater.com. Major downtown landmark that's bursting with frontier elegance and offers almost a hundred mostly small but appealing antique-furnished rooms, plus some rather wonderful suites. Great buffet breakfasts available, a reasonable restaurant, a lively Western saloon, and even regular performances of theatrical melodramas. **$187**

EATING

Main Avenue downtown, and the streets to either side, are filled with places to **eat**; some set their sights on affluent train passengers, others aim at young mountain bikers. There's at least one **espresso bar** on every block.

Chimayo Stone Fired Kitchen 862 Main Ave ☎970 259 2749, ⊛chimayodurango.com. Very stylish modern restaurant in a historic building, imaginatively revamped with curving concrete-walled booths and kitted out with stone hearth ovens that deliver perfect stone-fired pizzas for $13–19, and substantial $20–29 dishes like the delicious stuffed poblano chiles. Be sure to order the $6 house salad with jicama and pumpkin seeds. Mon–Fri 11.30am–10pm, Sat & Sun 10am–10pm; closed Mon mid-Nov to April.

Cyprus Cafe 725 E Second Ave ☎970 385 6884, ⓦcypruscafe.com. Friendly local bistro, a block east of Main Ave, with a spacious patio that features live jazz on summer evenings (Sun–Thurs). The largely Mediterranean menu emphasizes local, sustainable produce, and includes vegetarian options like Greek spanakopita (spinach-and-cheese parcels) as well as steaks, chops and seafood, with mains ranging $17–28. Mon–Sat 11.30am–2.30pm & 5–9pm.

Harvest Grill & Greens James Ranch, 33846 US-550 ☎970 676 1023, ⓦjamesranch.net. Organic farm, beside the highway 11 miles north of Durango towards Silverton, where you order at the counter then enjoy the superb burgers, sandwiches and salads at picnic tables near the river. The ranch marketplace, open the same hours, sells fresh vegetables, eggs and farm-made cheese. Late May to mid-Oct Mon–Sat 11am–7pm, mid-Oct to late May Sat 11am–5pm.

Jean-Pierre Bakery & Cafe 601 Main Ave ☎970 247 7700, ⓦjeanpierrebakery.com. It may seem a little incongruous in this Wild West building, but this classic French bakery/restaurant offers exquisite breads and pastries, plus lunchtime sandwiches, salads and quiches for $10–20, and full dinners like mussels or beef with crab for up to $37. Live music on Fri & Sat. Daily 7am–10pm.

Steaming Bean Co 915 Main Ave ☎970 385 7901, ⓦthebean.com. Early-morning espressos and pastries, as well as speciality drinks; sandwiches, soup and wraps; wi-fi; and live music later on. Mon–Sat 6.30am–9pm, Sun 7am–8pm.

DRINKING

Carver Brewing Co 1022 Main Ave ☎970 259 2545, ⓦcarverbrewing.com. Bustling brewpub, best known for its home-brewed ales, at $4.75 per pint, but also serving food all day, with a good menu of big eggy breakfasts, grilled specials like bison bratwurst and dinner options such as Navajo tacos, Thai salmon curry and steaks, for $10–25. Daily 6.30am–10pm.

Steamworks Brewing Co 801 E Second Ave ☎970 259 9200, ⓦsteamworksbrewing.com. Large brewpub, perched in a huge corrugated-iron shed a block above Main Avenue. In summer, the sunny open-air patio makes an ideal spot to enjoy their wood-fired pizzas (from $11) and daily specials; in winter you can always drink vast quantities of home-brewed beer in its bustling, cavernous interior. Mon–Thurs & Sun 11am–midnight, Fri & Sat 11am–2am.

The San Juan Skyway

North of Durango, the **San Juan Skyway** loops over two hundred miles through the Rockies, up US-550 and then back via Hwy-145 and US-160. En route, it passes through a series of compelling Wild West towns, including mining communities like **Silverton**, **Ouray** and **Telluride** that have reinvented themselves as year-round mountain resorts.

The Skyway's initial stretch, across invigorating high passes, is known as the **Million Dollar Highway**, for the amount of gold in the ore-bearing gravel used in its construction. As you skirt around the bald, red-striped **Engineer Mountain**, just beyond the Purgatory Ski Area, the views are spectacular.

Silverton

The first town along the San Juan Skyway, **SILVERTON** spreads across a small flat valley 9318ft up in the mountains fifty miles out from Durango, and marks journey's end for the narrow-gauge railroad. It's one of Colorado's most atmospheric mountain towns, with wide dirt-packed streets leading off towards the hills to either side of the one paved road, where the snow lingers year-round. Silverton's zinc- and copper-mining days only came to an end in 1991, leaving it dependent on tourism. The false-front stores along "Notorious Blair Street", paralleling the main drag, recall the days when legendary gunslinger Bat Masterson was the city marshal, and are the scene of frequent staged shoot-outs. Silverton is geared much more toward day-trippers than overnight guests, so even in summer it gets very sleepy at night, with a handful of Western saloons and steakhouses providing the only sign of life.

Without a 4WD vehicle – available for rent locally – it's hard to explore the mountains, but if instead of returning to the main highway you simply keep going beyond the end of

1

Silverton's main street, you can continue for several miles in an ordinary car. The dirt road usually starts to get difficult around the ruins of **EUREKA**, seven miles along the Animas River, which make a good starting point for hikes to nearby waterfalls. Check locally to ensure that this region is clear of the damage caused by the toxic spillage from the Gold King mine nearby in 2015. The crest of the mountain ridge to the east marks the Continental Divide, with the source of the Rio Grande on the far side.

Ouray

The attractive mining community of **OURAY** lies 23 miles north of Silverton, on the far side of 11,018-foot **Red Mountain Pass**, where the bare rock beneath the snow really is red, thanks to mineral deposits. The Million Dollar Highway twists and turns, passing abandoned mine workings and rusting machinery in the most unlikely and inaccessible spots. The best spot for an overview is the Red Mountain Overlook, where the relics of the Idarado Mine lie scattered below a magnificent red peak; tunnels once connected it with Telluride, little more than five miles west but sixty miles by road. Back roads into the mountains hereabouts offer rich pickings for hikers or 4WD drivers.

Ouray itself squeezes into a slender green valley at the head of the Uncompahgre River, with the **Ouray Hot Springs** ranged alongside the river at the north end of town. A mile or so south, a one-way loop dirt road leads to **Box Cañon Falls Park** (daily 8am–dusk; $4), where a straightforward 500-foot trail, partly along a swaying wooden parapet, leads into the dark, narrow Box Cañon. At the far end, the falls thunder through a tiny cleft in the mountain.

Ridgway

North of Ouray, the scenery changes abruptly, with the canyon of the Uncompahgre characterized by red rocks and sparse sagebrush. To complete the San Juan Skyway loop, turn west on Hwy-62 after eight miles at **RIDGWAY**, where the northern limits of the San Juan Mountains stand as a serrated ridge along the southern skyline.

Ridgway was a pivotal location for the 1968 movie *True Grit*. The 62-year-old **John Wayne**, who won his first Oscar as one-eyed Marshal Rooster Cogburn, met his young sidekick outside the town courthouse, while their subsequent adventures were played out against the magnificent backdrop of the **Wilson Peaks**, which you'll see if you continue west on the San Juan Skyway.

Telluride

As Hwy-62, the San Juan Skyway meets Hwy-145 23 miles southwest of Ridgway, and then turns sharply back eastward on Hwy-145 along the pretty, well-wooded valley of the San Miguel River. The former mining village of **TELLURIDE** is a 74-mile drive from Silverton, even though as the crow flies, across the mountains, the towns are barely ten miles apart.

Telluride was briefly home to the young Butch Cassidy, who robbed his first bank here in 1889. It's now best known as a **ski resort**, rivalling Aspen and Vail as a winter destination for the stars. Telluride has, however, achieved this status without losing its character – the wide main street, a National Historic District with low-slung buildings on either side, still heads directly up towards one of the most stupendous mountain views in the Rockies. Healthy young bohemians with few visible means of support but top-notch ski equipment form the bulk of the 2300 citizens, while most of the glitzy visitors hang out two miles above the town in **Mountain Village**, reached by a free year-round gondola service (daily 7am–midnight).

Although Telluride is generally cheaper to visit in summer than winter, prices do rise during the **Bluegrass Festival** in mid-June (Ⓦbluegrass.com), the **Jazz Festival** in early August (Ⓦtelluridejazz.org), and the **Film Festival** at the start of September (Ⓦtelluridefilmfestival.org).

1

SKIING AND SNOWBOARDING IN TELLURIDE

Telluride's winter season, which starts as the fall colours fade, usually in late November, continues until early April. The town also hosts US and world **snowboarding** championships, with many former ski trails now reserved for snowboarders.

Prospective visitors should visit ⓦ**telluride.com** for a wide range of lodging and package deals, plus local operators who rent out ski and snowboarding equipment. Guests in certain lodges get discounted lift tickets; otherwise a full-price lift ticket costs around $100 per day. The **Telluride Ski and Snowboard School** (ⓦtellurideskiresort.com) offers expert instruction for visitors of all levels.

Bridal Veil Falls

In summer, Telluride offers excellent **hiking** opportunities. One three-mile round-trip walk, which also makes a great if gruelling bike ride, switchbacks up a bumpy 4WD road from the head of the valley to reach Colorado's highest waterfalls, the 365-foot **Bridal Veil Falls**. To join it, follow the main highway all the way through town, park where it ends at Pioneer Mill, and set off uphill. Don't expect to be able to cool off with a swim in the falls, however; it's far too perilous for that.

INFORMATION   SAN JUAN SKYWAY

SILVERTON

Visitor centre 414 Greene St, at the southern edge of town (daily: May, June & Sept 9am–4pm; July & Aug 9am–5pm; Oct–April 10am–3pm; ☎970 387 5654 or ☎800 752 4494, ⓦsilvertoncolorado.com).

Tours and rentals San Juan Backcountry, 1119 Greene St (☎970 387 5565 or ☎800 494 8687, ⓦsanjuanbackcountry .com) rents out bikes, motorbikes, and 4WD vehicles, and offers guided tours around and beyond town, starting at $80 for a 4hr jeep tour and $110 for a 3hr ATV expedition.

OURAY

Visitor centre 1230 Main St, outside the hot springs (mid-June to Aug Mon–Wed 9am–7pm, Thurs–Sat 9am–6pm, Sun 10am–4pm; Sept to mid-June Mon–Sat

10am–5pm, Sun 10am–3pm; ☎970 325 4746 or ☎800 228 1876, ⓦouraycolorado.com).

Tours Switzerland of America, 226 Seventh Ave (☎970 325 4484 or ☎866 990 5337, ⓦsoajeep.com) rents out 4WD vehicles and offers guided jeep tours.

Hiking In summer, San Juan Huts arranges four-night self-guided hiking trips between Ouray and Telluride, Utah, with accommodation in mountain huts en route for $30 per person per night (☎970 626 3033, ⓦsanjuanhuts.com).

TELLURIDE

Visitor centre Telluride's visitor centre is in Oak Street Plaza, at the foot of the ski gondola up to Mountain Village (daily 9am–5pm; ☎888 605 2578, ⓦvisittelluride.com).

ACCOMMODATION

SILVERTON

Blair Street Hostel 1025 Blair St ☎970 387 5599, ⓦblairstreethostel.com. Tiny, tin-walled hostel, a block off the main street, that offers the cheapest accommodation in town, with dorm beds (bring your own sleeping bag) as well as a few bare-bones, private doubles that are progressively being revamped by new owners. Tent sites $18, dorms $26, doubles $56

Teller House Hotel 1250 Greene St ☎970 387 5423 or ☎800 342 4338, ⓦtellerhouse.com. Open since 1896, this Victorian guesthouse offers classy antique-furnished rooms, some of which – not just the cheapest –share bathrooms. $89

Triangle Motel 848 Greene St ☎970 387 5780, ⓦtrianglemotel.com. Behind its rather ugly facade, this motel at the south end of town is very well maintained, offering good facilities for the price, with two-room suites

available. $85

Wyman Hotel & Inn 1371 Greene St ☎970 387 4166 or ☎1 800 609 7845, ⓦthewymanhotelandin.com. Quirky historic hotel, where authentic Victoriana transforms the rooms according to themes such as Railroad and Steampunk. There's no elevator – it's been converted into a whirlpool tub in the eponymous Elevator room – but there is a private and very cosy railroad caboose. Rates include breakfast. $145

OURAY

Box Canyon Lodge 45 Third Ave ☎970 325 4981, ⓦboxcanyonouray.com. An old-style timber motel below the park, where guests can bathe in natural hot tubs. The guest rooms are cosy and snug, with good furnishings and fittings. $143

★ **Hot Springs Inn** 1400 Main St ☎970 325 7277 or

1

☏ 800 706 7790, ⊛ hotspringsinn.com. All the very pleasant rooms at this comfortable upscale modern inn, at the north end of town, have deck balconies facing the river, and the staff are hugely helpful with area recommendations. Closed mid-Oct to mid-May. **$175**

TELLURIDE
Manitou Lodge 333 S Fir St ☏ 970 728 3388 or ☏ 888 728 1950, ⊛ telluridehotels.com/manitou-lodge -telluride. While it calls itself a B&B, *Manitou Lodge* looks more like an outlying segment of an old-fashioned national park lodge. The cosy comforts of its 11 renovated rooms can't be faulted, though, and neither can its riverside setting – close to the ski lifts and just a short walk from the town centre, via a pedestrian bridge. There's a very pleasant outdoor deck, with a hot tub that's open to the elements when weather permits. **$149**

New Sheridan Hotel 231 W Colorado Ave ☏ 970 728 4351 or ☏ 800 200 1891, ⊛ newsheridan.com. Restored 1895 hotel in the heart of town, where the large, very luxurious rooms have stylish antique furnishings but modern bathrooms and fittings. The cheapest face inwards, but it costs little more to enjoy great mountain views. They even provide white noise machines to dampen things down when Telluride is in party mode. Closed late Oct to late Nov. **$228**

Victorian Inn 401 W Pacific Ave ☏ 970 728 6601 or ☏ 800 611 9893, ⊛ victorianinntelluride.com. Despite the name, this is a smart motel rather than a historic inn, with two decks of tastefully furnished rooms equipped with comfortable beds, and friendly staff. The location is unbeatable for the price, and it has its own sauna. **$149**

EATING AND DRINKING
SILVERTON
Avalanche Brewing Company 1067 Blair St ☏ 970 387 5282, ⊛ avalanchebrewing.com. A welcome contrast to Silverton's crop of rather ordinary Western steakhouses, this friendly hangout started out as a coffee bar, but now it's a microbrewery too, serving four home-brewed ales as well as morning espressos, lunchtime sandwiches, and substantial $10–13 pizzas from 3pm onwards. Daily 7am–9pm.

OURAY
Bon Ton 426 Main St ☏ 970 325 4419, ⊛ bontonrestaurant.com. Snug basement restaurant that offers Ouray's most satisfying special-occasion ambience and cuisine. As well as classic pasta dishes from $16, the menu features signature Colorado favourites such as grilled rack of lamb, costing up to $40. Mon–Sat 5.30–9pm, Sun 9.30am–1pm & 5.30–9pm; closed Wed mid-Oct to mid-May.

Maggie's Kitchen 705 Main St ☏ 970 325 0259. Hugely popular central diner, where every square inch (except for the spotless restroom) is covered in all-but-indecipherable graffiti. The blackboard lists grilled cheese, hot dogs and assorted sandwiches, but it's the fabulous burgers that draw in the crowds. Mon–Sat 11am–7pm, Sun noon–4.30pm.

RIDGWAY
Kate's Place 615 W Clinton St ☏ 970 626 9800, ⊛ www.katesplaceridgway.com. Bright, busy café, a block north of the main road west, that's a local legend for its emphasis on regional organic produce in general, and its big breakfast waffles in particular. The lunch menu includes inexpensive daily specials like a $12.50 lasagne, as well as sandwiches and salads. Daily 7am–2pm.

TELLURIDE
Baked in Telluride 127 S Fir St ☏ 970 728 4775, ⊛ bakedintel.com. Takeaway bakery-deli, just off the main drag, that's great for morning espressos and pastries, and has a tiny little front porch where you can enjoy your soup, sandwiches or pizza outdoors. Daily 5.30am–10pm.

The Butcher & The Baker 217 E Colorado Ave ☏ 970 728 2899, ⊛ butcherandbakercafe.com. Bright, friendly contemporary café/bistro, making extensive use of fresh organic produce to feed health-conscious locals. Often everything from breakfast eggs and burritos through to a dinner menu that takes in delicious "small plate" salads for $7–13 or burgers, brisket and chicken schnitzel for $14–22. Mon–Sat 7am–9pm, Sun 8am–2pm.

Chop House New Sheridan Hotel, 231 W Colorado Ave ☏ 970 728 9100, ⊛ newsheridan.com. This plush, upbeat Western saloon-style dining room makes a lovely setting for anything from a massive mountain breakfast to a meaty dinner. Prices are more reasonable for the morning brunch; an evening steak or chop – especially if you opt for elk or bison – can cost over $50. Daily 8am–2pm & 5.30–9pm.

Smugglers Brewpub 225 S Pine St ☏ 970 728 0919, ⊛ smugglersbrewpub.com. Lively, convivial evening hangout, with a wide-ranging menu of pretty good pub grub – the $9 "ancient grain" salad is excellent – and some exceptional house brews, including the likes of raspberry wheat beers. Daily 11.30am–9.30om.

1

Northwest New Mexico

Although **northwest New Mexico** formed the heart of the Dinétah, the Navajo's original homeland in the Southwest, the Navajo territories here are less visited than their more scenic equivalents in Arizona. Archeology buffs are drawn to **Chaco Canyon** and **Aztec Ruins**, which they rank among the most significant Ancestral Puebloan sites anywhere, but none of the towns nearby, whether on or off the reservation, holds any lasting interest.

Instead the region is notorious as the home of the **Four Corners Power Plant**, near Farmington. After this coal-fired generating station opened in the 1960s, it was said to be the single greatest source of pollution in the United States, emitting more noxious gases than either New York City or Los Angeles. Regulations have been tightened since then, but with the **Navajo Mine**, the largest open-pit coal mine in the West, just a mile away, and several other generating plants in the immediate neighbourhood, there's no incentive for outsiders to linger. For the Navajo, of course, who provide much of the industry's workforce, it's a different story.

Shiprock

By far the most striking landmark in the dusty red plains of New Mexico's far northwestern corner is the craggy monolith known as **Shiprock**. In Navajo legend, as *Tsé bitTaai* or "Rock Wing", this awesome 1500-foot peak was home to one or two monstrous birds, which were either killed by the hero Monster Slayer or turned into an eagle and an owl. To Anglo eyes, it resembled instead a mighty ocean-going ship. Navajo medicine men continued to use it in sacred ceremonies until 1939, when Shiprock was deemed to have been defiled by being climbed by Sierra Club members including David Brower, the "Arch-Druid" who later founded Friends of the Earth (see p.394).

Roadside signs on **US-491**, which runs within a few miles of Shiprock's vast, eerie bulk, explain that the mountain is a volcanic plug, the hard central core of a volcano that has itself eroded away. There's no point trying to approach it any closer; you can't even walk up to the base, let alone climb it. Neither is it worth stopping at the sprawling mining town six miles north, also known as **SHIPROCK**, other than in early October, when it hosts the **Northern Navajo Fair** (ⓦnorthernnavajonationfair.org).

Farmington

FARMINGTON, the largest town in northwestern New Mexico, lies fifty miles east of the Four Corners Monument; fifty miles southwest of Durango, Colorado; and, more to the point, a mere ten miles west of both the Navajo Mine and the Four Corners Power Plant. Formerly renowned as a definitive "edge-of-the-res" community, rife with racism and violence, Farmington has cleaned itself up and prospered accordingly. Developments like the **Animas Valley Mall**, 4601 E Main St, make it the principal business centre of a wide area.

Farmington's principal concession to tourism is its **museum**, in the Gateway Park on the northeast edge of town at 3041 E Main St (Mon–Sat 8am–5pm; free), which follows local history all the way from the geological "New Mexico Seacoast", via the trading-post era, up to modern-day mining and refining.

ARRIVAL AND INFORMATION   **FARMINGTON**

By plane Great Lakes Airlines (ⓦflygreatlakes.com) connects the Four Corners Airport, 2 miles northwest of town, with Denver, Prescott and Phoenix.

Visitor centre 3041 E Main St, in the museum (Mon–Sat 8am–5pm; ☎505 326 7602 or ☎800 448 1240, ⓦfarmingtonnm.org).

THE BEAST IS DEAD

Here is wisdom. Let him who has understanding calculate the Number of the Beast, for it is the number of a man: His number is 666. Revelation 13:18

Until 2003, 666 was not merely the Number of the Beast, and the number of a man; it was also the number of the main highway north through the Navajo Nation from Gallup to Shiprock. After being assigned the dreaded "666" in 1942, as the sixth major road to branch off Route 66, **US-666** swiftly acquired such nicknames as the "Devil's Highway" and the "Highway to Hell". Despite being largely straight, and doubtless paved with good intentions, it became renowned for an appalling accident record. *USA Today* rated it as the most dangerous highway in the country, while in 1995 the *Wall Street Journal* ran an article headlined "Beast of a Highway: Does Asphalt Stretch Have Biblical Curse?"

New Mexico's House and Senate passed a Joint Resolution in 2003 that declared:

WHEREAS, people living near the road already live under the cloud of opprobrium created by having a road that many believe is cursed running near their homes and through their homeland; and
WHEREAS, the number 666 carries the stigma of being the mark of the beast, the mark of the devil, which was described in the book of Revelation in the Bible; and
WHEREAS, there are people who refuse to travel the road, not because of the issue of safety, but because of the fear that the devil controls events along United States route 666; and

...the number of the road should be changed as soon as possible. A state highway official was reported as having no preference concerning the new designation: "As long as it's not 666 and it's nothing satanic, that's OK." The former US-666 therefore duly became **US-491**.

ACCOMMODATION AND EATING

Kokopelli's Cave 5001 Antelope Junction ☎ 505 860 3812, ⓦ bbonline.com/nm/kokopelli. This extraordinary cave dwelling, three miles north of town, was hollowed out in 1980, 75 feet below ground level but opening onto a cliff face balcony hundreds of feet above the La Plata River. It's rented out to groups of up to four people; breakfast ingredients are provided, but otherwise it's self-catering. To make the most of its glorious isolation, luxurious ambience, and features like the waterfall shower, stay two nights at least. $280

La Quinta Inn 675 Scott Ave ☎ 505 327 4706 or ☎ 800 753 3757, ⓦ lq.com. Presentable chain motel, near the Animas River on the east side of town, with a hundred decent rooms on two storeys, plus a heated pool and free breakfasts. $99

Three Rivers Eatery and Brewhouse 101 E Main St ☎ 505 324 2187, ⓦ threeriversbrewery.com. Sprawling and very central block-long complex that incorporates a brewery, tap room serving a huge range of speciality beers, a good-value pizzeria, and a lively, family-friendly restaurant serving the best (and most substantial) food you'll find for miles, including full meals, with mains at $15–27, as well as lunchtime sandwiches for under $10. Daily 11am–11pm.

Aztec

AZTEC, the county seat of San Juan County, straddles the Animas River fourteen miles northeast of Farmington, and 36 miles downstream from Durango. While lower-key and more enjoyable than its larger neighbour, its only real interest for visitors is the major Ancestral Puebloan site preserved in **Aztec Ruins National Monument**.

Aztec Museum and Pioneer Village

125 N Main Ave • May–Sept Tues–Sat 10am–5pm • $5 • ☎ 505 334 9829, ⓦ aztecmuseum.org

The quaint **Aztec Museum**, at the northern end of Aztec's leafy central thoroughfare, celebrates local history with displays on the oil industry and a mock-up barbershop. In its outdoor **Pioneer Village**, life-size mannequins hang out in frontier-style buildings like a schoolhouse, a jail and a bank.

1

Aztec Ruins National Monument

725 Ruins Rd, one mile north of Aztec, across the Animas River • Daily: summer 8am–6pm; winter 8am–5pm • $5 per person • ☎ 505 334 6174, ⓦ nps.gov/azru

The ancient pueblo now protected within **Aztec Ruins National Monument** was erroneously regarded by early Anglo settlers as the work of the dominant civilization of pre-contact Mexico. In fact, it's a large "outlier" Ancestral Puebloan settlement, built from 1111 onwards by people from the Chaco culture (see p.92), and connected with Chaco Canyon, 64 miles south, by a die-straight road now only visible from the air. Located halfway between Chaco and Mesa Verde, Aztec is thought to have been remodelled by a new wave of settlers from Mesa Verde around 1225.

From the visitor centre, which holds some interesting ancient artefacts, a short trail leads around and through the **West Ruin**, the only part of the site that has been excavated. This 500-room E-shaped structure held only one entrance and was entirely walled. The trail leads through room after room (you'll have to stoop to get through the low doorways) before culminating in the awesome **Great Kiva** – the term for a *kiva* used by an entire community rather than an individual clan or family.

Reconstructed in 1934, this is the only Great Kiva in the Southwest that can be seen in anything like its original state. Aspects of the restoration remain conjectural, but there's no disputing the circular chamber's sheer size, which measured fifty feet across. Its 95-ton roof was supported by four pillars that rested on 375-pound limestone disks, carried here from forty miles away. This *kiva* may have been in use when the *kachina* religion first developed, and its fifteen side rooms may have been changing rooms from

THE PUEBLITOS OF DINÉTAH

Although they now lie beyond the boundaries of the Navajo Nation, remote Largo and Gobernador canyons, southeast of Farmington and Aztec, were the original cradles of the **Dinétah**, the traditional Navajo homeland. The earliest known trace of a Navajo presence is a *hogan* in Gobernador Canyon, tree-ring dated to 1541, but the most significant era in its history followed the Pueblo Revolt of 1680. The refugees from the Rio Grande pueblos who fled west after the revolt were joined by further migrants when the Spaniards reconquered New Mexico from 1692 onwards.

Between 1680 and 1750, Navajo and Pueblo Indians combined to build around 130 stone fortresses in the region, known as the **Pueblitos of Dinétah**. Perched on high eminences close to the canyon rims, or tucked into alcoves just below, most of these "little pueblos" were too small to house an entire community; instead they were intended as lookouts, retreats for elders and religious leaders, and, above all, as shelters during raids. The Spaniards sent punitive expeditions into the area every summer between 1705 and 1716, while from the 1720s onwards Ute war parties threatened Navajo and Spaniard alike.

The *pueblitos* played a crucial role in forging a new synthesis of Navajo and Pueblo cultures. Many of the modern hallmarks of Navajo identity, from skills such as rug weaving and sheep-herding to religious beliefs, were acquired during this period. The driving force seems to have been the intermarriage of Navajo men with women from the pueblo of Jemez. Their union created the **Coyote Pass People**, still a prominent Navajo clan. Influences were also absorbed from further afield. Not only were Spanish metal-working techniques introduced, but in Three Corn Pueblito, abandoned in the 1750s, archeologists even unearthed a Qing dynasty plate from China.

While you can drive into both Largo and Gobernador canyons, along good-quality dirt roads used by gas-drilling companies, unless you have expert assistance you won't be able to reach or even spot the *pueblitos* themselves. Farmington's Bureau of Land Management office (6251 College Blvd; ☎ 505 564 7600, ⓦ blm.gov/nm) can provide directions to sites on BLM lands, but you'd do better to join an **organized tour** with Chaco Tours (☎ 505 632 2013, ⓦ chacotours .org), who charge $350 for an all-day 4WD trip for one or two people.

which masked figures emerged during ceremonies. You'll find details in the informative trail guide, written by an Indian from Santa Clara Pueblo quite possibly descended from the site's original inhabitants. A corresponding **East Ruin** lurks mysteriously beneath shapeless hillocks.

INFORMATION   AZTEC

Visitor centre 110 N Ash Ave, east of the river (daily 9am–4pm, closed Sun Oct–April; ☎505 334 9551 or ☎888 543 4629, ⓦwww.aztecnm.com). Their website provides directions to more than three hundred natural rock arches in the vicinity, the pick of which are highlighted in a free brochure.

ACCOMMODATION AND EATING

The Bistro 122 N Main Ave ☎505 334 0109, ⓦaztecbistro.com. This welcome little daytime stop, with an outdoor patio facing the museum, offers espresso coffee, breakfast bagels and burritos, and lunchtime salads, grilled sandwiches, and hearty green chile stew. Almost everything costs $10 or less. Mon–Fri 7am–2pm, Sat 8am–noon.

Step Back Inn 123 W Aztec Blvd ☎505 334 1200 or ☎800 334 1255, ⓦstepbackinn.com. Belying its modern exterior, the 39 pleasant rooms in this motel-cum-inn, where US-550 meets Main Avenue, are furnished with Victorian antiques. $72

ENTERTAINMENT AND LIVE MUSIC

Aztec Theater 104 N Main Ave ☎505 427 6748, ⓦcrashmusicaztec.com. Historic main-street theatre that's very much the centre of local nightlife, putting on live touring musicians one or two nights a week.

Bloomfield

BLOOMFIELD, eight miles south of Aztec or twelve miles east of Farmington, is an unattractive little desert crossroads at the axis of Hwy-64 and Hwy-550. It's notable for its **Salmon Ruins**, two miles west, and not much else. Several nondescript restaurants line Broadway Ave (Hwy-64), the main east–west road through town.

Salmon Ruins

6131 US-64, 2 miles west of Bloomfield • May–Oct Mon–Fri 8am–5pm, Sat & Sun 9am–5pm; Nov–April Mon–Fri 8am–5pm, Sat 9am–5pm, Sun noon–5pm • $4 • ☎505 632 2013, ⓦsalmonruins.com

The outlying Chacoan pueblo now known as **Salmon Ruins** was constructed between 1088 and 1094, twenty years before its neighbour at Aztec (see opposite). It may mark the first attempt to build a "new Chaco", which failed when the San Juan River proved too unruly to tame at this point, whereupon Aztec was built as a replacement. While much of the site consists of the exposed foundation walls of various structures, the central Great Kiva is undeniably impressive, much less fancifully restored than the equivalent at Aztec. Replicas of ancient pithouses and modern *hogans* offer insight into the region's successive inhabitants.

Bisti/De-Na-Zin Wilderness

Daily 24hr • No fees • ☎505 564 7600, ⓦblm.gov/nm/bisti

Yet another of the Southwest's seemingly infinite range of landscapes is on show in the **Bisti/De-Na-Zin Wilderness**, just under forty miles south of Farmington. A potential stop en route to or from Chaco Canyon, this 40,000-acre wilderness is more generally known as the **Bisti Badlands**, and as that name suggests has more in common with the badlands of the Dakotas than the red-rock country of New Mexico.

From a conspicuous parking lot just off Hwy-371, visitors can set off into a desolate grey wasteland composed of crumbling crevices and rounded hillocks of mud, shale and clay. Although there's no set trail, it's easy to follow in the footsteps of previous hikers, until you feel ready to turn back. Backcountry camping is permitted – you have to carry in all the water you'll need – but biking is not.

1

Chaco Canyon

Daily 7am–sunset • $12 per vehicle or $6 per individual • ☏ 505 786 7014, ⊛ nps.gov/chcu

The **largest pre-Columbian city** in North America, the **Ancestral Puebloan ruins** of **CHACO CANYON**, stand in extraordinary isolation amid the scrubby high-desert plains of northwest New Mexico. Now protected as **Chaco Culture National Historical Park**, they're a long, bumpy, twenty-mile ride off the nearest paved road, and more than double that from any significant town or facilities.

While the low-walled canyon itself can't match the likes of Canyon de Chelly for sheer beauty, there's still plenty about Chaco to take your breath away. Over 3600 separate sites have been logged here, of which the thirteen most important are open to visitors. Six of these, arrayed along the canyon's north wall, are what's known as **Great Houses** – self-contained pueblos, three or four storeys high, whose fortress-like walls concealed up to eight hundred rooms. The largest, **Pueblo Bonito**, is claimed to have been the largest single building in America until structural steel was developed in 1898.

Visitor centre

On the eastern side of the park, where the two approach routes meet • Daily 8am–5pm

An essential first stop, Chaco Canyon's **visitor centre** is the place to pick up maps and brochures, plus schedules of summer-only ranger-led tours. You can also watch videos such as *Sundagger*, which explains how rocks and petroglyphs atop nearby Fajada Butte were carefully sited to plot not only the annual solstices, but also the moon's 18.5-year cycle.

THE CHACO PHENOMENON

To archeologists, Chaco Canyon represents the apogee of Ancestral Puebloan achievement. However, what they call the **Chaco phenomenon** remains one of the Southwest's greatest puzzles. How can the canyon's apparent unsuitability for large-scale occupation – if anything, it was even drier in Ancestral Puebloan times than it is today – be reconciled with its massive structures and demonstrable influence over an "empire" that covered at least 25,000 square miles?

Although pithouses built by early Ancestral Puebloan Basketmakers are scattered around the canyon, Chaco's first surface pueblo appeared during the ninth century. Sophisticated masonry techniques, developed or introduced by migrants from the Mesa Verde region, enabled the construction of larger multistorey apartments such as Pueblo Bonito. The canyon's heyday came between 1050 and 1125; its last definite tree-ring date is 1132, and by 1200 it was abandoned. Prodigious work went into its construction. Upwards of 200,000 tree trunks, mostly ponderosa pines and corkbark fir, were carried here from hillsides fifty or more miles away, without the use of animals or the wheel.

Since Chaco became a national monument in 1907, estimates of its ancient population have repeatedly diminished. As few burials have been found, there's little sign that the upper floors were ever inhabited, and the canyon's soil is so poor, it's now believed that Chaco never held more than two thousand inhabitants.

Chaco was more of a **ceremonial centre** than a residential community; the Great Houses were not homes, but some combination of warehouses, temples and palaces. Huge quantities of **turquoise** have been discovered – harvester ants, who collect blue and green turquoise to adorn their nests, scavenged fifty thousand pieces in Pueblo Bonito alone. Still precious to contemporary Indian cultures, turquoise was the most valuable trading commodity in the ancient Southwest. The Chacoans acquired it raw from distant mines – mostly to the east, in the Cerrillos region (see p.128) – and crafted it into sacred and ornamental objects, which passed down trading networks into the heart of Mexico. Ninety percent of the turquoise found in Aztec Tenochtitlan was of Southwestern origin. Similarly, the parrots and scarlet macaws whose skeletons have been found here must have come from southern Mexico or beyond.

Chaco's primary significance, however, was much more local. Having started as a small trading settlement, it probably became a place of pilgrimage, where first individuals, and later large

The loop road

A nine-mile, one-way **loop road** provides the only access to the actual ruins in Chaco Canyon. Its gates are immediately north of the visitor centre, and open the same hours. The major stop is at the far end, where **Pueblo Bonito** can be explored on an easy half-mile trail.

Pueblo Bonito

Work on the four-storey D-shaped structure now known as **Pueblo Bonito** – which means "beautiful town" in Spanish, and is almost perfectly aligned east–west – started in 850 AD and continued for around three hundred years. Speculation that hordes of slaves were forced to build it have been deflated by precise dating of its parts; even during its busiest era, a workforce of just thirty men, cutting and hauling trees for a full month each year, and quarrying and shaping stone for four months every two years, could have done the job.

The half-mile trail around Pueblo Bonito heads first to the back of the structure, passing the spot where Threatening Rock, a colossal boulder whose collapse the ancient inhabitants staved off with prayer sticks and supporting walls, finally destroyed thirty rooms in 1941. Entering the ruin via its lowest levels, the path reaches its central plaza, which held at least three **Great Kivas** of the kind restored at Aztec (see p.90). From there, you can walk through the passageways and chambers of the pueblo proper, where the rows of neatly finished doorways, each framed by the next, are Chaco's most photographed feature.

crowds, would perform rituals and ceremonies to obtain sacred turquoise. For most of the year, Chaco held a small, high-caste population, and the upper floors of its pueblos were empty or used for storage; during regional **festivals**, they accommodated a large influx of guests.

An amazing 450-mile network of **roads** links Chaco with 75 "**outlier**" communities. Averaging thirty feet wide, they were far broader than ordinary human foot-traffic could require; they were more like causeways, built of hard-packed stone and running arrow-straight across cliffs, mesas and canyons. Most are now only visible from the air. The longest stretched all the way to Aztec Ruins, 64 miles north (see p.90), but if that same line is extended *south*, it makes a virtually perfect alignment with the site known as either **Casas Grandes** or **Paquimé**, over 300 miles away in Mexico. Roadside beacons may have been lit to summon pilgrims to major festivals.

Navajo legends relate that Chaco was ruled by the despotic **Great Gambler**, who was born to a poor Chacoan woman, taught to gamble by his father, the Sun, and won control over the canyon and all it held. When he was eventually defeated, he was shot into the sky, where he once more accumulated great wealth before returning in the shape of the Spanish invaders. Meanwhile, freed of their oppressor, the people of Chaco had dispersed.

Ferocious archeological debate has focused on the signs of large-scale **violence** at Chaco. Human remains found in two-thirds of the Great Houses appear to have been mutilated in a manner that suggests **cannibalism**. With no evidence of warfare, they're seen as possible victims of ritual slaughter. It has even been argued that a wandering group of Toltec refugees reached Chaco from the south around 900, and established a reign of terror by introducing the bloodthirsty Mexican practice of **human sacrifice**.

Trying to guess why the Chacoans left the canyon when they did – from 1230 onwards – is probably futile, although even a tiny reduction in rainfall might have been enough to drive them out. Where they went, however, is no great mystery. Both Aztec, at its peak between 1110 and 1275, and Casas Grandes, an even richer commercial centre occupied from 1250 to 1500, can be seen as successive "capital cities" of the same cultural tradition.

Acoma Pueblo (see p.99) is among the many modern pueblos that show a clear continuity with Chacoan culture. At least nine Hopi clans trace their origins back to what they remember as "the place beyond the horizon", while the Zuni say a medicine society known as the Sword Swallowers joined them from Chaco.

1

Chetro Ketl

A separate trail from the Pueblo Bonito parking lot heads to the smaller complex of **Chetro Ketl**, a quarter-mile east. Constructed over the course of a century, from 1010 onwards, this shows Chacoan masonry at its most sophisticated – or as some archeologists put it, at its most obviously influenced by Meso-American models. Its horizontal rows of large, squared-off stones are chinked with smaller, flatter stones and set into a bed of adobe mortar with mosaic-like precision. Many original beams (*vigas*) remain in place, while a vivid fragment of an ancient mural is protected behind glass.

Pueblo del Arroyo

The first stop along the loop road beyond Pueblo Bonito, **Pueblo del Arroyo** is the only Great House to stand right beside Chaco Wash. Although it rarely holds much water, the stream channel is much deeper and broader than it was in Ancestral Puebloan days. Only half the pueblo, raised on a small hillock and occupied between 1070 and 1105, has been excavated.

Casa Rinconada

Perched on a mound as the road heads back down the canyon from Pueblo del Arroyo, **Casa Rinconada** is the canyon's largest **Great Kiva**, at 62 feet across. It now lies open to the sun, the subtleties of its astronomical alignments lost but its central features still clearly identifiable. Archeologists are unsure whether the two large vaults in the *kiva* floor served as foot drums, or to propagate seedlings.

ARRIVAL AND INFORMATION   CHACO CANYON

By car Both the main approaches to Chaco Canyon entail driving at least thirteen miles over rough but passable dirt roads. They remain open all year, but should not be attempted during, or within a day of, a rainstorm.

From the south Leave I-40 at Thoreau, 28 miles northwest of Grants. Follow Hwy-57 north for another 28 miles, beyond Crownpoint, then turn right onto Arrowhead Hwy-9 for thirteen miles to Seven Lakes, where the twenty-mile dirt road to Chaco itself branches off to the left.

From the north or east Turn off US-550 three miles southeast of Nageezi, 36 miles south of Bloomfield; thirteen of the twenty miles from there are on dirt roads.

ACCOMMODATION

There's no indoor **lodging** at or near Chaco, and neither is **food** of any kind available.

Gallo campground Just east of the visitor centre ⊕505 786 7014; reservations ⊕877 444 6777, ⓦrecreation .gov. Backcountry camping being forbidden in Chaco Canyon, this basic campground is the only visitor facility in the park. Most of its 49 sites can accommodate RVs as well as tents; water is available, though it's not potable. No showers and no flush toilets between mid-Nov and Feb. Bring any firewood you require. Book ahead on summer weekends. $\underline{\$15}$

Crownpoint

CROWNPOINT, almost forty miles southwest of Chaco Canyon and 24 miles north of the I-40 town of **Thoreau**, is the principal town along the eastern flank of the Navajo Nation. Its chief appeal for tourists is as the site of the **Navajo Rug Auction**, held on the second Friday of each month, at Crownpoint Elementary School (⊕505 786 7386, ⓦcrownpointrugauction.com). Viewing is from 4pm until 6pm, with the auction at 7pm, and prices range from $100 up to perhaps $3000 (no credit cards).

Western New Mexico

Even if the reality of today's **I-40** may not match the romance of its predecessor, **Route 66**, crossing **western New Mexico** still has its rewards. The interstate passes through memorable desert scenery, while successive detours to the south lead to crucial sites in Southwestern history. At **Zuni Pueblo**, Spanish conquistadors first encountered the region's indigenous inhabitants, while **El Morro National Monument** records centuries of further incursions. Above all, **Acoma Pueblo**, the superbly sited "Sky City", makes it worth spending a night in the interstate towns of **Gallup** or **Grants**.

Gallup

As the largest town in I-40's 300-mile run between Albuquerque and Flagstaff, the famous Route 66 stop of **GALLUP**, 25 miles east of the Arizona state line, makes the obvious break in a long day's drive. That said, while cheap motels make it a handy overnight pit stop, there's little here to hold your interest.

Gallup sprang into being when the railroad arrived in 1881, and its role as the major railhead for the Navajo Nation was augmented by the arrival of first Route 66, and later I-40. The interstate and the railroad tracks still run east–west through the heart of town, paralleled by a ten-mile stretch of the former Route 66 that's lined with endless budget motels and fast-food outlets. Welcome splashes of colour are added by the large-scale **murals** scattered on prominent walls, some almost a century old and others added within the last few years.

Gallup remains a major commercial centre for the Navajo. An estimated eighty percent of all **silver jewellery** sold in the Southwest passes through the hands of traders like Richardson's Trading Company, 222 W 66 Ave (☎505 722 4762, ☻richardsontrading.com) and Shush Yaz, 1304 W Lincoln Ave (☎505 722 0130).

Inter-Tribal Indian Ceremonial

Red Rock State Park, 8 miles east of Gallup • Some free events, some ticketed, prices vary • ☎ 505 863 3896, ☻ theceremonial.com

In the week that culminates with the second weekend in August, the Navajo and other local Native Americans come together in Gallup for the **Inter-Tribal Indian Ceremonial**, a five-day extravaganza. The programme includes four days of rodeo and a three-day pow-wow plus craft shows, dancing and a Saturday-morning parade through town. Reserve accommodation well in advance.

ARRIVAL AND INFORMATION   GALLUP

By train Gallup's Amtrak station at 201 E 66 Ave sees one daily train towards Flagstaff and LA, at 7.08pm, and one east towards Albuquerque and Chicago, at 8.21am.
By bus Buses along I-40 call at the Amtrak station at 201 E 66 Ave, as do Navajo Transit services to Window Rock, Arizona (☎ 505 729 4002, ☻ navajotransit.com).

Information The Gallup Cultural Center, adjoining the Amtrak station at 201 E 66 Ave, sells crafts and souvenirs as well as providing local information (summer Mon–Sat 8am–5pm; winter Mon–Fri 8am–5pm; ☎ 505 863 4131, ☻ southwestindian.com).

ACCOMMODATION AND EATING

Comfort Inn Gallup 1440 W Maloney Ave ☎ 505 726 2700, ☻ choicehotels.com. Well-kept, good-value chain motel, immediately north of the main I-40 exit, across the tracks half a mile west of the centre. Decent rooms, indoor pool, and rates include breakfast. $103
Earl's Family Restaurant 1400 E 66 Ave ☎ 505 863 4201. This inexpensive diner, on the east side of town, serves chile-rich New Mexican specialities at prices that start below $10, and is usually bustling with Navajo crafts sellers. Mon–Sat 6am–9pm, Sun 7am–9pm.
★**El Rancho Hotel and Motel** 1000 E 66 Ave ☎ 505 863 9311, ☻ elranchohotel.com. *The* place to stay – if you prize Western historic charm over twenty-first-century luxury – this Route 66 roadhouse was built in 1937 by the

brother of movie mogul D.W. Griffith. From the murals in its Spanish Revival lobby to the signed photos of celebrity guests – Doris Day, W.C. Fields and Ronald Reagan among them – it's bursting with atmosphere, though the guest rooms are small, and the bathrooms even smaller. Some rooms are in the original ranch house, the rest in a less characterful two-storey motel building alongside. The decorative dining room (daily 6.30am–10pm) serves burgers named after John Wayne and Humphrey Bogart, plus (separate) Lucille Ball and Errol Flynn sandwiches, and the usual range of barbecue, steaks and shrimp priced at around $15, while the bar stays open until 1am. $113
Gallup Coffee Company 203 W Coal Ave ☎ 505 410 2505. If you simply want a snack or espresso as you pass

1

through, head for this lively central coffee bar, a block off the main drag. Mon–Sat 7am–8.30pm.

Red Rock State Park Hwy-566, just north of I-40, 8 miles east of Gallup ☎ 505 722 3839. This fully equipped campground, complete with showers and toilets plus a small supermarket, is the best place to camp near Gallup. Tents **$18**, RVs **$21**

Zuni Pueblo

Few tourists make the effort to visit remote **ZUNI PUEBLO**, 35 miles south of Gallup and a short way west of Hwy-602. However, it occupies a pivotal role in Southwestern history, as the first point of contact, almost five centuries ago, between the native peoples of the Southwest and the encroaching Spaniards. The invaders never found the gold they were seeking, but Zuni was a major trading centre, where the peoples of the Rio Grande exchanged turquoise for birds, feathers and shells from the west.

Much like the Hopi, the Zuni have since then found themselves restricted to an ever smaller area by Navajo, Apache, Spanish and Anglo newcomers. Today's **Zuni Indian Reservation** encompasses around three percent of ancestral Zuni lands and, with agriculture rendered marginal by erosion and over-grazing, the Zuni now depend for their livelihood on making **silver overlay jewellery**.

The dominant feature on the reservation, the red-and-white-striped mesa of **Dowa Yallane** or **Corn Mountain**, has long served as a refuge for the Zuni people in times of trouble. Immediately below, straddling Hwy-53 three miles west of Hwy-602, stands the main **village**. Now invariably known as **ZUNI**, it was founded as *Halona Idiwan'a*, or "Middle Place of the World", around 1700, when the Zuni came down from Corn Mountain after the Pueblo Revolt.

Simply driving along Hwy-53 through Zuni, it looks like just another run-down desert community. Almost none of the architecture is distinctive; although an ancient five-storey "apartment block", like those at Taos Pueblo (see p.151), still stands close to the centre, its bottom floors are now underground, while the upper levels are concealed beneath modern accretions. As even those buildings used for ceremonial purposes resemble new houses, the only traditional pueblo structures you'll see are the beehive-shaped bread ovens scattered around the plaza, and you get little sense that the traditional life of the pueblo is continuing. There are, however, several jewellery outlets, crafts shops and simple diners.

A:shiwi A:wan Museum and Heritage Center

02E Ojo Caliente Rd • Mon–Fri 9am–5pm; can be erratic, so call to confirm • Donations welcome • ☎ 505 782 4403, ⓦ ashiwi-museum .org • 3 blocks south of the highway from the only stoplight, along Pia Mesa Road

A former trading post refitted as an excellent modern museum, the **A:shiwi A:wan Museum and Heritage Center** reflects recent attempts by the Zuni to make their culture more accessible to visitors. Documenting Zuni history for tribal members as well as

---

FIRST CONTACT WITH THE ZUNI

It was at Zuni, in 1539, that the black African **Esteban** became the first outsider to enter the Pueblo world, and was promptly killed and cut into strips by the Zuni. Fray Marcos de Niza, following close behind him, fled for his life back to Mexico, to report that "this land … is the greatest and best of all that have been discovered".

The Zuni call themselves *A:shiwi*, "the flesh", and their country **Shi:wona**, "the land that produces flesh." Fray Marcos, who garbled that name into Cíbola, announced that the six Zuni towns were the **Seven Cities of Cíbola**. Spanish conquistadors had long sought the legendary Seven Cities of Antilla, founded by bishops who sailed west to escape the Moorish invasion of Portugal in 714 AD and said to be rich in **gold**. In 1540, therefore, a Spanish expedition led by Francisco Vásquez de **Coronado** returned to Zuni. Turned back from the now-abandoned town of **Hawikku**, the Spaniards defeated its inhabitants in the first battle ever fought between Europeans and Native Americans (see p.467).

> **THE SHALAKO DANCE**
>
> Apart from the **Zuni Tribal Fair** in late August, the one annual event that draws crowds to Zuni is the all-night **Shalako** dance, held in late November or early December. Anthropologists believe that this winter-solstice celebration, in which the *kachina* cult appears to blend with Aztec elements, was introduced by Mexican Indians left behind by Coronado.

tourists, it centres on a remarkable collection of artefacts that were excavated from the long-abandoned site of **Hawikku** during the 1920s, and only returned by the Smithsonian Institute in 2001. Enthusiastic staff will talk you through the displays, and provide local information of all kinds.

Our Lady of Guadalupe Mission Church

South of main road, not far east of A:shiwi A:wan Museum • Tours Mon–Sat 10am, 1pm & 3pm, Sun 1pm & 3pm; call to confirm • $10 • ☎ 505 782 7238, Ⓦ www.zunitourism.com

The adobe **Our Lady of Guadalupe Mission Church**, erected by the Spanish in 1629, has been restored to more or less its original appearance. In line with historical accounts, the interior once more holds "life-size" murals of Zuni *kachinas*.

Hawikku

Ojo Caliente Rd, 12 miles southeast of Zuni • Contact Zuni Visitor Center to arrange a 2hr 30min tour • $75 for 1 person, $25 for each extra person

The mound that conceals the ruins of the ancient settlement of **Hawikku** stands just west of the dirt road leading to the agricultural community of **Ojo Caliente**. Only visit with a guide supplied by the Zuni Visitor Center. Except for multicoloured potsherds poking from the rubble, there's little to see, but once you know the history it's an extraordinarily evocative site. Standing at the edge of the Pueblo world, you get a real sense of what a shock it must have been when first Esteban, and later Coronado, appeared across the infinite grasslands.

INFORMATION AND TOURS   ZUNI PUEBLO

Visitor centre The Zuni Visitor Center, 1239 Hwy-53 (no fixed hours; ☎ 505 782 7238, Ⓦ www.zunitourism.com), offers guided walks through the pueblo, typically costing $10 for 45min, plus longer visits to Zuni craftsmen and expeditions to archeological sites.

ACCOMMODATION AND EATING

Chu-Chu's Pizzeria 1344 Hwy-53 ☎ 505 782 2100. The pick of the simple restaurants along Zuni's main highway, with burgers, sandwiches and even blue-corn enchiladas to complement its decent pizzas. Daily 11am–10pm.

★ **Inn at Halona** ☎ 505 782 4547 or ☎ 800 752 3278, Ⓦ halona.com. Spending a night at the reservation's only accommodation option, tucked behind the Halona Plaza supermarket, is a memorable, indeed unmissable, experience for anyone with an interest in Zuni life. Eight charming and individually styled guest rooms, almost all en suite and sharing use of sitting rooms as well as a patio and library, are located in two separate buildings. The hospitable owners, who are not themselves Zuni but whose roots here go back over a century, provide excellent breakfasts, and are a mine of information. $80

El Morro National Monument

Hwy-53, 25 miles east of Zuni Pueblo and 42 miles west of Grants • Daily: visitor centre late May to early Sept 9am–6pm, early Sept to late May 9am–5pm; trail closes 1hr earlier • Free • ☎ 505 783 4226, Ⓦ nps.gov/elmo

Hidden away south of the Zuni mountains, **El Morro National Monument** feels as far off the beaten track as it's possible to be in the modern United States. It seems incredible, therefore, that this sheer sandstone cliff was a regular rest stop for international travellers before the Pilgrims landed at Plymouth Rock. The evidence is plain to see, however. It was first recorded by Spanish explorers in 1583 – *el morro* means "the headland" – and in

1

1605, **Don Juan de Oñate**, the founder of New Mexico, carved the first of the many messages that earned it the American name of **Inscription Rock**.

Translations and explanations of El Morro's graffiti are displayed in the **visitor centre**. You can see the real thing on a half-mile **trail**, access to which closes an hour before the visitor centre. El Morro is technically a cuesta, a long sloping mesa terminating in an abrupt bluff. The trail's first stop explains why so many people passed this way: a cool, perennial pool of water, collected beneath a waterfall that tumbles through a cleft in the pale pink cliffs. In such a self-evidently sacred spot, it's no surprise to see ancient **petroglyphs** scraped into the desert varnish nearby.

The optional and much more demanding two-mile **Headland Trail** climbs the cliff beyond the final inscription to see the **A'ts'ina Ruins**, up on top. Its builders, who abandoned it in 1350 AD, were among the ancestors of the modern Zuni.

EATING

Inscription Rock Trading mile-marker 46, Hwy-53. ☎ 505 783 4706, ⓦ inscriptionrocktrading.com. At this log-built cabin, at the foot of a mesa a mile east of El Morro, you can stop off for a snack and browse the Zuni crafts, or simply sit out on the patio to enjoy coffee, or on occasional summer evenings, live music. Tues–Sat 9am–5pm, Sun 10am–5pm.

El Malpais National Monument

El Malpais Information Center Hwy-53, 23 miles south of I-40 exit 81 • March–Sept daily 8am–5pm • ☎ 505 876 2783, ⓦ nps.gov /elma • **BLM ranger station** Hwy-117, nine miles south of I-40 exit 89 • Daily 8am–4.30pm • ☎ 505 240 0300, ⓦ blm.gov • Free

El Malpais being Spanish for "the Badlands", **El Malpais National Monument** preserves a tract of territory covered by **lava flows** from a volcanic eruption two or three thousand years ago – recent enough for the landscape to remain blackened and barren. Its designation as a federal park in the 1980s was bitterly opposed by neighbouring Acoma Indians, who lost, in part, because they preferred not to reveal the whereabouts of sacred shrines. For casual visitors, hiking any distance across the rough rock is a pretty miserable business, and it's not an especially worthwhile detour if your time is at all limited.

The map of El Malpais is a peculiar patchwork of desolate lava interspersed with pockets of grassland that the eruption missed. Highways 53 and 117 skirt the periphery, to the west and east respectively; in an ordinary vehicle you can only get from one to the other via Grants. On Hwy-117, the more interesting drive of the two, **Sandstone Bluffs Overlook** near the ranger station, commands views westwards across the flatlands to the jagged peaks of the **Cerritos de Jaspe** and north to Mount Taylor. Not far beyond, **La Ventana Arch** is a chunky natural window three-quarters of the way up a cliff face east of the highway.

Grants

In general, **GRANTS**, sixty miles east of Gallup on I-40, looks better by night than it does by day. Daylight exposes an air of ever-growing dereliction along its old Route 66 frontage that's concealed when the neon signs come on after dark. Even so, Grants has more character than Gallup and is a handy base for venturing off the interstate.

Like Gallup, Grants started out as a railroad town. In the 1950s, just as a half-hearted **carrot** boom fizzled out, it struck rich in a rather less wholesome way. A Navajo shepherd, Paddy Martinez, picked up some yellow rocks on nearby Haystack Mountain, and Grants found itself sitting on half the US's reserves of **uranium**. Both the Anaconda mining company, which opened an enormous mine, and the Santa Fe Railroad, which owned the land, made a fortune; Martinez got a monthly pension and the title "official uranium scout".

New Mexico Museum of Mining

100 N Iron Ave • Mon–Sat 9am–4pm • $3 • ☎ 505 287 4802, ⦿ grants.org

Grants' uranium years have receded into history, but they're enjoyably recalled in the **New Mexico Museum of Mining**. Visits consist of a faked descent into a mocked-up mine where you can poke around with no fear of radiation.

INFORMATION
GRANTS

Northwest New Mexico Visitor Center At the east end of town, just south of I-40 exit 85 at 1900 E Santa Fe Ave, this excellent National Park Service facility offers information on the region's public lands (daily 8am–5pm; ☎ 505 876 2783).

Visitor centre 100 N Iron Ave, adjoining the mining museum (Mon–Fri 9am–5pm; ☎ 505 287 4802, ⦿ grants.org).

ACCOMMODATION AND EATING

Holiday Inn Express 1512 E Santa Fe Ave ☎ 505 287 9252, ⦿ hiexpress.com. Grants' smartest motel offers the best rooms around, though that's not saying all that much; if you're just passing through and aren't too bothered about the size of your pool or TV, you could easily pay half this. **$116**

La Ventana Hillcrest Center, 110 Geis St ☎ 505 287 9393. The most popular place to eat in town, offering pretty much everything from $13 fajitas to $22 steaks, plus lighter sandwich lunches; the dining room is generally dark, so the patio seating can be welcome. Mon–Sat 11am–11pm.

Acoma Pueblo

The amazing **ACOMA PUEBLO**, south of I-40 fifteen miles east of Grants and fifty miles west of Albuquerque, encapsulates a thousand years of Native American history. Focused around the ancient village known as "**Sky City**", atop a magnificent mesa, it has adapted to repeated waves of invaders while retaining its own strong identity. Although the Acomans have long been happy to take the tourist dollar – so visitors seldom feel the awkwardness possible at other Pueblo communities – Acoma is the real thing, and its sense of unbroken tradition can reduce even the least culturally sensitive traveller to awestruck silence.

Five hundred years since the Spanish arrived, the **Acoma Indian Reservation** still has a population of six thousand. Most live in three communities that were originally sited for their proximity to fresh water but now stand conveniently close to I-40 – **ACOMITA**, **McCARTYS** and **ANZAC**.

For the most dramatic approach to Sky City itself, which stands twelve miles south of I-40 via any of three connecting roads, leave the interstate at exit 102 and drive in from the **west**. When the mesa comes into view, glowing in the sunlight as you drop down a hillside roughly three miles distant, you'll understand why the first Spanish explorers spoke of cities of gold.

Sky City

Cultural Center March–Oct daily 8am–7pm; Nov–Feb Sat & Sun 9am–4pm • **Tours** Hourly 8.30am–3.30pm, March–Oct daily; Nov–Feb Sat & Sun • Entire pueblo closed to all visitors June 24, June 29, July 9–14, July 25, first and/or second weekend in Oct, first Sat of Dec • Tours $23, plus $13 for photo permit, no camcorders or video • ☎ 505 552 7861 or ☎ 800 747 0181, ⦿ acomaskycity.org

All visits to Acoma begin at the **Sky City Cultural Center**, at road's end below the mesa. You can only see Sky City itself on a one-hour-thirty-minute **tour**; buses carry groups up from the Cultural Center at regular intervals. While you're waiting, it's well worth paying to see the displays on Acoma history and pottery in the centre's small but very informative **Haak'u Museum** (same hours as visitor centre; $4).

Once they reach the mesa-top, tour groups stroll more or less at will, with plenty of opportunities to buy handmade pottery or ears of multicoloured corn. Don't expect to enter any individual dwellings, however.

While the original walls of Sky City's oldest houses lie concealed beneath several centuries of replastering, the village's overall appearance has barely changed. The high windowless wall of the main pueblo, at the northern edge of the mesa, protected its

1

A HISTORY OF ACOMA PUEBLO

Only certain Hopi villages can rival the claim of **Sky City** to be the **oldest inhabited settlement** in the United States. This isolated mesa, 367ft high and 7000ft above sea level, was probably first occupied by Chacoan migrants at some point between 1100 and 1200, when the great pueblos of Chaco Canyon were still in use. The name Acoma means "people of the white rock"; by the sixteenth century, it's thought to have held around six thousand inhabitants, living in five hundred or so three- to four-storey houses.

The **Coronado** expedition of 1540 described the Acomans as "robbers, feared by the whole country round about". Noting the mesa's strong defences – it could only be reached by climbing ladders through a narrow crevice – the Spaniards commented that "no army could possibly be strong enough to capture the village".

In October 1598, **Don Juan de Oñate** visited Acoma in peace, while exploring his recently proclaimed colony of New Mexico. A month later, however, his nephew **Juan de Zaldivar**, following with reinforcements, arrived at the foot of the mesa, demanded food, and was rejected. Depending on which version you believe, the Spaniards either tricked their way onto the mesa, or the Acomans invited them up and then ambushed them. In the ensuing fight, all the Spaniards were killed, save four who survived being hurled off.

When a punitive Spanish force of seventy men, equipped with cannons, stormed the village in January 1599, over eight hundred Acomans died in a three-day house-to-house battle. Five hundred women and children and eighty men were taken prisoner. All were sentenced to twenty years of penal servitude, and each man had a foot publicly chopped off, in the plazas of the Rio Grande pueblos. Bitterness persists to this day; a statue of Oñate erected in Alcalde, New Mexico, in 1999 lost its right foot within days.

Oñate was eventually called back to Mexico City and removed from office for his savagery. By 1629, Acoma had a resident Spanish friar – Fray Juan Ramírez is said to have been accepted after he caught a child who fell off the mesa – and the Acomans were hard at work building a huge **mission church**. Although Ramírez's successors were driven out during the Pueblo Revolt, and a tyrannical eighteenth-century priest was thrown to his death, the pueblo was permanently converted to Catholicism.

The people of Acoma clearly never felt inclined to follow the architectural example of the mission, whose mighty beams were carried 25 miles from Mount Taylor without once touching the ground. Instead, they went on constructing the same multistorey stone and adobe houses that can still be seen today.

Only a dozen families, forty people in all, now live on the mesa itself. Others make daily trips to sell pottery or fry bread, while many more return to their ancestral homes for feast days and ceremonies. Eighty percent of Acomans call themselves Catholic, but the old religion endures; there are fourteen separate clans, and the Antelope Clan remains in charge of everything. Even now, the priest who serves the community is not himself Indian, and is only permitted to visit the mesa once a week, on Wednesdays.

inhabitants against both the chill north wind and potential invaders. Three or four storeys of terraced "apartments" face south to maximize the winter sun. Just one room still has its original tiny "windowpane" of translucent mica. Digging *kivas* down into the sandstone requires too much labour, so seven of the above-ground rooms are *kivas*, each shared by two clans and entered by a tall ladder pointing north. Acoma's sparse rainfall collects in natural depressions in the rock; beside the largest such cistern is the mesa's only tree, a slender cottonwood.

Legend has it that forbidding **Enchanted Mesa**, visible to the east, once held its own Pueblo community. The only access to the top was via a spider's-web of ropes strung between the mesa itself and an adjoining rock pillar. When that pillar collapsed one day while the men were away from the village, two women and a child on top were left stranded, their cries for help fading as they starved.

If you prefer, at the end of your tour you can walk rather than ride back down from Sky City, following the ancient footpath through clefts in the rock.

Church of San Esteban del Rey

The still-active mission church of **San Esteban del Rey**, the main stop on Sky City tours, measures 120ft long by 40ft wide. Its seventy-foot-high walls taper from ten-foot-thick at the base to six foot at the top. The floor is made of hard-packed earth, while the whitewashed interior walls hold a mixture of Christian images and Pueblo motifs. Acoma's greatest treasure hangs above the altar – a painting of **St Joseph**, said to answer prayers for rain, which was borrowed by Laguna Pueblo in 1800 and only returned after the Acomans took Laguna all the way to the US Supreme Court. As no photography is permitted in the vicinity of the church, you'll never have seen an image of the sublime view as you turn around from the altar, and won't be prepared for the glorious New Mexican light that streams in through the doorway to fill the cavernous space.

There's no soil on the mesa-top, so the adobe bricks of the church were made with mud carried up from below, and its **cemetery** was filled with endless basket-loads of sand. Only honoured elders can now be buried here – not in coffins, but "replanted", facing east. The churchyard wall looks crenellated, but in fact the bumps are "warriors", placed to guard the dead.

ACCOMMODATION AND EATING   **ACOMA PUEBLO**

Sky City Hotel Beside I-40 exit 102 ☎ 505 552 6123 or ☎ 888 759 2489, ⓦ skycity.com. The only accommodation available at Acoma is up by the interstate, in this large, comfortable, and reasonably stylish hotel. The adjoining tribal casino is best avoided, other than to eat the good-value food in its *Huwaka* restaurant, which offers cheap buffets as well as a full

menu (Mon–Thurs & Sun 7am–10pm, Fri & Sat 7am–midnight). $89
Y'aak'a Café Sky City Cultural Center, below Acoma mesa, 12 miles south of I-40 ☎ 505 470 0181, ⓦ acomaskycity .org. Good, inexpensive breakfasts and lunches; wraps and burgers cost $7–8, and a Pueblo taco – much the same as a Navajo taco – $9. Daily 9am–4pm.

Laguna Pueblo

LAGUNA PUEBLO, north of the interstate six miles east of Acoma and 44 miles west of Albuquerque, is New Mexico's **youngest** pueblo. It was established in 1698 by refugees from several pueblos, driven here by the disruption of the Pueblo Revolt and the threat of Navajo and Apache raids. It's also the **richest** pueblo, thanks partly to standing above the world's largest **uranium mine**, Anaconda's Jackpile mine, which closed in 1982, after operating for thirty years. **Contamination** from mining has left a sorry legacy of long-term health problems, but thanks to the pueblo-owned Laguna Construction Company, a major contractor with the US military, the tribe remains prosperous.

All of Laguna Pueblo, including its **San José Mission Church**, is visible from a rest stop on the westbound side of I-40, halfway between the tribe's two **casinos** at exits 108 and 140, where traders sell crafts. There's no reason to explore any further.

Santa Fe and northern New Mexico

TAOS PUEBLO

Santa Fe and northern New Mexico

Basking in the magical "light" beloved by artists and tourist boards alike, stretching beneath the flame-red peaks of the Sangre de Cristo mountains, northern New Mexico is the New Mexico of popular imagination, with its pastel colours, vivid desert landscape and adobe architecture. Quite apart from its ravishing beauty, nowhere else in North America can boast such a sense of unbroken history. Native American pueblos and Hispanic colonial settlements have stood side by side along the Rio Grande for over four hundred years, and the Yankees who arrived on the Santa Fe Trail still seem like relative newcomers.

State capital **Santa Fe**, the only city, more than lives up to its high-profile image as the epitome of Southwestern style, bursting with top-class museums, galleries and restaurants. Nonetheless, it remains less than a tenth the size of Albuquerque, and its central plaza is still recognizable as the frontier marketplace that welcomed trade caravans from Mexico and the Mississippi. **Taos**, 75 miles northeast and even smaller, is almost equally celebrated thanks to a remarkable twentieth-century influx of artists and writers such as **Georgia O'Keeffe** and **D.H. Lawrence**. It too has its share of museums and amenities and is a near neighbour to the Rio Grande's most striking pueblo, multistorey **Taos Pueblo**.

Both Taos and Santa Fe are surrounded by spectacular scenery, and detours away from the river are rewarded with glimpses of countless fascinating communities. These range from the ancient **cliff dwellings** of **Bandelier National Monument** on the Pajarito Plateau west of the river, to Hispanic villages such as **Chimayó** on the **High Road** to the east, Wild West towns like **Las Vegas**, and even the high-tech home of the H-Bomb, **Los Alamos**.

Santa Fe

SANTA FE has long ranked among the most desirable destinations in the US, a favourite for upmarket travellers in particular. There are very good reasons for that: founded by Spanish adventurers and missionaries a decade before the Pilgrims reached Plymouth Rock, it's one of America's **oldest** and most **beautiful** cities. Spread across a high plateau at the foot of the stunning **Sangre de Cristo** mountains, New Mexico's capital still glories in the adobe houses and baroque churches of its original architects, comple. mented these days by superb art museums and galleries. The busiest season is **summer**, when temperatures usually reach into the eighties Fahrenheit (high twenties centigrade); in winter, the average daytime high is a mere 42°F (5°C), though with snow on the mountains the city looks more ravishing than ever.

With well over a million tourists every year – not to mention twenty thousand daily commuters – descending on a town of just seventy thousand inhabitants, Santa Fe has inevitably grown somewhat overblown. It still offers a palpable, romantic continuity with the Spanish settlement of four hundred years ago, however. Despite the summer

SANTUARIO DE CHIMAYÓ

Highlights

❶ Palace of the Governors, Santa Fe Home to fascinating historical displays, the country's oldest public building flew the flags of three other nations before the Americans moved in. **See p.109**

❷ Museum of International Folk Art, Santa Fe The most enjoyable of Santa Fe's many fine museums; a wonderland of folk artefacts from around the globe. **See p.116**

❸ La Fonda de Santa Fe Splendidly atmospheric old hotel that once marked the end of the Santa Fe Trail. **See p.120**

❹ Coronado Historic Site When the fall colours are at their peak, the sunsets at this historic Pueblo settlement, beside the Rio Grande, are out of this world. **See p.127**

❺ Bandelier National Monument New Mexico's most appealing ancient site, where the ancestors of today's Pueblo peoples carved their homes into soft volcanic rock. **See p.132**

❻ Puyé Cliff Dwellings Seize this rare opportunity to tour ancient cliff homes with a pueblo guide descended from the peoples who built them. **See p.138**

❼ Santuario de Chimayó Exquisite adobe pilgrimage chapel beside the mountainous High Road from Santa Fe to Taos. **See p.145**

❽ Taos Pueblo Best experienced on its timeless, extraordinary feast days, this thousand-year-old pueblo centres on two amazing multitiered adobe dwellings. **See p.151**

HIGHLIGHTS ARE MARKED ON THE MAP ON P.106

SANTA FE AND NORTHERN NEW MEXICO

HIGHLIGHTS

1 The Palace of the Governors, Santa Fe
2 Museum of International Folk Art, Santa Fe
3 La Fonda de Santa Fe
4 Coronado Historic Site
5 Bandelier National Monument
6 Puyé Cliff Dwellings
7 Santuario de Chimayó
8 Taos Pueblo

0 — 25 miles

crowds, the downtown area – clustered around the city's venerable **plaza** – continues to have the peaceful ambience of a small country town, while holding an extraordinary array of cultural and historic treasures. Above all else, it's rare indeed for it to be such fun simply to stroll around a Southwestern city.

Once you've got your bearings in the plaza, the best places to get a sense of local history and culture are the **Palace of the Governors** and the **Museum of Fine Arts** downtown, and the museums of **Indian Arts and Culture** and **Folk Art** a couple of miles southeast. Two private museums, the **Museum of Spanish Colonial Art** and the **Georgia O'Keeffe Museum**, are also well worth seeing. Alternatively, set about exploring Santa Fe's distinct neighbourhoods, such as the old **Barrio Analco** just southeast of downtown, home to the **San Miguel Mission**; the **Canyon Road** arts district, just beyond; and funkier **Guadalupe Street** to the west, with its lively **Railyard** development.

Brief history

The first homes of **La Villa de Santa Fe** ("Holy Faith") were erected above an abandoned Native American pueblo around 1604. In 1610, after previous Spanish settlements to the northwest had been deemed unsuitable, Santa Fe became the third capital of the infant colony of **New Mexico**. It was laid out as an imposing administrative city; the *casas reales* or "royal houses" that commanded its parade-ground plaza went on, as the **Palace of the Governors**, to house Spanish, Pueblo, Mexican and American rulers.

Santa Fe was the base from which **horses**, introduced to North America by the Spanish, spread across the continent and were acquired by Native American peoples. During its first two centuries the city presented an inviting target for mounted Apache, Ute, and Comanche raiders. Relations with the **Pueblo** peoples were initially stable, but growing antagonism led to the **Pueblo Revolt** of 1680, when Santa Fe was besieged and conquered by an alliance of many different tribes. One thousand Spaniards fled south and lived in exile for twelve years at El Paso before returning under a new governor, **Don Diego de Vargas**. Their fight to regain control of the city is still celebrated in the annual **Fiesta de Santa Fe**.

Santa Fe was always a neglected outpost of the Spanish empire; at the time of Mexican independence in 1821, its garrison was armed merely with bows and arrows. Attempts to improve the economy thereafter focused on the ever-expanding United States. Although American goods were soon pouring across the plains on the **Santa Fe Trail**, US citizens were forbidden to settle in the city. In 1843, the Mexican president ordered that the Santa Fe Trail be closed altogether, but a mere three years later New Mexico passed

---

ADOBE

For many visitors, the defining feature of New Mexico is its **adobe architecture**, as seen in homes, churches, and even malls and motels. While ancient pueblo villages were constructed using blocks of mud, cut from the riverbeds and mixed with grass, it was early Franciscan missionaries who introduced moulded adobe **bricks**. The Spaniards had themselves learned the technique – in which a mixture of earth, sand, charcoal and chopped grass or straw is left to bake in the sun in a wooden frame known as an *adobero* – from the Arabs. Built into walls, the bricks are set with a mortar of much the same composition, and then plastered over with mud and straw. As the colour of the soil used dictates that of the final building, subtle variations can be seen throughout the state. However, adobe is far from being a convenient material: it needs replastering every few years and turns to mud when water seeps up from the ground, so many buildings must be sporadically raised and bolstered by the insertion of rocks at their base.

These days, most of what looks like adobe is actually painted cement or concrete, but even that looks attractive in its own semi-kitsch way. Superb genuine adobes include the remote **Santuario de Chimayó** on the High Road between Santa Fe and Taos, the formidable church of **San Francisco de Asis** in Ranchos de Taos, and the multitiered dwellings of **Taos Pueblo**.

into American hands. A discreet payment of $50,000 to Governor Armijo ensured that there was no opposition to the entry of the US Army on **August 18, 1846**.

The Yankees set about transforming the squat, dusty Mexican town into something more conspicuously American, building in wood rather than adobe, but Santa Fe remained largely unchanged for the rest of the nineteenth century. Even when the old buildings started to disappear, the city was promptly seized by the conviction that it could only retain its identity by turning the clock back again – a campaign inspired, ironically, by the romantic notions of Anglo newcomers as to how Santa Fe *ought* to look. Since the 1930s, almost every structure within sight of the plaza has been designed or redecorated to suit the **Pueblo Revival** mode. The rigorous insistence that every downtown building should look like a seventeenth-century Spanish colonial

SANTA FE AREA

EATING
Harry's Roadhouse	5
Jambo Cafe	3
Museum Hill Café	2
Tecolote Café	4
Tune-Up Café	1

ACCOMMODATION
Black Canyon Campground	1
El Rey Inn	2
Santa Fe KOA Cabins & Campground	4
Silver Saddle	3

NIGHTLIFE
Second Street Brewery	1

SHOPPING
Jackalope	2
Jambo Imports	1

SANTA FE FESTIVALS AND MARKETS

The first of the three major events in Santa Fe's annual calendar is **Spanish Market**
(W spanishcolonial.org), during the last week in July, when examples of the traditional folk arts
of Hispanic New Mexico are sold on the plaza, while contemporary works are on sale in the
Palace of the Governors.

Indian Market (W swaia.org) fills the plaza on the weekend after the third Thursday in
August, attracting over 100,000 buyers and craftspeople from all over the world for the premier
showcase of Southwestern Native American arts and crafts. A smaller-scale **Winter Indian
Market** takes place during the last weekend in November.

September's **Fiesta de Santa Fe** (W santafefiesta.org), which takes place over the weekend
after Labor Day, has been held annually since 1712 to celebrate the Spaniards' return after the
Pueblo Revolt. The ceremonial burning of *Zozobra* ("Old Man Gloom") in Fort Marcy Park on the
Thursday prior, which kicks off the parades and processions, is not a Catholic tradition; it was
invented in the 1920s by a group of high-spirited atheist intellectuals.

2

palace takes a bit of getting used to. This must be the only city in the world where it
would be illegal to build a gas station that didn't resemble an Indian prayer chamber,
and what on first glance appears to be a perfectly preserved ancient adobe turns out to
be a multistorey parking lot. As a result, though, Santa Fe today – at least at its core –
looks much more like its original Spanish self than it did a century ago.

The plaza

Santa Fe's central **plaza** has been the heart of the city since 1610, though the original
rectangular parade ground of the Spanish garrison was twice as large as the neat, leafy
square of today. As well as witnessing many turning points in New Mexican history –
from the public hanging of three "witch-doctors" in 1675 (which helped to trigger
the Pueblo Revolt five years later, when Pueblo Indians filled the plaza to lay siege
to the Palace of the Governors), to the nineteenth-century celebrations of Mexican
independence and annexation by the United States – it served as journey's end for
countless weary travellers on the Santa Fe Trail. Just how contentious the city's history
remains is illustrated by the **obelisk** at the centre of the plaza, where unknown hands
have chiselled the word "savage" out of an inscription that formerly honoured "the
heroes who have fallen in the various battles with savage Indians in the territories of
New Mexico".

The plaza now serves as a pleasant public park, where the trees are renowned for a
spectacular display of colours each fall. Visitors and office workers picnic on the grass
and listen to street musicians as they watch the latest bemused arrivals spill out of their
tour buses.

Under the arcade of the Palace of the Governors, along the plaza's northern flank,
Native American traders shelter from the summer sun or winter wind. They're strictly
licensed, so the price, authenticity and quality of their craftworks and jewellery compare
favourably with the stores and galleries that line the other three sides of the square.

Palace of the Governors

105 Palace Ave • May–Oct Mon–Thurs, Sat & Sun 10am–5pm, Fri 10am–8pm; Nov–April Tues–Sun 10am–5pm • $9, free Fri 5–8pm
May–Oct, under-17s free • ☎ 505 476 5100, W palaceofthegovernors.org

The oldest public building in the United States, the **Palace of the Governors**, fills
the north side of Santa Fe's central plaza. Now run as a fascinating **historical museum**,
in conjunction with the adjoining modern **New Mexico History Museum**, it was
constructed in 1610 as the headquarters of the Spanish colonial administration,
and first occupied by Governor **Pedro de Peralta**.

To call this long single-storey structure a "palace" may seem an exaggeration, but it was originally much larger, an imposing adobe, with two towers and a sod roof, which formed part of a bigger defensive complex. After the **Pueblo Revolt** of 1680, the palace was taken over by Pueblo peoples, who sealed its doors and windows, divided its rooms, and dug still-visible storage pits into the floor, but it was soon back in Spanish hands, and later became home to first Mexican, and then American, governors of New Mexico. By the time Governor **Lew Wallace** wrote part of *Ben Hur* here, during his term of office from 1878 to 1881, the palace had turned Victorian. Its balustrades, elaborate windows and wallpaper were removed after it ceased to be the official governor's residence in 1909, and was restored as part of the **Museum of New Mexico**. That it now looks so much like every other building in central Santa Fe is hardly surprising – it served as a blueprint for the remodelling of the city. It's also as much of a

■ **ACCOMMODATION**

El Paradero	6
Four Kachinas	8
Inn & Spa at Loretto	4
La Fonda de Santa Fe	2
The Madeleine	1
Old Santa Fe Inn	3
Hotel Santa Fe	7
Santa Fe Motel & Inn	5
Santa Fe Sage Inn	9

■ **NIGHTLIFE**

Cowgirl BBQ	2
Evangelo's	1

● **EATING**

Amaya	12
Cafe Pasqual's	8
Clafoutis	1
Downtown Subscription Coffee Bar	16
Eloisa	9
French Pastry Shop	6
Geronimo	15
La Boca	2
La Casa Sena	5
La Plazuela	7
Sage Bakehouse	13
Saveur	11
Sazón	10
The Shed	4
The Teahouse	14
Tia Sophia's	3
Vinaigrette	17

fake, in that until 1913, it was a typical, formal, territorial building with a square tower at each corner; its subsequent adobe "reconstruction" was based on pure conjecture.

Displays in its well-preserved interior are especially strong on Hispanic New Mexico. Starting with swords and helmets from the sixteenth-century Spanish *entrada* into the Southwest, they stress that the frontier experience of New Mexico lasted for three centuries, far longer than anywhere else in the United States. One room holds an idealized reconstruction of a nineteenth-century chapel, complete with a genuine 1830 altarpiece, and there's also a large collection of crucifixes and *santos*.

Be sure to visit the museum's well-stocked bookstore (which you can also access without paying admission), and to wander into the peaceful open-air courtyard beyond, where the Palace Print Shop sells hand-printed cards and booklets (daily 9am–4.30pm).

2

DOWNTOWN SANTA FE

● **SHOPPING**

Andrea Fisher Fine Pottery	1
Chile Shop	3
Collected Works Bookstore	2
Kowboyz	6
Nathalie	9
Pachamama	7
Seret & Sons	4
Silver Sun	11
Tom Ross Gallery	8
Travel Bug	5
Zaplin Lambert Gallery	10

New Mexico History Museum

113 Lincoln Ave • May–Oct Mon–Thurs, Sat & Sun 10am–5pm, Fri 10am–8pm; Nov–April Tues–Sun 10am–5pm • $9, free Fri 5–8pm
May–Oct, under-17s free • ☎ 505 476 5200, ⓦ nmhistorymuseum.org

Reached across a courtyard immediately behind the Palace of the Governors, a modern but surprisingly compatible extension houses the predominantly visual exhibits of the **New Mexico History Museum**. After racing through the pre-Hispanic period in a couple of cases, this tells the story of the shifting alliances, treacheries and compromises that went into creating modern New Mexico. Highlights include some fascinating letters from Billy the Kid, in the Kid's wonderfully elegant script, along with his spurs, and even the door of the jail from which he escaped in Lincoln (see p.183). There's also a good display on the **Fred Harvey** company, and its role in pioneering mass tourism throughout the Southwest a century ago.

New Mexico Museum of Art

107 E Palace Ave • May–Oct Mon–Thurs, Sat & Sun 10am–5pm, Fri 10am–8pm; Nov–April Tues–Sun 10am–5pm • $9, free Fri 5–8pm
May–Oct, under-17s free • ☎ 505 476 5041, ⓦ nmartmuseum.org

Santa Fe's **New Mexico Museum of Art** is housed in a particularly attractive adobe on the northwest corner of the plaza. Erected in 1917, this was Santa Fe's first example of the "Pueblo Revival" school of architecture, and remains unsurpassed to this day. It focuses around a beautiful garden courtyard with a fountain at its centre, and ornamental beams to all sides. One of the few major art museums to be established by artists rather than collectors, it continues to concentrate on changing exhibits of painting and sculpture by contemporary local artists. Selections from the permanent collection, displayed upstairs, usually include an O'Keeffe or two, while the room devoted to painter and printmaker Gustave Baumann is especially fascinating. A good shop sells Southwestern prints.

Georgia O'Keeffe Museum

217 Johnson St • Mon–Thurs, Sat & Sun 10am–5pm, Fri 10am–7pm • $12, under-19s free • ☎ 505 946 1000, ⓦ okeeffemuseum.org

Downtown Santa Fe's showpiece **Georgia O'Keeffe Museum** is home to the world's largest collection of O'Keeffe's art, including around 140 paintings. Highlights include many of the desert landscapes she painted near **Abiquiu**, forty miles northwest of Santa Fe (see p.139), where she lived from 1946 until her death in 1986. Entire rooms are devoted to paintings of particular motifs, be it scarlet poppies or pink seashells, all characterized by O'Keeffe's trademark close focus and voluptuousness. Among the more familiar sun-bleached skulls and iconic flowers, you may be surprised by earlier canvases such as her New York city scenes.

Precisely what's on show at any one time is liable to vary, as successive exhibitions are devoted to differing aspects of O'Keeffe's work, as well as other artists who have been influenced by, or paid homage to, New Mexico's favourite adopted daughter. O'Keeffe is also celebrated as an icon herself, via photos by her husband Alfred Stieglitz and others. The museum was rumoured to be on the point of undergoing major expansion as this book went to press, but no specific plans had been unveiled.

St Francis Cathedral

131 Cathedral Place • ⓦ cbsfa.org • Mass Mon–Sat 7am & 5.15pm, Sun 8am (Spanish), 10am, noon & 5.15pm

Santa Fe only acquired its first Catholic bishop in 1851, after New Mexico joined the United States and ceased to belong to the Mexican diocese of Durango. As described in Willa Cather's novel *Death Comes for the Archbishop*, the arrival of **Jean-Baptiste Lamy** – a Frenchman, previously resident in Kentucky – threw the overwhelmingly Hispanic church in New Mexico into turmoil.

Lamy's most lasting achievement, **St Francis Cathedral**, now makes an unlikely spectacle, looming two blocks east of the plaza at the top of San Francisco Street. Eschewing adobe, the first cathedral west of the Mississippi was built of solid stone, between 1869 and 1886, in the formal – and, frankly, dreary – Romanesque style of France. Its walls rose over and around those of its eighteenth-century predecessor, which was progressively removed as rubble. The interior is much brighter than you might expect, adorned with tiles, frescoes and *santos*.

In the only part of the original structure to survive, the side chapel of **Our Lady of the Rosary**, impressive *viga* beams remain conspicuous in its wooden ceiling. Pride of place within goes to a statue of the Virgin known as **La Conquistadora**. Brought from Mexico in 1625, she was credited by the Hispanic population of Santa Fe with facilitating both their escape from the Pueblo Revolt in 1680 and their subsequent reconquest of the province. A disingenuous caption in the chapel explains that while the reconquest may not have been peaceful, it was "less conflicting than it could have been". The statue itself looks more like a Victorian doll than a venerated religious artefact – an effect enhanced by the practice of dressing it in different clothes at different times of the year. She is still paraded through the city each June, on the Sunday after Corpus Christi.

Museum of Contemporary Native Arts

108 Cathedral Place • Mon & Wed–Sat 10am–5pm, Sun noon–5pm • $10, under-17s free • ☎ 505 983 8900, ⓦ iaia.edu/museum

The stimulating **Museum of Contemporary Native Arts** is housed in a modern building – which naturally looks like adobe – facing the cathedral. As they insist on telling you, "we're contemporary, not historical"; most of the artwork exhibited is less than a year old, so it's impossible to be specific as to what you'll see if you visit. Rest assured, though, that encompassing paintings, installations, collages and mixed-media pieces, it's all a long way from conventional stereotyped notions of Native American art. The sculpture garden is especially recommended.

Loretto Chapel

207 Old Santa Fe Trail • Mon–Sat 9am–4.30pm, Sun 10.30am–4.30pm • $2.50, ages 7–12 $2 • ☎ 505 982 0092, ⓦ lorettochapel.com

The **Loretto Chapel**, one block from the plaza, was built for the Sisters of Loretto from 1873 onwards, under the auspices of Archbishop Lamy. When the chapel was completed, it was realised that there was no way to reach the choir loft, twenty feet above the nave. Hence the legend of its **Miraculous Staircase**, an elegant wooden spiral – more of a spring, in a sense – that makes two complete 360-degree turns as it rises, and was built without a single nail or any support at either the centre or the sides. It's said to be the work of a mysterious carpenter who arrived in answer to the nuns' prayers and disappeared without demanding payment.

Sadly, the story is more entertaining than the reality. The chapel is now deconsecrated and belongs to the upmarket *Inn at Loretto*; when it's not in use as a wedding chapel, it tends to be packed with tourists. What's more, the nuns found the staircase too frightening to climb, so they disfigured it by adding banisters. The whole thing is now propped up with a metal brace.

San Miguel Mission

401 Old Santa Fe Trail • Mon–Sat 9am–5pm, Sun 1.30–4pm; Mass on Sun at 5pm • $1, under-7s free • ☎ 505 983 3974, ⓦ sanmiguelchapel.org

San Miguel Mission is said to be the oldest church in the United States to have remained in continuous use. The site is known to have been occupied in 1300 AD, while the church itself was built in 1610 by Tlaxcalan Indians from central Mexico,

2

KOKOPELLI

Time was when you could scarcely move in Santa Fe without someone trying to sell you a figurine of a turquoise coyote howling at the moon. These days, however, the coyotes have been superseded by a symbol more closely associated with Native American traditions – the hunchbacked flute player known as **Kokopelli**.

Although Kokopelli derives originally from ancient **rock art**, his image has been so extensively appropriated by non-Native artists that he's now become an all-purpose icon for the Southwest. He's usually depicted in silhouette, as a solid block of a single colour, whether printed, painted, cast in clay or cut from sheet metal. His flute is a simple extension of his face, each leg curves seamlessly from his trunk, and his head is crested with what might once have been feathers but are now often dreadlocks. You might see him cycling, skiing or dressed in strange costumes, but his basic shape remains instantly recognizable.

But who was Kokopelli? There's no single answer. While he's often referred to as an "Anasazi flute-player" – "Anasazi" being the term formerly used for the Ancestral Puebloans – he dates back longer than that. You can see him in the pictographs in Canyonlands' Horseshoe Canyon (see p.412), created by so-called Archaic peoples more than 1600 years ago. Other ancient cultures familiar with Kokopelli included the Mogollon, the Sinagua and the Hohokam.

While Kokopelli has been viewed in many, inconsistent ways, it's generally agreed that he was not physically deformed, but a trader whose "hunch" is really a pack on his back. As they carried their goods north from Mexico, such traders, possibly carrying seeds for sale, announced their arrival in each new pueblo by blowing a **flute**. Some see him as a benevolent deity who introduced agriculture to the Southwest, bringing new crops to each village and explaining the rituals necessary to their cultivation. Others see him as more of a trickster, a Pied Piper figure who used his flute to seduce impressionable women (hence the enormous phallus in many ancient images).

Today, Kokopelli is most associated with the Hopi, though even within that tribe different groups tell different stories. The Flute Clan, currently based at Walpi on First Mesa, marked their successive homes (they trace their migrations back to Mesa Verde) by depicting their clan symbol, Flute Player, in rock art. They regard Flute Player as distinct from the mischievous Kokopelli, who is remembered by other Hopi clans as a *kachina*, and also exists in a female version – or perhaps it's his wife – Kokolmana.

Authentic ancient depictions of Kokopelli can be seen near Santa Fe at the **La Cieneguilla Petroglyph Site**, accessible on a demanding hour-long hike that starts from Airport Road, a dozen miles southwest of the plaza. Pick up detailed trail information from the Public Lands Information Center (see p.118).

who had arrived with New Mexico's earliest Spanish settlers. Although its roof was destroyed during the 1680 Pueblo Revolt, parts of its graceful, sloping adobe walls survived. That said, before the church was "restored" to its current appearance in the nineteenth century, its external lines were much sharper than they are today; its rounded adobe look is not necessarily authentic.

Inside, a hole in the floor beneath the altar reveals the foundations of an ancient pueblo, belonging to a group known as the **Analco**, as well as the original steps of the sanctuary, while the pale green *reredos*, or altarpiece, above was painted in 1798 to frame a statue of San Miguel brought by missionaries from Mexico. The mission also holds a buffalo hide and a deerskin, painted with depictions of Jesus on the cross, which date from around 1630. In addition, its giftshop contains what's said to be the oldest bell in the US, cast in Spain in 1356.

The claims of a nearby adobe, immediately north of the church at 215 East de Vargas Street, to be the **oldest house in the United States** are generally dismissed. It too probably stands on the ruins of the former pueblo, though, and it's worth dropping in to take a look at its reconstructed rooms. This whole district, the **Barrio de Analco**, is now an appealing residential neighbourhood, abounding in two-hundred-year-old houses.

The Guadalupe District

A few blocks southwest of the plaza, the stretch of **Guadalupe Street** that runs south from the tiny Santa Fe river is the focus of the characterful little **Guadalupe District**. Traditionally this area catered more to local students and artists than to passing tourists, but in recent years, as home to the **Railyard**, it has mushroomed as an upscale shopping and nightlife destination.

Santuario de Guadalupe
417 Agua Fria St at Guadalupe • Mon–Sat 9am–noon & 1–4pm • Donation • ☎ 505 983 8868

The small **Santuario de Guadalupe** was built as a shrine between 1776 and 1795 to mark the end of the Camino Real, the trail from Mexico City that for centuries provided Santa Fe's only connection with the outside world. Remodelling in the 1880s added an incongruous New England-style spire and tall windows, and the church became a small museum of its own history to mark its (and the nation's) bicentennial in 1976. It now hosts regular Masses, including one at 12.12pm on the 12th of each month, as well as occasional concerts, usually of a religious nature.

The Railyard

During the late nineteenth century, the neighbourhood adjoining Guadalupe Street became the point of arrival into Santa Fe for trains on the Atchison, Topeka & Santa Fe, and Denver & Rio Grande railroads. Since it became Santa Fe's terminal for the Rail Runner system (see p.118), it has been redeveloped under the official name of **The Railyard**, with its former warehouses and small factories converted to house boutiques, art galleries and restaurants, along with a popular **Farmers Market** (Saturday mornings year-round, plus Tuesday morning in summer).

Canyon Road and Acequia Madre

Before Santa Fe ever existed, **Canyon Road**, which climbs a steady but shallow incline east from Paseo de Peralta, a few hundred yards east of San Miguel Mission, was an ancient trail that led to the pueblo at Pecos. Since the 1920s, however, it has been famous as the centre of Santa Fe's **art colony**. It's now dominated by expensive stores and galleries (see p.123), but even if you don't plan to buy anything it makes for an intriguing half-day stroll out from downtown.

Located at Canyon Road's far eastern end, the 1940 **Cristo Rey church** is the largest adobe building in the US. It's over three miles out, however, and most walkers prefer to double back along Canyon Road at some earlier point. You can also return to town via **Acequia Madre**, one block south. The name of this ancient street literally means the "mother ditch"; following the course of the city's first irrigation canal, it's lined with beautiful adobe homes.

Museum Hill
750 Camino Lejo

The raised plateau known as **Museum Hill** stands two miles southeast of downtown Santa Fe, enjoying magnificent views of the hills and mountains that all but surround the city. At its centre, Milner Plaza is a landscaped area that's home to two superb museums – one dedicated to **Indian Arts and Culture**, the other to **International Folk Art** – as well as a good café (see p.122), and a giant bronze statue of an Apache Mountain Spirit Dancer. Two further museums are located to the immediate north and south – the **Museum of Spanish Colonial Art** and the **Wheelwright Museum of the American Indian**.

2

2

Museum of Indian Arts and Culture

May–Oct daily 10am–5pm, Nov–April Tues–Sun 10am–5pm • $9, under-17s free • ☎ 505 476 1269, ⓦ miaclab.org

The excellent **Museum of Indian Arts and Culture** provides comprehensive coverage of all the major Southwest tribes, including the O'odham, Navajo, Apache, Pai, Ute and Pueblo peoples. Its centrepiece, a permanent exhibition entitled **Here, Now, and Always**, is intended as much for Native Americans themselves as for tourists – hence the taped messages that warn Navajo and Tewa visitors to skip certain sections in order to avoid contact with the world of their dead forebears. Myth and history are explained in copious detail. Ancient artefacts ranging from pots and pipes to bells, whistles and spearthrowers are drawn from sites that extend as far south as the Casas Grandes ruins in Mexico (see p.93), while contemporary realities are acknowledged in such forms as the inclusion of computer games, alongside music, architecture and language, in the exhibit on the modern Apache way of life. Different parts of the exhibit focus on the topography of the Southwest, explaining how native peoples have thrived in such differing terrains as canyons, river basins, mesas and deserts.

The museum also boasts an especially comprehensive array of Native American pottery, from pristine thousand-year-old Ancestral Puebloan and Mimbres pieces up to the works of modern revivalists.

Museum of International Folk Art

May–Oct daily 10am–5pm, Nov–April Tues–Sun 10am–5pm • $9, under-17s free • ☎ 505 827 6344, ⓦ internationalfolkart.org

The delightful **Museum of International Folk Art** centres on the huge **Girard Collection** of paintings, textiles and, especially, **clay figurines**, gathered from all over the world. These are arranged in colourful dioramas that include a Pueblo Feast Day, complete with dancing *kachinas* and camera-clicking tourists, and street scenes from countries such as Poland, Peru, Portugal and Ethiopia featuring fabulously ornate churches and cathedrals. The sheer scale of the place has to be seen to be believed – and it makes a pleasant change, for once, for there to be large signs that read "Please Do Take Photos".

An equally eclectic array of folk art objects is displayed in the Neutrogena Collection, where the specific artefacts on show change each year. The traditional New Mexican crafts in the **Hispanic Heritage Wing** are also fascinating. Alongside the expected *santos* (religious depictions of saints, whether carved figures or painted panels of wood), you'll encounter eerie skeletal wooden figures of "Death Personified", associated with the Penitente brotherhoods (see p.144). Excellent temporary exhibitions focus on more recent works such as *paños* – handkerchiefs decorated with religious and secular images in magic marker or pencil by often anonymous prison inmates.

Museum of Spanish Colonial Art

May–Sept daily 10am–5pm, Oct–April Tues–Sun 10am–5pm • $8, under-16s free • ☎ 505 982 2226, ⓦ spanishcolonial.org

Focusing on such traditional Hispanic religious artworks as *retablos* (painted images of religious scenes and figures) and *bultos* (carved wooden statues of saints), the **Museum of Spanish Colonial Art** makes a valiant attempt to place colonial art in a global context. Statuettes in its World of Art room are drawn from as far afield as Goa and Guatemala. Showcasing work by contemporary New Mexican schoolchildren, the Youth Gallery proves that local traditions are in no danger of dying out. The whole collection is appealingly laid out in a former private home, one room of which replicates the living room of an eighteenth-century Spanish captain in New Mexico, and reveals so-called "Santa Fe style" to be more than a mere home decorating invention.

Sadly, however, given the abundance of Hispanic colonial art on display throughout Santa Fe, and in particular the superior exhibits in the neighbouring folk art museum, there may be little here that isn't already familiar to you. In addition, being by definition largely vernacular, the pieces tend not to be of such exceptional quality as to merit a special trip.

Wheelwright Museum of the American Indian

Daily 10am–5pm • $5, under-12s free • ☎ 505 982 4636, ⓦ wheelwright.org

The original purpose of the large, private **Wheelwright Museum of the American Indian**, constructed in the 1930s to resemble a Navajo *hogan*, was to record Navajo sand paintings and ceremonials. These days, however, apart from the jewellery in its new Centre for the Study of Southwestern Jewellery, little of its permanent collection tends to be on show. It concentrates instead on changing exhibitions, largely of contemporary art that's similar to what you'll see in the galleries in town. The Case Trading Post downstairs sells jewellery, rugs and *kachinas* of very high quality, at very high prices.

2

Rancho de las Golondrinas

334 Los Pinos Rd, 15 miles south of Santa Fe, 3 miles from I-25 exit 276 • June–Sept Wed–Sun 10am–4pm; guided tours available by reservation, also on Mon–Fri in April, May & Oct • $6, ages 13–18 $4, under-13s free • ☎ 505 473 4169, ⓦ golondrinas.org

Once a fortified *paraje* (stopping place) on the Camino Real, the **Rancho de las Golondrinas**, or "Ranch of the Swallows", is now a living history museum. The adobe farmstead at its heart is thought to have welcomed the governor of New Mexico in 1698, and strongly resembles Pueblo architecture of the period. As La Cienaga Ranch, it belonged in the eighteenth century to Captain Manuel Delgado, whose living room is reproduced in Santa Fe's Spanish colonial art museum. He was wealthy enough to own a wardrobe of thirteen velvet, cashmere and silk suits.

Topped by a tall *torreon* (watchtower), the 200-acre farmstead incorporates a covered well and plenty of stables and livestock pens within its strongly defensive walls, while planted fields reach down to the river beyond. Other early Hispanic structures – many brought from elsewhere in New Mexico – include a watermill, a replica Penitente *morada* (see p.144), a smithy, and smaller farmhouses. The whole place is staffed by well-informed but unobtrusive "villagers" in period costume, with different sections maintained in the style of the seventeenth, eighteenth and nineteenth centuries. It's an absolutely lovely spot, ranged across the meadows and woodland to either side of the river and bursting with wildflowers and sweet-smelling herbs.

The best time to visit Las Golondrinas is during one of the **theme** or **festival weekends** (from $8), held on the first weekend of each month in summer, as well as several other weekends.

Santa Fe ski area

Hwy-475, 16 miles northeast of the city • Daily lift tickets $72 full-day, $58 half-day • ☎ 505 982 4429, ⓦ skisantafe.com • Served by RTD Mountain Trail Buses ($5; ⓦ ncrtd.org)

Santa Fe's **ski area** lies within the Santa Fe National Forest, off the winding and very scenic Hwy-475. Boasting a 12,075ft summit and 1725ft of vertical skiing, its 79 runs are usually open from late November until early April. Skiing is suitable for all levels, and it offers a ski/snowboard school as well as multi-day programmes and workshops for both children and adults. Equipment can be rented on site, but there are **no resort facilities** apart from a café and a grill that provide soups, burgers, sandwiches and the like.

Pecos National Historical Park

4 miles north of I-25 exit 397, 25 miles east of Santa Fe • Daily: summer 8am–6pm; winter 8.30am–4pm • $7 per person • ☎ 505 757 7241, ⓦ nps.gov/peco

The long, low ridge in the heart of the Sangre de Cristo mountains, east of Santa Fe, that's now preserved as **PECOS NATIONAL HISTORICAL PARK** served for over a thousand years as one of the most significant cultural rendezvous in the Southwest. Ninth-century Basketmakers (see p.462) were the first to inhabit this spot, but between 1450 and 1550, as the pueblo of **Cicuyé**, it was home to over two thousand people, including five hundred warriors. Protected behind four-storey walls, it was a **trading centre** where Pueblo peoples exchanged turquoise, axes and shells from as far west as the Pacific for bison meat, hides and wood for bows brought by Plains nomads who camped outside the walls. **Coronado** stayed here in 1541 and met a captive from the plains who lured his expedition east in search of the nonexistent gold of Quivira (see p.468).

After Franciscan missionaries built a church alongside what they called **Pecos Pueblo**, sixty years later, Spaniards too came to trade, but Apache and Comanche raids eventually forced Pecos into decline. Its last twenty survivors migrated 65 miles west to join Jemez Pueblo in 1838. Their descendants continue to elect a governor of Pecos Pueblo, and return for ceremonies. Excavations during the 1920s so precisely chronicled the changes in pottery and architecture that Pecos became the model for all other such digs, and is thus famed as the "birthplace of Southwestern archeology".

Visitor centre and trails

The whole Pecos story is well told in the **visitor centre**, from where a mile-long trail loops onto the ridge itself. Much of the former pueblo area remains unexcavated, though some walls are exposed, and large buried structures are obvious everywhere. Beyond it, the trail leads around and through the high roofless walls of the **mission church**, stark in the bright sunlight and surrounded by the ruined *convento* buildings where its priests once lived. The *kiva* in the heart of the church was dug as a deliberate act of sacrilege during the Pueblo Revolt. If you're pressed for time, spare yourself the hike from the visitor centre by following the signs off the approach road to the "picnic area", which will enable you to park close to the church.

Glorieta Pass

Two additional parcels of the park, accessible using a code available at the visitor centre and also on weekly guided tours (Sat 1.30pm; $2), incorporate the site of the **Battle of Glorieta Pass**. Fought on March 28, 1862, it was the turning point of the **Civil War** in the Southwest, when four thousand Union soldiers repelled three thousand Confederate invaders who had already briefly occupied Santa Fe.

ARRIVAL AND DEPARTURE   SANTA FE

By plane Santa Fe's small municipal airport, 10 miles southwest of downtown, is only served by flights from LA, Denver and Dallas/Fort Worth; the nearest major airport is in Albuquerque, 66 miles southeast.

By Rail Runner From the Santa Fe Depot, in the Railyard half a mile southwest of downtown, the Rail Runner train line connects Santa Fe with downtown Albuquerque (journey time 1hr 40min; $9 one-way, $10 all-day pass; ☏ 866 795 7245, ⓦ nmrailrunner.com); free shuttle buses link to Albuquerque airport.

By Amtrak Amtrak does not serve Santa Fe itself, but daily Southwest Chief trains between Chicago and LA stop at Lamy, 17 miles southeast, where they're met by Lamy Shuttle vans ($29 one-way; ☏ 505 982 8829).

By bus Greyhound no longer serves Santa Fe, but the El Paso–Los Angeles Limousine Express, which despite the name is a bus not a limo, stops four miles south of the plaza at the Giant Convenient Store, 2691 Sawmill Rd, en route between Denver and Albuquerque (☏ 866 691 7932, ⓦ eplalimo.com).

INFORMATION

New Mexico Tourism Department 491 Old Santa Fe Trail (Mon–Fri 8am–5pm, Sat & Sun 8am–4pm; ☏ 505 827 7336, ⓦ newmexico.org). This visitor centre is the best place to pick up maps and information on Santa Fe and the whole state.

Public Lands Information Center 301 Dinosaur Trail, 9 miles southwest of downtown, just south of I-25 at the top

of the Turquoise Trail (Mon–Fri 8.30am–4pm; ☏ 505 954 2002, ⓦ publiclands.org). Helpful advice on all New Mexico's public lands, including hiking trails close to Santa Fe.

Santa Fe CVB While the city visitor centre at 201 W Marcy St is not worth visiting, the official website, ⓦ santafe.org, is an excellent resource.

GETTING AROUND

By bus Free Santa Fe Pick-Up buses loop around downtown from the Rail Runner station (every 10min; Mon–Fri 6.30am–5.30pm, Sat 8.30am–5.30pm, Sun 10am–5.30pm), and out to Canyon Road and Museum Hill from the state visitor centre at 491 Old Santa Fe Trail (every 30min; daily 10am–5.30pm). In addition, the Santa Fe Trails bus operates ten routes from the Downtown Transit Center, a block northwest of the plaza on Sheridan Ave, charging a standard adult fare of $1, with one-day passes for $2 and monthly passes for $20 (Mon–Fri 6am–10pm, Sat 8am–8pm, Sun 8.30am–6.30pm; ⓦ santafenm.gov/transit). Route #2 goes up Cerrillos Road at 15min intervals, while route #M runs hourly to Museum Hill.

By taxi Capital City Cab (☎ 505 438 0000).

Bike rental Mellow Velo, 132 East Marcy St (Mon–Sat 10am–6pm; ☎ 505 995 8356, ⓦ mellowvelo.com).

TOURS AND ACTIVITIES

Bus tours The Loretto Line, based at the Loretto Chapel, 207 Old Santa Fe Trail, runs bus tours of the city, taking in Museum Hill and Canyon Rd as well as the plaza area (mid-March to Oct daily 10am, noon & 2pm; $16; ☎ 505 982 0092, ⓦ toursofsantafe.com).

Hiking The Santa Fe area holds excellent opportunities for hiking, with countless trails winding through the surrounding mountains. The greatest concentration can be found along Hyde Park Rd, which leads to the Santa Fe ski area; several trailheads dot either side of the road. On the left-hand side, 5.5 miles from the start of Artist Rd (which becomes Hyde Park Rd), is the trailhead for the Chamisa Trail (5 miles round-trip), a good introduction to the area's hiking possibilities, with plenty of expansive views as it passes alongside several of the region's native tree species, such as white pine, aspens and Douglas fir.

Horseriding Historic *Bishop's Lodge*, 4 miles north of the plaza at 1297 Bishop's Lodge Rd (☎ 505 819 4013, ⓦ bishopslodge.com), offers horseback rides through its thickly wooded 450 acres and the adjoining Santa Fe National Forest.

Mountain biking The more than twenty miles of trails of the Dale Ball network in the Sangre de Cristos offer numerous challenging rides, all within close proximity to the city centre. Mellow Velo (see above) can provide rentals as well as maps of this network and additional biking trails.

Santa Fe School of Cooking 125 N Guadalupe St (☎ 505 983 4511, ⓦ santafeschoolofcooking.com). Extensive programme of cookery classes, typically costing around $40 for a cookery demonstration class and $100 for a hands-on lesson, plus afternoon walking tours of four local restaurants, for around $115 including tastings.

Ten Thousand Waves The Zen-inspired Ten Thousand Waves spa, 10min drive east into the mountains at 3451 Hyde Park Rd (☎ 505 982 9304, ⓦ tenthousandwaves.com), offers treatments and services ranging from Japanese Anma massages to herbal wraps; many can be enjoyed outdoors and even under the stars. Its distinctive Japanese-styled main building and outlying lodges are prime specimens of organic architecture, and there's also an excellent Japanese restaurant.

Walking tours Historic Walks of Santa Fe runs regular 1hr 45min walking tours of downtown, starting from several hotels (March–Dec, schedules vary; $14; ☎ 505 986 8388, ⓦ historicwalksofsantafe.com).

Whitewater rafting Kokopelli Rafting, 802 Early St (☎ 505 983 3734, ⓦ kokopelliraft.com), leads half-day and full-day rafting tours on the Rio Chama and Rio Grande, ranging from gentle Class I floats to more adrenaline-fuelled Class IV trips in the Taos Box Canyon. All involve a long round-trip drive from Santa Fe, though, so if you're planning to stay in Taos during your trip, you'd do better to go rafting from there.

ACCOMMODATION

Santa Fe holds what has to be the finest array of accommodation in the Southwest. A dozen or more irresistible **hotels**, complemented by a plethora of exquisite **B&Bs**, stand within walking distance of the plaza, and embody the very essence of New Mexican style. Even in winter, you'd be lucky to find a room downtown for under $100, while in summer – when every bed in town is frequently taken – there's little under $150. **Cerrillos Road** (US 85), the main road in from I-25, holds most of Santa Fe's **motels** (and also its one hostel, which is not worth recommending).

B&BS

El Paradero 220 W Manhattan Ave ☎ 505 988 1177 or ☎ 866 558 0918, ⓦ elparadero.com; map pp.110–111. Converted Spanish-era farmhouse near Guadalupe St. The rooms, especially those that open onto the central courtyard, are relatively simple and furnished with colourful folk art; thirteen are en-suite, the remaining two share a bathroom and can combine to make a family suite. Good breakfast and helpful hosts. **$135**

Four Kachinas 512 Webber St ☎ 505 982 2550 or ☎ 800 397 2564, ⓦ fourkachinas.com; map pp.110–111. Very pleasant, welcoming B&B inn, in a quiet spot near the State Capitol, a short walk from the centre. Some of the six charming en-suite rooms – with varying themes such as Chimayó style or the prints of Gustave Baumann – have their own outdoor patios. The same owners run the similar, slightly more expensive *El Farolito* nearby. **$190**

The Madeleine 106 Faithway St ☎ 505 982 3465 or

☎888 877 7622, ⊛madeleineinn.com; map pp.110–111. Large Queen Anne inn, in a peaceful garden setting behind the cathedral. The mixture of rooms (not all en suite) and cottages are all furnished with Pueblo and Mexican artworks, and there's an on-site Indonesian spa. **$150**

HOTELS

Inn & Spa at Loretto 211 Old Santa Fe Trail ☎800 727 5531, ⊛innatloretto.com; map pp.110–111. Rising between the plaza and the river, this upmarket hotel is an extraordinary spectacle, designed with its seven tiers to resemble Taos Pueblo. As well as opulent rooms and public spaces, the high-class *Luminaria* restaurant, and adjoining Loretto Chapel, it hosts a top-quality spa. **$239**

★**La Fonda de Santa Fe** 100 E San Francisco St ☎505 982 5511 or ☎800 523 5002, ⊛lafondasantafe.com; map pp.110–111. Gorgeous old inn on the southeast corner of the plaza, marking the end of the Santa Fe Trail; guests have ranged from Kit Carson to John F. Kennedy. Built in 1920 to replace the century-old original, it features hand-painted murals and stained glass throughout, and plenty of nooks and crannies where you can sit and soak up the atmosphere. Each lavishly furnished room is different, with some lovely suites in the newer Terrace section, and there's the delightful *Plazuela* restaurant plus the *Bell Tower* rooftop bar. **$269**

Old Santa Fe Inn 320 Galisteo St ☎505 995 0800 or ☎800 734 9910, ⊛oldsantafeinn.com; map pp.110–111. Former Route 66 motor court, now an appealing inn; many of its tasteful, Mexican-themed rooms have their own gas fireplaces. Avoid the few rooms in the inadequately soundproofed two-storey buildings. **$189**

★**Hotel Santa Fe** 1501 Paseo de Peralta at Cerrillos Rd ☎505 982 1200 or ☎855 825 9876, ⊛hotelsantafe.com; map pp.110–111. Run by Picuris Pueblo, this attractive, elegant and very comfortable adobe hotel on the edge of downtown is within walking distance of the plaza, has its own good restaurant, *Amaya*, and stages free lectures by local historical and cultural experts. The suites in the adjoining "Hacienda" building are even more luxurious, and come with personal butler service. **$229**

MOTELS

★**El Rey Inn** 1862 Cerrillos Rd at St Michael's Drive ☎505 982 1931 or ☎800 521 1349, ⊛elreyinnsantafe.com; map p.108. This white-painted adobe compound, here since the 1930s, offers the most character and best value of the Cerrillos Road motels, with stylish, distinctive and large Southwestern rooms adorned with Art Deco tiles, semi-private patios, some nice suites, a pool and a large garden. Ask for a room away from the road. **$109**

★**Santa Fe Motel & Inn** 510 Cerrillos Rd ☎505 982 1039 or ☎800 930 5002, ⊛santafemotel.com; map pp.110–111. To call this delightfully stylish yet inexpensive little adobe complex a "motel" barely does it justice; even its most conventional rooms are appealingly furnished, and some have their own kitchens, while there are also several gorgeous little *casitas*. The staff are very friendly, and the rates, which are great for such a quiet, central location, include a full cooked breakfast. **$149**

Santa Fe Sage Inn 725 Cerrillos Rd at Don Diego ☎505 982 5952 or ☎866 433 0335, ⊛santafesageinn.com; map pp.110–111. Large, clean motel, very close to the edge of the Railyard District, with very helpful staff and good rates that include free local shuttle. **$119**

Silver Saddle 2810 Cerrillos Rd at Siler Rd ☎505 471 7663, ⊛santafesilversaddlemotel.com; map p.108. Busy, down-to-earth Western-themed motel, in the finest Route 66 tradition, four miles out from downtown. Each of the 27 rooms has a little patio, some have cooking facilities, and they feature all kinds of fun cowboy trappings. **$68**

CAMPING

Black Canyon Campground Hwy 475 ☎505 753 7331, ⊛fs.usda.gov/recarea/santafe, reservations on ⊛recreation.gov; map p.108. Attractive campground in the woods of the Santa Fe National Forest, seven miles northeast of central Santa Fe. Most of its 45 sites, unusual in offering advance reservations, are available to car campers or RVs; it has water and vaulted toilets but no electricity. Two much smaller and more basic campgrounds, free and open year-round (weather permitting), lie further along the same road: *Big Tesuque* and *Aspen Basin*. May–Sept. **$10**

Santa Fe KOA Cabins & Campground 934 Old Las Vegas Hwy ☎505 466 1419 or ☎800 562 1514, ⊛koa.com/campgrounds/santa-fe/; map p.108. The most appealing commercial campground near Santa Fe, a dozen miles southeast of town, near I-25 exit 294 on what was once Route 66. Each tent site has its own protective circle of trees, there's plenty of space for RVs, and there are also good-value rental cabins, but no pool. March–early Nov. Tents **$28**, RVs **$42.50**, cabins **$60**

EATING

Santa Fe has been renowned as one of America's most exciting places to **eat** since the early 1980s, when a stupendous feat of marketing managed to make dishes such as banana-crusted sea bass seem quintessentially Southwestern, and it's now said to have more high-end restaurants per capita than anywhere else in the US. There's certainly some memorable dining to be had, and it doesn't have to be wallet-busting. The sheer inventiveness of the city's menus makes up for its shortage of ethnic alternatives (though you will find the odd adobe sushi bar here and there).

THE PLAZA AREA

Cafe Pasqual's 121 Don Gaspar Ave ☎505 983 9340, ⓦpasquals.com; map pp.110–111. Lovely, lively and ever-innovative Old/New Mexican restaurant that serves top-quality organic food in an attractive tiled dining room, a block from the plaza. The dinner menu ranges from vegetarian enchiladas ($26), via *cochinita pibil* (slow-roasted pork $37), to grilled lamb chops with pomegranate molasses ($39). Appetizers include sauteed Vietnamese scallops ($16). They also serve large, tasty breakfasts, with typical menu items costing $15–17. Mon–Thurs & Sun 8am–3pm & 5.30–9.30pm, Fri & Sat 8am–3pm & 5.30–10pm.

Clafoutis 402 N Guadalupe St ☎505 988 1809; map pp.110–111. Hugely popular French café/bistro on the northwest edge of downtown (*not* in the Guadalupe Street district), open for breakfast and lunch only. Pastries, coffees and classic French snacks like *croque-monsieur* and *croque-madame* – both variations on a grilled cheese sandwich, costing around $8 – or meaty onion soup. Mon–Sat 7am–4pm.

Eloisa 228 E Palace Ave ☎505 982 0883, ⓦeloisasantafe.com; map pp.110–111. Returning from LA to his home state, dynamic chef John Rivera Sedlar has brought a contemporary Californian flair to this new hotel restaurant. Wonderful Southwestern creations stream from the big open kitchen, with the menu divided between $7–14 "small plates" such as steamed mussels with chorizo, or white and green corn with amaranth and quinoa, and "large plates" ranging from $22 duck enfrijoladas, served with a sumptuous grainy mole sauce and blue-corn tortillas, to lamb chops with ratatouille for $42. Mon–Thurs & Sun 11.30am–2.30pm & 5.30–9.30pm, Fri & Sat 11.30am–2.30pm & 5.30–10pm.

French Pastry Shop La Fonda de Santa Fe, 100 E San Francisco St ☎505 983 6697, ⓦthefrenchpastryshop.com; map pp.110–111. This conveniently central hotel café serves fabulous pastries and coffees, along with breakfasts, sandwiches and crêpes sweet and savoury; almost nothing costs as much as $10. Daily 6.30am–5pm.

La Boca 72 W Marcy St ☎505 982 3433, ⓦlabocasf.com; map pp.110–111. Enthusiastic locals squeeze into this little downtown bar/restaurant to enjoy excellent Spanish food, largely served in small tapas portions, including gazpacho, pork *pinchos* (kebabs) and delicious cheeses and hams. Most cost $6–13, but they're half-price in the afternoon, between 3pm and 5pm. The most substantial offering is a satisfying paella, containing chicken, chorizo and seafood, for $24 per person. There's also regular live music, including flamenco, and a similar, more intimate and informal, spin-off branch around the corner (*Taberna*; 125 Lincoln Ave). Mon–Sat 11am–9pm.

La Casa Sena 125 E Palace Ave ☎505 988 9232, ⓦlacasasena.com; map pp.110–111. Lovely courtyard restaurant, a block from the plaza. Zestful Southwestern lunches, with most mains priced at $14–16, are the best deal, while typical dinner specials cost $17–28, though opting for an antelope chop will set you back $41. At the adjoining, cheaper *La Cantina*, staff perform Broadway show tunes during dinner. Daily 11am–3pm & 5.30–10pm.

★**La Plazuela** La Fonda de Santa Fe, 100 E San Francisco St ☎505 982 5511, ⓦlafondasantafe.com; map pp.110–111. Delightful, beautifully furnished Mexican restaurant, which feels like an open-air courtyard even though it's covered by a glass ceiling. All the usual Mexican dishes are meticulously prepared and presented, with mains at $14–19 at lunchtime, and ranging, for pricier items such as lamb chops, up to $39 in the evening. Mon–Fri 7am–2pm & 5–10pm, Sat & Sun 7am–3pm & 5–10pm.

Sazón 221 Shelby St ☎505 983 8604, ⓦsazonsantafe.com; map pp.110–111. Stylish, high-quality cooking, courtesy of chef Fernando Olea, who takes an infectious delight in reinterpreting traditional Mexican cuisine. After sampling his three distinct mole sauces, diners can choose a meaty $30–40 main featuring their favourite. Be sure not to miss the $16 appetizer of *chapulines* – grilled grasshoppers. Mon–Sat 5.30–10pm.

★**The Shed** 113 E Palace Ave ☎505 982 9030, ⓦsfshed.com; map pp.110–111. Casual, family-owned New Mexican restaurant, decorated in primary colours and festooned with local art, and set in a rambling garden compound not far northeast of the plaza. The food itself is cheap, cheerful and above all tasty – be sure to try the *carne adovada* (slow-roasted pork), along with blue-corn tortillas and mocha cake. Mains cost around $10–12 for lunch, $12–18 for dinner. Reservations accepted for dinner only. Mon–Sat 11am–2.30pm & 5–9pm.

Tia Sophia's 210 W San Francisco St ☎505 983 9880; map pp.110–111. Spicy, very inexpensive Mexican diner, a block or two west of the plaza, that's hugely popular with lunching locals. Daily breakfast and lunch specials for under $10. Mon–Sat 7am–2pm, Sun 8am–1pm.

GUADALUPE DISTRICT AND THE RAILYARD

Amaya Hotel Santa Fe, 1501 Paseo de Peralta at Cerrillos Rd ☎505 955 7805, ⓦhotelsantafe.com; map pp.110–111. Warm, inviting restaurant in the lovely *Hotel Santa Fe*, serving a rich, hearty version of contemporary Southwestern cuisine. There's a lot of meat on the menu, with $26–36 mains including braised bison short ribs and Thai lamb chops. Breakfast too is a treat – be sure to try the $11 *Briowich*, a bacon and omelette sandwich in a butter brioche. Daily 7–10.30am, 11.30am–2.30pm & 5.30–10pm.

Sage Bakehouse 535 Cerrillos Rd ☎505 820 7243, ⓦsagebakehouse.com; map pp.110–111. No-frills bakery on the southern fringe of downtown, open early for delicious fresh-baked sourdough bread and coffees, best enjoyed on the small patio, plus $7–9 grilled sandwiches. Mon–Sat 7.30am–2.30pm.

Saveur 204 Montezuma Ave ☎505 989 4200; map pp.110–111. High quality café-cum-salad-bar not far west of the State Capitol, serving delicious cooked and raw specialities by the pound, and offering major discounts after 3pm. There's also a choice of three daily soups. Expect to pay $15–20 for a good lunch. Mon–Sat 7.45am–3.45pm.

Vinaigrette 709 Don Cubero Alley ☎505 820 9205, ⓦvinaigretteonline.com; map pp.110–111. The principal drawing card for this charming, bright "salad bistro" is its menu of organic salads, drawing on ingredients grown at the owner's farm, and given self-explanatory punning names like "nutty pair-fessor" and "all kale Caesar". Costing around $10, each is also served with fish, scallops, chicken or duck for $5–8 extra, and they have soups and sandwiches as well. Mon–Sat 11am–9pm.

CANYON ROAD

Downtown Subscription Coffee Bar & Newsstand 376 Garcia St ☎505 983 3085; map pp.110–111. Despite the name, this sprawling coffee bar, where the large outdoor terrace is usually commandeered by local intellectuals, is a 10min walk from downtown, being just south of Canyon Road. Inside, take your pick from a wide range of old-school papers and magazines. Daily 7am–7pm.

Geronimo 724 Canyon Rd ☎505 982 1500, ⓦgeronimorestaurant.com; map pp.110–111. With its separate small dining rooms, this converted ancient adobe, a mile from the plaza amid the galleries of Canyon Road, is Santa Fe's most intimate upmarket restaurant, with a streetfront patio and a cool inner courtyard. The menu is mostly contemporary fusion with the odd Mexican touch, with green miso sea bass or grilled lack of lamb priced at $30–52, and a vegetarian set menu at $60. Daily 5.45–9.30pm.

The Teahouse 821 Canyon Rd ☎505 992 0972, ⓦteahousesantafe.com; map pp.110–111. Large and very welcoming café at the far end of Canyon Road, with a pleasantly peaceful garden. The star attraction is the amazing range of white, green, black, flavoured and downright bizarre teas from all over the world, but it's also a good spot to unwind over a cooked $10–14 breakfast, lunchtime soup or sandwich, or $13–20 pasta or posole main. Daily 9am–9pm.

SOUTH OF DOWNTOWN

Harry's Roadhouse 96 Old Las Vegas Hwy ☎505 989 4629, ⓦharrysroadhousesantafe.com; map p.108. Much-loved diner on what was once Route 66, five miles south of downtown with some nice garden seating, where surprising twists on the predominantly burgers-and-burritos menu range from black rice and quinoa porridge for breakfast ($7) to Vietnamese caramelized catfish for dinner ($13.50). They only take reservations for parties of six or more, so you can expect a long wait at busy times. Daily 7am–9.30pm.

★**Jambo Café** 2010 Cerrillos Rd ☎505 473 1269, ⓦjambocafe.net; map p.108. Tucked away near Hobby Lobby in a modern mall, this large, colourful café is the brainchild of chef Ahmed Obo, who hails from an Indian-Ocean island off Kenya, and has accumulated devoted followers for his skilful adaptation of African and Caribbean traditions to suit Santa Fe tastes. The menu ranges from $12–16 goat, lamb or coconut lentil stews and curries to $10 plantain crab cakes and a $10 jerk chicken sandwich, with takeaway available. Mon–Sat 11am–9pm.

Museum Hill Café 705 Camino Lejo ☎505 984 8900, ⓦmuseumhillcafe.net; map p.108. Spacious café, enjoying fabulous mountain views from a terrace on the plaza between the Folk Art and Indian Arts museums southeast of town. Good, inexpensive sandwiches – turkey, tuna and steak all cost around $12.50 – plus tacos, *flautas*, burgers, pasta specials and salads, and a large brunch on Sundays. Tues–Sun 11am–3pm.

Tecolote Café 1616 St Michael's Drive ☎505 988 1362, ⓦtecolotecafe.com; map p.108. This local legend, recently transplanted to a new mall location a couple of miles southwest of downtown, is renowned for magnificent breakfasts – burritos, *huevos rancheros*, creamy eggs Benedict, or shirred eggs (poached on a bed of chicken livers). Typical dishes cost around $10. Tues–Sun 7am–2pm.

Tune-Up Café 1115 Hickox St ☎505 983 7060, ⓦtuneupsantafe.com; map p.108. The patio seating at the front of this informal restaurant, half a mile west of Guadalupe St, is especially popular with brunching locals. The crowd-pleasing menu covers American (buffalo, lamb or nut burgers costing $9–13) and Mexican classics (stuffed peppers or salmon tacos, $12–15), plus a nod to the owner's El Salvadorean roots in the form of banana-wrapped tamales served with corn tortillas. Mon–Fri 7am–10pm, Sat & Sun 8am–10pm.

NIGHTLIFE AND ENTERTAINMENT

While Santa Fe has the somewhat limited **nightlife** you'd expect in a small city, its **cultural scene** livens up during the summer tourist season. For current **listings**, check the local ticket agency (☎505 988 1234, ⓦticketssantafe.org), the free weekly *Reporter* (ⓦsfreporter.com), or the *Pasatiempo* section of Friday's *New Mexican*.

BARS AND CLUBS

Some of the most atmospheric places to drink in town are in the old hotels – in *La Fonda* on the plaza, both the

downstairs *La Fiesta* lounge and the rooftop bar are good bets – but otherwise conventional bars are surprisingly few and far between.

Cowgirl BBQ 319 S Guadalupe St ☎ 505 982 2565, ⓦcowgirlsantafe.com; map pp.110–111. Very busy country-themed restaurant and bar, with karaoke on Mondays and live music every other night, plus a billiard room. Mon–Thurs 11.30am–midnight, Fri 11.30am–1am, Sat 11am–1am, & Sun 11am–11.30pm.

Evangelo's 200 W San Francisco St ☎ 505 982 9014; map pp.110–111. The only good bare-bones bar in easy walking range of the plaza, with a pool table and a jukebox, plus occasional live music. Be sure to check out the *Underground* dive bar downstairs. Daily noon–midnight.

Second Street Brewery 1814 Second St ☎ 505 982 3030, ⓦsecondstreetbrewery.com; map p.108. This lively brewpub is too far from the centre to attract many tourists, which helps to explain why it's so popular with young locals; there's also live music several nights a week. There's another branch at the Railyard. Mon–Thurs 11am–10pm, Fri & Sat 11am–11pm, Sun noon–9pm.

LIVE MUSIC, THEATRE AND CINEMA

★**Jean Cocteau Cinema** 418 Montezuma Ave ☎ 505 466 5528, ⓦjeancocteaucinema.com. Having been defunct for several years, this much-loved repertory cinema has been rescued by new owner George R.R. Martin. As well as screenings of new and classic movies, it stages free preview showings of each *Game of Thrones* series, and puts on occasional gigs. It also holds a hip little cocktail bar/café, and a bookstore that sells signed copies of Martin's books.

Lensic Performing Arts Center 211 W San Francisco St ☎ 505 988 1234, ⓦlensic.org. All year round, this strikingly converted "Pueblo Deco" theatre downtown – originally a movie theatre – hosts musical and theatrical performances, by touring artists as well as local groups.

★**Santa Fe Opera** 1.4 miles northeast of US-84 exit 168 ☎ 505 986 5900 or ☎ 800 280 4654, ⓦsantafeopera .org. During its much-anticipated summer season, in July and August, the Santa Fe Opera stages five separate productions in a magnificent amphitheatre 7 miles north of Santa Fe. Ticket prices start at $31.

2

SHOPPING

With many visitors coming specifically to **shop**, central Santa Fe is bursting with stores and galleries. The city remains largely the preserve of independents, however; few of the international names that move in seem to last long. Don't expect to make an early start; most stores and galleries don't open until 10am. The best place to buy **Native American crafts**, and especially silver and turquoise **jewellery**, is from the predominantly Puebloan sellers outside the Palace of the Governors, ideally during August's Indian Market (see p.109).

CANYON ROAD

Nathalie 503 Canyon Rd ☎ 505 982 1021, ⓦnathaliesantafe.com; map pp.110–111. Little of the Western wear here would be at home on the range – it's all a little too chic and decorative for life on horseback – but it'll still look great when you wear it back home. There's also a good stock of homeware, glass and furnishings, some with distinctly French accents. Mon–Fri 10am–5pm, Sat 10.30am–5pm.

Pachamama 223 Canyon Rd ☎ 505 983 4020, ⓦpachamamasantafe.com; map pp.110–111. Unusually inexpensive Hispanic crafts, mainly from Mexico, including silver and yellow bronze *milagros*, *retablos*, statues and lots of tin. Mon–Sat 10am–5pm, Sun 11am–4pm.

Silver Sun 656 Canyon Rd ☎ 505 983 8743, ⓦsilversun-sf.com; map pp.110–111. A stand-out collection of beautiful turquoise jewellery, much of it at very affordable prices, complemented by selected other Native American arts and crafts. Mon–Sat 10am–5pm, Sun 11am–4pm.

Tom Ross Gallery 409 Canyon Rd ☎ 505 984 8434, ⓦtomrossgallery.com; map pp.110–111. Enjoyable fine art gallery, run by a children's book illustrator and specializing in very bright paintings and sculpture that blend the fantastic with the naive. Daily 10am–5pm.

Zaplin Lampert Gallery 651 Canyon Rd ☎ 505 982 6100, ⓦzaplinlampert.com; map pp.110–111. If you're looking for beautiful Southwestern art, this is the pick of the Canyon Road galleries, featuring works by most major Taos and Santa Fe artists, as well as original photos by the likes of Edward Curtis. An original Gustave Baumann print will cost $10,000–25,000 while paintings go up to $100,000. Tues–Fri 9am–5pm, Sat 9.30am–5pm.

THE REST OF SANTA FE

Andrea Fisher Fine Pottery 100 W San Francisco St ☎ 505 986 1234, ⓦandreafisherpottery.com; map pp.110–111. Museum-like gallery, a block west of the plaza, which specializes in Native American pottery and boasts one of the nation's largest selections of Maria Martinez pieces. Mon–Sat 10am–5pm, Sun noon–5pm.

Chile Shop 109 E Water St ☎ 505 983 6080, ⓦthechileshop.com; map pp.110–111. Plenty of downtown Santa Fe stores offer similar Southwestern souvenirs, from chile *ristras* (garlands) to spicy salsas, but it's worth a detour to the Chile Shop to buy Mimbreño china tableware, designed for the Santa Fe Railroad in the 1930s by Mary Jane Colter. Daily 9.30am–6pm.

Collected Works Bookstore 202 Galisteo St ☎ 505 988 4226, ⓦcollectedworksbookstore.com; map pp.110–111. This large central bookstore is a great source

2

for books on New Mexican history and culture, and has its own café. Check the website for upcoming author talks and other events. Mon–Sat 8am–8pm, Sun 8am–6pm.

Kowboyz 345 W Manhattan Ave ☎505 984 1256, ⓦkowboyz.com; map pp.110–111. Wonderful Western-wear store, across the street from the Railyard, with a great array of new and used hats, cowboy boots and men's and women's clothing; secondhand shirts start at just $10. Daily 10am–5.30pm.

Jackalope 2820 Cerrillos Rd ☎505 471 8539, ⓦjackalope.com; map p.108. A Southwestern legend for its pile-'em-high, sell-'em-cheap philosophy, this sprawling complex, centred on a disused church well out from downtown, completely takes the mystique out of purchasing folk art. However, the rock-bottom prices for its mostly Mexican and Peruvian arts, crafts and downright junk, make it an ideal spot to pick up inexpensive souvenirs. Mon–Sat 8am–6pm, Sun 10am–6pm.

Jambo Imports 2010 Cerrillos Rd ☎505 474 5252, ⓦjamboimports.com; map p.108. Two doors along from the popular *Jambo Café* (see p.122), this intriguing and unusual store holds arts and crafts from all over Africa, from carved drums to bead jewellery and woven baskets – some of

the motifs are remarkably similar to Native American designs – along with spices and chutneys. Mon–Sat noon–9pm.

★**Museum of International Folk Art** Museum Hill ☎505 827 6344, ⓦinternationalfolkart.org; map pp.110–111. This wonderful museum gift store stocks some of the best souvenirs in town, ranging from jars from Uzbekistan to tin toys from Zimbabwe. If you're interested in Hispanic folk art, take a look here before you shop downtown. Daily 10am–5pm; closed Mon Nov–April.

★**Seret & Sons** 224 Galisteo St ☎505 988 9151, ⓦstore.serets.com; map pp.110–111. Rather lovely, very upscale furnishings emporium, spreading through several adjacent storefronts, and selling sumptuous rugs, cushions and wooden furniture, from across Asia, and Tibet in particular. Mon–Fri 9am–5.30pm, Sat 9am–6pm, Sun 9.30am–5pm.

Travel Bug 839 Paseo de Peralta ☎505 992 0418, ⓦmapsofnewmexico.com; map pp.110–111. Tucked away behind the cathedral, a couple of blocks east of the plaza, this fabulous resource for travellers sells every imaginable map and guide book, hosts inspirational monthly travel talks, and has a café and snack bar. Mon–Sat 8am–8pm, Sun 8am–6pm.

South to Albuquerque

Travellers embarking on the sixty-mile drive southwest from Santa Fe to Albuquerque can choose between two routes. The **interstate**, I-25, is fast and reasonably scenic, but for atmosphere and Old West charm it doesn't begin to match the **Turquoise Trail**, which squeezes between the Sandia and Ortiz mountains to the east.

Along I-25

While commuters may not give it a second thought, the hour-long journey from Santa Fe to Albuquerque on **I-25** represents a major transition. When it drops down the escarpment known as **La Bajada**, twenty miles southwest of downtown Santa Fe, the interstate leaves the Rocky Mountains and enters the desert. To the north of La Bajada, the Rio Grande was traditionally known as the **Rio Arriba**, or Upper River, and cuts through a deep rocky gorge; to the south, the **Rio Abajo** or Lower River meanders across a broad floodplain.

La Bajada also marks the dividing line between the northern and southern **pueblos**. Below it, the interstate runs through three separate Indian reservations. In 1996, when state legislators considered banning the casinos that have finally brought the pueblos a degree of prosperity, pueblo authorities countered by threatening to place **toll-gates** at every boundary on the interstate.

Cochiti Pueblo

Hwy-22, 10 miles northwest of I-25 exit 259, a total of 24 miles southwest of Santa Fe • ☎505 465 2244, ⓦpueblodecochiti.org

COCHITI PUEBLO, at the foot of La Bajada, is home to a thousand Keresan-speaking Indians who trace their ancestry back to the cliff dwellers of Bandelier (see p.132).

In the Keresan language, its name is *Kotyete*, meaning "stone *kiva*". Visitors have free access to the pueblo in daylight hours; some residents sell crafts outside their houses, but there are no formal stores. The mission church of **San Buenaventura** still incorporates vestiges of its original adobe form, as built in 1628, but it has been greatly modified over the years, and the contemporary frescoes within are not all that enthralling.

A Cochiti potter, Helen Cordero, fashioned the first ceramic "**storyteller**" here in 1946. Each depicting a mother with up to thirty children, these rank among New Mexico's best-selling souvenirs and are made by over two hundred native craftspeople, including around fifty Cochiti.

Cochiti Lake

Visitor centre Mon–Fri 8.30am–3.30pm, Sat 10am–2pm, Sun noon–4pm • ☎ 505 465 0307

In the 1970s, Cochiti Pueblo was forced to lease some of its best agricultural land, and allow the federal government to create **Cochiti Lake** by constructing what was then the world's largest earthen dam across the Rio Grande. After a twenty-year legal struggle for redress, the tribe finally came to terms with the project, and now works in conjunction with the US Army Corps of Engineers. Though the dam itself remains something of an eyesore, the lake now attracts a million recreational users annually – almost exclusively New Mexico residents, with many windsurfers among them – and has a campground (March–Nov) as well as a small **visitor centre**.

Kasha-Katuwe Tent Rocks National Monument

Tribal Route 92, Cochiti Pueblo • Daily: mid-March to Oct 7am–7pm, last admission 6pm; Nov to mid-March 8am–5pm, last admission 4pm • $5 per vehicle, national park passes accepted • ☎ 505 331 6259, ⓦ blm.gov/nm • Follow signs from I-25 exits 264 or 259 to Cochiti Pueblo; at a painted water tower, 13 or 14 miles along respectively, turn right onto Tribal Route 92, and continue 4.5 miles

In 2001, a previously little-known corner of Cochiti Pueblo became **Kasha-Katuwe Tent Rocks National Monument**, jointly administered by the Bureau of Land Management and the pueblo. Kasha-Katuwe means "white cliffs" in Keresan and erosion has sculpted a canyon wall of pale, soft volcanic rock into cone-like shapes that range up to almost one hundred feet tall. Only a few are free-standing pinnacles; most are "hoodoos" that poke from the hillside.

To make the most of Kasha-Katuwe, allow at least three hours for the full detour off the interstate. That'll give you time to do more than simply hike the easy 1.2-mile **Cave Loop Trail**, which circles from the monument parking lot around the main formations. The much more exhilarating **Slot Canyon Trail** branches off at the furthest point of the loop, heading steadily upwards along the sandy floor of a narrow canyon. After a mile or so of squeezing past mighty boulders and scrambling over fallen tree trunks, you reach a final steep zigzagging ascent that brings you out atop the cliffs, with stupendous view over the tent rocks and across the full majesty of the Rio Grande Valley.

Kewa Pueblo

6.5 miles northwest of I-25 exit 259 • ☎ 505 465 2214, ⓦ santodomingotribe.org

KEWA PUEBLO, which officially changed its name in 2009 from **SANTO DOMINGO PUEBLO**, is the largest Keresan pueblo, with a population of just over 2500. For many centuries, its people have been renowned for making **jewellery**, and especially necklaces of delicate shell and turquoise *heishi* beads. By some accounts, they taught silversmithing to the Navajo in the nineteenth century, and they're now prominent among the Native American vendors in Santa Fe.

Kewa doesn't have a visitor centre or formal opening hours, but as well as an adobe church with a lovely painted facade, its central plaza holds several stores selling jewellery, pottery and other crafts.

San Felipe Pueblo

2.4 miles northwest of I-25 exit 252 • ☎ 505 867 3381

Until 1250 AD, the people of **SAN FELIPE PUEBLO**, six miles downriver from Kewa, were a single tribe with their fellow Keresan speakers now known as the Cochiti. Their subsequent migrations only ended in 1693, when they settled here for good after the Pueblo Revolt.

Daytime visits are always permitted here, but photography is not. On the pueblo's **feast day**, May 1, its plaza, worn down over the generations into a bowl-shaped depression, is thronged with dancers performing a day-long corn dance. The tribe runs a large **casino** and **travel centre**, both of which house restaurants, beside interstate exit 252.

Coronado Historic Site

US-550, 1 mile west of I-25 exit 242 • Daily except Tues 8.30am–5pm • $3 • ☎ 505 867 5351, ⓦ nmhistoricsites.org

Enjoying fabulous views of the Sandia Mountains from a spectacular setting on the west bank of the Rio Grande, **Coronado Historic Site** is located just outside **BERNALILLO**, an unexciting satellite community of Albuquerque, and five miles south of the languid riverside village of **ALGODONES**. The monument preserves what remains of the ancient pueblo of **Kuaua**. The Spaniards knew this region as **Tigüex**, and described it as a "broad valley planted with fields of maize and dotted with cottonwood groves". Francisco de Coronado spent the winter of 1540 in the vicinity, though there's no evidence it was at this precise spot. Kuaua was then a thriving community of well over a thousand rooms; now it's a ruin, of which archeologists have exposed a few eroded adobe walls. The central feature is a restored *kiva*, decorated with vivid reproductions of its multicoloured **murals**. The faded originals, preserved in the visitor centre, include scenes of a rabbit hunt. Rabbits often represent the **moon** in Pueblo art, as Pueblo peoples see a "rabbit in the moon" rather than a "man in the moon". The monument is especially ravishing from late October onwards, when the fall colours along the riverbank are unbelievable.

Rio Rancho

If you're unpleasantly surprised by the volume of traffic climbing US-550 past Coronado State Monument, that's probably because you've never heard of **RIO RANCHO**, reached via a turn-off a short way further up the hill. This ever-expanding community was founded in the early 1960s, after the AMREP Corporation purchased the Koontz cattle ranch for residential development. Though some of its earliest inhabitants, lured here from the East Coast by enticing advertising, were disappointed enough to sue AMREP (successfully) for fraud, Rio Rancho's population has mushroomed to over ninety thousand. With retirees joining Albuquerque commuters, and with Intel operating one of the world's largest semi-conductor plants here, Rio Rancho has become New Mexico's third-largest city. Although it holds half a dozen chain motels, there's no reason for tourists to visit.

Sandia Pueblo

I-25 exits 234 and 240 • ☎ 505 867 3317, ⓦ sandiapueblo.nsn.us

SANDIA PUEBLO, between Bernalillo and Albuquerque, dates back to around 1300 AD and was visited by Coronado in 1540. *Sandía* is the Spanish for watermelon; differing stories have it either that the Spaniards mistook the squashes they saw here for watermelons, or they thought that at sunset the mountains to the east resembled segments of pink watermelon. In its dusty central plaza, the village's Tiwa name – **Nafiat**, meaning "dry or sandy place" – seems more appropriate. After it was destroyed in 1692 by Spaniards returning after the Pueblo Revolt, many of its inhabitants took refuge with the Hopi, far to the west, and the settlement was not rebuilt for fifty years.

Today, the main preoccupation of the three hundred Sandians is protecting their sacred sites in the nearby mountains from blundering hikers. Being so close to Albuquerque, they've also been among the chief beneficiaries of the legalization of Indian gaming.

ALGODONES

Hacienda Vargas 1431 El Camino Real ☎505 867 9115, ⊛ haciendavargas.com. A relaxing rural B&B, set in a lovely adobe trading post not far from I-25 exit 248. All seven rooms have en-suite facilities, *kiva* fireplaces, and private entrances, and several have hot tubs. **$89**

BERNALILLO

While Bernalillo itself holds no accommodation, the nearby Santa Ana Pueblo is home to both the state's largest and most luxurious resort, the *Hyatt Regency Tamaya* (see p.135), and a top-quality restaurant, the *Prairie Star* (see p.136).

Range Cafe 928 Camino del Pueblo ☎505 867 1700, ⊛ rangecafe.com. One of New Mexico's finest restaurants, in a brightly decorated hall east of the river at the south end of Bernalillo; close to I-25 exit 240, it makes an easy

evening excursion from Albuquerque. Huge Mexican-style appetizers like chimichangas cost from around $10; strongly chile-flavoured main dishes, like the fabulous quesadillas garnished with blue-corn chips, a little more. As "brinner," they also serve breakfast items such as *huevos rancheros* in the evening. It's a very popular spot, so expect to wait. Mon–Thurs & Sun 7am–9pm, Fri & Sat 7am–9.30pm.

SANDIA PUEBLO

Sandia Resort 30 Rainbow Rd NE ☎505 796 7500 or ☎800 526 9366, ⊛ sandiacasino.com. The success of the adjoining 24-hour Sandia Casino, alongside I-25, has enabled the tribe to open this striking luxury hotel and conference centre, where full spa facilities complement its plush, opulently furnished rooms, and there's ready access to restaurants, cafés and lounges to suit all budgets. **$199**

SHOPPING

SANDIA PUEBLO

Bien Mur Indian Market Center 100 Bien Mur Drive NE ☎505 821 5400 or ☎800 365 5400, ⊛ sandiapueblo .nsn.us. As well as selling a broad range of Native American

ceramics, jewellery and other artefacts, this Pueblo-owned crafts centre, just off Tramway Road north of Albuquerque, commands views of a preserve that holds the tribe's herd of buffalo. Mon–Sat 9.30am–5.30pm, Sun 11am–5.30pm.

The Turquoise Trail

THE TURQUOISE TRAIL – less glamorously known as **Hwy-14** – is a modern name for what may be one of the oldest thoroughfares in North America, connecting **mines** along the eastern flanks of the Sandia Mountains with the settlements of the Rio Grande Valley. In the last two hundred years, these mines have yielded copper, coal and even gold, but **turquoise** production dates back perhaps ten times as far. Long before the coming of the Spaniards, traders carried local stone all over the Southwest and down into Mexico, and wealthy pueblos lined the nearby streams.

Until the recent influx of artists, craftworkers and small-scale entrepreneurs, communities along the trail had dwindled to become little more than **ghost towns**, but now funky **Madrid**, in particular, makes an appealing day-trip destination for visitors to Santa Fe.

Cerrillos

The northernmost Turquoise Trail town, **CERRILLOS**, just over twenty miles south of Santa Fe, is reached simply by continuing south on Cerrillos Road, which becomes Hwy-14, for fifteen miles beyond its intersection with I-25. The dusty rolling hillocks that surround it – the "little hills" of its name – hold one of the world's greatest concentrations of **turquoise**.

Archeologists estimate that ninety percent of the turquoise treasures seized by the Spaniards from the Aztec capital of Tenochtitlán were crafted using stone from this unprepossessing spot. Prehistoric miners scooped a hundred thousand tons of rock from **Mount Chalchihuitl**, two miles northeast, leaving a cavern 300 feet wide and 200 feet deep. Early Spanish settlers may have forced the local Puebloans to work for them; a mine collapse around 1680, which killed up to eighty Indians, helped to precipitate the Pueblo Revolt. By the time the Spaniards returned, the Puebloans had deliberately hidden many of the shafts, and tales of fabulously wealthy "**lost mines**" still abound.

Today's Cerrillos, nestled amid the giant cottonwoods along the bank of the broad but usually dry Galisteo River, has changed little since its last boom in the 1890s. Mining not only turquoise but gold, silver, copper and lead, it was briefly rich enough to support eight daily newspapers and numerous hotels and saloons. There's still a bit of life in the old town; as recently as 1983, robbers made off with $500,000 worth of gold from the nearby Ortiz Mines. In 1988, its unpaved streets and false-front wooden buildings made it an ideal location for the bratpack Western *Young Guns*.

Casa Grande Trading Post, Turquoise Mining Museum and Petting Zoo

17 Waldo St • Daily 9am–5pm • $2 • ☎ 505 438 3008

Cerrillos' one formal tourist attraction is the **Casa Grande Trading Post, Turquoise Mining Museum and Petting Zoo**. This endearing shop-cum-museum offers a random assortment of old bills and letters, porcupine quills, rattlesnake skins and petrified wood, plus the chance to pet a llama or pull on a string to make a plaster Indian hammer on a rock.

Cerrillos Hills State Park

Daily sunrise–9pm • $5 per vehicle • ☎ 505 474 0196, ⓦ emnrd.state.nm.us

For a first-hand look at Cerrillos' rich mining legacy, it's well worth venturing into the gently rolling hills of **Cerrillos Hills State Park**, which lies down a dirt road at the northeastern edge of the village. Hikers, mountain bikers and horse riders can explore over 35 miles of trails, some of which pass by long-shuttered mines, and enjoy expansive views of Mount Taylor (11,301ft) and the Ortiz Mountains.

Madrid

Between 1869 and 1959, the village of **MADRID**, three miles south of Cerrillos, made a good living from mining **coal**, with tunnels running directly beneath the main street. In the early days, coal was hauled by wagon as far as St Louis; later the Santa Fe Railroad consumed it in vast quantities.

Since the mine closed down, and the whole town was auctioned off piecemeal, the straggle of wooden cottages either side of the narrow highway have progressively been taken over by New-Agey newcomers. Several hold genuinely interesting crafts and antiques stores; if you're close enough to home to carry **furniture**, there are some real bargains to be had.

Old Coal Town Museum

Daily May–Oct only 9am–5.30pm • $5 • ☎ 505 473 0743, ⓦ themineshafttavern.com

At the **Old Coal Town Museum**, attached to the *Mine Shaft Tavern* at the southern end of Madrid, an abandoned mine shaft burrows straight into the hillside. The museum itself consists of several barns stuffed with ancient junk like obsolete X-ray machines and decrepit Model "T" Ford trucks. Its main entrance building doubles as the **Engine House Theatre**, which stages moustache-twirling **melodramas** on summer weekends, plus cabaret and assorted other performances in winter.

Golden

In 1825, **GOLDEN**, fifteen miles south of Madrid, was the site of the Wild West's first-ever gold rush. It has yet to revitalize to any great extent, and as the highway races down its former main street you might hardly notice that it's there. Look out, however, for the tumbledown **adobe church** on the hill at the north edge of town, which served the mining camp of **Tuerto** and has preserved its pioneer graveyard.

Sandia Crest and Cedar Crest

Ten miles south of Golden, the **Sandia Crest Scenic Byway** branches west from Hwy-14, to climb for eight tortuous miles up to the razorback ridge atop the Sandia Mountains. From the mile-high **observation deck** at road's end, you can survey the sprawling city of **Albuquerque**, with the Rio Grande flowing in from the north, and also look east across the endless plains, beyond the Ortiz Mountains. The adjacent *Sandia House* sells some fairly tasteless snacks and a fee of $3 is charged for day-use of the nearby trails, but most visitors stay for barely ten minutes before heading back down the hill; there's no through route to Albuquerque.

In winter, **skiers** exploring the eastern Sandia slopes base themselves down below, in **CEDAR CREST** at the foot of the Scenic Byway. The Turquoise Trail ends six miles south at the intersection with I-40, which sweeps the final dozen miles west to Albuquerque through **Tijeras** – "Scissors" – **Canyon**.

2

INFORMATION AND ACTIVITIES	THE TURQUOISE TRAIL

Useful website ⓦ turquoisetrail.org.
Horseriding Broken Saddle offer horse rides in Cerrillos

Hills State Park, including by moonlight (1–3hr; $65–115; ☏ 505 424 7774, ⓦ brokensaddle.com).

ACCOMMODATION AND EATING

MADRID

Java Junction 2855 Hwy-14 ☏ 505 438 2772, ⓦ java -junction.com. Attractive old mining home that houses a coffee shop downstairs, serving a limited array of bagels and pastries, and also has a very pleasant, bright B&B apartment upstairs, with kitchen and bathroom. $129
Mama Lisa's Ghost Town Kitchen/No Pity Cafe 2589 Hwy-14 ☏ 505 471 5769. Good home cooking, in all shapes and sizes, with $10 burgers ranging from green chile to salmon pesto as well as healthy salads and daily specials costing a little more. Summer daily 11.30am–2.30pm & 5.30–9pm; winter hours vary.
Mine Shaft Tavern 2846 Hwy-14 ☏ 505 473 0743, ⓦ themineshafttavern.com. This lively tavern, attached to the Old Coal Town Museum, claims to have the longest

bar in New Mexico. As well as serving a full menu of burgers, fajitas and the like – typically priced at $12–15 – until 7.30pm on weekdays and 9pm at weekends, it stays open late every night, with live music on weekends, and also offers three rental units in a nicely converted trailer home alongside. Sun & Mon–Thurs $76, Fri & Sat $85

CEDAR CREST

★ **Elaine's** 72 Snowline Rd ☏ 505 281 2467 or ☏ 800 821 3092, ⓦ elainesbnb.com. Very comfortable log-cabin-home B&B perched on the hillside in spacious rural grounds, half a mile west of Hwy-14 a mile south of the Sandia Crest turn-off. The five guest rooms are decorated according to varying schemes – the eccentric "Unicorn" room has its own hot tub – while Elaine herself is a very charming host. $109

West of Santa Fe

The **Jemez Mountain Trail**, which loops through the mountains west of Santa Fe, can be enjoyed as a long day's excursion or a roundabout route to or from Albuquerque. Potential stops range from modern **Los Alamos** – the top-secret "town that never was" – to the ancient dwellings of **Bandelier National Monument**, while the scenery encompasses mountain meadows and desert canyons.

The **Pajarito Plateau**, the dominant feature of the landscape, was created just over a million years ago, when colossal **volcanic eruptions** buried four hundred square miles beneath a thousand feet of ash. This solidified into **tuff**, which has eroded away ever since to form an intricate tangle of deep gorges and forested mesas. "Pajarito" means "little bird" in Spanish; it's a translation of the Tewa *tsirege*, the name of an abandoned local pueblo. Only one road climbs onto the plateau, **Hwy-502**, which branches west from US-84 near Pojoaque Pueblo, fifteen miles north of Santa Fe.

Visitors to both Los Alamos and Bandelier should try to avoid **rush-hour** traffic on Hwy-502, which heads westbound until around 9am, and eastbound from 3pm onwards.

Los Alamos

The wealthy enclave of **LOS ALAMOS**, eighteen miles up Hwy-502, is not so much a town as the overgrown campus of the **Los Alamos National Laboratory**. Home during World War II to the **Manhattan Project**, which first developed the atomic bomb, it remains the leading US centre for the research and development of nuclear weapons.

Los Alamos is a confusing place to visit. Sprawling along several "fingers" at the edge of the Pajarito Plateau, separated by deep canyons, its layout is bizarre in the extreme, and the fact that most of the complex is off-limits to the public doesn't help. If you attempt to explore the town, you can expect to be stopped repeatedly at checkpoints, so have ID ready. Most visitors simply call in at one of the two local **museums**, then head on to Bandelier.

Bradbury Science Museum

Central Ave & 15th St • Mon & Sun 1–5pm, Tues–Sat 10am–5pm • Free • ☎ 505 667 4444, ⓦ lanl.gov/museum

The **Bradbury Science Museum** presents the authorized version of the history of the Los Alamos National Laboratory. While opponents of nuclear proliferation are given space to state their case – forcefully argued rival displays debate the decision to drop atomic bombs on Japan – the overall line is extremely gung-ho. The central exhibits are full-sized 1940s replicas of "Little Boy", which devastated Hiroshima, and "Fat Man", dropped on Nagasaki. Be sure to take a look at the **visitors' book**, which is fascinating enough to have been published.

Los Alamos History Museum

1050 Bathtub Row • Mon–Fri 10am–4pm, Sat & Sun 11am–4pm • Free • ☎ 505 662 6272, ⓦ losalamoshistory.org

Housed in outbuildings of the former Los Alamos Ranch School, which were being refurbished as this book went to press, the **Los Alamos History Museum** combines the

THE TOWN THAT NEVER WAS: LOS ALAMOS AND THE BOMB

In 1942, the US and Britain decided to amalgamate the nine research efforts then racing to build the **atomic bomb**. Albert Einstein had suggested the idea to President Roosevelt three years earlier, and a team led by Enrico Fermi was achieving promising results beneath a disused football stadium in Chicago. The search was on for a suitable location in a sparsely populated area, away from the sea. **J. Robert Oppenheimer**, the scientific chief of the **Manhattan Project**, who had backpacked in New Mexico, recommended the exclusive Los Alamos Ranch School on the Pajarito Plateau, and the site was duly purchased. When its final class graduated in February 1943, the scientists moved in.

Working in the utmost secrecy – the words "Los Alamos" were forbidden, and newcomers were told merely to report to 109 Palace Avenue in Santa Fe – scientists took just over two years to make the bomb a reality. The first successful test took place at the **Trinity Site**, 200 miles south (see p.186), on July 16, 1945. Three weeks later, bombs were dropped on **Hiroshima**, on August 6, and **Nagasaki**, August 9; a complete Japanese surrender followed immediately.

For Oppenheimer, who described the development of the bomb with a quotation from the *Bhagavad Gita*, "I am become Death, the shatterer of Worlds", Los Alamos had served its purpose, and the laboratory could now close. Instead, as the Cold War set in, its energies were devoted toward the construction of the **H-Bomb**. Though security was more paramount than ever, ideologically motivated spies such as **Klaus Fuchs** and **David Greenglass** (whose sister and her husband, **Ethel** and **Julius Rosenberg**, were later executed) soon betrayed Los Alamos's secrets to the Russians. Paranoia grew to the point that employees were instructed to "Watch Your Liberal Friends", and Oppenheimer himself was barred by his successor Edward Teller from access to privileged information.

The gatehouse on the road up from Santa Fe that denied outsiders access to Los Alamos was finally removed in 1957. The laboratory business is still booming, spending well over half its two-billion-dollar annual budget on the research and development of nuclear weapons. While the lab has also drilled a 12,000-foot hole to "mine" heat from hot rocks deep in the earth and worked on the Human Genome Project, its public image remains firmly linked with nuclear experimentation.

Various wartime installations in Los Alamos, together with associated facilities in Hanford, Washington, and Oak Ridge, Tennessee, were jointly designated as the **Manhattan Project National Historical Park** in 2015. All the Los Alamos sites are, however, expected to remain out of bound to visitors.

kind of small-town history you might find anywhere with the extraordinary story of the bomb. Exhibits range from a 360-degree aerial photo of Hiroshima to prime specimens of atomic kitsch, such as a picture of the commander of the 1946 tests at Bikini cutting a mushroom-cloud-shaped cake, earrings made with "atomsite" fused glass from the Trinity site, and an A-bomb-shaped lamp.

INFORMATION   LOS ALAMOS

Visitor centre 109 Central Park Square (Mon–Fri 9am–5pm, Sat 9am–4pm, Sun 10am–3pm; ☎ 505 662 8105 or ☎ 800 444 0707, ⓦ visitlosalamos.org). Ask for their walking tour map.

ACCOMMODATION AND EATING

Los Alamos does hold a handful of chain motels and B&Bs, but it's not worth recommending as an overnight stop.

Blue Window Bistro 813 Central Ave ☎ 505 662 6305, ⓦ labluewindowbistro.com. The best-value place to eat in town, with lunchtime sandwiches and salads from $10, and tasty pasta or steak dinner mains ranging $16–28. Mon–Thurs 11am–2.30pm & 5–8.30pm, Fri 11am–2.30pm & 5–9pm, Sat 5–9pm.

Bandelier National Monument

10 miles south of Los Alamos, a total of 50 miles northwest of Santa Fe · $20 per vehicle · ☎ 505 672 3861, ⓦ nps.gov/band

Long before the scientists descended on Los Alamos, the "finger canyons" of the Pajarito Plateau were home to Native Americans. The Ancestral Puebloan inhabitants of what's now **BANDELIER NATIONAL MONUMENT** enlarged natural cavities in the soft volcanic rock to create **cliff dwellings**, and also built free-standing pueblos beside the streams on the valley floors. Set amid delightful woodlands and framed against the rose-pink canyon walls, Bandelier's intriguing remains provide an ideal introduction to New Mexico's past.

Although the Ancestral Puebloans are often said to have "disappeared" around 1300 AD, there's little mystery as to where they went. Bandelier is a "missing link", occupied between roughly 1150, as the Four Corners region was being abandoned, and 1550, when many of today's pueblos were established. As successive itinerant groups streamed in, perhaps fleeing drought or invasion, they may have merged here to create the modern Pueblo culture. The peoples of **Cochiti** and **San Ildefonso** in particular trace their ancestry back via Bandelier to Mesa Verde, and it was a Cochiti guide who led amateur archeologist **Adolph Bandelier** to this site in 1880.

Frijoles Canyon

The major sights of Bandelier National Monument are concentrated along a 1.5-mile loop trail through **Frijoles Canyon**, open daily from dawn to dusk. From the visitor centre, the trail leads swiftly to the remains of **Tyuonyi** on the canyon floor. Only the ground floor and foundations survive of this circular, multistorey, 400-room village, whose name means "place of agreement". It's seen as a centre for trade and storage, common to the **Keresan**-speaking peoples, whose pueblos lay to the south, and the **Tewa** speakers to the north. Local obsidian was traded as far as the Dakotas and the Mississippi. Despite the apparently large number of dwellings, the canyon's maximum total population is estimated at between five and seven hundred. Tyuonyi may have still been in use when Coronado's soldiers reached the Southwest (see p.467), though they didn't come this far.

A side path from Tyuonyi leads up to dozens of **cave dwellings**, their rounded chambers scooped into the warmer, south-facing wall of the canyon. (As artificial creations, technically these are "cavates" rather than caves.) Ladders and walkways mean visitors can scramble up to, and even enter, some of them, to peer out across the valley.

The main trail continues to the **Long House**, an 800ft-long series of two- and three-storey houses built against the cliffs. Though most of the upper storeys have collapsed to expose the plastered walls, you can still see the mortised holes that held their pine roof beams or *vigas*. Above these, rows of petroglyphs and pictographs depict figures and abstract symbols.

Though the main trail doubles back to the visitor centre, keen hikers can follow the stream for another half-mile, to the point where **Alcove House** nestles in a rocky overhang 150 feet above the canyon floor. Reaching it entails climbing three hair-raising ladders, as well as steep stairways hacked into the crumbling rock. At the top, *viga*-holes show that the cave once held several structures, but it's now bare except for a reconstructed *kiva*, set down in its sloping sandy floor, and entered by ladder.

Frijoles Canyon was devastated by both **fire** and **floods** in 2011. At the time of writing, the most visited areas had largely recovered, but several hiking trails that led further afield remained seriously affected. Check at the visitor centre to see what hikes are currently possible.

Tsankawi

Turn south off Hwy-502 onto Hwy-4, 5 miles east of Los Alamos; the Tsankawi parking lot is on the left, a little under a mile along

The small, separate **Tsankawi** section of Bandelier lies a dozen miles northeast of the monument visitor centre, just off Hwy-502 as it climbs from the Rio Grande Valley up to Los Alamos. Visits consist of an hour-long loop hike onto an isolated mesa-top that holds the almost indiscernible ruins of an ancient pueblo. If the site itself is disappointing, however, the trail is not; following the same route once used by the Ancestral Puebloans, it's worn waist-deep into the soft tuff in places, and includes a number of prehistoric "stairways", Assuming you're happy to negotiate a couple of short ladders, you're also rewarded with lovely views down into the valley, as well as glimpses of the mysterious Los Alamos laboratories closer at hand.

ARRIVAL AND INFORMATION   BANDELIER NATIONAL MONUMENT

By car Between late May and late October, private vehicles are only allowed to drive down into Frijoles Canyon before 9am or after 3pm daily, which is a strong incentive to set off by, say, 7.30am if you've spent the previous night in Santa Fe, or 7am from Taos. Otherwise, you'll have to park at the White Rock Visitor Center, on Hwy-4 in White Rock a couple of miles south of the monument's Tsankawi section, and catch one of the frequent free shuttle buses down to the canyon itself.

Visitor centre In Frijoles Canyon, at the bottom of a narrow switchback road down from Hwy-4 (daily: summer 9am–5.30pm, winter 9am–4.30pm). Displays of pottery and jewellery, models and reconstructions, century-old photographs, and an excellent film illuminate the Bandelier story and the region's fascinating geology, and snacks and safe drinks are on sale.

ACCOMMODATION

Juniper Family Campground Hwy-4 ☎ 505 672 3861, ⓦ nps.gov/band. While there's no roofed accommodation at Bandelier, the monument does operate this very pleasant campground, with restrooms but no showers or hook-ups, up on Frijoles Mesa at the start of the road down into the canyon. All except a couple of group sites are first-come, first-served, and there's almost always plenty of availability. $12

Valles Caldera National Preserve

Valle Grande Visitor Center Mile-marker 39.2, Hwy-4 • Daily: mid-May to Sept 8am–6pm, Oct to mid-May 9am–5pm • $20 per vehicle • ☎ 505 670 1612, ⓦ nps.gov/vall

West of Bandelier and Los Alamos, Hwy-4 climbs out of the forests before bursting unexpectedly into the open to skirt the long rim of **Valle Grande**. This 500-foot-deep, 13-mile-wide caldera was created 1.2 million years ago by a now dormant (but not extinct) supervolcano. Its wide meadows form a lush counterpoint to the dry-as-dust terrain of most of New Mexico, and the basin was much prized by ancient peoples both as prime hunting territory and as a source of obsidian, a volcanic glass that can be chipped to form ultra-sharp blades.

The national government purchased the huge Baca Ranch here for $101 million in 2000, to create the 89,000-acre **Valles Caldera National Preserve**; another 5000 acres of ancestral land was given back to neighbouring Santa Clara Pueblo. The original intention was to run the preserve as a self-sustaining wildlife reserve – it's home to a large elk herd in summer, as well as several rare bird species – that would be funded through commercial activities. That system never generated anything like enough revenue, however, so it passed into National Park Service control in 2015.

In practice, the preserve remains primarily a drive-through experience. Only if you venture along any of its **hiking trails**, some of which start from roadside pull-outs, do you have to pay the admission fee at the visitor centre on Hwy-4, where helpful staff can advise on the various possibilities. The altitude at 8750ft makes all physical activity here demanding, and lightning strikes are such a constant threat, thanks to the almost daily afternoon thunderstorms, that hikers are advised to leave the area by 2pm.

Spence Hot Springs

Hwy-4, between mileposts 24 and 25

Among the most irresistible of the many **hot springs** that bubble from beneath the ground close to Valles Caldera – the most obvious vestiges of the region's volcanic history – are the **SPENCE HOT SPRINGS**. Set on a promontory above the Jemez River, half an hour out of Los Alamos, it consists of half a dozen waterfall-connected pools that provide a range of temperatures to suit anybody, from the high nineties (Farenheit) in the lower pools to a blissful 104°F (40°C) at the top. Local custom calls for bathing suits on weekend nights, otherwise it's clothing optional. To get there, cross the river over a fallen tree and then climb up the canyon, keeping to the left for about a ten-minute walk uphill.

Jemez Springs

Five miles downhill from Spence Hot Springs, Hwy-4 runs past the enormous, bizarre and very smelly **Soda Dam**, where calcified deposits all but block the Jemez River, to enter **JEMEZ SPRINGS**. This appealing hamlet, where the river is lined by glowing cottonwoods and flows between high canyon walls that flame gold and red, was once the site of the Towa-speaking pueblo of **Giusewa**, the "Place of the Boiling Waters". The most active of its hot mineral springs was enclosed in the 1870s by a **bathhouse**, where you can enjoy an hour-long soak for $18, or a massage for $42 (Mon, Tues & Thurs–Sat 10am–6pm, Sun 10am–5pm; ☎575 829 3303, ⊛jemezspringsbathhouse.com).

Jemez Historic Site

Daily except Tues 8.30am–5pm • $3 • ☎575 829 3530, ⊛nmhistoricsites.org

The substantial shell of the mission church of **San Jose de los Jemez**, built by Franciscans in 1621 only to be destroyed almost immediately by Navajo raiders, is now preserved in **Jemez Historic Site**. Walls that once held bright frescoes are now just stumps, but the principal doorway has been reconstructed. Most of the ruins that surround it were convent outbuildings rather than pueblo dwellings, although you can still spot several subterranean *kivas*. Jemez Springs' religious tradition continues to this day, as it's home to large Christian monasteries as well as a Zen centre.

ACCOMMODATION AND EATING   **JEMEZ SPRINGS**

Cañon del Rio 16445 Hwy-4 ☎575 829 4377, ⊛canondelrio.com. Lovely B&B inn/retreat, in a splendid rural setting with its own pool and outdoor spa, where each of the five very comfortable en-suite rooms is

themed according to a different Southwestern tribe. No under-14s. $129

Laughing Lizard Inn ☎575 829 3410, ⊛thelaughinglizard.com. Four simple but appealing and inexpensive en-suite motel-style rooms, opening onto a nice terrace perched above both highway and river. **$70** **Los Ojos Restaurant and Saloon** ☎ 575 829 3547, ⓦ losojossaloon.com. Very much the social centre for

Jemez Springs, this late-opening roadside restaurant offers a full menu of pub food – burgers, wings and the like – for under $10 – as well as pool tables and cheap beer. Mon–Fri 11am–midnight, Sat & Sun 8am–midnight.

Jemez Pueblo

Walatowa Visitor Center Summer daily 8am–5pm, winter Wed–Sun 8am–4pm • ☎ 575 834 7235, ⓦ jemezpueblo.com

After Giusewa Pueblo, the site of modern Jemez Springs, was abandoned in 1630, its inhabitants built **JEMEZ PUEBLO** fifteen miles downstream. There they participated in the Pueblo Revolt of 1680, sacking their church and killing its priest; when the Spaniards returned, they briefly retreated northwest, establishing cultural and family links with the Navajo that endure to this day. They also assimilated the last twenty survivors of Pecos Pueblo in 1838 (see p.118). Jemez now has a population of around 3400 and is the only surviving Towa-speaking pueblo.

Home for the Jemez Indians is a gorgeous, lush canyon floor, surrounded by low cliffs of rich red rock. In honour of that scenery, they call themselves **Walatowa**, "people of the canyon", and that's also the name of their village. The pueblo itself is only open to visitors on feast days such as August 2, November 12 and December 12. The impressive **Walatowa Visitor Center**, three miles north on Hwy-4 at Red Rock, holds displays on their history, can arrange group tours and sells a wide range of crafts.

On a weekend in mid-October, the **Jemez Pueblo Open Air Market**, also at Red Rock, sells food and artwork.

Zia Pueblo

Visitor centre Mon–Fri 8am–noon & 1–5pm • Free • ☎ 505 867 3304

Six miles south of San Ysidro, reached by a short spur road off US-550, little **ZIA PUEBLO** overlooks the Jemez River. Now 750 strong, the Zia have occupied this spot since the sixteenth century. They're best known for the **sun symbol** that features on New Mexico's flag and licence plates. Though they've failed to persuade the courts to grant them royalties for its use, they do at least earn some money as a movie location; both *All The Pretty Horses* and *Ghosts of Mars* were filmed here.

There's little reason for outsiders to visit Zia, but the tribe does maintain a small **visitor centre** not far off the highway.

Santa Ana Pueblo

SANTA ANA PUEBLO, eight miles southeast of Zia Pueblo along US-550, and every bit as small, are, like their neighbours, Keresan speakers, who moved in after the Pueblo Revolt. Only since the advent of Indian gaming in the 1990s have they made any effort to welcome visitors. Profits from the roadside **Santa Ana Star Casino** (ⓦ santaanastar .com), which holds four restaurants and a large bowling centre, have enabled the tribe to branch out in several new directions. These include two top-quality golf courses, 22 soccer fields, and several crafts outlets.

From the end of the Jemez Mountain Trail, when Hwy-44 meets I-25 at **Bernalillo** (see p.127), downtown Albuquerque is a sixteen-mile drive south, while Santa Fe is a forty miles drive northeast (see p.104).

ACCOMMODATION	**SANTA ANA PUEBLO**

Hyatt Regency Tamaya Resort & Spa 1300 Tuyuna Trail ☎ 505 867 1234, ⓦ tamaya.hyatt.com. New Mexico's most prestigious luxury resort, a joint venture between Santa Ana Pueblo and Hyatt, is the most conspicuous consequence

of the tribe's recent gambling-based prosperity. As well as 350 opulent rooms and suites, it features three swimming pools, a fitness centre and spa, four restaurants, a championship golf course and its own stables. **$209**

Prairie Star 288 Prairie Star Rd, Santa Ana Golf Club ☎505 867 3327, ⓦmynewmexicogolf.com. Popular evening excursion for the affluent of Albuquerque, this excellent restaurant, set in an adobe mansion northwest of

the casino, offers contemporary Southwestern cuisine. Typical mains include pecan-dusted grilled salmon ($25) and lavender-infused rack of lamb ($35). Tues–Sun 5.30–9pm; closed Sun in winter.

From Santa Fe to Taos: the northern pueblos

The quickest route between Santa Fe and Taos follows **US-84** as far as the Rio Grande, then continues northeast beside the river on **Hwy-68** – not that the switch from one road to the other, at **Española**, is discernible. US-84 passes through the heartland of the **northern pueblos**. The most interesting of these tiny Tewa-speaking villages for casual visitors are **Nambé**, near the impressive **Nambé Falls**, and **Pojoaque** beside the highway, where a museum and visitor centre provide a quick taste of Pueblo culture. Serious collectors can head instead for **San Ildefonso**, in search of its famous pottery.

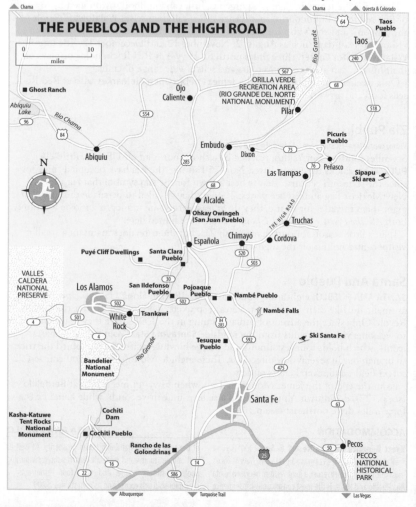

THE PUEBLOS AND THE HIGH ROAD

Tesuque Pueblo

Nine miles north of Santa Fe, west of US-84, and overlooked by the once seen, never forgotten **Camel Rock**, the traditional community of **TESUQUE PUEBLO** studiously turns its back on the city. Its name means "place of the cottonwood trees", and its people were the first to strike against the Spaniards during the Pueblo Revolt. There's no visitor centre, but the tribe operates the **Camel Rock Casino** (ⓦcamelrockcasino.com), which has a good buffet restaurant, and also holds a colourful open-air weekend **flea market**, selling everything from clothing to furniture to hot sauce (March–Dec Fri–Sun 9am–4pm; ⓦpueblooftesuquefleamarket.com).

2

Pojoaque Pueblo

POJOAQUE PUEBLO, twelve miles out of Santa Fe on US-84, was once one of the largest pueblos, but its original settlement was abandoned after a smallpox epidemic in 1895, and in terms of land it's now the smallest in the state. Though some ceremonial activities have resumed, most of the tribe's attention is devoted to running various commercial and cultural enterprises beside the highway. The **Cities of Gold** casino (ⓦcitiesofgold.com) has proved so lucrative that the tribe was able to buy the Santa Fe Downs racetrack, adjoining the pueblo, in order to close it down.

Poeh Museum

78 Cities of Gold Rd, alongside US-84 • Mon–Fri 9am–5pm, Sat 10am–5pm • Free • ☎ 505 455 5041, ⓦ poehcenter.org

Part of an ever-expanding complex, built in traditional adobe style and also incorporating a cultural centre, the **Poeh Museum** covers the history and culture of all the Tewa peoples. A walkway leads through a mocked-up cave to reach (uncaptioned) displays that trace Pueblo history from its nomadic origins to the construction of permanent villages and the development of weaving and agriculture. The coming of the Spaniards is represented by a crazy-eyed friar flogging a Puebloan, followed by a mission church ablaze, while the story ends rather poignantly with a vacant-faced Pueblo child staring at a big-screen TV.

ACCOMMODATION AND EATING   POJOAQUE PUEBLO

La Mesita 86 Cities of Gold Rd ☎ 505 455 7004, ⓦlamesitaeatery.com. Pueblo-run diner next door to the Poeh Museum, conspicuous for its distinctive ramada-style patio. Fried chicken, at $14, is the house speciality, but the menu also ranges through burgers, steaks and pasta specials. Tues–Sat 11am–9pm, Sun 11am–8pm.

Nambé Pueblo

☎ 505 455 4400, ⓦ nambepueblo.org

The most beautifully sited of the northern pueblos, **NAMBÉ PUEBLO** is reached by turning right on Hwy-503 just beyond Pojoaque. Keep going up the hillside beyond the Sacred Heart church, and turn right after three verdant miles. The pueblo itself, 1.5 miles along, is not visible from the road; apart from a large *kiva*, not much remains in its old plaza area.

The prime visitor attraction in the pueblo is a tribal park that lies another 3.5 miles along the road. When this book was being researched, however, the **Nambé Falls Recreation Area** was closed for reconstruction. Assuming it has reopened by the time you pass this way – check the website for the latest details – you can expect it to be accessible daily until sunset in summer (April–Oct), for an admission fee of around $10 per vehicle. The triple-decker **Nambé Falls** are reached by a steep five-minute hike up from the parking lot. At the top of the climb, you can admire the waters as they tumble through a jagged cleft in the surrounding red rocks, but the view is somewhat marred by the colossal concrete dam that towers above. There's no way to reach the foot of the falls, let alone swim there.

San Ildefonso Pueblo

$10 per vehicle, $10 camera, $20 video • ☎ 505 455 2273, ⓦ sanipueblo.org • **Tewa Visitor Center** Feb–Oct daily 8am–5pm; Nov–Jan Mon–Fri 8am–5pm • **Pueblo Museum** Mon–Fri 8am–4pm • No additional charge

SAN ILDEFONSO PUEBLO, located five miles west of Pojoaque, before Hwy-502 crosses the Rio Grande and climbs up to Los Alamos, is best known as the former home of potter **Maria Martínez**. From 1919 onwards, together with her husband Julian, she was responsible for revitalizing the Pueblo ceramic tradition; the finest collection of the pair's work is in Taos' Millicent Rogers Museum (see p.150).

The people of San Ildefonso trace their ancestry back to Mesa Verde, by way of the Pajarito Plateau. In 1694, when the Spaniards returned after the Pueblo Revolt, refugees from San Ildefonso and its neighbours held out on a nearby mesa, **Black Rock**, until they were starved down.

San Ildefonso now consists of two plazas, one of which holds a replica of its original mission church. Individual artisans sell pottery from their own homes – look for signs – or you can buy from the selection in the **Tewa Visitor Center** when you pay your admission fee. The nearby **Pueblo Museum** holds some of Martínez's original works.

Santa Clara Pueblo

SANTA CLARA PUEBLO, five miles north of San Ildefonso, or five miles west of Española, is known to its 1500 inhabitants as Kapo, "where the roses grow near the water". Like their neighbours, they too now sell pottery from houses around the central plaza, but the main reason to visit is to see where they *used* to live: the dramatic **Puyé Cliff Dwellings** in Santa Clara Canyon. The pueblo also runs the successful *Santa Claran* casino/hotel complex in Española (ⓦ santaclaran.com).

Puyé Cliff Dwellings

Check in and pay at Valero gas station on Hwy-30, 3 miles south of Santa Clara Pueblo, then drive 7 miles north on Santa Clara Canyon Rd to the ruins • Daily: April–Sept 8.30am–6pm, hourly tours 9am–5pm; Oct–March 9.30am–3pm, hourly tours 10am–2pm; closed week before Easter plus June 13 and Aug 12 • Cliff Tour $20, Mesa Top Tour $20, combined Puyé Adventure Tour $35 • ☎ 505 917 6650, ⓦ puyecliffs.com • If driving from Santa Fe, leave 1hr before your desired tour time

Like the similar but better-known ruins at Bandelier (see p.132), the ancient community that's now preserved as **Puyé Cliff Dwellings** – "Puyé" means "where the rabbits meet" – was set against the south-facing cliffs at the edge of the Pajarito Plateau, and occupied, presumably by descendants of the Mesa Verdeans, between 1250 and 1550. Two tiers of "apartments" were hollowed into the upper canyon wall – so soft that it could be shaped with wooden tools – while a large free-standing pueblo occupied the mesa-top just above.

Santa Clara Indians now lead hugely informative **guided tours** up to and around the complex, which provide the opportunity, rare indeed in the Southwest, to hear such a site interpreted by members of the same group that used to occupy it. The trail starts from a former Fred Harvey B&B at the base of the cliff that now serves as a visitor centre-cum-museum. Although in principle it's an easy walk, it can feel very exposed in the full heat of midsummer.

To see the whole thing you need to sign up for the full two-hour **Adventure Tour**, but most visitors will be content with the one-hour **Cliff Tour**, which involves climbing at least one steep ladder, as well as some deeply worn "staircases" in the rock. What seem like cosy little cave dwellings were originally interior rooms in larger complexes; each was fronted by several adobe-walled rooms, as the countless holes that once supported roof beams now testify. Intriguingly, petroglyphs above the entranceways appear to mark specific homes. The second hour of the Adventure Tour continues up onto the mesa, where the ruined foundations of the former pueblo are much less readily understandable. You can also go up there on the stand-alone **Mesa Top Tour**, but that's very much a second choice to the Cliff Tour.

Española

The only sizeable Hispanic settlement between Santa Fe and Taos is **ESPAÑOLA**, roughly halfway between the two and immediately south of the confluence of the Rio Chama and the Rio Grande. While most highway traffic continues northeast at this point toward Taos on Hwy-68, US-84 veers west across the river towards Chama (see p.158) and Colorado.

Other than watching the local youth cruising the streets in their customized "low-riders" or joining them in one of the dozens of neighbourhood fast-food joints, Española has little to offer tourists. However, it can make an alternative base to Santa Fe or Taos.

Abiquiu

O'Keeffe Home Tours June–Oct Tues–Sat 9am, 10.30am, noon, 2pm & 3.30pm, plus Behind the Scenes tour Wed & Fri 6pm; early March to May & Nov Tues, Thurs & Fri 9am, 10.30am, noon, 2pm & 3.30pm • Standard tour Tues–Fri $35, Sat $45; Behind the Scenes tour $65 • ☎ 505 685 4539, ⓦ okeeffemuseum.org

Twenty miles up US-84 from Española, the landscape erupts into a riot of red-rock splendour. Cliffs and mesas of Chinle, Entrada and Windgate sandstone soar above corrugated hillocks of grey, brown and red clays, all strongly reminiscent of southern Utah and the Navajo badlands of northeast Arizona. Surprisingly few visitors pass this way, but it's hardly little known. If it now appears definitively Southwestern, that's largely because the paintings of **Georgia O'Keeffe** have done so much to shape contemporary notions of the Southwest – and it was this very terrain that inspired those paintings. Of one peak, the **Pedernal**, O'Keeffe said, "God told me if I painted that mountain enough, I could have it."

From 1946 until she died, at age 98, in 1986, O'Keeffe's life centred on the pretty adobe village of **ABIQUIU** (pronounced *a-beh-cue*). Originally a settlement of *genízaros* (the Christianized descendants of Plains peoples captured by eighteenth-century Spaniards), Abiquiu village was a trading centre on a par with Taos in the late eighteenth and early nineteenth centuries, and was briefly New Mexico's third-largest town. These days, it consists of little more than a small plaza, surrounded by tumbledown adobes and centred by the beautiful, restored church of **Santo Tomás**; photography is not permitted.

O'Keeffe's former home, commanding magnificent views from its hilltop perch south of the highway and now known as the **Georgia O'Keeffe Home and Studio**, can be visited on guided tours. Reserve and pay in advance, providing full names and addresses of all participants. Most of the rooms are roped off, but you do get to stroll through her kitchen, and admire her garden.

ACCOMMODATION
ABIQUIU

★**Abiquiu Inn** 21120 Hwy-84 ☎ 505 685 4378, ⓦ abiquiuinn.com. Exceptionally peaceful B&B inn with wonderful views. A haven for O'Keeffe enthusiasts, it also makes a good base for explorations further afield. As well as a fine array of comfortable guest rooms and *casitas*, all en-suite with *kiva* fireplaces and Southwestern art, it's home to the excellent *Café Abiquiu* restaurant, open for all meals daily, where typical dinner mains such as seared tuna cost around $20. Doubles **$130**, casitas **$220**

Ghost Ranch

Hwy-84 • **Welcome Center** Daily: early March to Oct 7am–7pm; Nov to early March 8am–6pm • **Museums** Mon–Sat 9am–5pm, Sun 1–5pm • **Tours** O'Keeffe Landscape mid-March to late Nov Tues & Thurs–Sat 1.30pm, plus 3pm when necessary; late Nov to mid-March Thurs–Sat 1.30pm; O'Keeffe's Footsteps April–Nov Fri 9am; Archeology mid-April to mid-Oct Wed 10am; Movie mid-April to mid-Oct Thurs 10am; Paleontology mid-April to mid-Oct Sat 10am • Basic admission $5, Adventure Pass $39, Culture Pass $49, O'Keeffe Landscape $34, O'Keeffe's Footsteps $49; other tours $29 • ☎ 505 685 1000, ⓦ ghostranch.org

Standing in superb isolation 14 miles northeast of Abiquiu along US-84, Ghost Ranch has belonged to the Presbyterian Church since 1955, and is run as a centre for spiritual

VISITING THE RIO GRANDE PUEBLOS

In 1540, the first Spaniards to explore what's now New Mexico encountered a settled population of around a hundred thousand people, living in a hundred or so villages and towns. These inhabitants did not see themselves as a single people, but the Spaniards collectively named them **Pueblo Indians**, from the Spanish for "village". Smallpox, war and general disruption subsequently took their toll, but New Mexico is still home to around forty thousand Pueblo Indians, who live in nineteen autonomous pueblos, each with its own laws and system of government.

Fifteen pueblos are concentrated along the Rio Grande north of Albuquerque. There's a long-standing division between the seven southern pueblos, south of Santa Fe, most of which speak Keresan, and the eight to the north, which mostly speak Tewa (pronounced *tay-wah*). Together with the four pueblos that lie further afield, they jointly promote themselves through Albuquerque's **Indian Pueblo Cultural Center** (see p.173; Ⓦ indianpueblo.org).

Despite their fascinating history, most pueblos aren't the tourist attractions they're often touted to be. While the best known, **Taos** and **Acoma**, retain their ancient defensive architecture, the rest tend to be dusty adobe hamlets scattered around a windblown plaza. All the pueblos have to some extent incorporated **Catholicism**, as introduced by the Spanish, into their religious beliefs, and thus tend to centre on an old adobe mission church. Rarely, however, does Christianity amount to more than a syncretic imposition upon more fundamental traditional beliefs, and you'll also see *kivas*, or prayer chambers, nearby.

If you can time your visit to coincide with a **feast day**, a trip to a pueblo is an extraordinary experience. The spectacle of hundreds of costumed, body-painted tribal members of all ages, drawn from other pueblos as well as the host village, performing elaborate dances in such timeless surroundings, seems like a genuine glimpse of the ancient life of the continent. You won't be allowed to photograph or even sketch the ceremonies, but stalls selling food, jewellery, ceramics and other Pueblo crafts make it possible to take something away with you.

Otherwise, unless you are a knowledgeable shopper in search of Pueblo arts and crafts, visits can be disappointing. You'll certainly be made to feel unwelcome if you fail to behave respectfully – don't "explore" places that are off-limits, such as shrines, *kivas* or private homes.

Visitors to each pueblo are required to register at a visitor centre; some charge an admission fee of $3 to $10, and those that permit such activities at all charge additional fees of perhaps $5 for still photography, $10–15 for video cameras, and up to $100 for sketching. Many forbid the use of mobile phones.

SOUTHERN PUEBLOS

Cochiti (see p.124) Ⓦ puebalodecochiti.org
Jemez (see p.135) Ⓦ jemezpueblo.com
Kewa (see p.126) Ⓦ indianpueblo.org
San Felipe (see p.127) Ⓦ sanfelipecasino.com
Sandia (see p.127) Ⓦ sandiapueblo.nsn.us
Santa Ana (see p.135) Ⓦ santaana.org
Zia (see p.135) Ⓦ indianpueblo.org

NORTHERN PUEBLOS

Nambé (see p.137) Ⓦ nambepueblo.org
Ohkay Owingeh (see p.142) Ⓦ indianpueblo.org
Picuris (see p.146) Ⓦ picurispueblo.org
Pojoaque (see p.137) Ⓦ citiesofgold.com
San Ildefonso (see p.138) Ⓦ sanipueblo.org
Santa Clara (see p.138) Ⓦ indianpueblo.org
Taos (see p.151) Ⓦ taospueblo.com
Tesuque (see p.137) Ⓦ indianpueblo.org

PUEBLOS FURTHER AFIELD

Acoma (see p.99)	ⓦacomaskycity.org
Isleta (see p.175)	ⓦisletapueblo.com
Laguna (see p.100)	ⓦlagunapueblo.org
Zuni (see p.96)	ⓦwww.zunitourism.com

A PUEBLO CALENDAR

Jan 1	Turtle Dance	Taos
Jan 1	Corn Dance	Kewa
Jan 1	Cloud or Basket Dance	Ohkay Owingeh
Jan 6	Three Kings Day	Most pueblos
Jan 22–23	San Ildefonso Feast Day	San Ildefonso
Jan 25	St Paul's Feast Day	Picuris, Ohkay Owingeh
Feb 2	Candelaria Day	Picuris, San Felipe
Feb (1st weekend)	Governor's Feast	Acoma
Feb (2nd weekend)	Deer Dance	Ohkay Owingeh
March 19	St Joseph's Feast Day	Laguna
Easter	Dances	Nambé, San Ildefonso, Kewa, Zia
May 1	San Felipe Feast Day	San Felipe
May 3	Santa Cruz Feast Day	Taos
May 7	Santa Maria Feast Day	Acoma
June (1st Sat)	Blessing of the Fields	Tesuque
June 13	San Antonio Feast Day	Most pueblos
June 24	San Juan Feast Day	Ohkay Owingeh, Taos
June 29	San Pedro Feast Day	Kewa
July 4	Nambé Falls Celebration	Nambé
July (2nd week)	Taos Pueblo pow-wow	Taos
July 14	San Buenaventura	Cochiti
July (3rd week)	Northern Pueblo Arts & Crafts Show	Varying northern pueblos
July 25	Corn Dances	San Ildefonso, Taos
July 26	Santa Ana Feast Day	Laguna, Santa Ana, Taos
Aug 2	Santa Persingula Feast Day	Jemez
Aug 4	Santo Domingo Feast Day	Kewa
Aug 10	Pueblo Revolt Anniversary	Most pueblos
Aug 10	San Lorenzo Feast Day	Acoma, Picuris
Aug 12	Santa Clara Feast Day	Santa Clara
Aug 15	Assumption	Laguna, Zia
Aug (3rd week)	Indian Market	Santa Fe
Aug (3rd week)	Zuni Tribal Fair	Zuni
Aug 28	San Augustine Feast Day	Isleta
Sept 2	San Estéban Feast Day	Acoma
Sept 4	Isleta Pueblo Feast Day	Isleta
Sept 8	Corn Dances	Laguna, San Ildefonso
Sept 19	Laguna Pueblo Feast Day	Laguna
Sept 25	Santa Isabela Feast Day	Laguna
Sept 29–30	Feast of San Gerónimo	Taos
Oct (1st week)	Harvest Festival	Zuni
Oct 3–4	San Francisco Feast Day	Nambé
Nov 12	San Diego Feast Day	Jemez, Tesuque
early Dec	Shalako Ceremony	Zuni
Dec 12	Guadalupe Feast Day	Pojoaque
Dec 24–25	Matachina Dance	Most pueblos
Dec 26	Turtle Dance	Ohkay Owingeh
Dec 28	Children's Dances	Picuris, Santa Clara

2

and educational retreats. It owes its fame, however, to its previous incarnation as a dude ranch, where Georgia O'Keeffe spent several summers from 1934 onwards. O'Keeffe bought a small home here in 1940, which she continued to visit for many years after the rest of the ranch passed into Presbyterian hands.

Ghost Ranch now holds two small **museums**, one devoted to anthropology and the other to paleontology. The major appeal for visitors, however, is the staggering landscape hereabouts, which can be explored either on **guided tours**, some of which examine O'Keeffe's connections with the site, or on self-guided hikes. The demanding three-mile trail to and from **Chimney Rock**, a solitary red-rock pinnacle conspicuous from the highway, is especially recommended.

Visit the website for detailed schedules; sold on alternate days, the Culture Pass offers access to the museums and walking tours, while the Adventure Pass includes outdoor activities such as archery and kayaking.

Ohkay Owingeh

Mission Church Free • Photography by permission only

Set amid the cottonwoods on the east bank of the Rio Grande off Hwy-68, five miles north of Española, the largest Tewa pueblo, long known as **San Juan Pueblo**, has recently reverted to its Tewa name of **OHKAY OWINGEH**. This is the third village to have stood in this area since 1250, all of which have been called Ohkay, meaning "we are the brothers". The first two capitals of the colony of New Mexico were also built here in 1598. Before they relocated to Santa Fe in 1610, the Spanish took over Ohkay and called it San Juan, and then occupied nearby Yunge and renamed it **San Gabriel**. Later that century, San Juan was the birthplace of **Po'pay**, the medicine man who led the Pueblo Revolt.

The centrepiece of the plaza is the much-restored **mission church**, the first building in the Southwest to be made with adobe bricks as opposed to simple chunks of mud. It's flanked by two rectangular *kivas*, as well as a smaller Catholic chapel.

Embudo

The funky little village of **EMBUDO**, beside the Rio Grande 18 miles northeast of Española, has in recent years become something of an alternative artists' colony. Its handful of crafts and oddities stores include **Classical Gas**, whose forecourt display of 1950s gas pumps is a great little slice of Americana. Inside, you'll find what its owner calls the "shiny stuff", largely consisting of assorted neon and glass advertising signs from the Route 66 era. Open to no fixed hours, it's more of a museum than a shop, though some of the stock is for sale.

Río Grande del Norte National Monument

New Mexico's northernmost portion of the Rio Grande was designated as the **Río Grande del Norte National Monument** in 2013. Run by the Bureau of Land Management, the monument was created primarily to protect the region from exploitation, and covers a single contiguous area, stretching from the southern end of the **Rio Grande Gorge** all the way to the Colorado state line, and also taking in a tranche of the wilderness that extends away to the west. As far as visitors are concerned, however, it effectively consists of two distinct sections, southwest and northwest of Taos respectively: the **Orilla Verde** and **Wild Rivers** recreation areas.

Southern section: Orilla Verde Recreation Area

Rio Grande Gorge Visitor Center Late May to early Sept daily 8.30am–4.30pm, early Sept to late May Fri–Sun 10am–3pm • Day-use $3 per vehicle, camping primitive sites $5, vehicle sites $7, RV sites $15 • ☏ 575 751 4899, ⓦ blm.gov/nm

The most readily accessible section of **Río Grande del Norte National Monument** lies roughly fifteen miles southwest of Taos. Immediately south of **PILAR** on Hwy-68 here, you can pick up maps and details of the monument from the large **Rio Grande Gorge Visitor Center**. Pilar itself, incidentally, was originally a Jicarilla Apache farming village. On May 30, 1854, the Jicarilla defeated sixty US dragoons nearby in the Battle of Cieneguilla; several years of fighting ensued before they were finally confined to a reservation to the west (see p.159). Pilar is now a base for **rafting** trips (see p.154), and has a simple roadside diner.

Across from the visitor centre, a minor road drops down to the riverside **Orilla Verde Recreation Area**. An attractive six-mile drive leads along the eastern bank, passing a popular developed campground just before it crosses the river itself. To the north, the walls of the Rio Grande Gorge start to soar to either side and it's impossible to continue towards Taos along either bank; the road you're on is no longer paved as it climbs steeply up the western side, making **4WD** necessary if you want to meet up with US-285 beyond.

It is possible to **hike** on the west bank, however. The **Vista Verde Trail**, just over the bridge, is an enjoyable 1.25-mile hiking trail that leads across the sagebrush-topped mesa to an overlook above the Rio Grande Gorge. A longer trail, slightly further up the hillside, runs all the way to the Rio Grande Gorge Bridge (see p.156); at seven miles one-way, it's better tackled by bike or horse than on foot.

Northern section: Wild Rivers Recreation Area

Wild Rivers Visitor Center Late May to early Sept daily 9am–6pm; early Sept to late May varies with staff availability • Day-use $3 per vehicle, camping walk-in $5, vehicle $7 • ☎ 575 586 1150, ⓦ blm.gov/nm

To reach the main northern component of **Río Grande del Norte National Monument**, head northwest of Taos on first Hwy-68 and then Hwy-522, and turn west onto Hwy-378 at **CERRO**, a total of 28 miles along. Just under ten miles along, this access road divides in two to loop around the dry high mesa-top that towers over the spot where the Red River meets the Rio Grande, with the monument visitor centre located a couple of miles along its eastern segment.

Before the new monument was designated, this region was already known as the **Wild Rivers Recreation Area**, and equipped with some great hiking trails and campgrounds. The pick of the bunch, the **La Junta Trail**, drops directly down to the confluence from the southernmost tip of the mesa. That's a dramatic three-mile round-trip, which can be extended if you head north along the Rio Grande Gorge from the bottom, and return via the less demanding **Little Arsenic Trail** (total hike five miles) or **Big Arsenic Springs Trail** (eight miles).

The High Road

While the most direct route from Santa Fe to Taos heads straight up the Rio Grande Valley, the **"High Road"** over the forested Sangre de Cristo Mountains to the east makes a rewarding alternative if you have a couple of hours to spare. Winding through timeless **Hispanic villages**, it passes some splendid old **adobe churches** and offers good opportunities to sample traditional New Mexican food or buy local folk art. Shopping for crafts is a big deal year-round, reaching its peak in the **High Road Art Tour**, which takes place during the last two weekends of September (ⓦhighroadnewmexico.com).

Chimayó

The first and most famous of the High Road towns, **CHIMAYÓ** is 25 miles north of Santa Fe, eight miles northeast of **Pojoaque Pueblo** via the desiccated Hwy-592 and Hwy-503, or eight miles east of **Española** on Hwy-76. Stretching luxuriantly through the fertile upland meadows that line the Santa Cruz River, and backed by scrubby

2

THE PENITENTES

During the nineteenth century, the remote hills above Chimayó were renowned as the heartland of the mysterious Hispanic Catholic sect known as the **Penitentes**. Anglo newcomers claimed to have glimpsed hooded figures filing along the ridges at dawn, **whipping** themselves as they went.

A large grain of truth lay beneath the lurid speculation. Self-mortification – the infliction of pain in order to share the suffering of Christ – was widespread in medieval Europe. The Spanish expedition that founded New Mexico performed public self-flagellation on Good Friday 1598, as it marched up through Mexico, and similar acts by early Franciscan missionaries attracted Pueblo scorn. The Penitentes as such, however, emerged after Mexico achieved independence in 1821. Cut off from Spanish funding, the Franciscans vanished from New Mexico within twenty years, leaving the region almost devoid of priests. Hispanic Catholics formed **lay brotherhoods** to keep their faith alive.

The Penitentes – **Los Hermanos de Nuestro Padre Jesús Nazareno**, or the Brothers of Our Father Jesus of Nazareth – may well have modelled themselves on a Guatemalan example, introduced at the same time as the Guatemalan-influenced pilgrimages to Chimayó. From an initial emphasis on individual prayer and penance, they developed a complex system of rituals. While never administering the sacraments, they brought solace to Catholics obliged to live – and die – without priests. The Penitente brotherhood in each village became a mutual-aid society, a cultural and political force as well as a spiritual one.

When the Americans took over New Mexico in 1846, the Penitentes became outsiders not only in their own country but even in their own church. The first Catholic bishop of Santa Fe, Jean-Baptiste **Lamy**, had little sympathy for the unorthodoxies of his Hispanic flock, and denied the sacraments to their most prominent spokesman, Father **Martínez** of Taos. Forced into secrecy, the Penitentes began to gather at night in remote spots. Lacking access to church property, they met in plain adobe structures known as **moradas** – not necessarily distinguished with crosses or towers, but adorned with the handmade sacred images known as **santos**.

The focus of ritual activity was **Lent**, when all Catholics practise some form of self-denial, and the Penitentes attempted to experience the passion and death of Christ. For processions, they divided into *Los Hermanos de Luz* – the **Brothers of Light**, responsible for the candles and music – and *Los Hermanos de Sangre*, the **Brothers of Blood**, who scourged themselves with yucca whips or carried giant wooden crosses. Participants were hooded to ensure humility. Some re-enacted the **crucifixion**, albeit tied rather than nailed to the cross, while others dragged a **Death Cart** – a wooden wagon holding an effigy of Death, armed with a bow and arrow – laden with stones. The Death Cart also figured in the Penitentes' elaborate **funeral** processions. The wayside stone cairns, topped with crosses and seen throughout the High Country, are not graves, as outsiders supposed, but *descansos* – places where the coffin-bearers would pause to rest.

A century of conflict ended in 1947, when the Penitentes were officially recognized by the Bishop of Santa Fe. Those that remain now regard themselves as members of the **Third Order of St Francis**, a lay branch of the Franciscan monastic order, and the most lasting Penitente legacy in New Mexico is the *santero* tradition of religious folk art.

red-tinged hills, it feels more of a piece with the Rio Grande Valley below than with the mountains to the east.

Chimayó was founded in 1740 as a sort of penal colony for Hispanic troublemakers. In Tewa, the word *tsimayo* means "good flaking stone"; Indians from San Juan Pueblo quarried obsidian here, which they chipped to form sharp blades.

Chimayó has specialized in **weaving** since 1805, when two weavers sent as teachers from Spain chose to live here in preference to Santa Fe. Outlets scattered through the village, such as Centinela Traditional Arts (☎ 505 351 2180, ⓦ chimayoweavers .com), sell hand-woven goods; other galleries concentrate on wood carving and religious art.

Santuario de Chimayó

Daily: May–Sept 9am–6pm; Oct–April 9am–5pm; Mass Mon–Sat 11am, Sun 10.30am & noon • ☎ 505 351 9961,
ⓦ elsantuariodechimayo.us

Long before the Spaniards came to Chimayó, Tewa Indians held a dried-up hot
spring here sacred, on the basis that the mud from around it, when eaten, had healing
properties. That spring, now located in the *barrio* (neighbourhood) of **El Potrero**, at
the village's southern end, has become the site of a spell-binding colonial chapel, the
Santuario de Chimayó.

The church was built between 1813 and 1816, after a visiting priest told the
landowner, **Bernardo Abeyta**, about the shrine that had arisen at a similar spring
venerated by Indians at Esquipulas in Guatemala. As a result, Abeyta's church also
centred on a crucifix known as **Nuestro Señor de Esquipulas**, supposedly found locally
in 1810 (conceivably it had been buried during the Pueblo Revolt).

The church, the crucifix, and the still-exposed *posito*, or dust pit, swiftly became the
focus of **pilgrimage** not only for Hispanic peasants but also for Pueblo Indians, for
whom the sacred hole in the earth clearly echoed the ancient concept of the *sipapu*
(see p.463). To this day, it remains the "**Lourdes of America**", surrounded by an
ever-increasing array of parking lots and processional walkways.

While devout New Mexican Catholics see Chimayó as much more than a picturesque
tourist attraction, the Santuario itself is an undeniable delight to visit: a ravishing little
round-shouldered, twin-towered, tin-roofed adobe beauty set in a walled churchyard
beneath the rolling Sangre de Cristo foothills. At the heart of the altar within, the
crucifix is framed by a gorgeous *reredos*, with a small equestrian statue of Santiago to
the right. Two smaller **side chapels** are filled with mind-boggling votive offerings –
paintings, photographs, statues, press cuttings, even rows of discarded crutches.
The hole containing the "Holy Dirt" is in the floor at the rear; pilgrims are allowed
to take a scoop, as it's replenished regularly with earth from the hills.

The smaller **Santo Niño Chapel**, across the plaza and accessed via an extraordinarily
kitsch angel gate, contains a diminutive statue of Santo Niño, the Lost Child – more of
a doll, if truth be told – to whom expectant mothers bring offerings such as tiny pairs
of shoes.

ACCOMMODATION AND EATING   CHIMAYÓ

Casa Escondida 64 County Rd 100 ☎ 505 351 4805 or
☎ 800 643 7201, ⓦ casaescondida.com. Set back in six
acres of gardens on the edge of Chimayó, the "hidden
house" is a very tasteful B&B with nine comfortable rooms.
All feature *viga* ceilings, tiled floors, and *kiva* fireplaces, and
have their own private bathrooms. **$119**

Hacienda Rancho de Chimayó Hwy-98 ☎ 505 351
2222 or ☎ 888 270 2320, ⓦ ranchodechimayo.com.
Across the highway from the *Rancho* restaurant, and run by
the same management, this peaceful B&B inn offers seven

appealing en-suite rooms, arranged around a shared
courtyard; several have their own patio space. **$79**
★**Rancho de Chimayó** Hwy-98 ☎ 505 351 4444,
ⓦ ranchodechimayo.com. Join regulars like Robert
Redford at the best traditional New Mexican restaurant in
the state, which serves superb *flautas* and a mouthwatering
sopaipilla, stuffed with meat and chiles and costing $13, on
a lovely sun-drenched outdoor patio. May–Oct Mon–Fri
11.30am–9pm, Sat & Sun 8.30am–10.30am &
11.30am–9pm; Nov–April Tues–Sun 11.30am–8.30pm.

Truchas

By the time you reach **TRUCHAS**, eight miles northeast of Chimayó on Hwy-76, you're well
into the mountains; the views down and across the Rio Grande Valley are tremendous.
Villagers from Las Trampas, further up, were granted permission to establish Truchas in
1754, on condition that it was enclosed within a walled square, to defend against
Comanche attacks. The settlement took on its present form almost immediately, however,
consisting of separate individual farms arrayed along a high ridge above the Río de las
Truchas, or "river of trout". As one of New Mexico's least changed Hispanic communities,
it was the location for Robert Redford's 1987 movie *The Milagro Beanfield War*.

Hwy-76 makes a right-angle bend to avoid Truchas, but a detour east onto the minor road up the valley takes you along a narrow street of adobe homes and barns – interspersed with the odd incongruous art gallery – and past the fields toward the 13,103ft **Truchas Peak**.

Las Trampas

Truchas' parent community, the quiet hamlet of **LAS TRAMPAS**, is another eight miles northeast along Hwy-76. It started life as an outpost used by fur-trappers pursuing beaver – hence its name, "the traps" – which by attracting Comanche raids doubled as an early-warning system for Santa Fe. Las Trampas now holds a couple of gift stores, but nowhere to eat or sleep.

Five miles on from Las Trampas, Hwy-76 meets Hwy-75 ten miles west of Hwy-68 and the Rio Grande. The quickest route to Taos, twenty miles north, is via Hwy-73 to the east, and then Hwy-518 to the north; more Hispanic villages line the way, but none is of interest to tourists.

San José de Gracia

Though no longer walled, the dusty central plaza of Las Trampas, alongside the highway, still holds the evocative adobe church of **San José de Gracia**. Built in 1760, it features a choir loft that extends both inside and out, so that singers could accompany ceremonies on the square as well as in the church. Sadly, though, it's not open to visitors. Note the unattached *morada* – Penitente meeting place – beside the cemetery to the east.

Picuris Pueblo

Museum Daily 9am–5pm • ☎ 575 587 2519, ⓦ picurispueblo.org

Tiny **PICURIS PUEBLO** is tucked away in a side valley, half a mile towards the Rio Grande from the junction of Hwy-76 and Hwy-75. The last pueblo to be "discovered" by the Spanish, it proudly insists that it has never signed a treaty with any government, the US included. Its population has never risen much above two hundred, and Picuris remains just a cluster of adobe houses spreading across the hillside around a whitewashed church. The best-known tribal enterprise is the excellent *Hotel Santa Fe* in Santa Fe (see p.120).

There's a model of the pueblo and a reconstructed *kiva* in the village **museum** ($3 suggested donation). The same building also holds a gift store and a snack bar with views over a small blue lake.

EATING   PICURIS PUEBLO

Sugarnymphs Bistro 15046 Hwy-75, Peñasco ☎ 575 587 0311, ⓦ sugarnymphs.com. Unexpected but very welcome roadside café/bistro, in a small village, a mile or so east of where the High Road meets Hwy-75, serving delicious and largely organic, home-grown sandwich and salad lunches for around $10, and more substantial dinners for around $15. July–Sept Mon–Wed 11.30am–3pm, Thurs–Sat 11.30am–3pm & 5–8pm, Sun 11am–2.30pm; shorter hours in winter.

Sipapu

Five miles east of Picuris Pueblo, Hwy-75 meets Hwy-518. Turning left, north, takes you onto the final leg of the High Road to Taos; continue east on Hwy-518, however, and in a couple of miles you'll enter the tiny **ski resort** of **SIPAPU**, cradled in the pretty mountain valley known as **Tres Ritos Canyon**. Lift tickets in season, which generally runs mid-December through March, cost $44.

Sipapu Lodge Hwy-518, beside the Rio Pueblo ☎ 800 587 2240, ⓦ sipapunm.com. In assorted units to either side of the highway, this ski resort offers every conceivable grade of accommodation, from dorm beds to private camping cabins, motel rooms and luxury duplexes. Dorms $12, doubles $59

Taos

Home to one of the oldest of all Native American communities, and successively a Spanish colonial outpost, Anglo art colony and hangout for New Age dropouts, tiny **TAOS** is famous out of all proportion to its size. Not quite six thousand people live in its three component parts: **Taos** itself, focused around the old plaza; sprawling **Ranchos de Taos** three miles south; and the Indian village of **Taos Pueblo** two miles north. There's one restaurant for every 45 inhabitants, and a massage therapist for every thirty.

Like Santa Fe, Taos – pronounced to rhyme with "house" – stretches languidly across a glorious high-desert plateau. The approach from the south is especially spectacular, as you cross a final bluff on Hwy-68 to be confronted by the pine-forested Sangre de Cristo mountains soaring above the sun-bleached foothills. This far north, the **Rio Grande** is not yet meandering through a well-watered valley, but lies deep in a craggy canyon west of town, occasionally glimpsed as a crack in the plateau.

Taos is a delight to visit. As well as museums, galleries and stores to match Santa Fe, it still offers the unhurried pace and charm, and the sense of a meeting place between Pueblo, Hispanic and American cultures, that attracted the likes of Georgia O'Keeffe and D.H. Lawrence.

Downtown Taos still centres on the old Spanish **plaza**, which has been remodelled several times over the years, and has migrated slightly eastwards in the process. The tiny square is now ringed by galleries and souvenir stores, and its tree-shaded benches make a pleasant spot from which to watch the world go by. The Stars and Stripes have flown day and night from the flagpole at its heart ever since it was erected by Kit Carson during the Civil War; the nearby bandstand was a gift from Mabel Dodge Luhan.

While there's little to see on the plaza itself, a short walk along the narrow streets that meander away in all directions is rewarded with glimpses of Taos as it used to be. The best central museum is the **Kit Carson Home**, while the **Millicent Rogers Museum**, a few miles north, holds superb Native American and Hispanic artworks.

Brief history

Although the first Franciscan mission at the thousand-year-old **Taos Pueblo** (see p.151) was established in 1598, the modern town of Taos dates from the 1630s, when an uprising at the pueblo induced Spanish colonists to found the separate community of **Fernando de Taos** a few judicious miles south. Its early history was dogged by Pueblo rebellions, but the Spaniards and Pueblos eventually united to resist raids by "horse Indians" like the Apache and Comanche. During the early nineteenth century, despite attempts by the Mexican authorities to restrict contact with the outside world, Taos became the venue for annual **rendezvous**, at which "mountain men" and trappers from the Rockies would trade with Indians from the pueblos and plains, and New Mexican merchants.

After the US takeover of New Mexico, Taos' Hispanic and Pueblo citizens once more found common cause. In 1847, the territory's first American governor, Charles Bent, was killed in his Taos home, but the revolt failed to spread to Santa Fe, and the US Army launched an assault on the Pueblo that succeeded in suppressing further resistance.

Taos' role as an **arts colony** began at the end of the nineteenth century, with the arrival of the painter Joseph Henry Sharp. He was soon joined by two young New York artists, Bert Phillips and Ernest L. Blumenschein; legend has it their wagon lost a wheel outside Taos as they headed for Mexico in 1898, and they liked the place so much they never

2

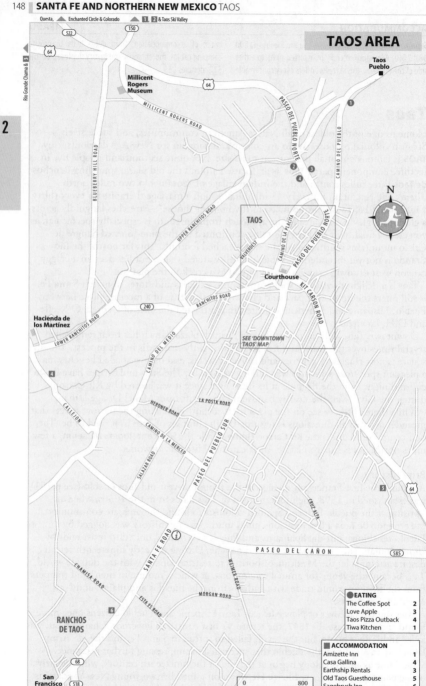

TAOS AREA

N

Taos Pueblo

Millicent Rogers Museum

MILLICENT ROGERS ROAD

PASEO DEL PUEBLO NORTE

CAMINO DEL PUEBLO

1

2 3
4

TAOS

BLUEBERRY HILL ROAD

UPPER RANCHITOS ROAD

CAMINO DE LA PLACITA

VALVERDEST

PASEO DEL PUEBLO NORTE

Courthouse

KIT CARSON ROAD

RANCHITOS ROAD

Hacienda de los Martínez

LOWER RANCHITOS ROAD

240

4

CALLEJON

CAMINO DEL MEDIO

SEE 'DOWNTOWN TAOS' MAP

HERDNER ROAD

LA POSTA ROAD

CAMINO DE LA MERCED

SALAZAR ROAD

PASEO DEL PUEBLO SUR

5

CRUZ ALTA

64

Rio Grande Chama & 3

Angel Fire & Carson National Forest

i

CHAMISA ROAD

SANTA FE ROAD

PASEO DEL CAÑON

585

WEIMER ROAD

MORGAN ROAD

RANCHOS DE TAOS

6

ESTA ES ROAD

ESPINOSA ROAD

68

San Francisco de Asís

518

Santa Fe   Las Vegas

0	800
	yards

● EATING

The Coffee Spot	2
Love Apple	3
Taos Pizza Outback	4
Tiwa Kitchen	1

■ ACCOMMODATION

Amizette Inn	1
Casa Gallina	4
Earthship Rentals	3
Old Taos Guesthouse	5
Sagebrush Inn	6
Snowmansion Taos Hostel	2

left. The three men established the **Taos Society of Artists** in 1915. Society heiress and arts patron Mabel Dodge turned up soon afterwards, and married an Indian from the pueblo to become **Mabel Dodge Luhan**. In turn, she wrote a fan letter to English novelist **D.H. Lawrence**, who visited in the early 1920s, and whose widow **Frieda** made her home in Taos after his death. New generations of artists and writers have "discovered" Taos ever since, the most famous being **Georgia O'Keeffe**, who stayed here in the 1920s before moving to Abiquiu (see p.139). Her renditions of the church at Ranchos de Taos in particular were a seminal influence on contemporary Southwestern art.

The influx of hippies who converged upon Taos in the late 1960s has been followed in subsequent decades by art-loving tourists, gallery-owning entrepreneurs, wealthy divorcées, eco-warriors and Hollywood exiles. Even as the urban area has grown larger and more commercialized, however, the population has remained minimal.

Governor Bent House and Museum

117 Bent St • Daily: April–Oct 9.30am–5pm, Nov–March 10am–4pm • $3 • ☎ 575 758 4945

Bent Street, a block north of the plaza, takes its name not from any irregularities but from the first American governor of New Mexico, Charles Bent. His former home is now privately run as the **Governor Bent House and Museum**. The imposition of American rule was resented by Taos' Hispanic and Indian population alike, and Bent was killed here by an angry mob on January 19, 1847. Most of his family attempted to escape through a still-visible hole hacked into the adobe walls; they were captured, but their lives were spared. The rest of the small house is a ramshackle museum of frontier Taoseño life, holding Indian artefacts, antiquated rifles, an eight-legged lamb, and, for some bizarre reason, a desiccated baby shark.

Kit Carson Home and Museum

113 Kit Carson Rd • Daily: March–Oct 10am–5pm, Nov–Feb 10am–4pm • $7 • ☎ 575 758 4945, ⊛ kitcarsonhomeandmuseum.com

The dusty but evocative adobe home of the legendary "mountain man", mason and part-time US cavalry officer **Kit Carson**, whose exploits were mythologized worldwide in the "dime fictions" that were the nineteenth-century precursors of Western movies, stands just east of the plaza, across the highway at the end of Taos' sole surviving stretch of wooden boardwalk. Born in Kentucky in 1809, Carson left home to join a wagon train to Missouri in 1826 – a one-cent reward was offered for the return of the teenage runaway – and spent the ensuing winter in Taos. He was to return repeatedly throughout his life, in between escapades like scouting for the 1840s Frémont expeditions and campaigning against the Navajo in the 1860s (see p.483).

Carson bought the house at the heart of today's museum in 1843, on his marriage to a local woman, Josefa Jaramillo. Sold after their deaths in 1868 to support their seven orphaned children, it now holds a small collection of press cuttings and photos relating to Carson himself, plus a mock-up of the family's living quarters, complete with *fogón de campaña*, a bell-shaped adobe fireplace.

Taos Art Museum at Fechin House

227 Paseo del Pueblo Norte • Tues–Sun: May–Oct 10am–5pm, Nov–April 10am–4pm • $10 • ☎ 575 758 2690, ⊛ taosartmuseum.org

Russian artist and woodcarver Nicolai Fechin (1881–1955) made his home in Taos between 1927 and 1933 – almost literally so, in that he sculpted and shaped virtually every inch of the interior. As the **Taos Art Museum at Fechin House**, it's now open to the public. Its ornate decorations are in themselves well worth a quick look, while its walls are adorned with choice pieces by Taos Society of Artists members, including a few lovely Gustave Baumann prints. The house makes a spectacular setting for chamber-music concerts on summer evenings.

Harwood Museum of Art

238 Ledoux St • Wed–Sat 10am–5pm, Sun noon–5pm • $10 • ☎ 575 758 9826, ⓦ harwoodmuseum.org

The **Harwood Museum of Art**, a complex of attractive interlinked adobes two blocks southwest of the plaza that was originally known as El Pueblito, started life as a combined library and exhibition space a century ago. Its educational mission now extends to displaying contemporary local art along with works by twentieth-century Taos artists such as Bert Phillips and woodcarver Patrociño Barelo, and *santos* and *retablos* by their nineteenth-century Hispanic counterparts.

Ernest L. Blumenschein Home and Museum

222 Ledoux St • Daily 10am–4pm • $8, $12 with Hacienda de los Martínez • ☎ 575 758 0505, ⓦ taoshistoricmuseums.org

The **Ernest L. Blumenschein Home and Museum** preserves the much-restored 1790 house of the co-founder of the Taos Society of Artists. Paintings by Blumenschein, his daughter Helen, and Zuni and Hopi artists such as Fred Kabotie (see p.310) are on display, but the real star is the house itself. Though Taos has grown to obscure its original uninterrupted views, Blumenschein's studio, made gloriously light by its raised ceiling and enlarged windows, still commands a fine prospect of the mountains.

D.H. Lawrence Forbidden Art

108 South Plaza • Irregular hours • $3 • ☎ 575 758 2211, ⓦ lafondataos.com

Known as **D. H. Lawrence Forbidden Art**, a gallery in *La Fonda* hotel on Taos Plaza holds a unique collection of nine paintings by the Nottinghamshire novelist. Although the hotel itself was built in 1937, well after Lawrence's death, the paintings were bought from his widow Frieda's second husband. Most were painted in Italy rather than Taos. One, *The Holy Family*, was his first-ever canvas – it shows. Apart from one landscape (a "collaboration" with Frieda and their friend Dorothy Brett), they depict sweaty, fleshy wrestlings such as *The Rape of the Sabine Women*. When first exhibited, in London in 1929, they were regarded as obscene and banned in Britain. They now seem tame, though the *Sunday Times*' original verdict remains accurate: "he can do rather less with a paintbrush than a child of seven without any natural flair."

Millicent Rogers Museum

1504 Millicent Rogers Rd, 4 miles north of the plaza • April–Oct daily 10am–5pm; Nov–March Tues–Sun 10am–5pm • $10, under-17s $2 • ☎ 575 758 2462, ⓦ millicentrogers.org

Focusing on both Native American and Hispanic art, and tracing how those cultures have been perceived, the **Millicent Rogers Museum** ranks among New Mexico's very finest galleries. Millicent Rogers herself – a former fashion model, granddaughter of a founder of Standard Oil and "close" to Clark Gable – lived here until her death in 1953.

The museum's highlight is the family collection of San Ildefonso Pueblo potter **Maria Martinez**, whose black-on-black ceramics are the most famous (and valuable) Native American artworks of the twentieth century. Fascinating photos show her creating a pot step by step. Displays also outline the unbroken thousand-year tradition of Pueblo pottery, from the prehistoric Mimbres and Ancestral Puebloan peoples onwards. Other crafts include Navajo blankets and turquoise jewellery, and there's also some impressive contemporary jewellery designed by Rogers herself.

The development of Spanish colonial religious art in the New World is shown through an array of rugs, looms, carved wooden furniture, *bultos* and *retablos*, plus a "**Death Cart**" (see p.144), in which a skeleton, known as Doña Sebastiana, rides in a rickety wooden carriage and brandishes a bow and arrow.

Taos Pueblo

Just over 2 miles north of Taos plaza, along either of two separate approach roads off Hwy-68 • Mon–Sat 8am–4.30pm, Sun 8am–4.30pm, but closed mid-Feb to March, and also frequently closed for tribal events • $16, under-11s free • ☎ 575 758 1028, ⓦ taospueblo.com

Tiwa-speaking peoples have lived at **TAOS PUEBLO** for almost a thousand years. While they may have originally arrived from the east, across the plains, and thus quite possibly not be of Ancestral Puebloan heritage, they have long been at the forefront of the **Pueblo Indian** cultural tradition. Together with Acoma (see p.99) and the Hopi

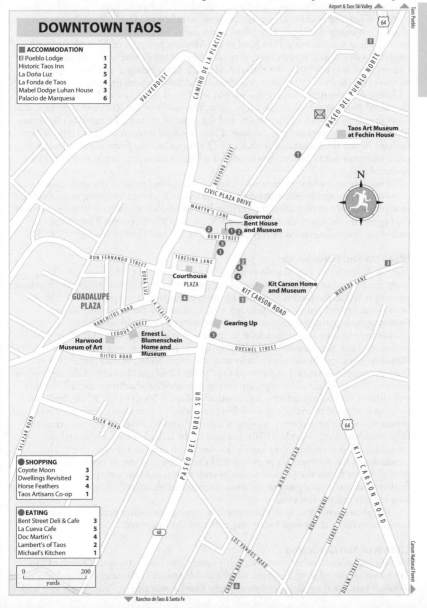

DOWNTOWN TAOS

■ **ACCOMMODATION**
El Pueblo Lodge	1
Historic Taos Inn	2
La Doña Luz	5
La Fonda de Taos	4
Mabel Dodge Luhan House	3
Palacio de Marquesa	6

● **SHOPPING**
Coyote Moon	3
Dwellings Revisited	2
Horse Feathers	4
Taos Artisans Co-op	1

● **EATING**
Bent Street Deli & Cafe	3
La Cueva Cafe	5
Doc Martin's	4
Lambert's of Taos	2
Michael's Kitchen	1

Airport & Taos Ski Valley

Taos Art Museum at Fechin House

Governor Bent House and Museum

Kit Carson Home and Museum

Gearing Up

Harwood Museum of Art

Ernest L. Blumenschein Home and Museum

Courthouse
PLAZA

GUADALUPE PLAZA

Ranchos de Taos & Santa Fe

0   200
yards

2

Taos Pueblo

Carson National Forest

mesas (see p.66), the pueblo can claim to be the oldest continuously occupied settlement in the United States. It's also stunningly beautiful, centring on two multistorey adobe "apartment blocks" framed beneath the shining forested peak of Taos Mountain.

The northernmost New Mexican pueblo, Taos is among the few not to have been displaced by the coming of the Spaniards. Its survival has required a long hard struggle; the pueblo was abandoned for two years in the 1630s, to escape retaliation after the killing of a priest, and it later played a central role in the **Pueblo Revolt** of 1680 (see p.469). When the Spanish subsequently reconquered New Mexico, Taos Pueblo was almost completely destroyed. It revolted again under both Mexican and American rule. In 1837, Taos Indians cut off the head of the Mexican governor of New Mexico and used it as a football. Ten years later, they were heavily implicated in the rebellion against Charles Bent (see p.149); when the retaliating US Army besieged and burned the pueblo's church, over 150 women, children and elderly non-combatants were killed.

During the twentieth century, the pueblo was forced to campaign for the return of the sacred **Blue Lake**, high in the mountains. The source of the Río Pueblo de Taos that flows through the heart of the village, and the focus of an annual three-day pilgrimage, Blue Lake was unexpectedly incorporated into a federal forest reserve in 1906. When Richard Nixon finally handed it back in 1970, it marked the first time that land had ever been returned to Native Americans for religious reasons; access is now forbidden to outsiders.

Although (camera-less) visitors are welcome throughout most of the year, only if you come on certain spectacular **feast days** and dances will you see anything more than the residents simply carrying on with everyday life. Most such events take place in summer; the biggest are the Corn Dances (June 13 & 24, July 25 & 26), the Taos Pueblo pow-wow (second weekend in July), and the Feast of San Gerónimo (Sept 29 & 30).

Hlaauma and Hlaukwima

The admission fee to Taos Pueblo entitles visitors to join one of the regular walking tours, led by Pueblo residents. While taking a tour may help overcome any awkwardness you might feel at the notion of intruding upon pueblo life, however, it won't take you beyond the limited public areas through which you're also free to wander alone. **Photography** is permitted, except on feast days and other special occasions.

Visits focus on the two large adobe complexes that stand to either side of the Río Pueblo de Taos, also known as Red Willow Creek. In their current form, both **Hlaauma**, the north house, and **Hlaukwima**, the south house, almost certainly date from the uncertain years that followed the Pueblo Revolt, at the start of the eighteenth century. This architectural design, consisting of individual dwellings stacked like dice and entered via rooftop ladders, was originally adopted for defence. While the homes have been adapted to include ground-level doorways and windows, their occupants still choose to live without toilets, running water or electricity. Both complexes remained fully inhabited until the mid-1970s, but due to the lack of conveniences and the constant tourist intrusion, they now hold a mere ten families between them. The remainder of the reservation's population of three thousand live in newer homes nearby. Several rooms facing the plaza function as **craft shops**, but you can't penetrate any further, and you'll only glimpse the *kivas* (ceremonial chambers), distinguished by their long ladders, from a distance.

In the plaza itself, what look like makeshift awnings to shelter parked cars are in fact *ramadas*, wooden racks used for drying corn and chile peppers.

Church of San Gerónimo

Visitors are encouraged to enter, but not photograph, the pretty little **Church of San Gerónimo** on the edge of the plaza. Murals inside feature traditional corn and sun motifs; Mass, open to all, is celebrated every Sunday morning at 7am. Tours also lead to the ruins of the pueblo's previous church, all but destroyed by the US Army in 1847. Its solitary bell tower, still adorned by its original bell, dominates a small dusty cemetery beside the adobe wall that surrounds the entire pueblo. Now just a few feet in height, the wall originally stood twelve feet tall.

Ranchos de Taos

The distinct community of **RANCHOS DE TAOS**, which spreads to either side of Hwy-68 three miles southwest of central Taos, was founded when Pueblo farmlands were taken over by the Spanish to grow the crops that fed the townspeople of Taos. Each *rancho* or farm had its own main house, or hacienda, and even today Ranchos de Taos retains the feel of a rural village; you can still buy fresh hay for your animals from lots along the highway.

San Francisco de Asis

In the small unpaved plaza of Ranchos de Taos, the mission church of **San Francisco de Asis** turns its broad shoulders, or more accurately its massive adobe buttresses, to the passing traffic on Hwy-68. Built around 1776, it's one of colonial New Mexico's most splendid architectural achievements, with subtly rounded walls and corners that disguise its underlying structural strength. Encountering genuine adobe, which crumbles away after heavy rain or snow, can come as a shock after so much fakery elsewhere in the state; the local congregation is obliged to replaster the whole thing yearly.

The ever-changing interplay of light and shade across the church's golden exterior has fascinated painters from **Georgia O'Keeffe** onwards. She observed in 1971 that "Everyone paints the Taos church. If you're in Taos for two days you have to paint the Taos church. I asked myself do I have to paint all that church? I'll just paint a little piece of it. That'll do just as well. And I did."

The church's **interior** is equally intriguing. Amid a clutter of devotional objects and artworks, a magnificently ornate green-and-red *reredos* (altarpiece) frames several individual paintings. It was painted by the nineteenth-century *santero* Molleno, also responsible for the altarpiece of the Santuario de Chimayó (see p.145).

Hacienda de los Martínez

708 Hacienda Way, off Lower Ranchitos Rd, 2 miles west of Hwy-68 • Daily 10am–4pm • $8, $12 with Blumenschein Home and Museum • ☎ 575 758 0505, ⓦ taoshistoricmuseums.org

One of the few Spanish haciendas anywhere to be preserved in something like its original state, the **Hacienda de los Martínez** was built in 1804 by Don Antonio Martínez, an early mayor of Taos who was also the father of Padre Antonio Jose Martínez (see p.144). Within its thick, windowless, adobe walls – the place could be sealed like a fortress against then still prevalent Indian raids – two dozen rooms are wrapped around two separate patios, holding animal pens and a well. Trade goods of the kind Don Antonio once carried south along the Rio Grande are displayed alongside tools, looms and simple furnishings of the era, while the rooms furthest from the entrance contain a superb collection of Hispanic religious art.

Taos Ski Valley

15 miles north of Taos • Daily lift tickets late Nov to mid-Dec and late March to early April $63, mid-Dec to late March $86 • Information ☎ 866 968 7386, reservations ☎ 800 776 1111, ⓦ skitaos.org

Located on the north flank of **Wheeler Peak** – at 13,161ft, New Mexico's highest point – the precipitous slopes of **TAOS SKI VALLEY** are reached via an attractive road that winds up through a narrow gap in the mountains from the village of **Arroyo Seco**. Its 110 separate runs, served by fifteen lifts, are usually open to skiers and snowboarders from late November until early April. Experts rate Taos one of the most challenging ski resorts in the Rockies – just over half the runs are for experts only – but the highly rated Ernie Blake Snowsports School teaches novices aged three and upwards on the nursery slopes.

The road up into the Ski Valley dead-ends at a massive parking lot that serves several **lodges**, **hotels** and **condo** blocks, as well as a number of cafés, restaurants and bars. Most accommodation and dining options remain open year-round, but there's little point staying in summer.

ARRIVAL AND INFORMATION   TAOS

By car Hwy-68, the main route up to Taos from Santa Fe and Albuquerque, passes first through Ranchos de Taos, then becomes an uninspiring commercial strip as it approaches downtown and is renamed Paseo del Pueblo Sur.
By bus Taos Express buses connect with Rail Runner trains to and from Santa Fe at weekends only (departs Taos Sat &

Sun 8.55am & 4.30pm; journey time 1hr 45min; $5 one-way, no reservations; ⓦ taosexpress.com). Greyhound does not serve Taos.
Visitor centre 1139 Paseo del Pueblo Sur, 2 miles south of the plaza where Hwy-68 meets Hwy-585 (daily 9am–5pm; ☎ 575 758 3873 or ☎ 800 348 0696, ⓦ taos.org).

GETTING AROUND

By bus On weekdays only, the Chile Line bus runs to and fro along a seven-mile stretch of Hwy-68, between Ranchos de Taos and Taos Pueblo, with a loop around the plaza in the middle (Mon–Fri 7.30am–5.30pm, every 35–45min; 50 cents one-way; ⓦ ncrtd.org); some services

continue up to the Ski Valley in winter only.
Bike rental Gearing Up, 129 Paseo del Pueblo Sur (☎ 575 751 0365, ⓦ gearingupbikes.com), also offer shuttle rides to biking trailheads.

TOURS AND ACTIVITIES

Cottam's Rio Grande Rafting Full-day whitewater rafting trips through the Taos Box Canyon of the Rio Grande, which offers rapids up to Class V (April–midsummer only, Mon–Fri $114, Sat & Sun $124; ☎ 800 322 8267, ⓦ cottamsoutdoor .com), plus shorter half-day trips on the Racecourse further south ($53). The same operators can also arrange biking, kayaking, and, in winter, snowmobiling expeditions.
Far Flung Adventures Half- and full-day rafting trips on the Rio Grande from Pilar, south of Taos, as well as through the Taos Box Canyon and on the Rio Chama (half-day $51; full-day $105; ☎ 800 359 2627, ⓦ farflung.com).

Pueblo Balloon Company Hot-air balloon flights over the Rio Grande gorge, with advance reservation only ($275 adults, $150 ages 13–18, $100 ages 6–12; ☎ 575 751 9877, ⓦ puebloballoon.com).
Taos Trolley Tours In summer, open-air trolley tours visit the main attractions (May–Oct daily 10.30am & 2pm from visitor centre, 10.45am & 2.15pm at plaza; ☎ 505 550 5612, ⓦ taostrolleytours.com; $33, including entry fees). All tours go to Taos Pueblo, except for those on Sunday and Monday afternoons, which visit the Millicent Rogers Museum and Hacienda de los Martínez instead.

ACCOMMODATION

Taos has accommodation to meet all needs, at prices well below those of Santa Fe. However, **high season** runs from Christmas to mid-April as well as mid-June to mid-October, so midwinter rates are no lower than midsummer, and can be considerably higher close to the ski area.

HOTELS, RENTALS AND HOSTEL
Earthship Rentals Hwy-64 ☎ 575 751 0462, ⓦ earthship.com; map p.148. Set on the high mesa a mile west of the Rio Grand Gorge, a full 14 miles northwest of Taos itself, the futuristic earthships of Taos are constructed on rigorous ecological principles. Though each 1–3 bedroom structure is quirkily different to the rest, all are walled and insulated using discarded rubber tires buried deep in the earth, catching water and deriving heat from the sun. Spending the night in a rental earthship is a real once-in-a-lifetime experience – unless of course you decide to buy or build your own, and join the community. **$130**

El Pueblo Lodge 412 Paseo del Pueblo Norte ☎ 575 758 8700 or ☎ 800 433 9612, ⓦ elpueblolodge.com; map p.151. Southwestern-themed 1940s fake-adobe motel, half a mile north of downtown near the Taos Pueblo, where the nicely furnished rooms have extra-large bathrooms, rates include hot breakfast, and there's a decent outdoor pool and hot tub. **$148**
★**Historic Taos Inn** 125 Paseo del Pueblo Norte ☎ 575 758 2233 or ☎ 888 518 8267, ⓦ taosinn.com; map p.151. Gorgeous, romantic central Taos landmark, consisting of several ancient adobes welded together to create an atmospheric and very Southwestern hotel. Each

of the 44 rooms plays some variation on the Pueblo theme, with varying degrees of luxury and a considerable range of prices; the *kiva* fireplaces are just for show, but a real fire burns downstairs, in the cosy, convivial lobby area that was once an open courtyard. Both the excellent *Doc Martin's* restaurant and the *Adobe Bar* are packed nightly. $119

La Fonda de Taos 108 South Plaza ☎ 575 758 2211 or ☎ 800 833 2211, ⓦ lafondataos.com; map p.151. Vintage 1930s hotel on the plaza that has been totally modernized to hold 24 luxurious suites, with Southwestern furnishings and tiled bathrooms. The lobby even holds a gallery of D.H. Lawrence paintings (see p.150). $149

Palacio de Marquesa 405 Cordoba Lane ☎ 575 758 4777 or ☎ 855 846 8267, ⓦ marquesataos.com; map p.151. Intimate and very luxurious little inn, set in adobe-walled gardens a couple of blocks southeast of the plaza. The eight rooms are themed to honour Southwestern women artists, and they also offer spa and message treatments. $237

Sagebrush Inn 1508 Paseo del Pueblo Sur ☎ 575 758 2254 or ☎ 800 428 3626, ⓦ sagebrushinn.com; map p.148. Attractive three-storey adobe inn, well south of the centre near Ranchos de Taos, which was briefly home to Georgia O'Keeffe and is filled with Southwestern arts and crafts. The hundred guest rooms themselves are nothing very special, but there's a pool and three hot tubs, and live music in the lobby bar most nights. $149

Snowmansion Taos Hostel Taos Ski Valley Rd, Arroyo Seco ☎ 575 776 8298, ⓦ snowmansion.com; map p.148. Pleasant, friendly hostel-cum-ski lodge, on a very tight curve in the road as you enter Arroyo Seco village on Hwy-150 up to the Ski Valley, five miles north of downtown. Office hours are daily 8–11am & 4–10pm, so don't arrive at midday. Two six-bed dorms, one for men and one for women, for which winter rates include breakfast; tipis that sleep up to six; and camping space out back; bargain private rooms and cabins come with and without en-suite facilities. Camping, May–Oct only $25; dorms $31; tipis, June–Sept only $55; private rooms $65; cabins $60

B&BS

Casa Gallina 609 Callejon ☎ 575 758 2306, ⓦ casagallina.net; map p.148. This hugely welcoming and very comfortable B&B, in a peaceful rural setting a couple of miles southwest of the plaza, consists of five separate, colourfully furnished adobe guesthouses, each holding from one to three bedrooms, in spacious gardens. Two-night minimum stay. $195

★ **La Doña Luz** 114c Kit Carson Rd ☎ 575 758 9000, ⓦ stayintaos.com; map p.151. Delightful, individually decorated Hispanic-flavoured rooms of differing sizes and prices in a peaceful adobe B&B a very short walk east of the plaza. All are lovely, and have en-suite facilities; some also have fully equipped kitchens and/or hot tubs. $84

Mabel Dodge Luhan House 240 Morada Lane ☎ 575 751 9686 or ☎ 800 846 2235, ⓦ mabeldodgeluhan.com; map p.151. This appealing 200-year-old adobe B&B complex, not far northeast of the plaza off Kit Carson Lane, isn't the most luxurious option in Taos, but its historic associations are certainly impressive, with rooms named in honour of former guests like Willa Cather and Ansel Adams. Two, including the light-filled solarium, share a bathroom painted by D.H. Lawrence; the cheaper lodge annexe has more modern fittings, though wi-fi is only available in the communal area. The inn regularly plays host to creative workshops. $116

Old Taos Guesthouse 1028 Witt Rd ☎ 575 758 5448 or ☎ 800 758 5448, ⓦ oldtaos.com; map p.148. Vintage adobe hacienda, a couple of miles east of the plaza, restored as a spacious B&B complex. Each of the ten rooms offers different facilities – all have private bath and hand-carved furniture, some have *kiva* fireplaces – and there's a massage room as well as an outdoor hot tub. $139

TAOS SKI VALLEY

Amizette Inn 1295 NM-150 ☎ 575 776 2451 or ☎ 800 446 8267, ⓦ amizetteinn.com; map p.148. Small but comfortable ski lodge, centred on a former post office building, just over a mile down the valley from the lifts, with an indoor hot tub and sweeping views from its verandas. $129

EATING AND DRINKING

Bent Street Deli & Cafe 120 Bent St ☎ 575 758 5787, ⓦ bentstreetdeli.com; map p.151. Open in daytime only, this airy, partly outdoor place, just north of the plaza, is always buzzing with locals and day-trippers. Good-value breakfasts, with chile-topped eggs Benedict at $9, are followed by sandwich or pasta lunches, with plenty of options for under $10. Mon–Sat 8am–4pm, Sun 10am–3pm.

The Coffee Spot 900 Paseo del Pueblo Norte ☎ 575 758 8556; map p.148. Welcoming and efficient coffeehouse, on the main road north of town, which serves a good array of coffee, chai and teas, plus decent pastries

and sandwiches. Roomy enough for locals to settle in with their laptops for hours at a time. Daily 6am–10pm.

★ **La Cueva Cafe** 135 Paseo del Pueblo Sur ☎ 575 758 7001, ⓦ lacuevacafe.com; map p.151. Tiny and very central adobe café, run by an energetic young couple and serving meticulously prepared Mexican classics, with meaty burritos and chimichangas at $8, seafood dishes like crab and shrimp enchiladas for $12, and lots of vegetarian options. Daily 10am–9pm.

Doc Martin's Historic Taos Inn, 125 Paseo del Pueblo Norte ☎ 575 758 1977, ⓦ taosinn.com; map p.151. Rich, inventive New Mexican food served in a fine old adobe inn, just east of the plaza. Typical lunchtime burgers and burritos cost $10–15, while in the evening, choices such as buffalo short ribs or mussels and clams in an Andouille sausage broth range up towards $30. Unusual options on the weekend brunch menu include the "Kit Carson" – poached eggs on yam biscuits, for $8.50. Mon–Fri 11am–10pm, Sat & Sun 7.30am–2.30pm.

Lambert's of Taos 123 Bent St ☎575 758 1009, ⓦlambertsoftaos.com; map p.151. Romantic restaurant snuggled into a historic adobe a block north of the plaza, with a classy but warm atmosphere. The cuisine is more New American than New Mexican, though there's a local-flavoured green chile stew appetizer for $9; sumptuous mains include Moroccan braised lamb shank for $30 and chipotle-glazed duck for $34. Lunchtime salads and sandwiches cost $10–15. Daily 11.30am–2.30pm & 5.30–9pm.

Love Apple 803 Paseo del Pueblo Norte ☎575 751 0050, ⓦtheloveapple.net; map p.148. This beautiful former chapel, open for dinner only, holds just thirteen tables, so you'll need to reserve well in advance to sample its locally sourced, partly foraged and mostly organic cuisine. Appetizers include succulent pâtés made from chicken livers or mushrooms with walnuts, while mains

range from with baked sweetcorn tamales in Oaxacan mole sauce for $16 to a very French beef bourguignon in puff pastry at £23. Tues–Sun 5–9pm.

Michael's Kitchen 304C Paseo del Pueblo Norte ☎575 758 4178, ⓦmichaelskitchen.com; map p.151. Inexpensive Mexican and Southwestern dishes served in an old adobe kitchen a few blocks north of the plaza. Breakfast is the busiest time, with a full meat'n'eggs menu plus pastries and cinnamon rolls baked on site. Mon–Thurs 7am–2.30pm, Fri–Sun 7am–8pm.

Taos Pizza Outback 712 Paseo del Pueblo; map p.148. Hard-to-find pizzeria tucked behind another building to the left of the highway a mile north of town. It has a welcoming youthful ambience and huge portions of great food – the 12-inch veggie pizza, at $14, makes a feast for two, and it's also available in a calzone version. Daily 11am–10pm.

Tiwa Kitchen 328 Veterans Hwy, Taos Pueblo ☎575 741 8128; map p.148. Indian-run, largely organic restaurant on the road into Taos Pueblo, serving strong chile-flavoured stews, blue-corn tortillas with buffalo meat from the pueblo's own herd, and traditional *horno*-baked bread, all costing under $10. April–Oct daily except Tues 11am–7pm.

SHOPPING

Coyote Moon 120C Bent St ☎575 758 4437, ⓦjohndunnshops.com; map p.151. A riot of colour, this is Taos' best selection of Mexican folk art, with plenty of Oaxacan carved animals and Day of the Dead souvenirs. Daily 10am–6pm.

Dwellings Revisited 10 Bent St ☎505 758 3377; map p.151. Eclectic store where the owners have imported trinkets, oddities, furniture and folk art from all over the world. Unusual Greek and Native American items sit alongside the more familiar Mexican stuff. Daily

10.30am–5.30pm.

Horse Feathers 109B Kit Carson Rd ☎575 758 7457, ⓦhorsefeathersintaos.squarespace.com; map p.151. A great source for all things Western, from Stetson hats and colourful cowboy boots at bargain prices to off-the-wall antiques. Daily 10am–6pm.

Taos Artisans Co-op 107A Bent St ☎575 758 1558, ⓦtaosartisansgallery.org; map p.151. Individually styled jewellery, clothing and sculpture, created by an assortment of Taoseño artists. Daily 10am–5.30pm.

West of Taos

Assuming your plans already cover Santa Fe and points south, the obvious day-trip drive from Taos follows the **Enchanted Circle** to the northeast (see p.159). However, a longer and wilder route heads **west** on US-64, across the Rio Grande and over the dramatic **San Juan Mountains**. Branching west off Hwy-68 four miles out of downtown Taos, this reaches the awesome 650-foot-high **Rio Grande Gorge Bridge** seven miles on. Be sure to take the time to park at the end and walk out to the middle, otherwise you'll barely get a glimpse of the narrow chasm as you drive across.

After a magnificent seventy-mile mountain run, punctuated by scenic overlooks, US-64 finally drops into **Chama Valley**. From there, either head south into Georgia O'Keeffe country around **Abiquiu**, or north to **Chama** itself, the base for excursions on New Mexico's best-known **steam railroad**.

Tierra Amarilla

US-64 meets the north–south US-84 in **TIERRA AMARILLA** ("yellow earth"), at the foot of the sheer, furrowed **Brazos Cliffs**. This pastoral village, founded in 1832 when the valley was prone to constant Ute, Apache and Navajo raids, provides a classic example of the consequences to New Mexico's Hispanic population of the American takeover of the territory. In 1860, the US Congress refused to recognize that shared grazing lands belonged to the community as a whole, and instead sold them off to a Yankee landowner from Santa Fe.

Bitter disputes have raged ever since, culminating in an incident that's commemorated by a defaced roadside marker in the heart of the village. In 1967, a group led by Chicano activist **Reies López Tijerina** seized a nearby campground in the Kit Carson National Forest. Declaring independence from the United States, they burned down Tierra Amarilla's Rio Arriba Courthouse, destroying land-grant records and injuring a policeman and a jailer. The government responded by sending in two hundred military vehicles, including tanks. After a series of trials, Tijerina eventually served two years in federal prisons.

While Tierra Amarilla remains the county seat, it has declined to the point where parts are all but derelict.

Tierra Wools

91 Main St, Los Ojos • April to late Oct Mon–Sat 9am–6pm, Sun 11am–4pm; late Oct to March Mon–Sat 10am–5pm • ☎ 575 588 7231, ⓦ handweavers.com

In the village of **LOS OJOS**, one mile west of Tierra Amarilla, a cooperative effort to revitalize the local economy has proved a resounding success. Based at the clearly signposted Los Ojos Trading Post, **Tierra Wools** maintains local **weaving** traditions by breeding Spanish Churro sheep in the valley, and selling hand-dyed rugs and clothing.

Chama

Tiny **CHAMA**, set in the meadows at the head of the Chama Valley, a dozen miles north of Tierra Amarilla and a total of 85 miles northwest of Taos, is a former mining camp that has reinvented itself as a base for summer hunters and winter skiers.

INFORMATION   CHAMA

Visitor centre At junction of US-64 with Hwy-17, 1.5 miles south of town (daily: summer 8am–6pm; winter 8am–5pm; ☎ 575 756 2306 or ☎ 800 477 0149, ⓦ chamavalley.com).

CUMBRES & TOLTEC SCENIC RAILROAD

The pretty yellow station just below Chama's nineteenth-century downtown core is the western terminus of the highest narrow-gauge railroad in the nation, the **Cumbres & Toltec Scenic Railroad** (late May to mid-Oct; ☎ 575 756 2151 or ☎ 888 286 2737, ⓦ cumbrestoltec .com). This exhilarating, if not entirely comfortable, 64-mile steam-train ride crosses the High Brazos mountains into Colorado by way of **Cumbres Pass**, then runs through the deep **Toltec Gorge** and out onto the plains before ending in **Antonito**, Colorado. Its many movie credits include the opening sequence of *Indiana Jones and the Last Crusade*.

It's not possible to do the entire round-trip by train in one day; passengers either go by van to Antonito and return by train (depart Chama 8.30am), or catch the train from Chama at 10am, and either go through the most scenic segment as far as Osier, and pick up a return train there, or ride the train all the way to Antonito, and catch a bus back from there. Each of those options costs $99 in coach class (child fare $49), $145 in Deluxe Tourist Class (child fare $79), or $185 in Parlor Class (no children allowed); all those fares include a buffet lunch. Reserve ahead to be sure of a place, and dress warmly; it gets pretty cold up in the mountains.

ACCOMMODATION AND EATING

High Country Restaurant & Saloon 2289 S Hwy-17 ☎ 575 756 2384, ⓦ thehighcountrychama.com. Come in from the cold at this top-quality Western diner, immediately north of the main highway intersection, south of downtown, where dinner mains range from pan-seared trout for \$14 up to a 12oz steak for \$26. Live music at weekends, outdoors in summer. Mon–Sat 11am–10pm, Sun 8am–10pm.

Vista del Rio 2595 US-64/84 ☎ 575 756 2138 or ☎ 800 939 9943, ⓦ vistadelriolodge.com. This is among the best of several very similar log-cabin riverfront lodges along the main highway into town, with 19 comfortable motel-style rooms. **\$100**

The Cumbres Pass and Antonito, Colorado

North of Chama, **Hwy-17** follows much the same route as the railroad, first climbing far above the single track and then crisscrossing it repeatedly as it makes its way up to the 10,022ft **Cumbres Pass**. In July 1848, legendary "mountain man" Bill Williams was injured here in a confrontation between the US Army and a combined force of Ute and Apache.

Beyond the pass, highway and railroad part company, not to meet again until they reach **ANTONITO**, Colorado, fifty miles out of Chama – a dreary little town that's home to the **Cumbres & Toltec Scenic Railroad** terminus.

Jicarilla Apache Indian Reservation

US-64 and US-84 join forces for the first twelve miles **west of Chama**, then once across the Continental Divide – not at all dramatic at this point – US-64 continues alone for another fifteen miles to **DULCE**, the headquarters of the **Jicarilla Apache Indian Reservation**. Today's three-thousand-plus Jicarilla are descended from separate Apache groups who lived further east, some as Plains nomads in the Cimarron area, and some in adobe villages near the pueblos of the Rio Grande. Their name is often said to come from the little baskets (*jicarillas*) they now sell to tourists, but the Jicarilla say they only started making baskets after they were confined to this remote reservation in the nineteenth century, and that the name comes from a Mexican word connected with chocolate.

There's little for tourists to see or do on the Jicarilla reservation, whose economy is based on oil and gas revenues and raising sheep. Dulce itself is just a very sharp dog-leg in the highway, where US-64 turns south rather than climb onto sheer Archuleta Mesa; after a few miles the road turns west again to head through Vaqueros Canyon and Gobernador Canyon (see p.90).

The Enchanted Circle

While the driving circuit through the Sangre de Cristo range northeast of Taos doesn't quite live up to its tourist-brochure billing as **THE ENCHANTED CIRCLE**, it does pass a handful of long-abandoned ghost towns amid the mountain scenery. Oklahomans and Texans flock to the closest **ski slopes** to home, but visitors from further afield are more likely to spin off east to the hard-bitten frontier town of **Cimarron**.

The Lawrence Ranch

Lawrence Ranch Rd, 1.5 miles east of Hwy-522 • Thurs & Fri 10am–2pm, Sat 10am–4pm • ☎ 575 770 4830, ⓦ dhlawrencetaos.org

Starting seventeen miles north of Taos on Hwy-522, a rutted, muddy road climbs for five miles east to the **Lawrence Ranch**. The English novelist **D.H. Lawrence** made three six-month visits to Taos in the early 1920s, having been enticed across the Atlantic by Mabel Dodge Luhan (see p.149). Staying at her mountain cabin, then known as Kiowa Ranch, he wrote "there are all kinds of beauty in the world, but for greatness of beauty

I have never experienced anything like New Mexico." **Georgia O'Keeffe** was also a guest here, in 1929, when she painted the tree right in front of the main cabin as *The Lawrence Tree*. The tree, as seen from below in the painting, looks more like a giant squid; the painting is usually on display in the Georgia O'Keeffe Museum in Santa Fe.

Lawrence died in France in 1930, but five years later his widow Frieda shipped his ashes back to New Mexico. They now rest in a small **shrine** that enjoys panoramic views of the upper Rio Grande Valley, at the top of a zigzag cement footpath cleared through the forest; according to some stories, the ashes were actually poured into a wheelbarrow of cement, to ensure they could never be taken away. Frieda is said to have acquired the ranch from Mabel Dodge Luhan in exchange for the manuscript of *Sons and Lovers* – which Mabel in turn used to pay her psychiatrist – and she lived in it until her death in 1956. It now belongs to the University of New Mexico, which holds weekend retreats in the main cabin. The shrine itself, however, is made accessible to visitors by a volunteer group, the D. H. Lawrence Ranch Alliance; hours tend to vary each year, so check ahead before you set off.

Questa

Half a dozen miles north of the turn-off to the Lawrence Ranch, as Hwy-522 gathers itself for the final climb into Colorado, the village of **QUESTA** bears the visible scars of opencast molybdenum mining, which ceased in 2014. It's currently transforming itself into both artists' retreat and overnight stop for visitors to the **Wild Rivers Scenic Area** section of the new **Río Grande del Norte National Monument** (see p.142), a total of 15 miles west via Hwy-522.

Red River

Hwy-38 branches off from Hwy-522 at Questa, and heads east beside the Red River. After twelve more attractive riverside miles, it reaches **RED RIVER**, a former gold-mining town whose rough-shod timber architecture is more authentic than it looks. Summer visitors hike in the surrounding forests, but Red River is at its busiest during the winter **ski** season, when there's cross-country skiing in the valley and a downhill resort in the mountains. The season typically lasts from late November until late March (lift tickets $68 per day; ☎575 754 2223, ⓦredriverskiarea.com).

Cimarron

East of Red River, Hwy-38 negotiates the 9820-foot **Bobcat Pass** – often closed in winter – then drops southwards, by way of the ruins of long-abandoned **Elizabethtown**, down to **Eagle Nest**. Just a cluster of cabins and RV parks, Eagle Nest sprang up around a lake formed when the **Cimarron River** was dammed in 1920, and is popular with fishing enthusiasts. US-64 parallels the river to enter impressive **Cimarron Canyon** four miles east, beneath the towering 800ft **Palisade Cliffs**. This route provided access to Taos for nineteenth-century travellers who split from the Santa Fe Trail's "mountain branch" at **CIMARRON** itself, 24 miles east of Eagle Nest.

Cimarron means "wild" or "untamed", and in its heyday the town was as wild as the West could be. It stood at the heart of the 1.7-million-acre **Maxwell Land Grant**, the largest private landholding in the US, accumulated by Lucien Bonaparte Maxwell after the American takeover of New Mexico. Maxwell's main business was cattle ranching, but with gold and silver mines booming and busting all over the mountains, Cimarron lured a vast profusion of gamblers, gunfighters, outlaws and cowboys. Its old downtown now stands relatively intact half a mile south of the main highway. Local history is lovingly chronicled in the **Old Aztec Mill Museum**, 220 W 17th St (Mon–Fri 10am–noon & 1–4pm; $3; ☎575 376 2417, ⓦaztecmill.com).

Angel Fire

The Enchanted Circle loops back to Taos from Eagle Nest along US-64, passing, after ten miles, through the part-**golf**, part-**ski** resort of **ANGEL FIRE** in Moreno Valley, developed in the late 1960s. Despite upgrading, Angel Fire shows few signs of maturing beyond its current brash, unappealing sprawl. The ski slopes are usually active between early December and late March, but they're considerably more suitable for novices here than at Red River, and there's also a snowboard park (lift tickets $68 per day; ☎575 377 6401, ⊚angelfireresort.com).

2

ACCOMMODATION AND EATING   THE ENCHANTED CIRCLE

RED RIVER

Alpine Lodge 417 W Main St ☎575 754 2952 or ☎800 252 2333, ⊚alpinelodgeredriver.com. This very central Red River option, handy for the ski lifts and downtown alike, offers spacious river-view cabins as well as hotel rooms and kitchenette apartment. Rooms $115, cabins $130

Anchovies Pizzeria 320 E Main St ☎575 754 6334, ⊚anchoviespizzeria.com. Ten-inch pizzas at this tiny but much-loved central restaurant range from the basic $14 Margherita up to the $19 Big Mountain Brisket. Mon–Thurs 4–9pm, Fri & Sat 11am–9pm.

CIMARRON

St James Hotel 617 S Collison St ☎575 376 2664 or ☎888 376 2664, ⊚exstjames.com. Built in 1873 by French chef Henri Lambert, who's said to have cooked for President Lincoln, Cimarron's most famous relic has witnessed 26 murders; names in the guest register include Jesse James and Buffalo Bill. It now has its own grand, tin-ceilinged restaurant, open for all meals daily and serving everything from $7 burgers and $13 *sopaipillas* to $32 steaks; twelve authentically furnished nineteenth-century rooms, not all en-suite; and ten more conventional motel-type rooms in a less romantic annexe. Shared-bath hotel room $85, motel room $95, en-suite hotel room $120

Northeast New Mexico

Successively traversed by Pueblo Indian traders, pioneers on the **Santa Fe Trail**, and passengers on the transcontinental railroad, the traditional route between New Mexico and the plains is now followed by the **I-25** interstate. The Wild West town of **Las Vegas** provides a good send-off into New Mexico's **northeast corner**, as the Sangre de Cristo mountains gradually recede below the western horizon and the Great Plains begin to unfurl in all their relentless monotony. There's no great reason to stray off the interstate until the Rockies start to loom above **Raton**, a hundred miles on, though with time to spare the detour to **Capulin Volcano** at that point is worth making.

Las Vegas

Now a sleepy backwater, **LAS VEGAS**, New Mexico, 73 miles east of Santa Fe, has more in common with its upstart Nevada namesake than may be immediately obvious. Once a lawless frontier outpost, where almost anything went, it consists of two distinct sections. The **old Plaza** area, above the fertile meadows (*vegas*, in Spanish) that line the Gallinas River, was established in 1835, when Hispanic settlers drove away the Comanche and set about capturing trade on the burgeoning **Santa Fe Trail**. When the **railroad** arrived in 1879, focus shifted across the river to the grid of streets around the new station. Incomers included the legendary **"Doc" Holliday**, who briefly owned a saloon on Center Street before scurrying back to Dodge City to escape a murder charge. In a single month, Las Vegas witnessed 29 gunshot deaths.

At the end of the nineteenth century, Las Vegas was the principal city in New Mexico, and almost all its buildings still date from the Victorian era. The conspicuous lack of adobe makes it easy to forget you're in the Southwest, but it ranks among the state's most authentic Wild West towns, and while it offers no particular stand-out tourist attractions, it's a delight to stroll around.

2

Theodore Roosevelt recruited around forty percent of his volunteer **Rough Riders**, who invaded Cuba in 1898, in Las Vegas. Their exploits, plus the minutiae of local history, are recorded in the **City Museum**, 727 Grand Ave (Tues–Sat 10am–4pm; $2 suggested donation; ☏505 426 3205, ⓦlasvegasmuseum.org).

Both Grand Avenue – the main business drag – and I-25 alike closely parallel the railroad, leaving the **plaza** high and dry a mile to the west. **Bridge Street**, which leads up from the highway, is lined with somewhat faded antiques stores and cafés, while the four-square layout of the plaza itself makes it resemble something from the Deep South, even if a Victorian bandstand rather than a courthouse stands at its centre. The only significant building on the perimeter is the *Plaza Hotel* (see below), which you may recognize from its prominent role in the Coen Brothers' movie, *No Country for Old Men*. Las Vegas is much used as a filming location, and currently serves as home to the *Longmire* TV series, which although nominally set in Wyoming is shot in the vicinity.

Local hopes for a revival in Las Vegas's fortunes are currently pinned on the restoration of the landmark **Castaneda Hotel**. Built for the Fred Harvey company, the *Castaneda* opened in 1899, just in time to host the first Rough Rider reunion, presided over by Teddy himself. Having lain defunct for more than half a century, it was bought in 2014 by Allan Affeldt, owner of the magnificent *Posada* hotel in Winslow, Arizona, and may have reopened by the time you read this. It only holds twenty rooms, so Affeldt plans to run it in conjunction with the *Plaza Hotel*, which he also owns.

Hwy-518 leads due north from Las Vegas into some of New Mexico's most appealing mountain scenery, and serves as an eighty-mile shortcut to **Taos**. The Hispanic farming village of **MORA**, thirty miles out, is the seat of Mora County, ranked by the *Wall Street Journal* as one of the three poorest counties in the US.

ARRIVAL AND INFORMATION   LAS VEGAS

By train Two Amtrak trains pull into Las Vegas each afternoon, one heading west to Albuquerque, the other east to Chicago.

Visitor centre 500 Railroad Ave (Mon–Fri 9am–5pm; ☏505 425 3707 or ☏800 832 5947, ⓦvisitlasvegasnm.com).

ACCOMMODATION AND EATING

Plaza Hotel 230 Old Town Plaza ☏505 425 3591, ⓦplazahotellvnm.com. Much the nicest place to stay in Las Vegas – at least until the *Castaneda* reopens (see above) – this historic hotel on the old plaza holds 71 very pleasant rooms, recently spruced up using furniture bought in from Santa Fe's legendary *La Fonda*. There's also the excellent *Gilded Age* restaurant, open daily for all meals (most dinner mains $18–22), and a saloon. **$99**

Raton

Appealing little **RATON** is tucked into the foothills of the Rockies a hundred miles north of Las Vegas on I-25, a mere eight miles south of the Colorado border. Once a way station on the Santa Fe Trail, it reached its present size after becoming the site of a railroad repair shop in 1880, and can have changed little since then.

Few passengers now bother to dismount from the two sleek Amtrak Starliners that pull into the Santa Fe Depot each day, but an hour or two's stroll in **downtown Raton** can be fun. Photos and oddments in the **Raton Museum**, 108 S Second St (May–Sept Tues–Sat 9am–5pm, Oct–April Wed–Sat 10am–4pm; free; ☏575 445 8979, ⓦtheratonmuseum.org), recall highlights from the town's first century. Until 1938, it was dominated by the seven-storey *Hotel Swastika*, which then "found it necessary to change its name" to the *Yucca*, and is now a bank.

Enchanted Grounds 111 Park Ave ☎575 445 2219, ⓦ egespressobar.com. The best place for a quick snack as you pass through Raton, this welcoming espresso café serves excellent coffee and fresh pastries, plus lunchtime sandwiches and, in summer, a daily hot soup special, all for under $10. They also have free wi-fi and a selection of books, and operate an espresso cart at the station nearby. Mon 7am–2pm, Tues–Fri 7am–4.30pm, Sat 7.30am–4.30pm.

Capulin Volcano National Monument

30 miles east of Raton on US-64/87, then 3 miles north on Hwy-325 • Gates open daily: late May to early Sept 7.30am–6.30pm; early Sept to late May 8am–4.30pm • $7 per vehicle • ☎ 575 278 2201, ⓦ nps.gov/cavo

The remote **CAPULIN VOLCANO NATIONAL MONUMENT** preserves the neatest and most symmetrical of a chain of cinder cones that last exploded around ten thousand years ago. Most people drive straight past the **visitor centre** on up the two-mile spiral of road that leads towards the summit. The road ends a thousand feet above the plains, at the lowest point on the rim. An easy short trail leads down to the vent where it all began, and you can also **hike** up to the highest point, and walk for a mile around its full 360 degrees, enjoying views to the Sangre de Cristo mountains in the west and Oklahoma to the east.

2

Albuquerque and southern New Mexico

ALBUQUERQUE INTERNATIONAL BALLOON FIESTA

Albuquerque and southern New Mexico

While New Mexico's best-known tourist destinations tend to be concentrated in its northern half, the state's often neglected central and southern portions hold many sites of interest. Prime among them is its largest city, Albuquerque, where the relics of its Route 66 heyday remain visible everywhere, and several stimulating museums celebrate a fascinating and varied history.

Much of the region remained dominated by the nomadic Apache until well into the nineteenth century. Even Albuquerque was founded long after Santa Fe, while towns such as **Silver City**, **Mesilla** and **Lincoln** only really got going after New Mexico joined the United States in 1846. All three went on to play significant roles in the career of **Billy the Kid**, and all still look today much like the frontier outposts Billy must have known. Together with the pre-Columbian remains of the **Gila Cliff Dwellings** in the remote southwest corner, they're the most appealing historic attractions in southern New Mexico. The region also holds a couple of **geological** wonders, however. The subterranean labyrinths of **Carlsbad Caverns National Park** lure a million tourists across the plains each year, while the dazzling dunes of **White Sands National Monument** make an extraordinary spectacle against the San Andres Mountains. Top-secret missile tests and bomb blasts give this desolate landscape an added sense of mystery, making its role in popular myth as the site of the notorious **Roswell Incident** a tiny bit more plausible.

Albuquerque and around

Sprawling at the heart of New Mexico, where the main cross-country road and rail routes cross both the Rio Grande and the old road south to Mexico, **ALBUQUERQUE**, with half a million people, is the state's only major metropolis, even if it isn't the capital. Though many tourists race north from the airport to Santa Fe without a thought for Albuquerque, the "Duke City" has a good deal going for it. Although, like Phoenix, it's grown a bit too fast for comfort, Albuquerque's original Hispanic core remains discernible, while its diverse, cosmopolitan population adds a rare cultural vibrancy. Above all, the city enjoys a magnificent setting, sandwiched between the Rio Grande to the west, lined by stately cottonwoods, and the dramatic, glowing **Sandia Mountains** to the east. Specific highlights for visitors include the intact **Spanish plaza**, the neon-lit **Route 66** frontage of Central Avenue, the fascinating **Indian Pueblo Cultural Center**, and October's **hot-air balloon** extravaganza.

Central Avenue, alive with flashing neon and arguably the most authentic remnant anywhere of the classic Route 66, threads for twenty miles through Albuquerque's various districts. **Old Town** remains the most interesting area for visitors. **Downtown**, two miles east, might be where the city conducts its daily business, but it holds little to detain tourists; unless you stay in a hotel nearby, or spend an evening in its bars and

WHITE SANDS NATIONAL MONUMENT

Highlights

❶ Albuquerque International Balloon Fiesta It's hard to imagine a more photogenic spectacle than hundreds of colourful hot-air balloons soaring above the Rio Grande on a crisp fall morning. **See p.169**

❷ Indian Pueblo Cultural Center Albuquerque's premier museum provides a great opportunity to learn about New Mexico's nineteen surviving pueblos. **See p.173**

❸ Lincoln This quintessential Wild West town has barely changed since Billy the Kid blasted free from the county courthouse. **See p.181**

❹ White Sands National Monument Hike, slide or simply play amid this utterly amazing

array of pure white sand dunes, etched against the azure sky. **See p.186**

❺ The Underground Lunchroom A perfect slice of 1950s Americana, this space-age subterranean cafeteria makes a surreal climax to a tour of Carlsbad Caverns. **See p.191**

❻ Silver City A wonderful Wild West relic, this mountain retreat from the heat of the desert is by far the most appealing town in southwest New Mexico. **See p.198**

❼ Gila Cliff Dwellings Remote ancient ruins, set in a lovely valley high in the mountains of southern New Mexico. **See p.200**

HIGHLIGHTS ARE MARKED ON THE MAP ON P.168

ALBUQUERQUE AND SOUTHERN NEW MEXICO

HIGHLIGHTS

1. Albuquerque International Balloon Fiesta
2. Indian Pueblo Cultural Center
3. Lincoln
4. White Sands National Monument
5. The Underground Lunchroom
6. Silver City
7. Gila Cliff Dwellings

TEXAS

MEXICO

ARIZONA

Amarillo

Odessa

Seminole

Hobbs

Lovington

Loving
White's City

Carlsbad

CARLSBAD
CAVERNS
NAT. PARK

Artesia

GUADALUPE
MOUNTAINS
NAT. PARK

Roswell

MESCALERO
APACHE
INDIAN
RESERVATION

Cloudcroft

Mescalero

Alamogordo

Capitan
Lincoln

Ruidoso

Carrizozo

Tularosa

Three
Rivers

Oscuro

Valley of
Fires Nat.
Rec. Area

WHITE SANDS
MISSILE RANGE
MUSEUM

White Sands
Missile Range
Museum

White Sands
Nat. Mon.

ORGAN
MOUNTAINS

DOÑA ANA
MNTS.

El Paso

Ciudad Juarez

Las Cruces

Mesilla

Rincon

Hatch

Fort Selden
Historic Site

Organ Mountains-
Desert Peaks
Nat. Mon.

Columbus

Deming

Lordsburg

Shakespeare

Silver City

Gila Cliff
Dwellings
Nat. Mon.

MOGOLLON
MOUNTAINS

MIMBRES MTS.

Kingston

Hillsboro

Truth or
Consequences

Elephant Butte

Spaceport
America

El Camino Real
International
Heritage Center

BOSQUE DEL
APACHE WILDLIFE
REFUGE

San Antonio

Socorro

Magdalena

Datil

Very
Large
Array

Quemado

Gallup

Zuni
Pueblo

El Morro
Nat. Mon.

El Malpais
Nat. Mon.

Acoma
Pueblo

Grants

Bernardo

Belen

Isleta
Pueblo

Albuquerque

SANDIA
MOUNTAINS

Santa Fe

Bernalillo

Golden
Madrid

Edgewood

Moriarty

Willard

Mountainair

MANZANO MTS.

Salinas National Monument

Quarai
Abó
Gran
Quivira

Corona

Vaughn

Santa
Rosa

Puerto
de Luna

Fort Sumner

Fort Sumner
Historic Site

Tucumcari

Clovis

Portales

Amarillo

SAN ANDRES MNTS.

JORNADA DEL MUERTO

Rio Grande

Trinity
Site

Safford

Tucson

Flagstaff

N

0   50
miles

clubs, you may bypass it altogether. The **University District** and the fashionable **Nob Hill** neighbourhood lie further east, across the I-25 interstate, while the Sandia Mountains, roughly ten miles beyond, finally call a halt to the Sunbelt sprawl. Albuquerque has instead pushed west of the Rio Grande, where only **Petroglyph National Monument** holds any appeal for tourists.

Albuquerque has acquired a higher profile in recent years as the setting to TV mega-hit **Breaking Bad**, and its spin-off *Better Call Saul*. Various tours explore sites from the series, though those tend to be ordinary back-street homes and businesses rather than major sights. Somewhat paradoxically, one reason the city is such a popular filming location is that the architecture of its residential neighbourhoods varies so enormously that it's possible to find buildings in the style of almost any region in the country.

Brief history

Three centuries ago, in 1706, Hispanic colonists named a new town beside a sweeping curve of the Rio Grande in honour of the Spanish **Duke of Alburquerque**. Albuquerque's earliest surviving adobe buildings, however, still the nucleus of **Old Town**, date from the 1790s, when it occupied a pivotal position on the **Camino Real** – the "Royal Road" from Mexico to Santa Fe, which later linked up with the **Santa Fe Trail** from Missouri. Modern Albuquerque began to grow with the arrival of the railroad in 1880, when its epicentre shuffled a couple of miles east towards the new station. Around that time, Albuquerque managed to lose its first "r," possibly thanks to a misspelling by a railroad sign-painter.

What really transformed Albuquerque was the decentralization of **defence** industries during World War II. Weapons research at **Sandia National Laboratories**, on the giant **Kirtland Air Force Base**, southeast of the city, brought a massive influx of money and jobs. In the 1950s, "Atomic City" was the best-educated city in the nation, in terms of PhDs per capita, and acquired enough federal offices to earn the nickname "Little Washington". It even achieved the dubious distinction of surviving an **H-bomb**: in 1957, a B-36 bomber accidentally dropped a 42,000-pound nuclear device near the air base. Its conventional explosives went off, creating a sizeable crater, but failed to trigger the intended one-megaton thermonuclear blast. Kirtland base these days is effectively a self-contained city, now more sealed off than ever from the rest of Albuquerque.

3

THE BALLOONS OF ALBUQUERQUE

First held in 1972 as a 50th anniversary stunt for a local radio station – that initial outing featured just thirteen balloons – Albuquerque's annual **International Balloon Fiesta** (ⓦ balloonfiesta.com) has grown to become the most important event in world ballooning. By a freak of geography, the "**Albuquerque Box**" offers ideal conditions for balloonists. After takeoff, the prevailing winds consistently blow balloons toward the east, until they clear the top of the Sandia Mountains. Then stronger winds propel them back westwards, making it possible to land more or less where they were launched. As a result, Albuquerque regularly hosts major gas and hot-air ballooning championships, such as the unlikely sounding Coupe de Gordon Bennett.

A photographer's dream, the Balloon Fiesta lasts from the first Saturday until the second Sunday of October. It attracts several hundred balloons and well over a million visitors, so book months in advance if you need a room, or even a rental car, in early October.

The fun focuses on **Balloon Fiesta Park**, half a mile west of I-25 and seven miles north of downtown. Admission costs $8 (under-13s free), with a further $12 for parking. The busiest times are the "mass ascensions" at 7am on the four weekend mornings, as well as the "Special Shapes" events, when balloons in shapes ranging from beer bottles to dumptrucks, and dragons to doughnuts, take to the air. Volunteers are always welcomed to help set the things up, and may be rewarded with a quick flight.

Various companies run hot-air balloon flights year-round, from around $160 per person, including World Balloon (ⓦ worldballoon.com) and Rainbow Ryders (ⓦ rainbowryders.com).

ALBUQUERQUE AREA

● EATING

Flying Star	6
Frontier	5
The Grove Cafe & Market	4
Pueblo Harvest Cafe	2
Sadie's	1
Scalo	6
66 Diner	3

■ ACCOMMODATION

La Quinta Inn Albuquerque Airport	2
Los Poblanos	1

■ NIGHTLIFE

Caravan East	1

Old Town

Albuquerque's tree-filled **Old Town plaza** may lack the cachet of its counterpart in Santa Fe, but it makes an appealing focus for the old Spanish settlement. Adobe buildings on all four sides have been restored as souvenir stores and tourist restaurants, with crafts sellers congregating under the porticos on the eastern side. The whole ensemble is still presided over by the twin-towered facade of **San Felipe de Neri church** to the north.

Albuquerque Museum

2000 Mountain Rd • Tues–Sun 9am–5pm • $4, free Sat 2–5pm, Sun 9am–1pm, all day on 1st Wed of each month, & 5–8.30pm on 3rd Thurs of month • ☎ 505 743 7255, ⓦ cabq.gov/museum

The **Albuquerque Museum**, a couple of blocks northeast of the plaza, makes a great introduction to the city's story. Before changing its name as part of a recent overhaul, this was the Albuquerque Museum of Art and History, and it still covers both briefs. As well as an impressive array of the armour and weaponry carried by the Spanish conquistadors – albeit largely drawn from sixteenth-century Europe rather than New Mexico – it displays delicate religious artefacts, along with exhibits that tell the story of weaving along the Rio Grande. Coronado brought five thousand sheep here in 1542, so the region has the longest tradition of sheep-rearing of anywhere in the US. The permanent collection also includes vernacular Hispanic artworks along with paintings from the big names of twentieth-century Southwestern art.

New Mexico Museum of Natural History and Science

1801 Mountain Rd NW • Daily 9am–5pm • $7 • ☎ 505 841 2800, ⓦ nmnaturalhistory.org

With its full-scale models of dinosaurs, and a replica of a Carlsbad-like snow cave, the **New Mexico Museum of Natural History and Science** is aimed primarily at kids. The main emphasis is on prehistoric monsters, complementing permanent displays of paleontology and geology with touring animatronic exhibits. Elsewhere, the fascinating "Start Up" exhibition uses Microsoft's origins in Albuquerque in 1977 as the springboard for a history of the computer revolution. Albuquerque was where the first Altair personal computer was developed, prompting an incredibly young-looking Bill Gates and Paul Allen to move here in 1977 and establish "Micro-Soft" to write software for the first generation of home-based programmers. A giant-screen theatre shows science-related movies for an additional charge.

American International Rattlesnake Museum

202 San Felipe St NW • June–Aug Mon–Sat 10am–6pm, Sun 1–5pm; Sept–May Mon–Fri 11.30am–5.30pm, Sat 10am–6pm, Sun 1–5pm • $5 • ☎ 505 242 6569, ⓦ rattlesnakes.com

The bizarre **American International Rattlesnake Museum**, southeast of the Old Town plaza, has live rattlers on display and rattlesnake curios for sale. Visits consist of walking through a small room at the back of the gift store, where spiders and scorpions as well as snakes are kept in tiny glass cases.

Turquoise Museum

2107 Central Ave NW • Guided tours only, by reservation, Mon–Sat 11am & 1pm • $10 • ☎ 505 247 8650, ⓦ turquoisemuseumcom

The intriguing little **Turquoise Museum**, half a block west of the plaza, looks like just another store. Step inside, however, on one of the one-hour-thirty-minute tours, and you'll find yourself in a fortified vault, filled with rare and beautiful turquoise nuggets. The story of worldwide turquoise production is told in detail, with advice on the tricks of the trade; unfortunately, the only definitive way to tell whether a piece of turquoise is genuine involves destroying it. Of course, visits end with the chance to buy trinkets.

The riverfront

The Rio Grande has shifted its course in the past three hundred years, so there's an unexpectedly low-key gap **west** of Old Town, much of it left undeveloped in deference

3

DOWNTOWN ALBUQUERQUE

OLD TOWN

DRINKING & NIGHTLIFE		EATING		ACCOMMODATION	
The Anodyne	3	Antiquity	1	Andaluz	4
Burt's Tiki Lounge	6	Artichoke Café	6	Bella Roma	3
Effex	5	Duran Central Pharmacy	2	Casas de Sueños	2
KiMo Theater	2	Java Joe's	3	Monterey Non-Smokers Motel	4
The Launchpad	4	Mas Tapas Y Vino	4	Route 66 Hostel	5
Marble Brewery	1				

to the unruly river. That allows space on the wooded eastern riverbank for some welcome natural attractions – the **ABQ BioPark**, home to an aquarium and botanical gardens, plus a separate zoo to the south, and the **Rio Grande Nature Center** further north.

ABQ BioPark

Aquarium & Botanic Garden 2601 Central Ave NW • June–Aug Mon–Fri 9am–5pm, Sat & Sun 9am–6pm; Sept–May daily 9am–5pm • **Zoo** 903 Tenth St SW • Same hours • $12.50 each section, $20 combined admission • ☎ 505 768 2000, ⓦ cabq.gov/biopark

In the **ABQ BioPark**, immediately north of the bridge where Central Avenue crosses the river, the **Albuquerque Aquarium** offers such diverse experiences as eating in a restaurant beside a glass-walled tank filled with live sharks, and walking through a tunnel surrounded by fierce-eyed moray eels. The whole place has been designed with a great eye for aesthetics, with sculpture outside and beautifully lit tanks filled with ethereal, wispy jellyfish within.

Across the park's central plaza, the **Botanic Garden** consists of two large conservatories – one holding rare plants from the Sonoran and Chihuahua deserts, the other more temperate Mediterranean species – plus a series of formal walled gardens. The river itself is not visible from either section.

A couple of miles south along the Rio Grande – buying a combined admission ticket entitles you to ride a miniature train to and fro – the **BioPark Zoo** holds everything from lions to polar bears, and posts a daily schedule of feeding times and other events.

Rio Grande Nature Center

2901 Candelaria Ave NW • Daily 8am–5pm • $3 per vehicle • ☎ 505 344 7240, ⓦ rgnc.org

Two miles north of Old Town, by way of Rio Grande Boulevard, the 270-acre **Rio Grande Nature Center** has informative displays describing local wildlife. Two short but pleasant nature trails, each around a mile long, follow the riverside, feeling far removed from the city.

The University District and Nob Hill

A couple of miles east of downtown, the campus of the **University of New Mexico** stretches along the northern side of Central Avenue. The 27,000-strong student body keeps the southern side of the highway lively around the clock with funky hangouts of all kinds, from bookstores and laundromats to cafés and diners. The similar but rather more affluent neighbourhood known as **Nob Hill**, home to upscale stores and restaurants, stretches another mile east along Central Ave.

Maxwell Museum of Anthropology

Tues–Sat 10am–4pm • Free • ☎ 505 277 4405, ⓦ unm.edu/~maxwell

Of the six museums on the campus of the University of New Mexico, non-academic visitors are most likely to enjoy the **Maxwell Museum of Anthropology**, which documents the peoples of the Southwest, past and present. There's some fine Mimbres pottery (see p.200), as well as material from Chaco Canyon, while the "Ancestors" segment traces human evolution from the three-million-year-old Lucy, just 3ft 7in tall, unearthed in Ethiopia in 1974.

Indian Pueblo Cultural Center

2401 12th St NW • **Museum** Daily 9am–5pm • $6 • **Gift store** Daily 9am–5.30pm • Free • ☎ 505 843 7270, ⓦ indianpueblo.org

The **Indian Pueblo Cultural Center**, north of I-40 a few blocks north of Old Town, is a highly informative **museum** that's collectively run by the nineteen New Mexican pueblos. Its horseshoe-shaped design deliberately echoes the architecture of the Ancestral Puebloan city of Pueblo Bonito, in Chaco Canyon.

This is the only major museum in New Mexico to be curated by Native Americans, and the displays in the two basement-level galleries have a clear and distinct point of view.

The shared heritage at the root of Pueblo culture is explained in detail, as is the impact of the Spanish conquistadors. Describing the Pueblo Revolt of 1680 as the "first civil war", it states that by allowing the defeated Spaniards to leave unharmed, the Pueblo peoples "showed them more mercy than they showed us". There's also as good an explanation as you're ever likely to get of a topic Pueblo Indians rarely discuss with outsiders: how indigenous Pueblo religion has managed to coexist with imported Catholicism. Films illustrate the work of Pueblo potter María Martínez and artist Pablita Velarde.

The larger **Shumakolowa gift store** upstairs, which you can visit without paying the museum admission fee, sells Pueblo pottery and jewellery, while a separate **art gallery** here, also free, hosts changing exhibitions of Native American art. The high-quality *Pueblo Harvest Café* (see p.177) opens off the main lobby. **Pueblo dances** are staged regularly in the central courtyard.

National Hispanic Cultural Center

1701 Fourth St SW • Tues–Sun 10am–5pm • $3 • ☎ 505 246 2261, ⦿ nhccnm.org

Whether or not you choose to visit the impressive **National Hispanic Cultural Center**, a mile south of Old Town in the Barelas neighbourhood, will probably depend on what's on in its spacious **art gallery**. Stimulating temporary exhibitions complement permanent displays that focus on "Hispanidad", with lots of New Mexican religious iconography. A good **café**, *La Fonda del Basque*, serves breakfast and lunch daily.

National Museum of Nuclear Science and History

601 Eubank Blvd SE • Daily 9am–5pm • $12 • ☎ 505 245 2137, ⦿ nuclearmuseum.org

Displays at the **National Museum of Nuclear Science and History**, outside Kirtland Air Force Base seven miles east of downtown, range from the early discoveries of Madame Curie, via newspaper advertisements promoting the health-giving properties of drinking the Radithor brand of radioactive water, to a 1953 *Life* magazine cover reading "we are in a life and death bomb race". You'll be soothed to learn how much more precise and sophisticated today's weapons are compared with the "primitive city-busting concepts" of the Cold War era, just how safe nuclear waste disposal can be, and a host of other little-known facts. A gift store sells space-age novelties.

Sandia Mountains

Sandia Peak Tramway Late May to early Sept daily 9am–9pm; early Sept to late May Mon & Wed–Sun 9am–8pm, Tues 5–8pm • $20 round-trip (ski season mid-Dec to mid-March, ski area open Fri–Mon only; lift tickets $55) • ☎ 505 242 9052, ⦿ sandiapeak.com

The forested **Sandia Mountains** tower 10,500ft over Albuquerque to the east; views from the summit are especially beautiful at and after sunset, when the city lights sparkle below. In summer it's a good 25°F cooler up here than in the valley, while in winter you can go downhill or cross-country **skiing**.

The most exciting way to reach the top is by riding the world's longest tramway, the 2.7-mile **Sandia Peak Tramway**, which departs from the end of Tramway Road a dozen miles northeast of town. During the uppermost 1.5 miles of its exhilarating 15-minute climb, not a single support tower interrupts the progress of the cable car.

If you'd rather **drive** to the top of the mountains, you have to circle around the back on I-40, then approach from the east, by way of the Turquoise Trail (see p.128).

Petroglyph National Monument

Unser Blvd NW • Daily 8am–5pm • Mon–Fri $1 per vehicle, Sat & Sun $2 • ☎ 505 899 0205, ⦿ nps.gov/petr

Set beneath a chain of burned-out cinder cones thrown up by a 150,000-year-old volcanic eruption, a low seventeen-mile escarpment west of the Rio Grande, protected as the **PETROGLYPH NATIONAL MONUMENT**, holds some unusually accessible ancient Native American **rock art**.

As the park **visitor centre**, reached by crossing the river on I-40 then driving four miles north on Unser Boulevard, stands in between its two main concentrations of petroglyphs, it's not an essential stop if your time is limited. In **Boca Negra Canyon**, three miles north, three easy trails lead up to the escarpment, which on close inspection turns out to consist of tumbled black lava boulders; only the half-hour **Mesa Trail** demands any energetic climbing. Most of the crudely scratched images you'll pass, ranging from simple spirals to masked figures and eagles with Bart Simpson hairdos, date from 1300 to 1680 AD. During the eighteenth century, shepherds from the nearby Hispanic settlement of Atrisco added a number of Christian crosses and symbols.

The one trail to the other important group of petroglyphs, in **Rinconada Canyon** 1.3 miles drive south of the visitor centre, is significantly longer; you'll need well over an hour to do the 2.2-mile round-trip justice. Apart from in the full heat of summer, though, it's not physically demanding, consisting of a level out-and-back route across the sandy canyon floor to and along the base of the escarpment. All the petroglyphs are at the far end; many were intricately shaped to follow the natural contours of the rock.

3

Isleta Pueblo

🕾 505 869 3111, 🖅 isletapueblo.com

The only New Mexican pueblo south of Albuquerque, **ISLETA PUEBLO**, lies just off the interstate a dozen miles from downtown, to which it's also connected by the Rail Runner light-rail system. The sole survivor of the many pueblos encountered by Spanish explorers along the lower Rio Grande, it served in the seventeenth century as a refuge where Tiwa peoples gathered to resist the threat of Apache raids. During the Pueblo Revolt, some Isletans accompanied the Spanish retreat southwards to found the pueblo of **Tigua**, outside El Paso, while others fled west to join the Hopi. Isleta itself was repopulated in 1718, and remains home to around three thousand people.

Although the tribal lands mark a verdant interruption amid the dormitory communities that line the interstate's first fifty miles, the reservation is plagued by river-borne pollution from the industries of Albuquerque. Economically, it's dependent on its huge neighbour; a high proportion of Isletans work in the city.

Every day during daylight hours, visitors have free access to the principal pueblo village – also known as **SHIAW-IBA** – where the main attraction is the white-walled **mission church** of San Agustín de Isleta. In addition, Isleta stages major festivals on August 28 and September 4, and runs a 24-hour **casino**.

ARRIVAL AND DEPARTURE

ALBUQUERQUE AND AROUND

By plane Albuquerque's International Sunport, four miles southeast of downtown, is served by all major US airlines. All the national rental car chains have outlets, while a taxi into town with Albuquerque Cab (🕾 505 883 4888, 🖅 albuquerquecab.com) costs from $15. Sunport Shuttle (🕾 505 883 4966, 🖅 sunportshuttle.com) runs door-to-door shuttles at similar rates. Many hotels and motels also run free shuttles. Buses also connect the airport with the Rail Runner network, Mon–Sat only (see below).

By train One daily train in each direction on Amtrak's Los Angeles–Chicago Southwest Chief service calls at the Alvarado Transportation Center, downtown.

By bus Long-distance Greyhound buses, heading north–south as well as east–west – use downtown's Alvarado Transportation Center. Note that there's no service to Santa Fe or Taos.

Destinations Denver (2 daily; 8hr 30min); Flagstaff (3 daily; 6hr); Las Cruces (2 daily; 3hr 20min).

GETTING AROUND

By train The Rail Runner light-rail system (fares from $2; 🕾 866 795 7245, 🖅 nmrailrunner.com) runs from its Downtown Albuquerque station, in the Alvarado Transportation Center at First and Central, both south to

Belen and north to Bernalillo, with continuing services all the way north to Santa Fe (see p.118). Connecting buses from the airport run to both the Downtown station and the first Rail Runner stop south of downtown, the Bernalillo

County station at 113 Rio Bravo SE, Mon–Sat only.
By bus Downtown's Alvarado Transportation Center is also the hub of the ABQ Ride city bus network (☎ 505 724 3100, Ⓦ cabq.gov/transit). Its free D-Ride route circles downtown, on weekdays only, while commuter buses further afield cost $1 a ride.

INFORMATION AND TOURS

Tourist information 303 Romero St NW, in the Old Town (daily: April–Oct 10am–6pm, Nov–March 9.30am–4.30pm; ☎ 505 842 9118, Ⓦ itsatrip.org), and at the airport (Mon–Fri 9.30am–8pm, Sat 9.30am–4pm).
Bike rental and tours Routes Rentals, 404 San Felipe St NW (☎ 505 933 5667, Ⓦ routesrentals.com), rents out bikes and offers city cycling tours, including a daily ride by the river ($35) and a *Breaking Bad* tour on Saturdays ($65).

Van tours Breaking Bad RV Tours, 1919 Old Town Rd NW (Thurs–Sun only, $75, ☎ 505 205 7292, Ⓦ breaking badrvtours.com), run group tours of *Breaking Bad* locations, using guides who worked on the series.
Walking tours The Albuquerque Museum, 2000 Mountain Rd, organizes walking tours of Albuquerque's historic Old Town (mid-March to mid-Dec, Tues–Sun 11am; ☎ 505 743 7255, Ⓦ cabq.gov/museum).

ACCOMMODATION

The twenty-mile length of **Central Avenue**, once Route 66, is lined with the flashing neon signs of cheap **motels**. Have a good look in daylight, to spot those that may turn scary at night. You'll have to pay a little extra to stay in the heart of **Old Town** – which has few accommodation options – or downtown. Larger convention **hotels** are congregated along the interstates and near the airport, while **B&Bs** are scattered across the city.

Andaluz 125 Second St NW ☎ 505 242 9090 or ☎ 877 987 9090, Ⓦ hotelandaluz.com; map p.172. This historic, elegant hotel was originally built in Mexican style by Conrad Hilton in 1939, as *La Posada de Albuquerque*. Long downtown's most appealing upscale option, it has been exquisitely revamped to the latest eco-conscious standards, while retaining its beautiful wood-panelled lobby and cosy bar, and hosting the top-class *Mas* restaurant (see opposite). **$163**
Bella Roma 1211 Roma Ave NW ☎ 505 400 4543, Ⓦ bellaroma.com; map p.172. Appropriately located on Roma Ave, within walking distance of the Old Town, this nineteenth-century Italianate home might look a little out of place in Albuquerque, but it's a delightful B&B. Two suites that sleep up to four each, and two double rooms, feature European themes, and gourmet breakfasts are served outdoors in summer. Doubles **$129**, suites **$169**
Casas de Sueños 310 Rio Grande Blvd SW ☎ 505 247 4560 or ☎ 800 665 7002, Ⓦ casasdesuenos.com; map p.172. Beautifully furnished, charming and friendly B&B, very close to Old Town, with themed adobe *casitas* (cottages) of varying degrees of luxury – some have kitchenettes and whirlpool baths. **$139**
La Quinta Inn Albuquerque Airport 2116 Yale Blvd SE ☎ 505 243 5500, Ⓦ lq.com; map p.170. Large,

relatively upscale motel, served by frequent shuttles from the nearby airport, and offering accommodation that's far from memorable but safe, good value and quiet. **$79**
★ **Los Poblanos** 4803 Rio Grande Blvd NW ☎ 505 344 9297, Ⓦ lospoblanos.com; map p.170. Set on an organic farm, five miles north along the river from the Old Town, this exquisite B&B offers lovely antique-furnished rooms in two different buildings. The delicious breakfast specials change daily, while the on-site *Merienda* restaurant serves dinner Wed–Sun only, using home-grown produce where possible; mains cost $20–26. **$210**
★ **Monterey Non-Smokers Motel** 2402 Central Ave SW ☎ 505 243 3554 or ☎ 877 666 8379, Ⓦ nonsmokersmotel .com; map p.172. Clean, fifteen-room motel, two blocks west of Old Town, run by a friendly Polish couple, and offering a pool and laundry, as well as, of course, as a strict non-smoking policy. **$72**
Route 66 Hostel 1012 Central Ave SW ☎ 505 247 1813, Ⓦ route66hostel.com; map p.172. Albuquerque's only hostel, a friendly place in what was once a private house, between Old Town and downtown, offers dorm beds and very plain but bargain-priced private doubles, plus kitchen facilities and abundant books and board games. Dorm **$20**, shared-bath double **$30**, en-suite double **$35**

EATING

Albuquerque is the place to come to grips with what real New Mexican food is all about. Family diners all over the city compete to create the spiciest *chile rellenos*, enchiladas, and *sopaipillas*.

CAFÉS AND DINERS
Duran Central Pharmacy 1815 Central Ave NW ☎ 505 247 4141, Ⓦ durancentralpharmacy.com; map p.172. Mexican dining counter attached to a working drugstore, not far from Old Town, with delicious, inexpensive tortillas,

enchiladas, and plenty of chile, both green and red. Mon–Fri 9am–6.30pm, Sat 9am–2pm.
Flying Star 3416 Central Ave SE ☎ 505 255 6633, Ⓦ flyingstarcafe.com; map p.170. Lively, crowded Nob Hill café serving eclectic international cuisine to a largely student

clientele. The menu ranges through breakfast specialities, salads and blue-plate specials like Vietnamese noodles, mac cheese or pasta pomodoro for $10. Other branches throughout the city. Sun–Thurs 7am–9.30pm, Fri & Sat 7am–10.30pm.
Frontier 2400 Central Ave SE ☎505 266 0550, ⓦwww .frontierrestaurant.com; map p.170. Legendary diner across from the university – no longer (quite) open around the clock – where an unceasing parade of characters chow down on burgers, burritos and great vegetarian enchiladas. As you enjoy your $7 *huevos rancheros*, see how many John Wayne portraits you can count on the walls. Daily 5am–1am.
The Grove Cafe & Market 600 Central Ave SE ☎505 248 9800, ⓦthegrovecafemarket.com; map p.170. With its emphasis on fresh organic ingredients, this is a great spot for breakfast, lunch or a bit of both – locals flock here for Sunday brunch. Pretty much everything, from poached eggs with ham and fresh fruit to lunchtime salads or sandwiches, costs around $10. Tues–Sat 7am–4pm, Sun 8am–3pm.
Java Joe's 906 Park Ave SW ☎505 765 1514, ⓦdowntownjavajoes.com; map p.172. On the western fringes of downtown this is as close as Albuquerque comes to having an "alternative" coffee shop, with wholesome breakfast specials and sandwiches and live music to go with its espresso drinks. *Breaking Bad* devotees will doubtless recognize the building as Tuco's HQ. Mon & Sun 7am–4pm, Tues–Sat 7am–9pm.
Pueblo Harvest Cafe Indian Pueblo Cultural Center, 2401 12th St NW ☎505 724 3510, ⓦindianpueblo.org; map p.170. While still serving Pueblo specialities like Indian fry bread at lunchtime, this unusual Native American restaurant is also open for breakfast (try the $10.50 cornmeal pancakes with bacon) and for fine dining in the evening, when braised bison ribs are among its $20–30 mains. Mon–Thurs 8am–8.30pm, Fri & Sat 8am–9.30pm, Sun 8am–4pm.
Sadie's 6230 Fourth St NW ☎505 345 5339, ⓦsadiesofnewmexico.com; map p.170. Huge, great-value Mexican restaurant – the stuffed *sopaipillas* are irresistible, as indeed are the margaritas. Giant screens make it too bright and loud to be romantic, but it's a good place to bring kids. Three other city locations. Mon–Thurs 11am–10pm, Fri &

Sat 10am–10.30pm, Sun 10am–10pm.
66 Diner 1405 Central Ave NE ☎505 247 1421, ⓦ66diner.com; map p.170. Classic Fifties diner near the university, with white-capped waiting staff, blue-plate specials, a soda fountain, and a lively late-night clientele. Mon–Thurs 11am–10pm, Fri 11am–11pm, Sat 8am–11pm, Sun 8am–10pm.

RESTAURANTS

Antiquity 112 Romero St NW ☎505 247 3545, ⓦantiquityrestaurant.com; map p.172. Old Town cottage turned dinner-only romantic restaurant. The menu consists largely of Mediterranean cuisine, albeit given a New Mexican twist here and there by a leavening of chile. Typical meat and seafood mains cost $24–35. Daily 5–9pm.
Artichoke Café 424 Central Ave SE ☎505 243 0200, ⓦartichokecafe.com; map p.172. Simple but classy restaurant in the heart of downtown, serving a good, varied menu of California-influenced modern American cuisine; typical mains cost $12–16 at lunch, $24–40 for dinner. Mon–Thurs 11am–2.30pm & 5–9pm, Fri & Sat 5–10pm, Sun 5–9pm.
Mas Tapas Y Vinos Hotel Andaluz, 125 Second St NW ☎505 242 9090 or ☎877 987 9090, ⓦhotelandaluz.com; map p.172. While primarily identifying itself as a tapas restaurant, this smart downtown dining room serves very substantial dinner mains like seafood paella ($28) and grilled steak ($34) in addition to its delicious $10–15 Spanish-style snacks and salads. It's also open for breakfast and lunch, with a popular Sunday brunch. Mon–Thurs 7am–10.30pm, 11am–2pm & 5–9.30pm; Fri & Sat 7am–10.30pm, 11am–2pm & 5–10pm; Sun 7am–2pm & 5–9.30pm.
Scalo 3500 Central Ave SE ☎505 255 8781, ⓦscalonobhill.com; map p.170. Large but romantic and stylish Northern Italian restaurant near the university. Antipasti like steamed mussels or beef carpaccio cost $10–12, mains such as seared halibut range up to $30, and there are plenty of pasta and vegetarian options. Mon–Thurs 11am–2.30pm & 5–10pm, Fri & Sat 11am–2.30pm & 5–11pm, Sun 11am–2.30pm & 5–9pm.

3

DRINKING AND NIGHTLIFE

Many of downtown Albuquerque's **bars** and **clubs** double as small theatres or music venues. The free weekly *Alibi* magazine (ⓦalibi.com) carries full listings of what's coming up or going down.

The Anodyne 409 Central Ave NW ☎505 244 1820, ⓦtheanodyne.com; map p.172. Downtown's most popular bar offers pool tables, pinball, a good jukebox, and an eclectic mix of customers, from beer guzzlers to martini sippers – but no food or live music. Mon–Sat 4pm–1.30am, Sun 7–11.30pm.
Burt's Tiki Lounge 313 Gold Ave SW ☎505 247 9735; map p.172. The Polynesian-cum-pirate decor in this tiki-bar cocktail-lounge makes a good backdrop for live bands

every weekend, though the Freaky Tiki Bass dance party, on the third Thursday of each month, is the biggest night. Wed–Sat 8.30pm–2am.
Caravan East 7605 Central Ave NE ☎505 265 7877, ⓦcaravaneast.com; map p.170. Enormous honky-tonk, where tenderfeet can do the two-step with throngs of urban cowboys, and the live music includes mariachi and conjunto as well as country. Tues, Fri & Sat 5pm–2am, Sun 6pm–midnight.

Effex 420 Central Ave SW ☎ 505 842 8870, ⓦ effexabq .com; map p.172. Huge, multistorey and very central gay club, across the street from the landmark KiMo Theater, with masses of room for shirtless posing as well as dancing. Tues–Sat 7pm–2am.

KiMo Theater 423 Central Ave NW ☎ 505 768 3544, ⓦ cabq.gov/kimo; map p.172. Gorgeous, city-owned "Pueblo Deco" theatre, dating from the late 1920s, which puts on an eclectic programme of opera, dance and theatre performances, kids' movies, and everything from burlesque to Beethoven, as well as regular live bands.

The Launchpad 618 Central Ave SW ☎ 505 764 8887, ⓦ launchpadrocks.com; map p.172. Dance and live music space that showcases touring indie and world music bands; besides the fabulous space-age decor, there's also a cluster of pool tables.

Marble Brewery 111 Marble NW ☎ 505 243 2739, ⓦ marblebrewery.com; map p.172. Bustling brewpub, just north of downtown. There's no kitchen, but takeaway food trucks park outside, and the (summer-only) outdoor patio makes a good place to eat. Mon–Sat noon–midnight, Sun noon–10.30pm.

East of Albuquerque

3

The first twenty miles of I-40's eastward run from Albuquerque are scenic, as the interstate threads between the Sandia Mountains. Once through the hills, however, anyone who doesn't turn north towards Santa Fe onto the **Turquoise Trail** (see p.128), is in for a long hard slog out into the plains. The only place before Texas that might pique your curiosity is **Fort Sumner**, which played a heart-rending role in Navajo history and also holds the grave of **Billy the Kid**.

Santa Rosa

A hundred unutterably boring miles east of the Sandia Mountains, weary drivers reach their first potential overnight stop. South and west of the interstate, a four-mile stretch of the former Route 66 runs through **SANTA ROSA**. Named **Parker Avenue** in the small downtown, and **Will Rogers Drive** further east, it's dotted with diners and motels, but there's little to see, apart perhaps from the restored classic cars at the **Route 66 Auto Museum**, 2866 Route 66 (April–Oct Mon–Sat 7.30am–6pm, Sun 10am–5pm; Sept–April Mon–Sat 8am–5pm, Sun 10am–5pm; $5; ☎ 575 472 1966). Thanks to the bright yellow car atop a pole outside, you won't have any difficulty finding it.

Blue Hole

Santa Rosa Dive Center • Sat & Sun 8am–dusk, weekdays by appointment • ☎ 575 472 3370, ⓦ santarosabluehole.com

Scuba divers desperate for a dip cross the plains to plunge into Santa Rosa's **Blue Hole**, a crystal-clear natural pool that's sixty feet across and eighty feet deep. To anyone who's seen the ocean, though, it may come as an anti-climax. You'll find it by turning left off Fifth Street, south of the main drag, and driving half a mile on Blue Hole Road. The on-site dive centre provides tank rentals.

Tucumcari

Sixty miles east of Santa Rosa, **TUCUMCARI** is the definitive Route 66 pit stop. Known at this point as Tucumcari Boulevard, Route 66 cuts a broad five-mile swathe through town. If you expect its abundant truck stops, diners and motels to yield a kitsch fascination, you'll be sorely disappointed, but their glittering neon signs make a welcome sight as dusk descends on the plains. No one stays two nights in Tucumcari. Once you've enjoyed the oddments and artefacts in the **Tucumcari Historical Museum**, which spreads through several outbuildings from a former schoolhouse at 416 S Adams St (Tues–Sat 9am–3pm; $5; ☎ 575 461 4201), it's time to hit the road again.

INFORMATION **TUCUMCARI**

Visitor centre 404 W Route 66 (Mon–Fri 9am–5pm; ☎ 575 461 1694, ⓦ visittucumcarinm.com).

ACCOMMODATION AND EATING

★**Blue Swallow** 815 E Route 66 ☎575 461 9849, ⓦ blueswallowmotel.com. Everyone loves the *Blue Swallow*, a classic, splendidly restored Route 66 motel where the appealing retro-furnished rooms are bursting with memorabilia. **$70**

Del's Family Restaurant 1202 E Route 66 ☎575 461 1740, ⓦ delsrestaurant.com. While dining choices in Tucumcari may be plentiful, they're also limited – this is as good a diner as you're going to find, serving New

Mexican specialities like *sopaipillas* as well as inexpensive chicken and steak dinners at $10–15. Mon–Sat 11am–9pm.

Historic Route 66 Motel 1620 E Route 66 ☎575 461 1212, ⓦ rte66motel.com. As well as simple clean rooms at great prices, this impeccably maintained old-fashioned motor court also offers the very friendly little early-morning *Circa Espresso Bar*, which serves excellent coffee and smoothies. **$42**

Fort Sumner

A 45-mile detour south of I-40 near Santa Rosa brings you to the small town of **FORT SUMNER**. This modern settlement is named after the nineteenth-century army outpost that stood to the southeast, and has been notorious ever since for its associations with **Billy the Kid** and the **Navajo**.

Fort Sumner Historic Site

3647 Billy the Kid Rd, 6 miles southeast of Fort Sumner • Daily except Tues 8.30am–5pm • $5 • ☎ 575 355 2573, ⓦ nmmonuments.org, ⓦ bosqueredondomemorial.com

What's now **Fort Sumner Historic Site** was infamous as the headquarters of the **Bosque Redondo Indian Reservation**, where nine thousand Navajo and Mescalero Apache captives were incarcerated during the 1860s after being rounded up by General James Carleton and Kit Carson and forced here on the Long Walk (see p.483). The idea was for the reservation to be self-sufficient and for the Indians to become accustomed to an agricultural lifestyle. In fact, the Pecos River proved too salty to drink, let alone use for irrigation. In the words of Navajo headman Barboncito:

Whatever we do here causes death. Some work at the acequias, take sick, and die; others die with the hoe in their hands; they go to the river to their waists and suddenly disappear; others have been struck and torn to pieces by lightning. A rattlesnake bite here kills us; in our country a rattlesnake before he bites gives warning which enables us to keep out of its way and if bitten, we readily find a cure – here we can find no cure.

The Mescalero escaped in November 1865, only to be chased by Carson and suffer further slaughter. The Navajo remained until General William T. Sherman arrived to replace Carleton on May 28, 1868; the treaty that allowed them to return home was signed on June 1. Over three thousand prisoners had died.

Only a low ridge of adobe bricks on the eastern riverbank remains of the fort the Navajo built for their captors, but the dead are honoured by a large visitor centre-cum-museum, the **Bosque Redondo Memorial**, which details the whole sorry story.

Old Fort Sumner Museum

3501 Billy The Kid Rd, 6 miles southeast of Fort Sumner • Daily 9am–5pm • $4 • ☎ 575 355 2942

After the Bosque Redondo reservation closed, rancher Lucien Maxwell bought Fort Sumner and the surrounding land. In 1881, **Billy the Kid** was hiding here in the bedroom of Maxwell's son, Peter, when **Pat Garrett** tracked him down and shot him dead (see p.182). His **grave** is located in the backyard of the **Old Fort Sumner Museum**, a few hundred yards east of the fort. Billy was buried alongside two fellow outlaws, Tom O'Folliard and Charlie Bowdre; all remain imprisoned to this day, as their joint tombstone, poignantly inscribed "*PALS*", is protected from would-be thieves behind steel bars. Originally erected by film director King Vidor, the tombstone was stolen so often that participants in an annual festival, held on the second weekend of June, now compete to "steal" an eighty-pound replica, and then throw it as far as possible.

3

The actual museum is less satisfying than the one in Fort Sumner itself; it holds jumbled items that may or may not have belonged to Billy, plus displays relating to local history.

Billy the Kid Museum

1601 E Sumner Ave, Fort Sumner • Daily 8.30am–5pm; closed Sun Oct to mid-May • $5 • ☎ 575 355 2380,
ⓦ billythekidmuseumfortsumner.com

While the **Billy the Kid Museum**, in the town of Fort Sumner, has no immediate connection with the life of the Kid himself, it's a vast and entertaining treasure house of Wild West relics that purportedly include his rifle, his spurs and even some of his hair. Pride of place goes to a photo that was authenticated in 2015 as showing Billy playing croquet with his friends at a wedding in 1878. Endless warehouses stretch back from the highway, filled with old cars, wagons, typewriters and other rusty hardware.

3 Southeast of Albuquerque

Although the Rio Grande Valley, south of Albuquerque (see p.192), has always held a larger human population, New Mexico's **southeast** quadrant offers greater scenic and historic appeal. Here you'll find the ancient pueblos of **Salinas National Monument**, the eerie gypsum wastelands of **White Sands**, and the mountain resorts of **Ruidoso** and **Cloudcroft**. Most compelling of all, however, is the rough-hewn frontier town of **Lincoln**. Scene of the bloodiest exploits of **Billy the Kid**, it has remained all but untouched since his death.

Salinas National Monument

Pueblos Daily: late May to early Sept 9am–6pm; early Sept to late May 9am–5pm • Free • **Visitor centre** On US-60 in Mountainair, 36 miles east of I-25 • Daily 8am–5pm • Free • ☎ 575 847 2585, ⓦ nps.gov/sapu

Early Spanish colonists ranked the precious salt deposits of **Salinas Valley**, east of the Manzano Mountains seventy miles southeast of Albuquerque, among New Mexico's greatest treasures. Franciscan missionaries targeted the Pueblo peoples of the valley, erecting massive churches atop their existing settlements, but due to epidemics and Apache raids, the entire region had been abandoned before the Pueblo Revolt of 1680. Three separate ruined pueblos now form **SALINAS NATIONAL MONUMENT**. Each has its own "contact station", and they share a **visitor centre** in little **MOUNTAINAIR**.

Only at the largest and most interesting Salinas pueblo, **Gran Quivira**, on a low hill 26 miles south from Mountainair along Hwy-55, has the pueblo itself been more than minimally excavated. That process revealed an impressive 300-room structure complete with hidden *kivas*, built in secret to avoid the wrath of the Spanish priests. The adjoining church probably remained incomplete when the pueblo was abandoned. Juan de Oñate, who visited Gran Quivira in 1598, reported that its inhabitants painted stripes on their noses.

The main feature of **Quarai**, a mile west of Hwy-55 eight miles north of Mountainair, is the fortress-like stone church of La Purísima Concepción, whose golden walls tower above the rubble-strewn mounds that conceal the pueblo village. At **Abó**, just north of US-60 nine miles west of Mountainair, the church of San Gregorio dominates an even more tantalizing expanse of ruins.

Carrizozo

Fifty miles southeast of Gran Quivira, where US-54 meets US-380, the parched desert outpost of **CARRIZOZO** replaced better-known Lincoln as the seat of Lincoln County in 1909. Other than a potential halt on a long drive, and the **Valley of Fires Recreation Area** nearby, there's nothing much to it.

Valley of Fires Recreation Area

US-380, 4 miles northwest of Carrizozo • Daily dawn–dusk • $3 per person, $5 for vehicle holding two or more • ☎ 575 648 2241, ⓦ blm.gov

The **Valley of Fires Recreation Area** preserves a jet-black river of lava that poured for over forty miles down the Tularosa Valley five thousand years ago. Though it ranges from four to six miles wide and up to 150 feet deep, the one trail across the lava is less than a mile long. It's so rough underfoot, and so exposed to the sun, that you're unlikely to want to hike any further, but there's a good **campground** alongside ($12). At its southern end, the lava flow abuts the utterly contrasting White Sands National Monument (see p.186).

Capitan

A twenty-mile drive up into the mountains east of Carrizozo brings you to the crossroads known as **CAPITAN**, notable only as the birthplace of a little bear named **Smokey**. Rescued from a forest fire in 1950, the five-month-old Smokey was taken to the National Zoo in Washington DC, where he survived another 26 years and became a national fire prevention symbol. His words of wisdom, seen on anti-fire billboards across the country – "Only YOU Can Prevent Forest Fires" – live on. Smokey's grave is the centrepiece of **Smokey Bear Historical Park**, which also features exhibits on his life and a short nature trail (118 W Smokey Bear Blvd; daily 9am–4.30pm; $2; ⓦ smokeybearpark.com).

Capitan is plagued, incidentally, by a running feud between people who say "Smokey Bear" (good) and wilful misfits who insist on "Smokey *the* Bear" (bad).

3

ACCOMMODATION AND EATING   CAPITAN

Smokey Bear Motel 316 Smokey Bear Blvd ☎ 575 354 2253 or ☎ 800 766 5392, ⓦ smokeybearmotel.com. Simple but appealing motel near the park, with cabin-style rooms. The adjoining restaurant, open for all meals daily, serves Mexican as well as all-American dishes for under $10. **$60**

Lincoln

Though not strictly speaking a ghost town, tiny **LINCOLN**, twelve miles east of Capitan on Hwy-380, is a perfectly preserved Wild West settlement. During the late nineteenth century, as both cattle-ranching centre and site of the army outpost of **Fort Stanton**, it was home to around 750 people, including **Billy the Kid**. Bypassed by the railroads, however, it soon dwindled, and time seems to have stood still ever since. No new buildings have joined the venerable false-front structures that line Main Street, and the entire town, including several sites not described in detail below, is now **Lincoln Historic Site**.

During the first weekend of August, the streets of Lincoln echo with gunfire once again during the three-day **Old Lincoln Days** festival, which features living history demonstrations, fiddle competitions and the like.

Anderson-Freeman Visitors Center

Daily 8.30am–4.30pm • $3.50, Joint admission to all Lincoln sites $5

The **Anderson-Freeman Visitors Center**, at the east end of Lincoln, offers the fullest displays on local history, including a short movie introduction to the town's complicated story. After exhibits covering Hispanics, cowboys, "Buffalo Soldiers" – the black cavalrymen stationed at Fort Stanton – and Apache, the museum moves on to the Lincoln County War. Its exhaustive account of Billy's life extends to the coroner's handwritten report on the men shot during his April 1881 escape; however, none of the artefacts definitely belonged to Billy himself.

Lincoln's oldest building, the **Torréon**, stands alongside. Despite resembling Ancestral Puebloan masonry, this circular tower was erected by Hispanic settlers during the 1850s, as a refuge against Apache raids. It's too small to admit visitors; a glance from the street makes it easy to imagine how cramped it must have been, and speaks volumes about the miserable, unglamorous reality of frontier life.

3

BILLY THE KID AND THE LINCOLN COUNTY WAR

The Hispanic farming community of Las Placitas del Río Bonito, founded during the 1850s, was renamed **Lincoln** in 1869, and became the seat of **Lincoln County**. At 27,000 square miles, this was the largest county in the United States, occupying a quarter of New Mexico. Rival Anglo ranchers and their political allies were then competing for economic control throughout the Wild West. What's been called the **Western Civil War of Incorporation** pitted large cattle-raising conglomerates, federal lawmen and Republican capitalists against small-scale Democrat ranchers and cowboys. Such tensions were everywhere exacerbated by individual antagonisms; Tombstone's **Gunfight at the OK Corral** is a classic example (see p.241).

The "ring" of men who dominated Lincoln centred on the mercantile, or store, of **Lawrence G. Murphy**, an Irish former theology student, Freemason and alcoholic whose business affairs were run by **James J. Dolan**. Their racketeering included rustling cattle from rancher **John Chisum** to supply beef to the US Army at nearby Fort Stanton. The arrival of a wealthy 23-year-old Englishman, **John Tunstall**, (born in Dalston, London), who opened a rival mercantile in Lincoln with lawyer **Alexander McSween**, triggered the **Lincoln County War**.

On February 18, 1878, Tunstall was murdered by Dolan's men on the road to Ruidoso. The young gunslinger **Billy the Kid**, one of Tunstall's hired hands, witnessed the slaying. Born Henry McCarty in Brooklyn in 1859, Billy had been brought west by his mother, who married William Antrim in Santa Fe in 1873. Within a year she had died in Silver City, and young Billy Antrim was cast adrift. A life of petty teenage crime culminated with the shooting in 1877 of a bullying Irish blacksmith in Fort Grant, Arizona. As **Billy Bonney**, the fledgling outlaw fled to Lincoln.

After Tunstall's death, his men formed the **Regulators** and were deputized by the local JP to seek out his killers. Ten of them, including Billy, killed the two chief culprits in March, then gunned down **Sheriff William Brady**, a Dolan man, on Lincoln's main street on April 1. That July, forty of Dolan's supporters laid siege to the Regulators in the adobe home of Alexander McSween; five days later, they summoned soldiers from Fort Stanton, who trained a Gatling gun on the house and set it ablaze. McSween and three Regulators were killed trying to escape, but Billy and ten others sprinted to safety.

Billy spent two years on the run, mostly rustling cattle near Fort Sumner, where he also dealt cards in the saloon of Texan buffalo hunter **Pat Garrett**. In 1880, New Mexico's governor **Lew Wallace** offered an amnesty to all participants in the Lincoln County War who would testify against Dolan. Billy accepted the deal and surrendered, only to escape when he realized that Wallace – then busy writing *Ben Hur* – did not intend to keep his word. Later that year, Garrett was elected as sheriff of Lincoln County, on a pledge to recapture Billy (who naturally lobbied for his opponent). Garrett knew exactly where to look. Just before Christmas, after ambushing and killing two of Billy's friends at Fort Sumner, he duly captured Billy himself at nearby Stinking Springs. Reporting his arrest, the *Las Vegas Gazette* made the first-ever reference to "Billy the Kid".

Billy was taken by train to Santa Fe and on to **Mesilla**, where he was convicted of Sheriff Brady's murder. As he awaited the hangman's noose in Lincoln's courthouse – the former Murphy store, its owner James Dolan having by now taken over the Tunstall mercantile down the street – Billy pulled off his most daring **escape**. Taking advantage of a trip to the outhouse, on April 28, 1881, he shot Deputy J.W. Bell with his own gun. Meanwhile, Marshal Bob Olinger, a long-time Dolan ally, was having lunch with prisoners at the *Wortley Hotel*. Hearing the shots, he raced across the street, to be felled by a blast from an upper window. Billy then struggled unsuccessfully for an hour to break his shackles, repeatedly falling off the horse he was attempting to commandeer, watched all the while by a crowd who dared not intervene.

With a **$500 reward** on his head, Billy fled back to Fort Sumner. Late on the night of July 14, Garrett crept into the bedroom of rancher **Pete Maxwell**, whose family owned Fort Sumner, to ask if he had seen his friend Billy. Moments earlier, Billy had climbed through the window to find out if Maxwell knew Garrett's whereabouts. Garrett recognized the voice that called "*quien es?*" (who's there?), and shot Billy dead.

The next year, Garrett wrote a bestseller, *The Authentic Life of Billy The Kid, the Noted Desperado of the Southwest*. He was not re-elected as sheriff, however, and embarked on a life of wandering that saw him ranching in Texas, a guest of Theodore Roosevelt at the White House, and a customs collector in El Paso, before he was eventually murdered for no apparent reason near Las Cruces in 1908.

Tunstall Store

March–Nov daily 9am–4.30pm • $3.50, Joint admission to all Lincoln sites $5

The **Tunstall Store**, a few yards west of the Visitors Center, is an extraordinary time capsule. The "mercantile" over which the Lincoln County War was fought must have failed to sell a single item in the ensuing century. It remains stocked with dusty date-expired groceries, plus Victorian paraphernalia like weighing scales and cash registers, cases of photos and artefacts, and even Lincoln County's first-ever light bulb, installed in 1914 and allegedly still capable of burning. The wounded Billy the Kid hid beneath the floorboards after shooting Sheriff William Brady on the street outside, on April 1, 1878.

Lincoln County Courthouse

Daily 8.30am–4.30pm • $3.50, Joint admission to all Lincoln sites $5

L.G. Murphy's original store, across the road and a hundred yards west from the Tunstall Store, became the **Lincoln County Courthouse** after James J. Dolan took over Tunstall's operation. It served as Billy's prison when he was brought back from Mesilla to be hanged. Billy felt he was being railroaded; his increasingly bitter letters to Governor Lew Wallace are displayed upstairs in the courtroom where his cell formerly stood. A bullet hole at the foot of the stairs shows where he shot Deputy Bell during his famous escape. You can stand at the window through which he then shot Marshal Olinger. Stones in the garden mark where the two men died. That the courthouse is now so old and musty only adds to the atmosphere of it all.

3

INFORMATION	LINCOLN

Anderson-Freeman Visitors Center ☎ 575 653 4372, ⌨ nmhistoricsites.org. Not all sites remain open through the winter.

ACCOMMODATION AND EATING

★**Ellis Store Country Inn** mile-marker 98, US-380 ☎ 800 653 6460, ⌨ ellisstore.com. Glorious old adobe farmhouse that's now a B&B, with luxurious en-suite rooms in the Main House plus cheaper but still very comfortable shared-bath rooms in the restored Mill House across the yard. A very fancy six-course dinner, costing $79, is available nightly except Sun. Mill House **$89**, Main House **$109**

Wortley Hotel US-380 ☎ 575 653 4300, ⌨ wortleyhotel.com. Once owned by Pat Garrett, this old-style roadside hotel, across from the courthouse and open in summer only (mid-May to mid-Oct), offers seven plain but appealing rooms, furnished with functional Victorian antiques and comfortable new beds. Its dining room serves breakfast and lunch Thurs–Sun only; the simple stews and sandwiches include the pot roast and mashed potatoes that constituted Marshal Bob Olinger's final meal. **$110**

Ruidoso

For visitors from the flatlands of west Texas and Oklahoma – not to mention nearby valley towns like Alamogordo – the hilltop community of **RUIDOSO**, nestling almost 7000 feet up in the forested Sacramento Mountains thirty miles southwest of Lincoln, offers an enticing retreat from the heat of summer. As a result, motels and mountain lodges line several miles of the Ruidoso ("Noisy") River. Tourists from further afield may feel it lacks interest, though it makes a reasonable overnight stop en route to Carlsbad.

In winter, attention turns to the 12,000ft slopes of **Ski Apache**, a downhill ski area 15 miles northwest of town (lift tickets $68; ☎ 575 464 3600, ⌨ skiapache.com). Though operated by the Mescalero Apache, it's not on tribal land.

Hubbard Museum of the American West

26301 US-70 • Mon & Thurs–Sun 9am–5pm • $7 • ☎ 575 378 4142, ⌨ hubbardmuseum.org

Outside the **Hubbard Museum of the American West**, alongside the Ruidoso Downs racetrack, stand eight sculpted galloping horses. Once within, though, the focus has shifted away from the original emphasis on matters equine, so you'll find displays on all aspects of Western history. Unexpectedly, it's the very local stuff that's the most interesting – prepare to be riveted by the photos of pretty much everyone who's ever lived in Ruidoso.

ALL-AMERICAN FUTURITY

Ruidoso's major claim to fame is the **All-American Futurity**, which was, until the 1980s, the world's richest **horse race** of any kind. With prize money totalling over $3 million, it remains the highest-paying event for quarter horses (so called because they excel at quarter-mile races.) The race takes place each Labor Day at the **Ruidoso Downs** racetrack, just east of town, as the climax of a 77-day season that runs from late May to early Sept (ⓦraceruidoso.com).

INFORMATION   RUIDOSO

Visitor centre 720 Sudderth Ave (Mon–Fri 8am–5pm, Sat 9am–3pm; ☏ 575 257 7395, ⓦ ruidosonow.com).

ACCOMMODATION AND EATING

Cornerstone Bakery & Cafe 359 Sudderth Drive ☏ 575 257 1842, ⓦ cornerstonebakerycafe.com. In addition to its coffee, bread and pastries, this friendly little café, open for breakfast and lunch only, serves good cooked breakfasts, including $7.50 *huevos rancheros*, and a great $5 green-chile stew. Daily 7am–2pm.

Grill Caliente 2800 Sudderth Drive ☏ 575 630 0224, ⓦ grillcaliente.com. As the name suggests, the speciality here is spicy New Mexican cuisine: $10–12 burgers smothered in chipotle or green-chile sauce, as well as $4–7 tacos, fiery pork chops for $24 and steaks at $26–30. Tues–Sat 11am–2pm & 5–9pm.

Inn of the Mountain Gods 297 Carrizo Canyon Rd ☏ 575 464 7059 or ☏ 800 545 9011, ⓦ innofthemountaingods .com. Glitzy resort, 3 miles southwest of central Ruidoso, which, like the ski resort, is owned by the Mescalero Apache, and holds a lucrative casino as well as luxury accommodation and restaurants to suit all budgets. $110

Shadow Mountain Lodge 107 Main St ☏ 575 257 4886, ⓦ smlruidoso.com. Central but exceptionally peaceful property, where the main wooden lodge holds 19 very comfortable rooms encircled by a wraparound veranda, and there are also four individual cabins with whirlpool baths and private decks. Doubles $129, cabins $159

Mescalero Apache Indian Reservation

Immediately south of Ruidoso, US-70 runs for around fifteen miles through the highlands of the **Mescalero Apache Indian Reservation**. The Mescalero trace their history as a distinct Apache group back to the early eighteenth century, when they were driven from the plains by the Comanche and turned to a lifestyle split between farming and raiding Pueblo and Hispanic settlements. In 1862 Kit Carson rounded up five hundred Apache to be confined with the Navajo at Bosque Redondo (see p.179). The Apache were eventually granted this small reservation in 1873, which was too high to grow or gather many traditional foods. The Mescalero were later joined by other Apache refugees, such as those remnants of Geronimo's Chiricahua who chose to return to the Southwest in 1913 from their enforced exile in Oklahoma.

Thanks to their successful investments in Ski Apache and the *Inn of the Mountain Gods*, the Mescalero's tribal economy has greatly strengthened in recent years. Tourists don't see much from the highway, and most roads leading off it are barred to outsiders. It's well worth driving through the open-range country between Ruidoso and Cloudcroft, however, where wildflowers dot the quasi-alpine meadows and Apache cowboys gallop in pursuit of their errant cattle.

Cloudcroft

Much smaller and cosier than Ruidoso, the picturesque mountain village of **CLOUDCROFT** – forty miles south, and almost two thousand feet higher – has been a vacation resort from the word go. It was built in 1898, after a railroad spur was pushed up into the Sacramento Mountains to carry timber down to El Paso, and immediately attracted day-trippers escaping the sweltering valley below. The railroad is long gone, but drivers still twist their way up US-82 from Alamogordo, leaving behind the bare sandstone hills, scattered with creosote bushes, as they penetrate the forested uplands. Once here, they find a pretty little Western community where the souvenir stores and cafés that line the boardwalk of **Burro Avenue**, one block north of the highway, get a bit more kitschy each year.

Hiking makes an enjoyable alternative to shopping. Cloudcroft stands at the heart of the southern segment of the Lincoln National Forest, which has several maintained and waymarked trails. Starting near the west end of town, the **Cloud Climbing Rail Trail** follows the old railroad route for a mile down to a vast ruined trestle that drivers on US-82 may have already noticed. Spectacular views extend right across the valley; it's usually possible to glimpse the White Sands (see p.186), as a thin white line at the foot of the San Andres Mountains on the far side.

ACCOMMODATION AND EATING CLOUDCROFT

Cloudcroft Hotel 306 Burro Ave ☎ 575 682 3414, ⓦ cloudcrofthotel.com. Renovated old hotel in the heart of town, with comfortable, antique-furnished rooms of widely varying sizes – some have kitchenettes – and balconies overlooking the main strip. $99

Cloudcroft Mountain Park Hostel 1049 US-82 ☎ 575 682 0555, ⓦ cloudcrofthostel.com. Located beside the highway six miles west of town, on the way down towards Alamogordo, this bright blue double-decker hostel is a smart motel-style affair that offers two dorms, two private shared-bath doubles, and one large family room that sleeps four. Cash only. Dorms $19, doubles $35, family room $60

The Lodge at Cloudcroft 601 Corona Place ☎ 800 395 6343, ⓦ thelodgeresort.com. Up in the woods, half a mile's climb south from the highway, the *Lodge* is a prestigious historic hotel. There are well-priced B&B rooms but also some absurdly plush suites and private cottages, plus the only fine-dining option in Cloudcroft, *Rebecca's* continental restaurant, which is open for all meals, with dinner mains at $26–38, along with and panoramic views. It even has its own golf course, at an elevation of 9000ft. $141

Alamogordo

Sprawled at the foot of the Sacramento Mountains seventy miles northeast of Las Cruces, **ALAMOGORDO** is, like Los Alamos, a child of the bomb. Once a quiet ranching centre, it has grown since World War II to a town of well over thirty thousand inhabitants, most of whom owe their living to the military bases and research facilities tucked away in the surrounding deserts. It's conservative enough to have held public burnings of the Harry Potter books in 2002.

Alamogordo's original central streets remain surprisingly unchanged, but they're a neglected backwater compared to the busy commercial activity along the five-mile strip of US-54, here known as **White Sands Boulevard**. Given pride of place at the **Alamogordo Museum of History**, 1301 N White Sands Blvd (Mon–Sat 10am–4pm; free) is an electric toaster salvaged from a defunct local cafe, which bears witness to quite how little ever happens around these parts.

New Mexico Museum of Space History

3198 Hwy-2001 • Daily 9am–5pm • Museum $6, movie theatre/planetarium $6; combined admission $10 • ☎ 575 437 2840, ⓦ nmspacemuseum.org

Any five-storey building in Alamogordo would probably count as a tourist attraction; that the gleaming glass cube on the hillside east of town holds the **New Mexico Museum of Space History** is gilding the lily. Displays inside trace the history of rocketry from eleventh-century China onwards, covering New Mexico-based pioneers Robert Goddard and Wernher von Braun all the way to the craft expected to offer the first commercial space flights. A diorama depicts the unfortunate Ham, the first chimp in space, who was trained at Alamogordo in 1961 by receiving electric shocks or banana-flavoured pellets according to which lever he moved. The adjoining giant-screen movie theatre doubles as a **planetarium**; there's also a "garden" of abandoned rockets outside.

INFORMATION ALAMOGORDO

Visitor centre Alongside Alamogordo Museum of History, at 1301 N White Sands Blvd (Mon–Fri 8am–5pm, Sat 9am–4pm, Sun 10am–3pm; ☎ 575 437 6120, ⓦ alamogordo.com).

ACCOMMODATION AND EATING

Magnuson Hotel & Suites 1021 S White Sands Blvd ☎ 575 437 2110, ⓦ magnusonhotels.com. Renovated veteran motel, previously known as the *Best Western Desert Aire*, and offering kitchenette suites as well as standard rooms, plus a sauna, hot tub and outdoor pool. **$89**

Memories 1223 N New York Ave ☎ 575 437 0077, ⓦ memories-restaurant.com. "Continental" restaurant set in a very floral old house in Alamogordo's sleepy downtown – quite a contrast to the highway – where mains such as steaks, salmon, or swordfish cost from around $20 including soup or salad. Mon–Sat 11am–9pm.

White Sands Motel 1101 S White Sands Blvd ☎ 575 437 2922 or ☎ 877 437 2922, ⓦ whitesandsmotel.biz. This old-fashioned roadside motel looks unremarkable from the outside, but it's well managed and cared for, while the accommodation itself is clean and spruce, and there are some great-value extra-large family rooms. Standard doubles **$70**, family rooms **$90**

White Sands National Monument

US-70, 14 miles west of Alamogordo • Visitor centre Daily: mid-May to mid-Sept 8am–7pm; mid-March to mid-May & mid-Sept to Oct 9am–6pm; Nov to mid-March 9am–5pm • ☎ 575 479 6124, ⓦ nps.gov/whsa

The glistening, towering dunes of **White Sands** fill 275 square miles of the broad Tularosa Basin, between the Sacramento and San Andres mountains. Though their whiteness is beyond dispute, they're not sand but fine **gypsum**, deposited on an ancient sea bed 250 million years ago. Anywhere else, the gypsum would have dissolved and been carried off by rivers; here, however, it's trapped in a riverless ring of mountains. The southern portion of this surreal landscape, immediately north of US-70 fourteen miles west of Alamogordo, has been set aside as **WHITE SANDS NATIONAL MONUMENT**. Be warned that roughly twice each week, US-70 **closes** for up to two hours while missile tests are under way.

Beside the highway, the **visitor centre** illustrates the unique life forms that populate this pallid environment. Access this far is free; you only pay the admission fee if you continue along the Dunes Drive into the park itself. While there's no developed **campground** at White Sands, backcountry camping is allowed, by permit only ($3 per person per night).

Once a month in winter, rangers lead vehicle convoys up to Lake Lucero, the actual source of the sands, for a guided 1hr 30min hike (Nov–April; $8).

Dunes Drive

Hwy-7/Carlsbad Cavern Hwy • Daily: summer 7am–9pm; winter 7am–sunset • $5 per person, under-16s free

The **Dunes Drive** heads into the heart of the dunes from the visitor centre. During its initial five miles, as you get your first glimpses of white sand beneath the scrubby

---

TRINITY SITE

Twice each year, sightseers make a peculiar pilgrimage to the **Trinity Site**, out on the **White Sands Missile Range** in the desert thirty miles west of Carrizozo (see p.180), where the first **atomic bomb** was detonated at 5.30am on July 16, 1945. Brought by road from Los Alamos in the back of a '42 Plymouth, the bomb, code-named **Fat Man**, was not dropped but placed atop a steel tower. As well as destroying a nearby "doom town" built to study its effects, the blast was strong enough to shatter windows in Silver City, 120 miles west, and to fuse the sands below "Ground Zero" into a thick slab of radioactive green glass known as **trinitite**. The eight-feet-deep crater it created was subsequently filled in to minimize radiation.

The Missile Range has witnessed thousands more weapons tests since then, and remains off-limits to non-military personnel except for the first Saturdays of April and October. Visitors on those days can either join a "caravan" that sets off from **Alamogordo** at 8am, or enter the range unaccompanied via the **Stallion Gate** (8am–2pm), on US-380 fifty miles west of Carrizozo. You're forbidden to stop or take photos other than at the site itself, or to make political speeches, and urged not to pick up any trinitite you may spot. Not only is it part of a National Historic Landmark, it's radioactive.

For more information on tours, and on the range itself, access ⓦ www.wsmr.army.mil – where the authorities helpfully explain "In the end, if it's a missile, we fire it" – or drop in at the White Sands Missile Range Museum (see p.187).

vegetation, you may wonder what the fuss is about. Unless you have either an abundance of time or walking difficulties, skip the unenthralling nature trail along the **Interdune Boardwalk**.

A little further along, the plants thin out, and you come to a bizarre world of dazzling white knife-edge ridges and graceful slopes. The drive now loops around a six-mile one-way labyrinth, where the roadway is at times hundreds of yards wide, and then narrows again to a slender channel, as the west winds that constantly replenish the dunes pile sand in your path in luxuriant drifts. Plentiful pull-outs, some equipped with fabulous 1950s-style curving picnic shelters, enable you to leave your vehicle and plough through pristine sand to the top of the ridges, which offer long-range mountain views. Slipping and sliding back down again is even better, and the visitor centre sells plastic disks that function as sledges.

Hiking off into the wilderness is all but irresistible. Although several trails are officially designated, however, they're not in fact marked or visible in the ever-shifting dunes. Be very careful not to lose your way, and above all take lots of **water**. One gallon per person is recommended. In a much publicized 2015 tragedy, a French couple who set off at noon on a summer's day along the Alkali Flats Trail, carrying a litre of water between them, died within a couple of hours; only their nine-year-old son survived.

White Sands Missile Range Museum

Hwy-213, 4 miles south of US-70 and 26 miles east of Las Cruces • Mon–Fri 8am–4pm, Sat 10am–3pm • Free • ☎ 575 678 8800, Ⓦ wsmr-history.org

A couple of miles north of the boundary of White Sands National Monument, on the top-security White Sands Missile Range – the largest military installation in the US – the **White Sands Space Harbor** held one of the three seven-mile runways where the **Space Shuttle** was able to land. While it was used extensively for training, it only welcomed one actual landing, in 1982.

For the full story, head for the **White Sands Missile Range Museum**, thirty miles southwest of the monument en route to Las Cruces. The open-air **Missile Park** alongside displays all the missiles ever tested at White Sands. These date back to "Vengeance Weapon 2", the **V2** rocket, almost four thousand of which were fired across the English Channel by the Nazis during World War II. After the war, the weapon's designer, Dr Wernher von Braun, directed the firing of sixty more V2s at White Sands – one went astray and crashed across the border near Ciudad Juarez, Mexico. He moved on to Huntsville, Alabama, in 1950.

Southeast New Mexico

East of the mountains, at the edge of the Great Plains, **southeast New Mexico** has little in common with the rest of the Southwest. It's not quite as dull as it looks, however; all its treasures are tucked away underground, from its oil and mineral wealth to the fairy-tale labyrinth of **Carlsbad Caverns National Park**. Traditionally, Carlsbad was the only reason tourists ever strayed this way, but these days a steady influx of pilgrims come to contemplate the extraterrestrial wonders of **Roswell**.

Roswell

The small ranching town of **ROSWELL**, 57 miles east of Lincoln and 75 miles north of the national park at Carlsbad, is renowned as the spot near which an **alien spacecraft** supposedly crash-landed on the night of July 4, 1947. The commander of the local air force base authorized a press statement announcing that the wreckage of a flying saucer had been retrieved and taken away for examination. Despite a follow-up denial within a day, claiming that it was in fact a weather balloon, the story of the so-called "**Roswell Incident**" has kept running. In 1997, as one hundred thousand *X-Files* fanatics gathered to mark its fiftieth anniversary, the US Air Force revealed that the errant balloon had been monitoring the atmosphere for evidence of Soviet nuclear tests. Witnesses were also said to have confused the balloon crash with parachute experiments in 1953, which involved dropping dummies from high-altitude planes.

Incidentally, considerable vagueness surrounds exactly where the crash took place. Since a local entrepreneur bought up one purported site, the original witnesses have started to "remember" that it all happened somewhere else entirely. With TV series such as *Roswell* and *Taken* having perpetuated the myth, Roswell's curious tourist boom shows no signs of abating.

International UFO Museum

114 N Main St • Daily 9am–5pm • $5 • ☎ 575 625 9495, ⓦ roswellufomuseum.com

Despite its best intentions, and the wishful thinking of the truly weird clientele who drift in from the plains, the **International UFO Museum** can't help but expose the tawdry tale of the Roswell Incident as transparent nonsense. Set up by the military press officer responsible for the 1947 announcement, it reveals such gems as that John F. Kennedy was shot because he was about to reveal the secret, and that Neil Armstrong, astonished at encountering flying saucers on the moon, blurted out "Boy, were they beige!" (You'd have to assume that "big" was the word he was fumbling for.) Murals depict "what might have happened", while the showpiece exhibit is a model of a so-called "**alien autopsy**". Note the "fiction" and "non-fiction" sections in the bookstore.

Roswell Museum

100 W 11th St • Tues–Sat 9am–5pm, Sun 1–5pm • Free • ☎ 575 624 6744, ⓦ roswellmuseum.org

The **Roswell Museum** boasts an excellent, multifaceted collection with nary an alien corpse to be seen. Its most sensational section celebrates pioneer rocket scientist **Robert Goddard** (1882–1945), one of whose early experiments prompted the newspaper headline "*Moon Rocket" Man's Test Alarms Whole Countryside*. His laboratory has been reconstructed, and entertaining footage shows him wheeling a rudimentary rocket in a wagon to the launch pad, then racing to escape the blast in a Model T Ford.

There's also a huge, top-quality **art gallery**, displaying Southwestern landscapes by Henriette Wyeth and Peter Hurd as well as a solitary Georgia O'Keeffe, *Ram's Skull With Brown Leaves*.

Carlsbad

Considering that a million tourists per year pass through **CARLSBAD** en route to Carlsbad Caverns National Park – covered below – the town itself is astonishing in its blandness. A century of ranching and potash-mining has given it a sizeable if characterless downtown area, which holds nothing whatsoever to see.

Quite the reverse, in fact – Carlsbad possesses the dubious distinction of being home to the totally invisible **Waste Isolation Pilot Plant** (ⓦ wipp.energy.gov). Hollowed from a thick layer of salt two thousand feet below ground level, this subterranean facility is the world's first repository for radioactive waste created during the production of nuclear weapons. A steady catalogue of reported leaks and alarms have ensured that its presence remains deeply controversial.

CLOCKWISE FROM TOP SILVER CITY (P.198); INDIAN PUEBLO CULTURAL CENTER, ALBUQUERQUE (P.173); INTERNATIONAL UFO MUSEUM AND RESEARCH CENTER, ROSWELL (P.188) >

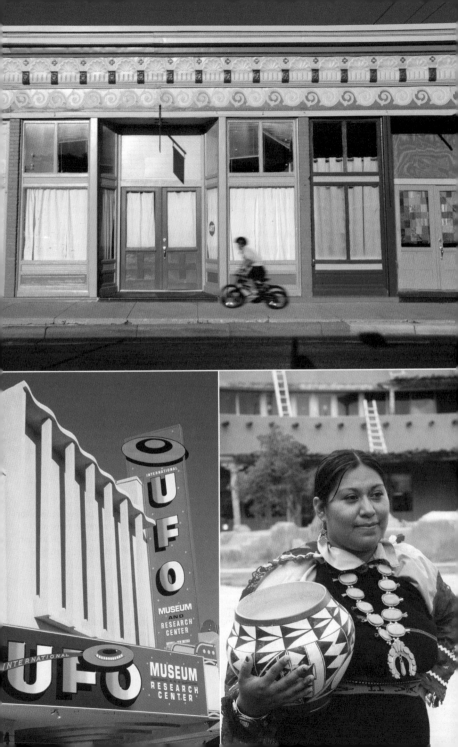

Living Desert Zoo and Gardens State Park

1504 Miehls Drive N • Daily: late May to early Sept 8am–5pm; early Sept to late May 9am–5pm; last admission 3.30pm • $5 • ☎ 575 887 5516, Ⓦ emnrd.state.nm.us

Carlsbad's one significant attraction is the **Living Desert Zoo and Gardens State Park**, a couple of miles northwest of town. This botanical garden of desert plants doubles as a zoo that houses elk, rattlesnakes, a prairie dog village and even "Maggie the Painting Bear", an adept, if so far strictly non-representational, watercolourist who only works on her ever-expanding oeuvre behind closed doors (but whose authorship nonetheless remains undisputed).

Carlsbad Caverns National Park

20 miles southwest of Carlsbad on US 62/180, then 7 miles west from White's City on Hwy-7 • $10 for 3 days, under-16s free; national park pass covers up to four adults; optional tours extra • ☎ 575 785 2232 (Mon–Fri only), tour reservations ☎ 877 444 6777, Ⓦ nps.gov/cave, tour reservations Ⓦ recreation.gov

CARLSBAD CAVERNS NATIONAL PARK consists of a tract of the Guadalupe Mountains that's so riddled with underground caves and tunnels as to be virtually hollow. Tamed in classic park-service style with concrete trails and electric lighting, this subterranean wonderland is now a walk-in gallery, where tourists come to marvel at its intricate limestone tracery. Before you decide to join them, be sure to grasp that the park is a *long* way from anywhere else – three hundred miles southeast of Albuquerque and 150 miles northeast of El Paso, Texas.

The Guadalupe Mountains are the remnants of the **Capitan Reef**, a 400-mile-long horseshoe-shaped reef that formed beneath a primeval ocean. Made up of algae and sponges rather than coral, it was thrust above the plains a mere three million years ago. Surface moisture has trickled through the resultant cracks ever since, gnawing at the rock within.

Almost all park visitors confine their attention to the main cave, **Carlsbad Cavern** itself, where the summer crowds can be intense. Strangely, though, that's part of the fun – coming to Carlsbad feels like a real throwback to the 1950s boom in mass tourism. If you're not convinced, wait until you see the gloriously kitsch **Underground Lunchroom**.

There's no **camping** at the national park; the nearest campgrounds and motels are at White's City and Carlsbad.

Visitor centre

Hwy-7/Carlsbad Cavern Hwy • Daily: late May to early Sept 8am–7pm; early Sept to late May 8am–5pm

Atop the mountains, and commanding sweeping views east across the plains, the **visitor centre** for Carlsbad Caverns National Park stands at the end of the narrow, twisting seven-mile road up from White's City. Part of a complex that also includes a restaurant, a gift store, a crèche and even a kennel, it's a compulsory port of call, in order to pay entrance fees and discover the day's schedule of tours.

LECHUGUILLA CAVE

Revealed in 1986, after cavers cleared a thirty-foot plug of bat dung and rubble in a little-known area of Carlsbad Caverns National Park, the astonishing **Lechuguilla Cave** system is not only deeper than Carlsbad Cavern but, at 1600ft, has turned out to be the deepest limestone cave in the US. Over 136 miles of tunnels have been mapped so far, but they're so dangerous that Lechuguilla is off-limits to all but the experts. It's expected to remain a "wilderness cave" – even its location is kept secret – so the rest of us will have to content ourselves with the marvellous pictures of its delicate crystalline formations displayed in the visitor centre.

THE BATS OF CARLSBAD

The recesses of Carlsbad Caverns are the summer home of approaching a million Mexican (or Brazilian) free-tailed **bats**. Each evening from April to mid-October, having slept all day suspended from the ceiling of the imaginatively titled **Bat Cave** – to which there's no public access – they emerge in cloud-like spirals at dusk or a little later, then disperse across the desert in search of delectable insects. Visitors watch the spectacle from the amphitheatre seating that faces the cave mouth; rangers can tell you what time sunset is due.

It was the bats that first brought the caves to human attention, in the 1890s. Miners employed to dig bat dung or **guano** as fertilizer started to explore what lay beyond the cave mouth. As word of their discoveries spread, sightseers began to arrive. Early visitors were dropped down in buckets and guided through on ropes. The present trail system was constructed after the caverns became a national park in 1930.

Carlsbad Cavern

Natural Entrance Route Daily: last entry late May to early Sept 3.30pm, early Sept to late May 2pm • **Elevator** Daily: summer first down 8.30am, last up 6.30pm; winter first down 8.30am, last up 4.55pm

3

The centrepiece of Carlsbad Cavern, the **Big Room**, lies 750 vertical feet below the visitor centre – as it's inside the mountain, it's also 400ft horizontally from the open air in some places. Measuring up to 1800ft long and 250ft high, it's festooned with stalactites, stalagmites and countless unnameable shapes of swirling liquid rock. All are a uniform stone grey; the rare touches of colour are provided by slight red or brown mineral-rich tinges, improved here and there with gentle pastel lighting. Most visitors take an hour or so to complete the reasonably level trail around its perimeter. Whatever the weather up top – summer highs exceed 100°F (37°C) – the temperature down here is always a cool 56°F (13°F), so dress warmly.

Direct **elevators** drop to the Big Room from the visitor centre. They arrive alongside the **Underground Lunchroom**, a vast formation-free side cave paved over in the 1950s to create a diner-cum-souvenir-store that sells indigestible lunches in polystyrene containers, plus Eisenhower-era souvenirs such as giant pencils and Viewmaster reels. To modern eyes, this strange installation seems absurd, but moves by the park service to close it down have repeatedly been stymied by its place in popular affections. Indeed, it has since 2004 been illegal in New Mexico to spend any money that "permits or requires" the closure of the lunchroom.

To get a better sense of the depth of the cavern, eschew the elevator and **walk** down via the **Natural Entrance Route**. This steep paved footpath switchbacks into the guano-encrusted maw of the cave, a short way from the visitor centre. It takes fifteen minutes to reach the first formations and another fifteen to reach the Big Room itself. All visitors are obliged to take the elevator back out.

The walk-down trail used to meander through beautiful side caves such as the **King's Palace**, filled with translucent "draperies" of limestone. However, formations were broken at the rate of two thousand per year, so these have long been closed to casual visitors. They're now open on guided tours only, which start from the Big Room (2–4 tours daily; $8). Additional tours can take you along the **Left Hand Tunnel** route down from the visitor centre ($7), or on a much more demanding descent into either **Spider Cave** or the **Hall of the White Giant** (both $20; under-12s not permitted).

Slaughter Canyon Cave

25 miles southwest of park visitor centre • Guided tours only, early March to Oct; schedules posted at ⓦ nps.gov/cave • $15, minimum age of 8

Much less frequented, and much less developed, than the main Carlsbad Cavern complex, **Slaughter Canyon Cave** can only be explored on strenuous guided tours. If you're physically fit, and up for a demanding (and claustrophobic) wilderness adventure on which you'll see spectacular formations in a relatively pristine state, these are well worth the effort.

Lasting almost six hours, the tours leave from the park visitor centre. Participants pool cars and drive to a point half a mile below the cave entrance, to start the steep hike up. You're provided with a flashlight, but expected to bring batteries, and you're not allowed to walk with a stick within the cave itself.

White's City

Twenty miles southwest of Carlsbad at the turn-off for Carlsbad Caverns, **WHITE'S CITY** is not a town but a privately owned tourist complex (ⓦhotelscarlsbadcaverns.com). A notorious eyesore, it was built in 1926 by entrepreneur Charlie White, who cannily anticipated mass automobile tourism and bought land at this crucial road junction without ever having seen it. Although White's City provides the closest accommodation and camping to the national park, none is currently worth recommending.

INFORMATION   **SOUTHEAST NEW MEXICO**

ROSWELL
Visitor centre 912 N Main St (Mon–Fri 8.30am–5.30pm, Sat & Sun 10am–3pm; ☎575 624 6860, ⓦseeroswell.com).

CARLSBAD
Visitor centre 302 S Canal St (Mon–Fri 8am–5pm; ☎575 887 6516, ⓦcarlsbadchamber.com).

ACCOMMODATION AND EATING

ROSWELL
Cattle Baron 1113 N Main St ☎575 622 2465, ⓦcattlebaron.com. Large, good-value steakhouse, with traditional Wild West decor, big slabs of meat, including steaks at $21–29, and an extensive salad bar. Mon–Thurs 11am–9.30pm, Fri & Sat 11am–10pm, Sun 11am–9pm.
La Quinta Inn 200 E 19th St ☎575 622 8000 or ☎800 753 3757, ⓦlq.com. Very dependable motel, just off the main through highway north of the centre; clean and well managed, with an indoor pool. **$144**

CARLSBAD
Thank to a boom in the local oil industry, accommodation prices in Carlsbad are much higher than you might expect; anything under $200 per night hereabouts currently counts as a bargain. Travellers on a budget would do better to visit the national park on a day-trip from somewhere much further afield.
Best Western Stevens Inn 1829 S Canal St

☎575 887 2851, ⓦbestwesternnewmexico.com. Large, old-fashioned roadside motel, a mile south of the centre, that's had a thorough makeover. The rooms are generally big but otherwise unremarkable, and there's an outdoor pool. Rates include a breakfast buffet at the on-site, similarly unremarkable *Flume Room* restaurant, open for all meals daily. **$152**
Blue House Bakery 609 N Canyon St ☎575 628 0555. Set on a sleepy residential road slightly northeast of downtown Carlsbad, this popular cottage café/bakery serves early-morning coffee and pastries, then salads and sandwiches if you're up for an early lunch. Mon–Sat 6am–noon.
★**Trinity Hotel** 201 S Canal St ☎575 234 9891, ⓦthetrinityhotel.com. An unexpected find for this part of New Mexico, this former bank in downtown Carlsbad has been beautifully converted into a nine-suite boutique hotel. Most rooms have walk-in showers, and there's also an excellent restaurant, open for all meals but, unlike the hotel itself, closed on Sundays. **$189**

The Rio Grande Valley

The 260-mile route between Albuquerque and the Mexican border at El Paso, Texas, follows one of America's oldest and most romantic trails. For 250 years, the **Camino Real** or "Royal Road" beside the Rio Grande offered New Mexico's Hispanic colonists their one tenuous link with the outside world. However, travellers on the Camino Real were so prone to Apache attack if they followed the curve of the Rio Grande between **Socorro** and **Las Cruces** that they preferred to leave the river and take a hundred-mile shortcut through the trackless desert that lies behind the mountains to the east. This route too had its perils – not least a complete lack of water – and became known as the **Jornada del Muerto** after Juan de Oñate's chaplain Fray Cristóbal de Salazar died here in the early 1600s. To this day there's no north–south road through the desert.

Never more than a rough wagon trail, the Camino Real has long since been superseded by I-25, a monotonous four-hour drive relieved only by distant views of the mountains. You don't even see much of the river itself, except where it's been dammed to form incongruous turquoise lakes. Of the old way stations en route, only **Socorro** in the north, the resort town of **Truth or Consequences** and **Mesilla** in the south are particularly worth visiting.

Socorro

Historic **SOCORRO**, eighty miles south of Albuquerque, received its unusual name – "help", in Spanish – from Don Juan de Oñate in 1598, after local Pueblo peoples fed his expeditionary party from their reserves of corn. The first Hispanic settlement was destroyed during the Pueblo Revolt of 1680, whereafter the site was abandoned for over a century. The picturesque **plaza** at its core, a block west of the main road, California Street, and the spruced-up adobe church of **San Miguel**, a couple of blocks north (daily 6am–6pm; free), were rebuilt during the 1820s. Sixty years later, triggered by the arrival of the railroads and the discovery of extensive **silver** deposits nearby, Socorro briefly became New Mexico's largest town. When the silver ran out, so too did most of the population, leaving behind some fine Victorian architecture.

Very Large Array (VLA)

US-60, 50 miles west of Socorro • Daily 8.30am–sunset; guided tours first Sat of month, 11am, 1am & 3pm • Free • ☎ 575 835 7410, ⓦ www.vla.nrao.edu

A must-see for astronomy enthusiasts and fans of the unusual, the aptly named **Very Large Array**, or VLA, spreads across the Plains of San Agustin fifty lonely miles west of Socorro. One of the world's most powerful observatories, it comprises 27 separate moveable radio dishes, each 25 metres across, which can be arranged in permutations that vary from a dense cluster to a twenty-mile line. Its visitor centre, clearly signed on Hwy-52 just south of US-60, holds assorted displays, but is usually not staffed. Instead, visitors simply follow a well-marked walking route that takes them closer, but not right up to, those dishes currently stationed nearby.

While the VLA makes a photogenic spectacle, reaching it requires a long detour from the interstate. Neither **Magdalena**, twenty miles east of the array, nor **Datil**, fifteen miles west, hold much for visitors apart from a basic diner or two, so the trek is probably only worth it if you're en route to or from Arizona.

Bosque del Apache Wildlife Refuge

8 miles south of San Antonio on NM-1 • **Refuge** Daily from 1hr before sunrise to 1hr after sunset • **Visitor centre** Late May to early Sept Mon–Fri 7.30am–4pm, Sat & Sun 8am–4.30pm; early Sept to late May daily 8am–4pm • $5 per vehicle • ☎ 575 835 1828, ⓦ fws.gov or ⓦ friendsofthebosque.org

Hispanic colonists heading south from Socorro along the Camino Real, beside the Rio Grande, would avoid the encampments at Bosque del Apache (forest of the Apache) by crossing the river twenty miles south of Socorro, and heading towards the Jornada del Muerto trail. This point off Hwy-1 is now the **Bosque del Apache Wildlife Refuge**, the Southwest's most spectacular **birdwatching** site. As many as twenty thousand sandhill cranes and almost fifty thousand snow geese migrate here in early December for the winter; and even in summer its riverine marshes and forests are bursting with birds and mammals. A twelve-mile, one-way road loops around the entire refuge, but to make the most of a visit you need to hike its trails, which range from one to four miles in length. Allow at least two hours in total.

THE FINAL FRONTIER

Appropriately enough, given its long-standing association with cutting-edge technology, frontier adventurism and strange alien spacecraft, New Mexico is due to host the world's first **commercial space flights**. The state government and Virgin Galactic have built **Spaceport America** (W spaceportamerica.com) in the empty desert of the Jornada del Muerto, 45 miles northeast of Las Cruces and 25 miles southeast of Truth or Consequences.

The craft to be used, SpaceShipTwo, is an updated version of the prototype that in 2004 became the first space vehicle to fly to an altitude of over 100km twice within two weeks, thereby claiming the $10 million Ansari X-Prize. Carried aloft by the WhiteKnightTwo launch plane, the ship is released and then fires its own rocket engines to reach suborbital space. Amazingly, it uses a combination of nitrous oxide – laughing gas – and solid rubber as fuel.

The projected date for flights to begin has been repeatedly postponed, most recently in the wake of a fatal crash of the VSS *Enterprise*, in 2014. Ultimately, however, Virgin Galactic hopes to operate a fleet of five spacecraft from New Mexico, each capable of carrying eight astronauts, and to offer its space voyagers a "five-star destination experience" on the ground as well. The actual flight will last around three hours, culminating in perhaps three minutes of weightlessness; it won't go into Earth orbit. Reservations for US$250,000 tickets can already be made via W virgingalactic.com.

On a more mundane but more affordable level, it's possible to join a half-day **tour** of Spaceport America itself, to learn all about what lies ahead. Reserve at least 24 hours in advance, online or via the visitor centre in Truth or Consequences from which the tours set off (see p.196; tours Mon & Thurs–Sun 9am, plus afternoon tours May–Sept Fri–Sun 1.30pm; $50; ☎ 844 727 7223, W spaceportamerica.com).

El Camino Real International Heritage Center

Exit 115 off I-25, 30 miles south of Socorro • Wed–Sun 8.30am–5pm • $5 • ☎ 575 854 3600, W elcaminoreal.org

The story of the Camino Real is recounted in lavish and fascinating detail at the impressive **El Camino Real International Heritage Center**, overlooking the Rio Grande thirty miles south of Socorro. The trail was the lifeblood of the Spanish colony of New Mexico, linking Santa Fe with Mexico City, 1500 miles south, and the exhibits stress ongoing cultural connections. Smaller-scale trails have been laid out nearby as short nature hikes.

Truth or Consequences

Until 1950, the small settlement seventy miles south of Socorro, where Apache warriors such as Geronimo once soaked away the worries of the warpath in natural thermal springs, was appropriately known as **Hot Springs**. Then the radio show *Truth or Consequences* promised that any community prepared to change its name would receive the meagre reward of hosting its tenth anniversary edition. Hot Springs prostituted itself for fifteen minutes of fame, and **TRUTH OR CONSEQUENCES** was saddled with the world's worst name – though locals habitually abbreviate it these days to "**T or C**". Its small downtown now consists of just a couple of blocks, sandwiched between two busy one-way streets, Broadway and Main Street.

Partly as a consequence of dam construction higher up the Rio Grande, T or C no longer holds any natural, free-flowing hot springs. There's still plenty of thermal activity hereabouts, though, which local hotels and resorts have tapped to create spas, hot tubs and other facilities. **Riverbend Hot Springs** (see p.196) has an especially delightful array of baths and pools, set into the riverbank and open to day visitors.

Geronimo Springs Museum

211 Main St • Mon–Sat 9am–5pm, Sun noon–5pm • $6 • ☎ 575 894 6600, W geronimospringsmuseum.com

Native American memorabilia, including Mimbres pottery (see p.200), forms a prominent part of the historical collection at the **Geronimo Springs Museum**. You can also learn fascinating snippets about **Ralph Edwards**, the presenter of the long-defunct

Truth or Consequences show, who managed to return each year for the first fifty times the **Truth or Consequences Fiesta** was celebrated, on the first weekend in May. He died aged 92 in 2005.

Hillsboro

Hwy-152 branches west from I-25 fifteen miles south of T or C, crossing the Mimbres Mountain en route to **Silver City** (see p.198). **HILLSBORO**, less than twenty miles off the interstate in the fertile foothills, is a former gold-mining settlement that has since turned its hand to apple growing instead, as celebrated in an annual **Apple Festival** held on Labor Day weekend in September. Now it is no more than a village, with a smattering of arts-and-crafts galleries.

Hatch

Forty miles south of T or C, along I-25 en route to Las Cruces, tiny **HATCH** is noteworthy only as the home of New Mexico's leading **chile farms**. All year, roadside stalls sell fresh peppers and the dried garlands known as *ristras*, while Labor Day weekend in September sees a **Chile Festival** (☎575 267 1095, ⓦhatchchilefest.com) with fiercely competitive chile cook-offs.

3

Fort Selden Historic Site

15 miles north of Las Cruces • Mon & Wed–Sun 8.30am–5pm • $3 • ☎575 526 8911, ⓦ nmhistoricalsites.org
Fort Selden Historic Site, on the east bank of the Rio Grande just south of **RADIUM SPRINGS**, preserves the ruined adobe walls of a US Army fort built to protect Las Cruces in 1865. Its small museum focuses largely on the black troops stationed here just after the Civil War, who became known as Buffalo Soldiers, and are commemorated by a bronze statue outside. The fort was decommissioned in 1891, so it basically consists of rounded stumps surrounding its former parade ground, but it comes alive on summer weekends during regular re-enactments.

Las Cruces

Named after the crosses that marked the graves of early travellers killed by the Apache, **LAS CRUCES** is now a major crossroads, where the east–west I-10 meets the north–south I-25. Once a riverside farming community, it has grown beyond recognition, though the boom in industrial and military employment has been at the expense of any scenic beauty it may once have possessed. As New Mexico's second-largest city, Las Cruces boasts a wide array of shops and services, but these days they're all housed in the malls that line I-25 to the east, leaving downtown a rather featureless sprawl.

New Mexico Farm and Ranch Heritage Museum

4100 Dripping Springs Rd, 2 miles east of I-25 exit 1 • Mon–Sat 9am–5pm, Sun noon–5pm • $5 • ☎575 522 4100,
ⓦ nmfarmandranchmuseum.org
Las Cruces' most interesting visitor attraction harks back to the city's agricultural roots. Part museum, and part working ranch, the **New Mexico Farm and Ranch Heritage Museum** is home to substantial herds of cattle, goats, sheep and horses, and puts on daily demonstrations of traditional skills.

Mesilla

The little-changed Hispanic village of **MESILLA** stands just south of I-10, an easy two-mile drive down Avenida de Mesilla from downtown Las Cruces. When New

Mexico passed into American hands in 1846, the Mesilla Valley still belonged to Mexico; Mesilla itself was founded in 1850 by New Mexicans who preferred to remain Mexican. Under the **Gadsden Purchase**, however, signed here in 1853, it passed to the US and soon became one of the Southwest's largest towns, with over eight thousand inhabitants. During the Civil War, Mesilla even served briefly as the Confederate capital of the territory of Arizona, but it went into swift decline when the railroad bypassed it in favour of Las Cruces in 1881.

Mesilla's Old West **plaza** has a real frontier feel, though most of the old adobes that surround it – including the former courthouse where **Billy the Kid** was tried and sentenced to death in 1881 – now house art galleries and souvenir shops.

Organ Mountains-Desert Peaks National Monument

Dripping Springs Visitor Center ☎ 575 522 1219, monument HQ ☎ 575 525 4300, ⓦ blm.gov/nm/omdp

Three distinct and entirely separate wilderness areas close to Las Cruces were jointly designated as **Organ Mountains-Desert Peaks National Monument** in 2014. Run by the Bureau of Land Management rather than the park service, the monument is primarily intended to protect the region from exploitation. Its **Desert Peaks** component, comprising the Robledo and Dona Aña mountains northwest of the city, and the even more remote Potrillo mountains to the southwest, remain largely inaccessible to visitors.

The **Organ Mountains**, on the other hand, which rise roughly five miles east of Las Cruces and run for around twenty miles south, parallel to the Rio Grande, already held some appealing hiking trails and recreation opportunities. For a wonderful **waterfall hike** that provides the best quick taste, park at the **Dripping Springs Visitor Center**, 10 miles east of I-25 exit 1, and follow the 3.5-mile round-trip loop along first the La Cueva Trail and then the Filmore Canyon Trail.

INFORMATION   **RIO GRANDE VALLEY**

SOCORRO
Visitor centre 217 Fisher Ave, a block west of the plaza (Mon–Fri 9am–5pm; ☎ 575 835 8927, ⓦ socorronm.org).

TRUTH OR CONSEQUENCES
Visitor centre 301 S Foch St (daily 8.30am–4.30pm; ☎ 575 894 1968, ⓦ geronimotrail.com). Supplies information on the Geronimo Trail National Scenic Byway, a driving route through the mountains to the west, and is the

base for tours to Spaceport America (see p.194).

LAS CRUCES
Visitor centre 211 N Water St (Mon–Fri 8am–5pm, Sat 8.30am–1pm; ☎ 575 541 2444, ⓦ lascrucescvb.org).

MESILLA
Visitor centre 2231 Avda de Mesilla (daily 9am–5pm; ☎ 575 524 3262, ⓦ oldmesilla.org).

ACCOMMODATION

SOCORRO
Holiday Inn Express 1040 N California St ☎ 575 838 4600, ⓦ ihg.com. Socorro holds pretty much all the national chains, but this well-run motel, just off I-25 exit 150, is the pick of the bunch, with large, comfortable rooms, and an indoor pool. $132

TRUTH OR CONSEQUENCES
Blackstone Hot Springs 410 Austin St ☎ 575 894 0894, ⓦ blackstonehotsprings.com. The seven spacious rooms in this downtown option are enjoyably themed in honour of 1950s TV shows, from *I Love Lucy* to *The Twilight Zone*. Each has its own spring-fed hot tub or shower, as well as a kitchenette, and some have patios. $75

★**Riverbend Hot Springs** 100 Austin St

☎ 575 894 7625, ⓦ nmhotsprings.com. As well as private and shared hot tubs, set into the banks of the Rio Grande, this lovely central lodge offers comfortable suites, plus RV parking, "budget doubles" that share bathrooms and can sleep up to four, and small, individually decorated "artist rooms". All guests must be aged 12 or over. RVs $50, Artist rooms $75, budget doubles $125, suites $160

Sierra Grande Lodge & Spa 501 McAdoo St ☎ 877 288 7637, ⓦ sierragrandelodge.com. Gorgeously restored 1920s lodge, now owned by Ted Turner, where each of the opulently furnished rooms and suites has its own private hot tub, and massages and spa treatments are available. $155

LAS CRUCES

★**Best Western Mission Inn** 1765 S Main St ☎575 524 8591 or ☎888 670 7234, ⓦbwmissioninn .com. The cream of Las Cruces' motels; it may not look all that special from the outside, but the large rooms are surprisingly attractive, featuring lovely Mexican tilework and murals. Rates include a full cooked breakfast, and there's a heated outdoor pool. The one drawback is its proximity to the railroad tracks. $85

Lundeen's Inn of the Arts 618 S Alameda Blvd ☎575 526 3326 or ☎888 526 3326, ⓦinnofthearts.com. Century-old B&B inn downtown, in which each of the twenty rooms is named for a regional artist, such as Maria Martínez or Georgia O'Keeffe, and furnished appropriately. The public spaces include two huge and impressive common rooms. $100

EATING AND DRINKING

SOCORRO

Socorro Springs Brewing Company 1012 N California St ☎575 838 0650, ⓦsocorrosprings.com. As well as a good range of beers, this conspicuous pub, run by a small-scale Colorado brewery, serves calzones and pizzas from its wood-fired oven, along with sandwiches, all priced around $8–12. Daily 11am–10pm.

TRUTH OR CONSEQUENCES

Latitude 33 304 S Pershing St ☎575 740 7804. Casual Asian-fusion bistro on a central side street, where the menu ranges from spicy peanut noodles to crispy orange chicken or pan-fried pork loin, with mains priced $10–16. Tues–Thurs 11am–2pm & 5–8pm, Fri & Sat 11am–8pm, Sun noon–7pm.

Passion Pie Cafe 406 Main St ☎575 894 0008, ⓦdeepwaterfarm.com. Friendly, hugely popular café in the heart of town, serving coffee, pastries and waffles plus lunchtime sandwiches and mixed Mediterranean-style plates with dishes like Greek *spanakopita* (filo-and-spinach parcels); everything costs under $10. Daily 7am–3pm.

HILLSBORO

Hillsboro General Store 100 Main St ☎575 895 5306, ⓦhillsborogeneralstore.com. The perfect pit stop as you pass through the village, this store has been in business since the nineteenth century, and now serves a tasty menu of home-made burgers and red- and green-chile enchiladas, at $5–7. Mon–Wed & Fri–Sun 8am–3pm.

HATCH

B&E Burritos 303 N Franklin St ☎575 267 5191. Absolute hole-in-the-wall place in New Mexico's chile capital that's renowned, not surprisingly, for its fiery Mexican cuisine ($6–10). Mon–Sat 8am–9pm.

LAS CRUCES

Nellie's Café 1226 W Hadley Ave ☎575 524 9982. The slogan – "Chiles with Attitude" – tells you what to expect: sublimely spicy Mexican food. All the classics are here, from *huevos rancheros* for breakfast to the burritos and green chile at lunchtime ($6–10). Tues–Sat 8am–2pm.

MESILLA

Double Eagle 308 Calle de Guadalupe ☎575 523 6700, ⓦdouble-eagle-mesilla.com. The smartest restaurant on the plaza, with indoor seating in a grand Victorian edifice, plus a courtyard. You can pay up to $47 for steaks, but most of the mains cost $24–30. Strictly speaking, at lunchtime, when it serves burgers, salads and Mexican dishes for $10–16, it goes by the name of *Peppers* – and to confuse things further, you can order from the *Peppers* menu in the evening as well. Mon–Sat 11am–10pm, Sun noon–9pm.

La Posta 2410 Calle de San Albino ☎575 524 3524, ⓦlaposta-de-mesilla.com. Mexican *cantina*, just off the plaza in a nineteenth-century adobe that was the former offices of the Butterfield Stage Coach. Expect your south-of-the-border specialities to cost $12–15, and arrive smothered in cheese and green chile. Mon–Thurs 11am–9pm, Fri 11am–9.30pm, Sat 8am–9.30pm, Sun 8am–9pm.

Southwest New Mexico

Most of New Mexico's sparsely populated **southwest corner** – also known as the "**Boot heel**" – consists of open rangeland. Interstate towns like **Deming** and **Lordsburg** are entirely forgettable, though a detour north into the mountains takes you to the historic mining town of **Silver City** and the ancient **Gila Cliff Dwellings**.

Deming

A bonanza of billboards sixty miles due west of Las Cruces announces your arrival at **DEMING**, a typical desert outpost scattered with motels and diners. Half-hearted attempts at agriculture have left their traces on the landscape, but the main sign of activity comes from the ever-present swirling dust devils (as the noncommittal highway signs would have it, "Dust Storms May Exist").

In Deming's biggest event of the year, late August's **Great American Duck Race** (ⓦdemingduckrace.com), live ducks waddle down a dry track and paddle down a wet one. If your duck wins – they're assigned by a lucky draw – you can win big money.

Deming Luna Mimbres Museum

301 S Silver Ave • Mon–Sat 9am–4pm • Free • ☎ 575 546 2382, ⓦ lunacountyhistoricalsociety.com

The highlight of Deming's downtown **Museum and Custom House** is an extensive collection of Mimbres pottery (see p.200), donated by local residents. The complex also includes the Harvey House restaurant that formed part of the town's old railroad station, and its original one-room "custom house".

INFORMATION	DEMING

Visitor centre 800 E Pine St (Mon–Fri 9am–5pm, Sat 9am–noon; ☎ 575 567 1962, ⓦ demingvisitorcenter.webs.com).

ACCOMMODATION AND EATING

★**Adobe Deli** 3970 Lewis Flats Rd SE ☎ 575 546 0361, ⓦ adobedeli.com. You won't regret it if you give downtown Deming's humdrum diners a miss, and drive a dozen miles east to hunt out this ramshackle old barn of a place, filled with stuffed animals and Western memorabilia. Huge lunchtime sandwiches cost around $7, while typical fish or meat dinner mains, like pork osso bucco or halibut, are more like $20. Mon–Sat 11am–5pm & 6–10pm, Sun 11am–9pm.

Holiday Inn Express 3601 E Cedar St ☎ 575 546 6500, ⓦ ihg.com. This large chain motel, near the eastern interstate exit, is as good as it gets in Deming, with clean rooms and an indoor pool. $78

Silver City

Six thousand feet up in the Mogollon Mountains, **SILVER CITY** stands roughly fifty miles from either Deming or Lordsburg on I-10. As you drive up from the interstate, however, it's easy not to notice that you're climbing – the region has been so extensively **mined** that many of the hills that once lay south of Silver City have now been completely carved away.

Ancient peoples knew this region as a source of top-quality **turquoise**, but the Hispanic settlement of La Cienaga de San Vicente was only founded in 1804, after friendly Apache showed a Spanish soldier where to find **copper**. The Santa Rita copper mine was repeatedly attacked by the Apache, however, and abandoned altogether in 1838. Only when **silver** was discovered after the Civil War was the town re-established, with a new name and a rip-roaring reputation. **Billy the Kid** spent most of his childhood here; he's said to have committed his first robbery – of a Chinese laundry – in Silver City, and also his first murder.

Things calmed down when the silver ran out, leaving Silver City as an appealing Victorian relic, scattered with ornate old buildings, antique shops and a couple of good museums. The 2500 students of Western New Mexico University, whose campus is on the western edge of downtown, keep things lively for most of the year, and they've been joined by a growing community of artists, outdoor enthusiasts and hipsters, as well as a large influx of tourists each summer. Copper mining, meanwhile, continues unabated; neighbouring Santa Rita, a fully fledged community that was the birthplace of Apollo 17 astronaut Harrison Schmitt, disappeared into the bowels of an open-pit copper mine in 1966.

A massive flood ripped out the heart of downtown Silver City in 1895, washing away its original Main Street. No buildings survive from the days of Billy the Kid; Wild West devotees have to settle instead for inspecting the places where they *used* to be. The former site of Main Street is now occupied by **Big Ditch Park**; stand on its eastern edge, at 11th and Hudson, and you're on the spot where Billy grew up, in a simple one-room cabin. His mother is buried in the town cemetery, on Memory Lane a couple of miles east. After her death, Billy found work as a busboy in the *Star Hotel*, which survives in much-altered form at Broadway and Hudson. Of course, he soon turned to crime; the jail where he was imprisoned stood at 304 N Hudson Street.

Silver City Museum

312 W Broadway • Tues–Fri 9am–4.30pm, Sat & Sun 10am–4pm • $3 • ☎ 575 538 5921, ⓦ silvercitymuseum.org

A classic little small-town gem, the **Silver City Museum** concentrates on the boom-and-bust mining years, with photos of the frontier era and personal accounts of the vanished community of Santa Rita. It also holds Indian pottery, rugs and basketry.

Western New Mexico University Museum

12th and Alabama • Mon–Fri 9am–4.30pm, Sat & Sun 10am–4pm; closed during university hols • Free • ☎ 575 538 6386, ⓦ wnmumuseum.org

The emphasis at Silver City's **Western New Mexico University Museum** is on an absolutely beautiful collection of the **Mimbres pottery** for which the region is famous (see p.200), tracing its development over a thousand-year period. Further displays cover more recent Native American ceramics and other artefacts, as well as Silver City's mining era.

3

INFORMATION

SILVER CITY

Visitor centre 201 N Hudson St, on Hwy-90 (April–Oct Mon–Fri 9am–5pm, Sat 10am–2pm, Sun noon–1pm; Nov–March Mon–Fri 9am–5pm; ☎ 575 538 5555, ⓦ silvercitytourism.org).

ACCOMMODATION

★ **Bear Mountain Lodge** 60 Bear Mountain Ranch Rd ☎ 575 538 2538, ⓦ bearmountainlodge.com. A 1920s adobe ranch house four miles northwest of downtown, where the eleven B&B guest rooms include four luxurious suites; the bathrooms are excellent, and there are cosy fireplaces aplenty (but no TVs). Breakfast is served in the on-site *Cafe Oso Azul*, which also serves lunch and, for $32 and with 24hr notice, dinner. **$160**

Holiday Inn Express 1103 Superior St ☎ 575 538 2525, ⓦ ihg.com. The best of Silver City's chain motels, with a heated spa and free continental breakfasts. Three miles east of downtown, it's hard to find, hidden behind a *Wendy's*. **$116**

★ **Murray Hotel** 200 W Broadway ☎ 575 956 9400, ⓦ murray-hotel.com. The biggest building in downtown Silver City, this Art Deco beauty originally opened as a hotel in 1938, but had lain defunct for twenty years before it was remodelled in 2012. So far, 56 refurbished guest rooms have been reopened, all with a knowing retro touch – the en-suite bathrooms are particularly tasteful – and the public spaces remain impressive. **$109**

★ **Palace Hotel** 106 W Broadway ☎ 575 388 1811, ⓦ silvercitypalacehotel.com. Nineteenth-century downtown hotel, nicely restored to suit budget travellers. Some rooms have showers instead of baths, and the lack of air conditioning can be a problem in high summer, as can weekend noise from the neighbouring bars. Doubles **$58**, suites **$94**

EATING AND DRINKING

Downtown Silver City has acquired an unlikely reputation for its **gourmet restaurants** in recent years, offering visitors a choice of cutting-edge culinary delights. The annual **Blues and Bikes Festival** attracts big names at the end of each May (ⓦ mimbresarts.org).

Buckhorn Saloon and Opera House 32 Main St, Pinos Altos ☎ 575 538 9911, ⓦ buckhornsaloonandoperahouse .com. Enjoyable Wild West-themed steakhouse in the ghost town of Pinos Altos, seven miles north of Silver City. Dinner mains range from pasta or chicken for around $20 up to as much as $40 for a big steak or surf'n'turf, and there's usually live music – generally folky singer-songwriters or acoustic indie bands – on Wed, Fri & Sat. Mon–Sat 3–10pm.

The Curious Kumquat 111 E College Ave ☎ 575 534 0377, ⓦ curiouskumquat.com. Chef Robert Connoley epitomizes Silver City's new-found foodie glory, serving an acclaimed five-course $49 dinner menu that changes nightly, but always features locally foraged ingredients along with prime organic meat and/or fish. Simpler lunch salads and sandwiches cost under $10. Tues–Sat 11am–4pm & 5.30–8.30pm.

Diane's Restaurant and Bakery 510 N Bullard St ☎ 575 538 8722, ⓦ dianesrestaurant.com. Welcoming downtown restaurant where the menu ranges from steak and meatloaf via Italian seafood stews to Thai green curries, pretty much all at $15–22; lots of wine by the glass, and they have their own bakery across the street. Tues–Fri 11am–2pm & 5–9pm,

Sat 9am–2pm & 5–9pm, Sun 11am–2pm.
Javelina Coffee House 117 W Market St ☎ 575 388 1350. Bright, friendly community rendezvous downtown,

open daily from very early, and attracting arty types who linger over their laptops drinking coffee and eating pastries. Mon–Sat 6am–7pm, Sun 6am–6pm.

The Mogollon and Mimbres mountains

North of Silver City, the volcanic **Mogollon** and **Mimbres mountains**, most of which belong to the **Gila National Forest**, rank among the remotest wilderness areas in the US. Until the late nineteenth century, this was an Apache stronghold; **Geronimo** was born at the headwaters of the Gila River and returned throughout his free adult life. Before that, the mountains were home to the **Mogollon** peoples, and the main reason to make the fifty-mile dead-end trip into the area on **Hwy-15** is to see the dramatic Mogollon ruins of the **Gila Cliff Dwellings National Monument**.

Hwy-15 is, however, a beautiful drive in its own right, albeit a slow one. It's never especially steep, let alone dangerous, but the twists and turns seem endless. Potential stops along the way include **Pinos Altos**, a fun little semi-ghost town in the woods a few miles out of Silver City, and the **Vista Viewpoint** above the Gila River near the far end.

Gila Cliff Dwellings National Monument

45 miles north of Silver City on Hwy-15 • **Visitor centre** Daily: summer 8am–5pm; winter 8am–4.30pm • **Dwellings access** Summer 8am–6pm; winter 9am–4pm • $5 per person or $10 per family • ☎ 575 536 9461, ⓦ nps.gov/gicl

Occupied for just a brief moment in history, between 1270 AD and 1300 AD, the Mogollon pueblo that's now preserved as the **GILA CLIFF DWELLINGS NATIONAL MONUMENT** is southern New Mexico's most spectacular archeological site. While not on the scale of the Ancestral Puebloan "cities" of the Four Corners region, it's much less

---

THE MOGOLLON AND THE MIMBRES

Archeologists identify the three major cultures of the prehistoric Southwest as the **Ancestral Puebloans** of the Colorado Plateau, the **Hohokam** of the Salt River Valley around modern Phoenix, and the **Mogollon**, based in the **Mogollon Mountains** of what's now southwest New Mexico. Thanks to their proximity to Mexico, Mogollon peoples were among the first to acquire both **agriculture** – in the shape of corn and squash, around 1200 BC – and **pottery** around 200 AD.

At its peak, between 100 AD and 1300 AD, the Mogollon culture extended well into modern Arizona and Mexican Chihuahua. Its heartland, however, remained the **Gila** and **Mimbres** rivers, north and east of modern Silver City. The Mogollon sub-group known as the **Classic Mimbres** culture is considered to represent the ancient Southwest's finest artistic flowering. Above all, the Mimbres people – the modern name by which they're known comes from the Spanish for "willows" – were superb **potters**. While the intricate stylized borders of their plates and bowls are typical of many pueblo peoples, their vivid naturalistic images of birds, insects and animals are quite extraordinary. Usually executed in black on white, they also hint at a complex mythology; some show bees or rabbits juxtaposed with strange humanoid creatures, others are what may be prototype *kachina* figures (see p.66), and there are even scenes of decapitation, suggesting human sacrifice.

The Mimbres culture reached its apogee around 1100 AD, when around five thousand people were farming beside the Mimbres River. While depictions of Pacific fish suggest that they travelled extensively, there's little evidence of trade. No Mimbres ceramics have been discovered elsewhere, and it's believed that the finest bowls were created for specific individuals at birth, used in ceremonies throughout their lifetime, and finally **buried** with them. The bowl would be inverted over the head of the corpse, always with a "**kill hole**" punched through it, which according to modern Pueblo Indians released its "spirit" to accompany that of the deceased. As a result, undamaged Mimbres bowls are extremely rare, and Mimbres pottery in general is so valuable that the few known Mimbres sites have been extensively looted, rendering the detective work of archeology almost impossible. As far as anyone can tell, the Mimbres stopped producing pottery around 1150 AD, and left the valley soon afterwards, possibly because overuse had depleted its soil.

visited, and you may well have the place to yourself. To modern eyes, ancient Southwestern peoples often seem to have chosen to live in inhospitable places, but here there's no such problem. The dwellings are tucked into sheltered south-facing recesses along the wall of a shallow canyon, a couple of hundred feet above a perennial creek and thus in earshot of running water and the constant rustle of small game. "Gila", incidentally, is pronounced "heela", and comes from an Apache word meaning "mountain".

Even when there's no traffic, Hwy-15 requires such care that driving the full 45 miles from Silver City is likely to take two hours. If you're coming from the east, Hwy-35, which branches off Hwy-152 fifty miles west of I-25, is not so slow or mountainous, but it's still a hell of a long drive. Either way, the final eight miles follow the broad valley of the Gila River to reach the **visitor centre**, poised near the confluence of the Gila's Middle and West forks.

The **trail** to the dwellings starts a mile further on, crossing the Gila on a long footbridge. Only half a mile along the creek do you get your first glimpse of the pueblo. What from below looks like three separate caves turns out after you climb the hillside to be a single, deep, long alcove with three entrances. Each of those entrances was sealed with stones and mortar, but behind them lay around forty interconnected rooms, sharing a communal – and presumably very dark – plaza at the rear. As the trail leads into and through the complex, keep an eye out for the pictographs that mark certain dwellings, as well as a granary that still holds a desiccated cache of tiny corn.

3

ACCOMMODATION   THE MOGOLLON AND MIMBRES MOUNTAINS

Forks Campground Hwy-15, 5 miles south of Gila Cliff Dwelling National Monument ☎ 575 536 2250, ⓦ fs .usda.gov. The northernmost of the two small, free campgrounds located either side of the Gila River, at the point where Hwy-15 crosses the river (the other is *Grapevine Campground*). Campers are dependent on water from the river itself. Another two undeveloped sites are located half a mile south of the monument. First come, first served. **Free**

Gila Hot Springs Ranch Hwy-15, 8 miles south of Gila Cliff Dwelling National Monument ☎ 575 536 9551, ⓦ gilahotspringsranch.com. Spreading comfortably amid verdant green meadows, this high-mountain ranch offers tent camping, RV hook-ups and a couple of large well-equipped rental units at bargain rates – they can sleep up to ten, with an extra per-person charge payable – and also has its own hot-springs pool. The owners offer single- and multi-day hunting and horseriding trips into the mountains. Tents **$15**, RVs **$20**, rental units **$92**

Lordsburg

Sixty miles down the interstate from Deming, 44 miles southwest of Silver City, and just twenty miles short of Arizona, **LORDSBURG** is southwest New Mexico's last gasp. John Wayne went to a lot of trouble to get here in *Stagecoach*, but the desultory strip of gas stations and motels today make you wonder why he bothered.

Far more redolent of the Old West is **SHAKESPEARE**, two miles south, a privately owned **ghost town** that's only open for infrequent guided tours (March–Dec only, on the second Sat & Sun of each month, plus occasional other weekends, 10am & 2pm; $4; ☎ 575 542 9034, ⓦ shakespeareghostown.com). If you go at any other time, there's no access to the site and nothing to see.

INFORMATION   LORDSBURG

New Mexico Welcome Center 191 Stagecoach Road, just south of I-10 exit 20 at the west end of town

(Mon–Fri 8am–4pm; ☎ 575 542 8149).

ACCOMMODATION AND EATING

Econo Lodge 1408 S Main St ☎ 575 542 3666, ⓦ econolodge.com. It would be hard to claim there's much to distinguish this large *Econo Lodge* from its similar neighbours along the few blocks of Main Street that lie south of I-10, but the mom-and-pop motels along Lordsburg's Motel Drive are so consistently dismal that you're better off

settling for one of the sizeable, bland rooms here. **$59**

Kranberry's 1405 S Main St ☎ 575 542 9400. The pick of a humdrum crop of diners, serving a tasty $9 green-chile stew that comes with two flour tortillas. Pretty much everything, from burritos to burgers, costs around $10. Daily 6am–10pm.

Phoenix and southern Arizona

OK CORRAL, TOMBSTONE

Phoenix and southern Arizona

Despite every conceivable geographic and climatic disadvantage, ninety percent of Arizonans live in Southern Arizona, mainly concentrated in two of the most unlikely cities on earth – Phoenix and Tucson. Not only does Southern Arizona for the most part lack the compelling scenery of the state's northern half, it also lacks the water to support either Phoenix or Tucson. However, although the very existence of either city defies normal logic, they have accrued sufficient political leverage to persuade the federal government to spend ever more money on vast canal projects to meet their needs.

Phoenix in particular can be seen as the bloated spider at the centre of the web, sucking the juices from the rest of the state. By far the largest city in Arizona, its tourist trade rests largely on the appeal of lounging by the pool in ultra-expensive resorts, but it does have several high-quality museums and gardens. **Tucson** has more of a spark of life, thanks to its long and fascinating history; it started out as a Mexican frontier outpost, and is still surrounded by such missionary relics as the churches of **San Xavier del Bac** and **Tumacácori**. It's also more at ease with its desert surroundings, accessible in **Saguaro National Park** and the **Arizona-Sonora Desert Museum**. Beyond Tucson, **southeast Arizona** is the one area of southern Arizona where the landscapes rival those of the Colorado Plateau. As well as intriguing flora and fauna, its "sky islands" hold evocative Wild West sites like **Tombstone**, now an entertaining if slightly tacky theme park of a town, and the mining settlement of **Bisbee**.

Phoenix's fragile grip on reality is highlighted by the fact that it was built on the ruins of a long-lost desert civilization. Until 1350 AD, the valleys of southern Arizona were home to the **Hohokam** people, and crisscrossed by sophisticated irrigation canals. The Hohokam eventually depleted the land too much for their way of life to endure. Their name means "people who have vanished" in the language of the **O'odham** (once known as the Pima and the Papago) who later took their place. The O'odham now occupy vast reservations in southwest Arizona, while their old enemies, the **Apache**, dominate the mountains to the east.

Phoenix and around

When it began life in the 1860s, as a sweltering little farming town, **PHOENIX** must have seemed like a good idea. Set in the heart of the **Salt River Valley**, which measures forty miles east to west and twenty miles north to south, with a ready-made irrigation system left by ancient native Americans, it had lots of room to expand. Within a century, however, Phoenix had turned into what writer Edward Abbey called "the blob that is eating Arizona", acquiring as it did so the money and political clout to grow way beyond its natural limitations. Today, Arizona's capital has filled the entire valley and is the sixth-largest city in the US. Over 1.5 million people live within the city boundaries, while more than four million inhabit the twenty separate incorporated cities, such as

THE HEARD MUSEUM, PHOENIX

Highlights

❶ Heard Museum Arizona's finest collection of Native American artefacts, including hundreds of superb Hopi *kachinas*. **See p.209**

❷ Musical Instrument Museum Providing a glorious visual as well as aural overview of music the world over, Phoenix's newest museum is absolutely irresistible . **See p.210**

❸ Saguaro National Park There's nowhere quite like it; hordes of towering multi-armed saguaro cactuses march across the desert hills of Tucson. **See p.227**

❹ Hotel Congress Downtown Tucson's hippest ·hangout; not just a hotel and a hostel, but also a great café and nightclub. **See p.230**

❺ San Xavier del Bac The spectacular "White Dove of the Desert" has to be the Southwest's most beautiful mission church. **See p.232**

❻ Tombstone From the OK Corral to *Big Nose Kate's*, Tombstone is an irresistible throwback to the wildest days of the West. **See p.239**

❼ Bisbee Atmospheric old mining town that has reinvented itself as a cosy, arty, mountain hideaway for overheated Arizonans. **See p.242**

❽ Chiricahua National Monument Apache such as Geronimo and Cochise once hid among the weird rock formations of this remote mountain fastness. **See p.244**

HIGHLIGHTS ARE MARKED ON THE MAP ON P.206

PHOENIX AND SOUTHERN ARIZONA

HIGHLIGHTS

1. Heard Museum
2. Musical Instrument Museum
3. Saguaro National Park
4. Hotel Congress
5. San Xavier del Bac
6. Tombstone
7. Bisbee
8. Chiricahua National Monument

Scottsdale, **Tempe** and **Mesa**, which together make up the metropolitan area. The entire Phoenix area is also known colloquially as the **Valley of the Sun**, but the term has no official meaning.

Perhaps the single most defining characteristic of Phoenix, even more than its sheer size, is that it's **hot**; between June and August daytime highs average over 100°F (38°C), making it one of the world's hottest cities outside the Middle East. While that may put off visitors in summer, when local room rates are at their lowest, tourists flock here from colder climes in winter, to enjoy temperatures that rarely drop below 65°F (18°C). They pay vast sums to warm their bones in the luxury resorts and spas, concentrated especially in Scottsdale, that are the modern equivalent of the 1930s dude ranches. Unlike golf, tennis and shopping in the city's plentiful upscale malls, **sightseeing** rarely ranks high on the agenda. Phoenix does hold a handful of must-see attractions, though, including the wonderful new **Musical Instruments Museum**, the **Heard Museum** with its excellent Native American displays, the cactuses at the **Desert Botanical Garden** and Frank Lloyd Wright's architecture studio at **Taliesin West**.

Brief history

Phoenix epitomizes the Western maxim that "water flows uphill to money"; its history revolves around its manoeuvrings to obtain ever more water, from ever further afield. The first Anglo-American settler in the Salt River Valley was John Smith in 1865, who supplied hay to Camp McDowell, thirty miles northeast. However, the obvious traces of over three hundred miles of canals dug by the ancient Hohokam people (see p.465) made it clear that the valley had once supported a large population. By clearing one such canal in 1867, Confederate deserter Jack Swilling established Phoenix. It was named by British adventurer "Lord" Darrel Duppa, who saw it as rising like the mythical bird from the ashes of the Hohokam civilization.

Phoenix was laid out in 1870 on a 98-block grid measuring one mile long by half a mile wide. Avenues and streets (now numbered) were named for Indian tribes, and cross streets for presidents. By 1889 it was **capital** of Arizona, and home to over ten thousand people. Catastrophic floods and droughts during the 1890s convinced the city-dwellers that their future depended on ensuring a safe, dependable source of water. The building of the **Roosevelt Dam** in the mountains to the east, in 1911 (see p.218), marked the first step in a process that culminated with the completion of the **Central Arizona Project**, a 336-mile aqueduct from the Colorado River to Phoenix and Tucson, in the 1990s.

By the 1920s Phoenix was promoting itself as the "winter playground of the Southwest", a healthy refuge from the smog-laden cities of the East. Its citizens were exhorted to landscape their properties with gardens, under the slogan "**Let's Do Away With the Desert**", and lavish resort hotels began to open. Exponential growth truly began during World War II, when the city acquired three major air bases, and **industrialization** continued apace during the 1950s. The development of **air conditioning** finally made the desert heat bearable, and the population quadrupled between 1950 and 1960 alone, to reach 439,000. As it swallowed a host of neighbouring communities, the city's endless sprawl swiftly covered the "golden fields of ripened grain" described in one 1940s guidebook. By the time it topped one million, around 1990, it had grown by over four hundred square miles in forty years.

Phoenix

Downtown Phoenix – defined as the few blocks east and west of Central Avenue and north and south of **Washington Street** – remains too hot and too spread out to walk around in any comfort. Determined efforts have been made to regenerate and revitalize the area, however, conspicuously including two massive side-by-side sports stadiums, the **Talking Stick Resort Arena** and **Chase Field** (home respectively to the Phoenix Suns and Arizona Diamondbacks).

What little remains of Phoenix's nineteenth-century architecture now constitutes **Heritage Square**, a couple of blocks southeast of the Arizona Center at 115 N Sixth St. Rather than original adobe ranch houses, it preserves a quaint assortment of Victorian homes converted into tea rooms and the like.

EATING	
Barrio Café	7
Coup des Tartes	4
Culinary Dropout	8
Durant's	5
Fry Bread House	3
Fuego Bistro	1
House of Tricks	10
Ncounter	9
Red White and Brew	6
Vincent Market Bistro	2

NIGHTLIFE	
Four Peaks Brewing Company	2
Marquee Theatre	1

Heard Museum

2301 N Central Ave • Mon–Sat 9.30am–5pm, Sun 11am–5pm; also open 6–10pm on first Fri of each month except March • $18; ages 6–17 $7.50 • ☎ 602 252 8840, ⓦ heard.org

Greatly enlarged while still showcasing its lovely old original buildings, the **Heard Museum** provides an excellent introduction to the culture of the **Native Americans** of the Southwest, and their arts and crafts in particular. A sumptuous pottery collection includes stunning Mimbres bowls (see p.200), clay dolls made by the

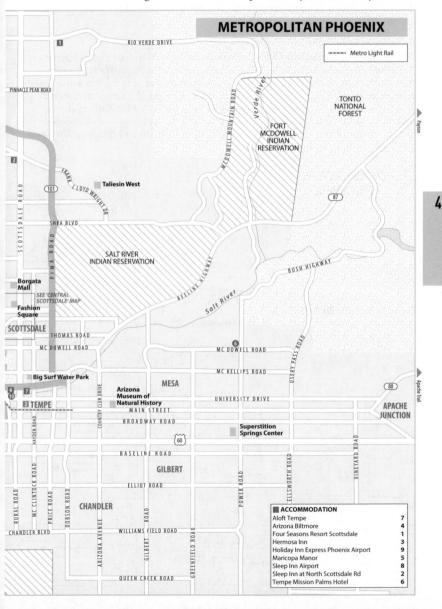

Quechan and Mohave peoples as souvenirs for nineteenth-century railroad passengers, and modern Hopi ceramics. You'll also find a complete Navajo *hogan* (see p.62), some fine old Havasupai baskets, Apache beadwork and painted buffalo-skin shields from New Mexican pueblos. Best of all are the Hopi **kachina dolls** (see p.66), four hundred of which were donated by arch-conservative Arizona senator Barry Goldwater. Additional galleries upstairs tell the heartbreaking story of how the federal government shattered traditional family life by shipping Native American children to boarding schools. The museum also holds a superb store, and a good café.

Phoenix Art Museum

1625 N Central Ave • Wed 10am–9pm, Thurs–Sat 10am–5pm, Sun noon–5pm • $15, ages 6–17 $6 • ☏ 602 257 1880, ⊕ phxart.org

The permanent collection at the vast and highly rewarding **Phoenix Art Museum**, a mile north of downtown, is sensibly rooted in an extensive array of Western art, with all the names you'd expect – Frederic Remington, Georgia O'Keeffe – and including an enjoyable room devoted to Arizona artist Philip Curtis. Anish Kapoor's black sculpture *Upside Down Inside Out* is another highlight, and temporary exhibitions range through all eras and styles. A top-quality gift store stocks Mexican crafts items and jazzy modern ceramics.

DOWNTOWN PHOENIX

■ NIGHTLIFE
Bar Smith — 2
Bikini Lounge — 1
Last Exit Live — 3
Monarch Theatre — 2

■ EATING
Alice Cooper'stown — 3
Green New American Vegetarian — 1
Pizzeria Bianco — 2

■ ACCOMMODATION
HI Phoenix – Metcalf House — 1
Hotel San Carlos — 2

---- Metro Light Rail

0   800
yards

Arizona Science Center

600 E Washington St • Daily 10am–5pm • $18, ages 3–17 $13; giant-screen movie theatre $9/$8 • ☎ 602 716 2000, ⓦ azscience.org

The ever-expanding **Arizona Science Center**, adjoining Heritage Square, is a hands-on museum that's targeted primarily at local schoolchildren. While it does its job very well, with plenty of interactive gimmicks as well as large models of how zits form and babies are born, there's not enough substance to make this a worthwhile stop for adults travelling without kids.

Pueblo Grande Museum

4619 E Washington St • Mon–Sat 9am–4.45pm, Sun 1–4.45pm • $6 • ☎ 602 495 0900, ⓦ phoenix.gov/parks

Set beside the Grand Canal – a nineteenth-century Anglo version of Phoenix's similar ancient waterways – the **Pueblo Grande Museum** preserves a Hohokam settlement that dates back 1500 years. In truth there's not very much to see, but the constant stream of planes heading to and from nearby Sky Harbor airport acts as an incongruous counterpoint to the ruins along the half-mile trail. Once mercifully back indoors, you can learn more about the Hohokam in the fascinating visitor centre.

Musical Instrument Museum

4725 E Mayo Blvd • Daily 9am–5pm • $20, ages 13–19 $15, ages 4–12 $10 • ☎ 480 478 6000, ⓦ mim.org

There's so much to see, listen to, and above all enjoy at the enormous **Musical Instrument Museum**, twenty miles northeast of downtown in Paradise Valley, that you could easily spend most of a day here. Founded by Robert Ulrich, former CEO of Target, it is as the name suggests an absolute treasure trove of extraordinary instruments from all over the world, from an armadillo-shell lute from Peru to ornate Ashanti drums from Ghana. An endless succession of rooms and galleries are devoted to every country and/or musical genre you could possibly think of – local boy Alice Cooper even gets his own special display. The real joy of the place, though, is that each section also features jaw-dropping, mind-bending video clips of performances both new and historical; it's all but impossible to tear yourself away until you've seen the whole lot.

Scottsdale

Now home to almost 250,000 people and stretching more than twenty miles from north to south, the town of **SCOTTSDALE**, founded ten miles northeast of Phoenix in the 1880s, is a remarkable success story in its own right. Despite being almost wholly subsumed into the metropolitan maw, it has carved itself an eccentric double niche as both the city's chic-est destination, home to opulent resorts and designer-led malls, and its most determinedly "Western" quarter.

Southeast of **Camelback Mountain** and the **Scottsdale Fashion Square** mall, downtown Scottsdale centres on a few pleasant blocks of sidewalk cafés and souvenir stores. West of Scottsdale

CENTRAL SCOTTSDALE

Main St Arts & Antiques District

● **EATING**
Arcadia Farms — 2
Bandera — 5
Cowboy Ciao — 1
Malee's Thai on Main — 3
The Mission — 4

■ **ACCOMMODATION**
Motel 6 Scottsdale — 1
The Phoenician — 2

Scottsdale Fashion Square

E. CAMELBACK ROAD

Arizona Canal

GOLDWATER BOULEVARD
STETSON DRIVE
SCOTTSDALE ROAD
DRINKWATER BOULEVARD
MILLER ROAD

68TH STREET
5TH AVE
3RD AVENUE
69TH ST
MARSHALL WAY
BROWN AVENUE
25TH ST

INDIAN SCHOOL ROAD

1ST AVENUE
OLD TOWN MAIN ST
Western Spirit: Scottsdale's Museum of the West
1ST STREET
2ND STREET
Scottsdale Museum of Contemporary Arts
4TH ST
5TH ST
6TH ST
4TH ST

OSBORN ROAD

0   400
yards

N

4

Road counts as the **Main Street Arts and Antiques District**; to the east, **Old Town** plays the Wild West theme for all it's worth.

Western Spirit: Scottsdale's Museum of the West

3830 N Marshall Way • Tues, Wed, Fri & Sat 9.30am–5pm, Thurs 9.30am–9pm, Sun 11am–5pm • $13, ages 6–17 $8 • ☎ 480 686 9539, ⓦ scottsdalemuseumwest.org

Despite being saddled with the world's most cumbersome name, **Western Spirit: Scottsdale's Museum of the West** is a sprightly modern museum that explores the art and history of the nineteen states it defines as constituting the American West. Its prime focus is on Western paintings, with major exhibitions that change each year devoted to such themes as the Lewis and Clark expedition, but there's also an impressive permanent collection of bits, spurs and revolvers, while written displays cover representations of the Wild West in literature and popular culture.

Taliesin West

114th St and Frank Lloyd Wright Blvd • Daily 9am–4pm; see website for tour schedules • Panorama Tour $28, Insights Tour $36, Extended Insights Tour $75 • ☎ 480 627 5340, ⓦ franklloydwright.org

The most notable among the many visionary designers who have worked in the Phoenix area was **Frank Lloyd Wright**, who arrived to work on the *Biltmore Hotel* and returned to spend the winter for most of the 25 years before his death in 1959. His studio, **Taliesin West** – at Scottsdale's far northeastern edge, a dozen miles from the Old Town – is now an architecture school and a working design studio, with exhibits of the man's life and work.

Eighty years since Wright first came here, Taliesin West is still a splendidly isolated spot, where his trademark "organic architecture" makes perfect sense. Wright and his students camped out and assessed the terrain long before building any permanent structures, and the complex blends seamlessly into the desert. It can only be seen on guided visits, the main options being the hour-long "Panorama Tour"; the one-hour-thirty-minute "Insights Tour", which grants access to Wright's private living area; and the three-hour "Extended Insights Tour". The expertise and enthusiasm of the guides makes the experience well worth the relatively high price.

Desert Botanical Garden

1201 North Galvin Parkway • Daily: May–Sept 7am–8pm; Oct–April 8am–8pm • $22, ages 3–12 $10 • ☎ 480 941 1225, ⓦ dbg.org

In **Papago Park**, at the south end of Scottsdale, the fascinating **Desert Botanical Garden** is filled with an amazing array of desert flora. Prime specimens include spineless "totem pole" cactuses from the Galápagos Islands and "living stone" plants from South Africa. Separate enclaves are devoted to **butterflies** – best seen in August and September – and to **hummingbirds**, of which Arizona boasts fifteen indigenous species.

Tempe

Phoenix's major recent success story has been the transformation of the community of **TEMPE** into the liveliest and most dynamic portion of the Valley of the Sun. It lies south of Scottsdale, across I-60, and six miles east of downtown Phoenix. The eighty thousand students of **Arizona State University** keep the cafés, clubs, stores and restaurants along the red-brick **Mill Avenue** constantly buzzing. Several minor museums and galleries are dotted across the college campus, immediately east, while a couple of blocks north the Salt River has been dammed and its surroundings landscaped to create an appealing park, the **Tempe Town Lake**.

Mesa

Built on the site of the Mormon settlement of Fort Utah, which lasted for three years from 1877, **MESA**, east of Tempe, is Arizona's third-largest city. Covering more than a hundred square miles, it has a population of well over 450,000. Spread among its endless broad boulevards are twenty golf courses, several large malls, some of Phoenix's most affordable residential districts, and dozens of cheap motels. With the Superstition Mountains rising to the east, it's not a bad base for passing visitors.

Arizona Museum of Natural History

53 N MacDonald St • Tues–Fri 10am–5pm, Sat 11am–5pm, Sun 1–5pm • $10, ages 6–12 $6 • ☎ 480 644 2230, ⓦ arizonamuseumofnaturalhistory.org

As well as displays on dinosaurs, including the fearsome animatronic models that prowl Dinosaur Mountain, the enjoyable **Arizona Museum of Natural History** features an intriguing reconstruction of a block of Mesa's Main Street as it looked a century ago. Other sections cover the Hohokam, and the story of the Lost Dutchman Mine (see p.218).

ARRIVAL AND DEPARTURE

PHOENIX AND AROUND

By plane Phoenix Sky Harbor International Airport is 3 miles east of downtown (ⓦ skyharbor.com). Free shuttles connect it with the nearest Valley Metro Rail station at 44th and Washington, while SuperShuttle (☎ 800 258 3826, ⓦ supershuttle.com) operates door-to-door shuttle buses costing around $15 for downtown destinations and more like $30 for Scottsdale. Arizona Shuttle Services runs shuttles to other towns in Arizona, including Tucson, Sedona and Prescott (☎ 800 888 2749, ⓦ arizonashuttle.com).

By train Amtrak doesn't serve Phoenix, but rail passengers who arrive in either Tucson or Flagstaff can catch connecting buses to Phoenix.

By bus Greyhound buses arrive at 2115 E Buckeye Rd (☎ 602 389 4200, ⓦ greyhound.com), close to the airport.

GETTING AROUND

By car Phoenix is so vast, and so utterly dependent on car travel, that it's much easier to drive than to use public transport – even driving, though, it can take hours to get across town.

By light rail The Valley Metro Rail system (one-way ride $2, one-day pass $4; ☎ 602 253 5000, ⓦ valleymetro.org) follows a 22-mile route, taking around 1hr 15min to get between Montebello Ave north of downtown Phoenix and Mesa Drive in Mesa. There are stations in downtown Phoenix and Tempe, and also close to the airport, but it's much more useful for commuters than visitors.

By taxi Yellow Cab (☎ 480 888 8888, ⓦ yellowcabaz .com). A cab from downtown Phoenix to Tempe, for example, is likely to cost over $30.

INFORMATION

Phoenix 125 N Second St, downtown (Mon–Fri 8am–5pm; ☎ 602 254 6500, ⓦ visitphoenix.com).
Scottsdale 4343 N Scottsdale Rd (Mon–Fri 8am–5pm; ☎ 800 782 1117, ⓦ experiencescottsdale.com).

Tempe 51 W Third St (Mon–Fri 8.30am–5pm; ☎ 866 914 1052, ⓦ tempetourism.com).
Mesa 120 N Center St (Mon–Fri 8am–5pm; ☎ 800 283 6732, ⓦ visitmesa.com).

ACCOMMODATION

Not only do room rates in Phoenix tend to be considerably higher than elsewhere in Arizona, but they rise considerably in **winter**, when snowbirds from all over the US fill the upscale resorts of **Scottsdale** in particular. Granted that any visitor to metropolitan Phoenix can expect to do a *lot* of driving, budget travellers should consider staying in less expensive areas like **Tempe**.

PHOENIX

Arizona Biltmore 2400 E Missouri Ave ☎ 602 955 6600 or ☎ 800 950 0086, ⓦ arizonabiltmore.com; map pp.208–209. Extraordinarily lavish 750-room spa resort, built under the influence of Frank Lloyd Wright in the 1930s and retaining its Art Deco trimmings and extravagant gardens despite subsequent renovations. Low-season rates can be a real bargain. Two golf courses, four restaurants, eight pools, plus afternoon teas, tennis and spa. Winter <u>$457</u>, summer <u>$197</u>

HI Phoenix – Metcalf House 1026 N Ninth St above Roosevelt St ☎ 602 254 9803, ⓦ phxhostel.org; map p.210. Friendly little "desert hostel" in a slightly run-down location in a residential district, 15min walk north of the Arizona Center. As well as two single-sex dorms, holding 4–10 beds, they offer a couple of private rooms. No curfew, plus use of kitchen and laundry; rates include continental breakfast. Check in 8–10am & 5–10pm, $3 discount for HI members. Cash only. Dorms <u>$27</u>, private doubles <u>$60</u>

Holiday Inn Express Phoenix Airport 3401 E University Drive ☎ 602 453 9900, ⓦ hiexpress.com;

4

map pp.208–209. This very presentable, good-value motel, between Phoenix and Tempe, may not be a place to spend very much time, but its large modern rooms make a handy overnight stop before or after a flight from nearby Sky Harbor – connected by free shuttles – and there's also an outdoor pool. Winter $189, summer $109

Maricopa Manor 15 W Pasadena Ave ☎ 602 264 9204 or ☎ 800 292 6403, ⓦ maricopamanor.com; map pp.208–209. The pick of the valley's B&Bs is handily poised between Phoenix and Scottsdale, near a light-rail station. Housed in a 1928 hacienda-style home, it holds six all-suite rooms, equipped with kitchenettes; they sleep up to four and are decorated to widely varying themes, from Arts and Crafts to Mexican, and there's a pool and hot tub. Winter $189, summer $119

Hotel San Carlos 202 N Central Ave ☎ 602 253 4121 or ☎ 866 253 4121, ⓦ hotelsancarlos.com; map p.210. To appreciate this historic very central 1920s hotel, you have to be the kind of traveller who positively prefers an old-fashioned, frazzled and often noisy downtown hotel with poor wi-fi connectivity to a crisp, new, deathly quiet motel. The rooms are tastefully furnished, if small – especially the often tiny bathrooms – and there's a nice Vietnamese restaurant, plus a rooftop swimming pool. $169

SCOTTSDALE

Four Seasons Resort Scottsdale at Troon North 10600 E Crescent Moon Drive ☎ 480 515 5700, ⓦ fourseasons.com/scottsdale; map pp.208–209. Magnificent desert resort, with very luxurious rooms and suites arrayed in separate *casitas* around spacious swimming pools in the cactus-studded mountains to the north of Scottsdale, plus a good spa and fine restaurants. Winter $529, summer $249

Hermosa Inn 5532 N Palo Cristi Rd ☎ 602 955 8614 or ☎ 844 267 8738, ⓦ hermosainn.com; map pp.208–209. This 1930s guest ranch, set in desert gardens halfway between Phoenix and Scottsdale in Paradise Valley, has been converted into a tranquil 35-room boutique hotel, with a genuine Southwestern ambience to its large, luxurious rooms and a good restaurant. Winter $378, summer $162

Motel 6 Scottsdale 6848 E Camelback Rd ☎ 480 946 2280, ⓦ motel6.com; map p.211. Cut-price lodgings are few and far between in Scottsdale, so this totally unremarkable budget motel, just off I-17 close to the Fashion Mall and downtown Scottsdale, is well worth considering. Winter $86, summer $56

The Phoenician 6000 E Camelback Rd ☎ 480 941 8200, ⓦ thephoenician.com; map p.211. Gorgeous 250-acre resort, spread out at the base of Camelback Mountain at the northern end of Scottsdale and offering every conceivable luxury, with golf course, waterfalls and lush gardens as well as lavish rooms and restaurants. Winter $493, summer $218

Sleep Inn at North Scottsdale Rd 16630 North Scottsdale Rd ☎ 480 998 9211 or ☎ 866 477 6424, ⓦ sleepinnscottsdale.com; map pp.208–209. Dependable, upscale chain motel, convenient for visiting Frank Lloyd Wright's Taliesin West, with a pool and hot tub. A free shuttle bus will take you anywhere within five miles, but downtown Scottsdale is ten miles south. Winter $139, summer $79

TEMPE

Aloft Tempe 951 E Playa Del Norte Drive ☎ 480 621 3300, ⓦ alofthotels.com/tempe; map pp.208–209. Aimed at younger, hipper travellers, the *Aloft* chain is a more affordable and frankly more likeable offshoot of the rather snooty designer *W* hotel group. With its bright palette and pool table in the lobby bar, it's a good fit for Tempe. The rooms themselves are spacious with high (loft-like) ceilings and rainfall showers. Winter $189, summer $99

Sleep Inn Airport 2621 S 47th Place ☎ 480 967 7100, ⓦ sleepinn.com; map pp.208–209. Above-average chain motel, three miles south of the airport but served by 24hr free shuttles. Winter $102, summer $68

Tempe Mission Palms Hotel 60 E Fifth St ☎ 480 894 1400 or ☎ 800 547 8705, ⓦ missionpalms.com; map pp.208–209. Very comfortable Southwestern-themed, largely business-oriented hotel in Tempe's revitalized Mill Ave district, with an opulent rooftop swimming pool. It's a pricey option in winter, but online summer deals can offer fantastic value. Winter $356, summer $113

EATING

Unless you're prepared to pay resort prices, it's hard to find a restaurant in Phoenix with very much atmosphere. Apart from a block or two in **central Scottsdale**, and Tempe's lively **Mill Avenue**, no areas are small enough to walk around while you look for a place to eat, but if you're happy to drive, neighbourhood diners – especially Mexican – can still be found.

PHOENIX

Alice Cooper'stown 101 E Jackson St ☎ 602 253 7337, ⓦ alicecooperstown.com; map p.210. This barbecue restaurant-cum-sports bar, owned by the rock star and local resident and filled with huge TV screens is alongside downtown's Talking Stick Resort Arena. While far from fine dining, the food's better than you might expect, with

barbecue sandwiches at $10 and mixed plates for $16, and the atmosphere is fun, with waiters in full Alice make-up and surprisingly frequent drop-ins by the man himself. Mon–Thurs 11am–9pm, Fri & Sat 11am–10pm, Sun 11am–4pm.

Barrio Café 2814 N 16th St ☎ 602 636 0240, ⓦ barriocafe.com; map pp.208–209. Reservations are not taken at this wildly popular little local Mexican place, but it's worth the wait – you can always bide your time sampling the huge array of tequilas, and there's live music Thurs–Sun. Enjoy authentic southern Mexican food, including succulent *cochinita pibil* (pork) for $13, and guacamole freshly made (and including pomegranate seeds) at your table. Tues–Thurs 11am–10pm, Fri & Sat 11am–10.30pm, Sun 11am–9pm.

Coup des Tartes 1725 E Osborn Rd ☎602 212 1082, ⓦnicetartes.com; map pp.208–209. Recently relocated in larger premises, but still offering the feel of home dining, this romantic restaurant serves classic French appetizers like baked brie with fruit ($12), mains from Moroccan lamb shank to apple-stuffed pork chop (both $24), and succulent French tarts ($9). For lunch, you can also get $12–17 sandwiches and sliders. Tues–Thurs 11am–2pm & 5–9pm, Fri 11am–2pm & 5–10pm, Sat 5–10pm, Sun 10am–2pm.

Durant's 2611 N Central Ave ☎602 264 5967, ⓦdurantsaz.com; map pp.208–209. This old-style downtown restaurant is a venerable institution for Arizona's elite, complete with red-leather banquettes and velvet wallpaper, and specializing in rich all-American food such as oysters Rockefeller ($19.50) and steaks, at $36 and up; if you can down the 48-oz Porterhouse, your name gets added to a plaque on the wall. The atmospheric central bar stays open for late-night drinks a couple of hours after food service ends. Mon–Thurs 11am–10pm, Fri 11am–11pm, Sat 5–11pm, Sun 4.30–10pm.

Fry Bread House 1003 E Indian School Rd ☎602 351 2345; map pp.208–209. You'll find fry bread on Native American reservations throughout the Southwest; in this no-nonsense café, though, Tohono O'odham chef Cecelia Miller raises it to fluffy perfection. Try it with either savoury (say, chile or chorizo) or sweet (chocolate) toppings, for $5–8. Mon–Thurs 10am–8pm, Fri & Sat 10am–9pm.

Fuego Bistro 713 E Palo Verde Rd ☎602 277 1151, ⓦfuegobistro.com; map pp.208–209. Delicious contemporary Latin American food, in a hard-to-find spot five miles north of downtown, with live music nightly from 6.30pm. Dinner mains like panko-crusted tilapia or the seafood-stuffed *chile relleno* cost $23–27, but lunch, of chicken tortilla soup for example, is less than half that. Tues–Sat 11am–2pm & 3–9pm.

Green New American Vegetarian 2022 N Seventh St ☎602 258 1870, ⓦgreenvegetarian.com; map p.210. Simple downtown café with a totally vegan, totally delicious menu. Order a "mock chicken" wrap or veggie burger at the counter – everything costs under $10 plus, perhaps, a craft beer or a glass of wine, then sit indoors or out on the patio. The associated *Nami* next door sells takeaway vegan ice cream and other desserts. Mon–Sat 11am–9pm.

Pizzeria Bianco Heritage Square, 623 E Adams St ☎602 258 8300, ⓦpizzeriabianco.com; map p.210. High-quality brick-oven pizzas at $13–18, in a very

convenient downtown location, with ultra-fresh ingredients including home-made mozzarella; no wonder it's so popular. No reservations. Mon 11am–9pm, Tues–Sat 11am–10pm.

Vincent Market Bistro 3930 E Camelback Rd ☎602 224 3727, ⓦvincentsoncamelback.com; map pp.208–209. Inexpensive, high-quality French-style bistro/deli, with a tiny outdoor seating area, squeezed around the back of *Vincent's* much more upscale fine-dining restaurant (also recommended). Lunchtime salads, omelettes and thin-crust pizzas cost $8–12, and dinner mains like coq au vin or beef bourguignon little more; specials include seafood kebab or paella. Note that when the adjoining farmers' market is in full swing, on Saturdays between Oct and May, there's no table service. They'll also deliver, as Vincent Van Go. Tues–Sat 7am–8pm, Sun 7am–2pm.

SCOTTSDALE

Arcadia Farms 7014 E First Ave ☎480 941 5665, ⓦarcadiafarmscafe.com; map p.211. The most popular lunch rendezvous in Scottsdale's Old Town – salads, sandwiches and hot dishes, including daily specials like crêpes, crab cakes and quesadillas, cost $12–16 – also serves healthy Southwestern breakfasts, and there's open-air courtyard seating. Check out their bakery and store alongside. Daily 8am–3pm.

Bandera 3821 N Scottsdale Rd ☎480 994 3524, ⓦbanderarestaurants.com; map p.211. Chicken cooked in the wood-burning oven ($19) is the speciality in this busy, inexpensive rotisserie on the southeast edge of downtown. Other meats and fish are almost as good, though the steaks do cost up to $43. Mon–Thurs & Sun 4–10pm, Fri & Sat 4–11pm.

Cowboy Ciao 7133 E Stetson Drive at Sixth ☎480 946 3111, ⓦcowboyciao.com; map p.211. With a decor that blends Old West roadhouse with an Italian feel, this hip downtown option serves "modern American food with global influences". At lunchtime, a burger or seared tuna sandwich costs $15–19; the $13 "Stetson" chopped salad is also available in the evening, when the exotic mushroom pan-fry is $25 and the bone-in pork chop is $32. Daily 11.30am–2.30pm & 5–10pm.

Malee's Thai on Main 7131 E Main St ☎480 947 6042, ⓦmaleesonmain.com; map p.211. Somewhat inconspicuous but very popular and dependably good Thai place downtown, serving all the usual items – pad thai noodles, chicken green curry – at reasonable prices (typically $15), in a smart date-night setting. Mon–Sat 11am–9pm, Sun noon–9pm.

The Mission 3815 N Brown Ave ☎480 636 5005, ⓦthemissionaz.com; map p.211. Named for the whitewashed adobe church alongside, and featuring stunning decor – including one wall made of salt blocks – that echoes its architecture, this "modern Latin" restaurant draws equally

4

on Old- and New-World cuisines. Classics like made-to-order guacamole ($12) are complemented by $28–34 meat and seafood dishes, prepared on either a wood-fired or flat-top grill. The tequila bar stays open until 2am. Mon–Thurs & Sun 11am–10pm, Fri & Sat 11am–11pm.

TEMPE
Culinary Dropout 140 S Farmer Ave ☎ 480 240 1601, ⓦ culinarydropout.com; map pp.208–209. Students and hipsters love this lively bar-restaurant, half a mile west of the centre in the so-called Farmer Arts District and part of a small local chain, for its cool laidback atmosphere, with bar games like shuffleboard and ping pong on the patio. The updated comfort food includes stellar Southern fried chicken for $16, pork ramen for $15, and burgers and salads for around $12. Mon–Wed 11am–11pm, Thurs & Fri 11am–1am, Sat 10am–1am, Sun 10am–10pm.

House of Tricks 114 E Seventh St ☎ 480 968 1114, ⓦ houseoftricks.com; map pp.208–209. Tiny Modern American place in the University district, named for chefs Robin and Robert Trick, with lots of vegetarian options and some lovely, well-shaded courtyard seating. In the evening

choose from $24 for squash and potato enchiladas up to $36 for beef tenderloin; simpler lunchtime sandwiches and specials, such as meatloaf, cost $12–15. Mon–Sat 11am–10pm.

Ncounter 310 S Mill Ave ☎ 480 968 9288, ⓦ ncounter.com; map pp.208–209. Large, very popular canteen in the thick of Tempe's buzzing downtown, with some outdoor seating. Open for breakfast and lunch only, it's an ideal stop-off for anything from a $5.50 stack of pancakes to a $9 Waldorf salad or grilled-cheese sandwich, or simply a $5 fresh-fruit smoothie. Daily 7am–3.05pm.

MESA
Red White and Brew 6740 E McDowell Rd ☎ 480 807 9393, ⓦ rwbaz.com; map pp.208–209. Small wonder that this mall restaurant, en route towards the Apache Trail at the east end of the valley, has such a good local reputation. There's something for everyone on the wide-ranging international menu, from mussels in wine for $12 to $14 pizzas and $16 tandoori shrimp, plus home-brewed beers. No reservations. Mon–Sat 11am–10pm, Sun noon–10pm.

NIGHTLIFE AND ENTERTAINMENT

Phoenix's **nightlife** has less of a Western identity than you might expect, with Tempe and Scottsdale respectively cultivating an alt-rock, college crowd, and a glitzier clubbing scene. For a rundown of what's happening, pick up the free weekly *New Times* (ⓦ phoenixnewtimes.com).

BARS AND CLUBS
Bar Smith 130 E Washington St, Phoenix ☎ 602 229 1265, ⓦ barsmithphoenix.com; map p.210. The best thing about this stylish downtown bar and lounge is its fabulous outdoor dance floor, upstairs. Wed–Sat 9.30pm–2.30am.

Bikini Lounge 1502 Grand Ave, Phoenix ☎ 602 252 0472, ⓦ thebikinilounge.com; map p.210. A real gem of a dive bar, this veteran tiki bar attracts a fascinating, eclectic mix of local characters. Daily 3pm–2am.

Four Peaks Brewing Company 1340 E Eighth St, Tempe ☎ 480 303 9967, ⓦ fourpeaks.com; map pp.208–209. The best brewpub in the metropolitan area, near the university a mile or so east of Mill Ave, with good beer and a full menu of pub grub, plus some outdoor seating. They have another outlet at 15745 N Hayden Rd in Scottsdale. Mon–Thurs 11am–1am, Fri & Sat 11am–2am, Sun 10am–1am.

Monarch Theatre 122 E Washington St, Phoenix ☎ 602 692 9633, ⓦ monarchtheatre.com; map p.210. Downtown Phoenix's hottest club styles itself a "bi-level beatshack", with plush lounge space upstairs, a huge dance floor, and a stage hosting the biggest names in EDM. Thurs–Sat, hours vary.

LIVE MUSIC VENUES
Last Exit Live 717 S Central Ave, Phoenix ☎ 602 271 7000, ⓦ lastexitlive.com; map p.210. Long a staple of the valley scene, this rock-oriented downtown venue continues to programme live music ranging from country-rock to local punks. Hours vary; doors typically open 7pm.

Marquee Theatre 730 N Mill Ave, Tempe ☎ 480 829 1300, ⓦ luckymanonline.com; map pp.208–209. The best venue to see big-name touring acts, with an open floor rather than seating, and good beer. Hours vary.

East of Phoenix

Almost two hundred miles of mountainous terrain stands between Phoenix and New Mexico to the east, much of which belongs to two huge **Apache reservations**. Although sweltering Phoenicians spend summer weekends in hill towns to the northeast, like Payson and Pinetop, there's little to detain ordinary tourists on the long drive east.

FROM TOP TRAILER AT SHADY DELL, BISBEE (SEE P.243); TALIESIN WEST (P.212) >

THE LEGEND OF THE LOST DUTCHMAN

The **Superstition Mountains** east of Phoenix are famous in Wild West lore as the site of the legendary **Lost Dutchman Mine**. The story goes that around 1870, two German prospectors, Jacob Waltz and Jacob Weiser, discovered rich deposits of gold, and turned up repeatedly in the town of Florence bearing priceless nuggets. Before his death in Phoenix in 1890, Waltz is said to have murdered not only Weiser but another seven men who tried to shadow him back to the motherlode. Ever since, expeditions have attempted to follow his deathbed directions to the mine – guarded, according to different accounts, by pygmies or a never-discovered group of Apache – and thirty gold-seekers are rumoured to have lost their lives.

US-60 and US-70 are the quickest routes to New Mexico, but if you want a quick escape from the desert heat, head instead up the **Apache Trail** into the **Superstition Mountains**, the supposed site of the **Lost Dutchman Mine**.

The Apache Trail

The closest accessible wilderness to central Phoenix lies along **Hwy-88**, which climbs northeast into the Superstition Mountains from **Apache Junction**, almost twenty miles east of Mesa and a good thirty miles from downtown Phoenix. Constructed in 1904 to reach the Roosevelt Dam, then being built at the confluence of Tonto Creek and Salt River, this fifty-mile highway was later renamed **The Apache Trail** to attract tourists. Still a popular scenic drive, it's a long, slow haul, taking around two hours from one end to the other.

Goldfield Ghost Town

4650 N Mammoth Mine Rd; 4 miles northeast of Apache Junction • Daily 10am–5pm • Attractions individually priced • ☏ 480 983 0333, ⓦ goldfieldghosttown.com

As the cactus-studded foothills of the Superstition Mountains start to rise, ramshackle **Goldfield Ghost Town** provides an appealing photo opportunity, complete with discarded mine machinery and a street of tumbledown timber-frame stores. Much of what you see is either fake or brought from somewhere else, but it's all quite atmospheric. **Activities** including descents into mine shafts and open-air train rides cost from around $8 per person, and various on-site businesses offer pricier jeep tours, horse rides and even helicopter flights. Alternatively, you can pick up coffee or a full steakhouse meal.

Canyon Lake

Many day-trippers go no further up the Apache Trail than **Canyon Lake**, fifteen miles along. Created by a more recent dam, it's a bit too narrow to satisfy pleasure-boaters, who find themselves having to turn around every time they get up a bit of speed. However, if you're happy to take it easy, a **steamboat cruise** aboard the *Dolly* (☏ 480 827 9144, ⓦ dollysteamboat.com) is an enjoyable way to pass a couple of hours. Daytime sightseeing cruises run up to three times daily in the peak winter season, and cost $23, while twilight dinner cruises, on Saturday nights and occasionally other nights as well, cost $65.

   TORTILLA FLAT, at the east end of Canyon Lake, is not so much a town as a hundred-yard stretch of boardwalk with an Old West flavour, equipped with a saloon, diner and souvenir store. Named for the nearby flat-topped boulders, Tortilla Flat has no connection with the Steinbeck novella.

Roosevelt Dam

Northeast of Tortilla Flat, as the Superstition Mountains finally start to get serious, Hwy-88 responds by turning to gravel. After a few hair-raising hairpin bends, with stomach-lurching views across the saguaro-studded canyons, it returns to undulating gently along beside the river. An optional detour drops down to **Apache Lake**, another busy boating and picnicking spot. Keep going to reach **Roosevelt Dam** itself, which was raised and strengthened during the 1990s to cope with Phoenix's bottomless thirst for water.

Tonto National Monument

Hwy-88, 3 miles east of Roosevelt Dam · Daily 8am–5pm · $5 per person · ☎ 928 467 2241, ⓦ nps.gov/tont

Set half a mile above Hwy-88, overlooking Theodore Roosevelt Lake, the **cliff dwellings** of **TONTO NATIONAL MONUMENT** are reached from the visitor centre along a very steep trail, which shuts an hour before closing time. Not a walk to schedule for the middle of a summer's day, it leads to the remarkably complete **Lower Ruin**, set in a deep alcove near the top of the rocky ridge, with great saguaro cactuses standing sentinel.

This large pueblo, dating from the mid-fourteenth century, was built by the **Salado** people, now regarded as less sophisticated than the Ancestral Puebloans to the north. Their masonry is much cruder, using lumps of rock that had fallen from the cliff face and were then thickly plastered with mud that still bears thousands of ancient fingerprints. Visitors can walk through several rooms of the ruin, some of which retain original beams and saguaro-rib ceilings. "Shelves" and storage niches are tucked into the cave walls, as well as notches that once supported additional rooms.

Between November and April only, rangers lead four-hour guided hikes to the similar, forty-room **Upper Ruin**, reached by a separate trail up the next ridge along.

Globe

4

The mining town of **GLOBE** stands where Hwy-88 meets US-60, the direct route east from Phoenix. Dating from the 1880s, when a twelve-mile strip of land on which a globe of pure silver had just been discovered was grabbed from the Apache reservation, it has made its living from copper since the silver and gold ran out.

Downtown Globe's few central blocks still hold several Victorian-era brick structures, though the claim that these include the last Woolworth's store in the West to close (in 1997) betrays quite how little there is of interest. On the third Saturday in October, Native Americans from all over the Southwest pour in for the **Apache Jii** fair.

If you prefer your Wild West utterly unvarnished and unromantic, head a mile or two west of Globe to the twin communities of **CLAYPOOL** and **MIAMI**. All but engulfed by monstrous mountains of copper-mine tailings, these flyblown towns are packed with gun stores, all-day saloons and pick-up trucks, and are certainly not a vacation destination to choose in preference to Miami, Florida.

Besh-Ba-Gowah

1324 S Jesse Hayes Rd; 1 mile southeast of Globe · July–Sept Wed–Sun 9am–4.30pm; May–June daily 9am–4.30pm · $5 · ☎ 928 425 0320, ⓦ globeaz.gov

The ruins of the ancient village of **Besh-Ba-Gowah** demonstrate that Native Americans lived in the mountains around Globe long before the Apache arrived. Home first to the Hohokam and later, between around 1225 and 1400, to the Salado, they take their modern name from the Apache for "metal-its-house". Visitors can enter reconstructed living quarters and a *kiva*.

INFORMATION	GLOBE

Visitor centre 1360 N Broad St (Oct–April Mon–Fri 8am–5pm, Sat & Sun 10am–4pm; May–Sept Mon–Fri 8am–5pm; ☎ 928 425 4495 or ☎ 800 804 5623, ⓦ globemiamichamber.com).

ACCOMMODATION AND EATING

Days Inn 1630 E Ash St ☎ 928 425 5500, ⓦ daysinn .com. Set just back from the highway, as it curves away east of the centre, this is the most salubrious of Globe's dozen or so motels, with an outdoor pool and hot tub. **$76**

Los Robertos 340 S Broad St ☎ 928 425 3040. A welcome addition to Globe's dining scene, this all-day diner, just south of the centre, offers conventional American breakfasts, then switches to serving the best Mexican food in town, with beef tacos and chicken enchiladas to die for, all costing under $10. Daily 7am–9pm.

Boyce Thompson Arboretum

US-60, Superior; 40 miles east of Apache Junction or 15 miles southwest of Miami • Daily: May–Sept 6am–3pm; Oct–April 8am–5pm; last entry 1hr before closing • $10, ages 5–12 $5 • ☎ 520 689 2723, ⓦ ag.arizona.edu/bta

The **Boyce Thompson Arboretum**, in the former silver-mining town of **SUPERIOR**, is a landscaped public garden that spreads through two parallel canyons, and contains desert plants from around the world. Cactuses are of course abundant, but there are also spectacular oddities like the towering boojum tree from Baja California. A brisk walk along the main hiking trail takes around an hour, though you could spend much longer exploring additional side trails like the themed "Plants of the Bible" walk. The fall colours are usually at their best from late November to early December.

San Carlos Indian Reservation

The two-million-acre **SAN CARLOS INDIAN RESERVATION**, which extends a hundred miles east and north of Globe, was created in 1872 to protect the **Apache** from such outrages as the Camp Grant massacre of 1871 (see below). In the words of one tribal member, the reservation was "the worst place in all the great territory stolen from the Apache. If anybody ever lived there permanently, no Apache knew of it. The heat was terrible. The insects were terrible. The water was terrible."

Around eight thousand Apache now live on the reservation, which offers few activities for tourists apart from sailing or fishing on **San Carlos Lake**, twenty miles east of Globe. After the original reservation town of **San Carlos** was drowned when the lake arose behind the new Coolidge Dam in 1930, the community previously known as **Rice**, ten miles north, was simply renamed San Carlos.

Aravaipa Canyon

Permits $5 per day, max 2-night stay • ☎ 928 348 4400, ⓦ blm.gov/az/aravaipa, permits at ⓦ recreation.gov

The beauty of **ARAVAIPA CANYON**, which lies just below the southern boundary of the San Carlos reservation, belies its sad history as the site of one of the most notorious tragedies in the whole sorry tale of Anglo–Apache relations. In 1871, when it was home to a semipermanent Apache encampment under the nominal protection of the US Army, 144 women and children were slaughtered in the **Camp Grant massacre**. Their killers were an unholy party of Tucson vigilantes who called themselves the Committee of Public Safety (see p.224).

Reached along a well-maintained eleven-mile dirt road that heads east from Hwy-77 fifty miles south of Globe, Aravaipa Canyon is now a **wilderness area**. The terrain ranges from sun-drenched hillsides covered with saguaros to the deep-red gorge carved by Aravaipa Creek – a rare perennial desert stream – and lined by giant cottonwoods. Visitors keen to experience the desert in its wild state need to come prepared; the canyon has no trails, no established campgrounds, and no signs, and is home to rattlesnakes and scorpions. Entry to the thirty-square-mile wilderness is by permit only, with only fifty permits sold for any one time.

From Phoenix to Tucson

The hundred-mile sprint from Phoenix to Tucson along I-10 ranks among Arizona's less inspiring drives. The chief distraction en route is the molar-shaped promontory of

Picacho Peak, at the base of which the roadside **Rooster Cogburn Ostrich Farm** (May to mid-Nov Mon & Fri–Sun 9am–5pm, mid-Nov to April daily 9am–5pm; Ⓦ roostercogburn.com) is as good a place to stretch your legs, and possibly buy a feather duster, as any. By taking a slightly more circuitous route, however, it's possible to break the journey at a couple of equally unlikely and enigmatic structures – ancient **Casa Grande** and ultra-modern **Biosphere 2**.

Casa Grande Ruins National Monument

Just outside Coolidge; 15 miles east of I-10 exit 185, or 20 miles north of I-10 exit 210 • Daily 9am–5pm • $5 per person • ☏ 520 723 3172, Ⓦ nps.gov/cagr

CASA GRANDE RUINS NATIONAL MONUMENT preserves the most substantial surviving example of **Hohokam** architecture. It shares its name – Spanish for "Great House" – but little else, with the town of Casa Grande, an I-10 pit stop thirty miles southwest, and the much larger ancient site of Casas Grandes, far south in northern Mexico.

The Casa Grande itself, a four-storey building completed early in the fourteenth century, is made of the concrete-like natural stone known as caliche. Spanish priest Father Eusebio Kino, who passed this way in 1694 – by which time the site had been abandoned for three centuries – said the main structure was "as large as a castle", and surrounded by thirteen smaller houses and many ruins. It was clear to him that "in ancient times there had been a city here." The house stood in a walled compound in the floodplain of the **Gila River**, where villagers used a network of canals to grow crops, harvested fruit from saguaro cactuses, and traded for shells and macaws with peoples from the south.

It's now protected beneath a spider's-web canopy; visitors can enter the compound but not the structure itself. Its exact purpose is unknown, though as its windows and wall niches are aligned with key moments in the cycles of both the sun and moon, archeologists think it was an astronomical observatory that doubled as a fortress.

4

THE UNBELIEVABLE STORY OF BIOSPHERE 2

When **Biosphere 2** was completed, in 1991, it was publicized as a major laboratory for environmental science. Containing five separate "**biomes**", or self-contained ecosystems – rainforest, marsh, savannah, desert, and a 25-foot-deep ocean – it was designed as a miniature working model of Biosphere 1, planet earth itself, and stocked like a real-life Noah's ark with almost four thousand species of plants and animals. Investigative journalists soon revealed, however, that it was staffed largely by ex-actors from an experimental theatre group, assembled by a certain "Johnny Dolphin" in the hope of colonizing Mars and thus escaping nuclear holocaust on earth. A hundred million dollars' worth of support from Texas oil tycoon Ed Bass got this far-fetched scheme off the ground, and top academics were recruited to add a veneer of respectability.

Eight "Biospherians" were sealed into Biosphere 2 in 1991, their "mission" being to survive in isolation for two full years. This they more or less did, growing 88 percent of their own food, and losing 13.65 percent of their body weight. Much of what transpired was replete with irony; hungry Biospherians found themselves planting bananas and papayas in what they had resolved would be the inviolate wilderness of the rainforest, and destroying parts of the desert to boost oxygen, while the ocean proved impossible to keep clean. As for their fellow inhabitants, the bush babies caught the hummingbirds, and the only birds to survive were unwanted sparrows that snuck in during construction. After "crazy ants" killed all the pollinating insects, all the plants had to be pollinated by hand.

By the time the next crew moved in, conditions had degenerated into farce. Two of the original crew, who had been acrimoniously fired, broke the Biosphere's seals from the outside, thus aborting the second mission after just six months; they later sued and won compensation for their dismissal.

Biosphere 2

Mile-marker 96.5 on Hwy-77; 30 miles north of Tucson or 8 miles southwest of Oracle • Daily 9am–4pm • $20, ages 6–12 $13 • ☏ 520 838 6200, ⓦ biosphere2.org

At one point, back in the twentieth century, the vast complex of Plexiglas pyramids known as **BIOSPHERE 2** ranked among Arizona's most popular tourist destinations. Decades have past since any would-be space adventurers were locked inside, however, and the crowds have dwindled. Run by the University of Arizona, it's primarily a historical attraction. Even so, the standard two-and-a-half-hour guided tours are still worth taking. Most of that time is spent peering into the greenhouses hoping to spot any sign of life larger than an ant, and marvelling at the fact that, whatever you may have assumed, Biosphere 2 is not solar powered but depends on an external natural-gas power plant. Tunnels take you down beneath the "Coral Biome"; the guides insist it isn't an aquarium, but it doesn't half look like one. Visitors are also allowed into the Biospherians' futuristic living quarters, tacked like a space capsule onto the back of the main block, where they appear to have suffered no privations whatsoever. An all-day café serves meals and snacks on an appealing terrace.

Tucson

For over two hundred years, under five separate flags, **TUCSON** has been southern Arizona's leading city. Spreading across a mountain-ringed basin at the northern limits of the **Sonoran Desert**, it's now the core of a metropolitan district where almost a million inhabitants pride themselves on being more cosmopolitan, cultured and liberal than those of its upstart rival Phoenix. Like Phoenix, the "Old Pueblo" has grown way past the point where the region's rivers, such as the Santa Cruz, could ever quench its thirst. All are now dry sandy washes for most of the year, though flash floods rage through the cross-town culverts after summer thunderstorms. However, Tucson embraces rather than denies the desert, eschewing lawns and fountains in favour of directing visitors toward the landscapes of **Sabino Canyon** and the **Arizona-Sonora Desert Museum**, and the cactus-strewn hillsides of **Saguaro National Park**.

By Southwestern standards, Tucson (pronounced *too-sonn*) is a diverse, attractive and lively city, home to the forty thousand energetic students of the **University of Arizona** as well as a large influx of retirees, and strongly influenced by its long association with Mexico, a mere sixty miles south. While prone to the same Sunbelt sprawl as Albuquerque and Phoenix, it still has a compact and recognizably historic centre, some good parks and museums, affordable accommodation and enjoyable restaurants, and decent nightlife.

Brief history

The valley of the Santa Cruz had already been inhabited for many centuries by the time Spanish priest Eusebio Kino visited the **Pima Indian** settlement of Stjukshon, or "dark spring", in 1700. Archeological excavations west of downtown have even suggested that this may be the oldest inhabited site in North America. In 1776, under the direction of **Hugo O'Conor** – one of the Catholic "Wild Geese" who had fled English-controlled Ireland to fight for Spain – the Spanish relocated their main Arizona fortress here from Tubac (see p.234). That forty-mile move northwards brought them closer to **Apache** territory, and the energies of the Hispanic and Pima citizens of **San Agustín de Tucson** were largely devoted to resisting Apache raids and sieges. The severed heads of Apache warriors were displayed as trophies on the city walls.

When Tucson was sold to the US in the **Gadsden Purchase** of 1854 (see p.473), the incoming Anglos were generally welcomed. Most of the valley's Mexican farmers remained in Arizona, and they were joined by more of their former compatriots. Soon, however, travellers were describing Tucson as "a place of resort for traders, speculators, gamblers, horse-thieves and vagrant politicians ... a paradise of devils."

METROPOLITAN TUCSON

● EATING

Beyond Bread	3
Blue Willow	4
Feast	6
Kingfisher	5
Tasteful Kitchen	7
Vivace	2
Wildflower	1

■ DRINKING & NIGHTLIFE

Nimbus Brewing	2
The Shelter	1

■ ACCOMMODATION

Adobe Rose Inn	8
Arizona Inn	6
Catalina Park Inn	7
Homewood Suites by Hilton Tucson	3
Lodge on the Desert	9
Loews Ventana Canyon Resort	2
Quality Inn Flamingo Downtown	4
Tanque Verde Ranch	5
Westward Look Resort	1

4

Although the **Confederates** who occupied southern Arizona in 1862 were swiftly driven away by Union forces from California, suspicions of lingering Confederate sympathies led to Tucson being passed over as capital of the new Territory. Conflict with the Apache continued, and a vigilante force of Mexicans, Anglos and O'odham Indians from Tucson was responsible for the notorious **Camp Grant massacre** of 144 Apache in Aravaipa Canyon in 1871 (see p.220). US Army commanders came to believe that a shadowy "**Tucson Ring**" of businessmen was deliberately provoking the Apache, in order to profit from the resultant military spending.

After the end of the Apache Wars in the 1880s coincided with the coming of the transcontinental **railroad**, trade with Mexico rapidly declined, and Tucson's wealthy Mexican merchants were driven out of business. Ever since, Mexican labourers have streamed back and forth across the border as the economy expands and contracts, but Tucson has become ever more American. Outstripped by Phoenix during the 1920s, and home to fewer than forty thousand people (in an area of just nine square miles) as recently as 1940, the city has nonetheless grown at a phenomenal rate.

Downtown Tucson

Downtown Tucson, which centres on the area where the east–west Congress Street and Broadway Boulevard cross the north–south Stone Avenue, is largely characterized by undistinguished modern architecture, though the 1928 **Pima County Courthouse** is an eclectic mix of Southwestern and Moorish influences. The adobe fortress of San Agustín de Tucson occupied what's now the four-block **El Presidio Historic District**, a couple of blocks northwest. None of its original structures is still standing, but several of their nineteenth-century successors have been restored as cafés, art galleries and B&Bs.

Tucson Museum of Art

140 N Main Ave • Tues, Wed, Fri & Sat 10am–5pm, Thurs 10am–8pm, Sun noon–5pm • $12, ages 13–17 $7, under-13s free • ☎ 502 624 2333, ⍵ tucsonmuseumofart.org

The **Tucson Museum of Art** devotes its main building to changing exhibitions of modern painting and sculpture, and the giftshop stocks interesting contemporary crafts. An adjoining adobe, the **Palice Pavilion**, displays magnificent pre-Columbian artefacts, including Mochica ceramics from northern Peru, with extraordinarily life-like faces; textiles from the later Peruvian Chancay culture; and gold from Colombia and Costa Rica. Mexican artefacts range from masks and effigies created by the ancient Olmec and Mixtec peoples to eighteenth-century religious pieces and nineteenth-century oil-on-tin family portraits.

The museum also controls access to much of the adjoining El Presidio complex. The oldest house there, **La Casa Cordova** at 175 N Meyer Ave (same hours), contains displays on the city's Mexican heritage.

Barrio Historico

Tucson's 1880s business district, now known as the **Barrio Historico**, stretches south from Cushing Street, on the southern fringes of the modern downtown. While the neighbourhood holds plenty of century-old adobes, its most notable landmark is the sidewalk shrine of **El Tiradito**, "the castaway". Said to mark where a young man was killed by his father-in-law for committing adultery with his mother-in-law, and then buried where he fell, it's famous as the **Wishing Shrine**. Light a candle that burns through the night, and your prayers will be answered.

The University District

Other than downtown, central Tucson's principal area of interest is the **University of Arizona**, which spreads between Sixth Street and Speedway Boulevard a mile east, and

DOWNTOWN TUCSON

— Sun Link streetcar

EAST FIFTH STREET

NORTH SEVENTH AVENUE

NORTH FOURTH AVENUE

WEST SIXTH STREET

NINTH AVENUE

TOOLE AVENUE

NORTH STONE AVENUE

EAST SIXTH STREET

NORTH SIXTH AVENUE

NORTH ARIZONA AVENUE

NORTH FIFTH AVENUE

NORTH HERBERT AVENUE

EAST SEVENTH STREET

WEST FRANKLIN STREET

NORTH MEYER AVENUE

NORTH COURT AVENUE

NORTH CHURCH AVENUE

WEST COUNCIL STREET

EAST COUNCIL STREET

EAST EIGHTH STREET

E STEVENS AVE

NORTH MAIN AVENUE

WASHINGTON ST

EAST ALAMEDA STREET

E NINTH STREET

La Casa
Cordova

EAST TOOLE AVENUE

Tucson
Museum
of Art ❷

WEST ALAMEDA STREET

Amtrak
Station

El Presidio
Park

Pima County
Courthouse

EAST PENNINGTON STREET ❸

ARIZONA AVENUE

WEST PENNINGTON STREET

WEST CONGRESS STREET

EAST CONGRESS STREET

❹❸🚏

❹

SOUTH FIFTH AVENUE

SOUTH HERBERT AVENUE

RAILROAD AVENUE

Greyhound
Depot

GRANADA AVENUE

ℹ️

WEST BROADWAY BOULEVARD

EAST BROADWAY BOULEVARD

N

WEST JACKSON STREET

EAST JACKSON STREET

Sosa-Carrillo-
Frémont House

WEST OCHOA STREET

EAST OCHOA STREET

SOUTH CHURCH AVENUE

EAST 12TH STREET

SOUTH FOURTH AVENUE

St Augustine
Cathedral

SOUTH SCOTT AVENUE

Armory
Park

SOUTH SIXTH AVENUE

Tucson
Convention
Center

W MC CORMICK ST

EAST 13TH STREET

EL PASO AVENUE

WEST CUSHING STREET

SOUTH STONE AVENUE

SOUTH ARIZONA AVENUE

SOUTH FIFTH AVENUE

SOUTH FOURTH AVENUE

❷

El
Tiradito

S MAIN AVENUE

SOUTH MEYER AVENUE

SOUTH CONVENT AVENUE

EAST 14TH STREET

● EATING	
Café à la C'Art	2
Café Passé	1
Café Poca Cosa	3
Cup Café	4

■ NIGHTLIFE	
Club Congress	3
IBT's	1
Rialto Theatre	4
Sky Bar	2

WEST SIMPSON STREET

EAST 15TH STREET

■ ACCOMMODATION	
Hotel Congress	1
Roadrunner Hostel	2

W KENNEDY STREET

0   200
yards

4

can be readily accessed using the new Sun Link **streetcar** system (see p.229). Park
Avenue, on its western side, is lined with funky cafés and stores that cater to students.

Arizona State Museum

1013 E University Blvd • Mon–Sat 10am–5pm • $5, under-18s free • ☎ 520 621 6302, ⊛ statemuseum.arizona.edu

In the **Arizona State Museum**, the highlight of the university campus, the Pottery
Project, traces the history of Southwestern ceramics. There's a stunning case devoted to

fabulous "burden carrier" pots made by the Hohokam between 850 and 1000 AD, as well as some very modern pieces that challenge all preconceptions about Native American pottery. The large **Paths of Life** exhibition illuminates the cultures of the major native peoples of the Southwest and northern Mexico, with a heavy emphasis on Arizona. They also have a wonderful collection of baskets.

Center for Creative Photography
1030 N Olive Rd • Tues–Fri 9am–4pm, Sat 1–4pm • Free • ☎ 520 621 7968, ⓦ creativephotography.org

The **Center for Creative Photography** holds one of the world's finest photography archives. **Ansel Adams** left his negatives, prints and journals to the university, and his collection has been complemented by images from all eras. Temporary exhibitions only show a tiny selection, however, and the archive is primarily intended for serious scholars.

UA Museum of Art
1031 N Olive Rd • Wed & Fri–Sat 9am–5pm, Thurs 9am–8pm, Sun noon–5pm • $8 • ☎ 520 621 7567, ⓦ artmuseum.arizona.edu

An eclectic affair, the **UA Museum of Art** has acquired its permanent collection via a number of unconnected bequests. Its treasures therefore include a somewhat morbid altarpiece from the cathedral of Spanish city Ciudad Rodrigo, along with prints, drawings and canvases by Rembrandt, Picasso and Warhol; a solitary O'Keeffe; and some fine cubist sculpture by Jacques Lipchitz.

Arizona Historical Society Museum
949 E Second St • Mon–Thurs 9am–4pm, Fri 9am–8pm, Sat & Sun 11am–4pm • $8 • ☎ 520 628 5774, ⓦ arizonahistoricalsociety.org

The **Arizona Historical Society Museum**, across Park Avenue from the UA campus, surveys the history of southern Arizona with a replica mine tunnel; exhibits on the Apache Wars that include a rifle that belonged to Geronimo; and a good "Oxcart to Auto" section, on travel in the frontier era. If it's specifically the history of Tucson itself that interests you, call in also at the museum's downtown offshoot, at 140 N Stone Ave (Thurs–Sat 10am–4pm; donation).

Sabino Canyon
5900 N Sabino Canyon Rd • Daily dawn–dusk • Free, but parking $5 • ☎ 520 749 8700, ⓦ sabinocanyon.org and ⓦ sabinocanyon.com

For an enjoyable taste of the **Santa Catalina Mountains**, which form Metropolitan Tucson's northern boundary, head to **Sabino Canyon**, in the Coronado National Forest ten miles northeast of downtown. The canyon was cut into the lower reaches of Mount Lemmon by Sabino Creek, which manages to flow for up to eleven months of the year, and is lined by green vegetation. Assorted trails lace into the hills from a four-mile riverbank road – barred to private vehicles, but served by jump-on, jump-off **tram rides** ($10) – that's popular with early-morning joggers.

Mount Lemmon
Mount Lemmon Ski Valley Mon & Thurs–Sun 9am–4pm • Full-day lift ticket $40; half-day $35 • Rentals available • ☎ 520 576 1321, ⓦ skithelemmon.com

The 9157ft summit of **Mount Lemmon**, which towers above Sabino Canyon, can be reached via a two-day hike beyond the canyon, or a one-hour drive on the scenic **Mount Lemmon Highway**. After branching off Tanque Verde Road, an eastward continuation of Grant Road, a few miles east of the Sabino Canyon turn-off, the highway winds for 25 slow miles up the mountain, with countless panoramic viewpoints to either side. The summit is largely given over to the **Mount Lemmon Ski Valley**, which holds more than twenty runs, including several black diamonds, and a few restaurants that collectively offer a surprisingly well-rounded portfolio of options.

Pima Air & Space Museum

6000 E Valencia Rd; 2 miles east of I-10 • Daily 9am–5pm • $15.50, ages 5–12 $9 • ☎ 520 574 0462, ⓦ pimaair.org

The **Pima Air & Space Museum** boasts an amazing collection of vintage and modern aircraft. Some exhibits, like the Wright Brothers' 1903 Flyer and the Apollo capsule, are replicas, but the great majority are the real deal, including plenty of World War II bombers, prototype helicopters and the superfast X-15 fighter. The whole place is so huge, with vast tracts of sun-scorched concrete between the various hangars, that you may well prefer to pay $6 extra to tour it by tram.

As you approach the museum, you pass rows of defunct aircraft lined up in the **Boneyard** of the adjoining Davis-Monthan Air Force Base. On weekdays, the museum offers bus tours that go in there as well, costing an extra $7.

Old Tucson Studios

201 S Kinney Rd, 12 miles west of downtown • Feb–April daily 10am–6pm; May Fri–Sun 10am–5pm; June, Aug & first weekend of Sept Sat & Sun 10am–5pm; Oct Fri–Sun 10am–4pm; Nov & Dec Fri–Sun 10am–5pm; closed July & last 3 weeks of Sept • $18, under-12s $11 • ☎ 520 883 0100, ⓦ oldtucson.com

The focus of **Old Tucson Studios**, an entertaining Wild West theme park, is a movie-set mock-up of nineteenth-century Tucson itself, constructed for the 1939 Western *Arizona*, and also used for TV shows and movies including *Tombstone* and *Geronimo*. Visitors can ride a stagecoach or a coal-fired steam train, and watch gunfights on Main Street or a bawdy show in the saloon. Old Tucson had to be almost entirely rebuilt after a fire in 1995, making it even more spurious, but kids love it all the same.

Arizona-Sonora Desert Museum

2021 N Kinney Rd, 14 miles west of downtown • March–May & Sept daily 7.30am–5pm; June–Aug Mon–Fri & Sun 7.30am–5pm, Sat 7.30am–10pm; Oct–Feb 8.30am–5pm • $20.50, ages 3–12 $8 • ☎ 520 883 2702, ⓦ desertmuseum.org

Part zoo, part garden, the **Arizona-Sonora Desert Museum** makes a hugely satisfying adjunct to visiting nearby Saguaro National Park. Displays in the museum proper explain regional geology and history, while dioramas are filled with tarantulas, rattlesnakes and other creepy crawlers. In enclosures along the loop path beyond – a hot walk in summer – bighorn sheep, mountain lions, jaguars and other seldom-seen desert denizens prowl in credible simulations of their natural habitats. An artificial cave is home to a colony of real bats, and hawks and bald eagles fly about a large aviary, thankfully separated from the greenhouse full of hummingbirds. Under the Raptor Free Flight programme, spectacular displays by free-flying Harris hawks are scheduled most winter afternoons. The outdoor terrace of the museum's restaurant is a great stop-off for a light lunch; it also has a good coffee bar.

Saguaro National Park

Admission to either or both sections, valid for a week, costs $10 per vehicle • ⓦ nps.gov/sagu • Backcountry camping by permit only

Flanking Tucson to either side, the two-part **Saguaro National Park** offers visitors a rare and enthralling opportunity to stroll through desert "forests" of monumental, multi-limbed **saguaro** (pronounced *sa-wah-row*) **cactuses**. Each section tends to be seen on a short foray from the city; neither area has any lodging, or even permanent campground, and in summer, it's far too hot to do more than pose for photographs, dwarfed beneath some especially eccentric specimen.

As saguaros prefer sloping foothills, which offer a little run-off after rain, to level desert, both sections of the park include rugged mountain tracts. Most of the **Rincon Mountain District** in the east, which became a national monument in 1933, is much higher, and the one road only penetrates its low-lying fringes. It was joined in 1961 by the **Tucson Mountain District** in the west, which incorporates the world's densest stand of saguaro.

The western park: Tucson Mountain District

15 miles west of downtown Tucson • Daily dawn–dusk • **Red Hill Visitor Center** 2700 N Kinney Rd, 2 miles northwest of Arizona-Sonora Desert Museum • Daily 8am–5pm • ☎ 520 733 5158

The **Tucson Mountain District** of Saguaro National Park is located on the western slopes of the Tucson Mountains, across the mountains from the city itself. Turn right off Kinney Road 1.5 miles beyond the **Red Hills Visitor Center** to set off along the six-mile **Bajada Loop Drive**, which although not fully paved is always passable to ordinary vehicles, and leads through a wonderland of weird saguaro, offering plentiful short hiking trails and photo opportunities. Although you can access the road at either of two intersections, less than half a mile apart, its central mile or so is one-way, so you can only complete a full loop if you start at the south.

The easiest walk, the **Desert Discovery Nature Trail**, sets off just before the one-way section. It follows a small gully before climbing onto a low brow for sweeping westward views, with abundant saguaro all around; in principle it's half a mile long, though you can choose how far you want to walk before you turn back. If you've only time for one hike, however, head further along the road and walk at **Signal Hill** instead, ideally timing your arrival to enjoy its magnificent sunset panoramas. You're not the first to pass this way; boulders at the top are marked with Hohokam **petroglyphs**. Gluttons for punishment can climb the longer **Hugh Norris Trail** up a ridge to the 4687ft summit of Wasson Peak.

Branching onto Golden Gate Road from the northeastern limit of the loop drive brings you in around five miles to Picture Rocks Road, which joins **Ina Road** a few more miles along and thus makes an alternative route back to northern Tucson.

The eastern park: Rincon Mountain District

Old Spanish Trail; 17 miles east of downtown Tucson • **Rincon Visitor Center** Daily 8am–5pm; Cactus Forest Drive Daily: April–Oct 7am–7pm; Nov–March 7am–5pm • ☎ 520 733 5153

To reach the eastern section of Saguaro National Park, the **Rincon Mountain District**, head east from downtown Tucson along first Broadway Boulevard and then Old Spanish Trail, turning south at the end to reach the **Rincon Visitor Center**. The eight-mile **Cactus Forest Drive** loops away beyond here, providing access to a couple

THE SAGUARO CACTUS – A DESERT SAGA

As the mighty, multi-armed **saguaro cactus** is unique to the Sonoran Desert, and Tucson stands near the desert's northeastern extremity, the Tucson region is one of very few places in the Wild West where real-life saguaro grow. Whatever you may have seen in the movies, you can drive a long way in Arizona without seeing a saguaro; finally encountering a thousand at once is a genuine thrill.

Each saguaro can grow up to fifty feet tall and weigh up to eight tons, but it takes a very long time to reach that size. A teenage cactus is a foot high, a fifty-year-old more like seven feet. At 75, it sprouts the first of what may amount to forty "arms", and it only reaches its full height at around 150, with perhaps another fifty years to go before it dies. Its roots radiate as much as a hundred feet in all directions, barely three inches below the surface, and can draw enough water from a single rainstorm to last for two years.

Each year from the age of thirty onwards, between late April and June, a saguaro grows up to a hundred **white flowers**, each of which blossoms for a single night and dies by the next afternoon. In its lifetime, each saguaro produces as many as forty million seeds, but few, if any, germinate and thrive. It's also home to an intricate community of birds, insects, mammals and reptiles. Woodpeckers and owls burrow holes into the trunk for their nests, which the cactus heals over with hardened "scar tissue" to create permanent hollows. The **Tohono O'odham** Indians traditionally cut away these depressions for use as bowls; they also mashed the saguaro's succulent **crimson fruit** to make jam, syrup and even wine, and used its long, wood-like ribs to construct dwellings and fences.

Thanks to the thriving black market in stolen saguaros, many cactuses in Saguaro National Park are now micro-chipped against theft.

of short trails that thread between mighty cactuses. The easiest is the level, quarter-mile **Desert Ecology Trail**, but rather more satisfying is the **Freeman Homestead Trail**, a mile or so south of the visitor centre along the road's only two-way segment. It drops down to the barely visible vestiges of a pioneer home, then follows the course of a gentle wash back up again, threading between abundant groups of towering saguaro.

Many visitors to the Rincon Mountain District come specifically to hike far from the road, up into the mountains. The saguaro cactuses thin out almost as soon as you start climbing the **Tanque Verde Ridge Trail** from just beyond the Freeman Homestead trailhead. It leads in due course to a hundred-mile network of remote footpaths through thickly forested canyons. Permits to use the district's six wilderness campgrounds, only accessible on foot or by horse, cost $6 per night. Water is seasonally available – check with rangers – but should be treated before you drink it.

ARRIVAL AND DEPARTURE
TUCSON

By plane Tucson International Airport, ten miles south of downtown (🌐 flytucsonairport.com), receives flights from all over the Southwest, but for long-distance services it's very much second fiddle to Phoenix. It's connected to central Tucson by the slow Sun Tran bus #25 ($1.50; 🌐 suntran.com) and the $25 shuttle vans of Arizona Stagecoach (☎ 520 889 1000, 🌐 azstagecoach.com). For taxi service, contact Discount Cab (☎ 520 200 2000, 🌐 discountcab.com).
By train The Amtrak station, downtown at 400 E Toole Ave, is served by three trains weekly in each direction between Los Angeles and points east; connecting Amtrak buses run north to Phoenix.
By bus Greyhound buses to and from destinations including Phoenix and LA stop centrally at 471 W Congress St (☎ 520 792 3475, 🌐 greyhound.com). Arizona Shuttle Services runs a shuttle-van service between Tucson and Phoenix's Sky Harbor airport (one-way $41; ☎ 520 795 6771 or ☎ 800 888 2749, 🌐 arizonashuttle.com).

GETTING AROUND AND INFORMATION

By streetcar The Sun Link streetcar system connects central Tucson with the university district, running west along Congress St and east along Broadway downtown (Mon–Wed 7am–10pm, Thurs & Fri 7am–2am, Sat 8am–2am, Sun 8am–8pm; 24hr pass $4, sold at stops but not on board; 🌐 sunlinkstreetcar.com).
Visitor centre 100 S Church Ave, in downtown's little La Placita mall (Mon–Fri 9am–5pm, Sat & Sun 9am–4pm; ☎ 520 624 1817 or ☎ 800 638 8350, 🌐 visittucson.org).
Maps and guides Tucson Map & Flag Center, 3239 N First Ave (Mon–Sat 9am–5.30pm; ☎ 520 887 4234, 🌐 mapsmithus.com), stocks Arizona's best selection of maps and local guides.
Bike rental and tours Tucson Bike Rentals (☎ 800 873 8828, 🌐 tucsonbikerentals.org) deliver rental bikes to any address in the city, and offer an extensive programme of guided and self-guided biking tours.

ACCOMMODATION

Tucson offers a broader range of accommodation than Phoenix, with plenty of reasonably priced **hotels** and **motels** downtown as well as some atmospheric **B&Bs** both in the historic centre and out in the surrounding desert. It also has its fair share of **resorts** and **dude ranches**. Rates drop when the mercury rises.

HOSTELS AND B&BS

★**Adobe Rose Inn** 940 N Olsen Ave ☎ 520 318 4644 or ☎ 800 328 4122, 🌐 aroseinn.com; map p.223. Charming, great-value B&B in a peaceful residential area near the university, with plenty of good restaurants nearby. The six en-suite rooms feature attractive fireplaces, tilework and ceramics, and the courtyard pool and outdoor seating areas are very welcome. The copious communal breakfasts are superb – the friendly hosts have their own scone business. June–Aug $90, Sept–May $140
Catalina Park Inn 309 E First St ☎ 520 792 4541, 🌐 catalinaparkinn.com; map p.223. Beautiful yet not overly fussy historic B&B across from a quiet park; all but one of the six en-suite rooms are large and some have hot tubs or private balconies. Within walking distance of the university and happening Fourth Ave. Closed June–Sept. $145
Roadrunner Hostel 346 E Twelfth St ☎ 520 940 7280, 🌐 roadrunnerhostel.com; map p.225. Small and very central independent hostel in a downtown home, popular with international travellers and in easy walking distance of eating and nightlife. Accommodation is in six-bed dorms or private doubles, with discounted weekly rates, and there's a communal kitchen and patio. Closed noon–3pm daily. Dorms $22, doubles $45

HOTELS AND MOTELS
Homewood Suites by Hilton Tucson 4250 N Campbell Ave ☎ 520 577 0007, 🌐 homewoodsuites.com; map

p.223. These large two-room suites, near the foothills north of downtown, are ideal for families. The hotel stands alongside St Philip's Plaza, which holds a number of good restaurants, and there's also a pool. Summer $118, winter $199

★ **Hotel Congress** 311 E Congress St ☎ 520 622 8848 or ☎ 800 722 8848, ⊚ hotelcongress.com; map p.225. Bohemian central, hotel, a short walk from Amtrak and Greyhound, with vintage Art Deco furnishings. In the 1930s, bank robber Dillinger was arrested here after pleading for his peculiarly heavy luggage to be rescued from a blaze on the third floor; now it offers forty plain en-suite guest rooms, with vintage radios rather than TVs. With the *Cup Café* (see p.231) and *Club Congress* (see p.231) downstairs, this is one of the hottest spots in town, with loud music and dancing at night; if you're simply looking for a quiet place to sleep, though, don't even dream of staying here. June–Aug $69, Sept–May $79

Quality Inn Flamingo Downtown 1300 N Stone Ave ☎ 520 770 1910, ⊚ flamingohoteltucson.com; map p.223. A much-loved Tucson fixture, the Western-themed *Flamingo* motel stands barely a mile north of downtown. From the outside it still looks straight out of the 1950s – Elvis himself slept here – but the rooms have nicely revamped in appropriate period style, and it has a reasonable pool and spa. $70

RANCHES AND RESORTS

Arizona Inn 2200 E Elm St ☎ 520 325 1541 or ☎ 800 933 1093, ⊚ arizonainn.com; map p.223. Elegant, family-owned desert oasis that's been a winter favourite for numerous presidents, Rockefellers, and the Duke and Duchess of Windsor, and still offers croquet on the lawn. With just 92 rooms, it remains surprisingly unstuffy and far from expensive in low season. Gourmet breakfasts included. Summer $129, winter $299

Lodge on the Desert 306 N Alvernon Way ☎ 520 320 2000, ⊚ lodgeonthedesert.com; map p.223. This 1930s adobe resort, a couple of miles east of downtown is tastefully restored to resemble a Mexican hacienda, with large, comfortable rooms and *casitas*, and a good restaurant, though the pool is somewhat small. Book well ahead for the best rates. Summer $99, winter $169

Loews Ventana Canyon Resort 7000 N Resort Drive ☎ 520 299 2020 or ☎ 800 234 5117, ⊚ loewshotels .com; map p.223. Grand red-brick resort, reaching majestically across a hundred acres at the foot of the Santa Catalina Mountains northeast of the city, with its own on-site waterfall. Four hundred rooms, four restaurants, two golf courses, plus tennis and spa, and the desert on your doorstep. Summer $164, winter $224

Tanque Verde Ranch 14301 E Speedway Blvd ☎ 520 296 6275 or ☎ 800 234 3833, ⊚ tanqueverderanch .com; map p.223. Arizona's most authentic dude ranch, an irresistibly romantic 400 acres adjoining Saguaro National Park twenty miles east of downtown. The accommodation in individual *casitas* is luxurious and the stable is home to more than a hundred horses; there's also tennis, swimming and hiking. Standard rates are for a room plus three meals; all-inclusive rates also include a full programme of rides, from early-morning cowboy cookouts to all-day pack trips. At times, during quiet periods, it's possible to stay on a room-only basis, for much cheaper rates. Three-day minimum. Summer standard $309, all-inclusive $450; winter standard $309, all-inclusive $550

Westward Look Resort 245 E Ina Rd ☎ 520 297 1151 or ☎ 800 722 2500, ⊚ westwardlook.com; map p.223. This fancy resort, in attractive landscaped grounds north of the city, retains its atmospheric 1912 core while modernized to eco-friendly standards, and holds almost 250 extra-large rooms and suites in very private low-slung *casitas*. Naturally, the emphasis on physical fitness, and tennis in particular, doesn't preclude having a top-quality restaurant. Summer $119, winter $229

EATING

Though downtown Tucson shuts down pretty early each evening – it's hard to find anywhere to eat after 9pm – the city has a fine selection of **restaurants**. Mexican joints and cowboy-style Wild West steakhouses abound in the central districts, while fancier restaurants congregate further north in the Foothills.

CAFÉS AND COFFEEHOUSES

Beyond Bread 3026 N Campbell Ave ☎ 520 322 9965, ⊚ beyondbread.com; map p.223. The most central of this hugely popular café-bakery's four Tucson outlets may lack atmosphere, but it's great for a takeaway sandwich (most of which from "classics" named for staff members like Bob's BLT to specials like a New Orleans-style shrimp po'boy, cost from $5 for a half-portion up to $9 for the whole thing) or for a breakfast omelette, or a hot special. Mon–Fri 6.30am–8pm, Sat 7am–8pm, Sun 7am–6pm.

Blue Willow 2616 N Campbell Ave ☎ 520 327 7577, ⊚ bluewillowtucson.com; map p.223. Tasty, fruity breakfasts – with nothing priced over $10, that's when it's most likely to

be crowded – and light lunches and dinners (mains like their signature meatloaf cost $15), served on a pleasant garden patio. Mon–Fri 7am–9pm, Sat & Sun 8am–9pm.

Café à la C'Art Tucson Museum of Art, 150 N Main Ave ☎ 520 628 8533, ⊚ cafealacarttucson.com; map p.225. With such a good café in the art museum courtyard, serving sandwiches, salads and daily specials for $9–13, museum visitors have no need to look further afield. Note, though, that it's also open at times – breakfast, for example – and even on days, when the museum itself is closed. Mon & Tues 8am–3pm, Wed–Sun 8am–3pm & 5–9pm.

Café Passé 415 E Fourth Ave ☎ 520 624 4411, ⊚ cafepasse.com; map p.225. Very friendly little

German-owned café, which as well as espresso drinks and bagel or granola breakfasts sells $10 lunchtime sandwiches with an emphasis on bratwurst sausages, including curried and even vegetarian versions . Be sure to check out the little record store – yes, genuine vinyl! – out back. Mon–Thurs & Sun 8am–8pm, Fri & Sat 8am–10pm.

Cup Café Hotel Congress, 311 E Congress St ☎ 520 798 1618, ⓦ hotelcongress.com; map p.225. Jazzy downtown café, straight out of the 1930s but updated to include an espresso bar. As well as making a good morning rendezvous, with eggy breakfasts for $10–12, it offers lunchtime sandwiches and salads at similar prices, and a full dinner menu that includes fish'n'chips for $17 and pot roast for $19. Mon–Thurs & Sun 7am–10pm, Fri & Sat 7am–midnight.

RESTAURANTS

★ Café Poca Cosa 110 E Pennington St ☎ 520 622 6400, ⓦ cafepocacosatucson.com; map p.225. Popular and stylish downtown café that serves tasty but inexpensive Mexican – or to be more precise, Sonoran – cuisine with a great deal of contemporary Southwestern flair. Typical highlights on the short blackboard menu include shredded beef, or cod with clams. Lunch mains cost around $10; at dinner they can top $20. Tues–Thurs 11am–9pm, Fri & Sat 11am–10pm.

Feast 3719 E Speedway Blvd ☎ 520 329 9363, ⓦ eatatfeast.com; map p.223. Thanks to its combination of top-notch modern cooking at affordable prices, plus takeaway if you'd prefer a picnic, this large, comfortable restaurant has gone from strength to strength. The menu changes monthly, but typical dishes include crispy duck salad ($12) and loin of venison ($26). Tues–Sat 11am–9pm, Sun 10am–9pm.

Kingfisher 2564 E Grant Rd ☎ 520 323 7739, ⓦ kingfishertucson.com; map p.223. Upmarket restaurant that serves seafood – from Maine lobsters and Maryland soft-shell crabs to Oregon oysters – with an eclectic mix of American cooking styles from Cajun to New Pacific. Typical fishy dishes include the $25 grilled sea bass and a $30 bouillabaisse, while meat-eaters can opt instead for roast chicken ($17) or ribs ($27). The reduced late-night menu (also, confusingly, served 3–5pm on weekdays) can be a life-saver. Mon–Fri 11am–midnight, Sat & Sun 5pm–midnight; closed first 2 weeks of July.

Tasteful Kitchen 722 N Stone Ave ☎ 520 250 9600, ⓦ thetastefulkitchen.com; map p.223. Excellent, inventive vegetarian restaurant, slightly north of downtown and open for dinner only, where the romantic little dining room has space for just 24 diners. All main dishes, like the seared cauliflower "steak", cost $16; don't miss the green pea ice cream, or the home-made, prickly pear "shrub sodas". You can bring your own wine, for a $7 corkage fee. Tues–Sat 5–9pm.

Vivace 6440 N Campbell Ave ☎ 520 795 7221, ⓦ vivacetucson.com; map p.223. High-quality northern Italian food in an attractive Italianate setting, with a large mountain-view terrace. It's particularly good value at lunchtime, when sandwiches and specials cost $12–18; in the evening, pasta costs $18–24, and more substantial mains like veal marsala or *osso bucco* range up to $47. Mon–Thurs 11.30am–9pm, Fri & Sat 11.30am–10pm.

Wildflower 7037 N Oracle Rd ☎ 520 219 4230, ⓦ foxrc .com; map p.223. While you can't help being wary of a place that calls itself a "progressive, on-trend restaurant concept", the fusion "New American" cuisine in this stylish mall restaurant, north of the centre, tastes nice – and that's all that matters. Choose between casual dining on the spacious patio, or nestle into the plush indoor seating, in sight of the open kitchen, and enjoy appetizers like edamame dumplings ($9); mains including lemongrass scallops with forbidden rice ($25); and the fabulous $5 butterscotch dessert. Daily 11am–9pm.

ENTERTAINMENT AND NIGHTLIFE

Downtown, Tucson **nightlife** focuses on Congress Street with its gaggle of arty cafés and nightclubs; most venues double as bars or restaurants, and the city has a reputation as being particularly **gay-friendly**. A handful of student places can be found near the university, while country saloons are scattered on the outskirts of town. Check listings in the free *Tucson Weekly* (ⓦ tucsonweekly.com).

Club Congress Hotel Congress, 311 E Congress St ☎ 520 622 8848, ⓦ hotelcongress.com; map p.225. Hip and hectic late-night bar with live music, including some surprisingly big names, three or four nights each week, and club nights on the rest. Nightly until late.

IBT's 616 N Fourth Ave ☎ 520 882 3053, ⓦ ibtstucson .com; map p.225. Tucson's premier gay downtown dance club features DJs most nights and also puts on drag acts and revue, with a huge dance floor indoors and another on the patio outside. Daily noon–2am.

Nimbus Brewing 3850 E 44th St ☎ 520 745 9175, ⓦ nimbusbeer.com; map p.223. Tucson's best local beer, served right in front of the brewery responsible, in the shape of pale, brown and red Nimbus ales and stouts (but no lagers); spend long enough here and you'll see the little monkey mascot dancing before your very eyes. Mon–Thurs 11am–11pm, Fri & Sat 11am–1am, Sun 11am–9pm.

Rialto Theatre 318 E Congress St ☎ 520 740 1000, ⓦ rialtotheatre.com; map p.225. This 1920s vaudeville theatre has been reincarnated as Tucson's hottest venue for touring bands. Hours vary, showtime usually 8pm.

The Shelter 4155 E Grant Rd ☎ 520 326 1345; map p.223. Take a trip back to groovier times in this round, windowless "go-go boot-wearing lounge"; all lava lamps, pinball machines and velvet paintings. It's barely changed since 1961, but still shakes up a mean martini, and has occasional live music and DJs. Daily 3pm–2am.

Sky Bar 536 N Fourth Ave ☎ 520 622 4300, ⓦ skybartucson.com; map p.225. While the USP here is astronomy, with telescopes set up on the (smoking allowed) patio so that patrons can learn about the night sky, it's a great bar in its own right, with live jazz on Tues, open mic on Wed, and Happy Hour all day on Sunday. They also serve smoothies and $1 coffees, and offer takeaway from *Brooklyn Pizzas* next door. Daily 9am–2am.

The Mission Trail

The first part of Arizona settled by the Spanish – who called it **Pimería Alta** – the southern tract between Tucson and the Mexican border remained its most populous region until well into the nineteenth century. Scattered **mission churches** and abandoned forts still testify to Spanish efforts to Christianize the **Pima** peoples from 1692 onwards. Epidemics and Apache raids meant that of the early towns, only Tucson grew to any size, but as recently as 1870, the Pima were still Arizona's largest ethnic group.

Now known as the **Akimel O'odham**, twelve thousand Pima survive on the **San Xavier reservation** a few miles south of Tucson. The magnificent church of San Xavier, and the Titan Missile Museum and artistic community at **Tubac** not far beyond, are the prime attractions for modern travellers who drive south on the I-19 interstate. Sadly, though, the notion of taking a day-trip to Mexico, via the border town of **Nogales**, is less appealing than it used to be.

San Xavier del Bac

1950 W San Xavier Rd; 9 miles south of downtown Tucson, just west of I-19 • **Church** Daily 7am–5pm • **Museum** 8am–4.30pm • Donation • ☎ 520 294 2624, ⓦ sanxaviermission.org

Even today, the white-plastered walls and towers of **San Xavier del Bac**, the best-preserved mission church in the US, seem like a dazzling desert mirage. How much more dramatic they must have been two centuries ago, when to Christian missionaries and Apache warriors alike they symbolized the Spanish quest to subdue and convert the native peoples of the Southwest.

Nicknamed the "White Dove of the Desert", the church stands on the eastern fringes of the arid San Xavier reservation. The Jesuit **Father Eusebio Kino** founded it in 1700, beside the Santa Cruz River and next to the Pima village of W:ak ("where the water emerges"), which in turn stood on the site of an ancient Hohokam settlement, and soon became known as simply Bac. Kino's church was destroyed by Apache in 1767; what survives is its replacement, built for the Franciscans between 1783 and 1797. No one knows the name of the architect responsible for its Spanish Baroque, even Moorish lines – it consists almost entirely of domes and arches, making only minimal use of timber – let alone the O'odham craftsmen who embellished its every feature.

As you approach the main entrance across the dusty plaza, with saguaro cactuses to the right and ocotillo to the left, take a moment to appreciate its ornate facade. On the top level, a cat squats on the spiral flourish to the right, eyeing a mouse in the corresponding position on the left. The tower on the right was never completed, possibly to avoid the need to pay a levy to the authorities back in Mexico.

Inside, the church is almost entirely adorned with weathered and fading frescoes. A huge gilded altarpiece dominates the main altar, the approach to which is guarded by two naive gilt-headed lions, representing the royal lions of León and Castille in Spain. The left alcove holds a recumbent, articulated statue of **St Francis Xavier**, covered with metal *milagros* (images of healed body parts). Devout Catholics can lean in and lift his head.

Still within the mission walls, to the right of the church, is a small **museum** that displays a gigantic illuminated sheepskin psalter and photos of other remote churches on the Tohono O'odham reservation.

OPENING THE HOUSE OF THE WIND

The little hillock immediately east of the church of San Xavier del Bac is now topped by a replica of the shrine of Saint Bernadette at Lourdes, France. Back in November 1699, however, Juan Mateo Manje, who accompanied Father Kino to W:ak, described finding a white stone on top of this hill:

We guessed it might be some idol that the heathen Indians worshipped, so with great effort we pulled out the stone, thereby exposing a large hole. At the time, we did not know what it could be. While we were coming down the hill, a great and furious hurricane developed. We could scarcely walk because of the terrific windstorm. None of the Indians had gone with us to the top of the hill; but when the furious wind arose they started to yell, saying in sort of rebellion, "Vbiriqui cupioca", which meant that the House of the Wind (god) had been opened.

Ramada-shaded stalls in the square-cum-parking lot in front of the church sell snacks and sodas. There's a constant stream of tourists, but the ideal time to come is on Sunday morning, when **Mass** at 8am, 11am and 12.30pm packs in parishioners from the reservation. This square also hosts the mission's major **feast days**, of St Francis of Assisi on October 4, and St Francis Xavier on December 3.

Titan Missile Museum

1580 W Duval Mine Rd, Sahuarita; I-19 exit 69 • Daily 8.45am–5pm • $9.50 • ☎ 520 625 7736, ⓦ titanmissilemuseum.org

The main attraction at the **Titan Missile Museum**, sixteen miles south of San Xavier, is an **underground silo** that, until 1982, held two Titan II nuclear missiles. Each was primed and ready to fire at a choice of three specific targets, as much as five thousand miles away; what those targets were remains classified even today, but they never changed during the 22 years that the site was operational. A total of 54 such missiles were deployed at 27 separate locations, in Arizona, California and Arkansas, but only this site survived the end of the Cold War. One of its missiles is still down there – no longer primed, of course – and can be examined close-up on hour-long subterranean **guided tours**.

The installation was designed to remain functional in a nuclear war. Its vast sliding door could open through eight feet of post-holocaust debris; the crew could live beneath the surface for up to thirty days; and the whole place could even operate on two 28-volt batteries in case of electrical outage. Tours culminate in the control room, still scattered with top-secret manuals, where two keys had to be turned simultaneously to fire the missile.

As you might imagine, inspecting colossal rocket launchers and other military hardware is very much a "guy thing". Casual visitors may well run out of steam before the excitable gun nuts in the tour group find time to draw breath. Check the website for schedules of the five-hour "Top-to-Bottom" tours (4–5 times monthly, starting 8am; $90).

Madera Canyon

11 miles southeast of I-19 exit 63, via White House Canyon Rd • Daily 24hr access • $5 per vehicle; national park passes valid • ☎ 520 281 2296, ⓦ fs.usda.gov/recarea/Coronado or ⓦ friendsofmaderacanyon.org

As you drive south on I-19, your eye is sure to be caught by the magnificent mountains that rise to the east. The best opportunity for a short hike hereabouts is in **Madera Canyon**, cut by a stream that flows down the flanks of the 9453ft Mount Wrightson. Protected in the Coronado National Forest, this gentle riparian environment is a haven for **birds**. Parking lots beside the access road make it easy to stroll down to the creek, which is punctuated by waterfalls. Once there, all you have to do is stand still, and you're sure to spot some of the 250-plus species that have been identified here, including flycatchers, tanagers and hummingbirds.

Tubac

These days, the village of **TUBAC**, fifty miles south of San Xavier, is a thriving **arts colony**. Originally, however, this was the first permanent Spanish settlement in Arizona, founded in 1752 as a **presidio** or fortress to guard against repetitions of the previous year's Pima Revolt against the Jesuits. In 1775, its commander, Juan Bautista de Anza, launched the expedition that established **San Francisco**, but Tubac soon declined, after its garrison was shifted to the new city of Tucson in 1776. For the next century, it was alternately abandoned and resettled as Apache raids permitted.

Tubac's reinvention has enabled it to grow almost beyond recognition. The broad streets in its central core are now paved and lined with studios, galleries, folk-art stores and boutiques, and surrounded by new real-estate developments that echo Taos and Santa Fe in their use of the faux-adobe architectural style. Most of what's on sale lies firmly within the established genres of contemporary Southwestern arts and crafts – lurid O'Keeffe-esque sunsets and blanket-swathed Native Americans, turquoise ironwork and the like – but there are also plenty of inexpensive imports, especially ceramics, from south of the nearby Mexican border.

Tubac Presidio State Historic Park

1 Burruel St • Daily 9am–5pm • $5 • ☎ 520 398 2252, ⓦ tubacpp.com

Although the foundations of Tubac's original adobe fortress now lie beneath an earthen mound, they can be admired in a cool underground viewing gallery in the **Tubac Presidio State Historic Park**. The excellent museum alongside displays items from all periods of Tubac's long history, including beautiful naive *retablos*, the press that was used to print Arizona's first newspaper, *The Weekly Arizonan*, in 1859, and a crucifix depicting the black "Christo Negro" – a Native American Christ.

Tumacácori National Historical Park

3 miles south of Tubac; I-19 exit 29 • Daily 9am–5pm • $5 per person • ☎ 520 377 5060, ⓦ nps.gov/tuma

A **Spanish mission** founded by Father Kino in 1691 is now the focus of the **Tumacácori National Historical Park**. Like San Xavier, its younger but more celebrated neighbour (see p.232), the church here was built at the end of the eighteenth century. It failed to withstand Apache raids, however, and was abandoned in 1848, five years before the region passed into US control.

Tumacácori is now an evocative ruin, topped by a whitewashed dome but home only to the birds that fly down from the Patagonia Mountains. Behind its weather-beaten red-tinged facade, the plaster has crumbled from the interior walls to reveal bare adobe bricks. Traces of a mural can be discerned in the raised sanctuary, but little remains of the priests' living quarters alongside.

A fascinating **museum** holds a replica of a banner carried by missionaries; one side depicts the Madonna and Child, the other shows an Indian burning in hell.

Nogales

NOGALES, an hour's drive south from Tucson and the largest of the Arizonan–Mexican border towns, consists in effect of two separate towns, one in the US and one across the border in Mexico, both of which were founded in 1880. The contrast between the sedate, ordered streets of the American town – the unlikely birthplace of iconoclastic jazz great **Charles Mingus** – and the jumbled whitewashed houses clinging to the slopes in Mexico hits you as soon as it comes into sight.

There's never been anything much to see either side of the border, and these days the tourist novelty of dipping into Mexico has become overshadowed, literally and metaphorically, by the construction of a huge security wall to deter illegal immigrants. While considerable numbers of people still cross the frontier every day, American

Nogales is now home to the second-largest Border Patrol facility in the country, while Nogales in Mexico has filled up with deportees who have nowhere else to go. The day-trippers who venture there – on foot, via a new pedestrian tunnel, as well as driving – tend to be looking for cut-price medicines or dental work rather than rugs or hammocks.

Patagonia and Sonoita

A longer but even more attractive route back from Nogales to Tucson avoids the interstate by following highways 82 and 83 northeast from Nogales through the lush **Sonoita Valley**, in the craggy mountains of the Coronado National Forest.

The appealing little Wild West mining and ranching community of **PATAGONIA**, laid out around a broad village green twenty miles up from Nogales, attracts weekend crowds of **birdwatchers**. Twelve miles further along, **SONOITA** itself is a wide-open desert crossroads, lined with a few false-front stores, at the point where Hwy-83 veers northwest to rejoin I-10, while Hwy-82 cuts east toward Tombstone, 35 miles away (see p.239).

Patagonia-Sonoita Creek Sanctuary

150 Blue Haven Rd, Patagonia • Wed–Sun: April–Sept 6.30am–4pm; Oct–March 7.30am–4pm • $6 per person • ☎ 520 394 2000, ⓦ nature.org/patagonia

At the far southwestern end of a mile-long dirt road that leads off Patagonia's Fourth Street, the **Patagonia-Sonoita Creek Sanctuary** is a dense riverbank stand of oaks and cottonwoods that's home to an amazing range of songbirds and raptors, including finches and flycatchers, kingbirds and kestrels, and woodpeckers and cardinals. With all this colourful collection to choose from, the sighting most prized by twitchers is in fact a drab little specimen called the northern beardless tyrannulet.

4

ARRIVAL, DEPARTURE AND INFORMATION   THE MISSION TRAIL

TO MEXICO
Crossing the border into Mexico from Nogales is straightforward, as only travellers heading more than 21km south of the border require Mexican visas. US citizens must, however, carry their passports, while foreign visitors should check that their visa status entitles them to re-enter the US; if you're on or eligible for the visa waiver scheme

(see p.41), you're fine. There's no need to change money; US dollars are freely accepted by stores and businesses in Mexico.

NOGALES
Visitor centre 123 W Kino Park (Mon–Fri 9am–5pm; ☎ 520 287 3685, ⓦ thenogaleschamber.org).

ACCOMMODATION AND EATING

MADERA CANYON
Santa Rita Lodge 1218 S Madera Canyon Rd ☎ 520 625 8746, ⓦ santaritalodge.com. Pleasant, very relaxing streamside lodge, with sizeable cabins, peaceful gardens and patios bedecked with hummingbird feeders, and hiking from its doorstep – but no restaurant, so guests have to bring their own food. **$130**

TUBAC
Shelby's Bistro 19 Plaza Rd ☎ 520 398 8075, ⓦ shelbysbistro.com. The best place to get a full meal in Tubac, with a long, consistently good menu that ranges from delicious black bean soup via pizzas up to substantial meat and seafood mains for $15–20 – but watch for bugs on the cooled outdoor patio. Mon, Tues & Sun 11am–4pm, Wed–Sat 11am–4pm & 5–8.30pm.

Tubac Country Inn 13 Burruel St ☎ 520 398 3178,

ⓦ tubaccountryinn.com. The nicest B&B in the heart of old Tubac, this timber-framed inn holds five very substantial en-suite rooms that share a common veranda and use of an attractive garden. A breakfast basket is delivered outside your door. **$130**

Tubac Deli & Coffee Company 6 Plaza Rd ☎ 520 398 3330, ⓦ tubacdeli.com. Busy coffeehouse, snack place and all-round community rendezvous, just off the main highway; salads and sandwiches to takeaway or eat in typically cost $8. Daily 6.30am–5pm.

NOGALES
Holiday Inn Express 850 W Shell Rd ☎ 520 281 0123, ⓦ hiexpress.com. This smart hundred-room motel, part of a cluster near the interstate three miles out from the centre, is considerably more appealing than the alternatives closer in. **$99**

PATAGONIA

Duquesne House 357 Duquesne Ave ☏ 520 394 2732, �🌐 theduquesnehouse.com. Century-old adobe boarding house that's been converted into a delightful little B&B. As well as three large suites that sleep up to four, there's a smaller studio apartment; each is en-suite, and has its own area of the tranquil gardens, which offer great birdwatching. Rates are $20 cheaper Mon–Wed, when the usual tasty breakfast is not available. **$130**

Gathering Grounds 319 W McKeown Ave ☏ 520 394 2097. This spacious coffeehouse/restaurant makes an ideal stop for a $10 lunchtime snack or sandwich, and also opens for dinner on the first and third weekend of each month, serving specials such as *clayuda*, a kind of Mexican pizza, at similar prices. Daily 7am–4pm.

Stage Stop Inn 303 W McKeown Ave ☏ 520 394 2211, ⍵ stagestophotelpatagonia.com. Despite appearances, this convenient hotel in the heart of old Patagonia was actually built as a Western-movie set in the 1970s. It holds a dozen retro-furnished rooms, some of which have private balconies and/or kitchenettes, plus the *Wild Horse* dining room (closed Sun evenings). **$89**

SONOITA

The Café 3280 Hwy-82, Sonoita ☏ 520 455 5044, ⍵ cafesonoita.com. This popular restaurant, just east of town, serves lunchtime burgers and sandwiches for around $10, and dinner such as chicken breast stuffed with green chiles for $15, or slow-roasted prime rib for $16–20. Mon–Wed & Sun 11am–2pm, Thurs–Sat 11am–2pm & 5–8pm.

Southeast Arizona

Although the I-10 interstate remains consistently dull as it crosses **southeast Arizona**, the rugged territory to the south holds some spectacular scenery and memorable historic sites. While the much-mythologized Wild West outpost of **Tombstone** does its best to entertain the hordes of cowboy fanatics who troop this way, the mining town of **Bisbee** is in many ways a more evocative relic of frontier times.

Further east are the **Chiricahua Mountains**, which witnessed the final saga of Native American resistance to federal encroachment, in the 1880s guerrilla campaign of Geronimo's **Apache**. The Chiricahua is merely one of around a dozen separate ranges that soar from the deserts, known as "**sky islands**" because each is sufficiently isolated to harbour its own unique ecosystem of plants, birds and animals.

Kartchner Caverns

Signposted west off Hwy-90, 7 miles south of Benson and 52 miles southeast of Tucson • Park gates open daily 6am–10pm • Discovery Center daily: June to mid-Dec 9am–5pm, mid-Dec to May 8am–6pm • Park entrance $6/vehicle, guided tours $23/person • ☏ 520 586 2283, ⍵ azstateparks.com • Reserve tours as far in advance as possible. You'll have to pay the full fee, which is not refundable, but you can change the time of your tour

The great difference between **Kartchner Caverns** and better known counterparts such as New Mexico's Carlsbad Caverns is that these caves are very unusual in being "live". They're still being hollowed out of the Whetstone Mountains by each new dose of rainfall, and the formations within are still growing. The caverns were discovered in 1974 when cavers Gary Tenen and Randy Tufts, investigating a strange-smelling hole in the mountainside, squeezed into what turned out to be a vast open space. Eventually the two explorers mapped out the subterranean complex at over two miles long, with around 13,000 feet of passageways. They told no one until 1987, whereupon it took a further twelve years for the Arizona state authorities to prepare the caverns for display as a state park.

The actual caves can only be seen on one of the two alternative **guided tours** detailed below. Overall numbers are limited, and during busy periods all tours may be fully booked months ahead, though two hundred unreserved "walk-ins" are allowed each day. If you're hoping to turn up without a reservation, call on your chosen day to assess your chances. If you fail to get in, you can at least content yourself with the displays in the large **Discovery Center** instead, but frankly the park is not really worth visiting without a place on a tour.

CLOCKWISE FROM TOP BIGHORN SHEEP, ARIZONA-SONORA DESERT MUSEUM (SEE P.227); TUMACÁCORI NATIONAL HISTORICAL PARK (SEE P.234); BIOSPHERE 2 (SEE P.222) >

The Rotunda/Throne tour

The shorter **Rotunda/Throne** tour follows a narrow, switchbacking cement trail for a third of a mile through the caverns' two upper "rooms". It lasts for something over an hour, including a tram ride to the cave entrance and 45 minutes spent underground. Formations en route include precarious **stalactites** (the ones that dangle from the ceiling) and towering **stalagmites** (which rise from the floor) – to add to the confusion, there's also a 21ft hollow **soda straw**, a combination of both that stretches from floor to ceiling. However, the most spectacular feature is the striated **colouring** of the cavern walls, created by eons of unseen flooding and illuminated by the dramatic sound-and-light show with which the tour culminates.

The Big Room tour

Available between mid-October and mid-April only, the **Big Room** tour delves deeper into the cave system than the Rotunda/Throne tour, and requires visitors to pass through no fewer than six separate airlock doors. Taking ninety or more minutes, it goes into a little more technical detail, while showcasing unusual wet formations such as a bizarre "fried egg".

Amerind Foundation Museum

1 mile southeast of I-10 exit 318 • Tues–Sun 10am–4pm • $10 • ☎ 520 586 3666, Ⓦ amerind.org

The privately run **Amerind Foundation Museum**, 65 miles southeast of Tucson in remote Texas Canyon, offers the one point of interest on the barren run east from Benson towards New Mexico on I-10. It's a rather highbrow affair, with the declared ambition to "increase the world's knowledge of ancient man by excavation and collection." Displays cover native cultures from North, Central and Southern America, but specialize in the Southwest, featuring fine Apache, Navajo and Hopi crafts, plus older pieces from the Mimbres and Hohokam peoples. While not quite on a par with the museums in Flagstaff, Phoenix or Santa Fe, it's worth an hour or two of your time if you're passing this way.

Sierra Vista

The characterless modern town of **SIERRA VISTA**, thirty miles south of Benson on Hwy-90, has grown in tandem with the army base at **Fort Huachuca**. One of the few nineteenth-century military outposts to remain active, the fort still employs over eighteen thousand people. As the headquarters of the United States Army Intelligence Center, it's widely reported to have played a major role in developing the interrogation techniques made infamous at Abu Ghraib – not that you'll find much on the subject in the **US Army Intelligence Museum** (Tues–Sat 9am–4pm; free).

Ramsey Canyon Preserve

Off Hwy-92, 7 miles south of Sierra Vista • Mon & Thurs–Sun: March–Oct 8am–5pm; Nov–Feb 9am–4pm • $6 per person • ☎ 520 378 2785, ⓦ nature.org

Owned by the Nature Conservancy, **Ramsey Canyon Preserve** squeezes into a slender gorge in the Huachuca Mountains, south of Sierra Vista. This well-watered spot is dedicated to safeguarding local wildlife in general, but the main reason everyone comes here is for its mind-boggling summer array of colourful **hummingbirds**, which reach their peak population in August. Guided walking tours explore the preserve in summer only (March–Oct Mon, Thurs & Sat 9am). Be warned that there's not much room for cars; the 23 parking spaces are first-come, first-served, so there's a risk you'll be turned away.

4

| ACCOMMODATION | SIERRA VISTA |

Ramsey Canyon Inn 29 Ramsey Canyon Rd ☎ 520 378 3010, ⓦ ramseycanyoninn.com. Just outside the namesake preserve, seven miles south of Sierra Vista and a mile above sea level, the *Ramsey Canyon Inn* is a plush B&B where all six rooms in the main house are en-suite; two separate suites, which sleep four and have a two-night minimum stay, and do not include breakfast, are the only options for families travelling with children. A battery of sugar-water feeders attracts countless hummingbirds in summer. Doubles $135, suites $150

Coronado National Memorial

5 miles south of Hwy-92, a total of 20 miles south of Sierra Vista • **Visitor centre** Daily 8am–4pm • Free • ☎ 520 366 5515, ⓦ nps.gov/coro

Tucked into the southernmost notch of the Huachuca Mountains, **Coronado National Memorial** commemorates the approximate spot where in May 1540 the expedition of **Francisco Vásquez de Coronado** first entered what is now the United States (see p.467). Displays in the **visitor centre** explain the history, but the memorial basically exists to offer a selection of scenic **hiking trails**. The best short hike climbs south from **Montezuma Pass**, the highest point along the washboard dirt road west of the visitor centre. The 0.4-mile **Coronado Peak Trail** culminates in huge views in all directions, and especially to the pyramidal Mexican mountains across the border.

Tombstone

Perhaps the most famous town in the Wild West, **TOMBSTONE** lies on US-80, 22 miles south of I-10 and 67 miles southeast of Tucson. Well over a century since its mining days came to an end, "The Town Too Tough to Die" still clings to an afterlife as a tourist theme park. With its dusty streets, wooden sidewalks, and swinging saloon doors, it's surprisingly unchanged, though these days the emphasis is on entertaining kids with tacky dioramas and daily shoot-outs. While much more commercialized than Lincoln, its counterpart in New Mexico (see p.181), to be honest, it's also more fun.

Prospecting in the Dragoon Mountains in 1877, **Edward Schieffelin** was told by soldiers stationed nearby that all he'd find would be his own tombstone. Hence the name of the town that rose from the desert after he made Arizona's largest **silver** strike, in March 1878. Schieffelin sold his stake for $500,000, but the mine yielded $30 million in seven years, and by 1880 Tombstone was home to over ten thousand people. Drifters arrived from the played-out goldfields of Canada and Australia, and gamblers came in from Dodge City, only for the mine to hit water 500 feet down in 1886, and be flooded beyond repair.

Most of the buildings that fill Tombstone's simple grid date from the early 1880s. Decaying wagons are parked on the street corners, and signs along the boardwalks mark the sites of famous shoot-outs. It's all quite surreal, as groups of disconsolate, ornery **gunslingers** still pace the streets, snarling at each other and generally creating enough trouble that the town council has repeatedly attempted to outlaw public gunfighting. As recently as 2015, two people were wounded when one such ne'er-do-well fired live ammunition rather than blanks. Assuming you visit when no ban is in place, whenever a posse of cowboys manage to round up enough tourists, usually at around $4 per head, they gun each other down on some appropriate vacant lot. During **Helldorado Days**, held on the third weekend of each October, you can hardly move for corpses.

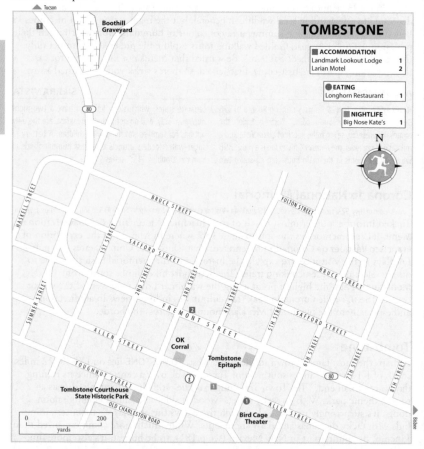

TOMBSTONE

ACCOMMODATION
Landmark Lookout Lodge   1
Larian Motel   2

EATING
Longhorn Restaurant   1

NIGHTLIFE
Big Nose Kate's   1

OK Corral

Allen St, between Third & Fourth • Daily 9am–5pm; gunfight schedule posted daily • $3.50, or $10 with gunfight • ☎ 520 457 3456, Ⓦ ok-corral.com

Although the real gunfight at the OK Corral in fact took place on Fremont Street, the **OK Corral** itself, on Allen Street, remains a big attraction. The first thing you see on entering is a contemporary hearse similar to those used to take the victims away. Crude dummies in the second of two baking-hot adobe-walled courtyards beyond show the supposed locations of the Earps and the Clantons.

The original studio of photographer **C.S. Fly**, famous for taking photos of Geronimo and his warriors, stands alongside, within the compound.

Bird Cage Theater

Allen St and Sixth Ave • Daily 8am–6pm • $10 • ☎ 800 457 3423, Ⓦ tombstonebirdcage.com

The **Bird Cage Theater** was Tombstone's leading venue for entertainment of all kinds. Seven "bird cages", much like theatre boxes but curtained off and used by prostitutes, hang from either side of the main hall. Those on the left were frequented by the Earps

THE GUNFIGHT AT THE OK CORRAL

Despite the fame of the **gunfight at the OK Corral**, which ended the feud between the **Earps** and the **Clantons**, how the clannish dispute began remains obscure. To Hollywood, the Earps have always been the heroes, with Wyatt Earp played by firm-jawed stars like Henry Fonda and Kevin Costner. They were, after all, officers of the law, although it was **Virgil** who was Tombstone's marshal, and his brothers **Wyatt** and **Morgan** merely temporary deputies. Ike Clanton, his brother Billy, and their "gang" were freebooting cattle rustlers, who raided Mexican ranches to feed Tombstone's hungry miners.

Such family-based clans were typical of the West, where individuals seldom prospered alone but trustworthy partners were few and far between. Just as typically, both factions had allied themselves with more powerful forces. Though the Earps dreamed of establishing their own cattle empire, they were the hired guns of Tombstone's **Republican** elite. For the owners and managers of the local mines, a federally imposed end to Arizona's frontier anarchy was essential for future investment. Their mouthpiece, Republican mayor John Clum, was also editor of the *Tombstone Epitaph*. The Clantons, like most cowboys and small-scale ranchers, were aligned with the county sheriff, **Democrat** John Behan.

In the spring of 1881, masked gunmen held up a stagecoach near Tombstone and killed two passengers. Some say the robbers were Clanton associates; others, that a familiar cough betrayed one as **John "Doc" Holliday**, a consumptive dentist from Georgia who was close to the Earps, and that the victims were Clanton's men. The hold-up may even have been a joint operation by both groups, who fell out when the plan went awry.

By October, each faction had sworn to shoot the other on sight. The final showdown came at 2pm on **October 26, 1881**. Virgil, Wyatt and Morgan Earp, together with Doc Holliday, confronted the Clanton brothers, Tom and Frank McLaury, and Billy Claiborne, not in the OK Corral itself, but on Fremont Street nearby. Two of the Clanton group were unarmed, whereas all the Earps had pistols, and Holliday was carrying a shotgun. The Earps fired first. When the shooting stopped, Billy Clanton and the McLaury brothers were dead; Virgil and Morgan Earp and Doc Holliday were wounded; and Ike Clanton had fled.

Under the headline "Three Men Hurled Into Eternity in the Duration of a Moment", the next day's *Tombstone Epitaph* reported that "the feeling among our best citizens is that the Marshal was entirely justified". However, Wyatt and Holliday were charged with murder and were held in jail before being acquitted towards the end of November.

In March 1882, Morgan Earp was killed as he played billiards in Tombstone's *Campbell & Hatch* saloon. Three days later, Wyatt Earp shot the chief suspect, Clanton associate Frank Stilwell, in Tucson. He also killed two more of the Clanton gang that summer before leaving Tombstone with his surviving brothers, and moving to Los Angeles. Lionized by early moviemakers, he died in 1929. Tombstone's Episcopalian minister at the time of the shoot-out, Endicott Peabody, went on to be Franklin Roosevelt's White House chaplain.

4

and their cronies, while the ones on the right were the preserve of Sheriff Behan and the Clantons. The theatre now holds a motley collection of curiosities, including a revolting foot-long "merman" from China and another ornate hearse, while downstairs you can see the old gaming tables and bordello rooms. It also serves as the base for after-dark "Ghost Tours".

Tombstone Courthouse State Historic Park

Third and Toughnut streets • Daily 9am–5pm • $5 • ☎ 520 457 3311, ⓦ azstateparks.com/parks/toco/

Centring on Cochise County's original red-brick 1882 courthouse, the **Tombstone Courthouse State Historic Park** holds displays on the Apache and early outlaws, and documents several rough episodes of frontier justice.

Boothill Graveyard

Half a mile north of downtown Tombstone on US-80 • Daily 7.30am–6pm • Free • ⓦ boothillgraves.com

Tombstone's fabled **Boothill Graveyard** closed in May 1884, having been filled by 276 burials. In keeping with the souvenir store that now guards the entrance, several of the graves bear dubious jokey epitaphs, and country music is piped from concealed speakers. The losers at the OK Corral, however, still rest in relative peace.

INFORMATION   TOMBSTONE

Visitor centre 395 E Allen (Mon–Thurs 9am–4pm, Fri–Sun 9am–5pm; ☎ 520 457 3929, ⓦ tombstonechamber.com).

ACCOMMODATION

Landmark Lookout Lodge 781 N US-80 ☎ 520 457 2223, ⓦ lookoutlodgeaz.com. Classy, tasteful Western-themed rooms (note the swinging saloon doors to each bathroom) with splendid mountain views. The one snag with this modern chain motel is that it's a mile north of downtown, out on its own with only the neighbouring

Holiday Inn Express for company. $99
★**Larian Motel** 410 E Fremont St ☎ 520 457 2272, ⓦ tombstonemotels.com. Much the best of the old-style motels in the middle of Old Tombstone, within walking distance of all the attractions. Clean well-maintained rooms and exceptionally friendly and helpful owners. $89

EATING

Longhorn Restaurant 501 Allen St ☎ 520 457 3405, ⓦ bignosekates.info/longhorn.html. Tombstone's oldest restaurant – once the *Bucket of Blood* – is a family steakhouse

rather than a saloon, serving all meals daily. Lunchtime barbecue hoagies cost $8, while dinner mains range from a $12 meatloaf to a $25 rib-eye steak. Daily 8am–9pm.

DRINKING

Big Nose Kate's 417 E Allen St ☎ 520 457 3107, ⓦ bignosekates.info. Very fancy Wild West saloon, with lots of stained glass and period fittings, where the waitresses wear period costume, country musicians

entertain most afternoons, and everyone strives to keep the atmosphere authentically raucous. It's more a place to drink than to eat, but they do serve burgers, pizzas and calzones, which start from around $8. Daily 10am–midnight.

Bisbee

Crammed into a narrow gorge 25 miles south of Tombstone, **BISBEE** is among Arizona's most atmospheric Victorian towns. Its fortunes were built on a century of mining mundane, dependable **copper** from the surrounding mountains, as opposed to a few ephemeral years of gold and silver, and its solid brick buildings testify to the days when Bisbee was the largest city between New Orleans and San Francisco. In 1910, its population stood at fifteen thousand, outstripping both Phoenix and Tucson, and it even started to develop its own suburbs.

George Warren, who first discovered copper in Mule Pass Gulch, the site of modern Bisbee, in 1877, swiftly lost his claim in a fit of drunken bravado, betting he could outrun a man on horseback. The Copper Queen and Phelps Dodge companies soon moved in, then amalgamated rather than fight over which owned a vast ore body found between their two mines. Phelps Dodge finally closed down in 1975, having extracted over six billion dollars' worth of metals. As the miners moved away, however, artists and retirees moved in, preserving Bisbee's original architecture while turning it into a thriving, friendly little community that caters to tourists without being overwhelmed by them.

Walking Bisbee's narrow central streets, lined with galleries and antiques stores, is a pleasure in itself, though you may grow weary of climbing the high staircases built as part of a federal public-works programme during the 1930s.

Bisbee Mining and Historical Museum

5 Copper Queen Plaza • Daily 10am–4pm • $8 • ☎ 520 432 7071, ⊕ bisbeemuseum.org

Excellent displays at the **Bisbee Mining and Historical Museum** explore every detail of local history. As well as a thorough account of the enforced deportation in 1917 of 1200 "Wobblies" – members of the International Workers of the World, who were seen by the mining corporations as communistic troublemakers – it has evocative photos of the town's early days, and lots of material on the immigrants who arrived here from all over the world.

INFORMATION AND TOURS
BISBEE

Visitor centre 478 Dart Rd, at the Queen Mine (Mon–Fri 9am–5pm, Sat & Sun 10am–4pm; ☎ 520 432 3554, ⊕ discoverbisbee.com).

Queen Mine Tours Hour-long underground tours of Bisbee's actual mines start from 478 Dart Rd; participants

wear full safety gear, including hard hats, and advance reservations are essential (daily: precise times vary, but typically 10.30am, noon, 2pm & 3.30pm; adults $13, ages 4–12 $5.50; ☎ 520 432 2071, ⊕ queenminetour .com).

ACCOMMODATION

Copper Queen Hotel 11 Howell Ave ☎ 520 432 2216, ⊕ copperqueen.com. Arizona's oldest hotel, in the heart of town, is more of a historic experience than an up-to-the-minute lodging option; the plumbing in particular remains antiquated. Its 48 rooms cover a very broad spectrum in terms of size and comfort; the smallest really are quite pokey, while those named for famous guests such as John Wayne or Teddy Roosevelt are sumptuous. There's also a plush bar and a good restaurant with terrace seating. $89

School House Inn 818 Tombstone Canyon ☎ 520 432 2996, ⊕ schoolhouseinnbb.com. Quirky B&B in a converted school a mile west of the centre, where the nine

attractively furnished en-suite rooms are still named for the original use – the History Room, the Library, even the two-room Principal's Office suite. They also have a large common lounge and serve high-quality breakfasts. $89

★**The Shady Dell** 1 Douglas Rd ☎ 520 432 3567, ⊕ theshadydell.com. Truly unique accommodation on the southern outskirts of town. The *Shady Dell* is home to nine beautifully restored, irresistibly kitsch 1950s trailers – each neatly fenced into its own desert-garden lot, and furnished with authentic period memorabilia – and even a 1947 yacht. This is not a place to bring your own RV, but a great opportunity to sample how a Southwest road trip used to be, complete with 1950s-style diner. $87

EATING AND DRINKING

Once-notorious **Brewery Gulch**, which runs north from Main Street, still holds a handful of spit-and-sawdust saloons and diners, while the less atmospheric **Copper Queen Plaza** mall to the south has its own brewpub and espresso café.

Café Roka 35 Main St ☎ 520 432 5153, ⊕ caferoka .com. Smart, very modern dinner-only restaurant in downtown Bisbee, where the menu changes twice monthly according to what's in season, including seafood as available. What you pay for your four-course set menu depends on the main course you choose; with grilled chicken breast, for example, it's $19.50, and with short ribs it's $27.50. Live jazz

on Friday nights. Thurs–Sat 5–9pm, Sun 3–8pm.

High Desert Market & Cafe 203 Tombstone Canyon ☎ 520 432 6775, ⊕ highdesertmarket.net. Part deli, part café, at the west end of town, this friendly hangout has indoor and patio seating, good salads and sandwiches for $8 – hummus on pitta, for example – and wholesome all-fruit smoothies for $5. Daily 7am–7pm.

4

Douglas

As you'll see if you drive south from Bisbee, the endless tailings that spill from the canyons hereabouts left little room to build in or near the town. In 1900, therefore, the new town of **DOUGLAS** was constructed 25 miles east, nestled against the Mexican border, to hold a smelter that processed copper from Bisbee's mines. Although Douglas has diversified into ranching and industry, the relocation of Phelps Dodge following a bitter 1980s strike hit the local economy too hard for it to make an appealing stop for tourists.

Illegal trade with the much larger city of **AGUA PRIETA** across the border – home to almost 100,000 people – is a major source of income. One notorious drug smuggler hired surveyors and labourers to dig a deep tunnel between his houses in either town, then had them executed in order to preserve his secret.

With its whitewashed adobe homes and churches, Agua Prieta is a considerably more attractive place to stroll around than Douglas, and offers plenty of opportunities to eat spicy Sonoran food and buy cheap souvenirs.

ARRIVAL AND INFORMATION   DOUGLAS

Crossing the border Cars and pedestrians alike can cross into Mexico at the foot of Pan American Avenue, a mile southwest of downtown Douglas; US citizens should carry passports.

Visitor centre 345 Sixteenth St (Mon–Fri 9am–4pm, Sat 10am–3pm; ☎ 520 417 7344, ⊛ visitdouglas.com).

ACCOMMODATION AND EATING

Gadsden Hotel 1046 G Ave ☎ 520 364 4481, ⊛ thegadsdenhotel.com. The one noteworthy building in downtown Douglas, this 160-room hotel opened in 1907, and still boasts an extraordinarily opulent lobby, with a white marble staircase leading to a 42ft Tiffany glass window. The guest accommodation is not nearly so classy, and the plumbing (and heating) unreliable, but both its *Saddle and Spur Lounge* and *Casa Segovia* restaurant, which serves simple meals for under $10, have a real frontier-town air. **$110**

Chiricahua National Monument

36 miles southeast of I-10 exit 340, Willcox, via Hwy-186 • **Visitor centre** Daily 8.30am–4.30pm • Free • ☎ 520 824 3560, ⊛ nps.gov/chir

Stretching northeast of Douglas towards New Mexico, the **Chiricahua Mountains** were the homeland and stronghold of the **Chiricahua Apache**. Led by legendary warriors like **Cochise** and **Geronimo**, the Chiricahua – the name means "land of wild turkeys" – were the last Native Americans to hold out against the US Army. The 25-year **Apache Wars** began at Apache Pass in 1861, when Cochise met Lt George Bascom under a flag of truce, and was falsely accused of kidnapping a 12-year-old boy. He escaped into the mountains, but his brother and two nephews were hanged, precipitating a vicious cycle of raids and killings that only ended with Geronimo's fourth and final surrender in 1886.

Had the small Chiricahua band not fought so long and hard, they might still be living on the **Chiricahua reservation**, established during a period of relative peace in

A FORTIFIED FRONTIER

Douglas has long been renowned as the number-one port of entry for **illegal immigrants** from Mexico. At its peak, in the late 1990s, 61,000 such entrants were arrested in Douglas in a single month – a rate of almost one hundred per hour, but nonetheless a small proportion of those who attempted the crossing. Those figures have dropped enormously since then, partly as a result of economic recession but also due to a major US crackdown that saw the construction of a permanent border wall. Head south anywhere in Douglas, and you'll soon find yourself confronted by a colossal, forbidding fence.

These days would-be migrants attempt to cross the fearsome Sonora Desert on foot, far from urban areas. Well over a hundred each year die of dehydration, while Douglas itself is racked by controversy, with unauthorized vigilante patrols vying with church and humanitarian groups to find distressed wanderers.

1872. Occupying the entire southeastern corner of Arizona, it was disbanded in 1876, when the Chiricahua were forcibly decamped to join their distant cousins on the San Carlos reservation to the north. No sign of the Apache presence remains, but the core of the former reservation now constitutes **CHIRICAHUA NATIONAL MONUMENT**. The monument was designated to protect the bizarre **rock formations** created in the 27 million years since volcanic eruptions covered the landscape with a 2000ft coating of dark rhyolite rock. That layer has now cracked and fragmented into strange towers and columns of stacked and balanced stones, a bewildering maze that always defeated army attempts to pursue the Apache into the mountains. The barely touched wilderness in this remote fastness serves as a sanctuary for rare animals and birds. These include a colony of thick-billed **parrots**, once common here and reintroduced in 1986. No food, gas or lodging is available in the monument, and overnight backpacking is forbidden.

Just one paved road – the eight-mile **Bonita Canyon Drive** – penetrates, but does not cross, the mountains, and stays open 24 hours. From the monument entrance it runs for two miles to the **visitor centre**, then follows Bonita Canyon east before climbing south to reach **Massai Point**, 6870ft up. This high vantage point looks out over the main concentration of rocky pinnacles, in **Echo Canyon** and **Heart of Rocks**. A short walk down to the promontory below the parking lot brings you to a viewing platform atop a rocky pedestal, while a paved trail also climbs up to a hilltop exhibit building and further viewpoints. **Cochise Mountain**, which resembles a warrior's face in profile, stands close at hand, while the **Cochise Stronghold** lies concealed in the Dragoon Mountains on the horizon forty miles west.

Hiking in Chiricahua

Massai Point is only a good spot from which to start **hiking** if you have a few hours to spare. It is possible to walk down into the labyrinth from the point, but then you're faced with either a long climb to get back out again, or a one-way walk of at least four miles to reach the visitor centre. If that appeals, reserve a seat in advance on the free **Hiker Shuttle**, which leaves the visitor centre at 9am daily.

For a shorter and easier stroll, set off instead along **Echo Canyon Trail**, which starts half a mile or so back down the road. This level footpath leads in ten minutes to some dramatic formations, and you can turn back whenever you've had your fill. The monument's highest peak, the 7310ft **Sugarloaf Mountain**, can be climbed on a separate mile-long trail, but it's a much less rewarding hike.

ACCOMMODATION AND EATING	CHIRICAHUA NATIONAL MONUMENT

Bonita Canyon Campground Chiricahua National Monument ☎520 824 3560, ⓦnps.gov/chir. Small, first-come, first-served campground that offers the only opportunity to spend the night in Chiricahua National Monument. All 22 sites remain open year-round, and tend to fill up every day during spring. **$12**

Sunglow Ranch 14066 S Sunglow Rd, Pearce ☎520 824 3344 or ☎866 786 4569, ⓦsunglowranch .com. This 475-acre guest ranch, twenty miles south of the monument, holds luxurious *casitas* of varying sizes, with bathrooms, fireplaces and private patios; six have one bedroom, and five have two. Rates include breakfast and dinner at the on-site *Sunglow Café*, which is also open for all meals to non-guests. **$299**

Fort Bowie

3203 S Old Fort Bowie Rd, 13 miles south of I-10 exit 366, at Bowie • **Visitor centre** Daily 8am–4pm • Free • ☎520 847 2500, ⓦnps.gov/fobo

The ruins of **Fort Bowie**, the original focus of the Chiricahua reservation and now a national historic site, lie just beyond the northern boundary of Chiricahua National Monument. They're reached by a demanding but exhilarating 1.5-mile trail that starts on the north side of **Apache Pass**, a total of 22 miles from the monument visitor centre.

Apache Pass today is an insignificant back route. The central nine miles of the **Apache Pass Road** across it are not even paved, though when it hasn't been raining they're usually passable to ordinary vehicles. This low saddle between the Dos Cabezas and Chiricahua Mountains is now overgrown with mesquite bushes, but when the Apache were here it ran through clear, open grassland. Its perennial natural **springs** made it a crucial way station for the **Butterfield Overland Mail**, which started regular runs through Apache Pass in 1857, as part of a 25-day, 2800-mile service between St Louis and San Francisco. The US Army soon established a permanent military presence at the pass.

Allow at least two and a half hours for the three-mile round-trip hike to and from the actual fort. The first significant relic comes half a mile up, with the stone walls of the **Apache Pass Stage Station**, built in 1858. Shortly after crossing the old stage route, now a mere furrow in the soil, you reach the **cemetery** where Little Robe, Geronimo's two-year-old son, lies alongside several US soldiers. Not far beyond, the trail reaches the glorious lush creek that flows from **Apache Spring** – the source of all the trouble, but now the preserve of playful coatis and bobcats.

There are no views as you climb; instead, the **fort** sits in a deep, broad bowl, ringed by mountains and dominated by a granite knob known as **Helen's Dome**. Only the rounded, sun-baked stumps of its adobe walls now survive, though a flag still flutters above the parade ground, and a **visitor centre** nearby provides much-needed shade and water. An optional, slightly longer route back continues up the adjacent hillside before circling down to the trailhead. En route, you step over the geological fault that created the springs, whereupon the vegetation transforms from yucca and flowering cactuses (on limestone) to beargrass (on granite).

Willcox

Only one significant community interrupts I-10 in its ninety-mile run east from Benson to the New Mexican border: **WILLCOX**, 36 miles out from Benson. In its small but atmospheric downtown area you'll find the **Chiricahua Regional Museum**, 127 E Maley St (Mon–Sat 10am–4pm; $2 donation; ☎ 520 384 3971), a storefront that holds informative displays on both Cochise and Geronimo.

INFORMATION

Visitor centre 1500 N Circle I Rd, close to I-10 exit 340 (Mon–Fri 8am–5pm, Sat 9am–4pm, Sun 9am–1pm; ☎ 520 384 2272 or ☎ 800 200 2272, ⓦ willcoxchamber .com).

ACCOMMODATION AND EATING

Big Tex Bar-B-Que 130 E Maley St ☎ 520 384 4423. Follow the giant sign for "The Dining Car", and you'll find yourself in a genuine old railroad dining car that's been cleverly opened up to form the focus of an efficient and very popular barbecue joint, where huge, tasty portions of ribs, brisket and pulled pork cost from $12.50. Mon–Thurs 11am–8pm, Fri & Sat 11am–9pm.

Bucko's 114 S Railroad Ave ☎ 520 384 2875. Very

welcoming espresso café housed in a charming old store opposite the railroad depot. Tues–Sun 9am–6pm.

Holiday Inn Express 1251 N Virginia Ave ☎ 520 384 3333, ⓦ willcoxlodging.com. This is the best equipped of Willcox's chain motels, out in the desert across the interstate from the old centre, offering clean rooms and a decent breakfast buffet. $90

Southwest Arizona

Two interstates, **I-8** and **I-10**, run west across central and southern Arizona towards California, set roughly 35 miles apart near Phoenix and more than twice that by the time they reach the state line. There's virtually nothing of interest in these vast desert plains, apart perhaps from the strange prototype military airplanes glimpsed above the

Barry Goldwater Air Force Range, which stretches south from I-8 to Mexico. A long detour south will take you to the wild terrain of **Organ Pipe Cactus National Monument**, but the only town you might conceivably want to visit is **Yuma**, a venerable river crossing on the far southwest border with California, whose mundane present fails to live up to its wild past.

Tohono O'odham Indian Reservation

Once known to the Spanish as **Papaguería**, the high country east of Tucson is now dominated by the **Tohono O'odham Indian Reservation** (formerly named the Papago Indian reservation). The **Tohono O'odham**, whose name means "desert people", are one of three related groups who together call themselves the **O'odham** – "The People". Unlike the **Akimel O'odham** (or Pima), the "river people" who lived in permanent villages, the Tohono O'odham were traditionally "two-villagers", who divided their time between a summer "field" village in the valleys and a winter "well" village near a spring in the foothills. Apart from the mission at San Xavier del Bac (see p.232), the O'odham are best known these days for the music they call *waila*, derived from Mexican accordion and polka music, which may be more familiar to visitors as "**chicken scratch**".

Around ten thousand Tohono O'odham now live on the reservation, which was established in 1916. They share it with the less numerous **Hia C–ed O'odham**, formerly known as the Sand Papago – desert nomads who in 1976 accepted $26 million as compensation for the loss of the lands now enclosed by Organ Pipe Cactus National Monument and the Barry Goldwater Air Force Range.

For tourists, the only reward in driving the hundred-mile width of the reservation, which starts 25 miles out of Tucson on **Hwy-86**, is its sheer sense of desolation. Most Tohono O'odham live far from the road, so there are few signs of human occupation, apart from a handful of roadside buildings at **Sells**, the administrative headquarters 56 miles southwest of Tucson, and **Quijotoa**, another 23 miles northwest.

Organ Pipe Cactus National Monument

Visitor centre Daily 8.30am–4.30pm • $12 per vehicle • ☎ 520 387 6849, ⓦ nps.gov/orpi

Located at the heart of the Sonoran Desert, right on the Mexican border, the five-hundred-square-mile **Organ Pipe Cactus National Monument** is a treasure trove of rare desert plants and animals, but focuses especially on the **organ pipe**, found almost nowhere else in the United States. Whereas the saguaro stands alone, the organ pipe grows in clusters of tubular "pipes", thrusting up from a shared central root system.

To reach the monument, detour south on Hwy-85 from the Y-shaped intersection, fifty miles south of Gila Bend, that has over the years acquired the formal name of **WHY**, then head for twenty miles along the straight, flat **Sonoyta Valley**, between the jagged ridge of the dry Ajo Mountains to the east and the lower Puerto Blanco Mountains to the west. The **entrance fee** is payable only if you leave the main road. From the **visitor centre**, just west of the highway, two separate **scenic drives** loop off into the mountains. Both are unpaved and steep, but generally passable for ordinary vehicles; the 21-mile **Ajo Mountain Drive** takes around two hours to complete, the 53-mile **Puerto Blanco Drive** at least half a day. This remote area is so prone to illegal border crossings that it receives virtually constant attention from security forces; roads are often closed altogether for significant periods, and even when they're not, the activities of the border patrols may make you feel too uncomfortable to linger.

In summer, **hiking** anything more than the hundred-yard nature trail at the visitor centre is far too gruelling to consider. Between October and April, however, you might feel more inclined to walk several short trails that lead further afield. The cooler months are also the only time when the first-come, first-served **campground** ($16), a mile south of the visitor centre, is likely to fill up.

4

Ajo

Located ten miles north of Why, almost halfway to Gila Bend and the interstate, **AJO** is a former copper-mining town that's much more appealing than the hideous open-pit mine to the south might suggest. Hispanic settlers were digging for copper here by 1750; they named the town in honour of the garlic (*ajo*) that grows wild in the hills nearby.

Since Phelps Dodge closed the mine in 1984, after a bitter state-wide strike, Ajo has clung to life by attracting a steady trickle of tourists and retirees. There's a welcoming bustle about its tidy, grassy plaza which is surrounded by palm trees and has two whitewashed Spanish-colonial churches, even if the streets behind hold little of interest.

ACCOMMODATION   AJO

Guest House Inn 700 Guest House Rd ☎520 387 6133, ⓦguesthouseinn.biz. Ajo's most central and comfortable lodging option was originally a mining-company guesthouse; now it's a comfortable B&B with four en-suite rooms featuring evocative antique furniture. $89

La Siesta 2561 N Hwy-85 ☎520 387 6569,

ⓦajolasiesta.com. This is the better of the two simple roadside motels that stand a couple of miles north of Ajo. As well as the conventional motel rooms visible from the highway, it also offers tiny wooden cabins, plus RV hookups and a small pool. Cabins $79, doubles $89

Gila Bend

At the intersection of Hwy-85 and I-8, **GILA BEND** is a minor farming community whose rather scanty history is celebrated in the tiny **museum** that adjoins its rudimentary **visitor centre** at 644 W Pima St (daily 8am–4pm; ☎520 683 2002, ⓦgilabendaz.org). The hundred miles between here and Yuma makes Gila Bend worth considering as a stopover, if not much else.

ACCOMMODATION   GILA BEND

Best Western Space Age Lodge 401 E Pima St ☎928 683 2273, ⓦbestwesternarizona.com. In this relic of the 1950s' obsession with all things space-related, the Sputnik motif extends to a neon flying saucer poised over the

run-of-the-mill on-site diner. The whole place had to be rebuilt after a fire; the actual motel rooms are less themed, and there are cheaper alternatives, but staying a night here is the one thrill that Gila Bend has to offer. $108

Yuma

The sheer size of **YUMA** surprises most visitors; even though its population remains under one hundred thousand, its numbered streets start a full fifty miles out from the centre. According to the *Guinness Book of Records*, it's also the sunniest place on earth, with less than three inches of rain per year and 339 sunny days. Average July highs are 107°F (42°C), while the record maximum is 124°F (51°C).

Yuma is not a vacation destination in the usual sense, but its warm, dry winters, when temperatures seldom drop below the mid-70°s F, have made it a goal for hordes of "**snowbirds**" who keep the fifty-plus local RV and trailer parks busy. During summer, on the other hand, Yuma is too much of an inferno for anyone to linger very long.

Although Yuma is much too large to explore on foot, its historic **downtown** has been spruced up in recent years, while **Gateway Park** immediately north offers appealing access to the riverside.

Brief history

Commanding the confluence of the Gila and Colorado rivers, the site of modern Yuma was recognized as being significant as early as 1540, when the naval wing of Coronado's expedition (see p.299), under **Hernando de Alarcón**, sailed past its high bluffs. It later became the major river crossing for California-bound travellers, though Spanish attempts to establish a permanent mission settlement were destroyed by the **Yuma**

Revolt of 1781, when **Quechan** Indians (known to the Spaniards as the Yuma) massacred over 150 settlers during Mass.

At the height of California's **Gold Rush**, sixty thousand passengers in a single year paid $2 each to be ferried across the Colorado at **Yuma Crossing**. This lucrative trade was at first controlled by the Quechan, but freebooting entrepreneurs wrested it out of their hands, with the US Army at Fort Yuma on hand to stifle Indian resistance. (A phenomenally bloodthirsty account of the struggle appears in Cormac McCarthy's *Blood Meridian*; see p.490.) Known initially as Colorado City, and later Arizona City, Yuma took on its current name in 1873, by which time it was experiencing a gold rush of its own.

Now that intricate hydraulic engineering has tamed the Colorado – one California-bound canal actually siphons beneath the river – it would take a major dam-burst to cause a repeat of the river's formerly devastating floods. In theory, Arizona could use its share of the Colorado's water to irrigate the land around Yuma and create a rival to California's nearby **Imperial Valley**, one of the world's richest farming areas. Instead, the vast bulk of the water is channelled across the desert to Phoenix and Tucson at astronomical expense.

Yuma Territorial Prison State Historic Park

1 Prison Hill Rd • June–Sept Mon & Thurs–Sun 9am–5pm; Oct–May daily 9am–5pm • $6 • ☎ 928 783 4471, ⓦ azstateparks.com

The best place to get a feel for Yuma's tempestuous past is the **Yuma Territorial Prison State Historic Park**, high above the Colorado east of downtown. Built in 1876, the "Hell Hole of Arizona" was the state's principal prison for 33 years. Its wooden guard tower gives great views of the green-lined river meandering in from the north; this spot originally marked the precise confluence of the two rivers, which has since shifted five miles upstream. The "Ocean to Ocean" bridge here was built in 1915, superseding the ferry and completing the southernmost transcontinental railroad route.

Displays inside the compound's adobe walls tell the stories of its three thousand prisoners. These ranged from teenage burglars to Harvard lawyers, and included nine Mormon polygamists, several Mexican revolutionaries, and women, such as the colourful Pearl Hart, who served five years for committing Arizona's last stagecoach robbery in 1899. You can also enter several cells.

Quartermaster Depot

201 N Fourth Ave • Daily 9am–5pm, closed Mon June–Sept • $4 • ☎ 928 783 0071, ⓦ azstateparks.com

All supplies originally reached Yuma via a fifty-mile river journey from the ocean via Port Isabel on the Gulf of California. Now a state park, the former **Quartermaster Depot**, near the river bridge, still holds two warehouses where Colorado paddle steamers used to moor. Various ancient wagons, carriages and even trains have been stabled indoors or set out to pasture on the lawns, but unless transportation history is your thing, it's not desperately exciting.

Camel Farm

15672 S Ave 1E, 4 miles south of town • Oct–May Tues–Sun 9am–5pm • $7 • ☎ 928 627 7511

Until you get within smelling distance, it's fiendishly difficult to find Yuma's most unusual attraction, the **Camel Farm**. Avenue 1E only starts, as a dirt road, south of the airport. Assuming you do manage to get here, you'll be able to inspect a large herd of slobbery, drooling dromedaries, bred for circuses and zoos – there's no camel riding – plus other wildlife such as ostriches, water buffalo and Watusi cattle.

Algodones and San Luis (Mexico)

Many visitors to Yuma take day-trips south into **Mexico**, whether to little **Algodones**, across the border from California, a mere ten miles east, or to the much larger city of **San Luis**, 23 miles south. Both offer the usual array of souvenir stores and restaurants, together with cut-price drugstores.

ARRIVAL AND DEPARTURE

By train Amtrak trains between LA and Tucson stop at 281 Gila St, at unsocial hours.
By bus Greyhound buses call at 1245 Castle Dome Ave

(☎ 928 783 4403).
Destinations Phoenix (2 daily, 4hr); San Diego (2 daily, 4hr 40min); Tucson (2 daily, 7hr 30min).

INFORMATION AND TOURS

Visitor centre Quartermaster Depot, 201 N Fourth Ave (daily 9am–5pm, closed Mon June–Sept; ☎ 928 783 0071 or ☎ 800 293 0071, ☺ visityuma.com).
Yuma River Tours Colorado cruises from Fisher's Landing, 32 miles upstream from Yuma (☎ 928 783 4400,

☺ yumarivertours.com), including trips on jet boats (four-hour $75, five-hour $95, both starting 10am daily) and a replica stern-wheeler (day cruise, $62, 11am daily; dinner cruise, $70, timings vary).

ACCOMMODATION

As well as a plethora of RV parks, the "business loop" that parallels the interstate for six miles through the heart of Yuma holds dozens of **hotels** and **motels**, with plusher chains along its east–west segment on **32nd Street**, and old-fashioned budget options on the north–south **Fourth Avenue** closer to the river.

Coronado Motor Hotel 233 S Fourth Ave ☎ 928 783 4453 or ☎ 877 234 5567, ☺ coronadomotorhotel.com. Veteran, nicely updated, central motel, within easy walking

distance of downtown, and built in appealing Mission Revival style, complete with a restaurant and small museum of pioneer life. $79

EATING

Garden Cafe 250 S Madison Ave ☎ 928 783 1491, ☺ gardencafeyuma.com. Tasteful café with indoor and outdoor seating, behind *Coronado Motor Hotel* that's open for breakfast and lunch only and serves salads, sandwiches, steaks and burritos for $8–14. Tues–Fri 9am–2.30pm, Sat & Sun 8am–2.30pm; closed June–Sept.
Lutes Casino 221 S Main St ☎ 928 782 2192, ☺ lutescasino.com. This downtown landmark may look like a dull old barn from the outside, but inside it's bursting with quirky oddities and paraphernalia, and does a brisk trade in surprisingly tasty $7.50 hamburgers, served with secret-recipe hot sauce, plus assorted

sandwiches. There's no gambling, but there are plenty of pool and domino players. Mon–Thurs 10am–8pm, Fri & Sat 10am–9pm, Sun 10am–6pm.
River City Grill 600 W Third St ☎ 928 782 7988, ☺ rivercitygrillyuma.com. Bright "international" restaurant, serving an eclectic and relatively expensive menu that concentrates on Asian-influenced seafood options like Thai crab cakes or seared *ahi*, with dinner mains priced at up to $28 (for mustard-crusted halibut) or $35 for steaks. Outdoor dining available. Mon–Sat 11am–2pm & 5–10pm, Sun 5–10pm.

North from Yuma

North of Yuma, three **wildlife refuges** – the Kofa, Cibola, and Imperial – line the Colorado River. Established to protect mule deer and bighorn sheep as well as migratory Canadian geese, the parks aren't really designed for visitors, and are virtually inaccessible without a four-wheel-drive vehicle. Granted that you'd rather not get caught up in the tank battles staged by the army in its enormous, 1300-square-mile **Yuma Proving Ground**, there's nowhere to stop on the main north–south highway, **US-95**, until you reach **Quartzsite**.

Quartzsite

With the Colorado now twenty miles west, **QUARTZSITE** is even bleaker and drier than Yuma, eighty miles south. While it has a nominal population of two thousand, it, too, experiences a major winter influx of snowbirds. Literally hundreds of thousands of RV-owners descend on this desert outpost between early January and mid-February each year, ostensibly to bargain for precious, semi-precious, and merely pretty stones, but also to ride out the coldest months with like-minded fellow retirees.

Despite, or perhaps because of, its endless expanse of RV parks, Quartzsite has just a couple of basic **motels**.

HI JOLLY'S FINAL CAMP

Topped by a brass camel, a pyramidal monument stands in Quartzsite's dusty central cemetery. Inscribed "The last camp of **Hi Jolly**, born somewhere in Syria about 1828, died Quartzsite December 16 1902", it marks the grave of Haiji Ali, who arrived at Indianola, Texas, in 1856, in charge of 33 **camels** that had been requisitioned by the then Secretary of War, Jefferson Davis.

Although the camels adapted well to the desert, army mule handlers and cowboys lacked the patience or inclination to care for them properly, and experiments to test their suitability as beasts of burden petered out during the Civil War. "Hi Jolly" became just another prospector; the abandoned camels bred in the wild into the twentieth century. To this day, it remains against the law to shoot a camel in Arizona.

Parker

Quartzsite's winter crowds spill over to **PARKER**, beside the river 35 miles north. The main activity here is boating on the placid waters downstream of the **Parker Dam**, a Depression-era project designed to divert Colorado water to the thirsty cities of southern California. Since 1985 the dam has also provided water for the **Central Arizona Project**, whose 336 miles of aqueducts stretch as far as Phoenix and Tucson. Almost twenty miles out of Parker, it's the deepest dam in the world, dug 235 feet into the riverbed. Jet-skiers glide up to its base for a closer look, but it's no longer open for tours.

ACCOMMODATION AND EATING   PARKER

Bluewater Resort & Casino 11300 Resort Drive ☎ 928 669 7000 or ☎ 888 243 3360, ⓦ bluewaterfun.com. Overlooking the Colorado just under two miles northwest of Parker, this huge casino resort, owned by the Colorado River Indians, has two hundred very comfortable guest rooms, plus three restaurants, including a steakhouse, a buffet, and one with a riverside patio, four pools, and its own indoor water park. Sun–Thurs <u>$75</u>, Fri & Sat <u>$130</u>

4

Flagstaff and central Arizona

PETRIFIED FOREST NATIONAL PARK

5

Flagstaff and central Arizona

With Arizona's northernmost hundred miles, from the rugged Navajo and Hopi reservations across to the Grand Canyon, impassable to east–west traffic, the I-40 corridor is the focus of a huge tract of the north and central parts of the state. Before the interstate was pushed through, the legendary Route 66 followed much the same path; before either road, there was the Santa Fe Railroad; and before the railroad arrived, not much more than a century ago, there were no significant Anglo settlements in the region at all.

Even today, of the I-40 towns, only charming, characterful **Flagstaff**, set in the world's largest stand of sweet-smelling ponderosa **pine forest**, amounts to much more than an overnight pit stop. It also makes a great base for visits not only to the Grand Canyon (detailed in Chapter 6) but to the dramatic ancient sites of **Wupatki** and **Walnut Canyon**, and the superbly positioned New Age mecca of **Sedona**.

The highlight of the long drive between Flagstaff and New Mexico is **Petrified Forest National Park**, where giant fossilized remains lie strewn like matchsticks across the eerie desert badlands. To the west, the road to California is less inspiring; it makes sense to detour south by way of the historic hilltop mining town of **Jerome** and pristine Victorian **Prescott** or, further west, to take a time-warp spin along Route 66 to the ghost town of **Oatman**.

New Mexico to Flagstaff

During its 150-mile run west from the New Mexico border to Flagstaff, **I-40** passes few towns of any size, let alone interest; **Winslow** is the one essential stop. The **landscape**, on the other hand, while barren in the extreme, is consistently beautiful, with double rainbows reaching across the desert plain and fiery dawns blazing along the horizon. The most accessible section of this **Painted Desert** lies within **Petrified Forest National Park**, which makes an intriguing half-day detour.

For many visitors, this relentless desolation is exactly what they came to see; few join the locals in escaping south to the cool uplands of the **White Mountains**.

Petrified Forest National Park

Straddling I-40, 108 miles east of Flagstaff and 25 miles east of Holbrook • $20 per vehicle, or $10 for motorcyclists, cyclists and pedestrians • ☎ 928 524 6228, ⓦ nps.gov/pefo

While the main function of **PETRIFIED FOREST NATIONAL PARK** is to protect an extraordinary prehistoric "forest" of **fossilized trees**, south of I-40, it also stretches north of the interstate to include picturesque stretches of the **Painted Desert**, an ill-defined area of multicoloured badlands that covers much of northeast Arizona. Its blue-tinged clays and crumbling sands support little vegetation or life, and continue to erode at a fearsome rate.

WUPATKI NATIONAL MONUMENT

Highlights

❶ Petrified Forest National Park As noteworthy for the bizarre coloured sands of the Painted Desert as for its namesake stony trees, this isolated park makes a great break on the long haul across Arizona. **See p.254**

❷ La Posada Glorious old restored hotel, straight from the heyday of Route 66, that's the one compelling reason to spend a night in Winslow. **See p.263**

❸ Downtown Flagstaff Flanking both sides of Route 66 and the Santa Fe Railroad, Flagstaff's bustling downtown streets abound with the flavour of the West. **See p.264**

❹ Museum of Northern Arizona Superb museum, just outside Flagstaff, that explains the history and geography of the Colorado Plateau in fascinating detail. **See p.265**

❺ Wupatki National Monument Extraordinary site northeast of Flagstaff, where the ancient Sinagua people raised multistorey pueblos out of the desert floor. **See p.271**

❻ Jerome Former mining town, now turned artists' colony, perched high on a hillside with magnificent views. **See p.279**

❼ Prescott Once the state capital, Prescott remains one of Arizona's most charming little towns. **See p.283**

HIGHLIGHTS ARE MARKED ON THE MAP ON P.256

FLAGSTAFF AND CENTRAL ARIZONA

HIGHLIGHTS

1 Petrified Forest National Park
2 La Posada
3 Downtown Flagstaff
4 Museum of Northern Arizona
5 Wupatki National Monument
6 Jerome
7 Prescott

Grand Canyon National Park

N

0   miles   40

NEW MEXICO

Gallup & Albuquerque

Clifton

Window Rock

Canyon de Chelly

Ganado

HUBBELL TRADING POST

NAVAJO INDIAN RES.

Keams Canyon

Old Oraibi

Second Mesa

HOPI INDIAN RES.

NAVAJO INDIAN RES.

Tuba City

Cameron

Chambers

PETRIFIED FOREST NATIONAL PARK

PAINTED DESERT

St. Johns

Springerville

Eagar

Alpine

Sunrise Ski Resort

WHITE MTNS.

Pinetop-Lakeside

Whiteriver

Fort Apache

SAN CARLOS INDIAN RES.

San Carlos

Peridot

Show Low

Snowflake

FORT APACHE INDIAN RES.

Black River

Mogollon Rim

HOMOLOVI RUINS STATE PARK

Holbrook

Winslow

Meteor Crater

Payson

Pine

Strawberry

Camp Verde

TONTO NATURAL BRIDGE STATE PARK

Cordes Jct.

SunsetCrater Nat. Mon.

Wupatki Nat. Mon.

Walnut Canyon Nat. Mon.

Flagstaff

San Francisco Peaks

Sedona

Oak Creek Canyon

Cottonwood

Montezuma Castle Nat. Mon.

Tuzigoot Nat. Mon.

Clarkdale

Jerome

Prescott

Williams

Valle

Grand Canyon Village

Tusayan

Colorado River

Ash Fork

Seligman

HAVASUPAI INDIAN RES.

HUALAPAI INDIAN RES.

Peach Springs

Skywalk

Diamond Bar Road

Colorado River

Nothing

Wickenburg

Phoenix

Hoover Dam

Las Vegas

Chloride

Kingman

Oatman

Bullhead City

Laughlin

Needles

Topock

Lake Havasu City

Lake Havasu

Parker

Quartzsite

Ehrenburg

Blythe

Colorado River

CALIFORNIA

NEVADA

Los Angeles

Los Angeles

5

STONE TREES IN THE SAND

Fossilized wood is not in fact all that rare; it's the sheer abundance of the stuff that makes **Petrified Forest National Park** so amazing. Each year, ongoing erosion exposes more and more lithified logs, lying in haphazard profusion on the barren slopes. The wood-bearing layer, also rich in dinosaur bones and other fossils, extends three hundred feet beneath the ground.

The **gigantic trees** of Petrified Forest, drawn from long-extinct species such as *Auracarioxylon*, *Woodworthia* and *Schilderia*, date back 225 million years. When alive, they resembled ponderosa pines. The park is not, however, the site of an actual forest. Its mighty trunks are horizontal, not vertical; they didn't grow here, they accumulated as a vast log jam in an ancient river. Settling onto the riverbed, they were buried by layers of silt and ash, thereby slowing decay. Bit by bit, silica seeped in and replaced the original wood cells, then crystallized into quartz.

Cross sections of petrified wood, cut with diamond saws and then polished, look stunning; prize specimens are displayed in the park's two visitor centres, while lesser examples, gathered outside the park, are sold in commercial outlets nearby.

Petrified Forest became a national park in 1962, when large-scale **pilfering** threatened to deplete its stocks altogether. A similar park in the Dakotas had to close in the 1930s after visitors carried off all its fossil treasures, and even today twelve tons of rock disappears from the Petrified Forest each year. In theory, rangers can search your vehicle as you leave and impose heavy fines on anyone caught with a pocketful of petrified wood-chips. They rarely bother, however, preferring the subtler approach of displaying letters in the visitor centres from repentant rock thieves who have been punished by the loss of hair, health, pets or progeny.

Petrified Forest effectively divides into three sections, with an area rich in ancient Native American remains separating the desert in the north from the forest in the south. To see its full range, you have to complete the entire 27-mile **Scenic Drive**, but there's no need to stop at every overlook along the way.

Although the eerie desertscape is never less than magnificent, the trees themselves, as seen on the ground from trails along the scenic drive, are not always as exciting as you might hope. Segmented, crumbling and very dark, they can just seem like a bunch of logs lying in the sand, even if they are stone logs. For the best viewing, stick around until late afternoon, when the setting sun brings out rich red and orange hues.

Exploring the park

Although the main road through Petrified Forest National Park crosses I-40, there's no access to or from the interstate at that point. Instead, the park has two separate entrances, at the north and south ends of its **scenic drive**. Which you use will depend on how much time you can spare, and which way you're heading.

If you're coming from New Mexico – or if you're heading east and only have time for a quick look – leave the interstate at exit 311, and within a mile you'll come to the **Painted Desert Visitor Center**. Anyone who's driving east and wants to see the entire park, however, would do better to leave I-40 at Holbrook and take US-180 for twenty miles southeast to the southern entrance, near the **Rainbow Forest Museum**.

Note that while you can pick up something to **eat** at either entrance, there are no **lodges** or **campgrounds** in the park. The only way to spend a night is to camp in the backcountry, with a free permit from the visitor centre.

Painted Desert Visitor Center

1 mile north of I-40 exit 311 • Daily: late Feb to late Sept 7am–6pm; late Sept to late Feb 8am–5pm

As well as displays on the geology of the park and forest, the **Painted Desert Visitor Center** holds most of the park's few facilities, including a *Fred Harvey* **restaurant** that serves overpriced café meals all day, a large gift store and a gas station.

5

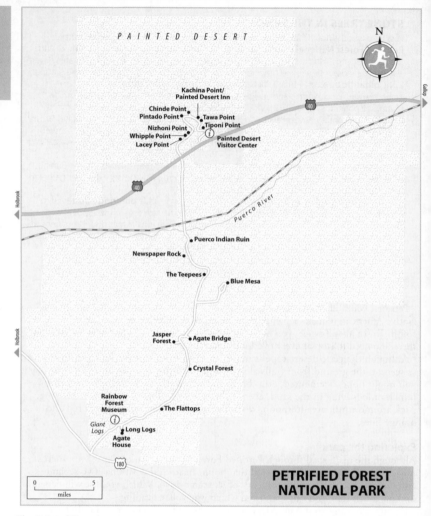

PETRIFIED FOREST
NATIONAL PARK

The Painted Desert

Assuming you enter the park in the north, continue beyond the Painted Desert Visitor Center and you'll soon find yourself skirting the edge of a giant mesa, which drops away northwards to reveal long-range views across the **Painted Desert** itself. At different times of day, the undulating expanse of clay-topped mounds takes on different colours, with an emphasis on blueish shades of grey and reddish shades of brown.

This astonishing vista is best admired through the panoramic windows of the **Painted Desert Inn**, a mile or two along, a long-defunct adobe hotel that has been restored as a museum (daily 9am–5pm; free). Murals inside, painted by Hopi artist Fred Kabotie in 1948, depict Hopi pilgrimages and dances, while a stone slab bears a thirteenth-century petroglyph depiction of a fierce-clawed mountain lion.

From the promontory behind the inn, **Kachina Point**, backcountry **trails** drop down into the Painted Desert Wilderness. Only by walking these can you truly appreciate the scale of the place, but even the shortest hike involves a hot climb back up again.

The scenic drive continues past several similar overlooks before crossing first the interstate, and then, in quick succession, the Santa Fe Railroad and the Puerco River.

Puerco Indian Ruin

At the **Puerco Indian Ruin**, immediately south of the broad but usually dry Puerco River, a short trail leads around a small, partially excavated pueblo, abandoned in 1300 AD by its Ancestral Puebloan inhabitants. Patches of black desert varnish on nearby rocks show well-preserved petroglyphs, including one you'd swear depicted a stork bringing a baby. A little further along, a bunch of bigger petroglyph-covered boulders – known collectively, like many such sites, as **Newspaper Rock** – lie at the foot of a rocky incline. Closer access is forbidden, but free spotting scopes allow you to peer at the indistinct scribbles. In time, some resolve themselves into male and female figures.

The Petrified Forest

The bizarre pyramidal hillocks of the **Teepees**, south of Newspaper Rock, mark the northern limit of the **Petrified Forest**. At roadside halts south from here, rough concrete walkways have been laid over the terrain – and often over the tree trunks too – so visitors can ramble through the larger concentrations of logs. At **Blue Mesa**, certain tree trunks are raised on muddy "pedestals" above the surrounding desert; at **Agate Bridge**, one even spans a little gully.

The park's busiest trail, the **Long Logs Walk** near the southern entrance, is so popular that its parking lot is closed in the mornings, and hikers have to walk a few hundred extra yards up from the Rainbow Forest Museum. Here at the edge of the desert, a little grass manages to survive, making the half-mile main trail especially surreal. The large, shattered logs are simply strewn across the grasslands, with not another stone or rock in sight. A side trail leads in another half-mile to a knoll holding the remains of a seven-hundred-year-old Indian pueblo constructed entirely from petrified wood. **Agate House** might sound amazing, but, thanks perhaps to its clumsy restoration, it's oddly banal.

When the Long Logs Walk looks crowded, the **Crystal Forest** trail, five miles north, makes a good alternative.

Rainbow Forest Museum

Off US-180, 20 miles southeast of Holbrook • Daily: late Feb to late Sept 7am–6pm; late Sept to late Feb 8am–5pm

The **Rainbow Forest Museum**, at the park's southern entrance, is the smaller of its two visitor centres. Along with exhibits on local history and the prehistoric past, it sells snacks. The short Giant Logs Trail, which starts just behind the museum, leads to some especially fine ancient specimens. During peak periods, when parking is hard to find, it makes sense to leave your car here while you hike the nearby Long Logs Walk as well.

Holbrook

From 1886 to 1900, **HOLBROOK**, halfway between Gallup and Flagstaff, was the rowdy headquarters of the "Hashknife" cattle outfit, the third largest in the country. Not much seems to have happened since, but traffic on Route 66 and I-40 has kept Holbrook ticking.

Unless you're ready to stop for the night, there's no great reason to stray off the interstate, though a romantic patch of Route 66 frontage survives along **Navajo Boulevard**, the main road through town.

Historic Courthouse

100 E Arizona St • Daily 8am–5pm • Free • ☎ 928 524 6558

Holbrook's **Historic Courthouse** offers pretty much the only diversion in town, in the form of a **museum** run by the Navajo County Historical Society. The appealing

5

small-town melange holds Ancestral Puebloan pots, fading photographs and dioramas of Wild West shoot-outs.

ACCOMMODATION AND EATING	HOLBROOK

Lexington Inn 1308 E Navajo Blvd ☎ 928 524 1466, ⓦ lexingtonhotels.com. Decent, unremarkable but clean and well-equipped chain motel, one of a clutch located up the hill north of the interstate at exit 286. **$79**

Mesa Italiana 2318 N Navajo Blvd ☎ 928 524 6696. The best bet for a good meal in town, this above-average roadside Italian joint offers pizzas and pasta mains like cheese ravioli or fettucini Alfredo for around $12, and veal or shrimp mains for $18. Mon–Fri 11am–2pm & 4–9pm, Sat & Sun 4–9pm.

★**Wigwam Motel** 811 W Hopi Drive ☎ 928 524 3048, ⓦ galerie-kokopelli.com/wigwam. By far the most unusual and exciting place to stay in Holbrook. Each room in this Route 66 relic – dating from 1950, it's one of three such *Wigwams* left in the country, the others being in Kentucky and California – is a miniature tipi of white concrete, filled with 1950s' furnishings and memorabilia. It's all enjoyably retro, and fortunately they've brought things up to date by buying new mattresses. **$62**

The Mogollon Rim

Although the spellbinding northern Arizona desert appears to stretch away forever to either side of I-40, in fact the southern limit of the Colorado Plateau lies just beneath the horizon to the south – the 2000ft escarpment of **The Mogollon Rim**, curving two hundred miles from west to east and extending well into New Mexico. Heading south from I-40 feels like you're heading into the back of beyond, but you're soon within a hundred miles of the megalopolis of **Phoenix** (see p.204).

For sweltering city-dwellers, the highland forests – especially in the **White Mountains**, near **Show Low** – make ideal destinations for weekend breaks. Visitors from beyond the Southwest rarely stray this way, and unless you're looking to hunt, fish or, inz winter, ski, the only point in doing so is to reach **southern Arizona** without passing through Phoenix. While no Mogollon Rim town amounts to more than the sum of its dreary parts, all do at least offer abundant motels. Both roads south, **US-60** and **US-191**, are exhilarating drives, passing through untamed mountainous terrain that evokes the early days of the Wild West.

Springerville and Eagar

The easternmost White Mountain towns, **SPRINGERVILLE** and neighbouring **EAGAR**, stand near the edge of the plains in **Round Valley**, a few miles west of New Mexico. They're only significant as base camps for trips into the mountains, which you'll encounter a couple of miles south on US-191, or ten miles west on Hwy-260, across the innocuous Little Colorado River.

Casa Malpais

2 miles north of Springerville; tours from visitor centre, 418 E Main St • **Museum** Mon–Fri 8am–4pm, Sat 9am–3pm • Free • **Tours** March–Nov Tues–Sat 9am, 11.30am & 2pm • $10, under-19s $5 • ☎ 928 333 5375, ⓦ casamalpais.org

Known as **Casa Malpais**, a pueblo that was built by the Mogollon people to exploit natural caves is located a couple of miles north of Springerville. It can only be visited on guided tours, which take around one hour thirty minutes, include some potentially demanding hiking, and lead you past the outline of a Great Kiva as well as individual homes. Tours leave from the local visitor centre, which also holds a small **museum** about the site that stays open year-round.

Coronado Trail Scenic Road

South of Springerville, the tortuous high-mountain US-191, designated the **Coronado Trail Scenic Road**, doesn't so much follow the route taken by Francisco de Coronado in 1540 (see p.467) as vaguely parallel it. Driving all the way to **Clifton**, 120 miles south, can take up to four hours, and it leads through stretches that were devastated by Arizona's largest-ever wildfire, the **Wallow Fire** of 2011, but much of it remains spectacular.

At the only village to interrupt the pine woods – **Alpine**, 25 miles south of Springerville – US-180 branches off west into New Mexico. Just a tiny T-junction in a meadow, Alpine is said to be the chilliest spot in Arizona. Beyond Alpine, snow frequently closes US-191 between mid-December and mid-March. When it's open, roadside trailheads, used mainly by hunters, make it possible to hike into the **Apache-Sitgreaves National Forest**, which also has several rudimentary campgrounds.

Show Low

SHOW LOW, fifty miles south of Holbrook on Hwy-77 and 43 miles west of Springerville on US-60, is the largest town on the Mogollon Rim. It stands on the site of a 100,000-acre ranch, whose cofounders played cards in 1876 to decide who should get to keep it. With the game all square, one invited the other to "show low and take the ranch"; his rival drew the deuce of clubs and duly took possession. He went on to sell the ranch to the Mormon church, which built a small settlement before selling it on again.

These days, Show Low amounts to little more than a strip of motels and diners ranged along US-60, or **Deuce of Clubs Avenue**. The nearby slopes of Sunrise Ski Park (⊛ sunriseskiparkaz.com) ensure it remains busy in winter too.

Fort Apache Indian Reservation

One reason why the mountains of eastern Arizona are not better known is that a large proportion of the central massif still belongs to the **Apache**. The Apache are not a single "tribe", however, so there are two separate but contiguous reservations here. The **Fort Apache Indian Reservation**, which starts just a mile or two out of Pinetop and Show Low, stretches south to the Salt and Black rivers; beyond it the **San Carlos Indian reservation** extends for another hundred miles past Globe.

The Fort Apache reservation is headquartered in the town of **WHITERIVER**, cupped in a mile-high valley twenty miles south of Pinetop. **US-60**, the only north–south road across the reservation, is also the most direct route between northeast Arizona and Tucson. All of its 87-mile run from Show Low to **Globe** (see p.219) is awe-inspiring, but the most dramatic moment comes fifty miles along, where it takes five miles of switchbacks to get to the bottom of gaping **Salt River Canyon**.

Fort Apache

Hwy-73, 5 miles southeast of Whiteriver • Summer Mon–Sat 8am–5pm; winter Mon–Fri 8am–5pm • $5 • ☎ 928 338 4625, ⊛ wmat.us

Fort Apache, at the confluence of the north and east forks of the White River, is a US Army outpost that was founded in 1870 to support the campaigns of General Crook. Even though he was allied with the White Mountain Apache, Crook wanted to keep an eye on them. Several surviving buildings hold displays on the period, and they're complemented by exhibitions on the Apache themselves in a modern museum known as **Nohwiké Bégowa**.

Payson

Until 1959, **PAYSON**, ninety miles west of Show Low on Hwy-260, was a sleepy cowboy town that had started out in a gold-rush frenzy and then relaxed into a yearly round of ranching punctuated by the odd rodeo. Then the paving of Hwy-87 placed Payson within two hours' drive of Phoenix, eighty miles southwest. It's now a mountain retreat whose population doubles or triples at weekends, as urban refugees flock to their second homes or at least rent cabins in the forest.

On first glance, Payson, if not exactly appealing, is at least mildly impressive in its quiet, bucolic prosperity. Somehow, however, as you drive down its long, broad streets, passing representatives of every national fast-food and lodging chain, you never seem to find a compelling reason to stop.

5

Tonto Natural Bridge State Park

Hwy-87, 14 miles north of Payson • Daily: late May to early Sept 8am–6pm; early Sept to late May 9am–5pm • $5 • ☎ 928 476 4202, ⓦ azstateparks.com

The world's widest and longest (but not quite highest) **travertine bridge**, formed from minerals deposited by constantly flowing springs, is preserved in **Tonto Natural Bridge State Park**. In 1877, a Scottish gold prospector, David Gowan, supposedly hid in a cave inside the bridge as he fled the Apache who used the surrounding meadows as a summer camp. He stayed and built a cabin nearby. When a description of the natural wonder appeared in an English newspaper in 1896, David Goodfellow spotted the name of his long-lost uncle and wrote to Gowan, who offered him the site. Goodfellow's ten-room lodge no longer accepts guests but still serves as the park's giftshop and visitor centre (same hours).

The bridge itself, reached by a network of short trails and spanning a gully that's roughly 150ft wide, is in truth more of a tunnel than a bridge, or a dank cave with openings at both ends. A steep but safe stairpath leads down to the base, and with care you can hike right through it.

INFORMATION

SPRINGERVILLE
Visitor centre 418 E Main St (Mon–Fri 8am–4pm, Sat 9am–3pm; ☎ 928 333 2123, ⓦ springerville-eagar chamber.com).

FORT APACHE INDIAN RESERVATION
Visitor centre Hwy-260, milepost 357, Fort Apache

THE MOGOLLON RIM

(summer Mon–Sat 8am–5pm, winter Mon–Fri 8am–5pm; ☎ 928 338 1230, ⓦ wmat.us).

PAYSON
Visitor centre 100 W Main St (Mon–Fri 9am–5pm, Sat & Sun 10am–2pm; ☎ 928 474 4515, ⓦ rimcountrychamber .com).

ACCOMMODATION AND EATING

SPRINGERVILLE
Reed's Lodge 514 E Main St ☎ 928 333 4323 or ☎ 800 814 6451, ⓦ k5reeds.com. Plain, no-frills old-fashioned motel, part of a complex that also includes a bookshop and gallery. The cheapest, "Bunkhouse" rooms are run-down, but a more comfortable option costs little more. $49.50
Safire 411 E Main St ☎ 928 333 4512. Something of a community centre, this friendly roadside diner serves meats and beers to match any hunter's appetite, with dinner plus salad bar for $15. Friday night is fish-fry night. Daily noon–10pm.
X Diamond Ranch CR4036, 8 miles southwest of Springerville ☎ 928 333 2286, ⓦ xdiamondranch.com. Six cabins, each with kitchen and sleeping 4–8 guests, on a working ranch beside the Little Colorado River. Also offers horseriding, a Wild West museum and an ancient Indian ruin. $115

SHOW LOW
KC Motel 60 W Deuce of Clubs Ave ☎ 928 537 4433 or

☎ 800 531 7152, ⓦ kcmotelinshowlow.com. Clean, efficient motel offering good-value central accommodation, with free, albeit simple, breakfasts. $64

PAYSON
Gerardo's Firewood Cafe 512 N Beeline Hwy ☎ 928 464 6500, ⓦ gerardosfirewoodcafe.com. Much the best restaurant in Payson, this friendly pizzeria emphasizes local organic ingredients. Weekenders from Phoenix dine Italian-style on sandwiches and simple pasta specials for $8–12 at lunchtime – there's an $8 all-you-can-eat pizza buffet on Wednesdays – and dinner mains like the $25 *cioppino* seafood stew plus a full menu of 12-inch pizzas for $11–17 all day. Tues–Thurs 11am–8.30pm, Fri & Sat 11am–9pm, Sun noon–8pm.
Quality Inn Payson 801 N Beeline Hwy ☎ 928 474 3241, ⓦ choicehotels.com. This former Best Western is everything a small-town motel should be: clean, comfortable and very dependable, with a nice rural feel. $70

Winslow

On I-40, 56 miles east of Flagstaff, **WINSLOW** is yet another Route 66 town kept alive by transcontinental truckers. It's also the closest the interstate comes to the Hopi mesas (see p.66), which jut from the desert across sixty miles of butte-studded wilderness to the north.

Winslow was founded as a railroad stop in 1882, not far from the recently established Mormon community of **Brigham City**, now lying derelict a mile northeast. If you only know of it thanks to the line about "standin' on the corner in Winslow, Arizona", in the Eagles' *Take It Easy*, you'll be glad there's an official **Standin' on the Corner Park** at Kinsley Avenue and Second, where you can have your photo taken with a bronze statue of a guitar-toting hitchhiker. Local history is recalled in the diverting **Old Trails Museum** at 212 Kinsley Ave (Tues–Sat 10am–3pm; free; ⊚oldtrailsmuseum.org).

La Posada

303 E Second St • ☎ 928 289 4366 • ⊚laposada.org

Winslow's landmark **La Posada**, the last and greatest of the railroad hotels built across the Southwest for the **Fred Harvey** company, closed in 1959 when the railroads had been superseded by private cars. Constructed in the late 1920s, it looks much older, because architect **Mary Jane Colter**, of Grand Canyon fame (see p.300), designed it to resemble a nineteenth-century Spanish hacienda. She even invented an entire fictional history of its former life.

La Posada still doubles as Winslow's Amtrak station, and reopened as a hotel in 1999, as part of an ongoing restoration project that's a true labour of love for a small group of enthusiasts who proclaim "we are not hoteliers – for us this is about art." Spending a night in one of its gorgeous **rooms** (see below), and dining in its *Turquoise Room* **restaurant** (see below) cannot be recommended too highly.

If you're simply passing through, though, be sure to drop in to explore *La Posada*'s public spaces. These include extensive galleries of paintings by co-owner **Tina Mion**, among whose brightly coloured (and undeniably morbid) works you'll find *A New Year's Eve Party in Purgatory for Suicides* and *Spectacular Death Spoons*. The gardens have been laid out to Colter's specifications, while the original train depot is being converted to hold the **Route 66 Art Museum** and the visitor centre for **Roden Crater** (see p.271), which will incorporate one of James Turrell's Sky Spaces.

Homolovi Ruins State Park

Hwy-87, 3 miles northeast of Winslow • Daily 8am–5pm • $7 per vehicle • ☎ 928 289 4106, ⊚azstateparks.com

Homolovi Ruins State Park holds four pueblo villages and hundreds of lesser sites that were occupied by the Hisatsinom people – the ancestors of today's **Hopi** – until perhaps the fourteenth century. Fascinating displays in the visitor centre explain the history of this location, and of the Hopi migrations. The ruins themselves, which lie beyond, remain largely unexcavated, so for casual visitors there's little to see.

ARRIVAL AND INFORMATION	WINSLOW

By train Winslow's Amtrak station welcomes one daily train west towards Flagstaff and one east to Albuquerque.

Visitor centre 523 W Second St (Mon–Fri 9am–5pm, Sat 9am–3pm; ☎ 928 289 2434, ⊚winslowarizona.org).

ACCOMMODATION AND EATING

★**La Posada** 303 E Second St ☎928 289 4366, ⊚laposada.org. Winslow's grandest accommodation option, a former Fred Harvey hotel designed by Mary Jane Colter (see p.300), is so totally magnificent – a worthy candidate for the best in the world, in fact – that it's worth going a very long way out of your way to spend a night here. It's an enormous place, abounding in earthy Southwestern style. Doors from the lobby lead straight to the old railroad station, while the beautifully carved beds and decorative fittings in the guest rooms feel like a real throwback to the heyday of transcontinental travel. All are named for illustrious former visitors ranging from Clark Gable to Roddy McDowell, and have en-suite baths or even whirlpool tubs, but lack phones. **$119**

★**Turquoise Room** La Posada, 303 E Second St ☎928 289 2888, ⊚theturquoiseroom.net. *La Posada*'s showcase restaurant is irresistible in terms both of its decor and contemporary Southwestern flair (even if chef John Sharpe does hail from Hartlepool, England). The dinner menu ranges from chile-tinged south-of-the-border specialities like grilled chicken breast with tomatillo sauce ($21) to Colorado elk medallions with huckleberries ($34), and it's all in a different league from anywhere else along a hundred-mile stretch of highway. Daily 7am–9pm.

5

Meteor Crater

6 miles south of I-40 exit 233, which is 18 miles west of Winslow and 38 miles east of Flagstaff • Daily: late May to early Sept 7am–7pm; early Sept to late May 8am–5pm • $18, under-18s $9 • ☎ 800 289 5898, ⓦ meteorcrater.com

Around 22,000 years ago, a meteorite slammed into northern Arizona, blasting a huge hole, nearly a mile across and over five hundred feet deep, into the scrubby plateau. The site of that impact, **Meteor Crater**, now lies six miles south of the interstate, almost forty miles east of Flagstaff.

Though the staff dress up in mock Park Service uniforms, Meteor Crater is privately owned and frankly offers poor value for money. A modern gallery beside the parking lot holds the small **Interactive Discovery Center**, filled with exhibits on meteorite impacts and craters all over the earth, and the moon too for that matter. The first men on the moon were trained on the cavity's otherworldly surface, indeed according to some sceptics this is where they faked their entire mission. Walkways climb from there to the lip of the abyss, where you'll probably find that there's a limit to how long you can spend staring at a featureless hole in the ground. Regular hour-long guided walking tours are included in the price, but you can't hike into the actual crater.

Flagstaff

Northern Arizona's liveliest and most attractive town, **FLAGSTAFF**, occupies a superbly dramatic location beneath the San Francisco Peaks, halfway between New Mexico and California. Straddling the I-40 and I-17 interstates, and a major way station for tourists en route to the Grand Canyon eighty miles northwest, it's also a worthwhile destination in its own right.

Flagstaff's little-changed **downtown**, where barely a building rises more than three stories, oozes Wild West charm. Its main thoroughfare, Santa Fe Avenue, used to be **Route 66**, and before that the pioneer trail west. During the 1960s, downtown Flagstaff had become run-down, and was about to be demolished to construct parking lots for Route 66 visitors; the flaw in the plan was that it would have left no Route 66 to visit. Instead restoration efforts brought the place back to life.

While the central few blocks hold no specific tourist attractions, old-style diners and saloons jostle for space with modern restaurants, brewpubs and espresso cafes, and souvenir stores selling Route 66 and Native American crafts stand alongside outfitters aimed at outdoor adventurers. Simply strolling around is gloriously evocative of the past. Cowboys and Indians share the sidewalks with liberal-minded students from Northern Arizona University, and with the tracks of the Santa Fe Railroad still dividing downtown in two, life in Flagstaff remains punctuated by an endless succession of passing trains (though they're no longer allowed to sound their horns).

Home to a population approaching seventy thousand, including over twenty thousand students, Flagstaff makes an ideal base for travellers. As well as the abundant amenities within easy walking distance of downtown, the national food and lodging chains pepper the interstates slightly further afield. There are also a couple of good museums nearby, together with wonderful scenery and ancient sites. Just one word of warning: at almost seven thousand feet above sea level, the nights may well be colder than you're expecting. It can even snow in July.

Brief history

Flagstaff's first settlers arrived in 1876, lured from Boston by reports of mineral wealth and fertile land. They soon moved on, disappointed, towards Prescott, having stayed long enough to celebrate the centenary of US independence by flying the Stars and Stripes from a towering pine tree. As this flagpole became a familiar landmark on the route west, the town became known as Flagstaff. Right from the start, it was a cosmopolitan place, with a strong black and Hispanic population working in the

▲ Museums & Grand Canyon

5

DOWNTOWN FLAGSTAFF

N

0   200
yards

■ DRINKING & NIGHTLIFE

Beaver Street Brewery	4
Flagstaff Brewing Company	3
Monte Vista Lounge	2
The Museum Club	5
Vino Loco	1

Lowell
Observatory

Amtrak Station

Northern
Arizona
University

▼ Sedona & Phoenix   ▼ & Airport

Cococino National Forest ▼

■ ACCOMMODATION				**● EATING**				
Grand Canyon International Hostel	5	Motel DuBeau	4	Black Bart's Steakhouse		Diablo Burger	2
Holiday Inn Express	7	Super 8 Conference Center		Brix	1	Downtown Diner	4
The Inn at Four Ten	1	NAU/Downtown	6	Charly's Pub & Grill	6	Macy's European Coffee	3
Little America	8	Hotel Weatherford	2	Coppa Cafe	2	House & Bakery	7
Monte Vista	3			Criollo	5	MartAnne's Burrito Palace	6

(originally Mormon-owned) lumber mills and the cattle industry, and Navajo and Hopi heading in from the nearby reservations in order to trade.

Museum of Northern Arizona

3101 N Fort Valley Rd, 3 miles northwest of downtown Flagstaff on US-180 • Mon–Sat 10am–5pm, Sun noon–5pm • $12, ages 10–17 $8 • ☎ 928 774 5213, ⓦ musnaz.org

Flagstaff's exceptional **Museum of Northern Arizona** makes an essential first stop for any visitor to the Colorado Plateau. Although it covers local geology, geography, flora and fauna – and the various theories regarding the origins of the Grand Canyon – the main emphasis is on documenting **Native American** life. It starts with an excellent run-through of the Ancestral Puebloan past, featuring stone knife blades still set in their wooden handles, an intact ancient loom and a collection of pottery miniatures whose purpose remains unknown. Attention then turns to contemporary Navajo, Havasupai, Zuni and Hopi cultures, with rooms devoted to pots, rugs, *kachina* dolls, and silver and turquoise jewellery. There are also temporary shows of local (not always Native American) arts and crafts, a well-stocked bookstore and a **nature trail** that runs through the small piñon-fringed canyon outside.

Ever since it was established, in 1928, the museum has actively encouraged traditional and even new skills among Native American craftworkers. The exquisite inlaid silver jewellery now made by the Hopi, for example, resulted from a museum-backed programme to find work for Hopi servicemen returning from World War II. During

5

its annual Heritage Festivals, every item is for sale; the **Hopi** show takes place on the weekend closest to July 4, the **Zuni** one in late May, and the **Navajo** one at the start of August. Late October sees the **Celebraciones de la Gente**, honouring local Hispanic traditions.

For details of **Museum of Northern Arizona Ventures**, an extensive programme of tours and expeditions, which include multi-day Grand Canyon trips, check the museum website, Ⓦ musnaz.org.

Pioneer Museum

2340 N Fort Valley Rd, 2 miles northwest of downtown on US-180 • Mon–Sat 10am–4pm • $6 • ☎ 928 774 6272,
Ⓦ arizonahistoricalsociety.org

Run by the Arizona Historical Society, and housed in what was once the county hospital, the **Pioneer Museum** holds a random but reasonably entertaining assortment of objects and images from old Flagstaff. The downstairs rooms focus on childhood, while an impressive steam train stands guard beside the highway outside.

Lowell Observatory

1400 West Mars Hill Rd, 1 mile west of downtown • Mon–Sat 10am–10pm, Sun 10am–5pm • $12, under-18s $6 • ☎ 928 774 3358,
Ⓦ lowell.edu

Flagstaff's **Lowell Observatory**, in the pine forest atop Mars Hill west of downtown, is famous as the place where the existence of Pluto was first confirmed. Many of the necessary calculations were performed by Dr Percival Lowell, who founded the observatory in 1894 and also deluded himself that he'd discovered canals on Mars. Lowell, whose gleaming 1911 automobile "Big Red" is displayed in the new Putnam Collection Center, died in 1916, and is buried in a small domed mausoleum of blue glass on the hilltop. Pluto was eventually spotted in 1930 by Clyde Tombaugh. Regarded for many years as the ninth planet, it was demoted to the status of dwarf planet or "plutoid" in 2006.

From the main **visitor centre**, where technically minded visitors will enjoy playing with computers and watching explanatory videos, the **Pluto Walk** footpath climbs up to the tiny original observatory. Signs tick off the relative positions of the planets; if it kept going on the same scale, it would have to extend over six hundred miles, beyond Boise, Idaho, to show the position of the nearest star, Alpha Centauri. Guided **tours** of the observatory campus leave hourly.

Astronomy remains a passion in Flagstaff, which is so dedicated to minimizing night-time light pollution that it became the world's first **International Dark-Sky City** in 2001. The observatory stays open after dark for **stargazing sessions**.

ARRIVAL AND DEPARTURE   FLAGSTAFF

By train Though the Santa Fe Railroad is still busy with freight, Amtrak's daily Southwest Chief between Chicago and Los Angeles is now the only passenger train that stops at Flagstaff's venerable wooden stationhouse, in the heart of town (Ⓦ amtrak.com). In summer, the eastbound service arrives from Los Angeles at 4.36am and the westbound arrives from Albuquerque at 8.51pm; winter times are one hour later.
By bus Greyhound, 880 E Butler Ave (☎ 928 774 4573, Ⓦ greyhound.com), runs five daily buses to Phoenix and

also heads east towards Albuquerque and west to Las Vegas, LA, San Diego and San Francisco. Arizona Shuttle (☎ 928 226 8060, Ⓦ arizonashuttle.com) offers buses to Phoenix (13 daily; $45), Sedona (2 daily; $39), and the Grand Canyon South Rim (see box opposite).
By plane Tiny Pulliam Airport, off 1-17 five miles south of downtown Flagstaff, at 6200 S Pulliam Drive, is connected several times daily with Phoenix on American airlines (Ⓦ aa.com).

GETTING AROUND AND INFORMATION

Car rental The least expensive local agency is Budget, 175 W Aspen Ave (☎ 928 213 0156, Ⓦ budget.com).

Bike rental Absolute Bikes, 202 E Route 66 (open daily; ☎ 928 779 5969, Ⓦ absolutebikes.net), rents out mountain

5

GETTING TO THE GRAND CANYON FROM FLAGSTAFF

Arizona Shuttle (☎928 226 8060 or ☎800 888 2749, ⓦarizonashuttle.com) runs daily buses from Flagstaff's Amtrak station, via Williams, to *Maswik Lodge* in Grand Canyon Village (one-way $30). Year-round, a bus leaves Flagstaff at 7.45am and reaches the *Maswik* at 9.30am, and another leaves Flagstaff at 3.45pm and gets to the *Maswik* at 5.45pm. Between March and October, a third bus leaves Flagstaff at 12.45pm and arrives at the *Maswik* at 2.45pm.

Flagstaff companies offering day-trip tours to the Grand Canyon, typically costing $120–150 per day, include All-Star (☎928 814 8887 or ☎800 940 0445, ⓦallstargrandcanyontours.com), Angel's Gate Tours (☎928 814 2277 or ☎800 957 4557, ⓦseegrandcanyon.com), and Touch The Southwest (☎928 226 1635, ⓦallaboutgrandcanyon.net).

A local **hostel**, *Grand Canyon International Hostel* (see below), also offers inexpensive Grand Canyon excursions.

---

bikes from $39/day.

Visitor centre Flagstaff's helpful visitor centre occupies half of the Amtrak station house at 1 E Route 66 (Mon–Sat 8am–5pm, Sun 9am–4pm; ☎928 213 2951 or ☎800 379 0065, ⓦflagstaffarizona.org). Even when it's not staffed, the building remains open for rail passengers, so visitors can still pick up brochures and discount motel coupons. To make hotel and hostel reservations, use the courtesy phone in the Amtrak lobby (daily 8am–5pm).

Outfitters Recommended outfitters offering equipment for outdoor activities and overnight expeditions include Peace Surplus, 14 W Route 66 (☎928 779 4521, ⓦpeacesurplus.com) and Aspen Sports, 15 N San Francisco St (☎928 779 1935, ⓦaspensportsflagstaff.com).

ACCOMMODATION

As Flagstaff is considerably more than just another interstate pit stop, its dozens of **motels** and **B&Bs** charge higher rates than its I-40 neighbours. They're still not bad value and **budget** travellers can choose between two hostels. Chain motels are clustered to the east, but staying close to downtown is much more fun. Plan ahead on summer weekends, when the town is likely to be booked solid.

CABINS AND HOSTELS

Coconino National Forest ☎928 526 0866, ⓦwww .fs.usda.gov/coconino, reservations on ☎877 444 6777, ⓦrecreation.gov. The national forest's "Rooms With A View" programme offers four separate century-old cabins, way out in the woods up to an hour's drive from Flagstaff, at rock-bottom rates. Each cabin is rented in its entirety, and sleeps six to ten guests, who have to bring their own food and bedding and, in low season, water too. Mid-April to mid-Nov only. $75

Grand Canyon International Hostel 19 S San Francisco St ☎928 779 9421 or ☎888 442 2696, ⓦgrandcanyonhostel.com. Long-standing independent hostel, under the same friendly management as the nearby *Motel DuBeau*. All the rooms, which include same-sex and mixed four-bed dorms as well as eight private doubles, share bathrooms. Rates include breakfast, and they also arrange Grand Canyon tours ($85; Tues, Thurs & Sat). Dorms $25, doubles $57

Motel DuBeau 19 W Phoenix Ave ☎928 774 6731 or ☎800 398 7112, ⓦmodubeau.com. Long known as "DuBeau International Hostel", now also styling itself a "travelers inn", this veteran motel, just south of the tracks, first opened in 1929. All its appealingly converted rooms have en-suite bathrooms; some serve as four-person dorms, the rest as private rooms ranging from doubles to family suites. Breakfast is free, but the common areas, complete with pool table, can get noisy at times. Contact them in advance if you plan to arrive between 12.30pm & 4pm. They also offer Grand Canyon tours, in conjunction with their sister property, the *International Hostel*. Dorms $25, rooms $57, suites $85

HOTELS AND B&BS

Holiday Inn Express 2320 E Lucky Lane ☎928 714 7130, ⓦhiflagstaff.com. Large motel in a rather characterless area just off the interstate, with a handful of diners nearby. While it's not one of this chain's newer properties, it's maintained to a good standard, has an indoor/outdoor pool, and offers free hot breakfasts. $153

★**The Inn at Four Ten** 410 N Leroux St ☎928 774 0088 or ☎800 774 2008, ⓦinn410.com. Bright Craftsman-style home, a very short walk up from downtown, that's now a luxurious antique-furnished B&B. All ten of its very sizeable rooms are en-suite, most with fireplaces and three with whirlpool tubs. On summer evenings, the porch and patio make welcoming, convivial retreats, while the breakfasts are superb. $180

Little America 2515 E Butler Ave ☎928 779 7900 or ☎800 865 1401, ⓦflagstaff.littleamerica.com. Large motel-cum-resort near the interstate, where the 1950s-style ambience conceals a higher standard of

5

accommodation than you might expect, with large rooms, pleasantly landscaped grounds and a good pool. **$180**

Monte Vista 100 N San Francisco St ☎ 928 779 6971, ⓦ hotelmontevista.com. Attractive landmark 1920s hotel in the heart of downtown. Its restored rooms, with and without attached bathrooms but with plenty of vintage fixtures and fittings, are named for celebrity guests, from Bob Hope to Jon Bon Jovi; Paul McCartney stayed here in 2008, but doesn't have his own room yet. Don't expect opulence, let alone tranquillity; in truth, the ambience is more like a hostel than a hotel. Many of the guests are young international travellers, drawn by the local nightlife, including the hotel's own bar (see p.269). Weekend rates typically rise by $20. Shared-bath **$85**, en-suite doubles **$115**

Super 8 Conference Center NAU/Downtown 602 W Route 66 ☎ 928 774 4581 or ☎ 800 800 8000, ⓦ super8 .com. The best-value chain motel that's at all near the centre, less than a mile southwest of downtown, just past the US-89 turn-off towards Sedona and adjacent to a Barnes & Noble bookstore. Focused on an enclosed swimming pool, it offers a decent standard of no-frills accommodation. **$80**

Hotel Weatherford 23 N Leroux St ☎ 928 779 1919, ⓦ weatherfordhotel.com. This old downtown hotel, with elegant wooden fittings, has been restored as a labour of love, though to appreciate it, you have to be here for period charm rather than modern luxury. The three finest "queen suites" offer tasteful accommodation, with antique furnishings and clawfoot tubs plus phones and TVs; a dozen more en-suite rooms are smaller and cheaper; and three large but basic ones share a bathroom. The upstairs lounge offers Wild West ambience, but can make for a noisy night – especially if you're in room 59, across the corridor. Shared-bath doubles **$55**, en-suite doubles **$95**, queen suites **$145**

EATING

While surprisingly short of high-end **restaurants**, central Flagstaff holds a lively assortment of both old-style Western **diners** and eclectic **budget** options. Thanks to all those students, the area around San Francisco Street, both north and south of the tracks, is filled with vegetarian cafés and espresso bars.

Black Bart's Steakhouse & Musical Revue 2760 E Butler Ave ☎ 928 779 3142, ⓦ blackbartssteakhouse .com. Enjoyable Western-themed steakhouse, across from *Little America* on the east edge of town, with waiting staff who sing and dance onstage between serving barbecued steak, ribs and chicken ($22–38). Daily 5–10pm.

Brix 413 N San Francisco St ☎ 928 213 1021, ⓦ brixflagstaff.com. Flagstaff's smartest contemporary restaurant, set in a former carriage house a couple of blocks up from the downtown hub, serves a seasonally changing menu of delicately prepared appetizers such as shrimp and grits ($12), and mains like grilled salmon ($27) or roasted duck breast ($31). Portion sizes tend to be significantly smaller than the Wild West norm. Daily 5–9pm, closed Mon in winter.

Charly's Pub & Grill Hotel Weatherford, 23 N Leroux St ☎ 928 779 1919, ⓦ weatherfordhotel.com. This café-restaurant is more a place to come to for its classy Western ambience than gourmet food, but it's open for all meals, with good $10–15 lunchtime sandwiches and dinner mains like "broken-hearted chicken" for more like $15. There's also live music (cocktail piano at lunch, bands at night). Daily 8am–10pm.

Coppa Café 1300 S Milton Rd ☎ 928 637 6813, ⓦ coppacafe.net. Cosy, quirky little bistro, in a rather anonymous setting near the university, a mile southwest of downtown towards Sedona. The wide-ranging Mediterranean cuisine takes in (Spanish) tortilla and chicken bruschetta for lunch, at around $10, steak or salmon at $30–35 for dinner, and cheese or cured meat platters for the whole table for $25. Wed–Sat 11am–8pm, Sun 10am–3pm.

Criollo 16 N San Francisco St ☎ 928 774 0541, ⓦ criollolatinkitchen.com. Smart, spacious restaurant, serving Latin American food worth lingering over. The full menu includes tapas as well as substantial dishes like pork belly tacos ($12) and a spicy Peruvian fish stew ($20). Mon–Thurs 11am–10pm, Fri 11am–midnight, Sat 9am–midnight, Sun 9am–10pm.

Diablo Burger 120 N Leroux St ☎ 928 774 3274, ⓦ diabloburger.com. Stylish burger joint in the centre of town, with outdoor seating beneath a great mural on Heritage Square. The $10–15 burgers feature exclusively local ingredients, most obviously free-range hormone-free cattle from the Diablo ranch. Cash only. Mon–Wed & Sun 11am–9pm, Thurs–Sat 11am–10pm.

Downtown Diner 7 E Aspen Ave ☎ 928 774 3492, ⓦ facebook.com/downtowndinerflag. Classic Route 66 diner a block north of the main drag, featuring leatherette booths and hefty burgers and sandwiches, mostly priced at or under $10. Mon–Sat 6am–9pm, Sun 7am–6pm.

Macy's European Coffee House & Bakery 14 S Beaver St ☎ 928 774 2243, ⓦ macyscoffee.net. Not merely superb coffee, but heavenly pastries to go with it, in a chaotic but friendly, student-oriented atmosphere. Breakfast is always busy – options even include couscous ($5) – while sizeable dishes later on, all vegetarian, include salads and a Mediterranean mixed plate ($8). There's a coin laundry next door. Daily: summer 6am–10pm, winter 6am–8pm.

MartAnne's Burrito Palace 112 E Route 66 ☎ 928 773 4701. This stylish, colourful, family-owned Mexican restaurant calls itself "the house that *chilaquiles* built", having built its reputation on serving irresistible breakfasts of fried corn tortillas with salsa; lunch and dinner is equally good, with mains from ceviche to shrimp tacos to red and green chile all priced around $12–15. April–Nov daily 7.30am–9pm, Dec–March Mon–Fri 7.30am–2pm, Sat & Sun 7.30am–2.30pm.

NIGHTLIFE

Milling with international travellers in summer and students the rest of the year, Flagstaff is the liveliest **nightspot** between Las Vegas and Santa Fe, and home to half a dozen brewpubs. Wander a block or two to either side of San Francisco Street downtown, and you can't go wrong.

Beaver Street Brewery 11 S Beaver St ☎ 928 779 0079, ⓦ beaverstreetbrewery.com. Popular micro-brewery that has won awards for its ales and lagers alike, and serves inventive and inexpensive food, including fondues. There's also a billiards room, and an outdoor BBQ in the beer garden on Wednesday nights in summer. Mon–Wed & Sun 11am–1am, Thurs–Sat 11am–2am.

Flagstaff Brewing Company 16 E Route 66 ☎ 928 773 1442, ⓦ flagbrew.com. Bustling downtown pub, with outdoor patio seating right by Route 66, big windows and live music Thursday to Saturday, plus a morning espresso bar. Daily 11am–2am.

Monte Vista Lounge Monte Vista, 100 N San Francisco St ☎ 928 779 6971, ⓦ hotelmontevista.com. Hip little bar and dance club in the basement of a venerable old hotel, with frequent live music and DJs. Daily noon–2am.

The Museum Club 3404 E Route 66 ☎ 928 526 9434, ⓦ themuseumclub.com. A real oddity, this log-cabin taxidermy museum, popularly known as "The Zoo", somehow transmogrified into a classic Route 66 roadhouse, saloon and country music venue – live bands typically Thursday to Saturday – that's a second home to hordes of dancing cowboys. Daily 11am–2am.

Vino Loco 22 E Birch Ave ☎ 928 226 1764, ⓦ vinolocoflag.com. Downtown wine shop that doubles as a lively and welcoming wine bar, serving a broad range of Arizona as well as international wines, by the bottle as well as by the glass. Mon–Wed & Sun 11am–9pm, Thurs–Sat 11am–midnight.

Around Flagstaff

Dominated by the striking **San Francisco Peaks**, the area around Flagstaff is extraordinarily rich in natural and archeological wonders. Three national monuments – **Sunset Crater**, **Wupatki** and **Walnut Canyon** – lie within 25 miles. All are generally seen as day-trips from Flagstaff; the monuments offer almost no practical facilities, with only **Sunset Crater** having so much as a campground.

The San Francisco Peaks

The **San Francisco Volcanic Field**, north of Flagstaff, consists of around four hundred distinct volcanic cones, which have formed over the past two million years. During that time, the region has also been covered by glacial ice on three separate occasions, shaving around 3000ft off the top of the volcanoes.

The serrated **SAN FRANCISCO PEAKS** are the remnants of a single mountain; their highest point today, at 12,643ft, is the summit of **Mount Humphreys**. They were named by Spanish missionaries in honour of St Francis of Assisi, though the Hopi already knew them as *Nuvatukya'ovi*, the home of the *kachina* spirits, and to the Navajo this was *Dook'o'oslíid*, one of the four sacred mountains. Seen from afar, topped by a semipermanent layer of clouds, it's obvious why the Hopi and Navajo regarded the peaks as the source of life-giving rain. Ironically, it's because the mountains were sacred sites for both tribes that they now belong to neither; as federal law stipulates that Native American reservations can only include lands of which one tribe has "exclusive use", the fact that both held them holy precluded either from claiming them, and left them open to Yankee exploitation. The Hopi in particular still make annual pilgrimages on foot from their mesas, 65 miles east, to shrines hidden in the mountains.

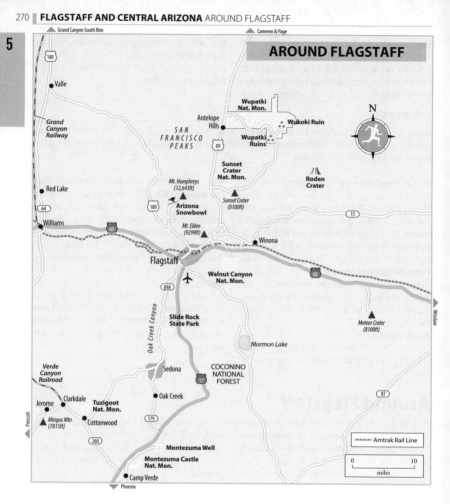

Arizona Snowbowl

9300 N Snowbowl Rd · Late Nov to early April · Lift tickets $69 · ☎ 928 779 1951, ⓦ arizonasnowbowl.com · At the end of a 7-mile spur road north of US-180

Considering that the San Francisco Mountain, which has not erupted for 220,000 years, is dormant rather than extinct, the time may come when the gods decide that Flagstaff's own **ski resort**, the **Arizona Snowbowl**, is a desecration no longer to be tolerated. For the moment, it survives, nestling between Mount Humphreys and Mount Agassiz and featuring ski runs such as "Boo-Boo" and "Bambi".

As there's not enough natural water to make artificial snow, the Forest Service fought Hopi and Navajo legal objections to be allowed to use waste water from Flagstaff's sewage system to make snow. The eventual Forest Service victory in the US Supreme Court in 2011 has lengthened the Snowbowl's annual ski season, and prompted further expansion.

Scenic Chairlift

Mid-May to mid-Oct Fri–Sun 10am–4pm · $19, under-13s $10 · ☎ 928 779 1951, ⓦ arizonasnowbowl.com

In summer, the Snowbowl's longest chairlift, which climbs to within a few hundred feet of the 12,350ft summit of Mount Agassiz, remains open as the **Scenic Chairlift**. To

5

protect the fragile vegetation, onward hiking is prohibited, but you'll find plenty of other day-use **trails** in these mountains, most of them also open to mountain bikers. One switchbacks to the summit of Mount Humphreys for seventy-mile views to the Grand Canyon and beyond. For more information, visit ⓦazhikers.org.

Sunset Crater National Monument

12 miles north of Flagstaff on US-89, then 2 miles east on FR-545 • **Visitor centre** Daily: May–Oct 8am–5pm; Nov–April 9am–5pm • $20 per vehicle, includes Wupatki National Monument; under-16s free • ☎ 928 526 0502, ⓦ nps.gov/sucr

The youngest of the San Francisco volcanoes provides the focus of **Sunset Crater Volcano National Monument**. Its most recent eruption, in 1065 AD, had a profound impact on the local population. Thick deposits of ash opened previously infertile land to cultivation, accelerating – if not triggering – a land rush that threw different Native American cultures into contact and competition for the first time.

John Wesley Powell named Sunset Crater for its multicoloured cone, which swells from a black base through reds and oranges to a yellow-tinged crest. Unfortunately, however, its shifting cinders are too unstable to allow hikers to climb up to the rim. Instead, after you've seen displays about the crater in the visitor centre, the one-mile **Lava Flow Trail** at its base offers a close-up look at the jagged black lava that streamed out across the desert. The steeper one-mile **Lenox Crater Trail** ascends a lesser cone nearby.

ACCOMMODATION	SUNSET CRATER NATIONAL MONUMENT
Bonito Campground Opposite Sunset Crater visitor centre ☎928 526 0866, ⓦnps.gov/sucr. Run by the Forest Service, this 44-site, summer-only campground	offers simple camping among the woods; running water available. Open May to mid-Oct. **$22**

Wupatki National Monument

20 miles north of Sunset Crater on FR-545, or 26 miles north of Flagstaff on US-89, then 14 miles east on FR-545 • $20 per vehicle, includes Sunset Crater • ☎ 928 679 2365, ⓦ nps.gov/wupa

A cluster of several exceptionally well-preserved ancient ruins, dramatically poised between the volcanoes and the desert north of Sunset Crater, jointly constitute **WUPATKI NATIONAL MONUMENT**. They appear to testify to a period in which different tribal groups lived side by side in harmony. At some time after the Sunset Crater eruption – though not necessarily because of it – the Sinagua people already present here, who surely witnessed the explosion, were joined by many others, including the

---

A SKYSPACE FOR THE AGES: RODEN CRATER

Roden Crater, a pristine cinder cone twenty miles east of Sunset Crater, is the focus of one of the most extraordinary **land art** projects in the world. Measuring three miles from rim to rim, and standing close to the Little Colorado River in an anomalous strip of the Painted Desert that's sandwiched between the national monuments to the east and the Navajo Nation to the west, it was acquired by artist **James Turrell** in 1977. Ever since then, Turrell has been transforming it into a sculptural installation-cum-astronomical observatory. He has created such "**Skyspaces**", designed to facilitate naked-eye viewing of celestial phenomena and consciously echoing ancient sites from Peru to Indonesia, all over the world. Roden Crater is destined to be the largest; at the time of writing, 6 of its 21 distinct tunnels and spaces had been completed, including the centrepiece Crater Eye. Some are aligned with annual events such as the summer and winter solstices, others celebrate the daily passage of sun, moon and stars.

Patrons of the arts have already started to pay $6500 for the privilege of **spending a night** within Roden Crater. For the moment there's no public access, but in due course that invitation will be extended to the world at large. A Skyspace is being constructed at Winslow's wonderful *La Posada* hotel (see p.263), which will serve as the gateway to the project.

5

Ancestral Puebloans and the Hohokam. When the rich new soil had been exhausted, around 150 years later, all moved on once more.

Visitor centre

FR-545, 21 miles east from the US-89 junction • Daily 9am–5pm

Although the first of the five separate pueblo complexes you see as you approach from Sunset Crater is Wukoki, it's best to start your visit at the monument's excellent **visitor centre**, slightly further along the highway. Displays explain the history of the Sinagua and their neighbours, placing them within the context of the traditional migration story of their modern descendants, the Hopi.

Wupatki Pueblo

Accessed via a paved loop trail that leads down from the visitor centre, the main three-storey, hundred-room pueblo block of **Wupatki** ("long cut house") is moulded to a sandstone hillock and conceals a number of natural caves. The site's most intriguing features, however, lie a little further along.

First comes what seems to be an amphitheatre, a walled circular plaza of unknown purpose. Beyond it is an oval **ball court**, the northernmost such court ever found. Similar arenas throughout central America were used for a game – part ritual, part sport – in which players tried to propel a rubber ball through a stone hoop high on a wall, using their knees and elbows alone, much like modern basketball (except that the losers were sacrificed at the end). Alongside the ball court, cracks in the ground have created a natural **blowhole**, through which air is either sucked or blown depending on pressure and temperature. The audible "breathing" of the earth made this a sacred shrine for Wupatki's ancient inhabitants.

Wukoki Pueblo

Wukoki, at the end of a 2.5-mile spur road near the visitor centre, takes its name from a Hopi word meaning "big house". Reminiscent of the castle-like structures at Hovenweep, it's within sight of a procession of rounded cinder cones, but was probably positioned for its commanding prospect of the Painted Desert to the north and east. Windows in its central tower – moulded to the contours of a red-rock outcrop, and built with bricks of the same material – look out in all directions. Some are precisely aligned to monitor the sunrise at significant moments. With the Little Colorado River five miles distant, the pueblo's inhabitants must have been desperately short of water.

The Citadel

The loop road past Sunset Crater and Wupatki rejoins US-89 twenty miles south of Cameron (see p.330). Outcrops along its final few miles hold more pueblos, such as **The Citadel**, perched on and fully occupying a hilltop. While its interior, which appears to contain a large circular *kiva*, remains unexcavated, much of its outer wall is still standing, incorporating striped bands of black lava boulders. It's dotted with tiny "windows" that may have served defensive or astronomical purposes.

Walnut Canyon National Monument

Just south of I-40, 10 miles east of Flagstaff • **Visitor centre** Daily: May–Oct 8am–5pm; Nov–April 9am–5pm • $8 • ☎ 928 526 3367, ⓦ nps.gov/waca

Between 1125 and 1250 AD, the shallow canyon now preserved as **WALNUT CANYON NATIONAL MONUMENT** was home to a thriving Sinagua community, who lived in small family groups rather than in communal pueblos. Literally hundreds of their **cliff dwellings** still nestle beneath overhangs in the canyon walls. They simply walled off alcoves where softer strata of rock had eroded away, and put up partitions to make separate rooms. No single dwelling is on the same scale as, say, the Sinagua pueblo of

Wupatki, and only a handful are accessible to visitors, but cumulatively they make an impressive spectacle.

A scenic window in the **visitor centre** gives an excellent overall view. **Walnut Creek** itself, diverted to provide Flagstaff's drinking water, now runs dry, but it's easy to see how fertile this valley was when the Sinagua first arrived. Trees cling to the porous rock to shade the ancient dwellings, and the vegetation thickens down to a valley floor dense with black walnut and oak.

Most visitors simply hike the Island Loop Trail around the main ruins, but each summer rangers lead two- to three-hour **guided hikes** to lesser-known and otherwise inaccessible sites.

Island Loop Trail

Only visitors who arrive an hour or more before closing time are allowed to set off down the mile-long **Island Loop Trail**; as the dwellings are at their most photogenic in late afternoon, that calls for careful timing. After dropping steeply from the visitor centre, the trail crosses a narrow causeway to an isthmus of rock high above a gooseneck of the creek. Once there, you can go inside a few Sinagua homes; note the T-shaped doorways, which could only be entered headfirst, and the ceilings blackened by smoke. Petroglyphs have been found in the other ruins visible on all sides, but none remain along the trail.

South of Flagstaff

US-89A threads its way south from Flagstaff down **Oak Creek Canyon** to emerge after 28 miles at **Sedona**, on the threshold of the extraordinary **Red Rock Country**. Up from the valley rise giant mesas and buttes of stark red sandstone, amid which author Zane Grey set many of his Wild West adventures. The boom-and-bust mining town of **Jerome** looks down from a mountainside to the south. Hwy-260 links both US-89A and I-17 and the haunting Sinagua ruins of **Tuzigoot** and **Montezuma Castle**.

Oak Creek Canyon

Local claims that **OAK CREEK CANYON**, the largest of several slender chasms that cut into the 2000ft escarpment of the **Mogollon Rim**, is a serious rival to the Grand Canyon are somewhat exaggerated. However, you *can* drive right through it, and with its sheer walls striped in vivid bands of colour, its sparkling streams and densely wooded glens, and its facilities for camping, eating and general playing around, this would be an unmissable attraction anywhere else.

While the canyon's narrow floor has been heavily developed, leisure facilities are hidden where possible by careful landscaping. **Lookout Point**, its northern end, appears suddenly a dozen forested miles south of Flagstaff on US-89A. Native American craft stalls surround the parking lot, and several nearby overlooks command prospects of the narrow gorge below. The road then switchbacks sharply down to run alongside **Oak Creek** itself. The lowest level in the rocks to either side, often obscured by maples, cedars, oaks and pines, is the bright-red Supai sandstone. Above that, layers of white sandstone, buff limestone, and finally black basalt testify to a geological history that has fluctuated from harsh desert to sea bottom. Temperatures are cool enough to make fishing, picnicking and hiking expeditions welcome escapes.

Slide Rock State Park

6871 N US-89A • Daily: Feb–April 8am–6pm; May–Oct 8am–7pm; Nov–Jan 9am–5pm • $20 per vehicle May–Oct; $10 Nov–April • ⓦ 928 282 3034, ⓦ azstateparks.com

Seven miles before US-89A reaches Sedona, **Slide Rock State Park** preserves what was originally a 43-acre apple orchard. The reason it's so full in summer, though, is that

5

Oak Creek at this point forms a natural water chute, where you can swim and slide across smooth boulders set in the riverbed. The absence of still water means that it's almost insect-free.

ACCOMMODATION   **OAK CREEK CANYON**

★ **The Canyon Wren** 6425 N US-89A ☎ 928 282 6900 or ☎ 800 437 9736, ⓦ canyonwrencabins.com; map opposite. Four large and hugely comfortable, private two-person cabins, each with a kitchen and a whirlpool tub, six miles north of Sedona; they're especially cosy in winter. No wi-fi. $165

Garland's Oak Creek Lodge 8067 N US-89A

☎ 928 282 3343, ⓦ garlandslodge.com; map opposite. The loveliest place to stay beside Oak Creek itself has to be in one of these individual log cabins, set in gorgeous gardens and reached across a small ford half a mile north of Slide Rock. Rates include breakfast and dinner in the top-quality dining room in the central lodge. Two-night minimum stay. Closed Sun, and late Nov to mid-March. $275

Sedona

There's no disputing that the New Age resort of **SEDONA** enjoys a magnificent setting, amid definitive Southwestern canyon scenery. Sadly, however, the town itself is a real eyesore, consisting of several miles of ugly sprawl to either side of a highway that's lined with hideous malls and seems always to be busy with traffic. Some visitors, particularly Europeans, experience a strong negative reaction, feeling that the Southwest holds plenty of beautiful landscapes that haven't been sullied by this sort of over-development. Other travellers, by contrast, absolutely love it, for its combination of luxurious accommodation and fancy restaurants, and almost limitless opportunities for active outdoor vacationing. In particular, artists, healers and wealthy retirees have flocked here in the last few decades. Whether you love or hate Sedona may depend on whether you share their wide-eyed awe for angels, crystals and all matters mystical – and whether you're prepared to pay over-the-odds prices for the privilege of joining them. Whatever your attitude, it's still an intriguing place to visit, where even the most hard-nosed commercial operation can seem a front for the real business of holding earnest conversations about the state of each other's psyches.

Established in 1902 by Theodore Schnebly and named after his wife, Sedona remained a small farming settlement for most of the twentieth century, unmarked on most maps. German surrealist painter **Max Ernst** moved here in the 1940s – the bizarre backdrops of his later canvases seem less surreal once you've seen where they were painted – and Hollywood moviemakers filmed in the area from the 1950s onwards. **Elvis Presley** shot his 27th movie, *Stay Away Joe*, hereabouts in 1967.

THE END OF THE NEW AGE?

Sedona's big break as a destination for **New Age** travellers came in 1981, when Page Bryant, author and psychic, "channelled" the information that Sedona is in fact "the heart *chakra* of the planet". After she pinpointed her first **vortex** – a point at which, it is claimed, psychic and electromagnetic energies can be channelled for personal and planetary harmony – the town achieved its own personal growth, and blossomed as a focus for New Age practitioners of all kinds.

However, Sedona's image as a spiritual centre suffered a devastating setback in 2009, when three people died of burns and dehydration during a sweat lodge exercise, and a further eighteen were hospitalized. Each had paid almost $10,000 to participate in a "Spiritual Warrior" retreat organized by self-styled guru James Arthur Ray, who was subsequently found guilty of negligent homicide and jailed for two years.

The tragedy served to focus attention on Native American views that New Age practitioners have grossly misrepresented Native American practices and beliefs. While Sedona still abounds in New Age tour operators and therapists, many have since toned down any claims to be associated with Native American spirituality.

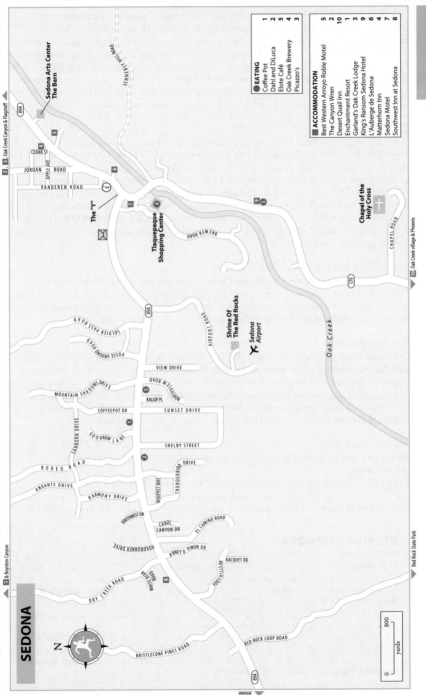

SEDONA

● EATING

Coffee Pot	1
Dahl and DiLuca	2
Elote Café	5
Oak Creek Brewery	4
Picazzo's	3

■ ACCOMMODATION

Best Western Arroyo Roble Motel	5
The Canyon Wren	2
Desert Quail Inn	10
Enchantment Resort	1
Garland's Oak Creek Lodge	9
King's Ransom Sedona Hotel	6
L'Auberge de Sedona	4
Matterhorn Inn	7
Sedona Motel	3
Southwest Inn at Sedona	8

Sedona Arts Center
The Barn

CEDAR ST
JORDAN ROAD
APPLE AVE
VANDEREN ROAD

The "Y"

Tlaquepaque Shopping Center

BREWER ROAD

Chapel of the
Holy Cross

CHAPEL ROAD

Shrine Of
The Red Rocks

✈ Sedona
Airport

AIRPORT ROAD
SOLDIER PASS ROAD
POSSE GROUND ROAD

Oak Creek

VIEW DRIVE
NORTHVIEW ROAD
MOUNTAIN SHADOWS DRIVE
KALLOF PL
COFFEEPOT DR
SUNSET DRIVE
SANBORN DRIVE
GOODROW LANE
SHELBY STREET
RODEO ROAD
WHIPPET WAY
THUNDERBIRD DRIVE
ANDANTE DRIVE
HARMONY DRIVE
SOUTHWEST DR
CAROL CANYON DR
EL CAMINO ROAD
ROADRUNNER DRIVE
ARROYO PINON DR
RACQUET RD
FOOT HILLS DR
DRY CREEK ROAD
WHITLOW ROAD
BRISTLECONE PINES ROAD
RED ROCK LOOP ROAD

N

0   800
yards

5

Don't assume that "New Age" equates with "alternative". Sedona is a profoundly conservative town – John McCain spends his weekends at a ranch here – where the pay-no-taxes ethos has ensured that most of the side roads off the main highways remain unpaved. That dovetails neatly, of course, with the booming business in **off-road tours**. Nonetheless, much of the best scenery is visible from the highway, and in any case many jeep roads are perfectly passable in ordinary vehicles. So long as you're happy to remain ignorant as to which rocks are really electromagnetic tuning forks vibrating in harmony with Alpha Centauri, there's no great need to take a commercial tour.

The "Y" and around

Sedona's one major road junction, known as the "**Y**", is poised above Oak Creek. Hwy-89A branches southwest towards Cottonwood, while Hwy-179 heads by way of the village of Oak Creek to meet I-17, fourteen miles south. The town itself holds little to detain sightseers, though strolling the two or so blocks that count as **uptown** – just north of the "Y," and the one area where the stores and businesses stand close enough together to make walking a possibility – is pleasant enough. Above the roaring traffic, you can usually still hear the synchronized chirruping of crickets in **Oak Creek** below, while your eyes are repeatedly drawn to the superb red rocks that tower above the banal buildings along Hwy-89A.

Airport Mesa and the Shrine of the Red Rocks

The closest **vortex** to town is on **Airport Mesa**. Turn left up Airport Road from Hwy-89A as you head west, a mile past the "Y," and the vortex is at the junction of the second and third peaks, just after the cattle grid. Further up, beyond the precarious airport, the **Shrine of the Red Rocks** looks out across the entire valley.

Boynton Canyon

Dry Creek Road, which heads north off Hwy-89 three miles west of the "Y", runs north past **Capitol Butte** to reach **Boynton Canyon**. While the lavish *Enchantment Resort* has impaired the magic of Boynton Canyon itself – which has its own vortex – several neighbouring canyons are ideal for short desert hikes. The resort office can provide trail maps marking Sinagua ruins in **Red Canyon**, or point the way to **Doe Mesa** or **Loy Butte Canyon**, both of which offer great views of the whole Sedona Valley.

Red Rock Loop Road

Red Rock State Park Daily: park 8am–5pm, visitor centre 9am–4.30pm • $5 per person, under-14s $3 • ☎ 928 282 6907, ⓦ azstateparks.com

Four and five miles west of Sedona's central "Y" on Hwy-89A respectively, are two successive turnings to the left that mark the Upper and Lower sections of the seven-mile **Red Rock Loop Road**, all of which is paved barring a bumpy but not too difficult

---

PARKING IN SEDONA

The major impediment to exploring the Sedona area in your own vehicle is the inconvenience of **parking**. The National Forest Service requires anyone parking in the forests around Sedona – which means anyone using the majority of roadside pull-outs in the vicinity for anything more than "incidental stopping", reckoned at fifteen minutes or more – to buy a **Red Rock Pass** (1-day $5, 1-week $15, 1-year $20). The passes are sold in local visitor centres, stores, motels and B&Bs, and also by vending machines in parking lots. Annual national park passes (see p.35) are also accepted, but must be displayed in the parked car.

To complicate matters further, four popular scenic spots – Banjo Bill, Grasshopper Point, Red Rock Crossing (site of Crescent Moon Ranch), and Call O' The Canyon (trailhead for the West Fork Trail) – are on private land, and charge their own fees of up to $10; a $40 **Grand Annual Red Rock Pass** covers those areas as well, but the national park passes do not.

mile in the middle. Its prime attraction is reached via a spur road a couple of miles down Lower Red Rock Loop Road.

Red Rock State Park may be the obvious name for a park in the Sedona area, but it's not in fact the best place to see red rocks. Instead it preserves a sweeping curve of **Oak Creek**, where the riparian environment survives reasonably intact. Its flora and fauna are explained in the prominent **visitor centre**, which holds stuffed hawks and owls and some live fish.

Two miles from the highway on Upper Red Rock Loop Road, a picturesque ford in Oak Creek known as **Red Rock Crossing**, which has featured in many movies, is alongside the Crescent Moon Picnic Area (daily 8am–dusk; $10 per vehicle). **Cathedral Rock**, on the far side of the stream, used to be called Courthouse Rock, and is another vortex.

The east bank of Oak Creek

To enjoy the Sedona area's most spectacular scenic drive, turn left off Hwy-179 as soon as it crosses Oak Creek south of the "Y," onto the unpaved **Schnebly Hill Road**. Ask locally about current conditions before you set off; in summer, the road remains open all the way to I-17, twelve rough miles east. Alternatively, continue south for three miles and then take Chapel Road to the left, which soon brings you to the **Chapel of the Holy Cross** (daily 9am–5pm). This tall and very narrow concrete chapel, whose facade is shaped like a massive cross, is squeezed into a cleft in the red cliffs. Another two miles down the highway is **Bell Rock**, on the east as you enter the village of Oak Creek, which is Sedona's fourth major vortex.

ARRIVAL AND DEPARTURE   SEDONA

By car Sedona is 28 miles south of Flagstaff on Hwy-89A, and 120 miles north of Phoenix. Its road system is utterly unable to cope with visitor levels; expect bumper-to-bumper traffic on weekends.

By bus Arizona Shuttle (☎ 928 226 8060 or ☎ 800 888 2749, ⓦ arizonashuttle.com) runs shuttles to Sedona from Phoenix (13 daily; $49) and Flagstaff (2 daily; $39).

GETTING AROUND AND INFORMATION

Bike rental Companies renting bikes include Bike & Bean, 75 Bell Rock Plaza, Hwy-179 (☎ 928 284 0210, ⓦ bike -bean.com), which has its own espresso bar.
Car rental Barlow Jeep Rentals, 3009 W Hwy-H9A (☎ 928 282 8700, ⓦ sedonajeeprentals.com) can provide

4WD vehicles.
Visitor centre 331 Forest Road at Hwy-89A, just north of the "Y" (daily 8.30am–5pm; ☎ 928 282 7722 or ☎ 800 288 7336, ⓦ visitsedona.com).

TOURS

Hillsboro Aviation ☎ 928 282 8903, ⓦ sedonahelitours .com. Helicopter flights, from the 12min Rim Dancer ($99) to the 30min Sinagua Majestic Deluxe ($179).
Northern Light Balloon Expeditions ☎ 928 282 2274 or ☎ 800 230 6222, ⓦ northernlightballoon.com. Exhilarating balloon trips from $220, with champagne picnics.
Pink Jeep Tours ☎ 928 282 5000 or ☎ 800 873 3662, ⓦ pinkjeep.com. You can't miss this lot in uptown Sedona. Quite exceptionally garish "4-wheelin' vehicles" crunch around in off-road tours, from $52.

Sedona Grand Canyon Air Tours ☎ 928 204 5939 or ☎ 888 866 7433, ⓦ sedonaairtours.com. Fly over Sedona in a helicopter – with the doors off, if you prefer – or take a fixed-wing tour over the Grand Canyon ($229) or to Grand Canyon West ($489).
Trail Horse Adventures ☎ 928 634 5276, ⓦ trailhorse adventures.com. Horseriding trips, largely geared around cowboy-style eating in Cottonwood's Dead Horse Ranch State Park, costing $65–205.

ACCOMMODATION

Home to a plethora of upscale **B&Bs** and full-service **resorts**, Sedona is an expensive place to stay. Oak Creek Canyon (see p.273), just north, also holds worthwhile alternatives, while budget travellers can get better deals at Cottonwood (see p.279) and Jerome (see p.282).

5

Best Western Arroyo Roble Motel 400 N US-89A ☎928 282 4001 or ☎800 773 3662, ⓦbestwestern sedona.com. This comfortable multitiered motel, stacked above Oak Creek not far north of uptown Sedona, has a separate deluxe wing, *Arroyo Roble North*, and a cluster of self-contained two-bedroom villas. Even the standard rooms have private patios or balconies, with fabulous views, and rates include good cooked breakfasts. $265

Desert Quail Inn 6626 Hwy-179 ☎928 284 1433 or ☎800 385 0927, ⓦdesertquailinn.com. Highway motel in the village of Oak Creek, seven miles south of the "Y" towards the interstate, offering relatively affordable and unexpectedly stylish rooms. $110

Enchantment Resort 525 Boynton Canyon Rd ☎928 282 2900 or ☎888 250 1699, ⓦenchantmentresort .com. Extremely luxurious resort, equipped with a spa plus four pools and seven tennis courts, that has taken over ravishing Boynton Canyon eight miles west of town. Accommodation is in fully equipped one- and two-bedroom adobe *casitas*. $301

King's Ransom Sedona Hotel 771 Hwy-179 ☎928 282 3132 or ☎877 480 0044, ⓦkingsransomsedona .com. Nicely refurbished upper-range motel, half a mile south of the Tlaquepaque mall, with rather small rooms – most with balconies – but a nice garden, a pool and spa,

and a highly recommended Mexican restaurant, *Elote Café* (see below). $104

L'Auberge de Sedona 301 L'Auberge Lane ☎928 399 7002 or ☎855 905 5745, ⓦlauberge.com. Plush two-part resort in the heart of the town, with fancy if somewhat incongruous French-themed motel rooms at road level looking out onto the red rocks, and a cable-car connection to the individual guest cottages ranged along the tranquil banks of Oak Creek below. $248

Matterhorn Inn 230 Apple Ave ☎928 282 7176 or ☎800 372 8207, ⓦmatterhorninn.com. Central motel, on the right as you come into town on Hwy-89A from the north, with two tiers of rooms that face across to the red rocks. $139

Sedona Motel 218 Hwy-179 ☎928 282 7187 or ☎877 828 7187, ⓦthesedonamotel.com. Small motel, amazingly inexpensive by local standards, in an ideal and attractive location close to the "Y" uptown, with a friendly atmosphere on its shared communal deck. $99

Southwest Inn at Sedona 3250 W US-89A ☎928 282 3344 or ☎800 483 7422, ⓦswinn.com. The classiest of Sedona's many highwayside motels, with very welcoming staff, an outdoor spa and comfortable soundproofed rooms; to get a view, though, you have to pay from $5 more. $152

EATING

Sedona is bursting with expensive Southwestern-style **restaurants**, not all of which are particularly good, but it still has a smattering of old-fashioned diners. There's a shortage of spots where you can just sit and watch the world go by over a coffee and a sandwich; most of its cafés are twee little places intended mainly to entice tourists into pastel-trimmed gift stores.

Coffee Pot Restaurant 2050 W Hwy-89A ☎928 282 6626, ⓦcoffeepotsedona.com. Sedona's largest, oldest diner – named for a nearby rock formation – serves a hundred kinds of omelettes ($7–11), and all the burgers ($7–10), Mexican dishes ($8–14), and fried specials you could hope for. Daily 6am–2pm.

Dahl and DiLuca 2321 W Hwy-89A ☎928 282 5219, ⓦdahlanddiluca.com. Northern Italian dinners served in a romantic mock-up of a Tuscan villa; specials like lamb, veal and prawn pasta can cost as much as $40, but standard, well-prepared pasta dishes are more typically priced around $20. Daily 5–10pm.

Elote Café 771 Hwy-179 ☎928 203 0105, ⓦelotecafe .com. High-quality Mexican restaurant a mile south of town, including delicious pepita-crusted snapper ($22),

buffalo ribs with mole sauce ($26.50) and smoked chicken enchiladas ($19.50). No reservations. Tues–Sat 5–9.30pm.

Oak Creek Brewery 336 Hwy-179 ☎928 282 3300, ⓦoakcreekpub.com. Sedona's first brewpub, in the mock-Mexican Tlaquepaque mall, closes remarkably early for a pub, but it offers a fine selection of lagers and ales, brewed on site, plus a full menu ranging from pork ribs for $16 to large pizzas for $21. No reservations. Daily 11.30am–9pm.

Picazzo's 1855 W Hwy-89A ☎928 282 4140, ⓦpicazzos.com. Part of an arty Arizona chain, this fancy organic pizza place enjoys pretty red-rock views, with outdoor seating on a shaded patio. Pizza flavours include fig gorgonzola ($17) and "meaty meaty" ($18.50), and they have plenty of vegetarian and even gluten-free options. Mon–Thurs & Sun 11am–9pm, Fri & Sat 11am–10pm.

Cottonwood

Describing **COTTONWOOD**, eighteen miles southwest of Sedona, the 1930s *WPA Guide to Arizona* wrote, "Familiar figures in the town are the cowboys from the range and the prospector or 'desert rat' who wanders in from his camp in the mountains to break the monotony of his lonely life." Today's Cottonwood is not nearly so romantic, though thanks to an influx of retirees it's much larger. It's not really even the same place, as the

VERDE CANYON RAILROAD

Although an unremarkable little place itself, the town of Clarkdale, three miles northwest of Cottonwood, is the starting point for Arizona's most scenic **vintage train ride**.

The **Verde Canyon Railroad** operates 25-mile round-trip excursions along the otherwise inaccessible Verde Canyon, heading as far as Perkinsville, with plenty of dramatic red-rock scenery and archeological ruins en route. The trips run year-round, almost always leaving at 1pm, and varying in frequency from twice weekly to daily in the peak spring and fall seasons. See the website for schedules, and note that the trains are powered by diesel engines, not steam ($65, ages 2–12 $45; ☎ 800 293 7245, ⊛ verdecanyonrr.com).

former downtown is stranded a couple of miles north of Hwy-89A, now lined by modern strip development.

Cottonwood does, however, make an inexpensive base for Sedona and Jerome, and its old main street still possesses a certain charm.

ACCOMMODATION AND EATING   **COTTONWOOD**

Old Town Red Rooster Cafe 901 N Main St ☎ 928 649 8100, ⊛ oldtownredrooster.com. This friendly café in downtown Cottonwood offers the perfect opportunity for latterday desert rats to break the monotony, with a breakfast coffee or pastry, or lunchtime soup, salad or sandwich ($6–10). Daily 8am–4pm.

Pines Motel 920 S Camino Real ☎ 928 634 9975 or ☎ 800 483 9618, ⊛ azpinesmotel.com. Good-value family-owned motel, just off Hwy-89A a short way south of the centre, with clean, good-sized rooms, some with kitchenettes, and a pool. You'd be lucky to find rates like this in Sedona. **$90**

Tuzigoot National Monument

2 miles northeast of Cottonwood on Hwy-89A, then 0.6 miles east on Tuzigoot Rd • Daily 8am–5pm • $10 per person, also valid at Montezuma Castle National Monument • ☎ 928 634 5564, ⊛ nps.gov/tuzi

During the fourteenth century, the valley of the Verde River, south of Sedona, held fifty major pueblo sites occupied by the ancient people now known as the **Sinagua**. One of the largest, perched on a hillock across the river from **Clarkdale**, now constitutes **Tuzigoot National Monument**.

The ground floor alone had 86 rooms; with fifteen more rooms on the upper level, it may have been home to some 225 people. Some archeologists think it was a final enclave, where the Sinagua gathered against encroaching drought before abandoning the area early in the fifteenth century. Artefacts displayed in the recently modernized visitor centre include turquoise mosaics and shell jewellery. Unfortunately, though, Tuzigoot is less satisfying than many such sites. When it was restored in the 1930s, a little too much work was done, and a broad cement trail was laid over, across and through the pueblo.

Jerome

The tiny mining-town-turned-arts-colony of **JEROME**, high above the Verde Valley on Hwy-89A, is conspicuous from quite a distance. Not only is an enormous letter "J" etched into the hillside above it, but a large chunk of that hill is missing altogether, having been blown apart for **opencast copper mining**.

As recently as the 1970s, Jerome was a **ghost town**, where it was possible to turn up and move into an empty house. Many who did so are still here, making a living from arts and crafts, and the town itself has made a dramatic recovery. While being solely geared towards the needs of visitors makes it something of a tourist trap, it's nonetheless fascinating to explore. Most of the shops only stock souvenirs, but there are some interesting crafts showrooms and art galleries around, as well as fine old saloons. Inevitably, the "ghost town" tag has been spun into stories that many of Jerome's fine old buildings are **haunted**, so there's a thriving trade in after-dark ghost tours.

5

Thanks to the steep angle of the hillside, Jerome's streets are stacked one atop the other, so its stone houses tend to have two storeys at the front and four or five at the back. Under the concussion of two hundred miles of tunnels being blasted into the mountainside, the whole town used to slip downhill at the rate of five inches per year; the **Sliding Jail** on Hull Avenue came to rest 225 feet from where it was built (it's still there, but it's not open to the public).

Brief history

Although Mingus Mountain abounds in mineral wealth – thick veins of copper are interspersed with gold and silver, and limestone is still extracted for cement – serious exploitation only started in 1876. The **United Verde** mine was partly financed by New Yorker **Eugene Jerome** (a cousin of Winston Churchill's mother, Jennie Jerome), who insisted the new town bear his name. The United Verde has been called "the richest mine ever owned by an individual"; it made entrepreneur William Clark $100 million, and by 1953 had produced enough copper to give a thirteen-pound lump to every person on earth. Until the tortuous highway was built, the only way up to Jerome was the rail line that corkscrewed down from the mine to the world's largest copper smelter, at Clarkdale.

Jerome was a hard-drinking, hard-living town. The young **Pancho Villa** started out in life by supplying its drinking water, using a relay of two hundred burros (small donkeys), and the International Workers of the World – the "**Wobblies**" – were briefly a strong presence; several hundred miners and "outside agitators" were literally railroaded out of town in 1917 and dumped in the remote deserts of southwest Arizona.

Harsh economic realities have always determined local fortunes. Plenty of copper remains in the earth; although the Depression hit hard, the mine was only closed in the 1950s, when cheap imported copper made it uneconomic to continue, and as prices rise, it may reopen. To keep the mineral rights from reverting to the state, the present owners are obliged to keep on researching and prospecting; in fact, they do more than they have to, and reportedly find enough gold to cover their expenses.

Jerome State Historic Park

100 Douglas Rd • Daily 8.30am–5pm • $5 • ☎ 928 634 5381, ⊛ azstateparks.com

Built for mine owner "Rawhide Jimmy" Douglas in 1917, the **Douglas Mansion**, below town, is now open as **Jerome State Historic Park**. Given the sweeping views, it can be hard to concentrate on the displays detailing the history of the mines and the lifestyles of the bosses.

Mine Museum

200 N Main St • Daily 9am–5pm • $2 • ☎ 928 634 5477, ⊛ jeromehistoricalsociety.com

Located in the former *Fashion Saloon*, in the heart of old Jerome, the **Mine Museum** displays an amateurish but enjoyable collection of Wild West oddities ranging from milk bottles to laundry machines and firearms. Its most memorable feature is the pressed-tin ceiling of the saloon itself.

ARRIVAL AND INFORMATION
JEROME

By car Though on paper Hwy-89A is a direct through route between Sedona, thirty miles northeast of Jerome, and Prescott, thirty miles southwest, the formidable Mingus Mountain makes reaching Jerome a slow business. Coming from Cottonwood, it's a painstaking switchback climb; if you approach from Prescott, you descend into Jerome, with gorgeous views of the valley spread out below. Hwy-89A branches in two in the heart of town, where a one-way system takes westbound traffic along Hull Avenue and eastbound along Main Street.

Visitor centre A tiny information shack at 310 N Hull Ave (Mon–Fri 9am–5pm; ☎ 928 634 2900, ⊛ jeromechamber.com).

FROM TOP GOLD KING MINE AND GHOST TOWN, JEROME (SEE P.279); DOWNTOWN FLAGSTAFF (SEE P.264) >

ACCOMMODATION

There's no room to build **motels** on Jerome's uncertain slopes, so accommodation is restricted to a couple of turn-of-the-century hotels and a few former homes converted into **B&Bs**.

Connor Hotel 160 Main St ☎928 634 5006 or ☎800 523 3554, �🌐connorhotel.com. Small central hotel, offering twelve attractive antique-furnished rooms, each with a tasteful tiled private bathroom, above the *Spirit Room* bar, which gets busy on weekends. **$105**

Ghost City Inn 541 N Main St ☎928 634 4678 or ☎888 634 4678, �🌐ghostcityinn.com. Century-old house, at the entrance to town as you come up from Cottonwood, with huge views from its wooden veranda. Some of the six guest rooms, which vary in price, are resolutely Western, others more flowery, but all have en-suite bathrooms. The owner is Jerome's police chief. **$105**

Jerome Grand Hotel 200 Hill St ☎928 634 8200 or ☎888 817 6788, �🌐jeromegrandhotel.com. Restored hotel, housed in a former hospital that spills down five storeys from the highest point in town; the views are fabulous, but the accommodation merely evokes bygone days, rather than being particularly luxurious. There's also a good on-site restaurant; see below. **$130**

Surgeon's House B&B 101 Hill St ☎928 639 1452, �🌐surgeonshouse.com. Smart, upmarket B&B, set in lovely gardens at the top of town; three of the four plush en-suite rooms enjoy dramatic views. **$175**

EATING AND DRINKING

Day-trippers tend to fill Jerome's **tea rooms** and **snack bars** at lunchtime – especially on weekends – but come the evening, when its **bars** come to life, you can still get a faint sense of its rip-roaring past.

★ **The Asylum** Jerome Grand Hotel, 200 Hill St ☎928 639 3197, ⍵asylumrestaurant.com. "Fun" restaurant that makes the most of its dramatic, quirky setting in a former hospital, while serving excellent Southwestern cuisine. All that plus a fabulous wine list and astonishing views – what more could you want? Dinner specials like maple leaf duck breast range $21–31; lunch salads and sandwiches cost $10–16. Daily 11am–3.30pm & 5–9pm.

Bobby D's BBQ 119 Jerome Ave ☎928 634 6235, ⍵bobbydsbbqjerome.com. Supposedly Arizona's oldest restaurant, built in 1899, the *English Kitchen* was successively an opium den and a meeting hall for the Wobblies. These days it specializes in barbecue, serving succulent pulled pork and smoked chicken, with "sammiches" for around $10, mixed plates more like $16, and takeaway available. The terrace offers commanding views over the valley. Mon–Thurs & Sun 11am–6pm, Fri & Sat 11am–8pm.

Flatiron Cafe 416 N Main St ☎928 634 2733, ⍵theflatironjerome.com. Small, friendly joint at the southern apex of the one-way system. Espresso coffees, scrambled-egg breakfasts, and fancy salad-and-sandwich lunches, with vegetarian options always available, for around $10. Mon & Thurs–Sun 7.30am–3pm.

Montezuma Castle National Monument

Two separate sites, just east of I-17, 40 miles south of Flagstaff and 20 miles southeast of Sedona

Towards the east end of the Verde Valley, two dramatic ancient sites, roughly ten miles' drive apart, jointly constitute **MONTEZUMA CASTLE NATIONAL MONUMENT**. If you only have time to see one, you'll find Montezuma Castle itself to be the more rewarding, but each offers a fascinating snapshot of the Sinagua culture.

Montezuma Well

4 miles east of I-17 exit 293 • Daily 8am–5pm • Free • ☎928 567 4521, ⍵nps.gov/moca

Montezuma Well, the northern component of Montezuma Castle National Monument, is a natural lake that measures 368 feet across by 55 feet deep. Set like a volcanic crater into a small hill, it formed when the roof of an underground cave collapsed 11,000 years ago. It's still fed by a spring that produces a phenomenal 1.5 million gallons of warm water per day, naturally heated to a constant 74°F.

Not surprisingly, the well was sacred to Native Americans; the **Yavapai** people (see p.324) say they emerged into the world here. The **Hohokam**, who arrived around 600 AD, were the first to divert its water for irrigation, while the **Sinagua** followed in 1125 AD. Traces of their ruined pueblos can be discerned on the hilltop, reached by a five-minute walk from the parking lot, while a more complete

5

cliff dwelling is set into the inner crater wall. It's inaccessible, though you get a good view from the staircase that leads down to the lakeside, where a couple more dwellings stand at ground level.

Montezuma Castle

1 mile east of I-17 exit 289 • Daily 8am–5pm • $10 per person, also valid at Tuzigoot National Monument • ☎ 928 567 3322, ⓦ nps.gov/moca

In an idyllic setting above Beaver Creek, **Montezuma Castle** is a superbly preserved Sinagua **cliff dwelling** dating from the twelfth century. Filling a hillside alcove with a wall of pink adobe, and originally reached by three separate ladders from the valley floor, its five storeys taper up to fit the contours of the rock. Apparently, the sycamore beams are still in place, and the fingerprints of the masons are still visible on the bricks, but visitors are not permitted to climb up.

The ruins of a much larger, though now much less photogenic, dwelling stand "next door". Once again you can't go inside, but holes in the limestone show that it had 45 rooms, as well as little "cupboards" recessed into the walls. It may have housed a hundred people, as opposed to thirty or so in the castle.

Displays on the Sinagua in the castle **visitor centre**, where you pay your entry fee, are stylish and modern, if not all that detailed. The collection includes a macaw skeleton, which suggests trade with the Mexican civilizations thousands of miles south. There's no connection with the Aztec ruler Montezuma, though the well is said to appear on a deerskin map that belonged to Cortes himself.

Prescott

The neat little Victorian town of **PRESCOTT** makes an unlikely sight in the Arizona wilderness, a hundred miles north of Phoenix by way of I-17 and Hwy-69 (which branches off the interstate at Cordes Junction). In 1863, when President Lincoln acceded to pressure from mining interests and granted Arizona territorial status, he chose to establish a new capital well away from the obvious choice, Tucson, which he saw as a hotbed of Confederate sympathizers. His first pick, **Fort Whipple**, was replaced in 1864 when gold was discovered near Prescott, which became the site of both fort and capital. It was named in honour of William H. Prescott, author of the classic *History of the Conquest of Mexico*, although he never visited the town.

Although Tucson duly supplanted it as capital within three years, Prescott survived, with cattle ranchers joining the gold miners to make it a rowdy, liquor-loving town. Those days are long gone, however, and while Prescott refused to die, neither has it grown. Instead, centring on its venerable courthouse square, it's a charming little town with a real Wild West flavour. While few out-of-state visitors find their way here, as it's not on any obvious itinerary, it makes a rewarding overnight stop, with plenty of hotels and restaurants.

Prescott was hit by an appalling tragedy in 2013, when nineteen local firefighters lost their lives in the **Yarnell Hill Fire**, in the forests 35 miles southwest of town towards Wickenburg.

Courthouse Square

Downtown Prescott focuses on the kind of **Courthouse Square** you'd expect to find in the Deep South. Apart from the courthouse itself, its central feature is the **Rough Rider Memorial Monument**, a bronze equestrian statue that commemorates William Owen "Buckey" O'Neill. While mayor of Prescott, this frontier character recruited many of Theodore Roosevelt's Rough Riders in 1898, and was killed in Cuba at the Battle of San Juan Hill. A colourful timeline set into the concrete footpath nearby traces local history from a visit by the Spanish explorer Espejo in 1581 up to the opening of the "Automated Flight Service Station" in 1985. Especially on summer weekends, the square plays host to community events and arts fairs.

Sharlot Hall Museum

415 W Gurley St • May–Sept Mon–Sat 10am–5pm, Sun noon–4pm; Oct–April Mon–Sat 10am–4pm, Sun noon–4pm • $7 •
☎ 928 445 3122, ⓦ sharlot.org

The **Sharlot Hall Museum**, a short walk west of Courthouse Square, is the best place to get a feel for Prescott's past. Sharlot Hall herself arrived here with her pioneer parents in 1882, aged twelve, and went on to become Arizona's official historian. She also started this collection, which now fills a dozen buildings and an entire city block. In its modern headquarters, you can admire the attractive flapper-esque gown of copper she wore when taking Arizona's three electoral college votes to Washington DC to elect Calvin Coolidge in 1925. Structures nearby include the 1864 Governor's Mansion and the contemporaneous Fort Misery, which became Arizona's first law office and courthouse as well as a church, general store and boarding house.

The main **Sharlot Hall Building** covers the town's early history and also explores the travails of the Yavapai, tracing their story from baskets, bows and arrows up to their current ownership of two casinos and the local Conference Center. The most popular section, the **Transportation Building**, holds a gorgeous Wells Fargo stagecoach, painted red with yellow wheels, which was in use – and held up by bandits – in Tombstone in 1881.

ARRIVAL AND INFORMATION   PRESCOTT

By bus Arizona Shuttle buses run from 740 N Montezuma St to Phoenix's Sky Harbor Airport (27 daily; $35 one-way; ☎ 928 442 1000 or ☎ 800 888 2749, ⓦ arizonashuttle.com).

Visitor centre 117 W Goodwin St, on Courthouse Plaza (Mon–Fri 9am–5pm, Sat & Sun 10am–2pm; ☎ 928 445 2000 or ☎ 800 266 7534, ⓦ prescott.org).

ACCOMMODATION

For a small town, Prescott has an ideal range of accommodation options. Besides historic hotels around the main square, small-scale B&Bs lurk in Victorian homes nearby. Chain motels can be found on the fringes, but it would be a shame to stay too far from the centre.

Hassayampa Inn 122 E Gurley St ☎ 928 778 9434 or ☎ 800 322 1927, ⓦ hassayampainn.com. Grand 1920s hotel just off the square, offering abundant Art Deco flourishes amid its overall Southwestern theme, and equipped with comfortable, individually styled guest rooms that vary considerably in size. The *Peacock Room*, open for all meals daily, serves upscale, expensive contemporary cuisine. **$109**

Hotel St Michael 205 W Gurley St ☎928 776 1999, ⓦstmichaelhotel.com. Atmospheric old downtown hotel – some say it's haunted – with a wide range of inexpensive rooms, all en suite, plus its own bistro and mall of antique and speciality stores. Rates include breakfast, and are at their cheapest on weekdays. **$89**

★**The Motor Lodge** 503 S Montezuma St ☎928 717 0157, ⓦthemotorlodge.com. While the *Motor Lodge*, a 10min walk south of downtown, might look like a vintage motel, its twelve individual en-suite cabins actually date from 1910. Playfully refurbished with colourful retro flourishes, equipped as a rule with gas fireplaces and/or private porches, they make an excellent and very memorable budget option. **$109**

Hotel Vendome 230 S Cortez St ☎928 776 0900, ⓦvendomehotel.com. Century-old lodging house, modernized in the ways that matter while retaining its period charm. Twenty en-suite rooms, spread over two storeys and sharing long verandas; rates include top-quality breakfasts. **$99**

EATING AND DRINKING

The streets around Prescott's Courthouse Square hold a plethora of places to **eat** and **drink** at reasonable prices. **Bars** are concentrated on Montezuma Street on its western side, in the block once known as **Whiskey Row**.

El Gato Azul 316 W Godwin St ☎928 445 1070, ⓦelgatoazulprescott.com. Actually bright yellow, this friendly little café, tucked away a block downhill from Courthouse Square, serves a wide-ranging menu that draws on Spanish as well as Mexican traditions. A delicious Spanish paella costs $18, pork carnitas $17, but many diners come simply for the tasty $6–10 tapas. There's indoor and outdoor seating, plus live jazz and acoustic music Thurs, Fri & Sun. Daily 11am–3pm & 4.30pm–late.

The Local 520 W Sheldon St ☎928 237 4724. Prescott's top breakfast and lunch (and of course brunch) spot, a few blocks northwest of Courthouse Square, is renowned for baked specials including an $8 vegetable pot pie, plus wholesome salads and sandwiches for around $10. Mon, Tues & Thurs–Sun 7am–2.30pm.

Lone Spur Cafe 106 W Gurley St ☎928 445 8202, ⓦthelonespur.com. Good old-fashioned Western diner, right on Courthouse Square and always busy in the daytime for massive pancake-and-eggs breakfasts, and burgers-and-steaks lunches. Dinner is only offered on Fridays, when options include Dover sole ($17) or a full rack of ribs ($21). Mon–Thurs, Sat & Sun 8am–2pm, Fri 8am–2pm & 4.30–8pm.

Palace 120 S Montezuma St ☎928 541 1966, ⓦhistoricpalace.com. This majestic old saloon, complete with double swinging doors, was originally the centrepiece of Whiskey Row. Still a genuine Western bar, it now also serves $10–14 lunchtime salads and burgers as well as full meaty dinners for $18–35. Mon–Thurs & Sun 11am–9pm, Fri & Sat 11am–10pm.

Wickenburg

WICKENBURG, sixty miles southwest of Prescott and as far northwest of downtown Phoenix, is another former mining and ranching town now kept humming by tourism. It's only a little higher, and a little cooler, than Phoenix, so the main visitor season is in winter, between November and April.

Wickenburg stands beside the **Hassayampa River**, whose Apache name, meaning "river that runs upside down", refers to the fact that it often flows underground. This spot marks the "pumpkin patch" where Prussian prospector Henry Wickenburg built a mill in 1864 to process the gold he'd discovered in the Vulture Mountains, fifteen miles south. His **Vulture Mine** was seldom profitable, and finally closed down in 1942. By then, however, Wickenburg had established a successful sideline running **dude ranches**, where well-heeled Easterners could dabble with the Wild West lifestyle for a few carefree days.

In general, Wickenburg is spruce and prosperous, with little sense of a desert outpost, though the wooden sidewalks and false-front stores along **Frontier Street** in the heart of town must look much as they did in Wickenburg's heyday. You can still see the mesquite tree that served as the original town "jail"; miscreants were simply chained to its trunk.

Desert Caballeros Western Museum

21 N Frontier St • Mon–Sat 10am–5pm, Sun noon–4pm; closed Mon late May to early Sept • $9, under-18s free • ☎928 684 2272, ⓦwesternmuseum.org

The principal focus in Wickenburg's large and consistently interesting **Desert Caballeros Western Museum** is on art, with paintings by the likes of Remington

5

and Russell displayed alongside lots of sculptures of noble native American warriors. Henry Farny's 1894 gouache portrait of Geronimo, signed by the Apache warrior himself, is a particular highlight. Local history, too, is comprehensively covered, with a reconstruction of a 1900s street scene that includes a fully stocked general store, along with several little dioramas, masses of spurs and bits and hats and chaps, and all the barbed wire you could want.

Vulture Mine

36610 N 355th Ave • Late Oct to early May, Sat 10am • $10, under-6s free • ⓦ vultureminetours.com

The long-abandoned workings of the **Vulture Mine** itself rear from the streets of the well-preserved ghost town of **Vulture City**, sixteen miles southwest of central Wickenburg. They can only be visited in the cooler months of the year, on once-weekly, two-hour guided tours. Stick to the walking trail as you wander round; the various buildings, which include a blacksmith's shop and the mine's head office, are not as sturdy as they appear.

INFORMATION   **WICKENBURG**

Visitor centre The friendly visitor centre, 216 N Frontier St (summer Mon–Fri 9am–5pm; winter Mon–Fri 9am–5pm, Sat 9am–2pm, Sun 10am–3pm; ☎ 928 684 5479, ⓦ outwickenburgway.com), hands out a sunny guide on local attractions.

ACCOMMODATION AND EATING

Best Western Rancho Grande 293 E Wickenburg Way ☎ 928 684 5445 or ☎ 800 780 7234, ⓦ bestwestern arizona.com. This is the most attractive of Wickenburg's conventional motels, part genuine adobe and part Spanish colonial mock-up, with good-sized rooms, some with kitchenettes, and a pool. **$73**

Flying E Ranch 2801 W Wickenburg Way ☎ 928 684 2690 or ☎ 888 684 2650, ⓦ flyingeranch.com. The only working cattle ranch in Wickenburg that still accepts paying guests spreads across twenty thousand acres. Rates include all meals in the central lodge (no alcohol served) but not riding; one 2hr ride costs $50, two cost $80. Nov–April only, min 2 nights. **$330**

Nana's Sandwich Saloon 48 N Tegner St ☎ 928 684 5539, ⓦ nanassandwichsaloon.com. The best place to pick up a good breakfast or lunch in Wickenburg backs onto the Desert Caballeros museum. As the name suggests, the menu is dominated by wholesome $7–8 sandwiches, but they also offer coffees, salads and ice cream. Mon–Sat 7.30am–4pm.

Joshua Forest Parkway

Northwest of Wickenburg, US-93 runs for 108 dramatic miles across some of Arizona's wildest and most scenic mountains, to meet I-40 twenty miles east of Kingman (see p.289). For anyone heading up from Phoenix, this slow two-lane highway bears witness to just how much of the state remains wilderness. Apart from the hamlet of **NOTHING** – which might sound enticing on the map, but really is nothing, other than the home base of a towing company that rescues unfortunate stranded motorists – there's almost no sign of human life. Instead, the vegetation is the main source of interest, with saguaro and ocotillo **cactuses** scattered across the impressive rocky outcrops. These eastern fringes of the Mojave Desert are among the few places in Arizona where you'll encounter an abundance of **joshua trees** – hence the road's official designation as the **Joshua Forest Parkway**.

West of Flagstaff

Though the two hundred miles of I-40 that run **west from Flagstaff** to California are kept busy by traffic heading to, from and between the Grand Canyon and Las Vegas, few towns along the way are especially interesting. However, most became reliant on tourism during the heyday of **Route 66**, and driving through any of them can bring on a frisson of that era's romance.

If you have the time to indulge your 1950s fantasies, then take the 120-mile side trip on the longest surviving section of what John Steinbeck called the "**Mother Road**", which starts at **Seligman**, loops back down to **Kingman**, and then crosses wild and mountainous country to the ghost town of **Oatman**. Otherwise, it makes little difference where or even whether you choose to take a break from the interstate.

Williams

Although Flagstaff is generally regarded as the obvious base for visitors to the Grand Canyon's South Rim, **WILLIAMS**, 32 miles west, is in fact the closest interstate town to the national park. While it can't boast the charm or pizazz of its neighbour, it's a nice enough little place, filled with Route 66-era motels and diners and retaining a certain individuality despite the stream of tourists. Its setting, cupped in a high grassy valley amid pine-covered hills, helps; the largest peak, the 9264ft **Bill Williams Mountain** to the south, was named for pioneer trapper and "mountain man" Bill Williams (1787–1849), and gave its name in turn to the town, founded thirty years after his death.

Like Flagstaff, Williams originally based both its architecture and its economy on the ponderosas of the surrounding forests. Since 1901, however, when the Santa Fe Railroad first connected it with the canyon rim, sixty miles due north, Williams has lived off tourism. Though the railroad went out of business in 1968, it reopened in 1989 as the **Grand Canyon Railway**, promoted as a fun ride rather than a serious means of transportation. Most people who spend the night in Williams are here to take the morning train up to the canyon.

The highlights of Williams's annual calendar are **Rendezvous Days**, on Memorial Day weekend in late May, when locals dress up as pioneer "buckskinners", and the Labor Day **rodeo**.

Route 66 and Railroad Avenue

Williams holds a romantic appeal as the very last town on the old **Route 66** to have been bypassed by the I-40 interstate. Until October 13, 1984, when Bobby Troup of (*Get Your Kicks On*) *Route 66* fame fronted a closing ceremony, the only stoplight on the interstate between Chicago and Los Angeles stood outside the Williams visitor centre. To this day, the town remains a major rendezvous for bikers, and on summer Saturdays especially it's usually thronging with Harley-Davidsons.

Much of the former Route 66 frontage remains barely changed, with quirky antiques stores selling vintage memorabilia alongside Native American crafts and jewellery. However, while it's fun to explore the central blocks along the two main one-way streets – Route 66, running west to east, is paralleled by the east–west **Railroad Avenue** – an hour's evening or morning stroll is enough.

ARRIVAL AND DEPARTURE   WILLIAMS

By train Amtrak's *Southwest Chief* train calls in at Williams Junction, three miles east of town, twice daily, heading east at 3.50am in summer, and west at 9.33pm. The *Grand Canyon Railway Hotel* runs free connecting shuttle buses into town.

By bus Greyhound buses do not serve Williams, but

Arizona Shuttle buses connect the *Railway Hotel* with *Maswik Lodge* in Grand Canyon Village (daily: March–Oct 8.15am, 1.30pm & 4.30pm; Nov–Feb 8.15am & 4.30pm; one-way $22; ☎ 928 226 8060 or ☎ 800 888 2749, ⓦ arizonashuttle.com).

INFORMATION AND TOURS

Visitor centre 200 W Railroad Ave, near the railroad depot (daily: summer 8am–6.30pm; winter 8am–5pm; ☎ 928 635 1418, ⓦ experiencewilliams.com). Also holds an entertaining museum of neighbourhood history, and

covers the nearby national forests as well.
Grand Canyon Railway The Grand Canyon Railway (☎ 303 843 8724 or ☎ 800 843 8724, ⓦ thetrain.com) departs daily from the Williams Depot in the centre of town (see p.318).

5

Guided tours Marvelous Marv's Tours run daily guided van tours of the Grand Canyon South Rim from Williams, with the $100 adult rate including park admission (☎ 928 707 0291, ⊛ marvelousmarv.com).

ACCOMMODATION

Williams's downtown streets are lined with **vintage motels** as well as the odd **B&B**, while national chains congregate near the interstate exits at either end of town.

Best Western Plus Inn of Williams 2600 W Route 66 ☎ 928 635 4400 or ☎ 800 635 4445, ⊛ bestwestern williams.com. Spacious, well-equipped motel-resort, perched near I-40 exit 161 at the west end of town, and generally a cut above usual chain standards. Large comfortable rooms plus a pool, hot tub and on-site restaurant. $189

Canyon Motel & RV Park 1900 E Rodeo Rd ☎ 928 635 9371 or ☎ 800 482 3955, ⊛ thecanyonmotel.com. The word "motel" hardly does this restored Route 66 relic justice. Perched on the edge of the forest east of downtown, it offers accommodation in individual brick cottages and, best of all, converted railroad cars; two 1929 cabooses sleep 5–6 each, while a larger carriage holds three separate en-suite units. Don't expect luxury, but it's a much more memorable experience than just another highway motel, and there are also fifty RV spaces. RV sites $38, motel rooms $79, carriage rooms $105, caboose $159

Grand Canyon Hotel 145 W Route 66 ☎ 928 635 1419, ⊛ thegrandcanyonhotel.com. Not to be confused with the much larger *Railway Hotel*, this restored downtown "boutique hotel" offers individual beds in a clean, crisp dorm, plus themed private doubles with and without en-suite facilities. Dorm $35, shared bathroom $69, en-suite $78

Grand Canyon Railway Hotel 1 Fray Marcos Blvd ☎ 928 635 4010 or ☎ 800 843 8724, ⊛ thetrain.com /lodging-food. The Grand Canyon Railway's flagship hotel opened in 1908 as the *Fray Marcos*. Rebuilt in a slightly different location, and renamed too, it lacks any particular flair, but the large open lobby is pleasant enough, and there's also an indoor pool, spa and saloon. All rooms provide two queen beds. $175

The Lodge on Route 66 200 E Route 66 ☎ 928 635 4534 or ☎ 877 563 4366, ⊛ thelodgeonroute66.com. Restored Route 66 motor-court motel in the heart of town, with spotless and very comfortable rooms and friendly management. $100

Red Garter Bed & Bakery 137 W Railroad Ave ☎ 928 635 1484 or ☎ 800 328 1484, ⊛ redgarter.com. Plush four-room B&B in a former downtown bordello, serving fresh-baked breakfasts from its own downstairs diner/ coffee shop – even if you don't stay, be sure to sample one of their amazing $3 raspberry turnovers. Closed mid-Dec to mid-Feb. $145

EATING

Williams's **restaurant** selection is frankly disappointing. A few spots conjure up the feel of its Route 66 heyday, but nowhere serves interesting food. That said, you will find filling meals and affable places to eat.

Cafe 326 326 W Route 66 ☎ 928 635 0777, ⊛ cafe326 .com. Funky, friendly café that serves espressos, juices and pastries, plus breakfast bagels and lunchtime sandwiches, all costing well under $10. It has a couple of outdoor tables and free wi-fi. Daily 7.30am–3pm.

Dara Thai Grand Canyon Hotel, 145 W Route 66 ☎ 928 635 2201, ⊛ thegrandcanyonhotel.com. Dependable outpost of Flagstaff's long-standing Thai restaurant, serving good Thai dishes for $8 at lunch, $10–12 at dinner. Mon–Sat 11am–2pm & 5–9pm.

★**Pine Country Restaurant** 107 N Grand Canyon Blvd ☎ 928 635 9718, ⊛ pinecountryrestaurant.com. Traditional, very central diner with friendly waitstaff, where the food is actually pretty good, and you can have a full dinner, like pork chops or country-fried steak, for $11, or simply stop by for an espresso coffee. An enticing glass cabinet is stacked with each day's fresh-baked delights; slices of the irresistible home-made pies – the menu lists around forty, in flavours like raspberry cream cheese – go for $4.59. Daily 6.30am–9pm.

Ash Fork

The ranching community of **ASH FORK**, stretched along a brief curving fragment of Route 66 north of the interstate twenty miles west of Williams, is smaller, less picturesque and far less involved in catering to travellers. By this point I-40 has pulled clear of the forests, so downtown Ash Fork is constructed not from timber but using the yellowish sandstone that's the basis of the local economy – it calls itself the "flagstone capital of the US". While the major motel chains haven't bothered to set up shop, Ash Fork holds a few run-down, homespun lodging alternatives.

Ash Fork Inn 859 Route 66 ☎928 637 2514. Sprawling, reasonably spruced up and rather pink old motel, at the west end of town near I-40 exit 144. The simple rooms can be cold in winter, but otherwise they're a pretty good deal. $42

Seligman

Starting a few miles west of Ash Fork, the old Route 66 parallels its modern replacement at a discreet distance for the twenty or so miles to **SELIGMAN**. This dusty desert halt now feels more than a little stranded, a mile or two north of the interstate, but if you're in the mood to be seduced by its kitsch diners and drive-ins, it makes a mildly diverting stop in a long day's drive. Every business strives to outdo the others with eye-catching displays – mannequins of Elvis and Marilyn waving from oddball parked vehicles and the like – and the passing traffic is worth watching, too, with all kinds of vintage roadsters making pilgrimages along the "Mother Road".

You might even choose to follow Route 66's original course as it curves northwards, through a dozen fading villages and part of the **Hualapai reservation** (see p.328), and back south to Kingman. That's a total drive of 88 miles, as opposed to the dreary 65-mile run west on I-40. It also provides access to **Havasu Canyon**, in the depths of the Grand Canyon, one of the Southwest's least-known marvels (see p.322).

★**Canyon Lodge** 22340 W Old Hwy-66 ☎928 422 3255 or ☎800 700 5054, ⓦroute66canyonlodge.com. From the outside, this blue two-storey structure on Route 66 might look like just another highway motel; each room, though, has been lovingly refurbished as a tribute to a different 1950s theme. The Elvis and Marilyn rooms are especially recommended. Rates include breakfast. $60

Delgadillo's Snow Cap 301 E Chino Ave ☎928 422 3291. Seligman's wackiest local diner, with a fine assortment of vintage jalopies and roadsters parked outside. Every malt or $5 burger comes with a side order of outrageous puns and put-ons. Daily March to mid-Nov 10am–6pm.

Kingman

With a population of almost thirty thousand, **KINGMAN**, 65 miles west of Seligman and thirty miles short of California, ranks second to Flagstaff among Arizona's I-40 towns. As all traffic between Phoenix or the Grand Canyon and **Las Vegas** – a mere hundred miles northwest on US-93 – is obliged to pass this way, Kingman's thirty-plus motels stay busy year-round. The best that can be said for it, however, is that it's not particularly ugly – apart from the long sprawl beside the railroad tracks, north of the interstate – and it's not lifeless. Apart from that, it's a humdrum pit stop with a slight tinge of Route 66 quaintness.

Kingman's main street, curving alongside the railroad tracks, is named in honour of native son **Andy Devine**, the actor who drove the eponymous *Stagecoach* in John Ford's 1939 movie. As a local brochure puts it, "there must be somebody who hasn't heard of Andy Devine, but that person sure doesn't live in Kingman". The year 1939 was clearly a big one for Kingman: Carole Lombard and Clark Gable were married here on March 29.

Route 66 and Electric Vehicle Museum

Powerhouse, 120 W Andy Devine Ave • Daily 9am–4.30pm • $5, same ticket as Mohave Museum • ☎928 753 9889, ⓦgokingman.com

Upstairs in Kingman's Powerhouse, which also holds the local visitor centre, the **Route 66 Museum** is much larger than it might seem at first glance, and, to be honest, considerably better too. Displays cover the original surveying and construction of Route 66 in these parts, with several fine old roadsters to admire, and good details on John Steinbeck's description of the Dust Bowl era in *The Grapes of Wrath*. A separate

5

section also traces the history of **electric vehicles**, the earliest of which dates back to 1909, while other exhibits illustrate mining in Oatman and Chloride, and there's even an old organ you can play.

Mohave Museum of History & Arts

400 W Beale St • Mon–Fri 9am–5pm, Sat 1–5pm • $5, same ticket as Route 66 Museum • ☎ 928 753 3195, ⓦ mohavemuseum.org

The **Mohave Museum of History & Arts** explores the various unlikely components of Mohave County's heritage, including the movie career of local boy Andy Devine and the culture and basketwork of the Hualapai. For no obvious reason, there's also a display of pictures of every American First Lady.

ARRIVAL AND INFORMATION   KINGMAN

By train Kingman's central Amtrak station still welcomes trains between Flagstaff and LA, but only at unearthly hours of the night.
By bus Greyhound buses, between Phoenix and Las Vegas as well as east–west, call at the USA Travel Center, 953 W

Beale St (☎ 928 753 1818).
Visitor centre Kingman's large Powerhouse visitor centre, at the western edge of downtown at 120 W Andy Devine Ave (daily 8am–5pm; ☎ 928 753 6106 or ☎ 866 427 7866, ⓦ gokingman.com), also sells lots of Route 66 memorabilia.

ACCOMMODATION

As you're unlikely to spend more than one night in Kingman – or linger in the morning, either – its ordinary but inexpensive **motels** should easily meet your needs.

Best Western A Wayfarer's Inn 2815 E Andy Devine Ave ☎ 928 753 6271 or ☎ 800 548 5695, ⓦ bestwestern arizona.com. Upscale hundred-room chain property, a couple of miles northeast of town near I-40 exit 53, charging reasonable rates for its smart if anonymous rooms, and offering a pool and indoor spa. **$110**
Hualapai Mountain Park 6250 Hualapai Mountain Rd ☎ 928 681 5700 or ☎ 877 757 0915, ⓦ mcparks.com. This beautiful county-run park, in the hills 15 miles southeast of Kingman, offers around 25 rental cabins,

which have fireplaces and en-suite bathrooms – though you have to bring your own bedding (and note that rates rise at weekends) – plus tent and RV camping. Tent sites **$17**, RVs **$39**, cabins **$70**
Quality Inn Kingman 1400 E Andy Devine Ave ☎ 928 753 4747 or ☎ 800 228 5151, ⓦ qualityinn.com. Standard motel half a mile from downtown, with small but adequate rooms, which offers a bit of character via a strong Route 66 theme, including a retro breakfast room and outdoor vintage gas pumps. **$56**

EATING

Most Kingman **restaurants** play on the Route 66 angle. It's too spread out to wander around comparing menus, but hop in your car and you'll find something.

Dambar & Steakhouse 1960 E Andy Devine Ave ☎ 928 753 3523, ⓦ dambarsteakhouse.com. Classic Western steakhouse atop the hill, all sawdust and bare timber, serving grilled and barbecued ribs and chicken, as well as massive steaks. Main dishes $20–27 at dinner, more like $8–14 at lunch. Daily 11am–10pm.
Mr D'z Route 66 Diner 105 E Andy Devine Ave ☎ 928 718 0066, ⓦ mrdzrt66diner.com. Loving re-creation of a classic Route 66 roadhouse, across from the visitor centre and bursting with memorabilia, neon and lurid moulded

trimmings. Good burgers and shakes, malts and floats, and fries with everything, all for less than $10, or more substantial pizzas, steaks and the like for $10–15. Daily 7am–9pm.
Redneck's Southern Pit BBQ 420 E Beale St ☎ 928 757 8227, ⓦ redneckssouthernpitbbq.com. Large portions of tangy Southern BBQ, ordered cafeteria-style and enjoyed in a family atmosphere. Beef, pork or chicken plates cost just under $10, ribs up to $25 for a full rack. Mon–Sat 11am–9pm; closed Mon in winter.

Chloride

Fifteen miles northwest of Kingman, as US-93 tears through the flat, prosaically named **Detrital Valley** toward Las Vegas, a paved road climbs away into the mountains to the right. Its goal, the former silver-mining centre of **CHLORIDE** four miles up, was established in 1864 and boasts Arizona's oldest still-functional post office. As well as silver, vast quantities of gold, copper, lead and turquoise were also extracted from the roadless **Cerbat Mountains** beyond, but Chloride these days lives by its wits, exploiting its ramshackle Wild West appearance to attract tourists.

Some of Chloride's erstwhile neighbours – such as **Cerbat** and **Mineral Park** – have become genuine **ghost towns**.

Bullhead City and Laughlin

While both the old Route 66 and the interstate head southwest from Kingman, Hwy-68 barrels due west for thirty miles to **BULLHEAD CITY** on the Colorado River. Built as a work camp for the construction of nearby Davis Dam, Bullhead City somehow survived the dam's completion in 1953 and is prospering these days due to its proximity to the casinos of **LAUGHLIN**, Nevada, just across the river.

In terms of temperature, **Bullhead** is the hottest town in the US, exceeding 120°F (49°C) day after day each summer. In most other respects, however, it's not the least bit hot. Almost forty thousand people now live along a ten-mile riverfront stretch of Hwy-95; why on earth you'd join them, even for a night, is hard to imagine.

Not that **Laughlin** is much better, despite the endless hype of its tourist authorities. If you've never been to Las Vegas, you may well be impressed by the huge, glittering **casinos** that jostle for position beside the Colorado. They lack the panache of their Vegas counterparts, however, as well as the will to cater to anyone other than hardened gamblers. The only real reason to come here is that **accommodation** rates are so cheap, though it is also fun to take a **paddle-wheeler cruise** on the Colorado, costing about $10 for a little over an hour, from the *Aquarius Casino*, the *Riverside Resort* or the *Edgewater Hotel*.

INFORMATION   LAUGHLIN

Visitor centre 1555 S Casino Drive (Mon–Fri 8am–4.30pm; ☎ 702 298 3321 or ☎ 800 452 8445, ⊚ visitlaughlin.com).

ACCOMMODATION AND EATING

Laughlin is home to nine enormous casinos, most of which offer well over a thousand rooms each, with weekday rates that can drop below $30 per night. Each holds several **restaurants** ranging from buffet joints whose all-you-can-eat specials start at under $5, to steakhouses and dimly lit Italian schmoozeries. It's really not worth eating anywhere other than where you're staying, however – it takes a long time to walk from one casino to the next, and you'll only find the same bland choices you had before you set off.

Don Laughlin's Riverside Resort Hotel 1650 S Casino Drive ☎ 702 298 2535 or ☎ 800 227 3849, ⊚ riverside resort.com. Laughlin's oldest casino traces its ancestry all the way back to an eight-room motel that opened in 1966. It has consistently kept pace with its neighbours, and now holds over 1400 rooms, plus around 740 RV spaces, a bowling alley, a movie theatre, and assorted restaurants and lounges.

Mon–Thurs & Sun $49, Fri & Sat $69
Golden Nugget 2300 S Casino Drive ☎ 702 298 7111 or ☎ 800 950 7700, ⊚ goldennugget.com/laughlin. The upscale, glittering *Golden Nugget* counts as Laughlin's top-of-the-range lodging option, with smart river-view rooms and a pool by the Colorado, and the classiest selection of restaurants around. Mon–Thurs & Sun $40, Fri & Sat $70

Oatman

If you're heading west from Kingman towards **Needles**, California, but don't mind how quickly you get there, following Route 66 over the **Black Mountains** to the south makes an enjoyable alternative route. It also has the bonus of passing through one of Arizona's most appealing **ghost towns**, the former gold-mining community of **OATMAN**. In total it's a drive of fifty miles to Needles if you head this way, as opposed to 64 on the interstate, but it's a long, slow drive, with lots of tricky mountain bends.

The eastern approaches to the mountains, at the edge of the Sacramento Valley, are guarded by a splendid solitary rock pinnacle that was a beacon to early travellers. Following a laborious climb up to a gap between the peaks, the road twists down the

5

LONDON BRIDGE IS FALLING DOWN

Californian chainsaw manufacturer **Robert P. McCulloch** moved his factory to the remote Arizona desert in 1964, to try out his new sideline in outboard motors on Lake Havasu. Three years later, he heard Johnny Carson mention that London Bridge was up for sale; in the words of the nursery rhyme, it really was falling down, unable to cope with all those newfangled automobiles. McCulloch bought it for $2,460,000, and painstakingly shipped ten thousand numbered blocks of granite across the Atlantic. Lacking any appropriate stretch of water for the bridge to span, he dug a channel that turned a riverbank promontory into the island of **Pittsburg Point**.

Despite the jibes that McCulloch thought he was buying London's picturesque Tower Bridge – the turreted one that opens in the middle – his investment in London Bridge, which was merely the latest in a long line of London Bridges and dated only from 1831, paid off handsomely. The bridge now ranks second among Arizona's tourist attractions, after the Grand Canyon, and Lake Havasu City has become a major vacation resort and retirement centre, with a population of over fifty thousand. For its part, London Bridge is listed in the **Guinness Book of Records** as the largest antique ever sold.

far side and eventually enters Oatman itself. Established in 1906, Oatman went bust in 1942, but a second career as a movie backdrop and tourist stop-off has ensured that it's never truly been abandoned.

Gift and craft stores now occupy most of the false-front structures along Oatman's raised wooden boardwalk. The streets are still roamed by semi-wild burros (small donkeys), descended from animals left by the miners; however much they imply to the contrary, you're not allowed to feed them.

Lake Havasu City

Forty miles southwest of Kingman on I-40, ten miles from the California border, a twenty-mile detour south on Hwy-95 brings you to the most incongruous sight of the Southwestern deserts. At **LAKE HAVASU CITY**, the old grey stones of **London Bridge** reach out across the stagnant waters of the dammed Colorado River. However, it's not often you see anything quite as boring in Arizona as London Bridge; unless you've never seen a bridge before, it's one to miss.

While Lake Havasu City has an undeniable attraction for the parched urbanites of cities such as Phoenix, who flock to fish on the lake or charge up and down in motorboats and on jet skis, it holds minimal appeal for travellers from further afield. Many of its copious clubs, bars and restaurants used to be heavily London-themed, but these days it's styled more like a generic tropical resort. What's more, between March and June, it's almost permanently filled with students on **Spring Break**, drinking and partying around the clock.

English Village

Only once you cross London Bridge to the island, and then look back, do you appreciate how large Lake Havasu City has grown, sprawling up the gentle slope away from the river. Most of those broad hillside streets are lined with condo blocks and minor malls; the only place tourists bother to visit is the **English Village**, a mock-Tudor shopping mall, which also holds a handful of river-view restaurants, at the base of the bridge. Several operators offer short **river cruises** from the quayside of the English Village – including tours of a series of miniature replicas of famous American lighthouses – and jet ski rentals are also widely available.

London Bridge Beach

Out on Pittsburg Point island, if you head south from the bridge you'll soon come to **London Bridge Beach**. The "beach" is more grit than sand, and few people swim from it. With its bizarre fringe of date palms, however, and its panorama of weird desert buttes and the Chemehuevi Mountains, it does at least linger in the memory.

INFORMATION   LAKE HAVASU

Visitor centre 422 English Village (daily 9am–5pm; ☎ 928 855 5655, ⊛ golakehavasu.com).

ACCOMMODATION AND EATING

Cha-Bones 112 London Bridge Rd ☎ 928 854 5554, ⊛ chabones.com. Buzzing bar/restaurant in the London Bridge Shopping Center, just north of the bridge on the mainland, with a good range of tasty $6–10 tapas as well as the more usual burgers and steaks. Mon–Thurs & Sun 11am–10pm, Fri & Sat 11am–11pm.

Heat Hotel 1420 W McCulloch Blvd ☎ 928 854 2833 or ☎ 888 898 4328, ⊛ heathotel.com. Lake Havasu isn't really the sort of place where you expect to find a boutique hotel, but there's really no faulting the stylish contemporary taste with which the *Heat Hotel*, next to the island end of the bridge, across from town, has been kitted out. Most rooms have private bridge views, and there's a communal "party patio" bar. Expect to pay a heavy premium at weekends. $129

London Bridge Resort 1477 Queen's Bay ☎ 928 855 0888 or ☎ 866 331 9231, ⊛ londonbridgeresort.com. This extravagant all-suite resort is basically a beach hotel, with a huge pool with waterslides, lively bars and restaurants, and lots of lake frontage too. Rates are usually higher on weekends. $129

Shugrue's 1425 W McCulloch Blvd ☎ 928 453 1400, ⊛ shugrues.com. The best place to combine eating with views over the bridge and lake, across from the mainland in the Island Fashion Mall, *Shugrue's* is a traditional, upscale American restaurant. Lunchtime salads, sandwiches and daily specials cost around $13, while in the evening you can get fresh halibut or tuna for around $25, and rack of lamb for $35. Mon–Thurs & Sun 11am–9.30pm, Fri & Sat 11am–10.30pm.

The Grand Canyon

SUNSET AT DESERT VIEW

The Grand Canyon

Although almost five million people come to see the Grand Canyon of the Colorado every year, it seems to remain beyond the grasp of the human imagination. No photograph, or set of statistics, can prepare you for such vastness. At more than one mile deep, it's an inconceivable abyss; varying in its central stretch from four to eighteen miles wide, it's an endless expanse of bewildering shapes and colours, glaring desert brightness and impenetrable shadow, stark promontories and soaring, never-to-be-climbed sandstone pinnacles.

While no one is disappointed with their first stunning sight of the chasm, visitors often struggle to understand what can appear as a remote and impassive spectacle. They race frantically from viewpoint to viewpoint, constantly imagining that the next one will be the "best", the place from which the whole thing will finally make sense. The secret to transcending that initial frantic excitement is to slow down, to appreciate whatever small portion of the canyon may be displayed in front of you at any one moment, and to allow enough time for the bigger picture to develop. And visiting the Grand Canyon doesn't have to be a passive experience. In addition to touring the **overlooks** along each rim, the views from all of which shift and change unceasingly from dawn to dusk, you can **hike** down into the depths; ride down on a **mule**; hover above the canyon in a **helicopter**; raft through the **whitewater rapids** of the river itself; spend a night at **Phantom Ranch** on the canyon floor; or swim beneath the waterfalls of the idyllic **Havasupai reservation**.

Mapping and defining precisely what constitutes the "Grand Canyon" has always been controversial; **Grand Canyon National Park** covers a relatively small proportion of the greater Grand Canyon area. Only in the past fifty years has it included the full 277-mile length of the Colorado River from Lees Ferry in the east to Grand Wash Cliffs near Lake Mead in the west, and even now it's restricted for most of that way to the narrow strip of the inner gorge. Ranchers whose animals graze in the federal forests to either side, mining companies eager to exploit the mineral wealth hidden in the rocks, engineers seeking to divert the river to irrigate the deserts, and the Native Americans who live in the canyon, have combined to minimize the size of the park.

The vast majority of visitors arrive at the **South Rim** – it's much easier to get to, holds far more facilities (mainly at **Grand Canyon Village**, inside the park), and remains open year-round. Another lodge and campground are located at the **North Rim**, which by virtue of its isolation can be a lot more atmospheric, but at one thousand feet higher this entire area is usually closed by snow from November until mid-May. Few people visit both rims on a single trip; to get from one to the other demands either a three-day hike down one side of the canyon and up the other, or a 215-mile drive. On both rims, the main activity

A VIEW OF WOTAN'S THRONE FROM CAPE ROYAL

Highlights

❶ Shoshone Point Little-known viewpoint, accessible only on foot, that feels a world away from all the other South Rim overlooks. **See p.308**

❷ Desert View Watchtower Circular mock-Puebloan tower, blending into the rocks at the east end of the South Rim, that provides stunning canyon views. **See p.309**

❸ The Bright Angel Trail Deservedly the most popular hiking trail within the park; a superb introduction to life below the rim. **See p.311**

❹ The South Kaibab Trail This hair-raising descent to the canyon floor offers the finest day-hikes in the park. **See p.314**

❺ El Tovar Hotel The jewel of Grand Canyon Village, this historic hotel provides the South Rim's best food and lodging. **See p.319**

❻ Havasu Falls Astonishing, lush turquoise waterfalls buried deep within the canyon on the Havasupai reservation. **See p.327**

❼ Cape Royal The perfect vantage point from which to appreciate the overall shape of the canyon. **See p.333**

❽ Toroweap Overlook The remotest canyon viewpoint within the national park offers unique views into the Granite Gorge. **See p.339**

HIGHLIGHTS ARE MARKED ON THE MAP ON P.298

PARK ADMISSION

Admission to Grand Canyon National Park, valid for seven days on either rim, costs $30 for one private, noncommercial vehicle and all its passengers; $25 per motorcycle with passengers; or $15 per pedestrian, cyclist or bus or train passenger. All park-service **passes** (see p.35) are sold and valid.

consists of gazing over the gorge from lookouts spaced along the canyon-edge roads. In the 1920s the average visitor stayed for two or three weeks, whereas these days it's more like two or three hours – of which forty minutes are spent actually looking at the canyon.

If you're visiting the Grand Canyon as part of a longer Southwest itinerary, you may be wondering whether you "should" visit both rims, or which rim is "better". That really depends on how much time you have and what time of year it is. Though wilderness enthusiasts tend to find the summer crowds at the South Rim unbearable, even there it's possible to escape the throngs, and there's great scope for day-hiking. The North Rim is convenient to Zion and Bryce parks and northeast Arizona and has nicer accommodation options. It's probably best to choose whichever rim fits in with your planned route, and not to feel you ought to see the other one as well.

Brief history

It may look forbidding, but the Grand Canyon is teeming with life – sheep and rabbits, eagles and vultures, mountain lions, and, of course, spiders, scorpions and snakes all thrive here. The earliest signs of any **human** presence are twig figurines of animals from around 2000 BC, found hidden in caves in the canyon walls and probably created to ensure successful hunting. Remains of later dwellings built by the **Ancestral Puebloans** are scattered throughout the canyon – the most accessible now is **Tusayan Ruin** (see p.309). Other tribal groups, including the **Havasupai** (see p.322) and the **Hualapai** (see p.328), had arrived by around 1300 AD.

The Spaniards arrive

In 1540 – less than twenty years after Cortés conquered the Aztecs of Mexico – the first **Spaniards** reached the Southwest. At the Hopi mesas, a detachment of Coronado's company were told of a great river not far west, inhabited by people with very large bodies (presumably the Havasupai, who tend to be bigger than the Hopi). A small party, led by **García López de Cárdenas**, was despatched to investigate. Their Hopi guides led them to a spot somewhere near Grandview Point, but chose not to reveal the trails down to the river. The Spaniards spent three days on the South Rim, only appreciating the scale of the canyon after an abortive attempt to reach the river. They identified the Colorado as being the Tíson or "Firebrand" River, up which a simultaneous naval expedition was attempting to sail (it managed 225 miles, reaching what's now the site of the Hoover Dam).

Mapping the canyon

When jurisdiction over the Grand Canyon passed from Mexico to the United States in 1850, it had never been surveyed and did not even have a fixed **name**. To the Havasupai, it was *Wikatata* ("Rough Rim"); Spanish maps showed it as *Río Muy Grande* ("Very Big River"); and trappers and prospectors knew it as the Big Cañon. The name Grand Canyon, first used on a map in 1868, was popularized by the one-armed Civil War veteran **John Wesley Powell**, whose expeditions along the fearsome and uncharted Colorado in 1869 and 1871–72 (see p.403) captured public imagination.

Mining, logging and the growth of tourism

As the Grand Canyon was being recognized as the most extraordinary natural wonder in the US, American settlers arrived nearby in ever greater numbers. Tensions have simmered ever since between this new permanent population, determined to survive in such an unforgiving environment, and visitors hoping to find unspoiled wilderness. Broadly speaking, **logging** and **grazing** interests retain control of the plateau forests, while in the canyon itself most attempts at **mining** were defeated by the difficulty of the terrain, and **tourism** soon proved a far more lucrative proposition.

When the **railroad** first crossed northern Arizona in 1882, visitors were taken by stagecoach from **Peach Springs**, the nearest station to the Grand Canyon, to stay at the *Diamond Creek Hotel* by the river. With the growth of the timber towns to the east, that site soon declined; by the 1890s, **Flagstaff** was the main terminus, connected with the canyon by three weekly stagecoaches. The railroad reached the canyon itself, via a branch line from **Williams**, in 1901. That triggered the growth of **Grand Canyon Village**, built by a subsidiary of the Santa Fe Railroad. The Fred Harvey Company's *El Tovar Hotel* – still the showpiece canyon-edge lodging – opened in 1905, and its early marketing strategies influence the experience of Canyon visitors to this day. Following an internal memo to "get some Indians to the Canyon at once", the Hopi House souvenir store was built, modelled on the Pueblo village of Old Oraibi (see p.69) and staffed with Hopi craftspeople. Similarly, Navajo weavers were exhorted to produce rugs to suit tourist tastes, using previously unfavoured "earth" colours such as brown. Pseudo-Pueblo architecture became the dominant theme, with a single architect, **Mary Jane Colter**, designing such structures as Hermit's Rest (1914), the Desert Watchtower (1932), and *Bright Angel Lodge* (1935).

A national park

Late nineteenth-century proposals to create a **Grand Canyon National Park** aroused vigorous local opposition. In due course, however, naturalist **John Muir** – who declared the Grand Canyon to be "unearthly … as if you had found it after death, on some other star" – found a powerful ally in President **Theodore Roosevelt**. Only entitled to protect sites of historical, rather than geological, interest, Roosevelt used the pretext of preserving Ancestral Puebloan ruins to proclaim Grand Canyon National Monument in 1908. Local politicians finally came round to the idea after Arizona achieved statehood in 1912. Even then, by the time the boundaries of the Grand Canyon National Park were fixed in 1919, they had trimmed away large tracts of grazing land. The new park covered around 1000 square miles and included just 56 miles of the actual canyon.

Meanwhile, tourism to the South Rim had not stood still. Exploiting bogus mining claims, **Ralph Cameron** charged a toll of $1 to riders on the Bright Angel Trail, and built his own hotel alongside the railroad terminal in 1905 – whereupon the Fred Harvey Company relocated the station out of sight of its upstart rival. Undeterred, and elected to the US Senate in 1920, Cameron spent the ensuing years hacking at the budget of the new national park. By the time his mining claims were finally invalidated, his presence had spurred the development of the **Kaibab Trail**, stretching from rim to rim by way of the Kaibab suspension footbridge (see p.334). Plans to pave that route never materialized, but a small enlargement of the park in 1927 permitted the construction of a road east to Desert View, which with the 1928 completion of Navajo Bridge, spanning Marble Canyon, reduced the previous 600-mile drive between the rims to a more feasible 215 miles.

The first **automobile** arrived at the Canyon in 1902, despite running out of gas twenty miles short. By 1926, more visitors were coming by car than by train, and Flagstaff was once again the major point of access. Advance reservations for both mule rides and lodging have been necessary since 1938; annual visitor numbers first exceeded a million in 1956, and ran at over five million through most of the 1990s.

As the millennium approached, it looked as though the village could no longer take the strain. An ambitious scheme was drawn up under which visitors would explore the South Rim using a **light-rail** network rather than their own vehicles. Visitor numbers, however, unexpectedly dropped, and the plan was abandoned. Instead, the spacious plaza built to serve the rail system, a mile or so east of the village, was kitted out with a new visitor centre and plentiful parking lots, served by free shuttle buses.

In recent years, with visitor numbers finally creeping back towards the five million mark, controversy over development has started to rage once more. The hottest debates have concerned sites beyond the national park boundaries. Environmentalist opposition has so far staved off schemes to open new **uranium mines** in the vicinity, while the proposed **Grand Canyon Escalade**, a cable car down to the confluence of the Colorado and Little Colorado rivers on the Navajo reservation, seems to have been definitively cancelled. However, it looks as though plans by an Italian consortium to transform the gateway community of **Tusayan** will go ahead, in which case the construction of more than two thousand homes, along with hotels and shops, will surely impact upon all future Grand Canyon visitors.

6

THE FORMATION OF THE GRAND CANYON

Although the Grand Canyon could be called the world's clearest geological textbook, scientists disagree over how to read the story written in the stone. Layer upon layer of different rocks, readily distinguished by colour, and each with its own fossil record, recede down into the canyon and back through time, until the riverbed lays bare some of the oldest exposed rocks on earth. Almost all the successive strata of sandstone and limestone were deposited during periods when the entire region was submerged beneath shallow primeval seas. The bottom layer, the two-billion-year-old **Vishnu Schist**, is so ancient that it contains no fossils; it dates back to the Precambrian era, when life had barely begun.

That same tale of sedimentation, of course, holds true for much of the planet. Two major factors transformed what was, until five million years ago, an unremarkable landscape into the Grand Canyon. First of all, the chronic shortage of rain in this desert area precluded the growth of vegetation to bind the brittle surface together. Secondly, there was the fast-flowing **Colorado River**, cascading down from the Rocky Mountains with a gradient over 25 times steeper than the Mississippi. In full flood, charged with mighty boulders, it can blast deep crevices into the earth.

However, a crucial mystery remains. The Colorado Plateau is not flat at this point; it's an enormous hill, known to the Paiute Indians as the **Kaibab**, or mountain with no peak, which slopes southwards from a ridge that runs roughly a dozen miles north of the North Rim. Thus the Colorado has eaten away a chunk of the hillside, around a third of the way up the southern slope – which explains why the North Rim is a thousand feet higher than the South. Why, or how, the Colorado River cuts straight through that hill, rather than flowing around it, has long perplexed geologists. The hypothesis currently in favour, "**stream piracy**", suggests that until five million years ago, the river did indeed skirt the Kaibab – along some unknown course – but was then "captured" by another river and began to flow through it instead. That may have occurred when a powerful stream, at the head of its own canyon, cut so far back that it breached the barrier that separated it from the Colorado. The Colorado then rushed through, abandoning its own course and usurping this alternative channel.

Crudely speaking, while the Colorado is responsible for the **depth** of the canyon – and continues to scour its way deeper – it did little to create its **width**, which owes more to flash-flooding along its tributary streams and extreme cycles of heat and cold. Vast slabs of stone are chiselled away when water that trickles into cracks in exposed rock later freezes and expands, thereby sculpting the fantastic pyramids and mesas that tower above the central gorge. Some layers of rock are much harder than others; thus the solid Tapeats Sandstone of the **Tonto Platform**, a mile-wide shelf above the river that runs through most of the national park, was left behind when the weaker Bright Angel Shale above it eroded away. Because the general slope of the Kaibab runs from north to south, rain that falls north of the canyon flows down toward the gorge, while rainfall to the south flows away. As a result, the North Rim is deeply cut by tributaries and pushed back further from the Colorado, while the lower South Rim is much more regular.

The most striking features were named for their supposed resemblance to the great temples of India and China – **Brahma Temple**, **Shiva Temple**, **Vishnu Temple** and so on – by Clarence Dutton, a student of comparative religion who wrote the first Geological Survey report on the canyon in 1881. The tradition was followed by later cartographers such as François Matthes, who named **Krishna Shrine** and **Walhalla Plateau**.

The South Rim

When someone casually mentions visiting the "Grand Canyon", it's almost certainly the **South Rim** to which they're referring. To be more precise, it's the thirty-mile stretch of the South Rim that's served by a paved road; and most specifically of all, it's **Grand Canyon Village**, the small canyon-edge community, sandwiched between the pine forest and the rim, that holds the park's principal **food** and **lodging** options. The reason nine out of every ten canyon visitors come here is not, however, because this is a uniquely wonderful spot from which to see the canyon; Grand Canyon Village

6

GRAND CANYON TOURS AND ACTIVITIES

PARK BUS TOURS

To reserve a guided South Rim **bus tour**, contact the "transportation desk" in any lodge, book on ⓦ grandcanyonlodges.com, or call ☎ 928 628 2631 or ☎ 888 297 2757. Accompanied under-17s travel free on all tours.

Desert View 52-mile, 4hr round-trip skirting the East Rim along Desert View Drive – a route open to private vehicles but not served by park shuttle buses. Stops include Yavapai Geology Museum, Lipan Point and Desert View at road's end. $49.50, or $65 with any other tour, not necessarily on the same day.

Hermit's Rest 2hr jaunt west of the village along the same route as the free Hermit's Rest shuttle bus (see p.318). $29.50.

Sunrise One-hour-thirty-minute early-morning tour east of the village. $23.

Sunset One-hour-thirty-minute late-afternoon tour west of the village. $23.

HORSERIDING

Apache Stables ☎ 928 638 2891, ⓦ apachestables .com. Based in Tusayan; $48.50 for a 1hr trail ride through the Kaibab Forest, and $88.50 for 2hr, plus evening campfire rides on horseback for $58.50, or by wagon for $25.50.

MULE RIDES

Joining a mule train from Grand Canyon Village is a fine old canyon tradition. Riders must be at least four feet seven inches tall (1.38m), speak fluent English and weigh not more than 200 pounds (90kg), fully clothed, for the overnight rides, or 225 pounds (102kg) for the day-trips. Places are limited, so make a reservation as early as possible, on ☎ 303 297 2757 or ☎ 888 297 2757. If you arrive without a reservation, put yourself on the waiting list at the *Bright Angel Lodge* Transportation Desk and turn up there at 6am on the morning you want to ride; there are usually a few last-minute cancellations each day. Precise timings vary.

Overnight Rides Spend the morning descending the Bright Angel Trail to the riverside *Phantom Ranch*, where you'll sleep in two-person cabins. Soon after sunrise the next day, the mules set off back up the South Kaibab Trail. You should be back at *Bright Angel Lodge* in time for lunch. Trip costs, including lodgings and all meals, are $539 for one person, $937 for two. Two-night rides, available between November and March only, follow the same route but stay another night down at the ranch, and cost $772 for one, or $1260 for two.

Day-trips Participants on the Canyon Vistas ride along the East Rim meet at the barn in Grand Canyon Village; the trip takes three hours in total, with an hour's round-trip to and from the trailhead and two hours in the saddle, enjoying the ever-changing canyon views. Mid-March to Nov 8am & noon, Dec to mid-March 9am; $121.

GRAND CANYON FIELD INSTITUTE

The **Grand Canyon Field Institute** offers well-priced, expert-led guided tours and hikes in and around the canyon (☎ 928 638 2485 or ☎ 866 471 4435, ⓦ www.grandcanyon.org/learn /grand-canyon-field-institute). Different tours, some restricted to women only, specialize in geology, history, natural history, photography, wilderness techniques and other topics. Most involve camping and backpacking, others include lodge accommodation or mule trekking; all are graded according to the difficulty of any hiking involved. Prices range from $645 for a three-night hike down to Indian Garden to $920 for a four-night rim-to-rim backpack.

just happens to be where the canyon's tourist facilities have been concentrated ever since the railroad arrived. While the village itself has changed remarkably little in the ensuing century, the initial point of arrival for most visitors has shifted in recent years, with the construction of a large open-air complex near **Mather Point** a mile or so to the east. Here you'll find four huge **parking lots**, as well as the main **visitor centre**, and the hub for the park's free **shuttle bus** system.

While certain canyon overlooks are not accessible by car year-round, it's perfectly possible to visit the South Rim using your own vehicle. The village may get clogged with traffic in summer, but it rarely comes to a standstill, and is a nicer and more attractive place to

6

FLIGHT-SEEING TOURS

Strict **regulations** surround flights above the national park. Airplanes and helicopters have to fly at different altitudes; no one can fly below the level of the rim; and 75 percent of the park, including the airspace above the South Rim lookouts and the central rim-to-rim "Corridor," is off-limits. All flights operate from Grand Canyon Airport at **Tusayan**, just south of the park.

By helicopter

Helicopters typically fly **three standard routes**: a 25-minute western tour, straight across the canyon and back a few miles west of the village, for around $200; a forty-minute eastern tour, flying along the rim as far as the confluence of the Colorado and Little Colorado rivers, for roughly $240; and a fifty-minute loop trip that combines the two by flying across the forest of the North Rim, for perhaps $300.

Grand Canyon Helicopters ☎928 638 2764 or ☎800 541 4537, ⊛grandcanyonhelicopter.com.
Maverick ☎928 638 2622 or ☎888 261 4414,
⊛maverickhelicopter.com.
Papillon ☎928 638 2419 or ☎888 635 7272, ⊛papillon.com.

By plane

"Flightseeing" or "fixed-wing" tours can cover much greater distances, but they're obliged to fly at least 1000ft above rim level, and thus don't offer quite such good views. Prices range upwards from $150 for 45 minutes to as long as you like for as much as you've got.

Grand Canyon Airlines ☎702 638 3200 or ☎866 235 9422, ⊛grandcanyonairlines.com.
Grand Canyon Scenic Airlines ☎702 638 3300 or ☎800 634 6801, ⊛scenic.com.

WHITEWATER RAFTING

Places on commercial **whitewater rafting trips**, which vary in length from three days to three weeks, tend to be reserved up to a year in advance. The main choice is whether to cut the 300-mile voyage from Lees Ferry to Diamond Creek in half by leaving or joining the expedition at Phantom Ranch. An estimated 161 sets of rapids interrupt the full route. You can also choose between a quieter, slower oar-powered trip or a motorized expedition; both tend to cost $250–350 per person, per day. For a list of operators, most of whom offer trips of both kinds, see ⊛nps.gov/grca/planyourvisit/river-concessioners.htm.

No **one-day** rafting trips are available within Grand Canyon National Park. There are two alternatives outside the park, however, one at either end of the canyon.

Colorado River Discovery ☎928 645 9175 or ☎888 522 6644, ⊛raftthecanyon.com. Based in Page, Arizona, and offering rafting (half-day, March–Sept; $92), motorized (full-day, March to mid-Nov; $112) and rowing (full-day, May & Sept to mid-Nov; $161) trips that start below Glen Canyon Dam. The motorized trips are also available from Grand Canyon Village through ⊛scenic.com, costing around $200 with coach transfers both ways, or $400 with a flight

one way and a coach the other.
Hualapai River Runners ☎928 769 2636 or ☎888 868 9378, ⊛grandcanyonwest.com. This tribal-run operation offers one-day trips (mid-March to mid-Oct; $350) plus overnight camping trips (weekends only; $650) on the Hualapai reservation near the west end of the canyon, starting at Diamond Creek. The price includes a helicopter flight back to the rim at the end of the trip.

spend time than you might imagine. The major drawback, or rather the price for keeping things bearable, is that all its accommodation tends to be booked up way in advance.

Grand Canyon Village and around

Naturally enough, the first thing that every visitor wants to do is to see the canyon. Where you see it for the first time doesn't actually matter all that much; of the twenty or so major, named viewpoints along the South Rim, plus any number of others in between, no single one can be said to be the "best". In any case, you don't have to move from place to place to obtain radically different views of the canyon; staying in one spot, and watching the colours and shadows change as the day progresses, achieves much the same end.

However, contrary to what you might expect, the views from **Grand Canyon Village** itself are not exceptionally good. To enjoy long-range panoramas, you have to head at least as far from the central village as **Maricopa** or **Yavapai** points. Both of those, as well as the majority of the overlooks along the two rim-edge sightseeing routes – **Hermit Road** to the west, and **Desert View Drive** to the east – make ideal vantage points from which to see an unforgettable canyon sunrise or sunset.

The Grand Canyon Village viewpoints

Grand Canyon Village ranges along the inner curve of a recess that cuts well back into the South Rim. Geologists call such features "arenas"; this one is also a "swale", in that the middle is significantly lower than the two sides. As a result, from the paved, railed terrace that follows the rim for the length of the village, you can only see straight across the canyon. The long promontories to either side end at **Grandeur Point** to the east, and **Maricopa Point** to the west, the ridge beneath which stretches into a sturdy sandstone mesa known picturesquely as the Battleship. Straight down below, the Bright Angel Trail threads through the oasis of Indian Gardens before disappearing into a deep crevice, while another long trail leads across the flat, pale-green Tonto Platform to its dead end at **Plateau Point**.

The defining absence in the view is the **Colorado River** itself. Although the mighty walls of the Granite Gorge – the chasm that holds the actual river – are visible on the far side, you can't see their full 1300ft depth, and the river remains out of sight at the bottom. Thanks to the Bright Angel geological fault, however, there is a gap in the gorge, where Bright Angel Canyon slices into the North Rim. Just to the left at the top is *Grand Canyon Lodge* (see p.336), though you're only likely to spot it after dark, when the lights come on.

Mather Point

Busy **Mather Point** – a short stroll from the visitor centre, with abundant parking nearby – centres on a pair of rocky outcrops that jut out just below the rim. When the crowds prove too much, there's always space somewhere along the railed rim trail nearby, with subtly changing views at every step.

Mather Point faces northeast, toward Bright Angel Canyon on the far side, which is the route followed by the North Kaibab Trail down from the North Rim (see p.335). Two other rim-to-river trails can be spotted closer at hand. To the east, the South Kaibab Trail zigzags down from Yaki Point, while the further west of the two visible stretches of the Colorado River marks the point where it's reached by the Bright Angel Trail. From there, the trail heads east to Phantom Ranch, which is also visible, nestling close to the other tiny patch of river.

Yavapai Point

Walk west along the rim for ten minutes from Mather Point, and you'll come to **Yavapai Point**, a stop on the orange Kaibab/Rim shuttle bus route that also offers parking for private vehicles. Long-range views are similar to those from Mather, meaning that the full range of pyramid-shaped buttes known as "temples" line up in front of the North Rim. Two different segments of the river are now on view, one of

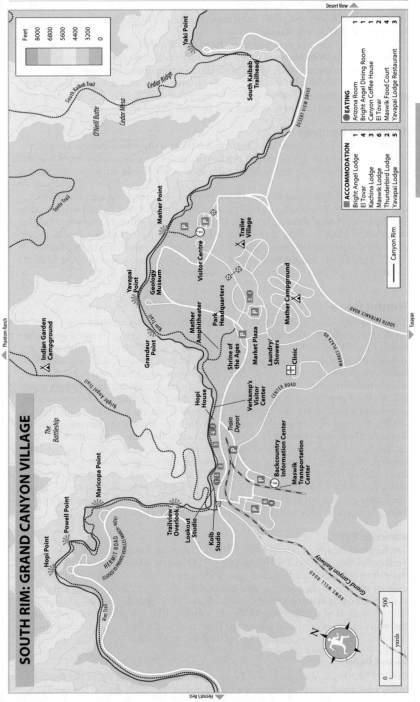

SOUTH RIM: GRAND CANYON VILLAGE

Feet	
8000	
6800	
5600	
4400	
3200	
0	

— Canyon Rim

ACCOMMODATION

Bright Angel Lodge	1
El Tovar	4
Kachina Lodge	3
Maswik Lodge	6
Thunderbird Lodge	2
Yavapai Lodge	5

EATING

Arizona Room	1
Bright Angel Dining Room	1
Canyon Coffee House	2
El Tovar	4
Maswik Food Court	3
Yavapai Lodge Restaurant	

6

Yaki Point

South Kaibab Trail

Cedar Ridge

O'Neill Butte

Cedar Mesa

South Kaibab Trailhead

DESERT VIEW DRIVE

Desert View

Tonto Trail

Mather Point

Visitor Centre

Yavapai Point

Geology Museum

Trailer Village

Rim Trail

Mather Amphitheater

Park Headquarters

Grandeur Point

Mather Campground

Shrine of the Ages

Market Plaza

Laundry/ Showers

Clinic

SOUTH ENTRANCE ROAD

Tusayan

MARKET PLAZA RD

CENTER ROAD

Indian Garden Campground

Phantom Ranch

Bright Angel Trail

The Battleship

Hopi House

Verkamp's Visitor Center

Train Depot

Backcountry Information Center

Maswik Transportation Center

Maricopa Point

Powell Point

Hopi Point

Trailview Overlook

Lookout Studio

Kolb Studio

HERMIT ROAD (CLOSED TO PRIVATE VEHICLES MARCH–NOV)

Rim Trail

ROWE WELL ROAD

Grand Canyon Railway

Hermit's Rest

N

0   500
     yards

which includes both the Kaibab Suspension Bridge, or "Black Bridge", across the Colorado, and Phantom Ranch.

Nearby, if you can tear your eyes away from the view through its tinted bay windows, is the **Yavapai Geology Museum** (daily: hours vary from 8am–8pm in summer down to 8am–5pm in winter; free), which holds illuminating displays on how the canyon may have been formed. It takes another ten minutes' walk west along the rim before rounding the corner of Grandeur Point brings you within sight of the village proper, and a good ten minutes more beyond that to reach Hopi House.

The historic buildings

Grand Canyon Village stretches a lot farther back into the woods than you might imagine and includes a well-hidden residential district for park employees. While those parts hold no interest for sightseers, the rim itself is lined by an attractive assortment of historic buildings.

Particular highlights include the **El Tovar Hotel**, a vast overgrown log cabin that opened in 1905; **Verkamp's**, originally a souvenir store and now an information centre; the triple-tiered **Hopi House**, also from 1905, a high-class gift store that was modelled on an actual Hopi dwelling in the village of Oraibi (see p.69); **Lookout Studio**, another gift store that appears to grow organically from a narrow protuberance just west of *Bright Angel Lodge*; and the **Kolb Studio**, a former photographic studio at the head of the Bright Angel Trail that now holds a bookstore and gallery.

Hermit Road

The seven-mile, dead-end scenic drive officially known as **Hermit Road** – and also unofficially as the **West Rim Drive** – starts a hundred yards west of *Bright Angel Lodge*, just as Grand Canyon Village peters out. Offering a succession of very different but consistently impressive canyon panoramas, it's the most obvious, and most enjoyable, half-day sightseeing trip from the village. As the only vehicles allowed access between March and November each year are the free Hermit's Rest Route **shuttle buses** (see p.318), the Xanterra bus tours (see p.302), and those displaying disabled permits, it also makes a welcome escape from the crowds and traffic elsewhere along the rim.

While for most of its length the road runs within a few yards of the canyon, it's paralleled by the **Rim Trail**, even closer to the edge. No one walks the entire seven miles, but since you can get on and off the bus at any of eight designated stops, the ideal way to explore is to combine shuttle bus rides with stretches of **walking**. Travelling the full length of Hermit Road without getting off the bus takes about 75 minutes. To allow for a couple of short hikes, and a stop at Hermit's Rest, give yourself perhaps three hours. Alternatively, you need never get on a bus at all; the four-mile round-trip hike from the village to Hopi Point, for example, takes under two hours, while **cycling** is permitted year-round.

Maricopa Point

The first two viewpoints along Hermit Road, known as **Trailview I** and **II**, show prospective Bright Angel Trail hikers (see p.311) exactly what they're in for, with its red-dirt switchbacks clearly etched against the canyon walls below. After just over a mile, as you round the corner to pass out of sight of Grand Canyon Village, the railed, rocky overlook at **Maricopa Point** commands an almost 360-degree view, though only the tiniest sliver of the churning Colorado is visible. This is a prime spot for identifying the majestic buttes on the far side of the river, such as the Brahma and Zoroaster "temples", each with its capping layer of hard red sandstone.

Powell Point

Beyond Maricopa, road and trail alike detour inland around the site of the **Orphan Mine**, which was America's largest uranium mine in the 1950s. At the headland

THE RETURN OF THE CONDOR

Of all the awesome spectacles along the South Rim, few can match the sight of a fully grown **California condor** soaring on the canyon updrafts. These magnificent birds, with a wingspan of more than nine feet and a lifespan of up to sixty years, were reintroduced to Arizona in 1996. Progress has been slow but steady, and over seventy free-flying, but tagged and monitored, condors now live in the Grand Canyon region, of which around eight were born in the wild. They can frequently be seen hovering above Grand Canyon Village, or perching just below the rim.

Although the birds were **native** to the canyon, and indeed to most of North America, their population is thought to have started to dwindle after the first humans arrived, around ten thousand years ago. The last condor in the Grand Canyon area was recorded as nesting near Lees Ferry in the 1890s, while a solitary bird was seen circling Williams in 1924. During the 1980s, the last remaining 22 individuals of the species were trapped in California to enable a **captive breeding programme** that reintroduced the birds first in California, and subsequently in northern Arizona. At the Arizona release site – on the **Vermilion Cliffs** fifty miles northeast of the South Rim – scientists keep contact between condors and humans to a minimum, so the birds don't learn to associate humans with food. Condors are very inquisitive creatures, however, and to the delight of tourists almost all the Arizona birds spend much of their time near the village, especially between late April and July. Project workers and park rangers discourage them from approaching too close, and leave animal carcasses for them in remote places. Natural scavengers, they also manage to find carrion by themselves.

immediately west, **Powell Point**, a short walk from the next shuttle stop leads to the spot where the park was officially dedicated on April 30, 1920. From the paved but rail-less viewing area on its far side, you can look across the river to the curious semicircular cliff wall of the "temple" known as the Tower of Set; shaped like an opening bracket, it's mirrored by a similar wall on Isis Temple to the east.

Hopi Point

Two miles out from Grand Canyon Village, **Hopi Point** is the busiest of the western viewpoints. Its reputation as the perfect place to watch the sunset rests on the fact that this promontory thrusts further north than any of its neighbours, with the vast panoply that spreads to the west forming just part of what's virtually a 360-degree canyon prospect.

The most dramatic of several visible stretches of the Colorado lies immediately below Plateau Point (see p.312). It's hard to believe that the river is 350ft wide down there, lying at the foot of gnarled and impossibly ancient walls of black schist, streaked through with vertical pink faults. To the west, the river threads its tortuous way towards the ocean between interleaved spurs of red rock, and a maze of lesser canyons twists among the mighty buttes.

Mohave Point and Pima Point

Road and trail curve gracefully west of Hopi Point for three-quarters of a mile to **Mohave Point**, a large railed promontory from which the long-range vista remains substantially unchanged. **Pima Point** is four miles further on, beyond a sheer-walled recess known as **The Abyss**. The river is by now less than two miles from the South Rim – look almost straight down to admire the three-quarter-mile Granite Rapid – but from the far bank it's another twelve labyrinthine miles to the North Rim.

Hermit's Rest

Way station Daily: summer 8am–7.30pm; otherwise 9am–sunset

Hermit Road ends slightly over a mile beyond Pima Point, at the **Hermit's Rest** way station, appealingly laid out in 1914 to evoke the dwelling of some imaginary canyon prospector, which sells gifts and simple snacks. The **Hermit Trail**, abandoned by the Santa Fe Railroad in 1931 but still popular with inner-canyon hikers (see p.317), starts a short way further along.

Desert View Drive

Desert View Drive, which runs for 23 miles east from Mather Point to Desert View itself, just inside the park's eastern boundary (and beyond that to Cameron and, potentially the North Rim), is the one part of the South Rim that's open year-round for self-guided driving tours. Allow two hours at the very least to get to the end and back. In addition to the formal viewpoints described below, the road occasionally runs very close to the rim; you're not supposed to stop for picnics and sightseeing, but plenty of people do.

6

Yaki Point
2 miles east of Yavapai Point

The first of the Desert View Drive lookouts, **Yaki Point**, is served year-round by free shuttle buses, but only accessible in your own vehicle between December and February. Two miles east of Yavapai Point, it commands much the same trans-canyon views as its neighbour.

The most prominent of several inner-canyon trails on show is the **South Kaibab Trail** (see p.314), which starts its quickfire descent to Phantom Ranch from its own separate parking lot nearby. From the main overlook, you can spot it far below, switchbacking down an exposed scree slope of red rock between two buttes. Scramble out onto the rocks beyond the viewpoint for clearer views down to the trail's principal staging post, O'Neill Butte.

Shoshone Point
Park 1.4 miles east of Yaki Point turn-off, or 6.4 miles west of Grandview Point

Shoshone Point is the least-known and least-visited of the South Rim viewpoints, for the simple reason that it's only accessible on **foot**, along an easy one-mile trail from Desert View Drive. It's an absolute gem of a place, offering beautiful views along with an unparalleled sense of peace and privacy. An hour's round-trip hike from the road

SUNSET AND SUNRISE

"**What's the best place to watch the sunset?**" is probably the single question Grand Canyon park rangers most tire of being asked. There is no best place, neither for sunset, nor for sunrise. How could there be? Each rim of the canyon is almost three hundred miles long. Every yard of the way, the views are different, while the weather, cloud cover and visibility change every day.

That said, the Grand Canyon *does* look especially dramatic at the start and end of each day. When the sun is high in the sky, the colours tend to be bleached out, and heat and dust diminish visibility. By contrast, when the sun is low, the rich reds and oranges of the sandstone formations emerge, etched against sharp black shadows, and the whole spectacle can be simply stunning.

It's definitely worth ensuring that you're at a major canyon viewpoint as sunset approaches, and, to a lesser extent, at dawn. On the South Rim, that means getting away from the village itself, to somewhere that commands long-range canyon views to either east or west, or ideally, both – like **Hopi, Mohave or Pima** points to the west, or **Yavapai, Yaki or Desert View** to the east. The most popular spots tend to be Hopi Point for the sunset and Yavapai for sunrise; the down side of that, however, is that often a thousand or more people cram into those single small areas at the relevant moment. It's always better to play things by ear, and simply hope to find a quiet area where you can wander at will, rather than jostle for position. Shoshone Point is strongly recommended; because it's a twenty-minute walk from the nearest road, it rarely sees more than a handful of visitors.

Bear in mind that it's not the sunset that's the spectacle, it's the canyon; if you arrive five minutes before the precise time the sun goes down, you'll see very little. To illuminate anything within the canyon itself, the sun has to be significantly above the horizon, so the finest viewing comes in the final hour or so before sunset, and it comes from looking east, away from the sun and towards those buttes and temples that continue to catch direct sunlight, not west into the shadows. Similarly, it doesn't matter if you miss the moment of dawn; it's the ensuing hour, in which the rising sun picks out the pinnacles one by one, that will live in your memory.

may well offer your only chance to be alone with the canyon on the South Rim, and it's arguably the finest viewpoint on either rim.

The trail to Shoshone Point begins from an unpaved parking lot 1.4 miles east of the turn-off to Yaki Point; look for a grey gate barring a dirt road, and a brown park notice reading "Site Use by Permit Only". The sign is there because the park service does not publicize Shoshone Point to casual visitors, as it's used for weddings in summer, but there's no system for issuing permits to hikers. Instead, you're simply asked to respect the privacy of any group that may be out there, and not to hike out at all if there are a lot of cars at the parking lot. The point itself is truly spectacular. A solitary pale hoodoo marks the tip of its slender neck, while the sublime views range along the full panoply of the North Rim.

6

Grandview Point
8 miles east of Yaki Point, 12 miles east of Grand Canyon Village

Grandview Point is thought to have been where Europeans first saw the Grand Canyon, in 1540 (see p.299). Their Hopi guides may have deliberately led them to a spot from which no trails were visible, to make the canyon appear even more impassable. Grandview was also the place where Grand Canyon tourism first took off, after prospector Peter Berry constructed the **Grandview Trail** (see p.316) down to his Last Chance copper mine in 1892, and visitors began to gravitate to the site.

In terms of views Grandview is unarguably superior to Grand Canyon Village. There's no need to set foot on the precarious trail itself to plot the sinuous course of the Colorado, which makes its broad and languorous entrance off to the east before disappearing into the stunning sandstone labyrinth. Down below, the twin prongs of **Horseshoe Mesa** reach out towards the North Rim. The left points to the mesa of Wotan's Throne, detached from the rim but still towering a couple of hundred feet taller than Grandview itself; in the centre is Cape Royal; and to the right Cape Final juts out at the far eastern end of the North Rim.

Tusayan Ruin
10 miles east of Grandview Point, 22 miles east of Grand Canyon Village

Tusayan Ruin, in the forest south of the highway (and not to be confused with modern Tusayan), is what remains of a genuine **Ancestral Puebloan pueblo**. One of two thousand known such sites in the Grand Canyon area, it's not comparable in scale to relics elsewhere in the Southwest, but its existence enabled President Theodore Roosevelt to accord National Monument status to the entire Grand Canyon. Only low stone walls survive of the original complex of buildings, occupied for perhaps 25 years by a group of up to thirty people, around 1185 AD. A small museum (daily 9am–5pm; free) holds displays on the contemporary Navajo and Hopi, as well as 4000-year-old twig figurines and Ancestral Puebloan pottery found nearby.

Desert View
Desert View, 25 miles east of Grand Canyon Village, is the last viewpoint along Desert View Drive. As Hwy-64, however, the road continues another 34 miles to meet US-89 at Cameron (see p.330), so Desert View also provides visitors approaching from the east with their *first* opportunity to see what all the fuss is about.

To the north, four miles distant, the Colorado River can be seen approaching its sudden westward turn. Just north of its last visible curve lies the confluence of the Colorado and Little Colorado rivers, proposed site of Grand Canyon Escalade. The stark cliffs known as the **Palisades of the Desert** delineate the South Rim, while above them the pallid plains of the **Marble Plateau** stretch to the horizon, beneath an overwhelming sky. Sixty-five million years ago, this entire landscape was buried beneath an additional four or five thousand feet of sandstone. Thanks to erosion, all that remains are a few tiny vestiges, such as reddish **Cedar Mountain**, a mile or two back from the rim.

6

THE BRIEF LIFE OF GRAND CANYON ESCALADE

The announcement in 2014 that a new billion-dollar tourist complex was to be built at the confluence of the Colorado and Little Colorado rivers prompted worldwide controversy. Located on Navajo land, outside Grand Canyon National Park but just ten miles north of Desert View, **Grand Canyon Escalade** was to consist of a cluster of hotels and shops atop the canyon rim, connected to the confluence itself, thousands of feet below, by a cable car. Thousands of visitors each day would be carried down to a riverside restaurant, cultural centre and open-air walkway.

Although the bulk of the proceeds would go to the Scottsdale developer responsible, the scheme was presented as potentially benefitting the Navajo in much the same way as the Hualapai-owned Skywalk attraction at the far west end of the Grand Canyon (see p.328). It would create a thousand or more jobs on the reservation, while the Navajo would also earn up to eighteen percent of the profits, in return for constructing the necessary thirty-mile access road from the nearest highway. However, the junction of the two rivers is not a uniquely Navajo site; it's sacred to other Native American peoples, including the Hopi, for whom it is the location of the *sipapu*, the hole through which they first reached this world. The plan also appalled environmentalists, wilderness advocates and the park service.

In the end, Grand Canyon Escalade turned out to have little support among the Navajo themselves. When Navajo Nation President Ben Shelly, who initially presented the project as very much a done deal, ran for re-election, he came a humiliating seventh. Russell Begaye, elected as his replacement in May 2015, immediately declared the scheme defunct. Instead, hailing the confluence as an "incredible treasure", he joined with leaders of the Hopi, Hualapai and Havasupai in calling for the creation of a new **Grand Canyon Heritage National Monument**, which would protect not just the confluence but a total of 1.7 million acres of tribal lands, from all forms of commercial exploitation, and especially uranium mining.

Over to the west, by contrast, the river disappears deep into the Granite Gorge, engulfed on all sides by buttes and mesas, temples, shrines and tabernacles. During the morning all of these present an extraordinary panoply of colours and shapes; the rich golds and reds are the first to go, leached out by the midday sun, while as dusk draws on they seem to lose all form as well, turning into mysterious interleaving shadowy screens, devoid of all three-dimensional quality.

Desert View Watchtower
Daily 8am–sunset • Free

Rather than the canyon itself, what immediately draws the eye is the remarkable **Desert View Watchtower** perched at its lip, built in Ancestral Puebloan style by Mary Jane Colter in 1932. Leased for many years as a gift store, it's now run once again by the park service, which has cleared the large circular chamber at its base so that visitors can once again enjoy original features like the fireplace, *kiva* ladder, and, of course, sweeping views. Stairs from there climb through three further rooms, which are decorated with murals by the Hopi artist Fred Kabotie, as well as reproduction petroglyphs.

South Rim hikes: into the canyon

Hiking any of the trails that descend into the Grand Canyon offers much more than just another view of the same thing. Instead you pass through a sequence of utterly different landscapes, each with its own climate, wildlife and topography.

Eight major trails lead into the canyon from the South Rim, but most either start from inaccessible places or are in poor condition. Traffic is heaviest on the **Bright Angel** and **South Kaibab** trails, the two "**Corridor Trails**" that link up in the gorge to lead to Phantom Ranch, and can be combined with the **North Kaibab Trail** (see p.335) to form a continuous route between the South and North rims. If you do want to hike from rim to rim, bear in mind that the Transcanyon Shuttle (see p.336) connects the two, so you can get back where you started. The Corridor trails also offer the best **day-hikes** in the canyon: down the Bright Angel Trail as far as **Indian Garden,** or at most out to **Plateau Point,** and down the South Kaibab Trail to **Cedar Ridge.**

Bright Angel Trail

Trailhead: Grand Canyon Village • Day-hike to Indian Garden 9.2 miles round-trip, 5–7hr; day-hike to Plateau Point 12.2 miles round-trip, 8–10hr; Phantom Ranch 9.6 miles one-way, 5–6hr descent, 7–9hr ascent

By far the busiest inner-canyon hiking route – with mules as well as hikers – the **Bright Angel Trail** starts in Grand Canyon Village, alongside the wooden shack that once served as the Kolb photographic studio. An old Havasupai route, it was improved by miners a century ago, and then operated as a toll trail when the mines failed to prosper.

Although the side canyon immediately below the village makes access to the Tonto Platform relatively straightforward, it's still a long, hard climb. Most **day-hikers** content themselves with walking to either of the two resthouses in the first three miles, but with an early start you should be able to manage the round-trip of nine miles to and from Indian Garden, or even twelve miles to and from Plateau Point. In summer, you can obtain water along the trail and only need to carry one quart (a litre) per person; in winter, when there is none, you should carry two. Only try to reach the river – 7.8 miles from the trailhead, with Phantom Ranch almost two miles beyond that – if you've reserved a campsite for the night.

The trail begins with a long, exposed set of switchbacks down the dry, rocky hillside, which changes from pale pink to sheer red. Two short tunnels punctuate its first mile. After another mile, you start to see more wildlife – deer, rodents and the ubiquitous ravens – and various rock surfaces with pictographs, all but obscured by graffiti. Both the basic 1930s **resthouses,** after 1.6 and 3.1 miles, have water in summer (May–Sept) and emergency phones, but only the 1.6-mile one has restrooms.

Jacob's Ladder and Garden Creek

Beyond the second resthouse, a set of switchbacks known as **Jacob's Ladder** carries you down the sheer Redwall cliff, a major obstacle throughout almost the entire canyon. Then, finally, the trail starts to level out, and the vegetation gets greener, with yellow- and red-blossomed cactuses scattered to either side. Soon you hear the astonishing sound of trickling water in **Garden Creek,** lined by dazzling green trees.

Indian Garden

The spring at **Indian Garden,** 4.6 miles from the rim, is the reason the Bright Angel Trail exists. Native peoples really did have a garden here, planted in prehistoric times and used by the Havasupai from around 1300 AD until the nineteenth century. Now

---

HIKING IN THE GRAND CANYON

While the canyon can offer a wonderful wilderness experience, it's a hostile and very unforgiving environment, gruelling even for expert hikers. Park rangers have one simple message for all would-be hikers: **Don't try to hike to the river and back in one day**. It might not look far on the map, but it's harder than running a marathon. Several hikers each year die in the attempt, and several hundred more receive emergency medical treatment. If you do want to reach the Colorado, it's best to reserve campgrounds for two nights, so you have a day to recover before the trek out.

The South Rim is 7000 feet above sea level, an altitude that most people find fatiguing in itself. Furthermore, all hikes start with a long, steep descent, and unless you camp overnight you'll have to climb all the way back up again when you're hotter and wearier. As a rule of thumb, keep track of how much time you spend hiking down and allow twice that much to get back up again. Average summer temperatures inside the canyon exceed 100°F; to hike for eight hours in that sort of heat, you have to drink an incredible thirty pints of water. Always **carry at least a quart (a litre) per person at all times** – and much more if there are no water sources along your chosen trail. You must have food as well, because drinking large quantities without also eating can cause water intoxication. Ideally, the best seasons to hike are spring and fall.

6

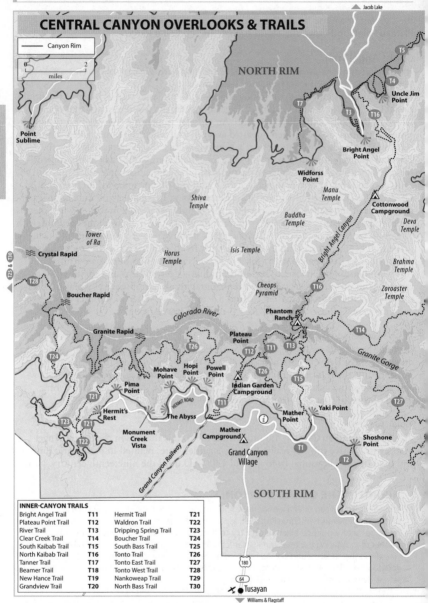

CENTRAL CANYON OVERLOOKS & TRAILS

Canyon Rim

0   2
miles

NORTH RIM

Jacob Lake

T5

T4

Uncle Jim
Point

T7   T3   T16

Bright Angel
Point

Point
Sublime

Widforss
Point

Manu
Temple

Shiva
Temple

Buddha
Temple

Cottonwood
Campground

Deva
Temple

Tower
of Ra

Crystal Rapid

Horus
Temple

Isis Temple

Cheops
Pyramid

Brahma
Temple

Zoroaster
Temple

T25 & T30

T28

Boucher Rapid

Colorado River

Phantom
Ranch

Granite Gorge

Granite Rapid

Plateau
Point

T16

T14

T26   T12   T11   T13

T24

Mohave
Point

Hopi
Point

Powell
Point

Indian Garden
Campground

T26

T15

T27

Pima
Point

Yaki Point

T21

Hermit's
Rest

HERMIT ROAD

The Abyss

T11

Mather
Point

T23

T21

Monument
Creek
Vista

Mather
Campground

i

Shoshone
Point

T22

Grand Canyon
Village

T1

T2

SOUTH RIM

Grand Canyon Railway

180

INNER-CANYON TRAILS			
Bright Angel Trail	T11	Hermit Trail	T21
Plateau Point Trail	T12	Waldron Trail	T22
River Trail	T13	Dripping Spring Trail	T23
Clear Creek Trail	T14	Boucher Trail	T24
South Kaibab Trail	T15	South Bass Trail	T25
North Kaibab Trail	T16	Tonto Trail	T26
Tanner Trail	T17	Tonto East Trail	T27
Beamer Trail	T18	Tonto West Trail	T28
New Hance Trail	T19	Nankoweap Trail	T29
Grandview Trail	T20	North Bass Trail	T30

64

Tusayan

Williams & Flagstaff

this unexpected little oasis holds a ranger station, restrooms, separate camping and day-use areas, and a staging post for mules.

Plateau Point

From Indian Garden, the Bright Angel Trail continues to the river, while the **Tonto Trail** runs both east and west for a phenomenal total of 92 miles along the flat, arid Tonto

Platform. A spur trail off the Tonto Trail – reached by heading left at Indian Garden, crossing Garden Creek, and then turning right at an obvious intersection three-quarters of a mile along – threads its way out to **Plateau Point**, a superb overlook above the Granite Gorge from which it is not possible to descend any further. Barren even by inner-canyon standards, the desert landscape is spectacular, with the mighty red buttes and mesas of the canyon now framed against the blue sky. Shortly after you get your first glimpse of the black tumbling walls of the gorge, the Plateau Point spur trail comes to an end. Precariously perched on the rocky outcrops, you can see a long stretch of the dark-green Colorado, but both the bridges lie out of sight around the next promontory to the east.

Devil's Corkscrew and the Colorado River

As it continues beyond Indian Garden, the Bright Angel Trail first drops through the fertile margins of Garden Creek, then switchbacks down the **Devil's Corkscrew**, hacked into the rock during the 1930s to create a shortcut to the river. Once beside the Colorado, dwarfed beneath thousand-foot walls of dark-grey granite, it undulates through sand dunes scattered with yucca and prickly pear.

Hikers can cross the river around a mile along, using the 1960s **Silver Bridge**; mules, which balk at the prospect of seeing the river between its slats, have to continue a little further. The 400ft **suspension bridge** they prefer was set in place in 1928; it hangs from twin cables that were carried down the Kaibab Trail on the shoulders of 42 Havasupai. Not far away on the other side – though you'll have to cross Bright Angel Creek twice to reach it – is **Bright Angel Campground**, with **Phantom Ranch** a short distance up beyond.

The temperature at river level tends to be around 20°F higher than on the South Rim, and there's significantly less rainfall. The **ecology** down here has changed since Glen Canyon Dam was completed in the mid-1960s (see p.395). Previously, up to a million tons of earth and rock hurtled past Phantom Ranch each day. Now it's more like forty thousand; trees that would previously have been swept away are establishing themselves, and fish that were perfectly adapted to such conditions are now becoming extinct.

Phantom Ranch

Bright Angel Creek flows down Bright Angel Canyon from the North Rim to meet the Colorado below Grand Canyon Village. John Wesley Powell named it in 1869, contrasting this "clear beautiful creek" with the muddy Dirty Devil River, upstream in Utah, and identified a small **Ancestral Puebloan ruin** that's still visible today.

This confluence now marks the only place where inner-canyon hikers and mule riders can not only cross the Colorado River but also camp and even sleep in a real bed at the bottom of the canyon. **Phantom Ranch**, beside Bright Angel Creek, consists of assorted cabins, corrals and outbuildings clustered around a central lodge and surrounded by huge cottonwoods and fruit orchards. Overnight accommodation is in individual cabins and dorms (see p.320), while the **Bright Angel Campground** is nearby (see p.320).

South Kaibab Trail

Trailhead: First shuttle bus stop on green route, around 500 yards before Yaki Point • Day-hike to Cedar Mesa 3 miles round-trip, 2–4hr; day-hike to Skeleton Point 6 miles round-trip, 4–6hr; Phantom Ranch 7.1 miles one-way, 4–6hr descent, ascent not recommended

The **South Kaibab Trail**, the most direct route from the South Rim to Phantom Ranch, is never as busy as the Bright Angel Trail. And no wonder – taking just six miles to drop to the river, it's an even steeper haul, while the trailhead lies three miles east of the visitor centre. If you plan to combine the Bright Angel and South Kaibab trails in hiking to and from Phantom Ranch, make the Kaibab the one you go *down*. Even if you can only spare the time for a short day-hike, however, you'll be rewarded by superb views.

The trail starts by descending slightly west of **Yaki Point**, but once past the end of the promontory it runs along the top of **Cedar Ridge**. This high crest surveys a thirty-mile stretch of the canyon in both directions and also faces straight up Bright Angel Canyon toward the North Rim. In the absence of any water en route, most hikers turn back after 1.5 miles. If you keep going, down a precipitous and very exposed slope, you reach another potential day-hike destination, **Skeleton Point**, 1.5 miles further along, and eventually meet the **Tonto Trail** a total of 4.4 miles down. A long, if level, trek east enables backpackers to connect with the Grandview Trail, but the obvious way to go is west. At a spot known as the **Tipoff**, a few hundred yards along, you're poised to plunge

OPPOSITE THE BRIGHT ANGEL TRAIL (P.311) >

down into the Granite Gorge. The river, and the 1928 suspension bridge that leads to Phantom Ranch, are little more than a mile away.

Grandview Trail

Trailhead: Grandview Point • Day-hike to Horseshoe Mesa 6.4 miles round-trip, 5–7hr

The **Grandview Trail**, down from **Grandview Point**, was built during the 1890s to aid copper mining on **Horseshoe Mesa**, which remains littered with abandoned mine

THE CORRIDOR TRAILS

INNER-CANYON TRAILS

Bright Angel Trail	T11
Plateau Point Trail	T12
River Trail	T13
Clear Creek Trail	T14
South Kaibab Trail	T15
North Kaibab Trail	T16
Tonto Trail	T26
Tonto East Trail	T27

RIM TRAILS

Rim Trail	T1
Shoshone Point Trail	T2
Transept Trail	T3
Uncle Jim Trail	T4
Ken Patrick Trail	T5
Widforss Trail	T7

NORTH RIM

Uncle Jim Point

Roaring Springs Canyon

Roaring Springs

Bright Angel Point

The Transept

Widforss Point

Shiva Temple

Manu Temple

Cottonwood Campground

Ribbon Falls

Buddha Temple

Deva Temple

Bright Angel Canyon

Isis Temple

Brahma Temple

Cheops Pyramid

Zoroaster Temple

The Box

Colorado River

Phantom Ranch

Black Bridge

Plateau Point

Silver Bridge

The Tipoff

Pipe Creek

Colorado River

Hopi Point

Indian Garden Campground

Maricopa Point

Skeleton Point

Mohave Point

Powell Point

Grandeur Point

Yavapai Point

O'Neill Butte

Cedar Ridge

Mather Point

Yaki Point

SOUTH RIM

Grand Canyon Village

Shoshone Point

DESERT VIEW DRIVE

Mather Campground

Feet	
	8000
	6800
	5600
	4400
	3200
	0

——— Canyon Rim

0   2
miles

workings. Although it's possible, by connecting with other trails, to use the Grandview to reach the Tonto Platform and thus eventually the Colorado, it's not itself a rim-to-river route. Instead, the hike down to the mesa and back is a popular **day-hike**. That doesn't mean it's easy, however; now officially "unmaintained", it's a very demanding trail with no water en route and a tendency to ice up in winter. Several of its switchbacks were constructed by inserting metal rods deep into the canyon wall, then covering them with juniper logs, stones and dirt. At times it can be a little hair-raising, but it has stayed surprisingly sturdy for well over a century.

6

Hermit Trail

Trailhead: Hermit's Rest · Day-hike to Santa Maria Spring 5 miles round-trip, 3–4hr; day-hike to Dripping Spring 6.5 miles round-trip, 3–5hr; Colorado River 9.7 miles one-way, 6–7hr descent, 7–9hr ascent

Although the **Hermit Trail**, built for mule riders in 1912 and abandoned in 1931, is considered an unmaintained trail, much of its engineering remains in good shape. Named in honour of Louis Boucher, a nineteenth-century prospector, it's now used mainly by solitary types, setting off on long backcountry camping expeditions away from the crowds.

From the Hermit's Rest parking lot at the end of Hermit Road (see p.307), the trail drops into a side canyon, then switchbacks into Hermit Gorge and slowly descends a high rock wall far above Hermit Creek. A detour less than two miles along allows for the popular day-hike to **Dripping Spring**, not recommended for anyone with a fear of heights. Alternatively, if you press on, rockfalls tend to make for slow progress, but the resthouse at **Santa Maria Spring**, 2.5 miles down from the trailhead, is a lovely day-hike destination. Beyond that, views of the Granite Gorge eventually open up. The *Hermit Camp* is not far west of the junction with the Tonto Trail, seven miles along. Turning right (north) shortly before the campground brings you to the Colorado itself, almost ten miles from the trailhead, at **Hermit Rapid**, where the wave-like surge of the river can reach over twenty feet high.

ARRIVAL AND DEPARTURE   THE SOUTH RIM

The South Rim is separated from I-40 by the sixty-mile expanse of the **Coconino Plateau**, which is covered by the largest **ponderosa pine forest** in the world. Crossing this undramatic landscape, you get no sense of the impending abyss until you reach the very edge of the canyon.

BY CAR
Driving to the Grand Canyon The vast majority of

visitors reach the park entrance at Tusayan by **driving** north from I-40. AZ-64 from Williams (52 miles south; see p.287),

---

BACKCOUNTRY CAMPING

Backcountry camping below the canyon rim is by permit only, with permits costing $10, plus $5 per person per night. Applications are accepted in person, by mail (Grand Canyon National Park Permits Office, 1824 S Thompson St, Suite 201, Flagstaff AZ 86001), or by fax (☏ 928 638 2125), but not by email or phone. Full details can be found at ⊕ nps.gov/grca.

All applications have to specify an exact itinerary, detailing where you'll spend each night – either named campgrounds or the wider-ranging "Use Areas" coded on official park maps, also available online. Between March and mid-November, there's a limit of two nights per party per campsite on the most popular trails.

Mailed or faxed applications are accepted for dates until the end of the fourth complete month after they're received; thus if you're planning a trip in the peak month of July, you'd better mail your application to arrive by March 1. Applications that arrive more than ten days early are ignored. To apply in person, turn up at either the **Backcountry Information Center**, near *Maswik Lodge* in Grand Canyon Village (daily 8am–noon & 1–5pm; ☏ 928 638 7875), or at the **North Rim Backcountry Office**, a quarter-mile north of the *North Rim Campground* (daily 8am–noon & 1–5pm; ☏ 928 638 7868). Even in peak season, your chances of a last-minute cancellation are pretty good. Your name is added to a waiting list, and each morning at 8am that day's cancellations are reassigned – though you have to be there on the spot to get one.

6

also known as the Bushmaster Memorial Highway, joins US-180 from Flagstaff (75 miles southeast; see p.264), at Valle, thirty miles south of the canyon itself. The route from Flagstaff, by way of the San Francisco Peaks (see p.269), is more scenic, and is followed by most commercial **buses**. It's also possible to drive to Grand Canyon Village from the east, by turning onto AZ-64 from US-89 at Cameron (see p.330).

BY TRAIN

Amtrak Amtrak trains come no closer to the South Rim than the stations at Flagstaff and Williams. In summer, westbound services, originating in Chicago, arrive at Flagstaff at 8.51pm and Williams Junction at 9.33pm daily, while eastbound trains, which start in LA, call at Williams Junction at 3.50am and Flagstaff at 4.36am daily. Times in winter are one hour later and there are bus connections year-round (see p.267).

Grand Canyon Railway Trains on the restored Grand Canyon Railway (☎303 843 8724 or ☎800 843 8724, ⊚thetrain.com) run for 64 miles from a separate station in the heart of Williams – *not* Williams's Amtrak station – to the picturesque station at Grand Canyon Village. The railway is a tourist attraction in its own right, with passengers riding in historic cars of varying levels of comfort and entertained by Wild West shoot-outs, hold-ups, pistol-packing marshals, singing conductors and the like. Diesel locomotives pull the trains; steam engines only operate on occasional "Steam Saturdays" in summer, detailed on the website. The scenery en route – part desert scrubland, part pine forest – is far from spectacular, and you never actually see the canyon from the train, but it's a fun way to make a short visit to the

park without having to drive. Services operate daily all year, leaving Williams at 9.30am and reaching the canyon at 11.45am, and then leaving the canyon at 3.30pm to arrive back in Williams at 5.45pm. Round-trip fares range from $65 (under-13s $29) in the Pullman Car up to $216 (under-13s not permitted) in the Luxury Parlor Car.

BY BUS

Arizona Shuttle Daily buses from Flagstaff's Amtrak station, via Williams, to *Maswik Lodge* in Grand Canyon Village (☎928 226 8060 or ☎800 888 2749, ⊚arizonashuttle.com; one-way $30; booking in advance recommended). Year-round, a bus leaves Flagstaff at 7.45am and reaches the *Maswik* at 9.30am, and another leaves Flagstaff at 3.45pm and gets to the *Maswik* at 5.45pm. Between March and October, a third bus leaves Flagstaff at 12.45pm and arrives at the *Maswik* at 2.45pm.

Tours Various companies operate one-day tours to the Canyon from Flagstaff (see p.267) and Williams (see p.288).

BY AIR

Tusayan airport The small airport (⊚grandcanyonairport. org) at Tusayan, six miles from the South Rim, just outside the park boundary, is used primarily by "flight-seeing" tour companies (see p.303). The only airlines that currently fly here offer excursions from Las Vegas; almost all passengers come on day-trips, but it is possible to arrange a one-way flight. The major operators are Grand Canyon Scenic Airlines (☎702 638 3300 or ☎800 634 6801, ⊚scenic.com), and Grand Canyon Airlines (☎702 638 3200 or ☎866 235 9422, ⊚grandcanyonairlines.com).

GETTING AROUND

BY CAR

Grand Canyon Village is always accessible to private vehicles and so, too, is the road east from the village to Desert View. The road west from the village to Hermit's Rest, however, is only open to cars during December, January and February, when the shuttle buses aren't operating.

BY SHUTTLE BUS

The park's free shuttle buses interconnect but do not overlap.

Village Route Coded blue on official park maps, the busiest shuttle bus route loops around Grand Canyon Village between the start of the Hermit's Rest route and the visitor centre, with stops including *Bright Angel*, *Maswik* and *Yavapai* lodges and *Mather Campground*. Starting an hour before sunrise, buses run at 30min intervals until 6.30am; at 15min intervals for most of the day; and 30min intervals in the evening until 9pm (Oct–April), 10pm (May & Sept) or 11pm (June–Aug).

Kaibab/Rim Route Coded orange, this loops between the visitor centre and Yaki Point and the South Kaibab

trailhead to the east, and with Mather and Yavapai points to the west. Buses start running at 30min intervals an hour before sunrise, increasing from 6.30am onwards to run at 15min intervals until an hour after sunset.

Hikers' Express For anyone planning to hike the South Kaibab Trail (see p.314), it's much quicker to catch this direct early-morning service to the Yaki Point trailhead from *Bright Angel Lodge*, via the Backcountry Information Center and visitor centre (daily June–Aug 4am, 5am & 6am; March & Nov 7am, 8am & 9am; April & Oct 6am, 7am & 8am; May & Sept 5am, 6am & 7am; Dec–Feb 8am & 9am). Note that you can also use a taxi on this route.

Hermit's Rest Route Coded red, this route operates between March and November only, and follows Hermit Road, a scenic seven-mile drive west of the village that holds eight canyon overlooks (see p.306). The whole point of the trip is to take your time and enjoy the views; allow at least 2hr. Buses run from an hour before sunrise until an hour after sunset, at 15min intervals through most of the day and at 30min intervals otherwise. Demand is always high for buses out from the village to see the sunset – be sure to get to the stop at least an hour in advance – and for the trip back to the village once the sun has gone down.

Tusayan Route Coded purple, and offering regular 20min runs between Tusayan, where there are four separate stops, and the visitor centre, between late May and late Sept only. The first bus leaves Tusayan at 8am daily, and the visitor centre at 8.25am; the last service back is at 9.30pm from the visitor centre, 9.45pm from Tusayan. All passengers entering the park must already have permits.

BY BIKE

Cycling is permitted on all paved and unpaved roads within the park, including Hermit Road itself, even when it's closed to private vehicles, and the Greenway Trail alongside Hermit Road, which starts at Monument Creek Vista, four miles west of the village, and runs for three miles west to Hermit's Rest. It's not, however, allowed on any portion of the Rim Trail. Park shuttle buses can carry two or three bikes.

Bright Angel Bicycles Based in its own espresso-and-snacks café alongside the visitor centre (daily: April 8am–5pm, May to mid-Sept 8am–6pm, mid-Sept to Oct 9am–5pm, Nov–March 10am–4pm; ☎ 928 638 3055, ⓦ bikegrandcanyon.com), Bright Angel rents bikes for $12/hr, $30/5hr, $40/8hr, $45/24hr, and $35/day for multi-day rentals, with reduced rates for under-17s. They also offer package deals that include one-way or round-trip shuttle rides to Hermit Road, trailers to pull children behind, and seasonally varying guided tours ($38–58).

INFORMATION

South Rim Guide Map The free *South Rim Guide Map*, handed out at the two entrance stations on AZ-64 (one's just north of Tusayan, the other a mile east of Desert View), list park facilities and shuttle bus routes. For details of current opening hours, however, and schedules of activities such as free ranger talks and guided hikes, you'll have to check online, or stop at a visitor centre or information desk.

Grand Canyon Visitor Center The official South Rim visitor centre is immediately north of the spur road that heads west into the village from AZ-64. Surrounded by parking lots and at the hub of the free shuttle bus network, the visitor centre itself holds very little information you can't find online, but is staffed by helpful rangers eager to advise on any topic you care to mention (daily: March–Nov

8am–5pm, Dec–Feb 9am–5pm; ☎ 928 638 7888, ⓦ nps .gov/grca). Across the plaza, there's an excellent separate bookstore.

Information desks Additional information desks are located at Kolb Studio, Verkamp's (see p.306), and Yavapai Geology Museum (see p.306).

Maps None of the free maps on offer at the park is adequate for backcountry hiking, so invest in the waterproof and tearproof maps published by National Geographic–Trails Illustrated. No. 261 focuses specifically on Bright Angel Canyon and the Corridor Trails, at 1:35,000, while nos. 262 and 263 cover the eastern and western portions of the canyon respectively, at 1:90,000 ($11.95 for set of three; ⓦ maps.nationalgeographic.com).

ACCOMMODATION

Roughly two thousand **guest rooms** are available close to the South Rim: half of them in and around **Grand Canyon Village**, and a further thousand in **Tusayan**, an unattractive strip-mall of a town that stands seven miles from Grand Canyon Village, a mile south of the park entrance. Given the choice, the best place to stay has to be on the very lip of the canyon, but very few rooms indeed enjoy canyon views, and they tend to be booked as much as two years in advance. In fact, in summer, you're very unlikely to find any same-day bookings available in the park, and often there's nothing for weeks or months ahead. While the more basic in-park lodges, away from the rim, still make more convenient bases than Tusayan, and the in-park rates often represent extraordinarily good value, the hotels in Tusayan do tend to be more modern and better equipped. If you're stuck, possibilities further afield include **Cameron** (see p.330), **Flagstaff** (p.267), and **Williams** (p.288).

GRAND CANYON VILLAGE

For all hotels in the park itself, **wi-fi** is available in the lobbies only, not in the rooms.

★ **Bright Angel Lodge** Grand Canyon Village same-day ☎ 928 638 2631, advance ☎ 303 297 2757 or ☎ 888 297 2757, ⓦ grandcanyonlodges.com. Designed by Mary Jane Colter and built in 1935, the *Bright Angel* complex consists of an imposing central lodge and a westward sprawl of rustic but delightful detached log cabins, of which only the Rim Cabins enjoy canyon views. Though reasonably sized and appealingly furnished, many of the lodge rooms share bathrooms and/or toilets; a few do offer private showers. Best of all is the Buckey O'Neill

Suite, which boasts a large living room with working fireplace and two front doors that open on the rim, and can only be booked by phone. Lodge rooms $81, Historic Cabins $134, Rim Cabins $176, Buckey O'Neill Suite $426

★ **El Tovar** Grand Canyon Village same-day ☎ 928 638 2631, advance ☎ 303 297 2757 or ☎ 888 297 2757, ⓦ grandcanyonlodges.com. Named for an early Spanish explorer, this log-construction rim-side hotel remains the centrepiece of Grand Canyon Village, and exudes the same combination of rough-hewn charm and elegant sophistication that made it the very peak of fashion when it first opened. Only three suites offer extensive canyon views; the rest of the 78 tastefully furnished guest rooms come in two different

6

sizes, but are otherwise very similar. Most provide just one bed. Standard $207, larger $251, suites $337

Kachina Lodge Grand Canyon Village same-day ☎ 928 638 2631, advance ☎ 303 297 2757 or ☎ 888 297 2757, ⊛ grandcanyonlodges.com. Anonymous but perfectly adequate motel-style rooms, each with two queen-size beds and full bath, set in a low and utterly undistinguished two-storey block separated by just twenty yards of grass from the rim. The upper-floor rooms on the canyon side – which cost $17 extra – provide great panoramas. $215

Maswik Lodge Grand Canyon Village same-day ☎ 928 638 2631, advance ☎ 303 297 2757 or ☎ 888 297 2757, ⊛ grandcanyonlodges.com. This large complex, a few hundred yards back from the rim, includes two distinct blocks of motel-style rooms; the Maswik North building is much nicer than the smaller, cramped Maswik South. Maswik South $107, Maswik North $205

Thunderbird Lodge Grand Canyon Village same-day ☎ 928 638 2631, advance ☎ 303 297 2757 or ☎ 888 297 2757, ⊛ grandcanyonlodges.com. Built of grey brick in the 1960s and intended to last only ten years, the *Thunderbird* is still going strong without being in any way distinctive. Of its 55 rooms, 37 are on the canyon side of the building and cost $17 extra; all have full bathroom. $215

Yavapai Lodge 11 Yavapai Lodge Rd, Grand Canyon Village property direct ☎ 928 638 4001, reservations ☎ 801 449 4139 or ☎ 877 404 4611, ⊛ visitgrandcanyon .com. The largest in-park lodge, set back in the woods half a mile from the rim, and twice that from the heart of Grand Canyon Village, *Yavapai* has been modernized and expanded since being taken over by new concessionaires. The rooms themselves offer perfectly decent motel-style accommodation, most with twin beds, and are housed in two similar sections, the air-conditioned Yavapai East, and Yavapai West, which has ceiling fans only. Pets are welcome. Yavapai West $147, Yavapai East $183

TUSAYAN

Best Western Grand Canyon Squire Inn 74 Hwy-64 ☎ 928 638 2681 or ☎ 800 622 6966, ⊛ grandcanyonsquire .com. Most rooms in Tusayan's most lavish option are spacious and comfortable, but even if it does have its own four-lane bowling alley, this is still an upscale chain rather than anything more remarkable. Paying a little extra gets you an enormous deluxe room with oval bath. $210

The Grand Hotel 149 Hwy-64 ☎ 928 638 3333 or ☎ 888 634 7263, ⊛ grandcanyongrandhotel.com. The overall look of this modern hotel, run by the main park concessionaires, Xanterra, is a nod towards traditional park lodges. Once you get past the smart public spaces, however – designed with tour groups in mind – the rooms themselves are not as good as you'd hope for these sort of prices. There is a nice figure-of-eight indoor pool, though, and it's home to the *Canyon Star Steakhouse* and saloon. $309

Red Feather Lodge 106 Hwy-64 ☎ 928 638 2414 or ☎ 800 538 2345, ⊛ redfeatherlodge.com. This long-established motel was joined a few years back by a large new hotel block. They share a pool, the rates aren't bad and the newer rooms offer a reasonably high standard. $135

Seven Mile Lodge AZ-64 ☎ 928 638 2291. Tusayan's last roadside motel, this twenty-room place is very plain beyond its Pueblo-style doorway and hanging flowers, but it's the least expensive option around. Reservations are not accepted; rooms are simply doled out from 9am daily. Despite the slight premium charged for housing three or four guests in the same room, it's still great value for groups of (close) friends. $121

PHANTOM RANCH

★**Phantom Ranch** Colorado River ☎ 303 297 2757 or ☎ 888 297 2757, ⊛ grandcanyonlodges.com. Located at river level, beside Bright Angel Creek near the bottom of the Bright Angel, South Kaibab and North Kaibab trails, *Phantom Ranch* can only be reached on foot or mule. First call on its fully equipped individual cabins goes to mule riders (see p.302), but they're also let to hikers when available, which is more likely in winter. Otherwise, hikers can get beds in one of the four ten-bunk, single-sex dormitories – two for men and two for women – with bedding, showers, towels and soap provided. Reservations are essential, while cancellations are handed out first-come, first-served, at *Bright Angel Lodge* early each morning. All supplies reach *Phantom Ranch* the same way you do, so family-style meals in its restaurant cost $20 for breakfast and $29–45 for dinner. Dorms $47, cabins $135

CAMPING IN THE PARK

★**Bright Angel Campground** Phantom Ranch area, Colorado River; details on ⊛ nps.gov/grca; reserve via Backcountry office PO Box 129, Grand Canyon, AZ 86023 ☎ 928 638 2125. Accessible only on overnight backpacking trips, the beautiful *Bright Angel Campground*, amid the cottonwoods alongside Bright Angel Creek a quarter of a mile up from its confluence with the Colorado, holds 32 separate sites, each with its own picnic table. Camping is by backcountry permit only (see p.317); do not hike down without a reservation. $5

Desert View Campground Desert View ⊛ nps.gov /grca. The park opens up this simple campsite, set back from the rim 25 miles east of Grand Canyon Village, in summer only (mid-April to mid-Oct), on a first-come, first-served basis, with no RV hook-ups available. No reservations. $12

Mather Campground Grand Canyon Village ☎ 928 638 7851, advance reservations ☎ 877 444 6777, ⊛ recreation.gov. Year-round tent and RV camping (without hook-ups), south of the main road through Grand Canyon Village, not far from Market Plaza. Sites holding up to two vehicles and six people can and should be reserved up to six months in advance for dates between March and mid-Nov. In winter, they're first-come, first-served. Cheaper walk-in sites for hikers and bikers are available March to Mid-Nov only. Walk-in sites $\overline{\$6}$, vehicle sites March to mid-Nov $\overline{\$18}$, mid-Nov to Feb $\overline{\$15}$

Trailer Village Adjacent to Mather Campground, Grand Canyon Village ☏ 928 638 1006 or ☏ 877 404 4611, ⊕ visitgrandcanyon.com. Exclusively RV sites with hook-ups, open all year round. Basic rates are for two people, with charges for each additional adult. $\overline{\$35}$

CAMPING OUTSIDE THE PARK

Camper Village 549 Camper Village Lane, Tusayan

☏ 928 638 2887, ⊕ grandcanyoncampervillage.com. Commercial campsite, just east of AZ-64 in central Tusayan, in easy walking distance of restaurants (though not the canyon itself) and equipped with its own small store. Open year-round. Tents $\overline{\$29}$, RVs $\overline{\$46}$

Ten-X Campground AZ-64, 2 miles south of Tusayan ☏ 928 638 2443, ⊕ fs.usda.gov; reservations ☏ 877 444 6777, ⊕ recreation.gov. Minimally equipped campground, with no hook-ups or showers, run by the Kaibab National Forest and enjoying a peaceful forest setting, 55 of its seventy sizeable sites are first-come, first-served – and seldom full – while the remaining fifteen can be booked in advance. Closed Oct–April. $\overline{\$10}$

EATING AND DRINKING

Grand Canyon Village offers a reasonably wide choice of places to **eat**, and prices in the budget cafeterias are not bad. Summer crowds can lead to endless queueing, though, so it's worth bringing at least some food with you. A few stores – notably the Canyon Village Marketplace, which has a pretty good **deli counter** (summer daily 7am–6pm, otherwise daily 8am–5pm) – sell basic supplies. Tusayan has several fast-food options in addition to the places listed below. Both the *Bright Angel* and the *El Tovar* have atmospheric **bars** open until 11pm nightly.

Arizona Room *Bright Angel Lodge* ⊕ grandcanyon lodges.com. Informal, plain but good-quality restaurant, just a few yards from the rim; no views to speak of, but you do get a strong sense of the vast space nearby. The open kitchen serves conventional meat and seafood meals, with sandwiches, salads and simple main dishes costing $9–13 at lunchtime, and typical dinner prices including baby back ribs for $19, a 10oz steak for $27, or a marinated chicken breast for $17.50. No reservations; nip in a little before sunset, or you may have to wait in the bar for up to two hours. Daily 11.30am–3pm (closed Nov & Dec) & 4.30–10pm.

Bright Angel Dining Room Bright Angel Lodge. Straightforward, windowless diner that serves pretty much anything you might want, from snacks and salads for around $10 to steaks at up to $26. No reservations. Daily 6am–10pm.

Canyon Coffee House Bright Angel Lodge. Early-morning organic coffees and scones, served in the *Bright Angel's* bar. Daily 6–10am.

★ El Tovar El Tovar Hotel ☏ 928 638 2631 ext 6432 ⊕ grandcanyonlodges.com. Very grand, very classy dark-wood dining room, with subdued lighting and great big windows that focus all attention outwards, especially at sunset – though only the front tier of tables have actual canyon views. Reservations, accepted for dinner only, tend to be grabbed long in advance. The food itself is rich and expensive, especially at dinner, when main dishes such as roast duck or salmon tostada cost around $26, and steaks more like $35. Appetizers are a bit more imaginative, with a "crab tower" at $12 and French onion soup at $8. Lunchtime sandwiches, tacos and so on cost more like $12–17. Daily 6.30am–11am, 11.30am–2pm & 4.30–10pm.

Maswik Food Court Maswik Lodge ⊕ grandcanyon lodges.com. Self-service fast food, aimed especially at tour groups, with separate Mexican and Italian sections, as well as burgers and standard plate lunches. Breakfast costs $6–8, while main dishes at lunch and dinner are closer to $10. There are two spacious seating areas plus an adjoining "Pizza Pub", with sports TV and a substantial menu of $20, 16-inch pizzas, also available by the slice. Daily 6am–10pm; pub daily 11am–11pm.

Yavapai Lodge Restaurant 11 Yavapai Lodge Rd, Grand Canyon Village ⊕ visitgrandcanyon.com. Large cafeteria, where you have to order using touch screens before you even get to see quite how ordinary the food is; if you're not staying here, it's not worth a special trip. Sandwiches and burgers for under $10, half a rotisserie chicken for $13.50, steaks up to $22. Beyond the central dining area, which has a dull canteen-like feel, there's a nicer glassed-in annexe. There's also an espresso bar and takeaway deli alongside. Summer daily 6am–10pm; shorter hours in low season.

DIRECTORY

Bank In Market Plaza, with 24hr ATM machine. Mon–Thurs 9am–5pm, Fri 9am–6pm.

Camping equipment For sale or rent at Canyon Village Marketplace. Daily: summer 7am–8.30pm, spring & fall 8am–8pm, winter 8am–7pm.

Internet access Wi-fi access in lobbies of all lodges; free wi-fi and public computers in Park Headquarters, near Market Plaza.

Laundromat Near *Mather Campground*. Daily: summer 6am–11pm; spring and fall 7am–9pm; winter 8am–6pm.

6

Medical help Call ☎911 for emergencies; ☎928 638 2551 for the village clinic (daily 8am–6pm; emergencies only at other times); ☎928 638 2460 for the pharmacy; and ☎928 638 2395 for dentist.

Petrol The closest gas stations to the South Rim are in Tusayan and at Desert View.

Post office In Market Plaza. Mon–Fri 9am–4.30pm.

Showers Coin-operated showers, available to all visitors, are located in the laundromat building (hours as above).

Travellers with disabilities Download the *Accessibility Guide* from ⓦnps.gov/grca, or pick up a copy at visitor centres and lodges. At either park entrance station, you can obtain a permit enabling you to drive on Hermit Road. All shuttle buses except those along Desert View Drive are wheelchair accessible.

The Havasupai Indian Reservation

92 miles north of I-40 exit 123, via AZ-66 and Arrowhead Hwy-18, then 8 miles on foot, horseback or helicopter • No entry to reservation without advance lodging reservation • Entrance fee $35 • ☎928 448 2121, ⓦhavasupai-nsn.gov

Havasu Canyon, one of the most spellbindingly beautiful places in the entire Southwest, nestles deep in the Grand Canyon, a mere 35 miles west of Grand Canyon Village as the condor flies. The only road access is from the southwest, however, so it's a drive of almost two hundred miles from the South Rim; south to I-40, west, and then, for the final ninety miles, back northeast across the endless Coconino Plateau.

Those visitors who brave the eight-mile desert hike down into the canyon are rewarded by a stunning oasis of **turquoise waterfalls** and lush vegetation, a Shangri-La that has been home for centuries beyond record to the same small group of Native Americans. They're here thanks to a geological fluke; although the canyon receives only nine inches of rain each year, all the water that falls for three thousand square miles around funnels down into this one narrow gorge, to create the year-round torrent of Havasu Stream. The down side of that is that the canyon is prone to repeated, devastating **flash floods**. The major flood in 2008, which caused immense damage and carved out a new set of waterfalls, was the fifth such in twenty years.

Havasu Canyon forms the heart of **The Havasupai Indian Reservation**, said by a 1930s anthropologist to be "the only spot in the United States where native culture has remained in anything like its pristine condition." Since then, tourism has become the mainstay of the tribal economy, but visitor numbers are kept deliberately low, at about 35,000 per year. Suggestions of building a road – or even a tramway – down into the canyon have always been rejected, to minimize the impact on the traditional way of life. Instead, the five hundred or so Havasupai earn their keep by ferrying non-hikers up and down the trail on horses and pack mules, and by operating a thriving **campground** beside the stream as well as a comfortable lodge in the village of **Supai**. Although visitors should not expect sweeping views of the Grand Canyon itself – or to have much interaction with the tribal members – for spectacular desert scenery and sheer romance, the Havasupai reservation is beyond compare.

The road to the reservation

The only way to get to the Havasupai reservation is via I-40, turning off at Seligman if you're coming from Flagstaff or Grand Canyon Village, or at Kingman from Las Vegas or California. In total, it takes between three and four hours to drive from Flagstaff, more like five from Las Vegas. Stock up with food, water and gas when you leave the interstate, then follow AZ-66 – the only surviving segment of Route 66 not superseded by newer roads – to the poorly marked intersection with Arrowhead Hwy-18, six miles east of Peach Springs.

Hwy-18 runs for its entire sixty-mile length with hardly a building in sight, across bare sagebrush desert interrupted by patches of thick ponderosa forest. Eventually it starts to wind down through burgeoning canyonlands, coming to an end at the large plateau known as **Hualapai Hilltop**.

At an elevation of 5200ft, the plateau commands a long view of the white-walled Hualapai Canyon, cutting into the tablelands as it stretches north towards its meeting with Havasu Canyon. Although the hilltop holds no more than a small cluster of dilapidated shacks, with no accommodation, food or gas available, there are usually far more vehicles parked here than you might anticipate for such a remote spot.

THE HAVASUPAI INDIAN RESERVATION

6

The trail to Supai

From the end of the parking lot at Hualapai Hilltop, the **Hualapai Trail** to Supai village zigzags steeply down the hillside to the right, and can then be seen threading its way across the valley floor below. Beyond its initial switchbacks, the trail is not especially difficult. It is, however, a long eight-mile walk, with no shade for the first three miles and no reliable water source until very near the end. Allow around three hours to reach **Supai village** (and four or more to come back up again); only set off if you have already reserved accommodation; and be sure to carry enough food and water for a day in the desert.

The route is very obvious and kept busy throughout the day with small supply trains of mules and horses. Once on the valley floor, the trail follows the bed of a dry wash between red-rock walls that slowly but inexorably climb to form a deep, narrow canyon. The sand underfoot is so thick that it shifts at every step, but the potential for flash floods is clear from the much-scoured rocks to either side. Mighty boulders occasionally all but block the path, while solitary cottonwoods reach up towards the thin strip of sky overhead.

After almost seven miles, the trail reaches the intersection where Havasu Canyon comes in from the right; until a disastrous flood in 1910, this was the site of Supai village. Be sure you don't continue straight ahead into Cataract Canyon at this point – it took three weeks to find a dehydrated camper who did so in 1975. Bear left instead, at a dense cluster of small trees. The sound of rushing water soon signals the emergence of Havasu Stream from hidden crevices in the rock; before long it's flowing through the parched landscape in all its blue-green splendour.

THE HAVASUPAI

The **Havasupai** – the "people of the blue-green water" – trace their occupation of Havasu Canyon back at least as far as 1300 AD. The word "**Pai**", which means "people", refers to a Yuman-speaking group that reached the Southwest via California well over a thousand years ago. They soon quarrelled, splitting to form the **Hualapai** ("People of the Tall Pines") of northwest Arizona, and the **Yavapai** ("Almost-People", who no longer quite deserved to be regarded as people) who settled along the Colorado further south. The Hualapai established close links with Pueblo groups such as the Hopi and Zuñi, from whom they eventually acquired the art of raising sheep and horses, as well as the seeds and skills to grow such crops as peaches. Until the Havasupai were allocated their own reservation toward the end of the nineteenth century, they regarded themselves not as a separate "tribe" but as just another band of Hualapai.

Although the Havasupai took their name from the turquoise river that watered their fields, they only lived on the canyon floor in summer, in houses of hide-covered branches. In winter, the canyon made a cold, miserable home, lacking big game and wood for fuel and receiving as little as five hours of sunlight per day. Instead, the Havasupai moved up onto the plateau to hunt deer, elk and antelope. Their territory extended beyond the San Francisco Peaks (near modern Flagstaff), and took in the region now occupied by Grand Canyon Village.

In the summer of 1776, as the Declaration of Independence was being signed in Philadelphia, the Havasupai welcomed their first white visitor, **Father Francisco Tomás Garcés** from San Xavier del Bac near Tucson (see p.232), with five days of feasting. Describing the Grand Canyon as a "calaboose of cliffs and canyons", he dubbed it the Puerto de Bucareli in honour of the viceroy who had despatched him; more enduringly, he was the first to name the Río Colorado. Meanwhile, as Garcés explored the canyon, the rest of his expedition blazed a trail to California, where they founded San Francisco.

The Havasupai then remained undisturbed for eighty years, until Anglo prospectors and surveyors began to enter the region. Conflict arose in 1866, when Congress granted the Atlantic and Pacific Railroad company ownership of swathes of land adjoining its tracks across northern Arizona. Native resistance escalated into **war**, after which the defeated Hualapai spent several years confined to a reservation near Ehrenberg on the Colorado. Because the Havasupai did not participate in the fighting, they were allowed to remain in their traditional territory. In negotiations over the extent of a permanent Havasupai reservation, the US government was

Not far beyond a footbridge across the creek, you cross a low rise to be confronted by the meadow that holds the modern village. Two red-rock pillars, known as the **Wigleeva**, watch over Supai from the high canyon wall on the far side. These twin sentinels, of which one is considered to be male and the other female, are regarded as the guardian spirits of the Havasupai.

Supai

Though located in a superb natural setting – a wide flat clearing surrounded on all sides by forbidding walls of red sandstone – the village of **SUPAI** is not in itself attractive. The Havasupai were only obliged to build a year-round settlement down in the canyon after losing their lands on the plateau above, and this site was their second choice after the first proved prone to flooding. It too has suffered repeated flood damage ever since, and therefore consists of just a scattering of basic timber-frame houses and prefabricated cabins. Even the name is a flimsy fabrication; "Supai" is a meaningless abbreviation of "Havasupai," invented by the US Post Office.

Once the Hualapai Trail, running alongside irrigation ditches, has shepherded you into the village, the first building you come to holds the tribal **registration office**. Only campers are obliged to pay the $35 reservation **entrance fee** here; for lodge guests, it's added to their bill. A back room holds a small **museum** (daily 7am–7pm; donations welcome), which has an interesting assortment of early twentieth-century photos and

as usual only prepared to acknowledge Native American "ownership" of land that held permanent settlements and cultivated fields. Fearful of being deported themselves, the Havasupai settled in 1882 for a tiny 518-acre plot at the bottom of Havasu Canyon. Restricted to a fraction of their former range, they were obliged to farm as intensively as possible.

During the ensuing century of hardship, the Havasupai repeatedly petitioned to have their reservation enlarged. Suffering great spiritual uncertainty, both the Havasupai and Hualapai took part in the 1890s **Ghost Dance** movement, joining in trance-like rituals designed to ensure that white men would vanish from the land and the old ways would return. The Havasupai also briefly adopted the rain-making *kachina* dances of the Hopi (see p.66), until a catastrophic **flood** on January 1, 1910 destroyed their village, which then stood half a mile from its current site.

At first, the creation of **Grand Canyon National Park** placed yet more restrictions on Havasupai use of traditional lands. The Havasupai survived largely through disobeying whatever unenforceable regulations outsiders sought to impose, continuing to spend their winters up on the plateau. Many Havasupai in due course found jobs in Grand Canyon Village, while tourism to Havasu Canyon itself became an important element in the tribal economy.

After endless legal battles, the Havasupai finally won their struggle in 1975. Almost 200,000 acres were added to the reservation, the largest tract of land ever returned to Native Americans. It came only just in time; almost immediately, the Grand Canyon region experienced a boom in **uranium** mining, with over 3500 claims filed in the Arizona Strip during the ensuing decade.

In 1988, Energy Fuels Nuclear was granted rights to develop **Canyon Mine**, at a site outside the reservation, close to **Red Butte** in the Kaibab National Forest, which is sacred to the Havasupai as *Mat Taav Tijundva*. Despite fears that the mine might contaminate Havasu Creek, Havasu Canyon and ultimately the Colorado itself, federal courts blocked Havasupai attempts to stop it. The mine was built, but did not go into operation at the time, thanks to a drop in world uranium prices. Although the US Secretary of State imposed a twenty-year ban on the opening of any new uranium mines in the Grand Canyon region in 2012, Energy Fuels Nuclear continues to assert its right to start operations at Canyon Mine in the near future. Not surprisingly, the Havasupai are among the most enthusiastic advocates of the proposed **Grand Canyon Heritage National Monument**, which would forbid uranium mining altogether (see p.310).

6

cuttings. The Havasupai are famous for crafts such as basket-making, so there's a case of assorted baskets, one of which has been coated with pine pitch to make it waterproof. Ancient artefacts have become too expensive for the museum to afford, though, so the finest old Havasupai baskets in Arizona are in Phoenix's Heard Museum (see p.209).

Fifty yards further on, beyond the only post office in the US that still receives its mail by pack mule, lies Supai's dusty, wind-blown **plaza**. Benches outside the village's one **grocery store** form its main social centre, where the older Havasupai gather each evening. The younger set, together with a vast population of dogs, are more likely to be found on the terrace of the **café**, opposite. Once past that, the trail skirts the village school, then branches left down towards the campground. Visitors are forbidden to wander off the main trail into the surrounding farm lands.

Below Supai: the falls

All the **waterfalls** for which the Havasupai reservation is famous lie further down the canyon beyond Supai. To get there, follow the footpath out of the village from near the lodge; it takes several minutes to get clear of the straggle of farms and homes.

New Navajo Falls and Rock Falls

The riverbed immediately below Supai village is forever being reshaped by flash floods and fresh erosion. Thus a catastrophic flood in 2008 scoured out a great new chasm, well

HAVASUPAI HORSES, HELICOPTERS AND HIKING TOURS

HORSE AND MULE RIDES

It's possible to ride rather than walk down the Hualapai Trail, or to have your bags carried while you hike, though, you may well be disturbed to see that many of the horses and mules used are in alarmingly poor condition. Each day, the mule train leaves the hilltop at some point between 10am and noon; advance reservations are essential. If you arrive any later than noon, you won't be able to ride down, and you'll lose both your reservation and your deposit. To ride as far as the **village** costs $70 per person one-way and $120 round-trip, and should be arranged via the lodge (☎928 448 2111); riding to the **campground** costs $93.50 each way, and is arranged by the camping office (☎928 448 2121 or 2141); full details on ☻havasuwaterfalls.net. Riders' baggage weighing over ten pounds has to be carried separately; one animal can carry up to four packs, again for $70 one-way, $120 round-trip.

HELICOPTER SHUTTLES

A **helicopter shuttle** service connects Hualapai Hilltop with Supai village, run by AirWest Helicopters (mid-March to mid-Oct Thurs, Fri, Sun & Mon 10am–1pm, mid-Oct to mid-March to Fri & Sun 10am–1pm; ☎623 516 2790). Passengers are carried on a first-come, first-served basis, without any advance reservations, for a one-way fare of $85. If you register between 10am and 1pm on a day the service is operating, at either the hilltop or the village, they guarantee you will definitely be taken.

It's also possible to charter a helicopter from the South Rim to the reservation, for around $600 per person, via Papillon (☎928 638 2419 or ☎888 635 7272, ☻papillon.com).

GUIDED TOURS

Arizona Outback Adventures ☎480 945 2881 or ☎866 455 1601, ☻aoa-adventures.com. Three- to five-day trips with accommodation at their own "Base Camp". Prices start at $915, with extra charges if you ride or fly rather than hike.
Discovery Treks ☎480 247 9266 or ☎888 256 8731, ☻discoverytreks.com. Three-day trips with a choice of hiking, horseriding and helicopter rides, and camping or staying in the lodge. Prices range upwards from $895.
Grand Canyon Field Institute ☎928 638 2481 or ☎866 471 4435, ☻grandcanyon.org /fieldinstitute. Three highly recommended four-day hiking and camping tours each summer, costing $795; one is reserved for women only.

over 100ft deep. Leaving the former Navajo Falls high and dry, it created two spectacular new cascades. The first you come to, known as **New Navajo Falls**, is a short walk left of the trail roughly a mile down. Tumbling over a wide cliff face in countless separate strands, it shrouds a regrowth of young ferns and saplings in a mist of white spray.

From the foot of the falls, Havasu Creek has carved a new course. The riverbed itself is extraordinarily green and verdant, but scores of dead aspens, whose roots no longer reach the water table, look down forlornly from the high cliffs on its far side.

Another quarter-mile along, the second of the new falls, **Rock Falls**, usually consists of a single expansive cascade. The full width of the river roars over a 20ft drop, immediately before making a sharp turn; it's possible to swim in the pool immediately below the falls.

6

Havasu Falls

When the trail appears to divide, half a mile beyond Rock Falls, take the left fork and follow it down to a footbridge over the creek. You're now approaching the stupendous double cascade of **Havasu Falls**. First seen from an overlook more or less level with the top, this is a breathtaking sight. The creek foams white as it hurtles over a 150ft cliff, to crash into shallow terraces filled with limpid turquoise water. The rock formations all around are formed from water-deposited limestone known as **travertine** – the same stuff that creates the stalactites of Carlsbad Caverns, and clogs the inside of domestic kettles. It's the light travertine coating on the riverbed that gives the water its astonishing blue-green glow. Be sure not to walk barefoot on it, however; travertine is horrendously sharp stuff.

In the days when it was known to the park service as **Bridal Veil Falls**, Havasu Falls used to be a long broad expanse of water, which explains the solidified sheets and curtains of travertine that run right across its wide brim. Then a flash flood punched out a notch right in the centre, through which the falls now gush to either side of a small outcrop that's knitted together by a frail cottonwood sapling.

Side trails off the main path lead down to an idyllic shaded "beach" beside the largest, deepest pool, where the ceaseless roar makes conversation difficult, but swimming is all but irresistible. Cross to the far side of the river, traversing the travertine dams that divide the various terraces, to reach a group of picnic tables standing in a cottonwood grove at the mouth of a side canyon.

Havasu Campground

A short distance beyond Havasu Falls, two miles down from Supai village, you finally reach **Havasu Campground**, set in an especially narrow and high-walled segment of the canyon. Once a tribal burial ground, this site was only added to the reservation in 1975, having originally been considered to be too rich in mineral deposits to be left to the Indians.

Today, the campground stretches for around three-quarters of a mile, through an area where the cottonwood trees are finally recovering after major damage in the 2008 flood. Although villagers are barred from the campground in summer, groups of horses stand tethered at the entrance, waiting to carry campers back up the hill.

Mooney Falls and the Colorado River

Havasu campground is brought to an abrupt end by the precipitous, and once again luridly turquoise, 196ft **Mooney Falls**. This natural barrier was long regarded, even by the Havasupai, as impassable. Its modern name comes from an unfortunate prospector who fell to his death here in 1880, after a rope snagged as he was being lowered to the bottom. It took several months before his companions managed to bore through the travertine to retrieve his body, which lay by then beneath a fresh coating of limestone.

The trail to the bottom remains little better today. Having scrambled down travertine ledges to reach the two successive tunnels that drop through the cliff face, you come to a sheer section that was blasted away in a 1993 flood, and now consists

6

of a vertical series of footholds aided by an iron chain fixed into the rock. The prospect of having to climb back up is terrifying enough to make many hikers turn back at this point; if you press on, there are also two steep ladders to contend with. Assuming you do make it to the bottom, you'll find that the pools and swimming holes at the foot of the falls are once again gorgeous.

A long day-hike from the campground continues on for three miles to **Beaver Falls**, a quick-fire set of rapids that's as far as the Havasupai recommend any visitors should try to go. Negotiating an onwards route involves climbing up to and along a high ledge, after which it takes four more miles to reach the Colorado itself. Quite possibly, you'll be greeted by river-runners who prefer to get here the easy way, shooting 157 miles of whitewater from Lees Ferry (see p.303).

ACCOMMODATION AND EATING   HAVASUPAI RESERVATION

Note that accommodation prices do not include the $35 entrance fee.

Havasu Campground Havasu Canyon ☎ 928 448 2121 or ☎ 928 448 2141. Facilities in the creekside campground, which holds around three hundred campers, are primitive in the extreme, though at least safe drinking water is provided by fresh springs in the canyon wall, and a snack stand at the entrance sells fry bread. Tents can be pitched to either side of the creek, which is usually shallow and is in any case crossed by makeshift footbridges; the nicest sites tend to be the furthest from the entrance. There are no showers or phones, and fires are not permitted. Reservations are compulsory. $23.70
Havasupai Lodge Supai Village ☎ 928 448 2111 or ☎ 928 448 2101. Set slightly apart from things on the

edge of the village, close to the canyon wall behind the school, this simple two-storey structure, a functional motel rather than an atmospheric park lodge, holds plain but adequate air-conditioned rooms, without phones or TVs. All sleep four people. Advance bookings are compulsory, and very hard to get between May and October. $159.50
Tribal Café Main Plaza, Supai Village ☎ 928 448 2981. The food, in the only place to get a meal in Supai, is far from exciting, with fried breakfasts, and a lunch or dinner of beef stew, Indian fry bread, or burritos; pretty much everything seems to cost around $10, a little more if you want grated cheese on top. Daily: summer 6am–7pm, winter 8am–5pm.

The Hualapai Indian Reservation: Grand Canyon West

Immediately west of the Havasupai reservation, and similarly inhabited by descendants of the Pai people, **THE HUALAPAI INDIAN RESERVATION** spreads across almost a million acres, bounded to the north by a 108-mile stretch of the Colorado River.

A cluster of overlooks above that river frontage is promoted as **Grand Canyon West**, and also sometimes known as the "**West Rim**" of the Grand Canyon. While it's been tremendously hyped since the construction of the glass-floored **Skywalk** over the

FLYING TO GRAND CANYON WEST

Flight-seeing tours to Grand Canyon West from **Las Vegas** start at around $150 by plane (without landing) or $250 by helicopter. Expect to pay at least $250 by plane or $300 by helicopter for a tour that includes walking on the Skywalk, and around $500 for a helicopter tour that lands down by the river as well.

Note that many flights depart not from Las Vegas itself, but from Boulder City, thirty miles southeast.

Grand Canyon Airlines ☎ 792 835 8484, ⓦ grandcanyonairlines.com.
Maverick ☎ 702 261 0007, ⓦ maverickhelicopter .com.

Papillon ☎ 702 736 7243, ⓦ papillon.com.
Scenic Airlines ☎ 702 638 3300, ⓦ scenic.com.
Sundance ☎ 702 736 0606, ⓦ sundancehelicopters .com.

canyon, it's very far from being a must-see attraction – and it's also extraordinarily **expensive** and time-consuming to visit. If you're an outdoors type, eager to immerse yourself in the magnificent desert wildernesses of the Southwest, this probably isn't for you. If you're happy to pay premium prices for a once-in-a-lifetime thrill, on the other hand, it may be.

Grand Canyon West bears no relation to the canyon at its best. This far west, the canyon is starting to peter out; it lacks the colossal depth and width of its central section, and holds none of the towering mesas, buttes and temples so conspicuous from the South or North Rim viewpoints. Instead, it's essentially a canny piece of marketing aimed at Las Vegas' forty million annual tourists. This is the closest spot to Las Vegas where it's possible to see the Grand Canyon, and most of its visitors are day-trippers who don't realize that this isn't the canyon proper. That said, the West Rim is undeniably an impressive spectacle, and offers several unique experiences, including helicopter flights down to the Colorado, and short river trips, as well as the Skywalk.

6

The one entrance to Grand Canyon West is at the **airport**, a few hundred yards short of the rim. Whether you fly in, or drive yourself this far, you have to join a **bus tour** to reach the Skywalk and other viewpoints, further down the road.

The Skywalk
Eagle Point, a short distance from Grand Canyon West airport

The **Skywalk** is a horseshoe-shaped glass-bottomed walkway that juts out a short way from the rim, four thousand feet above the canyon floor. Whatever impression the publicity may give, it's not on the main canyon rim, and not directly above the Colorado, but on one rim of a narrow, unnamed side canyon, the cliff face on the other side of which bears an uncanny resemblance to a massive eagle with its wings outstretched. Supposedly to protect its glass floor, **cameras are forbidden** on the walkway, so you have to pay an official photographer if you want to capture the big moment.

Guano Point
At the dead end of the road, two miles from the terminal, the unfortunately named **Guano Point** surveys long stretches of the Colorado in both directions. Though the Grand Canyon looks as if it could go on forever, in fact it comes to an end not far beyond the next bend in the river to the west, where it bisects the Grand Wash Cliffs.

The Colorado River
No hiking trail connects Grand Canyon West with the Colorado River below, but many visitors take the four-minute **helicopter** ride down from the terminal. The flight in itself is a major adventure, and it's also a real thrill to find yourself walking down by the river in the depths of the inner gorge.

THE SHEER COST OF VISITING GRAND CANYON WEST

Any independent traveller planning to visit Grand Canyon West needs to be aware that it's much more **expensive** than any other outdoors destination covered in this book. The following charges apply to all independent visitors to Grand Canyon West; if you buy a flight-seeing or other tour from Las Vegas, check exactly what the quoted price includes.

All visitors have to buy at least the $41 Hualapai Legacy package, which covers use of the shuttle buses to reach Eagle Point, Guano Point and Hualapai Ranch, but not the Skywalk, which would cost $15 if bought separately or any food (you're forbidden to bring your own food or drink onto the reservation). The $76 Legacy Gold package additionally includes a ticket for the Skywalk, plus one meal at any of the viewpoints. Having your photo taken on the Skywalk – you can't take your own camera – costs another $20, while a helicopter flight down to the river, where you take a pontoon boat ride, costs $188. Tribal taxes of around ten percent are added to all prices.

Full details can be found on Ⓦ www.grandcanyonwest.com.

A short footpath leads down from the landing site to the river's edge, where wooden jetties act as the base for the pontoons and jet boats that sweep visitors out for a quick swirl on the river. The adjoining beach is the terminus for the Hualapai's one-day rafting trips (see p.303); participants fly out from here.

6

ARRIVAL AND DEPARTURE   GRAND CANYON WEST

By car The best routes to Grand Canyon West approach not from the east via Peach Springs, but on two separate paved roads from the west and south. The busier Pearce Ferry Road heads northeast from US-93, thirty miles north of Kingman and forty miles south of the Hoover Dam. Twenty-eight miles along, you'll turn east on Diamond Bar Road. The other paved route to this same spot, the forty-mile Stockton Hill Road, runs due north from central Kingman to meet Pearce Ferry Road around twelve miles short of Diamond Bar Road. Diamond Bar Road itself climbs for fourteen rocky miles to reach the Hualapai reservation, where the airstrip and Grand Canyon West headquarters lie five miles farther up the road.

Peach Springs

The only town on the Hualapai reservation, **PEACH SPRINGS**, is fifty miles southeast of Grand Canyon West as the crow flies, but not connected to it by road. Instead you have to reach it along Route 66 from I-40, by heading either fifty miles northeast of Kingman, or 35 miles northwest of **Seligman**. Home to just under a thousand of the total Hualapai population of around 1500, Peach Springs is no more than a straggle of buildings along the highway.

ACCOMMODATION   PEACH SPRINGS

Hualapai Lodge 900 AZ-66, Peach Springs ☎ 928 769 2230 or ☎ 888 868 9378, ⓦ www.grandcanyonwest.com. This shiny, modern lodge, prominent in the heart of Peach Springs – *not* at Grand Canyon West – holds sixty good-sized motel bedrooms and a reasonable restaurant, open for all meals. $149

Hualapai Ranch Grand Canyon West ☎ 928 769 2636 or ☎ 888 868 9378, ⓦ www.grandcanyonwest.com. As well as offering horseriding, cowboy-style entertainment and cookouts, this Wild West ranch offers the only overnight accommodation at Grand Canyon West, in well-equipped wooden cabins. Rates shown do not include the Hualapai Legacy package or any other entrance option to Grand Canyon West. $150

The road between the rims

Although the South and North rims of the Grand Canyon stand just eleven miles apart, the shortest driving route between them takes 215 miles, and at least four hours. Very few towns lie along the way, but the scenery is consistently spectacular. Starting from Grand Canyon Village, you follow first Desert View Drive and then AZ-64 east, which runs close to the gorge of the **Little Colorado** (look out for Navajo trinket stalls) until it meets US-89 at **Cameron**. Head north to cross **Marble Canyon** on Navajo Bridge, then continue west on US-89A to **Jacob Lake**, where you take AZ-67 44 miles south to the North Rim. As most of this route is on the Navajo reservation, which observes daylight savings time, for six months of each year clocks at any establishment en route are set one hour later than at the Grand Canyon.

Cameron

Tiny **CAMERON**, which amounts to little more than a handful of buildings, lies a mile or so north of the intersection of AZ-64 and US-89, on the south side of the suspension bridge spanning the Little Colorado River.

The **Cameron Trading Post** here, established in 1911, stocks a huge array of Southwest arts and crafts, from mass-produced trinkets and jeans to genuine Hopi *kachinas* and museum-quality Navajo rugs. While busy with tourists in summer, it remains at heart a trading centre for the Navajo Nation, still conducting some of its business by barter.

Marble Canyon and Navajo Bridge

Fifteen miles north of Cameron, US-160 branches northeast towards Monument Valley, southeast Utah and Colorado via **Tuba City** (see p.51). Continuing north, after another forty miles of emptiness US-89 climbs up the mesa to the right, heading for Page and Glen Canyon Dam (see p.397). US-89A, however, presses on at the foot of the **Echo Cliffs**, to reach **Navajo Bridge** after a further fifteen miles.

There are in fact two Navajo Bridges. The 1929 original is now reserved for pedestrians only; a wider facsimile opened 150ft downstream in 1995. The Colorado at this point cuts through the chasm of **Marble Canyon** – it's such a narrow interruption in the vast flat plains that you can't tell it's there until you're right on top of it.

On the west bank, the **Navajo Bridge Interpretive Center** (daily: April–Oct 9am–5pm; ☎928 355 2319, ⓦglencanyonnha.org) is not so much a visitor centre as a good bookstore, stocking literature about the Glen Canyon region (see p.394).

Lees Ferry

Before the construction of Navajo Bridge, ferries struggled across the river at **LEES FERRY**, six miles north. Mormon elder **John Doyle Lee** was sent to this remote spot – the only place within hundreds of miles to offer easy land access to both banks of the Colorado – in 1871, to set up a ferry service for Mormon missionaries en route south into Arizona. Lee was on the run after the **Mountain Meadows Massacre** in Utah in 1857, when a wagon train of Yankee settlers was slaughtered by a white band clumsily disguised as Indians, Lee among them. He was finally arrested in 1874 and executed in 1877, but his (seventeenth) wife Emma remained here. Determined not to honour Lee, Congress passed a special act to remove the apostrophe from what used to be "Lee's Ferry".

The ferry service was always perilous, with the boats in constant danger of being swept downstream, and was finally abandoned after a fatal accident in 1928. A crucial piece of equipment needed to finish the bridge on the left bank was stranded on the right bank; the only way to get it across was to take it eight hundred miles by road, via Las Vegas.

Lees Ferry marks the confluence of the Paria River with the Colorado; **Paria River Beach**, at the foot of the gently sloping road from Marble Canyon, is the official start of the Grand Canyon. To the south, the broad Colorado picks up speed as it squeezes into Marble Canyon. All Grand Canyon **whitewater rafting** expeditions (see p.303) set off into the canyon from a large parking lot a few hundred yards north, across the Paria; the first point at which boats can get out again is at Diamond Creek, twelve days away by muscle power.

Lonely Dell Ranch

John Lee lived not at the ferry site, but in the much more congenial surroundings of the **Lonely Dell Ranch**, nestled in a fertile curve of the Paria River half a mile up from the confluence. His original **log cabin** stands not far beyond a replanted approximation of his **orchards**, rich with apple, pear, plum and peach trees. For serious backpackers, this marks the end of an epic four- to six-day hike that traces the full length of **Paria Canyon**, starting at the White House trailhead off US-89 between Kanab and Page (see p.366).

The Vermilion Cliffs

West of Marble Canyon, US-89A curves beneath the southernmost section of the **Vermilion Cliffs**, whose soaring sandstone walls glow a magnificent red at sunrise and sunset. Once past the southernmost promontory of the cliffs, the highway runs straight as an arrow across the broad sagebrush desert. Just under forty miles from the river, it hits the Kaibab Mountains and climbs through thick forest for the final eleven miles to Jacob Lake.

Jacob Lake and DeMotte Park

Deep in the pine forest 44 miles north of the North Rim, the crossroads community of **JACOB LAKE** looks more like a Canadian logging camp than anything you'd expect to find in Arizona. In winter, when AZ-67 down to the Grand Canyon is closed by snow, Jacob Lake goes into hibernation; in summer, however, it makes a good living from the constant stream of tourists.

Jacob Lake is named for Jacob Hamblin, a Mormon missionary to the Paiute and Navajo. The Mormons made little use of the forests to the south, however, apart from grazing their cattle in large meadow-like clearings such as **DEMOTTE PARK**, 27 miles from Jacob Lake, along the road to the canyon. The national park entrance is another five miles down the road, with visitor facilities nine miles beyond that.

6

ACCOMMODATION AND EATING — THE ROAD BETWEEN THE RIMS

CAMERON

Cameron Trading Post 466 US-89, Cameron ☏ 928 679 2231 or ☏ 800 338 7385, ☜ camerontradingpost.com. All the rooms in this large motel complex, surrounded by landscaped gardens, are smart; those on the upper floors have large balconies that look out across the Little Colorado. A pleasant dining room with tin ceiling and large fireplace serves all meals, though the food itself is nothing special, with Navajo tacos at around $13 and steaks more like $25 (daily: summer 6am–9.30pm; otherwise 7am–9pm). **$119**

MARBLE CANYON

Marble Canyon Lodge US-89A, not far west of Navajo Bridge, just past the turn-off for Lees Ferry ☏ 928 355 2225 or ☏ 800 726 1789, ☜ marblecanyoncompany.com. More than sixty conventional motel-style rooms, with TVs but no phones, in low-slung buildings in a romantic desert-outpost setting at the foot of the cliffs. In the adequate but unexciting restaurant, open for all meals daily, main dishes cost $10–15, and a Navajo taco salad is $10. **$90**

VERMILION CLIFFS

Cliff Dweller's Lodge US-89A, 6 miles west of Lees Ferry Lodge ☏ 928 355 2261 or ☏ 800 962 9755, ☜ cliffdwellerslodge.com. Built in 1890 as a mocked-up "ancient ruin", now run as a standard-issue Western motel, this little place is geared primarily towards river-runners, and also runs river fishing expeditions, so its restaurant – which has an attractive shady patio – serves a very early start (daily: summer 5am–10pm, winter 6am–9pm). **$90**
Lees Ferry Lodge US-89A, 3 miles west of Marble Canyon Lodge ☏ 928 355 2231, ☜ vermilioncliffs.com. Besides ten appealingly rustic guest cabins of varying sizes,

in a very pretty location, this 1929 compound centres on a friendly little restaurant that serves good food, with main courses costing up to $20, washed down with an extraordinary range of bottled beers (daily: summer 6.30am–10pm; shorter hours in winter). **$90**

JACOB LAKE

Jacob Lake Campground US-89A, just west of intersection ☏ 928 643 7395, ☜ fs.usda.gov. Lovely wooded campground that caters to tent campers only, and is run by the Forest Service, which also has a visitor centre nearby. Closed mid-Oct to April. **$18**
Jacob Lake Inn intersection of US-89A and AZ-67 ☏ 928 643 7232, ☜ jacoblake.com. Sprawling but welcoming complex of timber-frame buildings at the road junction, open year-round. Simple motel rooms and log cabins plus a gas station, a general store, an old-fashioned diner counter, and a restaurant where chicken, trout, or steak dishes cost under $20. Cabins **$108**, doubles **$126**

DEMOTTE PARK

Kaibab Lodge AZ-67, 27 miles south of Jacob Lake ☏ 928 638 2389 in summer, ☏ 928 526 0924 in winter, or ☏ 800 525 0924, ☜ kaibablodge.com. Three different kinds of cabin – cosy older ones with bare wooden floors and paper-thin walls, a few slightly more expensive ones with motel-style trimmings, and three larger family units with their own sitting rooms – set at the edge of an idyllic meadow. A simple restaurant that's open for all meals daily, from breakfast blueberry pancakes to $27 dinner steaks. Closed late Oct to mid-May. Old cabins **$90**, newer cabins **$130**, family units **$185**

The North Rim

Higher, bleaker, and much more remote than the South Rim, and receiving barely a tenth as many visitors, the **North Rim** of the Grand Canyon is accessible to travellers for about half the year. Even in peak season, it offers a sense of splendid isolation; you won't have the place to yourself, but you can still feel as though you're venturing into unexplored wilderness. The canyon itself is significantly different this side of the Colorado. Erosion is much more active: twice as much rain falls, and it freezes more often. As the Kaibab Plateau slopes south, the water flows towards the rim, which has cut twice as far back from the river, so the North Rim is far more indented with massive side canyons. The basic experience of visiting, however, is the same, with a cluster of venerable park-service buildings at **Bright Angel Point**, where the main highway reaches the canyon, and another rim-edge road, on the **Walhalla Plateau** to the east, where drivers can take their pick from additional lookouts.

Once **AZ-67**, the only road in, has been blocked by the first major snow of the winter, the North Rim remains **closed** until the following spring. Although that first snow used to arrive toward the end of October, annual snowfall has been decreasing; these days the closure tends to come at the end of November, and has even been as late as December 19. The one accommodation option on the North Rim, *Grand Canyon Lodge*, continues to operate to a more rigid schedule, opening during the second week of May and closing on October 15. After it closes, the park itself remains open until the snow comes, but no food, gas or lodging other than camping is available, and visitors must be prepared to leave at a moment's notice.

Bright Angel Point

All visitor activity on the North Rim focuses on the rambling, romantic *Grand Canyon Lodge*, a glorified log cabin in classic national park tradition. A short paved trail leads from its left side to the very tip of **Bright Angel Point**. In places, the trail fills the full width of this slender spit of land, with sheer drops to either side. After four hundred yards, you reach the sanctuary of a railed viewing area, backed by massive boulders that daredevils climb in search of solitude. Everyone understandably regards the prospect ahead as one of the great Grand Canyon panoramas, but strictly speaking the canyon itself is all but obscured by the long straight gorge of Bright Angel Canyon, cutting at an oblique angle across your entire field of vision.

Away to the right, you can just about see where it joins the Grand Canyon proper, but none of the Granite Gorge, let alone the Colorado River, is visible. You may hear the sound of rushing water, but it's coming from **Roaring Springs**, much closer to hand at almost 3500ft below, which supplies all the water used by the park on both rims.

Mentally extending the line of Bright Angel Canyon across to the far side reveals the fault continuing up to the South Rim, though it's hard to spot a sign of life at Grand Canyon Village, eleven miles away, until the sun goes down and the lights start to flicker. That simple turn of the head also traces the easiest trans-canyon hiking route – the **North Kaibab Trail**, which drops down to the Colorado on this side via Roaring Springs and Bright Angel canyons, and climbs up via the matching Bright Angel Trail across the river. On foot, that's a 24-mile one-way hike.

On a clear day, looking directly ahead, you can see far beyond the South Rim to the San Francisco Peaks near Flagstaff. The highest point on the horizon, Mount Humphreys, is 62 miles distant and 12,633ft high.

Cape Royal Road

Apart from Bright Angel Point, all the North Rim's **canyon overlooks** are ranged along the eastern edge of the **Walhalla Plateau**. This long, high headland is reached by turning east onto **Fuller Canyon Road**, three miles north of *Grand Canyon Lodge*. At a junction five miles along, **Point Imperial Road** branches off to the left, while **Cape Royal Road** winds into the cool dense woods to the right.

Even if your time is limited, it's well worth driving the full fifteen miles from the junction to **Cape Royal**, at the end of Cape Royal Road. From there, an even, paved footpath leads first to **Angels Window**, a natural archway just below the top of a rocky

6

spur. As you approach, you can look through it all the way down to the Colorado River. An extremely narrow railed pathway that detours off the main trail a little further along leads onto the top of the "window", for views across to the flatlands of the Navajo reservation. Two broad, green-trimmed stretches of river are visible from this point, including the foaming Unkar Creek Rapid.

Views from **Cape Royal** itself, a couple of hundred yards further along the main trail, extend much further west – virtually the full 360 degrees, though the intervening ridge immediately west obscures Bright Angel Point. This is the only Walhalla viewpoint from which you can see the central portion of the Grand Canyon, with major landmarks like Wotan's Throne and Vishnu Temple straight ahead, and Brahma and Zoroaster temples off to the right. The canyon is much narrower here, so flat-topped **Cedar Mountain** is very conspicuous, just above the South Rim.

Other possible halts along Cape Royal Road include **Walhalla Overlook**, a mile or so from the end, where a very short forest trail ends at the foundation walls of a small Ancestral Puebloan dwelling place. **Roosevelt Point**, halfway between Walhalla and Fuller Canyon Road, looks across Marble Canyon toward the Echo Cliffs.

6

Point Imperial

The highest spot along either rim of the entire canyon, at 8803ft, **Point Imperial** is reached by a spur road that climbs three miles northeast from the intersection of Fuller Canyon and Cape Royal roads. A long red sandy ridge pokes out from beneath the overlook, with a stark butte at the end, while to the right is the thickly wooded ridge that ends at Cape Royal. Looking down, the landscape is as dry as dust, a labyrinth of spurs and buttes in which it's virtually impossible to guess which is the main gorge of the Colorado. The plateau of the Navajo reservation on the far side is almost three thousand feet lower, so it seems to stretch forever, pierced by further chasms and gorges. To the southeast, at the site of the proposed Grand Canyon Escalade (see p.310), the Little Colorado emerges from its own canyon to join the main onward rush of the Colorado.

North Rim hikes

Hikers on the Grand Canyon's North Rim should take the same precautions – and be as aware of their capabilities – as their counterparts on the South Rim (see p.311). There tends to be less scope for getting into difficulties here, however, as almost all the North Rim trails suitable for day-hiking stay atop the plateau. On the only route that descends into the canyon itself, the **North Kaibab Trail**, hiking to the river and back in a single day is completely out of the question – it's a 28-mile round-trip with a 6000ft change in elevation.

North Kaibab Trail

Trailhead: 2 miles north of Grand Canyon Lodge • Day-hike to Supai Tunnel 4 miles round-trip, 3–5hr; day-hike to Roaring Springs 9.4 miles round-trip, 7–9hr; Phantom Ranch 14 miles one-way, with overnight stop at Cottonwood Campground 6.8 miles down

Some version of the **North Kaibab Trail**, following Bright Angel Creek down to the Colorado, has been in use for over a thousand years. Its current route, which starts by descending through Roaring Springs Canyon from a roadside trailhead, was established in the late 1920s. Parking at the trailhead is limited, but an early-morning **hiker shuttle** service leaves *Grand Canyon Lodge* at 5.45am and 7.10am daily, until the road closes for the winter, costing $8 for the first person in each group, plus $5 per additional passenger.

Planning a day-hike on the North Kaibab, it's easy to be overambitious; the distances might not sound that large, but the gradient is steep from the word go. Many people go no further than the **Coconino Overlook**, just 1.4 miles down through the fir forests, a high rocky vantage point from which you can see the junction of Roaring Springs and Bright Angel canyons. The gorgeous waterfalls at **Roaring Springs** come after another 3.6 miles, during which the trail burrows through the **Supai Tunnel**, crosses the suspended **Redwall Bridge**, and makes some spectacular cliffside traverses. Water from the springs is pumped up to the *Lodge* and also piped over to the South Rim, but there's enough left over to tend the "gardens" downstream that were originally planted by the Ancestral Puebloans.

The well-shaded **Cottonwood Campground**, 2.5 miles beyond the springs, is a major way station for trans-canyon hikers. The highlight of the final seven-mile segment to **Phantom Ranch** (see p.314) is lacy **Ribbon Falls**, reached via a short spur trail a mile past the campground.

Rim-edge trails

The ten-mile **Ken Patrick Trail**, the best canyon-edge trail near Bright Angel Point, alternates dramatic views with dense forest as it leads from the North Kaibab Trailhead all the way to Point Imperial. The four-mile **Uncle Jim Trail** branches off it half a mile along, to reach a viewpoint that overlooks the North Kaibab Trail, while the **Widforss Trail** heads the other way, west from the inland end of Bright Angel Point to the tip of the next headland along.

6

ARRIVAL AND DEPARTURE

By car The only road to the North Rim – AZ-67, which leaves US-89A at Jacob Lake – is usually blocked by snow for most of the winter.

By public transport The only public transportation to serve the North Rim is the Transcanyon Shuttle (☏ 602 638 2820, ⓦ trans-canyonshuttle.com). Schedules vary, but in recent years two vans have been in operation daily, one leaving Grand Canyon Village on the South Rim in the morning, reaching *Grand Canyon Lodge* on the North Rim around midday, and then returning to the South Rim in the afternoon, and the other making the equivalent round-trip from the North Rim to the South and back again. A one-way trip takes 4hr 30min and costs $85, while the round-trip is $160; reservations required.

INFORMATION AND TOURS

Visitor centre At the entrance to *Grand Canyon Lodge* (mid-May to mid-Oct daily 8am–6pm; ☏ 928 638 7864, ⓦ nps.gov/grca).

Permits Request or pick up backcountry camping permits (see p.317) at the North Rim Backcountry Office, just over a mile up the highway from *Grand Canyon Lodge*, not far north of the campground. Daily 8am–noon & 1–5pm; ☏ 928 638 7868.

Tours No organized sightseeing tours are available at the

THE NORTH RIM

North Rim, and there's no equivalent to the viewpoint shuttle buses that operate along the South Rim.

Mule rides A desk in *Grand Canyon Lodge* handles reservations for mule rides (☏ 435 679 8665, ⓦ canyonrides.com). A one-hour rim-edge ride costs $40, while two half-day options – either along the rim to Uncle Jim Point or down the North Kaibab as far as the Supai Tunnel – cost $80. No full-day rides or overnight trips.

ACCOMMODATION AND EATING

Deli in the Pines Grand Canyon Lodge ☏ 928 638 2611. Little windowless cafeteria, serving deli sandwiches or salads for around $7 and pizza either by the slice or whole pie ($15–20). Daily: mid-May to Aug 10.30am–9pm, Sept to mid-Oct 11am–8pm.

★ **Grand Canyon Lodge** ☏ 480 337 1320 or ☏ 877 386 4383, ⓦ grandcanyonforever.com. Guest rooms are not in the lodge itself but in individual cabins and larger motel-style blocks. Most are ranged over the quiet, well-wooded hillside beside the approach road. Each of the well-appointed Western Cabins has a full-size bathroom and a porch and can sleep up to four people; the four that stand close enough to the rim to offer canyon views cost $10 extra per night, which makes them fabulous value, but very difficult to reserve. The more spartan Frontier Cabins can accommodate three guests each and have smaller bathrooms, while the similar Pioneer Cabins have two separate bedrooms. In addition, a couple of two-storey blocks located furthest from the lodge hold twenty motel rooms apiece, each with a queen bed and private bathroom. Only the Frontier Cabins and the motel rooms have telephones. Reservations for all are available up to thirteen months in advance, and are absolutely essential. Cancellations are often available at short notice, so keep calling if you can't

get a room or the precise kind of room you want. Motel rooms $130, Frontier Cabins $138, Pioneer Cabins $181, Western Cabins $207

Lodge Dining Room Grand Canyon Lodge ☏ 928 638 2611, or ☏ 928 645 6865 out of season, ⓦ grandcanyonlodgenorth.com. The room itself, with its soaring timber ceiling, is elegant and impressive, and if you get a window table (assigned at random), you'll enjoy awesome canyon views. As for the classy resort cuisine, mains such as grilled salmon with prickly pear cactus or shrimp pomodoro cost around $20, and prime rib and steaks more like $30. Lunch options, at $10–12, centre on sandwiches, light grilled specials and salads, though there's also an all-you-can-eat buffet, while breakfast can either be a full buffet for $14 or à la carte. Service is friendly rather than formal, and the staff seem admirably keen to answer the same old canyon queries from every table. Reservations are accepted only for dinner, when they're essential; book your table as early in the season as possible, as trying to do so once you arrive is liable to be way too late. Daily 6.30–10am, 11.30am–2.30pm & 4.45–9.45pm.

★ **North Rim Campground** 1 mile north of Grand Canyon Lodge, reservations ☏ 877 444 6777, ⓦ recreation.gov. This very pleasant campground holds

87 car-camping sites spaced out through the forest, but no RV hook-ups. Although all vehicle sites are often reserved in advance, additional room is always available for walk-ins and cyclists without their own vehicles. Closed Nov to mid-May. $18

Rough Rider Saloon Grand Canyon Lodge ☎ 928 638 2611. This rough-hewn bar, stocked with a wide range of beers and liquor, has a separate early-morning incarnation as an espresso bar doling out coffee and pastries. Daily 5.30–10.30am & 11.30am–11pm.

DIRECTORY

Camping equipment Sold at the General Store, opposite *North Rim Campground*.
Laundromat and showers Near *North Rim Campground*. Daily, laundry 7am–10pm, showers ($1.50) 7am–8pm.
Medical help There is no health clinic on the North Rim.

Call ☎ 911 for emergencies.
Petrol Near *North Rim Campground* (daily 8am–5pm).
Post office In *Grand Canyon Lodge* (Mon–Fri 8am–noon & 1–5pm).

The Arizona Strip

By any logic, you'd expect the **Arizona Strip** – the anomalous area sandwiched between the North Rim of the Grand Canyon and the Utah state line – to belong to Utah rather than Arizona. In 1864, Mormon leader Brigham Young called on Congress to grant the Mormons all territory that lay within two degrees of latitude of either side of the Colorado; the boundary was drawn instead along the 37th parallel, and that remains the Utah–Arizona border. Repeated attempts to incorporate the Strip into Utah failed, largely because this remote region became a stronghold of renegade Mormons who didn't accept their church's abandonment of multiple marriage (see p.475). Effective isolation from the state authorities of both Utah and Arizona suited these die-hard polygamists just fine.

Virtually no roads cross the Strip, and those that do link just a few tiny, secretive and often semi-derelict hamlets. Although you have to pass this way to complete a full tour around the Grand Canyon, the majority of visitors tend to be racing between the Grand Canyon and the national parks of southern Utah. Few are aware that they're missing perhaps the most spectacular section of Grand Canyon National Park: the **Tuweep** district, home to two stunning overlooks at **Toroweap Point** that provide a rare opportunity to see the canyon's innermost core.

Le Fevre Overlook

Between mile-markers 590 and 591 on US-89A

At the point where Hwy-67 north of Jacob Lake drops off the edge of the Kaibab Plateau, the roadside **Le Fevre Overlook** offers tremendous views across southern Utah. Tier upon tier of cliffs rise one behind the other into the distance, making it clear why geologists call the entire region the **Grand Staircase**. First comes the red sandstone of the Vermilion Cliffs, the formation pierced by Zion Canyon (see p.352); next are the White Cliffs, which form the Kolob Canyons district of Zion National Park; and beyond them, forty miles away, stand the softer Pink Cliffs, sculpted into the hoodoos of Bryce Canyon (see p.368).

Fredonia

The largest town on the Arizona Strip, **FREDONIA** stands thirty miles northwest of Jacob Lake on US-89A. With the bigger and much more interesting community of **Kanab** a mere seven miles north, across the Utah border (see p.364), it's hard to see why anyone would choose to spend the night here, but Fredonia does have a few small motels.

Pipe Spring National Monument

Just off AZ-389, 13 miles west of Fredonia · Daily 8am–5pm · $7 per person · ☎ 928 643 7105, ⓦ nps.gov/pisp

Pipe Spring National Monument marks the site of one of the very few water sources on the Arizona Strip. Ownership of this precious spring has been much contested; Mormon rancher Dr James Whitmore, who appropriated it from the Paiute in 1863, was killed three years later by Paiute and Navajo raiders. The Mormons subsequently enclosed the spring in a fort, known as **Winsor Castle**. They retained control until it was declared a national monument in the 1920s, as much because it stood halfway between the Grand Canyon and Zion national parks as for any intrinsic interest.

Pipe Spring is surrounded by, but distinct from, the **Kaibab Paiute Indian Reservation**. The buildings remain in good condition and serve as a rather unenthralling museum of early ranching life, of most appeal to students of Mormon history.

Colorado City

AZ-389 continues northwest from Pipe Spring, making it the most direct route from the North Rim to the I-15 interstate between Las Vegas and Salt Lake City. A mile or so before it reaches Utah, a spur road to the right runs up to **COLORADO CITY**, set beneath the towering bluffs of the Vermilion Cliffs. This tiny community is renowned as the stronghold of a breakaway group of **Mormon polygamists**, who have been able to live outside the law thanks partly to their sheer remoteness, and partly to their ability to flit across the state line to the linked community of **Hildale** in Utah.

A surreal-looking place, Colorado City is laid out with a small grid of extremely broad streets that see very few cars but plenty of gingham pinafores. Massive homes built to house multiple marriages and even more multiple families stand on every corner, and with much of the male population currently in jail, on the run or hounded out of town, you're only likely to see female faces. As young women are forbidden to cut their hair before marriage, most are surmounted by extraordinary swept-back quiffs. Everyone will assume that you're a magazine journalist hoping to write a sensational article about polygamy, and there's no encouragement to linger.

Toroweap

61 miles southwest of AZ-389 via BLM road 109, the Sunshine Route, or 90 miles southeast of St George, Utah, on the Main Street Route · ⓦ nps.gov/grca

The Arizona Strip holds one tremendous prize for visitors equipped to venture off the paved highways: **Toroweap Point**, the only place where you can drive to the very lip of the canyon's Granite Gorge and peer down sheer 3000ft cliffs to the Colorado River. As the crow flies, it's slightly under sixty miles west of Bright Angel Point, but by road it's almost 150 miles. Even a fleeting visit requires at least six hours of painstaking driving on gravel roads, which for most of the year are passable only in **high-clearance 4WD vehicles**. Conditions vary day to day, so check at national park visitor centres and on the park website before you set off. If you get the go-ahead, carry plenty of food, water and gas, plus whatever you'd need if forced to spend a night in the backcountry, and of course pack a spare tyre and emergency repair kit.

There are two main routes. The eastern **Sunshine Route**, which remains open all year, starts by following **BLM road 109** south from AZ 389 seven miles west of **Fredonia**, then runs for 61 miles southwest, while the more scenic but longer western **Main Street Route** takes a total of ninety miles from **St George**, Utah, but is closed by snow in winter. Both routes eventually converge to enter the **Tuweep Area** of Grand Canyon National Park. Five very rough miles on, a free **primitive campground**, where no water is available, holds nine sites, for which you have to have a backcountry camping permit (see p.317), specifically designated for *Tuweep Campground*.

THE EXTRAORDINARY SAGA OF COLORADO CITY

In the early years of the twenty-first century, exposé after exposé revealed that despite its dependence on state and federal funding, Colorado City was the virtual fiefdom of the **Fundamentalist Church of Latter Day Saints**, run by the self-styled "Prophet" **Rulon Jeffs**. Not only did he assign the town's young women, often in their early teens, as brides to his middle-aged and already multiply married cronies – and conduct the wedding ceremonies himself – but he also presided over a system in which hundreds of young men, their own children, were run out of town as they came of age so they could not become rival bridegrooms. Many ended up as homeless addicts in neighbouring communities.

After Rulon's death in 2002, his son **Warren Jeffs** succeeded him as Prophet, and within a week married all but two of his father's nineteen wives (though not his own mother). After a federal warrant for Warren's arrest was issued in 2005, on charges of sexual conduct with a minor and conspiracy to commit sexual conduct with a minor, he spent fifteen months on the run, on the FBI's "Ten Most Wanted" list.

Along with many of the town's menfolk, Jeffs fled to a linked polygamist community in Eldorado, Texas. He was, however, arrested in Nevada in 2006, and found guilty in St George in 2007 of two charges of first-degree rape for authorizing the marriage of a fourteen-year-old girl to her nineteen-year-old cousin. His Utah conviction was overturned in 2010, but he was then extradited to Texas, where he was sentenced to **life imprisonment** in 2011 on two charges of sexual assault of a minor.

Colorado City itself is still in complete chaos. Evidence of widespread financial fraud resulted in the dismantling of the church's property holdings, but its inhabitants and law enforcement officials continue to refuse to implement or respect court decisions, and Jeffs' influence is said to remain as strong as ever.

Toroweap Overlook
1 mile beyond Tuweep Campground

What doesn't quite sink in until you reach the end of the road at Toroweap is that this is an utterly unique segment of the Grand Canyon. Everywhere else, there are effectively two canyons in one, consisting of a towering rim that's separated by mighty cliffs and, as a rule, a broad plateau, from the deep, narrow chasm that holds the Colorado River. Here, that high outer rim is absent on the north side of the river, and the road extends right to the brink of the Granite Gorge.

This wide, rocky hilltop, a mile beyond the campground, is the **Toroweap Overlook**, which at 4600ft is the lowest viewpoint within the national park. The view may lack the usual buttes and pyramids or labyrinthine spurs and mesas, but tiptoe to the southern edge of the parking lot, and the ground suddenly drops 3000ft from your feet. Though you can see the river approaching from the east and flowing away to the west, it's so directly below that you may have to lie full length and peep over the edge to see it right here.

Lava Falls Overlook
5 minutes' hike west from Toroweap Overlook

The view of the Colorado River from the west-facing **Lava Falls Overlook**, turning from green to blue as it recedes towards the horizon, and interspersed with churning white rapids, is so spellbinding that you may not at first notice the most awesome feature of the landscape. Straight ahead, a colossal black **lava cascade** spills over the North Rim and pours down to within a few feet of the Colorado. On at least eight separate occasions, volcanic eruptions here have filled the Grand Canyon to a depth of as much as 2330ft, and thus blocked the Colorado. The largest flow, around 1.2 million years ago, created the long-vanished Prospect Dam, which backed the river up to form a lake that stretched all the way east to Lees Ferry. It took an estimated 23 years to fill to the brim; then the Colorado burst over the top and, eventually, wore the dam entirely away.

Southern Utah

ANGELS LANDING, ZION NATIONAL PARK

Southern Utah

Southern Utah is a peculiar combination of the mind-boggling and the mundane. Its scenery is stupendous, a stunning geological freak show where the earth is ripped bare to expose cliffs and canyons of every imaginable colour; unseen rivers gouge mighty furrows into endless desert plateaus; and strange sandstone towers thrust from the sagebrush. With one or two honourable exceptions, on the other hand, the tiny Mormon towns scattered across this epic landscape tend to be boring in the extreme. Each has its cluster of characterless motels and dull-as-ditchwater diners; they're not unfriendly places, but finding ways to while away your evenings can truly tax the imagination.

Most visitors therefore spend as much time as possible **outdoors**. Southern Utah has the greatest concentration of **national parks** in the US; in fact there have been serious proposals for the entire area to become one vast national park. The five parks that currently exist are not necessarily the most beautiful or spectacular spots – their boundaries, the result of devious behind-the-scenes wrangling, exclude lands prized by the ranching and mining conglomerates. Taken together, however, they make an ideal focus for a tour of Utah, each with its own well-maintained infrastructure of hiking trails and scenic overlooks.

In southwest Utah, **Zion National Park** centres on an awe-inspiring and richly fertile canyon, backed by barren highlands of sun-scorched white sandstone, while **Bryce Canyon** is a roaring inferno of flame-like orange pinnacles. Over to the east, **Arches** holds an eroded desertscape of graceful red-rock fins and spurs, on a more manageable scale than the astonishing hundred-mile vistas of neighbouring **Canyonlands**. Both lie within easy reach of **Moab**, a dishevelled former mining town that's now Utah's hippest destination. The fifth park, **Capitol Reef**, stretches down the massive rainbow-tinted Waterpocket Fold in the heart of the region, pierced by slender, ravishing canyons.

Lesser-known but equally dramatic wildernesses include **Dead Horse Point** and **Muley Point**, on the eastern side of the state, and vast **Grand Staircase–Escalante National Monument** to the west. The most spellbinding wonder of all, **Glen Canyon**, has been drowned since the 1960s beneath **Lake Powell**, an elongated reservoir whose turquoise waters, lapping desultorily against the red desert rocks, have become a playground for houseboaters and jet-skiers.

MULEY POINT

Highlights

❶ **Zion Canyon** Whether you admire it from the roadside, or hike up its soaring walls, Zion is pure magic. **See p.352**

❷ **Bryce Canyon** Towering incandescent sandstone hoodoos make this one of the most extraordinary-looking places on earth. **See p.368**

❸ **Calf Creek Falls** An easy trail leads to a magnificent waterfall that's the gem of Grand Staircase–Escalante National Monument. See **p.384**

❹ **The Great Gallery** Eerie ancient pictographs, hidden deep in a remote section of Canyonlands National Park. **See p.412**

❺ **Sunset at Delicate Arch** The hike up to this free-standing natural arch is the crowning glory of a visit to Arches National Park. **See p.420**

❻ **Rafting in Canyonlands** Penetrate the mysterious wilderness at the heart of Utah on float trips down the Green or Colorado rivers. See **p.427**

❼ **Muley Point** Though not in a national park, this seldom-visited viewpoint is perhaps the finest in all of Utah. **See p.434**

❽ **Goosenecks State Park** The convolutions of the San Juan River near Monument Valley have to be seen to be believed. **See p.435**

HIGHLIGHTS ARE MARKED ON THE MAP ON PP.344–345

SOUTHERN UTAH

0 — 25
miles

HIGHLIGHTS

1 Zion Canyon
2 Bryce Canyon
3 Calf Creek Falls
4 The Great Gallery
5 Sunset at Delicate Arch
6 Rafting in Canyonlands
7 Muley Point
8 Goosenecks State Park

N

▲ Salt Lake City

28

89

650

50

70

● Fillmore

257

FREMONT
INDIAN
STATE PARK

● Richfield

● Sevier

Loa

24

Bicknel

15

89

62

● Beaver

Junction

21

62

U T A H

20

AQUARIUS
PLATEAU

Hell's
Backbone
Road

130

● Parowan

● Panguitch

Escalante

148

Red
Canyon

12

Cedar
City

Brian
Head

143

12

Hatch

Tropic

56

Cedar Breaks
Nat. Mon.

BRYCE
CANYON
NAT.
PARK

2

● Cannonville

KAIPAROWITS
PLATEAU

Mountain
Meadows
Massacre
Site

Kolob
Canyons

14

KODACHROME
BASIN
STATE PARK

Grand
Staircase-
Escalante
National
Monument

● Pine Valley

ZION NAT.
PARK

1

Glendale

Skutumpah Road

18

● Virgin

Orderville

9

● Pahreah

Snow
Canyon

Hurricane

Springdale

Mt. Carmel
Junction

89

9

Rockville

St. George

59

Coral Pink
Sand Dunes

● Kanab

Coyote
Buttes

● Paria Canyon

Wahwe

Virgin River

Las Vegas

● Colorado City

● Fredonia

Pipe Spring
Nat. Mon.

89A

Vermilion
Cliffs
National
Monument

Lees
Ferry

89

KAIBAB-PAIUTE
INDIAN RESERVATION

389

Grand
Canyon-
Parashant
National
Monument

A R I Z O N A

Jacob Lake ●

CLOSED IN WINTER

GRAND
CANYON
NAT. PARK

89A

89

67

Colorado
River

Grand Canyon South Rim & Flagstaff ▼

Grand Canyon North Rim

> The time in **Utah** is one hour later than **Nevada** all year round, and one hour later than **Arizona** between April and October; from November to March, it's the same as Arizona.

The defining topographical feature of southwest Utah is the **Grand Staircase**. Named by pioneer river-runner John Wesley Powell, it consists of a series of plateaus, stacked tier upon tier, that climb from the North Rim of the Grand Canyon. The **Chocolate Cliffs**, near the Arizona state line, are followed by the dazzling **Vermilion Cliffs**, then the **White Cliffs** – a 2000ft wall of Navajo Sandstone, best seen at Zion Canyon – the **Grey Cliffs**, and finally the **Pink Cliffs** of Bryce Canyon. Although these rocks took a billion years of sedimentation to form, the staircase itself has only been created in the last twelve million years, by the general upthrust of the **Colorado Plateau**, which stretches away to the east.

7 The southwest corridor

Now the most accessible and densely populated area of southern Utah, the far **southwestern corner** was a forbidding prospect for early explorers. In October 1776, close to modern Cedar City, two Spanish priests, fathers Domínguez and Escalante, despaired of finding their way to California and headed back towards Santa Fe. Not until 1830 did the **Old Spanish Trail** establish a permanent route west, and it was another twenty years before Brigham Young ordered Mormon settlers to establish a string of towns at the foot of the **Hurricane Cliffs**.

The largest of those towns, **St George** and **Cedar City**, stand fifty miles apart on I-15, the busy interstate that links Las Vegas with Salt Lake City. Both depend on tourism for their livelihood, catering especially to visitors to Zion National Park.

St George

Spreading beneath a long sandstone escarpment, nine miles north of Arizona, the venerable Mormon town of **ST GEORGE** has grown from a population of ten thousand in 1970 to almost eighty thousand today. While this influx, largely of retirees, has made St George cosmopolitan by Utah standards, anywhere else it would seem like a conservative backwater, albeit with a surprising number of motels.

St George was named not for England's dragon-slaying patron but for a Latter-day saint, Apostle George A. Smith, who was sent with 309 families to establish a colony here in 1861. With the original plan being to make Utah self-sufficient in **cotton**, this appropriately southern region became known as "**Utah's Dixie**". However, cotton from the Deep South flooded the market after the Civil War, and St George switched to other crops instead. It also became a winter refuge for ageing Mormon elders such as Brigham Young, whose much-restored adobe **Winter Home** still stands at 200 North 100 West, complete with period furnishings and artefacts (daily 9am–dusk; free).

Mormon Temple

490 South 300 East • **Temple** Closed to visitors • **Visitor centre** Daily 9am–9pm • Free • ☎ 435 673 5181, ⓦ ldschurchtemples.com /stgeorge

Pride of place among St George's broad thoroughfares and sturdy well-spaced homes belongs to the gleaming white **Mormon Temple**, the only LDS temple completed during Brigham Young's lifetime. Young presided over its dedication shortly before his death in 1877, and half fortress, half cathedral, it was a defiant statement that the settlers were here to stay. As with all Mormon temples, non-Mormons can't go inside the building itself; staff in the adjoining **visitor centre**, however, may be so eager to convert you as to make the problem how to get out, not how to get in.

TRAVELLING AMONG THE MORMONS

For many visitors, a trip to Utah serves as their first encounter with the **Mormon Church**, which claims something over sixty percent of the state's three million residents, and fifteen million adherents worldwide. The word "Mormon" is no more than a widely accepted nickname for members of the **Church of Jesus Christ of Latter-Day Saints** (hence the adjectival abbreviation **LDS**), taken from their main work of scripture, the Book of Mormon.

The two most obvious ways in which Utah's Mormon heritage impacts upon travellers are in its notoriously arcane **alcohol laws** and its ponderous if logical system of **addresses**. Although tourists in small-town Utah can still find it hard to get a drink, regulations regarding the sale of alcohol have been relaxed in recent years. In most towns, at least one **restaurant** is licensed to sell beer, wine and mixed drinks to diners, and it may also be licensed to sell beer in its bar or lounge. However, you won't be shown a cocktail menu, or even offered a drink, unless you specifically ask. With the exception of low-strength beer, sold in supermarkets and grocery stores, takeaway bottled drinks can only be purchased in State Liquor Stores and Package Agencies. For full details, see ⓦ abc.utah.gov/laws.

Most Mormon towns are laid out on a **grid**, usually centred on the intersection of Main and Center streets. Streets north and south of that point are named "100 North", "200 South", and so on, and similarly to east and west. Thus the **address** "165 North 300 West" pinpoints a spot on 300 West, between 100 North and 200 North.

7

ARRIVAL AND DEPARTURE   ST GEORGE

By bus 2 daily Greyhound buses between Las Vegas and Salt Lake City stop outside *Texaco Minute Mart* at 1572 S Convention Center Drive (☎435 673 2933), while the St George Shuttle connects with Las Vegas a dozen times daily (☎435 628 8320, ⓦ stgshuttle.com; $39).

INFORMATION AND TOURS

St George Welcome Center 1835 S Convention Center Drive, near I-15 exit 8 (Mon–Sat 10am–6pm; ☎435 634 5747 or ☎800 869 6635, ⓦ utahstgeorge.com). It's in the foyer of the Rosenbruch Wildlife Museum (ⓦ rosenbruch.org), an unremarkable collection of taxidermied animals.

Bus tours Red Rock Shuttle (☎435 635 9104, ⓦ redrockshuttle.com) offers one-day bus tours to Zion ($100) and Bryce ($150), plus cheaper shuttle trips.

ACCOMMODATION AND EATING

With forty-plus motels along St George's main drag, finding a room is usually easy, though summer weekends get busy. Dining out tends to be a question of which highway steakhouse or fast-food outlet catches your eye; there's plenty of choice, but not much excitement.

Best Western Coral Hills 125 E St George Blvd ☎435 673 4844, ⓦ coralhills.com. Central chain motel, a local veteran kept nicely up to date, with sizeable rooms and indoor and outdoor pools. $83

Dixie Palms 185 E St George Blvd ☎435 673 3531, ⓦ dixiepalmsmotel.com. St George's best-value budget motel, a simple family-run place with fifteen freshly remodelled rooms. $50

★Hawaiian Poke Bowl 170 W 900 South ☎435 628 7653, ⓦ hawaiianpokebowl.net. That's *poke* as in the delicious Hawaiian speciality of marinated raw tuna, cut into succulent boneless chunks and served over hot rice,

starting at $9 per substantial bowl. This friendly, lunch-only fast-food joint also offers barbecued *kalua* pork. Mon–Fri 11am–3pm.

The Pizza Factory 2 W St George Blvd ☎435 628 1234, ⓦ stgeorgepizzafactory.com. The pick of assorted lively restaurants in the central Ancestor Square development (including the same owners' *Pasta Factory*); opt for a special like garlic chicken, or pick your own toppings. With typical pizzas or calzones costing $15, it's relatively expensive, but the ambience makes it worth it. Mon–Sat 11am–9.30pm.

Snow Canyon State Park

Hwy-18, 7 miles north of downtown St George • Daily 6am–10pm • $6 per vehicle • ☎435 628 2255, ⓦ stateparks.utah.gov

One of Utah's most attractive state parks lies within ten minutes' drive of St George. Don't expect to see snow in **Snow Canyon State Park**; it's a classic red-rock canyon, where the most distinctive feature is the layer of jet-black lava that flakes off the tops of its sun-baked sandstone pinnacles, left by a volcanic eruption 10,000 years ago.

The park's six-mile **scenic drive** drops left from Hwy-18, winding down past overlooks and rounded monoliths to reach the **park headquarters** after a couple of miles. An excellent hour-long (1.5-mile) round-trip hike, the **Hidden Pinyon Trail**, starts a hundred yards further on. After cutting between the craggy outcrops into a peaceful meadow, it zigzags up and over a ridge to enter a heavily eroded landscape reminiscent of Canyonlands' Needles District (see p.413).

If it's too hot to hike, pull off another two miles on instead, where a cluster of lurid **red sand dunes** threatens to drift across the road. Kids especially will enjoy sliding down the slopes, which doubled for central Asia in Howard Hughes' movie *The Conqueror*, which starred John Wayne as Genghis Khan. When it was filmed in 1954, the Nevada Test Site, just ninety miles west, was at its busiest; Wayne, Hughes and three-quarters of the cast died from cancers widely believed to have been caused by fall-out from the nuclear explosions.

ACCOMMODATION   SNOW CANYON STATE PARK

Snow Canyon Campground Alongside park headquarters ☎800 322 3770, ⓦutahstateparks .reserveamerica.com. Reservations for this pleasant, shaded 36-space campground are recommended in spring and fall, but things get quieter during the hottest months. Without hook-ups **$20**, with water and electricity **$25**

Cedar City

CEDAR CITY, 53 miles northeast of St George on I-15 – and twenty miles north of the Kolob Canyons section of Zion National Park (see p.362) – is now half the size of its upstart rival. Like St George ten years later, it too was founded in Mormon Utah's precarious early years, as the church bid for self-sufficiency. The Mormons urgently needed **iron**, so when scouting parties discovered iron ore in southern Utah, the **Iron Mission** was dispatched to establish Cedar City in November 1851. Most of its first inhabitants were British miners; they soon succeeded in smelting iron from the hills to the west, but the venture ultimately failed, and ore mined locally has been shipped out for processing ever since.

Cedar City's major tourist attraction is the summer-long **Utah Shakespeare Festival**, a semi-professional event held on the campus of the Southern Utah State University since 1962.

Frontier Homestead State Park Museum

585 N Main St • Daily: June to early Sept 9am–6pm; early Sept to May 9am–5pm; closed Sun Nov–Feb • $3 • ☎ 435 586 9290, ⓦ utah.com/frontier-homestead-state-park

Historical markers dotted around Cedar City detail the former locations of its social hall, hospital, brickyard and flour mill, but only the **Frontier Homestead State Park Museum** offers much insight into local history. Apart from rusty nuggets, this warehouse-like museum is filled with nineteenth-century horse-drawn vehicles, including wagons, sleighs and hearses.

INFORMATION AND FESTIVAL   CEDAR CITY

Visitor centre 581 N Main St (Mon–Fri 8.30am–5pm, Sat 9am–5pm; ☎435 586 5124 or ☎800 354 4849, ⓦscenicsouthernutah.com).

Utah Shakespeare Festival Southern Utah State University 351 W Center St (tickets $23–68; ☎435 586 7878 or ☎800 752 9849, ⓦbard.org). Running from late June to end of Oct each year, this prestigious festival usually features nine or so productions, with three or four Shakespeare plays among assorted others.

ACCOMMODATION AND EATING

Abbey Inn 940 West 200 North ☎435 586 9966 or ☎800 325 5411, ⓦabbeyinncedar.com. Very well equipped modern motel, just off the interstate at exit 59, with almost a hundred good-value rooms and an indoor pool. **$140**

Best Western Town and Country Inn 189 N Main St ☎ 435 586 9900, ⓦ bwtowncountry.com. Smart chain motel, north of the centre, charging reasonable rates for spacious rooms in separate wings either side of 200 West St, and holding a large heated indoor pool. **$130**

The Grind Coffee House 19 N Main St ☎ 435 867 5333. Busy, very central local rendezvous, serving pastries and sandwiches for under $10 as well as coffee, and putting on regular live music. Mon–Sat 7am–6pm, Sun 8am–2pm.

Cedar Breaks National Monument

Scenic drive Late May to mid-Nov (or first heavy snowfall) • **Visitor centre** Late May to mid-Oct daily 9am–6pm • $5 per person • ☎ 435 586 0787, ⓦ nps.gov/cebr

The most direct route to Bryce Canyon from Cedar City, **Hwy-14**, climbs steadily onto a densely wooded plateau via a narrow gorge east of town. While Cedar City itself stands at an elevation of 5800ft, the plateau rises a further five thousand feet. The scenery along Hwy-14 is therefore spectacular, with views that stretch south to encompass all of Zion National Park.

Fifteen miles along, shortly after the highway enters the **Dixie National Forest**, the pink, white and orange rocks of **Cedar Breaks National Monument** stand immediately below the forest that tops the high ridge to your left. Cedar Breaks is a sort of pocket version of Bryce Canyon, where erosive forces have scooped a natural amphitheatre into the hillside and filled it with brilliantly coloured limestone formations. While it lacks Bryce's opportunities for hiking, it's well worth seeing if you're in the area.

7

The road through Cedar Breaks, **Hwy-148**, branches north from Hwy-14 nineteen miles out of Cedar City. When it's clear – it's usually snowbound between late October and mid-May – you can choose between four similar cliff-edge viewpoints. The southernmost, **Point Supreme**, is the best, with pinnacles rising from the orange canyon floor at your feet and sweeping views to the south and west. The park's small and very scenic **campground** stands nearby; fifteen of its sites are first-come, first-served, the other ten can be reserved (mid-June to mid-Sept; $18; ⓦ recreation.gov).

Although you can hike for short distances along the rim at both Point Supreme and **Chessmen Ridge**, a mile or so north, no trails descend into the formations.

The road to Zion

The main approach to Zion National Park is via **Hwy-9**, a lovely thirty-mile drive that heads east from I-15 seven miles northeast of St George (see p.346). None of the pioneer villages along the way is especially exciting, but the scenery is great, with the cottonwood-fringed Virgin River to the south and gigantic sandstone cliffs to the north. Be warned that you have to pay the admission fee to Zion if you want to continue east beyond the park on Hwy-9.

Hurricane and around

The westernmost town along Hwy-9 is **HURRICANE**, ten miles east of the interstate at the junction with Hwy-59. While not actually on the Virgin River, it's connected to it by a seven-mile canal, conceived in 1863 but not completed until 1906. Only then was the town site settled, and it's still much the same agricultural community more than a hundred years on. Seven miles **east** of Hurricane, close to the foot of the **Kolob Terrace Road** north into the Zion backcountry (see p.362), is tiny little **VIRGIN**, which is notorious for having introduced a law making gun ownership compulsory.

Southeast from Hurricane, Hwy-59 takes twenty miles to reach the Arizona border, marked by the polygamist community of **Colorado City** (see p.338). The **North Rim** of the Grand Canyon is a hundred miles beyond (see p.332).

Rockville and around

By the time you reach **ROCKVILLE**, ten miles beyond Virgin, you're getting very close to the wonders of Zion, and it's hard to keep your eyes on the road at all. Rockville is nevertheless a pretty little town, with several small-scale B&Bs along its tree-lined central avenue.

South across the river from Rockville, turn right off Bridge Road onto an unpaved track, to reach the photogenic little ghost town of **GRAFTON**. Mormon farmers abandoned the struggle against floods and Indians around 1900, but Rockville residents have kept an eye on it ever since. It's also been touched up by Hollywood crews shooting movies like *Butch Cassidy and the Sundance Kid*; this is where Paul Newman rode a bicycle to the tune of "Raindrops Keep Fallin' On My Head".

Just beyond Rockville, Hwy-9 veers north at the confluence of the North and East forks of the Virgin River, and heads for the maw of Zion Canyon.

7

Springdale

SPRINGDALE, the last town before Zion, spreads along a leafy three-mile stretch of the Virgin River just south of the park entrance. Rounding the final corner into town presents you with your first stupendous view of Zion Canyon itself. Settled at the same time as the canyon, in the 1860s, Springdale is now almost exclusively devoted to pampering tourists.

With its clashing, discordant architecture, Springdale is a classic national park gateway community, but somehow it still has considerable appeal. Here and there green fields nestle right up to the highway – some even hold grazing cattle – while the occasional private home punctuates the motels, inns and restaurants. The whole ensemble is dwarfed into insignificance by the magnificent canyon walls that loom on either side of the river. By the time you've driven up and down the only road, Zion Park Boulevard, a couple of times, you'll have seen everything Springdale has to offer, but this lively, friendly community makes by far the nicest base in southwest Utah, and spending three or four nights here is no hardship whatsoever.

ACCOMMODATION

SPRINGDALE

As Zion Park Boulevard runs straight between the burgeoning canyon walls towards the park, all the **motels** and **B&Bs** along the way offer the same attractive views. Although Springdale remains busy between late April and late October, only in high summer does it tend to sell out completely. Standards are high, but with the word about Springdale's many charms well and truly out, so too are prices. It's also possible to stay in the park itself, either at *Zion Lodge* (see p.361), or in the two large campsites near the park entrance (see p.361).

Cliffrose Lodge & Gardens 281 Zion Park Blvd ☎ 435 772 3234 or ☎ 800 243 8824, ⓦ cliffroselodge.com. The closest motel to the park makes a pretty place to stay, with separate units spreading down the hillside to the cottonwoods that line the Virgin River. It also has its own pool and wild gardens. **$209**

★**Desert Pearl Inn** 707 Zion Park Blvd ☎ 435 772 8888 or ☎ 888 828 0898, ⓦ desertpearl.com. Absolutely gorgeous hotel, ranged alongside the Virgin River just outside the park, with superb views. From the parking areas it may look like a regular motel, but the rooms themselves are extremely stylish, with high ceilings, wooden floors, huge windows and balconies, and face a lovely turquoise pool with hot tubs. **$229**

Harvest House 29 Canyon View Drive ☎ 435 772 3880, ⓦ harvesthouse.net. Very classy B&B in a modern home, tucked beneath the sandstone cliffs. Four en-suite rooms, pleasant gardens, an outdoor hot tub, and gourmet breakfasts. **$135**

Holiday Inn Express Springdale 1215 Zion Park Blvd ☎ 435 772 3200, ⓦ hiexpress.com/springdale. Modern convention-style hotel at Springdale's southern end. Built as the *Best Western Zion Park Inn* and now entirely refurbished, it offers spacious rooms with panoramic windows, plus a heated swimming pool. **$202**

Zion Canyon Campground 479 Zion Park Blvd ☎ 435 772 3237, ⓦ zioncamp.com. Set beside the river half a mile outside the park, this commercial campground shares both its site, and facilities like its laundry, pool and pizzeria, with a *Quality Inn* motel. Very much dominated by RVs, it makes a poor choice for tent campers. Tent sites **$39**, RVs **$49**

EATING

Baby Sumo 792 Zion Park Blvd ☎435 233 2103, ⓦbabysumospringdale.com. This Japanese steakhouse and sushi joint, which has indoor seating plus a large patio, adds a welcome dash of variety to Springdale's dining scene; pretty much any combination of meat and seafood is likely to cost $20–30. Mon–Sat 4.30–10pm.

Bit & Spur Restaurant & Saloon 1212 Zion Park Blvd ☎435 772 3498, ⓦbitandspur.com. Hectic dinner-only Mexican restaurant and bar, facing the red-rock cliffs at the south end of town, where the food has a creative edge, and the margaritas are top-notch. Chillie-rubbed steak costs $28, and a *chile relleno* (stuffed chillie) just $14. From the outdoor patio, you can watch the moon rise over the mountains. Daily 5–10pm.

Deep Creek Coffee 832 Zion Park Blvd ☎435 767 0272. The perfect place to greet the new day in Zion, this friendly coffeehouse is buzzing from early morning onwards, serving $6–9 home-made scones, waffles and sandwiches, and fresh smoothies to go with its powerful java. Daily 6.30am–2pm.

Spotted Dog Cafe Flanigan's Inn, 428 Zion Park Blvd ☎435 772 0700, ⓦflanigans.com. Reasonably priced restaurant, attached to a motel at the park end of town, that's much larger than it looks – the open-air patio is just the tip of the iceberg. Dinner specials such as braised lamb shank ($21) or trout ($18) have a zesty, continental feel, and they also offer a substantial breakfast buffet. Daily 7–11am & 5–10pm.

Whiptail Grill 445 Zion Park Blvd ☎435 772 0283, ⓦwhiptailgrillzion.com. Central diner that spreads across a broad streetfront patio from a former gas station, and serves tasty Mexican dishes like squash and goats'-cheese enchiladas, or fish tacos, typically costing around $12–16, with organic and wheat-free options. Be sure to try the home-made chips and salsa. Daily noon–9pm.

Zion National Park

Zion National Park is divided into two main sections: Zion Canyon (see p.352) and Kolob Canyons (see p.362) • $30 per vehicle, $25 motorcyclists, $15 cyclists and pedestrians; valid 7 days • ☎435 772 3256, ⓦnps.gov/zion

With its soaring cliffs, riverine forests and cascading waterfalls, **ZION NATIONAL PARK** is Utah's most conventionally beautiful park. On first glance it's also the least "Southwestern", in that its centrepiece, **Zion Canyon**, is a lush oasis that feels far removed from the otherworldly desolation of Canyonlands or the downright weirdness of Bryce. Like California's Yosemite Valley, it's a spectacular gorge, squeezed between mighty walls of rock and echoing to the sound of running water. Also like Yosemite, it's prone to be crowded in summer, though a seasonal shuttle bus system alleviates traffic problems.

Too many visitors see Zion Canyon as a quick half-day detour off the interstate, as they race between Las Vegas and Salt Lake City. Beautiful though the **Scenic Drive** through the canyon may be, Zion deserves much more of your time than that. Even the shortest **hiking trail** within the canyon can help you escape the crowds, while a full day-hike will take you away from the deceptive verdure of the valley and up onto the high-desert tablelands beyond. In addition, two less-used roads – **Kolob Canyons Road** and the **Kolob Terrace Road** – lead into remoter sections of the park.

With elevations varying from under 4000ft at the visitor centre to almost 9000ft at Kolob Peak, Zion is home to a bewildering array of **flora and fauna**. Its vegetation ranges from the cottonwoods and box elders along the Virgin River to the ponderosa pines and stunted piñons that cling to the high sandstone mesas. Desert flowers and cactuses provide unexpected flashes of colour in the uplands, as do darting hummingbirds. Resident animals include the bank beaver (so named because it doesn't build dams) and the generally retiring Western rattlesnake.

Summer is by far the busiest season, and that's despite temperatures that frequently top 100°F (38°C), and the violent thunderstorms, concentrated in August and a week or so to either side, that bring most of Zion's scant fifteen inches of annual rainfall. If you can, come in April or May to see the spring flowers bloom – though

7

the mosquitoes are also at their peak – or in September and October, to enjoy the fall colours along the river. The park remains open throughout the winter, but daytime highs drop below 40°F (4°C) in January, while the nights tend to be freezing from November to March.

Zion Canyon

The North Fork of the **Virgin River** has taken thirteen million years to carve **Zion Canyon** into the southern edge of the Markagunt Plateau. For most of the year, the Virgin meanders placidly along the valley floor, en route to the Colorado. After summer thunderstorms, however, run-off from the mesa-tops is channelled down into the canyon, turning it into a torrent that carries as much as 600,000 cubic yards of rock and sand – a good-sized city block – in a single day. Each winter, the canyon walls grow further apart, as water that seeps through the porous sandstone turns to ice and shears mighty chunks off the cliffs.

As you approach from the south on Hwy-9, thirty miles east of I-15, it's abundantly clear that the **Markagunt Plateau** – named for a Paiute word meaning "highland of trees", it's one of the seven high plateaus that make up the Colorado Plateau in southern Utah – constitutes the next rung of the **Grand Staircase** (see p.337). Zion Canyon serves as a handy cross section to display the different layers of rock. At the lowest level, around the South Entrance, the thick red **Vermilion Cliffs** rise from a barely discernible bed of the even older and darker Moenave and Kayenta strata, deposited at the bottom of swampy seas 200 million years ago. The 2000ft walls of the canyon itself are composed of rusty **Navajo Sandstone**, once a mass of drifting sand dunes.

The first of the colossal peaks that crown the chasm look down from either side of the South Entrance. The **West Temple** is one of two similar mountains here whose summits consist of neat little box-shaped mesas crowned with pine trees, while the **Watchman** stands guard to the east. At this point, the walls stand well over a mile apart; officially the canyon doesn't begin for another few miles, but within just ten miles north it dwindles to a mere twenty feet wide.

Whether you access Zion Canyon using the park shuttle buses, or visit in winter when you're free to use your own vehicle, you'll garner your first impressions from the highway. The main road – **Hwy-9**, which becomes the **Zion–Mt Carmel Highway** – passes plenty of dramatic formations as it climbs east towards Bryce, but Zion's most memorable monoliths are ranged on either side of the dead-end **Scenic Drive**, which runs for six miles north alongside the Virgin River.

Zion Canyon visitor centre

Immediately inside the South Entrance • Daily: late April to late May & Sept to mid-Oct 8am–6pm; late May to Aug 8am–7.30pm; mid-Oct to late April 8am–5pm • Free • ☎ 435 772 3256, ☏ nps.gov/zion

As well as providing detailed information on all aspects of Zion, the park's spacious and partly open-air **visitor centre** is the base for its two **shuttle bus** routes (see p.361), and thus an essential stop for all visitors. In summer, when the parking areas alongside are usually full by 9am, you may well have to park in Springdale and take a shuttle from there. Free handouts include the park newspaper and maps; the bookstore stocks detailed guides; permanent displays explain geology and history; and there's a detailed schedule of talks, slide shows and guided hikes.

7

A HISTORY OF ZION CANYON

Zion Canyon may seem like an oasis, but it has never held much of a **human** population. Its earliest inhabitants were probably semi-nomadic hunter-gatherers, who from 500 AD onwards grew crops beside the Virgin River. Known to archeologists as the **Virgin Anasazi**, they are regarded as less sophisticated cousins of the Ancestral Puebloan groups to the east; living in small bands, they never built "cliff palaces" or pueblos. By 1250 AD, drought had driven them out of Zion, leaving isolated pictographs on the canyon walls as their only monument.

During the ensuing centuries, **Paiute Indians** migrated seasonally throughout southern Utah, harvesting the few resources the desert could offer. They saw Zion, however, as the abode of Wai-no-Pits, the evil one, who cursed them with disease, and Kainesava, the God of Fire, whose lightning blazed from its high peaks. When **Mormon missionary** Nephi Johnson arrived in 1858 to explore the Upper Virgin River, the Paiute would lead him no further than Oak Creek, at the canyon entrance.

Isaac Behunin, who set up a log cabin in 1862 where *Zion Lodge* now stands, dubbed the canyon "**Little Zion**" in the hope that it would serve as a place of refuge for beleaguered Mormons. Some of his fellow farmers were soon taking things too easy; Brigham Young thundered that their indulgence in tobacco and wine made the name "**Not Zion**" more appropriate. In the long run, Zion Canyon proved too narrow to support farming, and its main commercial role was simply as a route through which timber sawn on the high mesas could be shipped out to the plains. Between 1900 and 1930, logs lowered from "Cable Mountain" built the fine homes of such towns as St George.

John Wesley Powell's second Colorado expedition in 1872 (see p.403) had brought the scenery of Zion to national attention, under the Paiute name of "Mukuntuweap Canyon". The canyon itself was set aside in 1909 as Mukuntuweap National Monument; a larger area became Zion National Park in 1919, and the Kolob Canyons district was added in 1956.

Although most visitors assume Mormon settlers gave Zion's pinnacles and promontories their portentous names – the **Court of the Patriarchs**, the **Great White Throne**, **Angels Landing** and so on – they were coined by a visiting Methodist minister in 1916.

In its first full year, 1920, the park attracted fewer than four thousand visitors. Trails and campgrounds remain little changed since their construction during the 1930s, but visitor numbers have climbed to well over three million per year.

ZION CANYON

EATING
Red Rock Grill 1

ACCOMMODATION
South Campground 2
Watchman Campground 3
Zion Lodge 1

7

Zion Human History Museum

Left of Hwy-9, not far north of visitor centre • Daily: mid-March to late April & Oct–Nov 10am–5pm; late April to late May 10am–6pm; late May to Aug 9am–7pm; Sept 9am–6pm • Free • ☎ 435 772 3256, ⓦ nps.gov/zion • Served by Canyon Shuttle bus route

Despite its name, the **Zion Human History Museum** does not focus exclusively on people. Instead, the photo displays inside concentrate as much on plants and animals as they do on humans, and while it's not an essential stop, it does hold some interesting background material.

The Scenic Drive

Served by Canyon Shuttle bus route; accessible to private vehicles between November and mid-March only, precise dates vary each year

It's possible simply to drive through the southern end of Zion Canyon and continue east towards Bryce. To see its full glory, however, you have to follow the **Scenic Drive** north beside the Virgin River for the full six miles until the canyon walls squeeze so tight together that it can't continue any further. Only in winter can you do so in your own vehicle; for most of the year, you're obliged to use the canyon **shuttle buses** instead (see p.361).

For half a mile north of the visitor centre, Hwy-9 parallels the west bank of the river. The highest of the peaks to the left, collectively known as the **Towers of the Virgin**, is the **Altar of Sacrifice**, named somewhat gruesomely for the blood-like streaks of rust that seem to flow from its flat crest.

The highway crosses the river just beyond its confluence with **Pine Creek**. Guarded by the **Sentinel** to the west and the **East Temple** to the east, this marks the start of Zion Canyon proper. It's also the site of the Canyon Junction shuttle stop, and the northern trailhead of the **Pa'rus Trail** (see p.357). The **Scenic Drive** branches left on the far side of the bridge, while Hwy-9 carries on eastwards.

From here on north the canyon is so narrow, and its walls so steep, that there's barely room to squeeze in a road. Erosion remains as active as ever, and the Scenic Drive has had repeatedly to be rebuilt after landslides. The first major roadside pull-out comes after 1.7 miles, facing the **Court of the Patriarchs**, where peaks named for Abraham, Isaac and Joseph stand arrayed around a small canyon west of the river. A mile further on you reach the meadows of **Zion Lodge** (see p.361). In the height of summer, the crowds can be overwhelming, but for most of the year it's a pleasant, shady place to break the day, perhaps enjoying an ice cream or snack on the lawns. It's also the trailhead for the popular **Emerald Pools Trail** (see p.357).

Zion Canyon's one designated picnic spot is the **Grotto**, less than a mile beyond the lodge near the foot of the **West Rim Trail** (see p.357). To one side stands **Red Arch Mountain**, named for a natural archway created in 1880 when a vast chunk of the mountain suddenly collapsed and obliterated a cornfield. To the other, the long western flank of the **Great White Throne** looks from this angle neither white nor especially dramatic.

During the next mile the road passes the trailhead for **Weeping Rock** (see p.359) and the **East Rim Trail** (see p.359), as well as several unnamed pull-outs where paths lead down to the river. The best views of all come just under five miles from the start of the Drive, as it completes its long curve around the river's "Big Bend". The lookout here faces the northern aspect of the Great White Throne, framed between the slender neck of **Angels Landing** (see p.358) to the right and the pipe-like formations of the **Organ** to the left. Glowing at sunset, the throne is utterly majestic.

A mile or so on, the Scenic Drive – and the shuttle bus route – comes to an end at the start of the mile-long **Riverside Walk** (see p.359) toward the Narrows. This general area is known as the **Temple of Sinawava**, after a wolfish deity of the Paiute Indians; the most prominent single rock is the **Pulpit**, standing alone near the west bank of the river.

Zion–Mount Carmel Highway

Open all year • Visit ⓦ nps.gov/zion for current travel restrictions and/or fees for oversized vehicles – such as RVs – and cyclists

The side canyon formed by Pine Creek, half a mile north of the visitor centre, enables Hwy-9 to continue east, a route known as the **Zion–Mount Carmel Highway**. At first it heads straight for the **East Temple** – topped like its larger twin by a forested mesa – but it's soon forced to start tacking its way up the hillside. At the eastern end of each extravagant switchback comes a better view of the enormous **Great Arch** at the head of the canyon. Measuring 720ft wide by 580ft high, this is not in fact an arch at all, but simply a deep alcove, or what's known as a "blind arch".

Finally, the highway burrows into the rock, entering the first and longer of two remarkable **tunnels** that were blasted through the canyon walls in the 1920s. Five "windows" punctuate its one-mile length to let in air and light, but you can't stop to admire the views. All the rubble from the excavation tumbled into Pine Creek far below; the river may seem innocuous, but it cleared the whole lot away within a single year.

Easily seen on the enjoyable **Canyon Overlook Trail** (see p.360), the hot dry plateau beyond the eastern end of the main tunnel feels far removed from the lushness of Zion. These pale, smoothly undulating rocks, capped here and there by strange beehives and hoodoos, are the lithified remains of ancient sand dunes. One huge specimen, crisscrossed with stress lines from eons of erosion and resembling some long-abandoned pyramid, is known as the **Checkerboard Mesa**. It looms south of the highway at a clearly marked turn-off five miles beyond the second tunnel, a quarter of a mile short of the park's East Entrance.

Hiking in Zion Canyon

Every visitor to Zion Canyon should **hike** at least one of its many clearly marked and signposted trails. However, almost all trails except the short Riverside Walk require a stiff climb away from the canyon floor, and with summer temperatures in excess of 100°F (38°C) and elevations of well over 6000ft, it's all too easy to overdo things. Carry plenty of food and drink, and don't simply assume that because you have no trouble walking five miles at home you can do it here, straight up a cliff. Water is available on most trails – although not until around five miles along the West or East Rim trails – but must be purified before use.

As for specific **routes**, avoid the sun by hiking the east side of the canyon in the morning and the west in the afternoon. If you're reasonably fit and have just one day, the best combination is probably an hour or two along the **Riverside Walk** plus a longer climb either to **Angels Landing** on the West Rim Trail or **Hidden Canyon** on the East Rim Trail.

All the trails detailed below set off from either Hwy-9 or the Scenic Drive, but some of the longer ones leave the canyon altogether and end up on backcountry dirt roads. If you're planning a one-way hike, look at the **shuttle board** in the visitor centre, to see if you can swap vehicles with hikers coming in the opposite direction. Both *Zion Lodge* and the Zion Adventure Company (see p.361) also operate commercial **hiker shuttle services**.

Watchman Trail

Trailhead: Visitor centre • 2.7 miles round-trip; 2hr • Elevation change 368ft

Just inside the South Entrance, a right turning leads across the river to the *Watchman* campground and the start of the **Watchman Trail**. This steep mile-long climb switch-backs up a side canyon below Bridge Mountain, then heads back south to loop around a flat promontory below the Watchman itself. Thankfully, it doesn't go right to the top, but its views up the canyon, as well as across to the West Temple and back down to Springdale, tucked among the trees, are a good way to get your bearings when you first arrive. Until around 10am, the canyon walls keep most of the route in shade; later on, it's liable to be baking hot.

ZION HIKING PERMITS

Hiking permits are required for all **overnight** trips in Zion National Park, and for all hikes that require technical equipment, most obviously the **Zion Narrows** (see p.358). Permits are issued for specific wilderness campsites and trails; they do not entitle you to go wherever you choose on the day. They cost $10 for one or two people, $15 for three to seven, and $20 for eight up to the group maximum of twelve. You can pick them up at any visitor centre the day before you hike, and reserve up to three months in advance via the park website, ⓦnps.gov/zion. At the very busiest periods, for the most popular routes, you may have to enter an online lottery to make a reservation (incurring an extra application fee of $5), but around a third of all sites are kept free for walk-in visitors, and made available one day in advance.

Pa'rus Trail

Trailheads: Visitor centre and Canyon Junction • 1.8 miles one-way, 3.5 miles round-trip; 40min one-way, 1hr 20min round-trip • Elevation change 50ft

The gentle, paved **Pa'rus Trail**, also open to cyclists, is a level stroll of almost two miles that connects the two campgrounds either side of the visitor centre with the shuttle bus stop at Canyon Junction. Along the way, it repeatedly crisscrosses the Virgin River. While it lacks the glamour or rewarding destinations of other, more demanding trails in the park, it's a truly delightful walk, especially enjoyable around sunset at the end of a hard day.

Emerald Pools Trail

Trailhead: Zion Lodge • **Lower pool** 1.2 miles round-trip; 1hr • Elevation change 69ft • **Upper pool** 2.2 miles round-trip; 1hr 40min • Elevation change 200ft

The **Emerald Pools Trail**, which starts conveniently from *Zion Lodge*, is every bit as pretty as the name implies. It's also suitable for walkers of all levels, as the lowest of the pools can be seen on a gentle round-trip stroll of little more than a mile, while the highest makes a good objective for a more energetic hike.

On the far side of the footbridge that crosses the Virgin River from the lodge, the pink-paved trail to the right is the direct route to the **lower pool**. After an easy climb through the forest, with views straight up the main canyon, it cuts left into Heaps Canyon, and soon reaches a huge overhang of red rock, streaked black by a broad cascade of water. The almost constant flow collects in pools that tend be muddy red rather than emerald green; the overhang is deep enough for the trail to circle inside them, running behind the waterfall. Be very careful if you attempt to wade across a flowing stream at any stage; several hikers have been swept to their deaths after slipping on algae, even in just a few inches of water.

From this point, the trail becomes confusing, with countless possible routes made by lost or blundering hikers. If you're pressed for time, head back the way you came; alternatively, continue straight ahead, along the shelf on the canyon wall, and in just over half a mile you'll drop back to cross the river at the Grotto picnic area, half a mile north of *Zion Lodge*.

Most hikers head instead for the **upper pool**, by following a narrow path through a cleft in the gigantic split boulder to the left. Having first doubled back to the top of the waterfall, where the stream bubbles out of the woods to spill across a lip of slickrock, you then take the spur trail to the right on the far side.

A hot, hard climb of not much more than five minutes is rewarded by a delightfully cool seep-fed pool at the foot of the monumental outer walls of the canyon. Climbing any higher is out of the question, but this is a good place to linger, with its small sandy "beach" and plenty of shade.

Angels Landing and the West Rim Trail

Trailhead: The Grotto • **Angels Landing** 5.4 miles round-trip; 4hr • Elevation change 1488ft • **Horse Pasture Plateau** 11 miles round-trip; 10hr • Elevation change 2813ft

Serious hikers and backpackers rate the **West Rim Trail** as Zion's most compelling challenge. Even if you have nothing to prove, its views and variety make it well worth attempting, but it's not a hike to undertake lightly. The first couple of miles involve a gruelling 1500ft climb out of Zion Canyon, while to reach the obvious day-hike destination, **Angels Landing** – a five-mile round-trip from the valley floor – you have to brave a terrifying knife-edge ridge.

The trail starts across the river from the Grotto picnic area, half a mile north of the lodge. As it winds ever more steeply towards the sheer canyon wall, it seems that no onward route could possibly exist, but in the end it switchbacks several times and cuts back into a crack in the rock. Unless you've made a very early start, you'll have been out in the sun for a long time by now, and the cool shade of this narrow crevice comes as a merciful relief.

However, things soon get worse; beyond the brief flat stretch of **Refrigerator Canyon** you're confronted by a severe set of switchbacks known as **Walter's Wiggles**. Constructed during the 1920s, these serve as a ladder up an otherwise impassable cliff. At the top lies **Scout Lookout**, a tranquil patch of sand with views up and down Zion Canyon and a population of scavenging chipmunks that feast on the remains of countless well-earned picnics.

Daredevil day-hikers are invariably drawn to the spur trail from Scout Lookout to **Angels Landing**. What you're letting yourself in for is obvious from the outset; the trail sets off along the top of the steep promontory straight ahead, with awesome drop-offs to either side, and only token stretches of metal chain offer the illusion of security. If you think you're the brave one, take a look to see if there are any climbers scaling the sheer rock face on your left. Your goal is a knee-shaking half-mile on, with a

HIKING THE ZION NARROWS

Hiking the **Zion Narrows** – the slender gorge through which the Virgin River enters Zion Canyon from the north – has acquired a reputation as *the* thing every Zion visitor simply must do. Don't underestimate the challenge, though. It's a very demanding **wilderness experience**, much more suitable for extreme-sports devotees than for casual hikers.

A ravishing "slot canyon" squeezed between mighty sandstone cliffs and interspersed with fertile grottoes, the Narrows is undeniably spectacular. However, you can only trek its full length by following the river downstream from a remote trailhead that's usually only accessible in a four-wheel-drive vehicle. For at least ten of the sixteen miles of hiking from there, you can expect to be wading thigh- or even shoulder-deep in **cold, fast-flowing water**, struggling with every step to find a foothold on the slippery rounded boulders of the streambed. While it's possible to complete the whole hike in a single, gruelling day – the average hiking time is **twelve hours** – it's more realistic to plan to camp overnight along the way.

Specialist **equipment** is essential, in the form of waterproof, super-grip footwear, neoprene socks, and a walking stick or two, complemented between October and May by a drysuit. As it's not a question of whether, but of how often, you'll fall over, you'll also need zip-lock plastic bags for everything you carry, and since the water isn't drinkable, you'll have to lug that along too.

Though it doesn't have the same kudos among the adventure-sports fraternity, you can also sample the Narrows as a **day-hike** by pushing your way upstream, against the current, from the end of the Riverside Walk, and turning back when you've had enough (the furthest you're allowed to go is the five miles to Big Spring, making a ten-mile round-trip). However, you'll still need all the gear – don't even dream of setting off without it.

For anything more than a day-hike upstream, you have to have a **permit** (see p.356) to hike the Narrows. The park service issues a maximum of eighty such permits per day, of which around half can be reserved in advance, while the rest are available first-come, first-served the day before. Making a reservation does not necessarily mean you'll be allowed to hike; the Narrows is always liable to be closed due to flash floods or wildfires. In principle, the **best times to hike** are in June or from September until early October. July and August see frequent thunderstorms, so the risk of flash floods then is at its highest. In addition, the road to the trailhead is often closed altogether between December and April.

The Narrows is just one among many wonderful hikes on offer in the park, most of which don't require nearly so much planning, expertise, or expense. According to park rangers, its recent popularity is largely due to being heavily promoted by commercial companies. As the Narrows lies inside the national park, local operators can't offer guided trips, but they do rent **equipment** and run **shuttle services** (see p.361).

If you have your own 4WD vehicle – or if rangers advise you that road conditions are suitable for ordinary vehicles – you can get to the trailhead, at Chamberlain's Ranch, by turning left 1.7 miles east of the East Entrance (just east of milepost 46 on Hwy-9), and then following North Fork Road, which in due course becomes a rough dirt track, for around seventeen miles north. The total thirty-mile drive from Zion Canyon takes about one hour thirty minutes.

quarter-mile drop to the canyon floor at your feet and the Great White Throne towering a further thousand feet above you on the far side of the river.

Beyond Scout Lookout, the West Rim Trail climbs steadily out of the canyon. After crossing an expanse of slickrock, perilously close to the rim, it descends into a spectacular high-country valley. This is another side of Zion altogether, rimmed with white cliffs, "checkerboarded" by cross-bed hatching, and scattered with rounded outcrops of layered sandstone. For a couple of miles, the trail picks its way gingerly across the valley and up the far side, twice crossing streambeds that nurture forest glades. Finally, it runs into the monumental wall of red sandstone that marks the head of **Behunin Canyon**, a huge side canyon off Zion Canyon (itself by now way out of view). Doubling back, it clings to the cliff face on an exposed switchback that comes out atop **Horse Pasture Plateau**, three miles up from Scout Lookout. A hundred-yard side trail from the broad overlook at the top leads to the muddy little **West Rim Spring**.

Just to set foot on Horse Pasture Plateau is a stiff target for a day-hike from the floor of Zion Canyon. In the full heat of summer even that would be too much to take on, but the trail continues north for another ten miles, to **Lava Point** off the Kolob Terrace Road (see p.362), with plenty of potential scenic detours en route. This is Zion's most popular overnight backpacking trip, usually done as a two-day expedition, starting from Lava Point and working down, and camping near the southern edge of Horse Pasture Plateau. As with any such overnight hike, a backcountry camping permit is required (see p.356).

Riverside Walk

Trailhead: Temple of Sinawava • 2.2 miles round-trip; 1hr 30min • Elevation change 57ft

Not least because it involves no climbing, the mile-long **Riverside Walk** at the end of the Scenic Drive is Zion's best-loved trail. Having watched the canyon walls converge ever closer, the urge to find out what happens beyond the end of the road is irresistible. You may well have more company than you'd prefer, but the views from the gentle paved footpath are too beautiful for that to matter. While it's easy enough to complete the round-trip in under an hour, you'll enjoy it more if you allow much longer.

Walls of deep red sandstone soar to either side of the river, which is flanked by shimmering cottonwoods that turn a rich gold in the fall. There are even patches of low-lying "desert swamp", where bullfrogs bellow in the rushes and willows thrust from the mud.

Riverside Walk ends where the Virgin emerges from **the Narrows**, overlooked by the mighty **Mountain of Mystery**. For eight miles upstream from this sandy little beach, the river fills the entire gorge, often less than twenty feet wide and channelled between vertical cliffs almost a thousand feet high. As explained in the box opposite, it's possible to wade upstream, against the current, to see the Narrows for yourself, while if you arrive towards sunset, you'll also doubtless encounter plenty of bedraggled backpackers who have hiked here sixteen miles downstream, from Chamberlain's Ranch.

Weeping Rock

Trailhead: Weeping Rock • 0.4 miles round-trip; 30min • Elevation change 98ft

As one of Zion Canyon's easiest short walks, the paved half-mile hike to and from **Weeping Rock** is prone to be overcrowded in summer. Eaten from the canyon wall by a perennial spring, this damp alcove is filled with ferns and tiny flowers; while it comes as a surprise in the desert, however, it's not as beautiful as you may be led to expect.

Hidden Canyon and the East Rim Trail

Trailhead: Weeping Rock • **Observation Point** 8 miles round-trip; 6hr • Elevation change 2148ft • **Hidden Canyon** 3.4 miles round-trip; 4hr • Elevation change 850ft

Rewarding hikes of almost any length can be enjoyed by taking the **East Rim Trail**, which sets off from the Weeping Rock trailhead. Only backpackers who camp overnight on the mesa-top attempt its full 10.5-mile length, and they normally prefer to start from the far end, near the park's East Entrance. However, the strenuous two-mile climb out of Zion Canyon is its most exhilarating segment, and offers the alternative options of continuing all the way up to **Observation Point** if you fancy a full day's hiking, or taking the separate trail into **Hidden Canyon** for a half-day excursion.

After half an hour of ascending along a cement pathway, enjoying ever-improving views of Weeping Rock itself, the East Rim Trail reaches a stiff set of switchbacks. By the time you reach the top of those, you've climbed about half a mile up the face of Cable Mountain, but you're still only halfway up to the mesa. A stone bench here makes a good place to ponder the decision as to whether you should keep on going, or head instead for **Hidden Canyon**, a "hanging canyon" that has yet to cut its way down to the floor of Zion. To reach it, follow a spur trail for a further half-mile, beyond a brief stretch of forest and a hair-raising segment, clinging to a wall of rock, which is enough to deter many would-be canyoneers. The broad "lip" of the canyon, perched 700ft above Zion, turns into a waterfall after heavy rain, while the rounded holes scoured into the slickrock fill with water and life. Strictly speaking, the trail ends here; it's just about feasible to press on into the canyon, but only expert rock climbers have any hope of approaching its head.

If Hidden Canyon sounds too intimidating, you may prefer to keep on switchbacking up the East Rim Trail beyond the Hidden Canyon turn-off. A mile or so further on, deep in wafer-thin Echo Canyon – a "slot canyon" with beautiful walls that drop far below the trail as well as towering above it – the **East Mesa Trail** climbs steeply off to the left, while the East Rim Trail itself continues straight on. Reaching **Observation Point**, two miles along the East Mesa Trail, involves quite a bit more climbing, switchbacking up a mighty sandstone cliff face on a very narrow red-dirt path. Eventually you pick your way through the woods atop the plateau, to be rewarded with breathtaking views all the way down Zion Canyon. The massive cliffs of Cable Mountain and the Great White Throne stare you full in the face, while Angels Landing towers proudly on the far side.

Hikers who choose to stay on the **East Rim Trail** rather than heading for Observation Point also face another mile of climbing out of Echo Canyon, with the possibility of having to negotiate streams en route. Once on top of the mesa, walking becomes much easier, as the trails follow former logging roads. **Stave Spring**, the only perennial water source on the East Rim Trail, is roughly halfway between Zion Canyon, five miles west, and the East Entrance, slightly further southeast. Overnight campers can head southwest at this point, along a trail that soon forks to the summits of **Cable Mountain** – where you can take a closer look at the century-old workings that hauled timber down into Zion (see p.353) – or Deertrap Mountain. Either hike is a six-mile detour from Stave Spring.

Canyon Overlook Trail

Trailhead: Zion–Mt Carmel Highway • 1 mile round-trip, 1hr • Elevation change 163ft

At the eastern end of the long tunnel on the Zion–Mount Carmel highway, alongside the ranger station, steps cut into the rock mark the start of the **Canyon Overlook Trail**. So long as you don't mind edging along the brink of a precipice – at one point the trail consists of wooden planks braced against the cliff face – this offers a fascinating variety of terrain in the space of just half a mile. It's also the only trail described here for which you can access the trailhead in your own vehicle year-round – though so little parking is available that that may turn out to apply in theory only. The scenery en route ranges from fern-filled grottoes fed by seeping water to a bare slickrock mesa topped by tiny hoodoos.

The trail ends at a railed viewing area at the head of Pine Creek Canyon; though you can't see it, you're directly above the Great Arch. Only one of the tunnel's five "windows" is visible in the rock wall to your left, but the road emerges below to zigzag into the valley. Straight ahead is the west wall of Zion Canyon; a helpful sign labels the peaks ranged along the far side of the river, from the ruddy tree-capped West Temple to the paler Sentinel.

ARRIVAL AND DEPARTURE — ZION CANYON

By car Hwy-9 follows the Virgin River for 30 miles east of I-15, and enters the park via the South Entrance, just north of Springdale. Half a mile north, it abandons the river and heads east, to tunnel its way out of the canyon (see p.355).

GETTING AROUND

Between mid-March and late October, and also on weekends in November – precise dates vary each year – all visitors to Zion Canyon, other than guests staying at *Zion Lodge* (see below), have to leave their vehicles either in Springdale or at the main visitor centre and use shuttle buses instead. Frequent services run on two separate loops and are free, and you can get on and off as often as you like.

Zion Canyon Shuttle The in-park shuttle runs between the visitor centre and the end of the Scenic Drive, with nine stops including *Zion Lodge*. It operates between 6am and 9.15pm from mid-May until late September, between 7am and 8.30pm in spring and fall, and from dawn until sometime after dusk in winter.

Springdale Loop Connects Springdale with the visitor centre, with nine stops en route, between 7.10am and 9.45pm in summer, 8.10am and 8.45pm in spring, and 8.10am and 7.45pm in fall. A short walk connects the different shuttle bus systems at the visitor centre; the Springdale buses stop just outside the park, so passengers have to pass through entrance gates on foot to reach the visitor centre and canyon shuttles.

TOURS AND ACTIVITIES

Canyon Trail Rides ☎ 435 679 8665, ⊛ canyonrides .com. Horseback rides in the canyon itself, starting from *Zion Lodge* (March–Oct; daily 3hr rides at 9am & 1.30pm, $90, minimum age 10; daily four 1hr rides $45, minimum age 7).

Zion Adventure Company 36 Lion Blvd, Springfield ☎ 435 772 1001, ⊛ zionadventures.com. Assorted activities just outside the park, such as tubing on the Virgin River, and guided biking, photography, climbing and canyoneering trips, plus Narrows equipment rental from $23 per day; and hiker shuttles, including to Chamberlain's Ranch for $37.

Zion Canyon Field Institute ☎ 435 772 3264 or ☎ 800 635 3959, ⊛ zionpark.org. Hikes, excursions and lectures in the park, covering topics that range from reptiles to basketry, photography to solar energy, and costing from around $45 for a morning class up to $100 for a full day.

Zion Rock and Mountain Guides 1458 Zion Park Blvd, Springfield ☎ 435 772 3303, ⊛ zionrockguides.com. Guided climbing, biking and canyoneering trips in the vicinity of the park; Narrows equipment rental for around $20/day in summer, $35 in winter, and daily hiker shuttles, including to Chamberlain's Ranch for $35.

ACCOMMODATION AND EATING

Red Rock Grill Zion Lodge, Scenic Drive, Zion Canyon ☎ 435 772 7760, ⊛ zionlodge.com. Whether or not you stay at the lodge, it's well worth stopping to eat in its bright, cool, upstairs dining room. The river views will probably linger longer in your mind than its standard breakfasts and lunches, both costing $9–13. Dinners are slightly more sophisticated, featuring steak or trout for $18–27. Cheaper snacks are available all day, downstairs. Daily: summer 6.30–10.30am, 11.30am–3pm & 5–10pm; winter 7–10am, 11am–2pm & 5.30–8pm.

Zion Lodge Scenic Drive, Zion Canyon. Advance reservations ☎ 303 297 2757 or ☎ 888 297 2757, same-day reservations and property phone ☎ 435 772 7700, ⊛ zionlodge.com. This appealing if often overcrowded complex of low-slung wooden buildings, occupying pride of place on lush well-shaded lawns a couple of miles up the Scenic Drive, offers the only food and lodging within the canyon. Stay if you can in one of the forty en-suite cabins, which have gas fireplaces and private porches; the 72 motel rooms are plainer, but still have porches or balconies. Open all year; reserve well in advance, especially in summer. Cabins **$210**, doubles **$220**

CAMPING

South Campground Zion Canyon ☎ 435 772 3256, ⊛ nps.gov/zion. Located, despite the name, just north of the park visitor centre, in a gloriously lush but inevitably somewhat crowded setting alongside the river and the Pa'rus Trail, this first-come, first-served campground is open between late Feb and late Nov only. Arrive early in summer, when it tends to fill by noon daily. Flushing toilets and cold running water, but no showers. **$20**

Watchman Campground reservations ☎ 877 444 6777, ⊛ recreation.gov. Although it's open year-round,

7

this large campground, in a verdant location amid the cottonwoods south of the visitor centre, accepts reservations between March and late November only.

Flushing toilets and cold running water, but no showers. 18 walk-in, tent-only sites; the rest can hold one RV or two ordinary cars. Basic site $20, with electric hook-up $30

Kolob Terrace Road

The only road access to the central uplands of Zion National Park is along **Kolob Terrace Road**, which branches inconspicuously north from Hwy-9 at tiny **Virgin**, fifteen miles west of the park's South Entrance. Especially in its earlier stages, it's a dramatic drive, but unless you have a high-clearance 4WD vehicle, you won't manage the full 43 miles to meet I-15 just south of Cedar City. As ordinary cars have to turn back after just over twenty miles, only long-distance hikers or tourists with a spare afternoon tend to come this way. In addition, the entire road is closed to all traffic in winter.

The road starts by climbing through a dry desert valley, heading for two pyramidal mountains that dwarf the cliffs on the horizon. It reaches Zion after just over seven miles, only to exit almost immediately, and then dips repeatedly in and out of the park. As it next re-enters the park, you get superb views north across **Hop Valley** to the russet and white pinnacle of **Burnt Mountain**. Keen backcountry campers can hike to Kolob Arch from here along the **Hop Valley Trail**, but it's not as easy as it looks; you have to plough through thick sand for most of the way, so the fifteen-mile hike is even more difficult than the route from Kolob Canyons (see p.363).

Soon after you leave the park yet again, twenty miles up from the highway, a dirt road to the right leads 1.7 miles to **Lava Point**, back within the park. As well as being the trailhead for the West Rim Trail, which takes fourteen miles to drop down into Zion Canyon (see p.359), this is a superb vantage point in its own right. Poised four thousand feet higher than the visitor centre, it overlooks a panorama that stretches north to Cedar Breaks and southeast to the Kaibab Mountains, with the monoliths of Zion Canyon mere incidental details in the foreground. There's a **picnic area** and a free, first-come, first-served, six-site primitive **campground** with no water nearby (June–Oct only).

Kolob Canyons

Just off I-15, 161 miles northeast of Las Vegas and 20 miles south of Cedar City • $30 per vehicle, $25 motorcyclists, $15 cyclists and pedestrians; valid for 7 days • ☎ 435 586 9548, ⓦ nps.gov/zion

Despite being easier to reach than Zion Canyon, the **Kolob Canyons**, which have formed part of Zion National Park since 1956, receive far fewer visitors. In all honesty, they're less immediately impressive than Zion Canyon, and you'll only get the most out of the area if you can spare the time and energy to **hike**. If you stay in your car, you can drive to the end of the five-mile road, admire the view of the red-rock canyons, and be back on the interstate within the hour, wondering what the fuss is about.

Kolob Canyons Road twists alongside Taylor Creek and then up through Lee Pass, with countless trailheads and roadside viewpoints en route. Its final parking lot faces across the riverbed to a succession of narrow, red-walled "finger" canyons cut into the west rim of the Markagunt Plateau. Each was carved by a separate tiny stream; one, Hanging Valley, is interrupted by a sheer 1500ft cliff, stranding an isolated patch of thick forest far above the valley floor. In the distance, you may just be able to make out the West Temple, above Zion Canyon.

Footpaths on the far side of the lot lead to a picnic spot in the woods. From here, the half-mile **Timber Creek Overlook** trail runs through low trees along the top of the ridge, to end at a rocky promontory with views over the endless rolling forests.

Taylor Creek Trail

Trailhead: Kolob Canyons Rd, 2 miles from visitor centre • 5 miles round-trip; 4hr • Elevation change 450ft

The **Taylor Creek Trail** follows the Middle Fork of Taylor Creek on a five-mile round-trip to **Double Arch Alcove**, passing long-abandoned cabins built by early homesteaders. The trail grows progressively less distinct before it culminates by climbing into the lush hollow in the canyon wall that lies beneath the Double Arch itself.

Kolob Arch Trail

Trailhead: Lee Pass Trailhead, Kolob Canyons Rd, 3.5 miles from visitor centre • 14 miles round-trip; 8hr • Elevation change 1037ft

Among Zion's very finest hikes, the fourteen-mile round-trip route to **Kolob Arch** only makes an appropriate day-hike for confident, experienced desert hikers. Starting from Lee Pass, it initially follows the **La Verkin Creek Trail** along the drainage of Timber Creek. It can be muddy going, but at least there's usually plenty of water en route (which must be purified before drinking). The first couple of miles, heading south, feature superb close-up views of the finger canyons; you then veer east to meet **La Verkin Creek** itself, just above a waterfall.

Kolob Arch, seven miles along and accessed by the short spur trail that's officially named the **Kolob Arch Trail**, may or may not be the world's longest natural rock span. Like Landscape Arch, in Arches National Park (see p.421), it's approximately 300ft across; no one agrees how to measure arches any more precisely than that, so they're generally considered equals. Camping somewhere nearby (by prior arrangement at the visitor centre) makes for a less gruelling hike and gives you the option of exploring the remote regions that lie farther along La Verkin Creek.

INFORMATION   **KOLOB CANYONS**

Visitor centre Exit 40, I-15 (daily: mid-April to late May and Sept to mid-Oct 8am–5pm; late May to Aug 8am–6pm; mid-Oct to mid-April 8am–4.30pm; ☎ 435 586 9548). As well as providing free hiking advice, rangers also allot 24 numbered backcountry campsites (permit required). No gas or food is available.

East from Zion: US-89

As soon as you leave Zion National Park via its eastern entrance (see p.363), you're out in flat, open ranching country. Eleven nondescript miles further on, Hwy-9 meets **US-89** at Mount Carmel Junction. Turn **north** here if you're heading towards Bryce Canyon, to follow the broad **Long Valley** cut by the **Sevier River**. The only real point in heading **south** on US-89 is to reach Arizona, with the North Rim of the Grand Canyon (see p.332) almost exactly a hundred miles away. A century ago, when Mormons from Arizona would come this way to be married in the temple at St George, this route was known as the **Honeymoon Trail**. The largest town along the highway, **Kanab**, retains a strong Mormon identity, but it also has a back-of-beyond frontier feel and makes a good overnight stop.

Mount Carmel Junction

The eastward progress of Hwy-9 stops when a north–south wall of red cliffs rears up on the far side of the Virgin River. **MOUNT CARMEL JUNCTION** here, at the junction of Hwy-9 and US-89, is a bucolic spot, with cottonwoods lining the river and horses grazing in the meadows to the north. Unless you're ready to stop for the night in one of its two **motels**, however, there's little reason to get out of the car.

ACCOMMODATION   **MOUNT CARMEL JUNCTION**

Best Western East Zion Thunderbird Lodge Hwy-9 & US-89 ☎ 435 648 2203 or ☎ 888 848 6358, ⓦ zionnational-park.com. The larger and fancier of the pair of motels at this isolated road junction, with large rooms plus

a pool, spa, restaurant and even half a golf course. $170
Golden Hills Hwy-9 & US-89 ☎ 435 648 2268 or ☎ 800
648 2268, ⓦgoldenhillsmotel.com. Plain, low-slung

little motel, where some rooms are right beside the river. A
basic diner is open for all meals, with lunchtime sandwiches
well under $10, and dinner mains costing up to $20. $57

Coral Pink Sand Dunes State Park

15 miles south of Mount Carmel Junction • Daily dawn–dusk • $8 per vehicle • ☎ 435 648 2800, ⓦ stateparks.utah.gov/parks/coral-pink •
Access roads leave US-89 4 and 9 miles southeast of Mount Carmel Junction, to meet just before the park itself

Few areas in the Southwest conform so exactly to the popular notion of a desert –
graceful dunes of fine sand, their parallel crests sweeping towards the horizon – as
Coral Pink Sand Dunes State Park. This pseudo-Saharan landscape, a dozen miles
south of Mount Carmel Junction, can be reached via two separate paved
roads off US-89.

The only dune field in the Colorado Plateau lies at the foot of a seven-mile bluff of
the Vermilion Cliffs, which here unusually face northwest. Its sand grains are eroded
from Navajo sandstone, itself originally deposited in the form of dunes.

Hikers who launch themselves from the boardwalk near the park visitor centre usually
find a few minutes of wading knee-deep in sand enough to sate their *Lawrence of
Arabia* fantasies. However, in marked contrast to Utah's federal parks, **off-road vehicles**
are positively encouraged. The park was created in response to campaigns by local
off-road enthusiasts, and plays host to countless formal and informal **dune buggy races**,
most notably each July 4.

ACCOMMODATION   **CORAL PINK SAND DUNES STATE PARK**

Campground Alongside the visitor centre ☎ 800 322
3770, ⓦutahstateparks.reserveamerica.com. The well-
shaded campground remains open all year, though it only
has water in summer. Spending a night here offers the

enticing prospect of seeing not only tiny kangaroo rats,
named for their squatting postures, but, more to the point,
the snakes that prey on them, which are not a danger to
humans. $20

Kanab

Until new roads were pushed through the region in the 1950s, **KANAB**, seventeen miles
southeast of Mount Carmel Junction and just two miles north of the Arizona state line,
was renowned as the most inaccessible town in the US. Now it's a significant tourist
rest stop, poised halfway between the Grand Canyon's North Rim, eighty miles
southeast, and Bryce Canyon, 83 miles northeast.

Kanab started life in 1864 as **Fort Kanab**, a frontier outpost so prone to Indian attacks
that it was abandoned after just two years. Jacob Hamblin founded the town itself in
1870 as a God-fearing ranching community with a sideline in harbouring Mormons
who fell afoul of the federal government, among them several perpetrators of the
Mountain Meadows Massacre. Pulp novelist Zane Grey later cultivated that lawless
image, setting many of his Westerns nearby. Kanab's rugged surroundings also drew
Western film greats, from Tom Mix, who filmed *Deadwood Coach* here in 1924, to
Clint Eastwood, who swept into town with *The Outlaw Josey Wales* in 1976. Kanab
earned the nickname "Utah's Little Hollywood".

With ranching in decline, and the prospect of large-scale coal mining on the
Kaiparowits Plateau to the northeast thwarted by the establishment of Grand Staircase–
Escalante National Monument, Kanab now survives by catering to tourists. US-89 is
lined with an above-par assortment of motels and restaurants, especially concentrated
where it briefly doglegs to run east–west along **Center Street**. A few blocks south,
US-89 proper branches off east towards Page, while US-89A continues south towards
Fredonia in Arizona.

Apart from shopping in its Western-themed souvenir stores, there's almost nothing to
do in Kanab, though hikers may enjoy the views from the **Squaw Trail**, which climbs the

escarpment just north of town. It takes six miles – a hike of up to four hours – to loop back to Kanab, but if time is short you can simply turn around when you've had enough.

INFORMATION

KANAB

BLM field office 669 S US-89A (mid-March to mid-Nov daily 8am–4.30pm; mid-Nov to mid-March Mon–Fri 8am–4.30pm; ☎435 644 1200, ⓦblm.gov/ut). Information on nearby public lands and current driving conditions given out by the Bureau of Land Management.

Grand Staircase–Escalante National Monument visitor centre 745 E Hwy-89A (daily 8.30am–4.30pm; closed Sat & Sun early Dec to early March; ☎435 644 1300,

ⓦblm.gov/ut). If you wake up in Kanab and wonder where everyone is, look no further. First thing in the morning, they're right here, waiting for the daily lotteries for permits to hike Coyote Buttes and Paria Canyon (see box, p.366).

Visitor centre 78 S 100 East (March–Oct Mon–Fri 9am–7pm, Sat 10am–6pm, Sun 9am–4pm; Nov–Feb Mon–Fri 8am–5pm, Sat 8.30am–4.30pm; ☎435 644 5033 or ☎800 733 5263, ⓦvisitsouthernutah.com).

ACCOMMODATION

Aiken's Lodge 74 W Center St ☎435 644 2625 or ☎877 644 2105, ⓦaikenslodge.com. This low-slung option may not look desperately pretty, but it's the ideal budget motel: crisp and clean, right in the heart of town, and with its own pool. **$96**

Canyons Lodge 236 N 300 West ☎435 644 8888 or ☎844 322 8824, ⓦcanyonslodge.com. Vintage motel that's been attractively spruced up with a knowing retro edge, and has an outdoor pool, spacious lawns and free

bicycles for guest use. **$89**

Parry Lodge 89 E Center St ☎435 644 2601, ⓦparrylodge.com. Opened in 1931, Kanab's oldest motel has an undeniable air of romance. Photos of celebrity guests festoon the lobby and restaurant, while nameplates identify the rooms where they slept; you can even bathe in John Wayne's extra-large bathtub. Although it's being progressively upgraded by new owners, *Parry's* isn't *that* great, and some rooms can be dingy and noisy. **$100**

EATING

Nedra's Too 310 S 100 East ☎435 644 2030, ⓦnedrascafe.com. Informal local hangout at the junction of US-89 and US-89A on the south side of town, with a sister restaurant in Fredonia (see p.337). The unifying factor of the Mexican/American menu is the fryer; even the ice cream comes deep-fried. Mexican dishes cost $11–13, steak and seafood $18–22. Daily 7am–9pm.

Rocking V Café 97 W Center St ☎435 644 8001, ⓦrockingvcafe.com. This valiant and largely successful bid to improve Kanab's culinary reputation is housed in a former bank, one of the town's oldest buildings. Burgers, sandwiches and daily "taste of the Planet" specials, like Thursday's chana masala vegetarian stew, go for around $12 at lunch; dinner mains like salmon creole cost $23. Daily 11.30am–10pm; closed Tues & Wed in winter.

East of Kanab: US-89 and Paria Canyon

US-89, which heads due east out of central Kanab, curves northwards into the southern reaches of Grand Staircase–Escalante National Monument (see p.375) as it makes its spectacular 73-mile run to **Page**, Arizona (see p.396). Though not as popular with visitors as the broadly parallel US-89A further south, which allows access to the North Rim of the Grand Canyon, it's still a dramatic drive and has its own potential diversions in the shape of the hikes into **Coyote Buttes** and **Paria Canyon**.

Exploring these or any other off-highway areas requires you to drive down dirt roads that become very treacherous in bad weather, while even the shortest hike leads swiftly into remote backcountry. Be sure to pick up detailed, current advice on conditions, either at the BLM office in Kanab (see above) or at the BLM's **Paria Contact Station** (see p.366), 43 miles east.

Coyote Buttes

A conspicuous but unmarked dirt road leads south from US-89, between mileposts 25 and 26, along a high ridge, towards the **Coyote Buttes** area. Since 2000, this has formed part of **Vermilion Cliffs National Monument**, but despite that enhanced status it remains relatively untrampled by human feet. Its guardians, the BLM, are so determined to keep it that way that hiking is rigidly controlled, by permit only (see box, p.366).

7

PERMITS FOR COYOTE BUTTES AND PARIA CANYON

Day-hikers who stay within the upper reaches of Wire Pass, Buckskin Gulch, and Paria Canyon do not require **permits**, though they still must pay $5 per person per day at the trailheads. For overnight stays in those areas, and for day-hikes as well as overnight backpacking trips further afield, including to Coyote Buttes, permits are essential. With just twenty issued per day for Coyote Buttes North ($7 per person) and another twenty for Coyote Buttes South ($5), they're very hard to come by.

Only half of these places can be booked **online**, at ⓦ blm.gov/az/paria. For **Coyote Buttes North**, you have to suggest three possible dates, four months in advance, and are entered into a lottery that's drawn on the first day of each month; thus in March, you can put your name down for three dates in July, and the lottery will be drawn on April 1; as a rule, you have a five percent chance of success in spring or fall, ranging up to more like 25 percent in winter. For **Coyote Buttes South** and **Paria Canyon**, applications open on the first day of each month for specific dates at least three full months ahead, so on March 1 you can apply for dates in June. If you apply on the first possible date, you have a good chance of getting a permit. The remaining permits are allocated each morning to **walk-ins** who enter the daily lotteries at the Grand Staircase–Escalante visitor centre in Kanab (see p.365); applications for The Wave in Coyote Buttes North are accepted 8.30–9am, and those for Coyote Buttes South and Paria Canyon 9.30–10am.

What everyone is so eager to see is a rock formation known as **The Wave**, an extraordinary, disorienting ripple of sculpted sandstone atop a hard-to-find prominence known as **Top Rock**, just south of the Arizona–Utah state line in the north section of the buttes. As there's no fixed trail, you'll need good advice to complete the seven-mile round-trip hike in a single day. The BLM requests that specific instructions not be published, in order to discourage unauthorized or poorly equipped hikers; if you're lucky enough to get the necessary reservation, they'll provide you with a detailed map. Both the Coyote Buttes and Buckskin Gulch routes start from the **Wire Pass Trailhead**, just over eight miles south into the wilderness from US-89.

INFORMATION   COYOTE BUTTES

BLM field office The Paria Contact Station (mid-March to mid-Nov daily 8am–4.30pm; ☏ 435 644 4628), is four miles east of the highway turn-off; if you're approaching from Page, remember it's an hour later here in Utah than it is in Arizona.

Paria Canyon

The same restrictions on backpacker permits as for Coyote Buttes (see box above) also apply to hikers intending to make the remote and demanding four- to six-day trek down **Paria Canyon**, which ends at the start of the Grand Canyon at Lees Ferry, Arizona (see p.331). While it's possible to access the route by first hiking down Buckskin Gulch from the Wire Pass Trailhead mentioned above, most hikers start at the **White House Trailhead**, two miles south of US-89 just east of the Paria Contact Station. A basic **campground** near the trailhead charges $5 per night.

The road to Bryce Canyon

Drivers heading from Zion to Bryce Canyon should turn **north** on US-89 from Mount Carmel Junction (see p.363), rather than heading south to Kanab. For just over forty pretty but uneventful miles, punctuated by the occasional Mormon hamlet, the road remains within **Long Valley**, with the Markagunt and Paunsaugunt plateaus rising to either side. Then you're faced with the choice of either continuing north towards Salt Lake City, or veering east towards Bryce, and Utah's other national parks.

Orderville and Glendale

Tiny **ORDERVILLE** stands four miles north of Mount Carmel on US-89. Despite its historical significance as the longest-lasting of several experiments in communitarian living organized by the **United Order**, a nineteenth-century Mormon group that believed all property should be held in common, modern Orderville is not worth an extended stay. Aside from two gas stations and a couple of shabby motels, it has little to attract passing tourists. The almost equally insignificant hamlet of **GLENDALE**, however, nestled amid a cluster of apple orchards five miles further north of Orderville, makes a pleasant overnight stop.

Hatch

Long Valley steadily dries out north of Glendale, so travellers from Cedar City who pick up US-89 at the east end of Hwy-14 (see p.349) encounter further upland forests rather than farmland. At 7000ft up, little **HATCH**, 25 miles on, makes a cool overnight stop in summer, but that's the only time its handful of motels are at all busy.

Red Canyon

The only road in a hundred miles that manages to climb through the wild country east of US-89 is **Hwy-12**, which was blasted into the rocks ten miles north of Hatch to provide a route to **Bryce Canyon** and beyond. It starts by climbing through **Red Canyon**, a small-scale precursor of the joys ahead.

7

Four miles along on the left, the short Pink Ledges **hiking trail** sets off from a parking lot that also holds a Dixie National Forest **visitor centre** (summer daily 9am–5pm; ☎435 676 2676); longer trails leave from the first-come, first-served *Red Canyon* **campground** ($15), half a mile further on. Immediately beyond that, the highway tunnels through two artificial red-rock arches, before topping out on top of the Paunsaugunt Plateau, with another ten miles to go before Bryce.

Panguitch

The spruce, squeaky-clean and oddly endearing Mormon town of **PANGUITCH** – 24 miles from Bryce, seven miles north of the intersection of Hwy-12 and US-89, and fifty from Mount Carmel Junction – was established in 1864 and named for no good reason after the Paiute term for "Big Fish". After an uncertain start, Panguitch became, and remains, the largest town along the Upper Sevier Valley. That was originally due in part to the brick factory responsible for the distinguished brick homes that still adorn its streets, but Panguitch today depends heavily on passing tourism for its bread and butter. It's a bit too chilly to linger in the off season, but in summer, the pumps at the eight local gas stations rarely stop spinning, and twenty-odd budget motels and restaurants are kept busy.

INFORMATION

THE ROAD TO BRYCE CANYON

PANGUITCH
Visitor centre 55 S Main St (daily May–Oct 9am–5pm; ☎435 676 8585 or ☎800 444 6869, ⓦbrycecanyoncountry .com). They can provide a walking tour of the town's

historic homes, but you'd have to be more than a little weird to spend your morning doing that rather than setting off into the wondrous deserts of Bryce Canyon.

ACCOMMODATION AND EATING

GLENDALE
Smith Hotel 295 N Main St ☎435 648 2156 or ☎800 528 3558, ⓦhistoricsmithhotel.com. This white clapboard house, complete with a large upstairs veranda, looks much like the rest of Glendale's homes, but it's actually a welcoming wayside inn, with six bright and very pleasant en-suite B&B rooms. $89

HATCH
Riverside Resort & RV Park 594 N Hwy-89 ☎435 735 4223, ⓦriversideresort-utah.com. Don't let the word

"resort" raise your hopes too high, but if you're happy to get an ordinary motel room for half what you'd pay nearer the parks, or to park an RV or set up a tent in a field near the river, this complex a mile north of Hatch should suit you fine. Tents $15, RVs $35, rooms $79

PANGUITCH
Cowboy's Smokehouse Bar-B-Q 95 N Main St ☎435 676 8030, ⓦcowboyssmokehousecafe.com. This Victorian-era saloon is much the best of Panguitch's half-dozen humdrum restaurants, with moderately priced

barbecued meats (half a rack of ribs for $20) and huge fruit pies, plus regular live music. Mon–Sat 7am–9pm.
Harold's Place Intersection of US-89 and Hwy-12, 7 miles south of Panguitch ☏435 676 8886, ⍟haroldsplace.net. Twenty log cabins lined up side by side, of which two sleep six people, plus 32 motel rooms in

a separate inn. Closed Nov to April. $89
Purple Sage Motel 132 E Center St ☏435 676 2659 or ☏800 241 6889, ⍟purplesagemotel.biz. Great value, well-run little budget motel, a block from the town centre. $89

Bryce Canyon National Park

Hwy-63, 3 miles south of US-89, 86 miles northeast of Zion Canyon (2hr drive), or 120 miles southwest of Capitol Reef (over 3hr drive) • $30 per vehicle, $25 for motorcyclists, $15 cyclists and pedestrians; valid 7 days • ☏435 834 5322, ⍟nps.gov/brca

Few more freakish landscapes can exist than those confined within **BRYCE CANYON NATIONAL PARK**. From the safety of the park's rim road, visitors gaze down upon a throng of red, yellow and orange pinnacles of rock, eating like the flames of a forest fire into the thickly wooded plateau. Braver souls can hike down into the inferno and thread their way between the top-heavy towers, to explore a barren desert that's aglow with almost psychedelic colours.

Paiute Indians, who hunted in the vicinity, had an elegantly precise word for the landscape: *Unkatimpe-wa-Wince-Pockich*, "red rocks standing like men in a bowl-shaped recess." The current name comes from the Mormon settler **Ebenezer Bryce**, who established a short-lived homestead nearby in 1874 and memorably declared that this was "a helluva place to lose a cow". In fact, however, "Bryce's Canyon" is not a canyon at all but a row of crescent-shaped amphitheatres, hollowed into a twenty-mile stretch along the eastern edge of the **Paunsaugunt Plateau**. At up to 9000ft above sea level, this marks the final and most spectacular rung of the Grand Staircase as it climbs through southern Utah (see p.337). Between sixty and forty million years ago, the **Pink Cliffs** were deposited in layers of varying thickness and strength on the beds of shallow lakes. Some are limestone, some siltstone; all were dyed and stained with combinations of red, white, orange, blue or yellow by different concentrations of minerals, especially iron.

Since it became a national park in the 1920s – with irregular boundaries designed to minimize the impact on local ranchers – Bryce Canyon has deservedly ranked as a must-see attraction for any visitor to Utah. If you're at all stretched for time, however, this is one park that you can realistically hope to see in a single day, or even an afternoon. Just be sure to take at least a short **hike** into the technicolour ravines – far more vivid than the Grand Canyon, as well as much more human in scale. Most visitors pass through between June and August, but the park is, if anything, even more inspiring in the stillness of winter, when the hoodoos rear their heads from a blanket of **snow**.

Although Hwy-12 runs within the northern boundaries of the national park on its way across southwest Utah, you won't see Bryce's rock formations unless you turn south onto Hwy-63 thirteen miles east of US-89, or eight miles northwest of Tropic (see p.374).

HOW TO MAKE A HOODOO

Conditions at Bryce are perfect for rapid erosion, with ice forming overnight and thawing in the morning over two hundred times per year. Water seeps into cracks in the ground, then expands as it freezes, to wedge the cracks ever wider. Spurs emerge from the cliff face as it recedes, then dwindle to slender fins and eventually break into separate standing columns. When the topmost rock of a column is hard enough, lower levels erode away beneath it at a much faster rate. A mighty boulder left precariously perched on a tall, narrow pillar is known as a **hoodoo**. At Bryce, thousands upon thousands of hoodoos are crammed into each successive amphitheatre, to form a menagerie of multihued, contorted stone shapes. The best known, and most precarious, is **Thor's Hammer**, near Sunset Point.

BRYCE CANYON NATIONAL PARK

Panguitch & Zion

Tropic & Escalante (33 miles)

Tropic (1 mile)

0   3
miles

ACCOMMODATION
Lodge at Bryce Canyon	4
North Campground	3
Ruby's Inn	1
Ruby's Inn Campground	2
Sunset Campground	5

Canyon Rim
Canyon Area

7

DIXIE
NATIONAL
FOREST

PAUNSAUGUNT PLATEAU

Visitor Centre ℹ

Fairland
Point

PINK CLIFFS

Fairyland Canyon

Rim Trail

Fairyland
Loop Trail

Tropic Valley

Sunrise
Point

**Bryce
Amphitheater**

Sunset
Point

Inspiration
Point

Bryce
Point

SEE INSET BELOW

Paria
View

Swamp
Canyon

Swamp Canyon
Connecting Trail

Whiteman
Connecting Trail

Under-the-Rim Trail
(Bryce Point to Rainbow Point)

N

Piracy
Point

Fairview
Point

Natural
Bridge

Agua
Canyon

Ponderosa
Point

Rainbow
Point

Yovimpa
Point

Bristlecone
Loop Trail

Riggs
Spring
Loop Trail

ℹ Visitor Centre

Fairyland Loop Trail

0   1
mile

3

Queen's Garden
Trail

Sunrise
Point

QUEEN'S GARDEN

**Bryce
Amphitheater**

Lodge at
Bryce Canyon 4

Thor's
Hammer

Sunset
Point 5

SILENT
CITY

Wall St

Navajo
Loop Trail

Peekaboo
Loop Trail

Inspiration
Point

Rim Trail

Bryce
Point

N

Visitor centre

Hwy-63, immediately beyond park fee station • Daily: May–Sept 8am–8pm; April & Oct 8am–6pm; Nov–March 8am–4.30pm • Free • ☎ 435 834 5322, ⊛ nps.gov/brca

For drivers and shuttle passengers alike, the park **visitor centre** makes a logical first stop, even though it's not within view of the canyon itself. A valuable source of information on current weather and hiking conditions, it's also the place to pick up $5 **permits** if you plan to camp in Bryce's **backcountry**. All the designated backcountry sites are south of Bryce Point below the rim, well away from the main trails.

Bryce Amphitheater

Most visitor activity at Bryce is concentrated around **Bryce Amphitheater**, the largest and most accessible of the indentations in the Pink Cliffs. Whether you park your own car off the loop road that leaves Hwy-63 half a mile south of the visitor centre, or get dropped off by the shuttle bus, a brief walk will bring you to the brink of the crescent-shaped depression, which is paralleled for its full length by the paved **Rim Trail**. En route, you can also drop in at the *Lodge at Bryce Canyon*, where the main lobby holds a fascinating large-scale relief model of the park, and there are several souvenir stores and snack bars as well as a restaurant (see p.372) and hotel accommodation (see p.372).

Precisely where along the Rim Trail you get your first blast of the incandescent rocks makes little difference. Of the two official overlooks, five hundred yards apart, **Sunrise Point** to the north attracts fewer of the tour-bus crowds than **Sunset Point** to the south. Neither name is particularly appropriate; both face east, so you won't see the sun set, while the best place to catch the dawn is **Bryce Point**, a mile or so further south. Here at the southernmost tip of the amphitheatre, you can look back west as the first rays of the sun strike the toy soldiers below. Although dawn and dusk are the prime times to **take photos** at Bryce, the views to the east and north are astonishing at any time of day, ranging as much as a hundred miles to encompass the Aquarius Plateau and the Henry Mountains.

Scenic Drive

Beyond Bryce Amphitheater, **Hwy-63** – also known as the **Scenic Drive** – meanders south along the rim of the Paunsaugunt Plateau for another fifteen miles. It's a slow drive, passing a succession of substantially similar viewpoints; there's no need to stop at them all, though each has its merits. Look out for the huge **Natural Bridge**, which spans a steep gully approximately halfway along the route, very close to the eponymous lookout. Suspended far above the forest, it doesn't cross running water, so technically it's not a bridge but an 85ft-long arch.

Hwy-63 steadily climbs another thousand feet higher as it continues south, until finally the ridge that it's following narrows to a slender neck, and the road is forced to end at the highest viewpoint of all, **Rainbow Point** (9115ft). While that faces east, nearby **Yovimpa Point** commands sweeping views south, to Navajo Mountain and the Kaibab forest that fringes the Grand Canyon.

As you leave the park, bear in mind that **Fairyland Point**, reached via a separate turn-off a mile or so north of the visitor centre, is one of Bryce's quietest yet most scenic viewpoints.

Hiking in Bryce Canyon

The **Rim Trail** follows the lip of the plateau for just over five miles, skirting Bryce Amphitheater between Sunrise and Sunset points, and extending both north and south. Die-hard overnight backpackers can continue beyond its southern limit, at Bryce Point, all the way to Rainbow Point, 22.6 miles on, along the **Under-the-Rim Trail** (which has designated camping spots).

By far the most popular trails in the park, however, are those that drop into Bryce Amphitheater itself. With several alternative routes to the bottom, and a choice of connections once you're there, you can tailor a hike to suit whatever time you have, from a couple of hours to a full day.

The basic experience is much the same whichever trail you take. The rock stratum that has eroded to form the hoodoos, just below the rim, averages from 300 to 500ft thick, so hiking consists of descending between them until you reach the flatter pine forest beyond, walking through the woods, and then climbing back up again. At an elevation of almost two miles, even a brief hike involves considerable effort; you'll need good footwear and plenty of water.

Navajo Loop Trail

Navajo Loop Trailhead: Sunset Point • 1.3 miles round-trip; 1–2hr • Elevation change 550ft • **Navajo/Queen's Garden combination** 2.9 miles round-trip; 2–3hr • Elevation change 600ft

For a concentrated burst of Bryce at its best, the **Navajo Loop Trail** is ideal. The shortest and busiest trail of all, it plummets abruptly from Sunset Point into formations known as the **Silent City**, then circles back up to complete a hike of 1.3 miles. Allow plenty of time to enjoy the whole round-trip without exhausting yourself. Taking the trail's steeper right-hand branch as you set off makes for an easier hike, and also brings you, by way of precipitous switchbacks, straight into the cool crevice of **Wall Street**. In places, this awe-inspiring gulf of orange rock is less than twenty feet wide, but it's too deep for the 800-year-old Douglas firs that grow from its sandy floor to poke their heads above the cliffs.

Beyond Wall Street, you swiftly reach a small sandy wash. The return leg of the Navajo Loop Trail starts a short way to the left and follows a slightly gentler incline back to Sunset Point, passing **Thor's Hammer** and other humongous hoodoos en route. Alternatively, continue northwards on the level footpath just above the wash, pausing perhaps to rest in the shade of the pines and junipers. The basin known as the **Queen's Garden** is something over a mile along. Named for an almost translucent fin that's topped by a rocky pile bearing a vague resemblance to Queen Victoria, it's connected by a mile-long trail up the hillside to **Sunrise Point**. During its climb, the path cuts repeatedly through limestone fins and spurs, with each tunnel framing yet another irresistible photograph. Most of the horseriding expeditions in the park pass this way. Dwarfed beneath the ludicrous, multicoloured spires and turrets, the horses make an especially surreal spectacle.

ARRIVAL AND DEPARTURE

BRYCE CANYON NATIONAL PARK

By plane Charter and sightseeing flights from elsewhere in the Southwest land at Bryce Canyon Airport on Hwy-12, to no fixed schedule (⊚ brycecanyonairport.com). Oddly enough, this is one of the oldest airports in the US, with pine-log hangars built by the Works Progress Administration (WPA) in the 1930s.

On foot Keen hikers should note that it's possible to avoid the crowds by walking into the park from Tropic (see p.374).

GETTING AROUND AND TOURS

Shuttle buses Although visitors can drive to all the scenic overlooks year-round, the park runs free shuttle buses to reduce traffic congestion (daily: late April to mid-May & early Sept to early Nov 8am–6pm; mid-May to early Sept 8am–7pm). The bus route connects the *Ruby's Inn* complex, just south of the intersection of Hwy-12 and Hwy-63, with the overlooks in Bryce Amphitheater. If that's as far as you want to go – and for most people, even enthusiastic hikers, it's entirely sufficient – then there's no reason to use your own car. The shuttles don't go as far south as Rainbow Point, but it's normally served by two free bus tours each day, departing from six stops including *Ruby's* and the visitor centre (reserve ahead, on ☎ 435 834 5290).

Horseriding Canyon Trail Rides, contactable via the desk at the *Lodge At Bryce Canyon* (☎ 435 679 8665, ⊚ canyonrides.com), arranges horseback rides into the canyon (2hr rides starting at 9am & 2pm, minimum age 7, $65; half-day rides at 8am & 1pm, minimum age 10, $90). Ruby's Horseback Adventures, based at *Ruby's* (☎ 866 782 0002, ⊚ brycecanyonhorseback.com), offers a wider range of rides, at broadly similar prices.

Flight-seeing tours Bryce Canyon Airlines & Helicopters, based at *Ruby's* (☎ 435 834 8060, ⊚ rubysinn .com/scenic-flights/), offer flights over Bryce Canyon and further afield, with rates starting at around $100 for a 17min flight.

ACCOMMODATION

INSIDE THE PARK

Lodge at Bryce Canyon 100 yards from the rim between Sunrise and Sunset points ☎ 435 834 8700 or ☎ 877 386 4383, ⊕ brycecanyonforever.com. This venerable stone-and-timber lodge offers the only accommodation within the park itself. Furnished in its original 1920s style, it consists of a handful of luxurious suites, some more basic studios, a row or two of rough-hewn but very comfortable individual cabins, and about seventy relatively ordinary motel rooms, which are the only options that remain open all winter. All have en-suite bathrooms but no TVs, and tend to be reserved several months in advance. Studios $160, doubles $208, cabins $228, suites $256

North Campground Walking distance from the visitor centre ☎ 877 444 6777, ⊕ recreation.gov (reservations) & ⊕ nps.gov/brca (information). This year-round park-service campground, stretching alongside the Rim Trail a short walk from the visitor centre, offers 86 sites on a first-come, first-served basis only, and is usually full by early afternoon. Each site holds up to ten people, in two vehicles, with three tents. No hook-ups are available, but some sites are also open to RVs, while a further 13 sites, open to RVs only, can be reserved between mid-March and November only. The closest showers are the coin-operated ones by the General Store in the *Lodge* complex. Tents $20, RVs $30

Sunset Campground Near Sunset Point ☎ 877 444 6777, ⊕ recreation.gov (reservations) & ⊕ nps.gov /brca (information). Seasonal campground, across the highway from the *Lodge* near Sunset Point, where all sites hold up to ten people, in two vehicles. Eighty of its 100 sites are available first-come, first-served – all tend to be taken by early afternoon – while the remaining twenty can be reserved in advance, between early May and late Sept only. RVs can stay, but there are no hook-ups; the closest showers are the coin-operated ones by General Store in the *Lodge* complex. Closed mid-Oct to April. Tents $20, RVs $30

NEAR THE PARK

Half a dozen accommodation options loiter just outside the park along highways 12 and 63; the cluster at the intersection has rather ludicrously taken to calling itself Bryce Canyon City. All remain open year-round, with considerably reduced rates in winter. Otherwise, both Panguitch (see p.367) and Tropic (p.374) nearby offer motels.

Best Western Plus Bryce Canyon Grand Hotel 30 N 100 East, Bryce Canyon City ☎ 435 834 5700 or ☎ 866 866 6634, ⊕ brycecanyongrand.com. Large chain motel, just off Hwy-63 a mile short of the park, with good comfortable rooms and an outdoor pool and hot tub. $260

Bryce Canyon Pines Hwy-12 milepost 10 ☎ 435 834 5441 or ☎ 800 892 7923, ⊕ brycecanyonmotel.com. Reasonable if anonymous motel, three miles west off the road junction on Hwy-12, with a strangely shallow swimming pool in a separate shed. They also have an RV park and campground in the woods alongside. Tents $25, RVs $45, doubles $140

Ruby's Inn 26 S Main St, Bryce Canyon City ☎ 435 834 5341 or ☎ 866 866 6616, ⊕ rubysinn.com. Large, unattractive motel complex on Hwy-63, a mile or so outside the park. Fifty of the 368 rooms feature whirlpool baths, and there's a heated indoor swimming pool. Paying extra to be housed in the main lodge, rather than one of the outlying sections, only makes sense in the depths of winter. The food in the dining room (open daily for all meals) is consistently atrocious. $185

Ruby's Inn Campground 26 S Main St, Bryce Canyon City ☎ 435 834 5341 or ☎ 866 878 9373, ⊕ brycecanyoncampgrounds.com. This is the nearest commercial campground to the park, in the woods adjoining *Ruby's Inn*. As well as tent sites and RV hook-ups, they also have basic cabins, each holding two double beds, and tipis that sleep 6–8 guests, although the prices shown here are for two. Closed Nov to late March. Tents $30, tipis $41, RVs $49, cabins $65

EATING

All the accommodation options near the park have their own unenthralling restaurants, but the *Lodge* is the only option inside the park itself.

Lodge at Bryce Canyon 100 yards from the rim between Sunrise and Sunset points ☎ 435 834 5361, ⊕ brycecanyonforever.com. This high-ceilinged and reasonably high-quality dining room is open to the public for all meals. Lunchtime salads and sandwiches are typically priced at around $12, though there are more

expensive daily specials, and richer dinner mains like slow-cooked short ribs or marinated pork tenderloin cost up to $30. Reservations can be made for dinner only, and only on the same day. Daily 7–10am, 11.30am–3pm & 5.30–10pm; closed Dec to mid-March.

East of Bryce Canyon

Continue east from Bryce Canyon, and you're leaving civilization firmly behind. This central region of southern Utah is almost entirely given over to wilderness, and there's barely time to draw breath after Bryce before you plunge into Grand Staircase–Escalante National Monument. A few tiny communities cling to the fringes, however, and **Tropic** offers a few creature comforts as you brace yourself for what lies ahead.

Tropic and around

The first community east of Bryce along Hwy-12, **TROPIC**, stands eight miles from the Bryce Canyon National Park turn-off. Among the migrants from Panguitch who settled this tiny hamlet in the 1880s – naming it for its allegedly superior climate – was Ebenezer Bryce himself (see p.368). His restored log cabin is now the centrepiece of the *Pioneer Village* motel.

Tropic may turn its back on the flamboyance of Bryce Canyon, ranged along the ridge above it, but it has little appeal of its own; the main street consists of a row of motels and fast-food joints, and strolling around the centre is unrewarding. However, the unmarked road that leads west from Bryce's log cabin reaches the park boundary in a couple of miles, from where it's a further two-mile hike up to the main formations.

Five miles south of Tropic, at the village of **CANNONVILLE**, Hwy-12 veers east across the Paria River en route towards Capitol Reef National Park.

INFORMATION   TROPIC AND AROUND

Cannonville Visitor Center 10 Center St, Cannonville, 5 miles south of Tropic (mid-March to mid-Nov daily 8am–4.30pm; ☎ 435 826 5640). A useful stop to pick up information on Grand Staircase–Escalante National Monument.

ACCOMMODATION AND EATING

The one reason to stay in Tropic rather than closer to the park is price. Few of its motels have facilities – for example pools – that might entice you to hang around during the day. As for the limited array of **restaurants**, no one would make a special trip to eat in Tropic, but once you're here it's not worth driving anywhere else either.

Bryce Canyon Inn 21 N Main St ☎ 435 679 8502 or ☎ 800 592 1468, ⓦ brycecanyoninn.com. Standard motel rooms, plus 18 large, newer log cabins, available in summer only, and a decent pizzeria. Doubles $75, cabins $129

Buffalo Sage B&B 980 N Hwy-12 ☎ 435 679 8443 or ☎ 866 232 5711, ⓦ buffalosage.com. Modern, purpose-built B&B perched on a bluff at the northwest end of town, enjoying great views from a wraparound deck and offering four comfortable en-suite rooms. $80

Grand Staircase Inn 105 N Kodachrome Drive, Cannonville ☎ 435 679 8400, ⓦ grandstaircaseinn .com. Simple but adequate highway motel five miles south of Tropic, attached to a grocery store and gas station. $89

Stone Canyon Inn 1380 W Stone Canyon Lane ☎ 435 679 8611 or ☎ 866 489 4680, ⓦ stonecanyoninn.com. Upscale complex of bungalows, cottages and cabins in a peaceful and pretty spot 1.5 miles west of the town centre, and managed by friendly owners. $235

Kodachrome Basin State Park

Cottonwood Canyon Road, 13 miles south of Tropic • Daily 6am–10pm • $8/vehicle • ☎ 435 679 8562, ⓦ stateparks.utah.gov/parks /kodachrome

From **Cannonville**, five miles south of Tropic, choosing to head south along Cottonwood Canyon Road through Paria Valley will bring you in eight miles to **KODACHROME BASIN STATE PARK**, where the pavement runs out. This assortment of contorted rocky columns, tucked beneath the cliffs that climb to Kaiparowits Peak, was named by a *National Geographic* photographer in 1948 in honour of the latest Kodak film; he felt the area's existing name of Thorny Pasture was too prosaic.

By the standards of Utah's national parks, however, Kodachrome Basin is not especially worth making an effort to see. Its main focus is a unique geological phenomenon, not found anywhere else on earth: its 67 **sand pipes**. Each of these misshapen pillars was formed as an underground geyser, created by an earthquake, which was then blocked with tough calcite sediment. When the softer rock that surrounded them eroded away, they were left towering as high as 150ft above the scrubby plain.

After paying the **fee** at the entrance station, follow the road for a couple of miles to the left to reach the park's attractive **campground** ($19 tents, $28 RV hook-ups). Trailheads along the way mark the start of short hikes among the formations. Alternatively, there's an unpaved road that forks right from the entrance station and ends after a little over a mile at the trailhead for **Shakespeare Arch**. A pleasant quarter-mile walk brings you to a small high natural arch, from where you can get good views across the valley to the Pink Cliffs of Bryce Canyon.

Grand Staircase–Escalante National Monument

7

Free • ⓦ ut.blm.gov/monument • Visitor centres in Escalante (see p.379), Kanab (see p.365) and Cannonville (see p.374)

Created by presidential decree in 1996, **GRAND STAIRCASE–ESCALANTE NATIONAL MONUMENT** is, at 1.9 million acres, the largest US national monument outside Alaska. Though its staggering landscape unquestionably merits such recognition, it's not so much a homogeneous entity as the final piece in a jigsaw puzzle, placing the leftover lands between Bryce, Capitol Reef, the Dixie National Forest and Glen Canyon NRA under federal control. From the Aquarius Plateau in the north (as the highest segment of the Colorado Plateau, the top rung of the "staircase") to Lake Powell in the south, only the farming valleys around towns such as Tropic, Escalante and Boulder remain in private ownership.

Although **Hwy-12** dips in and out of its northern flanks, **US-89** runs briefly through its southern extremities, and the rudimentary **Burr Trail** leads into Capitol Reef from its eastern end (see p.390), no paved roads cross this magnificent wilderness. True, dirt tracks provide limited access to the backcountry, but even they don't begin to penetrate the extraordinary canyon country at its heart, and all are in any case rendered impassable by poor weather. What's more, there's only one maintained hiking trail in the whole huge expanse.

Created to "maintain the unspoiled nature" of the region, rather than "develop" it for tourism, Grand Staircase–Escalante was the first national park or monument to be administered not by the National Park Service but by the Bureau of Land Management. No new paved roads have been built, and all facilities are located in existing towns, primarily **Escalante** itself.

Most of the million visitors who pass this way each year arrive with little idea of what to do other than simply drive the hundred-mile stretch of **Hwy-12** between Bryce Canyon and Capitol Reef. Only completed in 1980, thanks to the difficulty of the terrain and the lack of towns en route, this is indisputably the most scenic of southern Utah's fifteen or so designated "Scenic Byways". No driver could fail to be awed by the highway's ever-changing panoply of red-rock canyons, crystal-clear rivers, and shimmering oases, but it's well worth taking the time to get out of your car and explore at least a little on foot.

The **Escalante River**, which drains this whole region, was the last river to be named, let alone explored, in the continental US, and to this day most maps show the area as a vast blank. However, the back roads and trails now bustle with venturesome tourists, who tend to stay two or three nights rather than just one, spending perhaps one day exploring the remarkable **slot canyons** along rugged **Hole-in-the-Rock Road**, and

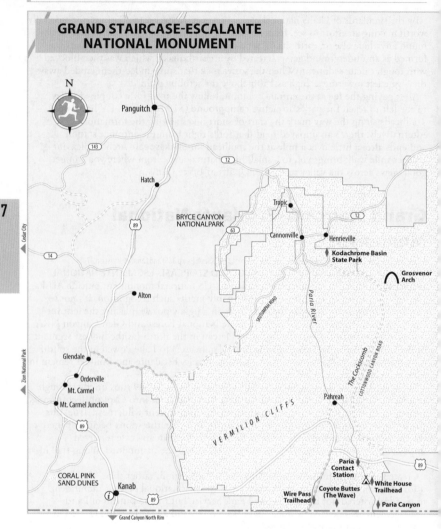

another in and around delightful **Calf Creek**. For multi-night backpackers, the options are all but infinite, though the sandstone bridges and arches on the lower reaches of **Coyote Gulch**, and the Escalante River itself, are the prime attraction.

Skutumpah and Cottonwood Canyon roads

Two long, lonely, mostly dirt roads cut north–south trajectories through the western end of Grand Staircase–Escalante, branching off from the paved road to Kodachrome Basin (see p.374). In principle, both can be travelled in ordinary two-wheel-drive vehicles, but check conditions with rangers before setting off. Even slightly adverse weather can make the going impossible, while in winter the roads will almost certainly be not only impassable, but potential deathtraps. Unless you have a 4WD, don't base your itinerary on the assumption you'll be able to get through.

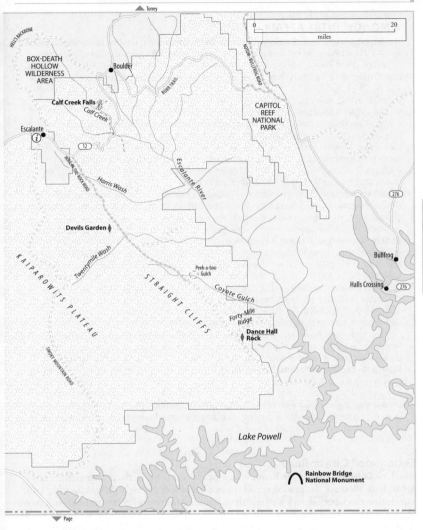

Skutumpah Road

Skutumpah Road, the better maintained of the two north–south roads through Grand Staircase–Escalante, starts three miles south of Cannonville and takes 52 miles to reach US-89, nine miles east of Kanab. Both the first sixteen and the last sixteen of those miles are paved (the latter part as Johnson Canyon Road), but that still leaves twenty difficult unpaved miles, as the road picks its way across **Bull Valley Gorge** and through the **White Cliffs**. One of the best hikes comes early on, before the terrain becomes difficult: the five-mile round-trip stroll though the narrows of **Willis Creek**. From the **trailhead**, six miles down Skutumpah Road, it only takes a few minutes' walking before canyon walls begin to climb to either side of the wash, and they swiftly close in to stand just a few feet apart.

A MONUMENTAL AFFAIR

The first proposal to create **Escalante National Monument** was submitted to Franklin Roosevelt in 1940. Its boundaries would have enclosed 4.5 million acres, stretching from Lees Ferry as far as Moab and Green River, and taken in 280 miles of the Colorado River, 150 miles of the Green River, and 70 miles of the San Juan. That vast expanse was then crossed by just one road, and no bridge spanned the Colorado. Although Roosevelt saw himself as an environmentalist, the greenery of the Hudson River Valley was far more to his taste than the red rocks of the West. In the face of vociferous Mormon opposition in Utah, the idea was quietly dropped.

When Canyonlands National Park was created in the 1960s, it included only a small proportion of that suggested tract. Glen Canyon on the Colorado River was by now submerged beneath Lake Powell (see p.394), while the **Kaiparowits Plateau**, which stretches south from Escalante to the lake, remained outside federal protection. That was thanks to southern Utah's business community, acutely aware that the so-called Fifty-Mile Mountain stands atop the world's largest known deposits of **coal**.

Rumours surrounded plans to mine the Kaiparowits Plateau for well over fifty years. The closest any came to fruition was in the 1970s, when the Southern California Edison Company announced its intention to open a 6000-acre mine, complete with an on-site electricity generating plant. Controversy over the scheme pitted its supporters, the so-called **Sagebrush Rebels** – an informal grouping of Utah's Mormon-dominated business elite, plus the workers whose livelihoods were at stake – against environmentalists from across the nation. Although its abandonment in 1976 was largely due to slackening demand for electricity, communities such as Kanab, desperate for jobs, took out their anger by burning effigies of green activists in the streets.

In 1980, a study commissioned by Congress showed that almost 400,000 acres on the Kaiparowits Plateau had already been logged to clear the way for mines. Much of that timber was processed at a mill in Escalante, and when green opposition resulted in a moratorium on tree-felling, Escalante too witnessed its own share of public "hangings".

By the mid-1990s, however, the pro-mining lobby was merely a vociferous minority, and President Clinton chose to delight environmentalists in every state rather than appease the business community in Utah. In 1996 he therefore declared the creation of the **Grand Staircase–Escalante National Monument**. Utah legislators condemned it as "the mother of all land grabs", and the ropes came out once again, this time to "hang" both Clinton and his Interior Secretary Bruce Babbitt. However, the move was welcomed elsewhere, and once the die was cast, even Escalante accepted it. After years of insisting that they'd rather be farming, logging and mining than running motels, the predominantly Mormon local population has at least been guaranteed a secure economic future, even if it's not the one it anticipated.

Cottonwood Canyon Road

Much of **Cottonwood Canyon Road**, which heads east from Kodachrome Basin, runs across bare **slickrock**. Its graded gravel surface becomes extremely dangerous after rain, but during drier periods, it's well worth continuing for ten miles beyond the park to see the intricate double **Grosvenor Arch**. At that point, the road turns south, to meet **US-89** thirty miles on, roughly halfway between Kanab and Page. En route it threads its way between the dark pyramidal fins of the **Cockscomb**, a bizarre geological oddity resembling the armour-plated back of a stegosaurus, which forms the boundary between the Grand Staircase and the Kaiparowits Plateau.

Escalante

Hwy-12 climbs northeast from Cannonville, passing through the speck that is **Henrieville** and then ascending the clay cliffs known as "The Blues". Once atop the cliffs you're confronted by the unexpected sight of the high but fertile **Upper Valley**, kept well watered by snowmelt from the Aquarius Plateau.

Mormon militiamen who pursued Indian raiders through the Upper Valley in 1866 noted the rich meadowland beyond, and dubbed the region "Potato Valley" in honour of its abundant wild sweet potatoes. Within ten years, several returned to establish a ranching and farming community. They called it **ESCALANTE**, despite the fact that the Spanish explorer-priest Fray Silvestre de Escalante (see p.472) never came within a hundred miles of this spot.

Life was harsh during Escalante's early years; the pioneers spent their first winter huddled in primitive dugouts. Then came a period of deceptive ease, as their sheep and cattle multiplied on the open range. By 1910, however, the native grasses on which they grazed were gone forever. The land has never recovered, and Escalante has remained frozen at much the same size and appearance ever since.

Escalante is a neat enough little town, with its main street gently sloping down from west to east and with a couple of blocks of four-square brick and timber homes to either side. It's also a screamingly dull place to spend the night, though the wilderness that stretches away in every direction more than makes up for that.

INFORMATION

ESCALANTE

Escalante Interagency Visitor Center 755 W Main St (daily 8am–4.30pm; closed Sat & Sun mid-Nov to mid-March; ☎ 435 826 5499, ⓦ ut.blm.gov/monument). Up-to-date information on hiking and mountain biking in the public lands in and around Grand Staircase–Escalante National Monument, plus free permits for backcountry camping.

ACCOMMODATION

Canyons Bed & Breakfast 120 E Main St ☎ 435 826 4747, ⓦ canyonsbnb.com. Behind this ordinary town house you'll find four attractive en-suite guest rooms, each with its own little patio. Rates include a decent continental breakfast. Closed Nov to mid-March. $150

Circle D Motel 475 W Main St ☎ 435 826 4297, ⓦ escalantecircledmotel.com. Basic old-style motel, perched at the west end of town, with assorted rooms arrayed off a long wooden veranda; ask for one of the newer rooms. $74

Escalante's Grand Staircase B&B 280 W Main St ☎ 435 826 4890, ⓦ escalantebnb.com. Somewhere between a motel and B&B, with eight spacious, bright and cheerfully decorated rooms. No children under 12. $145

Escalante Outfitters 310 W Main St ☎ 435 826 4266 or ☎ 866 455 0041, ⓦ escalanteoutfitters.com. Hikers' and campers' supply store where each of the seven attractive little log cabins out back has heating but no phone or TV. They share use of a bathhouse. There's also tent camping. Closed Nov to mid-March. Tents $16, cabins $45

Prospector Inn 380 W Main St ☎ 435 826 4653, ⓦ prospectorinn.com. Escalante's largest motel offers spacious, comfortable and good-value twin-bedded rooms. $125

EATING

Restaurants struggle to survive in Escalante, so it sustains just a handful of nondescript diners, where it's hard to stretch a night on the town much beyond twelve and a half minutes.

Circle D Eatery 425 W Main St ☎ 435 826 4297, ⓦ escalantecircledeatery.com. Faux-adobe diner/steakhouse, specializing in home-smoked, locally raised meats like beef brisket ($18) and pork ribs (full slab $24). Lunchtime burgers and sandwiches cost $10–12. Mon & Wed–Sun 7.30am–9pm, Tues 5–9pm.

Esca-Latte Escalante Outfitters 310 W Main St ☎ 435 826 4266, ⓦ escalanteoutfitters.com. Small-scale espresso bar in an outfitters' store, which serves light snacks, $10–13 salads and $13–18 pizzas as well as coffee, smoothies and home-brewed beer. Service is brusque in the extreme, but it's still the best lunch spot around. Summer daily 8am–10pm; winter Tues–Sat 8am–6pm.

Hell's Backbone

While Hwy-12 is by far the quickest route between Escalante and Boulder, summer thrill-seekers can choose instead to take a two-hour, forty-mile trip across the top of the Aquarius Plateau, along the old "Upper Road". Turn north on the 300 East block in Escalante, and the paved **Forest Road 153** heads up Pine Creek Canyon, to reach the appealing mountain-set **Posey Lake** fourteen miles on.

Turn east at the lake, onto Hell's Backbone Road, and the fun begins. Having crawled up the flanks of the 10,000ft Roger Peak, this dirt track teeters along the slender ridge known as **Hell's Backbone**, with sheer drops down to Sand Creek on one side and

7

THE HOLE-IN-THE-ROCK EXPEDITION

These days, **Hole-in-the-Rock Road** is emphatically a dead end, its progress blocked by tumbled boulders high above the waters of Lake Powell. When it was created, however, this was intended to become the most direct route across southern Utah.

In November 1879, the 230 Mormon pioneers of the **San Juan Mission** gathered outside Escalante. Intent on reaching their new home, almost two hundred miles east, they were convinced they'd find a shortcut along the uncharted east flank of the Kaiparowits Plateau and across the Colorado. Even when confronted with the abyss of Glen Canyon, their faith saw them through. In the space of six weeks, they dynamited a narrow slit in a fifty-foot cliff – the **Hole-in-the-Rock** itself – until it was wide enough to squeeze through. Despite snow and ice, they then used ropes to lower 83 wagons down a precipitous "road" that descended 1800ft to the river. Once there, they ferried the whole lot across the Colorado on makeshift rafts, then repeated the entire process to escape the canyon on the far side. A mere hundred more miles of desert brought them to **Bluff** (see p.435), which they established on April 6, 1880. All 230 members of the party lived through the trek, joined by three babies born en route.

Death Hollow on the other. The best views come at the hair-raising bridge halfway along. The bizarrely named **Box-Death Hollow Wilderness** far below can only be penetrated on foot and is southern Utah's most difficult hiking region. Tracing its full length necessitates eighteen miles of wading in ice-cold water and takes between four and seven days; don't even consider setting off without talking to the rangers at the visitor centre in Escalante.

For the last ten miles, as it descends through the woods to Boulder, Hell's Backbone Road is paved, but the backcountry section is usually closed by snow between October and late May.

Hole-in-the-Rock Road

The most popular route into Grand Staircase–Escalante National Monument, **Hole-in-the-Rock Road**, turns south from Hwy-12 five miles east of Escalante. Following a route established by Mormon pioneers, it continues for more than fifty hard miles to stop just before Lake Powell. While it has never been paved, its first forty miles are passable for ordinary vehicles for most of the year. It's a long, slow drive, however – allow three hours to get as far as Dance Hall Rock and back, and carry water and emergency supplies – and despite the build-up it's not nearly as dramatic as Hwy-12. That said, the **hiking trails** that branch away from it make the effort worthwhile; the best for day-trippers is the loop down to the Peek-A-Boo and Spooky **slot canyons**. Staff at the visitor centre in Escalante can provide leaflets and simple maps, but if you're planning anything substantial, buy a proper topographical map.

Devils Garden

12 miles south of Hwy-12 on Hole-in-the-Rock Road · Free

For its first five miles, Hole-in-the-Rock Road crosses mundane, level ranching country. It then climbs to reveal a first glimpse of the red rocks of Escalante Canyon away to the east, and the surface changes from gravel to mud. As you continue across a sagebrush-strewn plateau, there's no incentive to get out of your car before **Devils Garden**, twelve miles along. The one official picnic area en route, this small valley, below the highway to the west, is scattered with rounded, clay-ish hoodoos and arches, reminiscent of Goblin Valley (see p.402). Countless trails and footpaths weave among the excrescences; none leads anywhere in particular, but it's a great place to play hide-and-seek.

In winter, after the snow has set in – usually some time in December – Hole-in-the-Rock Road is normally blocked beyond Devils Garden.

Slot canyons of Dry Fork

1 mile along Dry Fork Road, which starts 26 miles south of Hwy-12 on Hole-in-the-Rock Road • Free

Apart from crossing the occasional bouncy, sandy wash, Hole-in-the-Rock Road remains uneventful as you continue beyond Devils Garden. Now and then, vistas of the colour country open up, and 24 miles along you begin to see rounded slickrock domes perched above the canyon. Just as the thought of what lies to the east is becoming seriously frustrating, however, you finally get the chance to see what's down there.

Head east on **Dry Fork Road**, a couple of miles along Hole-in-the-Rock Road – something over 45 minutes' driving from the highway – and after five hair-raising minutes you'll come to a makeshift parking lot on the edge of a shallow canyon. A steep, sandy and rather hard-to-follow trail takes roughly twenty minutes to switchback down from here into the Dry Fork of Coyote Gulch, where you'll find a couple of Utah's most accessible **slot canyons**, **Peek-a-Boo Gulch** and **Spooky Gulch**. Scoured by fierce desert storms, these kind of impossibly slender and delicate canyons have become hugely popular of late, mainly because they look so utterly gorgeous in photographs. In real life, they're breathtaking, but they're also very dangerous. If there's the slightest threat of rain anywhere nearby, don't go in – and as if that weren't enough, they're also home to midget rattlesnakes.

7

Peek-a-Boo Gulch

Although **Peek-a-Boo Gulch**, the first slot canyon you come to on the Dry Fork of Coyote Gulch, is facing you as soon you reach the canyon floor, you might not recognize it. It's *not* the sandy-bottomed canyon heading off to your left, which isn't quite narrow enough to count as a "slot". Peek-A-Boo instead is on the far side, with its mouth at first glance appearing to be blocked by a "chimney" of slickrock. Just to enter it, you have to haul yourself up a couple of chest-high ledges, which serve as a foretaste of several more to come. Exploring is irresistible, however, as each twist and turn reveals some new arch, bridge or tunnel to scramble through or over. The walls to either side are never all that high, and it doesn't take long to get all the way through, but the elegant swirls and patterns in the storm-gouged rock make it a constant delight.

Spooky Gulch

Spooky Gulch, fifteen minutes' walk down Dry Fork beyond Peek-A-Boo Gulch, is by contrast downright intimidating. It starts narrow and just keeps on getting narrower and darker. To keep going at all, you have to crawl early on beneath a big fallen boulder, and after that it becomes a very tight squeeze indeed. Soon it's only possible to walk sideways, with serious pressure on your rib cage and back, and a sandpaper-like rasping at your clothes.

Coyote Gulch

Hurricane Wash, 33.5 miles south of Hwy-12 on Hole-in-the-Rock Road • Free

Beyond Dry Fork, the surface of Hole-in-the-Rock Road becomes sandier and more uneven, and progress that much slower. A mile or so after the solitary finger of **Chimney Rock** appears on the edge of the mesa, a parking lot on the right signals your arrival at **Hurricane Wash**. This is the starting point for the monument's most popular multi-night **backpacking** route, the three- to four-day round-trip hike down through **Coyote Gulch** to the Escalante River. If you plan to attempt it, ask someone at the visitor centre in Escalante to talk you through the route before you set off.

Strictly speaking, the trail proper begins a quarter-mile down a dirt track to the left of Hole-in-the-Rock Road, but even if your vehicle can get that far, there probably won't be space to park. From there, it's five miles' walk along the sandy but ever-narrowing bed of Hurricane Wash before you reach Coyote Gulch, and then a further eight miles until that meets the Escalante in turn.

Coyote Gulch itself is a spellbinding creek, cutting through a slickrock canyon that's lined with gorgeous sandstone bridges and arches, and punctuated by dramatic waterfalls. Most of it actually lies within the Glen Canyon NRA, but this is the only way to reach it on land. When Lake Powell is at its maximum high-water level, the lake extends all the way up the canyon of the Escalante to its confluence with Coyote Gulch, which means there's no scope for hikers to see, let alone explore, the Escalante River itself. However, in recent years, the waters have tended to remain considerably lower than that. In 2016, for example, the surface of the lake was around 3600 feet, exposing roughly eight miles of the Escalante River below the Coyote Gulch confluence, so it was possible to hike to long-submerged side canyons as well as beside the river.

The day-hike from Forty-Mile Ridge

Starting from Hurricane Wash, there isn't time to hike to any significant features of Coyote Gulch and back within a single day. However, it is possible to snatch a glimpse on a **day-hike** from the end of **Forty-Mile Ridge**, an almost pure-sand "road" that leaves Hole-in-the-Rock Road another couple of miles further on. The first snag is that if you don't have 4WD, you'll probably only be able to drive the first five miles of Forty-Mile Ridge, and thus face an extra two-mile hike to reach the trailhead at its far end. The second snag is that the trail itself enters Coyote Gulch, two miles along, through the **Crack in the Wall**, an incredibly tight squeeze between sandstone boulders perched above a towering cliff that is every bit as alarming as its name suggests. And the final snag: it's much more difficult coming back the other way, so only climb down if you're certain you can climb up again.

Assuming you can cope with these obstacles, the rewards are tremendous. Before you drop down into the gulch, you cross some fabulous slickrock slopes with colossal views out over the wilderness. Once there, Cliff Arch, Coyote Natural Bridge and the huge Jacob Hamblin Arch all lie within reach.

Dance Hall Rock

36 miles south of Hwy-12 on Hole-in-the-Rock Road • Free

Under normal conditions, two-wheel-drive vehicles should go no further along Hole-in-the-Rock Road than **Dance Hall Rock**, a mile beyond Forty-Mile Ridge. The 1879 Mormon party camped alongside this superb natural amphitheatre while they worked out how to get across the Colorado, creating evening entertainment to keep up their spirits. An easy walk from the roadway enables you to tread the same stage, and it's also worth exploring the rolling slickrock hills immediately behind. In a couple of places, natural tanks have been scooped deep into the rock, each sheltering a solitary tree on its sandy floor.

Hole-in-the-Rock

51 miles south of Hwy-12 on Hole-in-the-Rock Road • Free

Beyond Dance Hall Rock, the gravel surface gives way to bare slickrock, only negotiable in high-clearance vehicles. The original **Hole-in-the-Rock** lies just past the final parking lot, fifteen miles on. Keen hikers can scramble over the rocks that block it and pick their way down to the lake, which, depending on its current level, obliterates some or all of the lowermost thousand feet of the pioneers' primitive pathway.

Upper Escalante River

While driving Hole-in-the-Rock Road certainly offers the thrill of venturing into the back of beyond, several wonderful hikes start right alongside Hwy-12. If your time is at all limited and you'd rather spend it on the trails than behind the wheel, there's a lot to be said for staying on the main road until it reaches the **Escalante River**.

The first sighting of the Escalante system comes from a roadside lookout at an extravagant curve five miles east of the Hole-in-the-Rock turn-off. From here, the highway takes five more miles to drop down to the river itself, which it crosses very close to its confluence with Calf Creek, on a low bridge that's designed to allow floodwaters to flow harmlessly over. Immediately on the far side, a parking lot serves as the trailhead for exhilarating hikes both up- and downstream.

While this can be the starting point for major, multi-night **backpacking** trips in either direction – Escalante town is two days' walk upstream, while Lake Powell lies at least ten days' hike downstream – intriguing natural features much closer at hand serve as obvious **day-hike** destinations. Whichever way you go, trailside notices announce "Yup, You Gotta Get Wet"; be prepared to ford the river several times. If you're just going a short distance there's no great need to keep pulling your boots on and off – the riverbank is sandy enough to walk barefoot. That said, the whole concept loses its appeal in winter, when the river can freeze right over.

Upstream: Escalante Natural Bridge

7

Trailhead: Escalante River bridge, Hwy-12, 13.3 miles east of Escalante or 14.6 miles south of Boulder City • 3.2 miles round-trip; 2hr

The shorter of the two potential Escalante River day-hikes from Hwy-12 heads **upstream** as far as **Escalante Natural Bridge**. Having started by following the river away from the highway bridge, you're soon obliged to wade over to its south bank. The canyon here is broad and open, and the trail gentle. Once you've crossed the river four times, meaning you're now back on its northern side, you'll see the bridge open up on its southern wall. Although it's 100ft wide and 130ft high, it spans a mere trickle, dribbling down from a little side canyon.

Downstream: Maverick Bridge and Phipps Arch

Trailhead: Escalante River bridge, Hwy-12, 13.3 miles east of Escalante or 14.6 miles south of Boulder City • 6.6 miles round-trip; 5hr

Heading **downstream** from Hwy-12 – the trail is accessed by walking beneath the road bridge, then crossing a footbridge over Calf Creek – is slightly heavier going than heading upstream. Much of the valley floor belongs to private farmers, so you have to scramble and dodge to stay outside their fences, but it's still a lovely walk.

The best day-hike in this direction is twice as long as its upstream equivalent, at nearly seven miles for the round-trip. The route leaves the Escalante 1.6 miles along, heading south into sandy **Phipps Wash**. There are no signs or marked trail, so look for footprints and carry a good map. After another half-mile, you'll see two prominent knobs of Navajo sandstone atop the canyon wall to your right. A hundred yards before you reach the larger of the two, head right again, up a sandy slope into a side canyon. One hundred yards along, pick your way onto a ledge on your left to avoid a deep sinkhole; another hundred yards after that, you'll come to **Maverick Bridge**, spanning the wash in front of another round cavity.

Return to Phipps Wash, then keep going south for half a mile until another side canyon opens up to your left. Now things get difficult; to reach the stark, mesa-top **Phipps Arch**, you have to scramble up a steep slickrock ledge, and there's no way to tell whether you've got the right one until you're up there. The views are so good that it doesn't really matter, but make sure you keep track of how to get down again.

ACCOMMODATION AND EATING   THE UPPER ESCALANTE RIVER

★ **Kiva Koffeehouse** Mile 73.86, Hwy-12 ☎ 435 826 4550, ⓦ kivakoffeehouse.com. Solitary little café in as spectacular a setting as it's possible to imagine, perched on a rocky eminence immediately below the Escalante River lookout. Through panoramic windows or from the flowery patio, you can enjoy fabulous views along the river while enjoying simple snacks such as granola, sandwiches, or enchiladas. A separate cottage nearby holds two very comfortable guest rooms, named Sunset and Sunrise for obvious reasons. Mon & Wed–Sun 8.30am–4.30pm, closed Nov–March. $190

Calf Creek Falls

The two most enjoyable hiking trails along Hwy-12 lead from separate trailheads to two entirely distinct but similar waterfalls on **Calf Creek**, the tributary stream that meets the Escalante River alongside the highway bridge. The trail to **Lower Calf Creek Falls** is more popular, but if your time is limited, the hike to the smaller **Upper Calf Creek Falls** makes a quicker, if more physically challenging, alternative.

Lower Calf Creek Falls

Trailhead: Calf Creek Recreation Area, milepost 75 on Hwy-12, 1.1 miles north of Escalante River bridge • Day-use fee $5 • 6.2 miles round-trip; 3–4hr

The magnificent six-mile round-trip walk to the 125ft **Lower Calf Creek Falls** is one of the very best **day-hikes** Utah has to offer. To reach the trailhead, look out for the parking lot for the **Calf Creek Recreation Area** on Hwy-12. There's a nice little **campground** right here, with minimal facilities ($15 per night), but most visitors simply come to hike. Summer sun and deep sand can make it more effort than you might expect, but this would be a lovely canyon walk even if it didn't culminate with the falls.

The clearly marked trail heads upstream between the high red walls of Calf Creek Canyon, following a perennial creek, interrupted by beaver ponds, that feeds a lush riparian environment. Fremont pictographs testify to a long-standing human presence. It takes around ninety minutes to reach the falls themselves, which are absolutely stupendous. Spilling over the pouting lip of a crevice in the centre of a vast sandstone amphitheatre, they spread over a mossy slope of golden stone, iridescent with permanent rainbows. The (utterly freezing) water that collects in the pool below is fringed by a shaded beach where you can rest before you hike back out again.

Upper Calf Creek Falls

Trailhead: Between mileposts 80 and 81 on Hwy-12, 22.4 miles northeast of Escalante or 5.5 miles south of Boulder City • 2 miles round-trip; 1hr 30min • Elevation change 600ft

The **Upper Calf Creek Falls**, a photogenic pocket version of the better known Lower falls, cannot be accessed from Calf Creek Recreation Area. Instead, the trail starts just off Hwy-12 six miles north – watch out for a white-painted roadside boulder, which marks the start of a short and bumpy 100-yard dirt road to the parking lot. From here, you have to make your way for a mile across exposed open slickrock, following a trail that's steep and not clearly marked. The slope may seem intimidating, but with good boots it's not too hard, and the views are amazing. As you descend, fix a landmark back on the rim in your mind, so you'll have a target to aim for when you return.

When you get low enough to sense the location of the stream bed, don't head straight there, but keep going to your right. Eventually, the trail forks: one strand goes to the top of the 50ft falls, the other to the bottom, where a lovely pool awaits.

If you have the choice, do the hike in the late afternoon, when the light hits the falls at the optimum angle, and the climb back to the trailhead is cooler.

Boulder

BOULDER, thirty miles beyond Escalante, is not so much a town as a group of farms scattered across a pleasant high-mountain valley. Cattle ranching in this remote spot started in 1889, and during the fifty years it took for it to be connected by road with the outside world, it acquired a reputation as Utah's own little Shangri-La. Now that it's just another stop on the highway, what magic it may once have had has largely gone.

As the western terminus of the **Burr Trail** (see p.390), Boulder makes an ideal launching point for explorations into the backcountry of Capitol Reef, but few visitors spend much time in the valley itself.

Anasazi State Park

460 N Hwy-12 • Daily: March–Oct 8am–6pm; Nov–Feb 8am–4pm • $5 • ☎ 435 335 7308, ⓦ stateparks.utah.gov/parks/anasazi

On a shallow knoll beside Hwy-12 in the heart of Boulder, the small **Anasazi State Park** holds the excavated remains of an ancient pueblo. Its 83 rooms were occupied by the Kayenta Anasazi, an Ancestral Puebloan subgroup, from 1129 AD until 1169, when the complex was destroyed by fire; charred stumps still poke from the ruins. A good little museum, and a six-room replica at the start of the short ruins trail, do a good job of illustrating their daily life, farming along Boulder Creek – and the fact that modern farms still stand alongside helps make the site particularly evocative.

ACCOMMODATION AND EATING	BOULDER

Boulder Mountain Lodge 20 N Hwy-12 ☎ 435 335 7460 or ☎ 800 556 3446, ⓦ boulder-utah.com. Twenty comfortable rooms, including some with kitchenettes and some two-room suites, at the point where Hwy-12 meets the Burr Trail. Open all year. Doubles $135, suites $204

★ **Hell's Backbone Grill** 20 N Hwy 12 ☎ 435 335 7464, ⓦ hellsbackbonegrill.com. Highly recommended local bistro, facing the highway on the grounds of *Boulder Mountain Lodge*, where the wholesome and very tasty international cuisine draws heavily on produce from their

own organic farm. Lunchtime quesadillas or meatloaf range $14–18, while dinner main courses like pork chops or braised beef are more like $25–30. Daily 7.30am–2.30pm & 5.30–8.30pm; closed late Nov to mid-March.

Pole's Place 465 N Hwy-12 ☎ 435 335 7422, ⓦ boulderutah.com/polesplace. Simple, friendly family-run motel, opposite the state park, with its own café and store. It's by no means luxurious – the least expensive rooms are not en suite, but share access to a locked bathroom cabin outdoors, and there's no wi-fi. Closed Dec–Feb. $86

North to Capitol Reef

Although Hwy-12 leaves Grand Staircase–Escalante for good as it heads north of Boulder, the scenery remains every bit as sublime. The 35-mile link between Boulder and Torrey, across the eastern segment of the Aquarius Plateau, also known as **Boulder Mountain**, takes around an hour to drive. Once Hwy-12 has climbed out of Boulder Valley, successive roadside lookouts face fabulous vistas to the east, across a sea of gold and red sandstone outcrops to the Waterpocket Fold and beyond.

Torrey

Poised at the intersection of highways 12 and 24, eleven miles west of Capitol Reef National Park, **TORREY** has thrown its lot in firmly with the tourist trade. Quietly prospering while so many of its neighbours have faltered, it still consists of little more than one tree-lined central avenue – measuring well over a mile north to south, so a little too far to walk, and surrounded by golden meadows grazed by contented cows – plus a handful of slightly stark brick motels on a ridge to the west. However, for visitors who see their evenings as opportunities to meet other travellers, Torrey is the most exciting prospect for at least a hundred miles.

ACCOMMODATION	TORREY

Austin's Chuck Wagon Motel 12 W Main St ☎ 435 425 3335 or ☎ 800 863 3288, ⓦ austinschuckwagonmotel .com. Well-kept motel, beside a tiny church in the town centre, offering small rooms in the main streetfront

building, larger conventional motel rooms further back, and some newer two-room log cabins. Closed Dec–Feb. Doubles $61, cabins $153

Capitol Reef Inn & Cafe 360 W Main St ☎ 435 425 3271,

ⓦ capitolreefinn.com. Long-established but crisply maintained little motel, just off the highway in the heart of town, looking south to Boulder Mountain. On-site restaurant and small bookstore. $64

Capitol Reef Resort 2600 E Hwy-24, 3 miles east of Torrey ☎ 435 425 3761, ⓦ capitolreefresort.com. Well-equipped modern motel-style hotel, with great views and a good pool, and some large new stand-alone cabins. Doubles $139, cabins $249

Rim Rock Inn 2523 E Hwy-24 ☎ 435 425 3398 or $135

☎ 888 447 4676, ⓦ therimrock.net. Modern, wood-built hotel, across the highway from the *Capitol Reef Resort* three miles east of Torrey, and offering perfectly acceptable and much cheaper rooms plus two restaurants. $74

Skyridge Inn 1012 E Hwy-24 ☎ 435 425 3222, ⓦ skyridgeinn.com. Six en-suite B&B rooms – three of which have hot tubs – in a tasteful, imaginatively furnished modern home with expansive grounds. Head towards central Torrey from the intersection of highways 12 and 24. $135

EATING

Whether it's the pressure of competition or just a little local pride, the **restaurants** and **diners** of Torrey make more effort to please than you may have come to expect of southern Utah.

★**Café Diablo** 599 W Main St ☎ 435 425 3070, ⓦ cafediablo.net. Inventive modern restaurant, offering a slight Southwestern twist to meats and fish, with rosemary-crusted beef sirloin at $30, pumpkin trout for $24, and even "free-range rattlesnake patties", served with aioli, for $12. The food is good without being incredible, but that's enough to keep it packed out every night in summer; they cope with the crowds very efficiently, but it's advisable to reserve ahead. Mid-April to Oct, daily 11.30am–10pm.

Capitol Reef Inn & Cafe 360 W Main St ☎ 435 425 3271. Bright café that serves pretty good diner food, using fresh ingredients like just-caught local trout. Full pork ($18) or chicken ($13) barbecue dinners, while the amazing ten-vegetable salad ($4.60 or $9) can form part of a real vegetarian feast, with sumptuous banana pies to follow. Avoid the coffee, though. April–Oct, daily 7am–9pm.

Rim Rock Restaurant 2523 E Hwy-24 ☎ 435 425 3398, ⓦ therimrock.net. This hotel actually has two separate dining areas, both serving better food than its rustic log-cabin decor might suggest. In the main dining

room, open for dinner only, the $18 turkey mole is recommended, while the menu also roams the wilds of "Spaghetti Western" dishes like "Lee Van Cleef spaghetti and meat boulders" for $18, and steaks cost up to $33. The Patio section serves cheaper pizzas and Mexican favourites, for lunch and also later into the night. Daily noon–11pm.

Robbers Roost 185 W Main St ☎ 435 425 3265, ⓦ robbersroostbooks.com. Rustic central bookstore, complete with hammocks and a wooden deck, that's an invaluable resource for information on the parklands, and also serves great coffee, pastries and breads. Mon & Wed–Sun 8am–6pm.

The Saddlery Cowboy Bar 422 W Main St ☎ 435 425 2424, ⓦ saddlerycowboybar.com. As well as serving everything from $18 meatloaf to $38 bone-in bison rib-eye steaks, and offering five pool tables, this colossal purpose-built barn puts the country in Utah, with live bands playing beneath the gaze of mounted longhorn hands every Fri & Sat. It really is a saddler; you can buy a hand-tooled saddle for around $4000. Late May to Mid-Oct Wed–Sun 5pm–1am.

Capitol Reef National Park

Hwy-24, 11 miles east of Torrey, 120 miles northeast of Bryce Canyon, and 100 miles southwest of Green River • $10/vehicle, $7 pedestrians and cyclists • ☎ 435 425 3791, ⓦ nps.gov/care

CAPITOL REEF NATIONAL PARK is the second largest of Utah's five national parks and also the least visited. Life might be different if it bore the name originally proposed by locals – **Wayne Wonderland**, this being Wayne County. As it is, that word "reef" seems to confuse visitors. It refers to the fact that the hundred-mile rock wall thrust up by the **Waterpocket Fold** presented an almost impenetrable obstacle to nineteenth-century travellers, who therefore likened it to a reef on the ocean. Add the resemblance of the rounded "knobs" of white sandstone that top its central section to the US Capitol in Washington, and you have "Capitol Reef".

Capitol Reef is very much of a piece with the Southwest's other national parks. Within its 378 square miles lie hidden canyons, verdant valleys and strange rock formations that draw their colours from an extravagant palette of golds and greens,

CAPITOL REEF NATIONAL PARK

■ ACCOMMODATION
Cathedral Valley Campground   1
Cedar Mesa Campground   3
Fruita Campground   2

7

reds and whites. Despite stretching for over a hundred miles north to south, the park is often less than ten miles wide. The one east–west highway, **Hwy-24**, crosses it in under twenty miles, following the gorge of the Fremont River. It's an impressive drive, but that's nothing rare in southern Utah, and unless you time your arrival from the west to coincide with the daily magnificent sunset, you could easily pass straight through Capitol Reef without feeling any great urge to stop. Only if you take the time to explore will you get a sense of the magic of the place, and why it fully deserves its national park status.

Even a couple of hours is enough to admire the western cliffs from the dead-end **Scenic Drive**, south of the park headquarters at **Fruita**. Given half a day or more, you could venture all the way south to Lake Powell on the unpaved **Notom–Bullfrog Road**, tracing the eastern flank of the Waterpocket Fold, or loop back westward via the **Burr Trail**, halfway along. With **hiking trails** of all lengths and levels setting off into the wilderness, it would be easy to spend a week in this one park.

The best **seasons** to visit Capitol Reef are spring, when the fruit trees blossom and the wildflowers bloom, or fall, when the crowds have gone, the cottonwoods change colour and hiking conditions are at their peak. Midsummer temperatures can reach 100°F (38°C), and August in particular is prone to flash-flooding, but so long as you set your sights appropriately low – say, to lazing on your back in the orchards, eating fresh fruit – a summer visit is not such a bad idea.

Brief history

Although traces of human occupation date back ten thousand years, Capitol Reef's first known inhabitants were an Ancestral Puebloan subgroup, now known as the **Fremont Anasazi**, who farmed along the Fremont River from 700 AD until climate changes forced them to move on around 1300 AD. Archeologists distinguish them from their more sophisticated cousins to the southeast by the fact that they lived in pithouses dug into the hillsides, and didn't keep domesticated dogs or turkeys. The most enduring signs of their presence are the intriguing **petroglyphs** still visible on the canyon walls.

After many centuries when only the occasional Paiute hunter passed this way, a small group of Mormons established a permanent settlement beside the Fremont in 1878. The orchards they planted transformed the landscape, and when the post office insisted they gave their community a proper name, a few years later, **Fruita** seemed the perfect choice. The population of the fledgling town never rose above fifty, however, and it was soon suggested that the region had more future as a park than a home. The immediate vicinity of Fruita became Capitol Reef National Monument in 1937, and that was upgraded to national park status when it was enlarged to include the entire Waterpocket Fold in 1971. Former Fruita townspeople and their heirs are still entitled to graze cattle within the park, but ranching is slowly being phased out.

THE GEOLOGY OF CAPITOL REEF

The **Waterpocket Fold**, which slopes from north to south for the full hundred-mile length of Capitol Reef National Park, is what geologists call a **monocline**, created when layers of sedimentary rock buckled under pressure sixty million years ago. Within the last ten million years, it has in turn been lifted a mile or so above sea level by the general raising of the Colorado Plateau. Most of the original fold has long since eroded away; the reef itself is just the rump. Its western face consists of a long, jagged cliff of hard rock; it rises more gently from the east, in multicoloured waves of sandstone that the Navajo called the "Land of the Sleeping Rainbow".

Here and there, the fold is pierced right through by deeply incised **canyons**. Often hundreds of feet deep but less than twenty feet wide, these slender gorges were mostly blocked by fallen rocks until Mormon pioneers cleared a way through. After summer thunderstorms, rainwater can cascade through the canyons in fearsome flash floods. At other times, it collects in depressions worn into the rock – the "**waterpockets**" for which the whole mighty edifice is named.

Hwy-24 through the park

At its simplest, driving through Capitol Reef on **Hwy-24** takes less than half an hour. However much of a hurry you may be in, pause once or twice en route. Rather than a token pit stop at the visitor centre, try taking a five-minute hike from one of the clearly marked trailheads. Only if you turn south of Hwy-24 onto the Scenic Drive (see p.390) do you have to pay the $10 park entrance fee.

Gooseneck Point and Sunset Point

Capitol Reef's westernmost scenic viewpoint lies south of Hwy-24, roughly three-quarters of the way from Torrey to the visitor centre. There's a parking lot beside the highway, signed "Panorama Point", but continue for roughly a mile along the dirt road beyond to reach the larger parking lot where it comes to an end. The brief climb to **Gooseneck Point** from there is rewarded with a 500ft view down into the canyon of Sulphur Creek, an "entrenched meander" that once curved across a flat floodplain but has been etched deep into solid rock by the uplifting of the Colorado Plateau.

Reached by walking ten minutes along a different trail from the same parking lot, **Sunset Point** is as you'd expect a fabulous vantage point to watch the cliffs glow gold and red as the sun goes down.

Visitor centre

52 Scenic Drive, 11 miles east of Torrey • Daily: May–Oct 8am–6pm; Nov–April 8am–4.30pm • ☎ 435 425 3791, ⓦ nps.gov/care

The point where the park's Scenic Drive branches south from Hwy-24 is overshadowed by a huge, fluted red-rock butte known as the **Castle** on the highway's north side. Across the road to the south, the **visitor centre** holds displays on the park and its history, stocks all sorts of free handouts, and can advise on current driving and hiking conditions.

Fruita

The defunct village of **FRUITA** ranges for a mile or so around the confluence of Sulphur Creek and the **Fremont River**, at the heart of Capitol Reef National Park. Spreading alongside both Hwy-24 and the Scenic Drive, eleven miles east of Torrey, it now consists of a cluster of restored barns and houses that serve as homes for park employees, while overnight visitors camp out in the **orchards** that are Capitol Reef's crowning glory.

A waxy, luxuriant green against the towering red cliffs, they hold almost three thousand trees planted by the pioneers. The cherries and peaches **blossom** in the first half of April, the apples slightly later, while the **harvest** lasts from the second half of June until well into October. So long as you stay in the orchards, you can eat as much fruit as you like; you only pay for what you take away. Be sure to stop at the **Gifford House**, a former farmhouse a mile along the Scenic Drive, which sells fabulous takeaway fruit pies ($6) plus pastries and coffees (daily mid-March to Oct 8am–6pm).

Back on Hwy-24, drop by Fruita's former **schoolhouse**, just north of the highway where the rivers meet. It was built in 1896, and hasn't had a pupil since 1941; park rangers, not a Mormon schoolmarm, keep it spick-and-span.

A short distance down the highway beyond the schoolhouse is the **Fremont Culture Walk**, an easy boardwalk amble beside a canyon wall crammed with ancient **petroglyphs**. As well as stylized representations of goats and bighorn sheep, some show how the Fremont people may have seen themselves – unless of course these strange helmeted figures, with triangular bodies and massive shields, really did come from other planets.

East of Fruita

Hwy-24 crosses the Fremont two miles east of the visitor centre, near the start of the **Hickman Bridge Trail** (see p.392). Only beyond this point does **Capitol Dome**, high above the north bank another half-mile ahead, resolve itself into a dome; so far you've seen it from the side, as a slender fin. By now Fremont Canyon is at its deepest, and it's joined within the next couple of miles by **Chimney Rock Canyon** from the north and

Grand Wash from the south (see p.391). A mile past Grand Wash stands the sandstone cabin of one of Fruita's earliest settlers, **Elijah Behunin**, with the eastern boundary of the park another 2.5 miles down the road.

The Scenic Drive

Other than Hwy-24, the only paved road in Capitol Reef is the **Scenic Drive**, which parallels the golden cliffs of the Waterpocket Fold for eight miles south from the visitor centre. Once past Fruita, and the fee station just beyond, the road undulates through the desert, dipping into dry sandy washes and then climbing scrubby rolling hillocks. Successive individual pinnacles, such as **Fern's Nipple** and the **Egyptian Temple**, line the crest of the red-rock battlements to the east.

Until Hwy-24 was pushed through Fremont Canyon in 1962, this unlikely route was southern Utah's main east–west thoroughfare. It now ends at a large parking lot, facing a crack in the cliffs that marks the start of **Capitol Gorge**. For a century, traffic squeezed its way between the narrow walls beyond, but now the gravel continuation known as the Capitol Gorge Road peters out just over two miles in. Hikers, however, can keep going on foot, to see the Pioneer Register where early wagon-drivers carved their names (see p.392).

Notom–Bullfrog Road

If you'd rather survey the Waterpocket Fold from the comfort of your car than sweat it out on foot, the long drive south along the **Notom–Bullfrog Road** is Capitol Reef's best option. Just be sure to stock up on gas and water; you'll have to drive at least seventy miles to find any facilities.

The road leaves Hwy-24 nine miles east of the visitor centre, not far outside the park. Only its first eleven miles – which include the tiny but well-irrigated settlement of **NOTOM**, now home to half a dozen ranchers, four miles along – are paved. Thereafter, its rough surface repeatedly ripples into a "washboard" as it follows a dry-as-dust bench above Sandy Creek, with the eerie badlands of the Waterpocket Fold to the west and the volcanic **Henry Mountains** to the east.

So long as it hasn't been raining – in which case the surface turns to treacherous mud – ordinary vehicles should have no problem negotiating the full length of the Notom–Bullfrog Road, which re-enters the park twenty miles along and then leaves it again in the southeast corner fifteen miles on. Seventy miles from the highway, after a final paved 25-mile segment where you find yourself constantly stopping to swoon at the turquoise expanse of Lake Powell on the southern horizon, you come to the marina at **Bullfrog** (see p.399).

Burr Trail

Most drivers who set off south on the Notom–Bullfrog Road don't go all the way to Bullfrog, but branch onto the **Burr Trail** roughly halfway to Lake Powell, and complete a loop around the Waterpocket Fold. The only road actually to cross the fold, rather than slice through it, this was originally a rutted wagon trail, but was upgraded by uranium prospectors in the 1940s and 1950s. The four miles within the national park are still **unpaved**, but the remaining thirty, running west to **Boulder** (see p.384), were paved during the 1980s. Wilderness advocates argued that increased road use would irreparably damage one of Utah's least-spoiled regions; Garfield County authorities, keen to grab a piece of the Capitol Reef action, went ahead anyway. From their point of view, they were just in time; the area now belongs to Grand Staircase–Escalante National Monument, so there'll be no further road construction.

The panorama that unfolds as you set off along the Burr Trail, ascending the fearsome set of switchbacks that climb west from the Notom–Bullfrog Road 29 miles south of

Hwy-24, is out of this world. Looking back east, you see the top of Swap Mesa and the stark Henry Mountains. Once past the topmost ridge, the Upper and Lower sections of **Muley Twist Canyon** stretch to north and south through the heart of the fold. Both make excellent multi-day backpacking expeditions, starting from near the highway. As you leave the park and enter the national monument (where the pavement begins), an extraordinary procession of reefs marches south, with the white canyons of the Waterpocket Fold in the foreground and four or five craggy red cliff faces beyond, leading on to Lake Powell.

The oval plain just west of the park, ringed by the Circle Cliffs, was described by the nineteenth-century geologist Clarence Dutton as "a spot which is about as desolate as any on earth". The Burr Trail leaves it by way of the deep **Long Canyon**, then struggles on to reach Hwy-24 immediately south of Boulder.

Cathedral Valley

Capitol Reef's least accessible section is **Cathedral Valley**, north of Hwy-24. Like the Notom–Bullfrog Road, it parallels the eastern side of the Waterpocket Fold, but the territory here is much more forbidding than the sagebrush plain to the south. In among the heavily eroded red, blue and grey hills lie deep canyons and primeval gardens, populated by strange stone monoliths. Unless you have your own 4WD or high-clearance vehicle, you'll only see it by joining a guided 4WD tour (see p.392).

Two roads run north into the backcountry from Hwy-24, 11.5 and 18.6 miles east of the visitor centre. The first, **River Ford Road**, traverses the Fremont River by means of a crude ford a few hundred yards along. If you're planning a loop drive, come this way first – it's not safe to cross when the water's more than a couple of feet deep, and you wouldn't want to find that out at the end of a sixty-mile drive. The second route, the **Caineville Wash Road**, meets the first – by now Hartnet Road – at the far end of Cathedral Valley. Several more dirt roads leave the park at this northern extremity, connecting with I-70 to the north or joining Hwy-72 above Loa to the west.

Hiking in Capitol Reef

You can't drive far in Capitol Reef without feeling the backcountry beckoning. Choosing which of the many, mostly short, **trails** to hike is largely a matter of whether you feel up to climbing; only a few, such as the walks through the Capitol Gorge or Grand Wash, remain on level ground, while the rest demand mountain-goat-style scrambling up the slickrock.

If you do choose to stick to the canyon floors, bear in mind the danger of **flash floods** after rain, and don't pause where there's no clear escape route.

Grand Wash Trail

Trailheads: 4 miles southeast of visitor centre on Grand Wash Road, and 4 miles east of visitor centre on Hwy-24 • 2.5 miles each way; 1hr

Capitol Reef's busiest trail connects the Scenic Drive with Hwy-24, along the gravelly bed of the **Grand Wash**. The western trailhead is at the end of the unpaved Grand Wash Road, which leaves the Scenic Drive a mile past Fruita, while its eastern end is on Hwy-24 a mile or two beyond Capitol Dome.

As a one-way walk, the **Grand Wash Trail** takes around an hour, but unless you arrange a pick-up at the far end you'll have to double back. In the half-mile stretch known as **The Narrows**, the vertiginous 800ft canyon walls close in to a mere sixteen feet apart.

Cassidy Arch Trail

Trailhead: 4 miles southeast of visitor centre on Grand Wash Road • 3.4 miles round-trip; 2hr • Elevation change 670ft

Although **Butch Cassidy** and his gang are said to have used the tangle of side canyons that lead off Grand Wash as hideouts, there's no evidence that Butch ever saw **Cassidy**

Arch, which is reached by a steep climb that branches off from the left, north side of the Grand Wash Trail, 0.2 miles along from its southeast end.

It takes half an hour of hiking back along a ledge that parallels the Grand Wash Trail below before you round a corner and get your first view of the arch itself, carved in a perfect smooth crescent into a layer of red rock. Continue another twenty minutes, following an ill-defined cairned route across the slickrock, and you'll suddenly realize that you're now above the arch. If you're feeling brave, you can hike across its broad, level top; otherwise, content yourself with gazing down through it back to the sandy bed of the wash.

Capitol Gorge Trail

Trailhead: end of Capitol Gorge Road, 2 miles beyond end of Scenic Drive • 2.5 miles round-trip; 1hr

The **Capitol Gorge trail**, reached by driving the full length of the Scenic Drive, is every bit as claustrophobic as the Grand Wash. It's a short and easy walk, providing you spare yourself an extra 4.6-mile round-trip by parking not at the foot of the Scenic Drive but at the end of the gravel road beyond.

In the space of a mile, the trail inches all the way through a crack in the Waterpocket Fold, though hikers have to turn back when they reach the private land on the far side. From 1871 onwards, this "**Blue Dugway**" was a major trans-Utah thoroughfare, as the painstaking inscriptions on the **Pioneer Register**, carved into the canyon wall halfway along, will testify.

A couple of twists of the canyon past the Register, side canyons start to open up to both left and right. Not far along, a sign on the left reads "Tanks 0.2". Climb up the cairned trail here to reach, within a few hundred yards, a succession of natural circular "tanks". Early travellers would break off from the laborious haul through the gorge, hoping to find fresh water in such clifftop "**waterpockets**".

Golden Throne Trail

Trailhead: end of Capitol Gorge Road, 2 miles beyond end of Scenic Drive • 4 miles round-trip; 2hr 30min • Elevation change 730ft

The strenuous but exhilarating **Golden Throne Trail** launches itself north from the Capitol Gorge trailhead, straight up the side of the canyon. It then threads its way west, parallel to the dirt road below and climbing consistently all the way back to the mouth of the gorge. En route, it weaves in and out of countless side canyons before finally emerging on the slickrock flatlands that cap the Waterpocket Fold, and command huge views to Boulder Mountain in the west. The dominant feature up here, however, is the towering yellow Navajo-sandstone butte known as the **Golden Throne**, beneath which the trail peters out.

Hickman Bridge Trail

Trailhead: Hwy-24, 2 miles east of visitor centre • 2 miles round-trip; 2hr • Elevation change 400ft

While not the easiest of Hwy-24's roadside trails, the **Hickman Bridge Trail** makes a supremely rewarding hike. Setting off along the north bank of the Fremont River, it meanders briefly through the cottonwoods before climbing a brisk stairway out of the canyon to the shadeless heights up top.

Once you've marvelled at Capitol Dome, off to the east, fork left at the junction ahead. Pockmarked black boulders strewn on all sides, incongruous against the red, pink and cream sandstone, testify to ancient lava flows. Three-quarters of a mile along, the path loops around and through the arching span of **Hickman Bridge**. A hundred feet high, a hundred feet wide, it's a genuine natural bridge, worn through the rock by a side channel eager to reach the Fremont below. The rocky chaos beneath somehow complements the grace of the bridge itself.

ACTIVITIES AND TOURS   CAPITOL REEF NATIONAL PARK

Hondoo Rivers & Trails Torrey ☎ 435 425 3519 or ☎ 800 332 2696, ⊚ hondoo.com. Jeep tours, starting from your motel – half-day $115 per person, full-day $165 – plus guided hikes, and longer tours including horseriding adventures.

Redrock Adventure Guides Torrey ☎ 435 425 3339,

ⓦredrockadventureguides.com. Guided hikes in the park, at $350 for one or two people; canyoneering for $400; and overnight backpacking trips.

CAMPING

There are no motels or lodges inside the park; the closest **accommodation** is in Torrey (see p.385). In addition to the three **campgrounds** listed below, you can camp in Capitol Reef's backcountry, with a free permit from the visitor centre (see p.389).

Cathedral Valley Campground Cathedral Valley ⓦnps.gov/care. Six-site primitive campground, 25 miles north of Hwy-24 along either the Hartnet Road (which requires you to ford the Fremont River) or the Caineville Wash Road. Picnic tables and pit toilets but no water. First-come, first-served. Free

Cedar Mesa Campground Notom–Bullfrog Road ⓦnps.gov/care. Five-site primitive campground, 22.5 miles south of Hwy-24, with picnic tables and pit toilets but no water. First-come, first-served. Free

Fruita Campground Scenic Drive ⓦnps.gov/care. The park's only developed campground operates on a first-come, first-served basis, with no reservations. Set amid the orchards, a mile south of the visitor centre, it's a great overnight stop even if you never see the rest of the park. All its 71 RV/tent sites are usually taken by early afternoon in spring and fall. No hook-ups or showers. While it remains open all year, in winter it can be without water altogether. $20

Lake Powell

Until the early 1960s, it was all but impossible to travel between southwest and southeast Utah. In the unseen heart of the endless desert, the mighty Colorado River churned its way towards the Pacific through a series of yawning canyons. Here and there boatmen might ferry the occasional passenger across, and a few adventurous souls even rafted down the river itself, but there was no highway for two hundred miles north of Arizona.

Now the Colorado has gone, submerged beneath the huge, docile **LAKE POWELL**. For many people – especially those who knew the sublime **Glen Canyon** that it destroyed – the lake is a loathsome abomination. Many more see it as a thing of beauty, and Lake Powell has become Utah's number-one tourist attraction, drawing more than three million visitors per year – by tradition, over half a million on Labor Day alone – and matched in popularity in the Southwest only by the Grand Canyon. It is, undeniably, an extraordinary spectacle, its turquoise waters rippling against its stark red-rock rim and cradling islands that once were buttes and mesas. No one could ever mistake this for a natural landscape, however, and you don't have to be an out-and-out environmentalist to be disturbed by the transformation of America's last great wilderness into a playground. The concessionaires of the **Glen Canyon National Recreation Area** invite you to "think of Lake Powell as a 160,000-acre bathtub and consider our boats, floats, boards, and tubes as your toys." Beyond the unappealing rhetoric, there's some truth in what they say; granted that the lake exists, if you're going to come here at all, the best way to enjoy your visit is to get out on the water.

Five of Lake Powell's six **marinas** are accessible by road. Two are south of the state line in Arizona: the largest, **Wahweap**, lies just west of the dam itself and the purpose-built town of **Page**, while **Antelope Point** is on Navajo land immediately east of Page. The remaining four are in Utah. **Bullfrog** and **Hall's Crossing**, northeast up the lake from the dam, are connected by a ferry service. **Hite** is in theory at the northeast limit of the lake, though low water levels have left it stranded high and dry, and it's not currently in operation. The sixth and final marina, **Dangling Rope**, is a refuelling station that can only be reached by boat.

There's surprisingly little accommodation on land; it's assumed you'll want to join the armada out on the water, either in your own vessel or in a rented **houseboat**. For a quick taste, join a **guided tour** at either Wahweap or Bullfrog – the trips to **Rainbow Bridge** are by far the most popular – or take the **ferry** between Bullfrog and Hall's Crossing.

LAKE POWELL: CONTROVERSY AND COMPROMISE

The western half of the United States would sustain a population greater than that of our whole country today if the waters that now run to waste were saved and used for irrigation.

President Theodore Roosevelt, State of the Union address, 1901

The twentieth-century growth of the American West was largely the story of the "taming" of the **Colorado River**. If the Colorado were to run dry, Los Angeles, Las Vegas and Phoenix would die, and the exodus from the Southwest would dwarf anything from the Dust Bowl era.

In terms of volume, the Colorado does not rank among the top 25 rivers in the US. However, the sheer aggression with which it hurtles from 13,000ft up in the Rockies makes it the fastest and fiercest of them all. That's why it's responsible for so many magnificent canyons; and that's also why civil engineers couldn't bear to leave it alone, yearning instead to harness its energy with hydroelectric dams, and divert its flow to irrigate the desert.

Early in the twentieth century, the sparsely populated southwestern states began to fear that southern California's ever-increasing thirst might drain them dry. The **Colorado River Compact** of 1922 divided the river between an **Upper Basin**, consisting of Utah, Wyoming, Colorado and New Mexico, and a **Lower Basin** – Arizona, Nevada and California. Each basin was to receive 7.5 million acre-feet of the estimated annual flow of 16.8 million, with the dregs left over for Mexico. This was the first of fifteen such agreements over the next fifty years, largely necessitated because the estimates were wrong; the long-term average is thought to be more like 13.9 million acre-feet.

The task of distributing the water fell to a new federal agency, the **Bureau of Reclamation**. Its engineers saw their mission as being to "reclaim" the West; the main tool at their disposal was the **dam**. They began in 1935, by damming Black Canyon, on the doorstep of California, with the **Hoover Dam** (see p.459). That project inspired a dam-building spree, in the US and all over the world. The Bureau's subsequent plans for the Colorado Plateau were clear from the subtitle of one report: *A Natural Menace Becomes A Natural Resource*. Proposals included damming the Green River in northwest Colorado, the San Juan in New Mexico, and the Colorado itself in both Bridge Canyon in Arizona and Utah's Glen Canyon.

In 1869, John Wesley Powell was entranced by the idyllic canyon that stretched southwest from the confluence of the Green and Colorado rivers: "A curious ensemble of wonderful features – carved walls, royal arches, glens, alcove gulches, mounds, and monuments ... We decide to call it **Glen Canyon**." Those few river-runners who subsequently passed this way described a cool, tranquil haven, bursting with luxuriant vegetation and desert wildlife, and a far cry from the cataract-filled canyons both up- and downstream. Theirs were lone voices in the wilderness, however; too little known to receive federal protection, Glen Canyon's remoteness was to work against it.

The environmental movement was in its infancy in the 1950s, and its strategy concentrated on defending national parks. The Green River dam-site lying within Dinosaur National Monument, **David Brower**, the executive director of the Sierra Club, told Congress that damming Glen Canyon was a far better idea – in fact, he originally endorsed construction

Brief history

Lake Powell's success as a wet'n'wild theme park has been a surprise spin-off from its real purpose. Glen Canyon Dam was constructed to regulate the flow of water along the Colorado River. Half is kept back to irrigate the deserts of the plateau, while the rest gushes through its turbines, generating electricity as it makes for Arizona and California. Demand is so precisely monitored that the level of the lake fluctuates according to whether it's dinnertime in Phoenix. Hence its closest resemblance to a bathtub – the scummy dirty-bath tidemark that sullies the sandstone around its edge.

The whole vast system cost $300 million to build. When full, Lake Powell is 550ft deep at the dam and holds enough water to cover all of Arizona five inches deep. It stretches back up 186 miles of the Colorado River and 72 miles of the San Juan, as well as inundating 96 side canyons formed by rivers such as the Escalante and the Dirty of a dam in the Grand Canyon *on condition* that a dam was built in Glen Canyon as well. Conservationists prided themselves on a job well done when it was decided to dam the Green River outside Dinosaur, at Flaming Gorge to the northwest, and to go ahead with damming Glen Canyon. The one concession to "the abominable nature lovers", as one Utah senator termed them, was that water would not be allowed to encroach upon Rainbow Bridge National Monument.

President Eisenhower triggered the first blast at the dam-site in 1956. Meanwhile, with Glen Canyon doomed but not yet drowned, archeologists, artists and photographers chronicled its disappearing treasures. These included the glowing, fern-dripping alcove known as the **Cathedral in the Desert**, and the **Crossing of the Fathers**, where the Spanish priests Domínguez and Escalante forded the river in 1776.

On January 21, 1963, the same day that the Colorado River was brought to a halt, Secretary of the Interior Stewart Udall – great-grandson of John D. Lee, of Lees Ferry (see p.331) – announced plans to build two further dams within the Grand Canyon. By now, the Sierra Club had realized its mistake; and it promptly made another, arguing for building coal-burning power stations instead of hydroelectric dams. The Navajo, thinking nuclear power might soon render its mineral resources worthless, decided to cash in by permitting the strip-mining of Black Mesa (see p.55), and the hideously polluting Navajo Generating Station was constructed outside Page.

It took seventeen years for Lake Powell to fill to the brim, on June 22, 1980. By now, David Brower, who left the Sierra Club to found Friends of the Earth in 1969, was describing his support for Glen Canyon Dam as "the greatest sin I have ever committed". Shortly before his death, in 2000, the 87-year-old "Archdruid" hosted a "Day of Action Against Dams" at the dam-site, and called for Lake Powell to be drained so the canyon could regenerate. One original argument for the dam had been that the Colorado would otherwise fill **Lake Mead**, behind the Hoover Dam, with silt within a few years; Brower argued that the floodgates at Glen Canyon should remain open until that really does happen, perhaps two hundred years from now. Other activists went further. In *The Monkey-Wrench Gang*, Edward Abbey fantasized about dynamiting the dam, and he was among the demonstrators who in 1981 signalled the birth of the **Earth First!** movement by suspending a 300ft strip of plastic down its face to simulate an almighty crack. To some extent, the argument has been won; no major dam has been built since the 1960s, and the general consensus is that Glen Canyon Dam will be the last.

The debate over the future of Lake Powell was given an extra spin by the ongoing **drought** of the early twenty-first century (see below), which threatens to restore Glen Canyon by default, and has demonstrated how swiftly flora and fauna can re-establish themselves. Some argued that the lake would never refill, others that this latest dry spell was typical of long-term weather patterns, and showed precisely why the dam is necessary. In any case, though drought may be a natural phenomenon, the level of the lake is dictated by political decisions, and specifically the amount of water released to the Lower Basin states. A five-year "trial agreement" between the US and Mexico, signed in 2012, finally guaranteed Mexico 1.5 million acre-feet of water per year, in the hope that the Colorado might once more flow all the way to the sea.

Devil. The total shoreline of 1960 miles is longer than the entire US Pacific coast. Despite the searing sun, the lake is officially claimed to lose a mere 2.5 percent of its volume each year to evaporation.

The fullest the lake has ever been was in 1983, when water flowed over the top of the dam, and an emergency release had to be instigated. As recently as 1999, the level was just four feet below the maximum, but drought set in from 2000 onwards, and by 2005 the waters had dropped 146 feet, with the reservoir a mere one-third full. That was enough for Glen Canyon to begin to reappear, and backcountry hikers flocked to marvel at such long-submerged wonders as the Cathedral in the Desert. The lower reaches of the Escalante River sprang back to life; the banks were host once more to 25-foot trees, while the thick layer of sediment deposited on the lake bed steadily washed away. Levels have risen somewhat since then, but in 2016, for example, the lake remained only half-full, 100 feet below maximum.

Page

Home to around 7500 people, **PAGE** – which is actually just south of the state line in Arizona, but is the only town of any size on the periphery of Lake Powell – is the largest community in a 720-mile stretch of the Colorado River. Before Glen Canyon Dam was constructed four miles west, this all but barren mesa belonged to the Navajo Nation. Thanks to a small spring, however, it made the best site to house the dam's workforce. The Navajo agreed to swap it for a similar-sized chunk of desert between Bluff and Hatch in southeast Utah, a new road was blasted through the Echo Cliffs, and the town was born on Thanksgiving Day 1958.

Although Page seemed destined to wither away once the dam was completed, it gained a new lease of life when Congress decided that rather than build more dams, the Southwest could meet its power needs by burning coal instead. The **Navajo Generating Station**, which creates electricity using coal from Black Mesa and pumps water from Lake Powell to Phoenix, went up four miles southeast of town, and has kept Page in work ever since.

The view as you descend towards Page is utterly surreal. The three power plant chimneys stand silhouetted amid sandstone outcrops, while lines of pylons march off across the desert and the misty hump of Navajo Mountain rises in the distance. As you approach, the waters of Lake Powell emerge from the haze, with drowned buttes poking their heads here and there above the surface. Page itself, on the other hand, resembles a dull suburban mall writ large; if it has a redeeming feature, you'll have a hard time finding it.

Powell Museum

6 N Lake Powell Blvd • April–Oct Mon–Fri 9am–5pm; Nov–March Mon–Fri 10am–3pm • $3 • ☎ 928 645 9496, ⓦ powellmuseum.org

The only sight of any interest in Page is the **Powell Museum**. As well as charting the exploits of John Wesley Powell, the first man to raft down the Colorado (see p.403), the museum celebrates later river-runners and recounts Page's own brief history. It also holds a locally excavated plesiosaur fossil and an amazing collection of fluorescent rocks.

Antelope Canyon

Mile-marker 299, AZ-98, 2 miles southeast of Page • Guided tours only; $48–58 for 1hr 30min, $95 for 2hr 30min with recommended operator Antelope Slot Canyon Tours (☎ 928 645 5594, ⓦ antelopeslotcanyon.com); mid-March to Oct daily 8am–5pm; Nov to mid-March daily 9am–3pm • ☎ 928 698 2808, ⓦ navajonationparks.org/htm/antelopecanyon.htm

Antelope Canyon, a couple of miles southeast of Page, is Arizona's most famous – and irresistibly, astonishingly beautiful – **slot canyon**. The canyon actually comprises two separate sections, on either side of AZ-98, both of which are on Navajo land. The closest to the highway, **Lower Antelope Canyon** immediately north, became world famous in 1997, when the tragic deaths of eleven hikers in a flash flood proved just how dangerous such places can be. Since then, the Navajo have realized what an invaluable tourism asset Antelope Canyon represents, and now control all access, with visits by **guided tour** only.

Much the most popular destination for tours is **Upper Antelope Canyon**, a two-mile dirt-road drive down from the highway. Shuttle buses deposit visitors outside a slender, unprepossessing crack in a red sandstone wall. Stepping inside is like entering both a cathedral, in that you find yourself in a majestic chamber adorned with delicate glowing colours, and a pinball machine, in that you feel as though any second some mighty and unavoidable boulder will come thundering down the narrow passageway. Walking the full length of the canyon and back takes barely twenty minutes, even with frequent pauses to admire the interlacing fins of multihued rock that swirl overhead, in places to a height of 120ft. Flash floods can fill the slot to the brim with water and spill over the top; once such a flood recedes, on the other hand, it leaves the canyon floor scrubbed bare of its usual eight-foot layer of fine soft sand.

Be warned that while Antelope Canyon is every bit as ravishing as photos suggest, it offers little of the wilderness feel of other desert highlights. It's both short and narrow enough to get *very* crowded at busy times, and as the main priority for all visitors is to take photographs, it can feel more like a working set than a place to contemplate beauty.

Horseshoe Bend
Just south of mile-marker 545 on US-89, 3 miles south of Page • Daily dawn–dusk • Free

An easy self-guided hike not far south of Page leads to an amazing view of **Horseshoe Bend**, where the Colorado River makes an extravagant 180-degree turn in the depths of Marble Canyon, roughly halfway through its short course between Glen Canyon Dam and the official start of the Grand Canyon at Lees Ferry.

To reach the overlook, turn west off US-89, exactly 2.6 miles south of *Wal-Mart* in Page, onto a dirt road that ends at the foot of a small sandy hill. Climb the railed path to the top of that hill, then down another 0.4 mile to the lip of the gorge. The river itself is only visible from the very edge, which is unrailed, windy and pretty hair-raising. The huge curving sweep far below barely fits into the widest-angled lens. Carry water, and allow about an hour for the exposed round-trip hike.

7

INFORMATION

Visitor centre In the Powell Museum, 6 N Lake Powell Blvd (April–Oct Mon–Fri 9am–5pm, Nov–March Mon–Fri 10am–3pm; ☎ 928 645 9456, ⓦ visitpageelakepowell.com). Several other offices that purport to be information centres are in fact tour operators offering trips to Antelope Canyon (see opposite).

ACCOMMODATION

Courtyard Page at Lake Powell 600 Clubhouse Drive ☎ 928 645 5000, ⓦ marriott.com. Page's most incongruous splash of luxury – a 153-room resort, complete with golf course – is below the mesa in view of the dam. **$289**
Lake Powell Motel 750 S Navajo Drive ☎ 928 645 3919. Page's best-value budget motel; the huge, well maintained rooms are more like apartments than standard hotel offerings, complete with kitchenettes and living rooms. Closed Nov–March. **$69**
LuLu's Sleep Ezze Motel 208 N Lake Powell Blvd ☎ 928 608 0273 or ☎ 800 553 6211, ⓦ lulussleepezze motel.com. Tiny, very welcoming little motel in central Page, with simple but nice rooms. **$98**

EATING

Beans Gourmet Coffee House 800 Elm St ☎ 928 645 2825. Espressos and light snacks, plus picnic lunches to go. Daily 6am–5pm.
Bonkers 810 N Navajo Drive ☎ 928 645 2706, ⓦ bonkerspageaz.com. Something for everyone, with a full menu of Italian specialities – pesto shrimp and veal parmesan both cost just over $20 – plus burgers and sandwiches. Mon–Sat 4–9.30pm, closed Nov–Feb.
Dam Bar & Grille Dam Plaza 644 N Navajo Drive ☎ 928 645 2161, ⓦ damplaza.com. Themed diner and bar, appealingly designed to echo the days when Page was populated solely by dam-building hard-hats; it serves pizza and pasta for around $20 and steaks for up to $30. Daily 11am–11pm.

Glen Canyon Dam
US-89, 2 miles northwest of Page • **Hayden Visitor Center** Daily: March to mid-May & mid-Sept to Oct 8am–5pm; mid-May to mid-Sept 8am–6pm; Nov–Feb 8am–4pm • Dam tours $5 • ☎ 928 608 6072, ⓦ nps.gov/glca

Glen Canyon Dam plugs **Marble Canyon** (see p.331) not at its narrowest point, but at its northern end, just downstream from Wahweap Creek. As US-89 crosses Glen Canyon Bridge outside Page, the vast curve of the dam is to the north, while Marble Canyon drops 700ft below you.

You can't stop on the bridge; for a better look, drop by the **Carl Hayden Visitor Center** on the west bank, which doubles as the main source of information on the **Glen Canyon National Recreation Area**. Guided **tours** of the dam itself take 45 minutes to drop via two elevators first to the walkway along the top, and then a further 500ft to the generating

> ### RENTING A HOUSEBOAT
>
> To rent a **houseboat** on Lake Powell, contact Lake Powell Resorts and Marinas in Wahweap (☎928 645 2433 or ☎888 896 3829, ⓦlakepowell.com). The smallest Expedition houseboat, capable of sleeping six, costs $1836 for three days, while the luxury twelve-berth Odyssey class of boat costs $15,000 per week.
>
> **Package deals**, offering different combinations of time on houseboats, in the marina lodges and on guided tours, are also available. Many houseboat users like to **camp** overnight onshore; regulations insist that anyone who camps within a mile of the lake must carry and use portable toilets.

station at the bottom. Beneath the roar of the 1.3-million kilowatt turbines, a digital counter steadily ticks off the billions of dollars earned thus far by the sale of power.

Just before the bridge, a spur road on the east bank tunnels down through the cliffs to the river; rafters use it as an access point for the gloriously lazy fifteen-mile **float trip** down to Lees Ferry (see p.303). There's no whitewater along the way, and strictly speaking you never enter the Grand Canyon, but it's still a very pleasant drift between imposing high-canyon cliffs.

Wahweap

Unlike Page, **WAHWEAP**, a couple of miles west of Glen Canyon Dam, has never become a town. Lake Powell's principal **marina** has, however, grown steadily since it was established in 1963, coordinating the boat rental and tour business and also offering several hundred motel rooms.

To the fury of the federal authorities, the first man to appreciate Wahweap's potential did so long before the dam was ever built. Art Greene, the original owner of *Marble Canyon Lodge* (see p.332), ran boat trips upriver to Rainbow Bridge from the 1940s onwards; when he got wind of plans to dam Glen Canyon, he shrewdly leased the land at the mouth of Wahweap Creek at a knockdown rate. Knowing that it made the perfect site for a marina, Greene refused to budge, and wound up making a killing as official concessionaire.

TOURS
WAHWEAP

Boat tours In addition to Rainbow Bridge trips (see below), Lake Powell Resorts and Marinas (☎928 645 2433 or ☎888 896 3829, ⓦlakepowell.com) runs boat tours that range from 1hr 30min water-only Antelope Canyon excursions ($45 adults, $30 under-13s) to a dinner cruise (Tues & Sat, late May to Sept; $80/$35).

ACCOMMODATION AND EATING

Lake Powell Resort Wahweap Marina ☎928 645 2433 or ☎888 896 3829, ⓦlakepowell.com. Only half the rooms in this very plush resort actually overlook Lake Powell. Its *Rainbow Room* restaurant, however (closed Nov–Feb), has huge lakeside windows and serves breakfast buffets for $10 or $15, plus full dinners for $21 (roast chicken) to $31 (steak). The same management also operates the adjacent first-come, first-served campground, and an RV park. Tents $26, RVs $48, rooms $291

Rainbow Bridge National Monument

Accessible by boat, on 100-mile round-trip tours from Wahweap • March Thurs & Sat 8am; April–Oct daily 7.30am; Nov–Feb Sat 9am • $125, under-13s $90 • ☎928 645 2433 or ☎888 896 3829, ⓦlakepowell.com

Millions of tourists have Lake Powell to thank for providing access to the world's largest natural bridge, the magnificent **RAINBOW BRIDGE NATIONAL MONUMENT**. The Navajo, seeing this formerly sacred site swarming with visitors, are far less enthusiastic, though at least the height of Glen Canyon Dam, and thus the level of the lake, was mandated to ensure that Rainbow Bridge was not drowned – unlike the nearby and equally revered confluence of the Colorado and San Juan rivers.

Both the Navajo and the Paiute knew of Rainbow Bridge long before the first university-sponsored expedition reached it in 1909. Within a year, it was declared a national monument, but it remained far off any beaten track until the construction of Lake Powell made it accessible by **boat**. The bridge now lies a couple of miles down **Forbidding Canyon**, a side canyon located around fifty miles by water from Glen Canyon Dam.

Tours from Wahweap operate year-round. Schedules are open to considerable variation, however, as the length of the trip depends on the level of the lake, which determines which deep-water channels are navigable. What used to be a half-day excursion now takes between six and eight hours; check in advance, though, as the waters might just have risen sufficiently for the tour boats once more to make two round-trips each day. For much of the year, tours are booked far in advance, so reserve before you finalize your accommodation.

Even with the water low, Lake Powell remains a broad expanse, spread beneath a huge sky. When you reach Forbidding Canyon, on the other hand, you enter another world; it's a beautiful high-walled slot canyon that twists mysteriously away from the lake proper. Eventually, the tour boats moor at a floating jetty, the precise location of which varies. A walk from here that's currently over a mile leads to the astonishing sandstone gateway of the bridge, climbing nearly 300ft high. It's also almost 300ft wide, with Navajo Mountain visible through its superbly smooth curve. The upper section, including the forty-foot-thick span, is composed of Navajo sandstone, while the base belongs to the harder Kayenta formation, not so easily cut by flowing water. When the lake is full, the bridge spans open water, but these days the former streambed is usually dry. What were once waterfalls nearby have also been exposed; what a spot this must have been. The Park Service asks visitors to consider not walking right up to, or beneath, the bridge itself, out of respect for Navajo spiritual traditions. Almost everyone goes anyway.

7

Hiking to Rainbow Bridge

Hiking permits from Navajo Parks & Recreation $5, plus $12/person/night • ☎ 928 968 2808, ⓦ navajonationparks.org • Route information on ⓦ glencanyonnha.org

With considerably more difficulty than the boat trip, Rainbow Bridge can also be reached **on foot**. Two fourteen-mile trails start respectively 38 and 42 miles up Arrowhead Hwy-16, which runs north from Hwy-98 from a junction 57 miles southeast of Page. They loop to either side of Navajo Mountain, then join for the last half-mile. Only experienced canyoneers should attempt this hike, having obtained the compulsory permits from Navajo Parks & Recreation.

Bullfrog

The marina at **BULLFROG** is slapped atop the slickrock on the west side of Lake Powell, seventy miles upstream from Wahweap, or seventy miles southeast of Capitol Reef National Park on the Notom–Bullfrog Road (see p.390). It's the focus of a small community that now proudly boasts its own high school, as well as a Glen Canyon NRA **visitor centre**.

INFORMATION   BULLFROG

Visitor centre Bullfrog marina (May to early Oct daily 8am–5pm; ☎ 435 684 7423, ⓦ nps.gov/glca).

ACCOMMODATION AND EATING

Defiance House Lodge Bullfrog Marina ☎ 435 684 3000 or ☎ 800 528 6154, ⓦ lakepowell.com. While this mesa-top motel, marked by a houseboat on stilts above the road, holds some very comfortable rooms, the best place to enjoy the big lake views from is its *Anasazi* restaurant (open daily for all meals), even though the food itself is indifferent. The park concessionaires also have some fully furnished but deeply unatmospheric three-bedroom "family units" (similar to trailers) for rent, and there's a year-round RV park too. RVs $46, doubles $142, family units $296

THE LAKE POWELL FERRY

Schedules for the 25-minute **ferry crossing** between Bullfrog and Hall's Crossing have become too irregular in the last few years to make it appropriate to publish a detailed timetable. In particular, it would only take a small additional drop in water levels to force the ferry to stop running altogether. If the latest schedule manages to operate, however, you can expect four sailings per day in each direction between mid-May and Sept; four on Fri–Sun only from April to mid-May and Oct–Nov; and four on Sat only Dec–March. The one-way fare for ordinary cars, with all passengers, is $25.

For the latest information, contact the Utah Dept of Transportation (☎ 435 893 4747, ⊛ udot .utah.gov), or Glen Canyon visitor centres.

Hall's Crossing

Hall's Crossing, on the east shore of Lake Powell, now plays second fiddle to its larger neighbour Bullfrog to the west. As the name suggests, it was the base of a river ferry operator long before the lake existed. **Charles Hall** started out by building his own boat at Hole-in-the-Rock, 35 miles downstream (see p.382), in 1870. Business there was so bad that he moved here in 1881, only to give up altogether when the transcontinental railroad rendered his service redundant. Hall charged $5 per wagon and 75¢ per passenger; the going rate for a family car on the **Lake Powell Ferry** these days is $25.

When they finally get around to colonizing Mars, the first settlement should look much like the airstrip on the bare red mesa that rises above Hall's Crossing. Hwy-276 to the east makes an exhilarating drive, dropping down the **Clay Cliffs** with views across the red plains to Monument Valley, and running for forty empty miles to meet Hwy-95 near Natural Bridges (see p.432).

Accommodation possibilities are limited to family units in a glorified trailer park, while if you're looking for a meal, you can either take your pick from a small assortment of Twinkies on sale at the local gas station, or a marginally wider range of groceries at the marina store. There's nothing at all at the ferry ramp, just over a mile beyond the marina.

Hite

Lake Powell's northernmost marina, at **HITE**, is reached via **Hwy-95**, which branches off Hwy-24 halfway between Capitol Reef and I-70 to run for 122 miles southeast to Blanding. The only highway to cross the Colorado between the Glen Canyon Dam and Moab, Hwy-95's most dramatic segment is the twenty-mile stretch as it approaches the river from the west, rattling along beside the North Wash.

At the mouth of the North Wash canyon, the highway climbs to the windswept hilltop that holds **Hite Overlook**. You'll almost certainly be confronted here by the fact that while Hite remains accessible by road, it's no longer on the lake. Thanks to the ongoing drought, Lake Powell receded out of sight several years ago; the waters might just have returned by the time you read this, but don't bet on it.

Hite has always felt like a godforsaken spot, and even more so now that it's lake-forsaken as well. Beyond the overlook, Hwy-95 loops north to cross first the Dirty Devil River and then the Colorado. Reaching the ramshackle **Hite Marina** itself involves a detour of a couple of miles on the far side. At the time of writing, no boats could reach Hite, so all the marina facilities were shut. There's still a small gas station and a grocery store (open 11am–2pm only); it's even possible to rent a "family unit" like those at Bullfrog (see p.399), but that would be a seriously bad idea.

Between Capitol Reef and Canyonlands

No direct route crosses the tract of craggy sandstone and eroded clay that stretches for a hundred miles **east of Capitol Reef**. Travellers making the circuit of Utah's parks are obliged to make a giant detour to the north or south, either crossing Lake Powell via the bridge at Hite or taking **Hwy-24** up to meet I-70, and then looping back down to Moab – a total drive of around 150 miles.

The scenery along Hwy-24 is consistently awesome, beginning with the **badlands** twenty miles beyond Capitol Reef, where the 1500ft **Factory Butte** rises above corrugated humps of greyish-blue clay reminiscent of Arizona's Painted Desert (see p.258). Only small sections of the backcountry are at all accessible, however, and the interstate town of **Green River** is the only community of any size the whole way to Moab.

7 Hanksville

Forty miles east of Capitol Reef, Hwy-24 turns sharply north toward I-70, while Hwy-95 runs south towards Lake Powell. The tiny farming community of **HANKSVILLE** stands at the intersection, a few miles south of the confluence where the Fremont and Muddy rivers join to form the Dirty Devil.

Hanksville is only a dot on the map, but with the next dot a good fifty miles away in any direction, it draws in enough weary drivers to keep it ticking.

ACCOMMODATION AND EATING   **HANKSVILLE**

Blondie's Eatery 3 N Hwy-95 ☏ 435 542 3255. Poised on a low bluff close to the intersection, with an expansive veranda, this cheerful diner is better than it looks, serving burgers for $5–9, ham and eggs or fried chicken for $10, and steak and eggs for $12. Daily 8am–9pm.

Luna Mesa Oasis Milepost 101, Hwy-24 ☏ 435 456 9122. Inexpensive but dependable restaurant, in the middle of nowhere 16 miles west of Hanksville; enthusiastic young owners serve both Mexican and American cuisine. March–Oct Mon–Sat 8am–9pm.

Rodeway Inn Capitol Reef 25 E Hwy-24, Caineville ☏ 435 456 9900, ⓦ cainevilleinn.com. Small, comfortable and gloriously isolated motel with an outdoor swimming pool, out in the badlands facing a spectacular butte at milepost 99 on Hwy-24, around 18 miles west of Hanksville. **$100**

Whispering Sands Motel 90 S Hwy-95 ☏ 435 542 3238, ⓦ whisperingsandsmotel.com. This clean and welcoming family-run motel at Hanksville's main intersection, across from *Blondie's*, fills quickly each evening as the sun goes down. **$89**

Goblin Valley State Park

Temple Mountain Rd, 32 miles north of Hanksville, 48 miles southwest of Green River • Daily 6am–10pm • $10/vehicle • ☏ 435 275 4584, ⓦ stateparks.utah.gov/parks/goblin-valley • Branch west from Hwy-24 near milepost 137, drive 5 miles on Temple Mountain Road, then 7 miles south on a paved spur road

Utah's quirkiest park, **Goblin Valley State Park**, nestles at the foot of the San Rafael Reef, twelve miles west of Hwy-24 around halfway between Hanksville and the interstate. This small patch of barren desert became a park for the simple reason that its clay-like rock formations are funny. The man who first noticed them, in the 1940s, called it Mushroom Valley, but "goblin" is as good a name as any. In the 1999 movie *Galaxy Quest*, Goblin Valley doubled plausibly as an alien planet, with its rocks coming to life in one fabulous sequence.

Past the entrance kiosk, the road ends beside a sheltered overlook, poised above a slim valley whose sandy floor is completely devoid of vegetation. It's filled instead with parallel fins of pale Entrada sandstone, each topped by a ridge that's indented with weird eroded figures. Some hoodoos also stand alone, while larger buttes and columns loom around the periphery.

A couple of formal trails lead down into the valley, but no one bothers to follow them, preferring to slither at random from one misshapen masterpiece to the next.

Once you're on the valley floor, a typical monster in the maze will rise a few feet over your head; some really do look like goblins, complete with eyes and ears.

ACCOMMODATION

Goblin Valley Campground Goblin Valley State Park ☎ 800 322 3770, ⌨ utahstateparks.reserveamerica .com. Away from the main valley, but still engulfed by stunted sandstone sprites, the park's well-equipped campground has running water, toilets and showers, and also a couple of yurts, with bunk beds that sleep up to five but are not equipped with bed linen. Open year-round. Tents $\underline{\$23}$, yurts $\underline{\$80}$

San Rafael Swell

Fronted by the "reef" that soars immediately northwest of Goblin Valley, the **San Rafael Swell** is one of southern Utah's least known but most tantalizing wilderness areas. With so many mapped and tamed parklands hereabouts offering such instant and abundant

JOHN WESLEY POWELL

7

Until **John Wesley Powell** led the first expedition to float down the full length of the Green and Colorado rivers, the Colorado Plateau was a vast blank at the heart of maps of the American West. No one knew how the region's mountains and waterways fitted together, or whether falls larger than Niagara might prevent river traffic completely.

Born in Ohio in 1834, the son of a travelling preacher, Powell spent his youth making solo forays along the Ohio, Mississippi and Illinois rivers. He lost his right arm fighting for the Union at Shiloh, where he formed a lasting friendship with future president Ulysses Grant. Once the Civil War was over, the veteran major headed west to explore the Colorado Plateau.

Powell, his brother Walter, and a volunteer crew of eight frontier types set off in four flat-bottomed wooden boats from Green River, Wyoming, on **May 24, 1869**. Powell was lashed to an upright wooden chair in the leading vessel. Not long after entering the Uintah Mountains, by way of **Flaming Gorge**, one boat was smashed to smithereens in Lodore Canyon. They then whisked through Green River, Utah, and plunged into the desert, encountering their biggest challenge so far in the shape of **Cataract Canyon**, soon after the Green met the Grand to form the Colorado. Wherever possible, they carried their boats around the fiercest rapids, and with prodigious energy Powell repeatedly climbed out of the canyon to get his bearings. After several terrifying days, they burst out of the gorge, for an idyllic period of respite in **Glen Canyon**.

Three members of the party became demoralized in the depths of the **Grand Canyon**, when the blackness of the walls to either side seemed to presage further ferocious rapids ahead. They decided to hike their way out, only to be murdered mysteriously – some say by suspicious Mormons, others by Shivwits Indians. Powell, however, made it through the remainder of the canyon with unexpected ease; it took him merely one more day to reach the **Grand Wash Cliffs**, at the confluence of the Colorado and Virgin rivers (now beneath Lake Mead) on August 30. Two of his crew continued all the way to the Pacific, but Powell and his brother left the river, after almost a hundred days afloat.

Now a national celebrity, Powell returned for a better-funded and more leisurely trip two years later. Starting this time from Green River, Utah, he documented his experiences in much greater detail, and used them as the basis of a bestselling book. During the voyage, he left the canyon at every opportunity, and even returned to Washington DC for the winter, while his crew holed up in Kanab.

In later years, Powell became director of both the Smithsonian Institution's **Bureau of Ethnology** and the **US Geologic Survey**. His forceful opinions as to how the federal government should administer the limited resources of the West – and especially its water – are now regarded as prophetic. Refusing to accept the then-current adage that "rain follows the plow", he argued that state boundaries should be drawn along natural watersheds, to prevent water issues from bedevilling the region's political future. His advocacy of federally funded water projects led the bureaucrats to name **Lake Powell** in his honour, but one can't help imagining that Powell himself would prefer Glen Canyon as it was in the beginning.

rewards, few out-of-state visitors add this difficult, mountainous terrain to their itineraries. A glimpse of it from I-70, as the interstate plunges east down its craggy foothills toward Green River, usually suffices.

In the past, most of the swell was only safely accessible in 4WD vehicles. Now a significant number of dirt roads have been upgraded, and local tourist authorities issue lavish booklets and maps of potential driving tours. If you're driving an ordinary two-wheel-drive vehicle, it's still essential to enquire locally, in Green River or Goblin Valley, before attempting to explore on your own. Conditions vary month to month; many roads become impassable every winter, and are only fit for conventional use in early summer, when the latest winter's damage has been repaired.

A couple of highlights are detailed below; others, for which you're more likely to need 4WD, include **Little Wild Horse Canyon**, a slot canyon that cuts into the reef seven sandy miles west of Goblin Valley, and the swell's highest point, the **San Rafael Knob**, a four-hour round-trip hike from the end of Copper Globe Road, which heads south from I-70 at exit 114.

Black Dragon Canyon

Milepost 147 I-70, 3 miles west of junction of Hwy-24, and 17 miles west of Green River • Free

The most accessible part of the San Rafael Swell, spectacular **Black Dragon Canyon**, immediately north of I-70, can only be approached from the interstate's westbound lane. Pull directly off the highway just past milepost 147, and go through the gate, closing it behind you. Drive straight ahead for a mile on a dirt road, ignoring a possible west turn, then follow the sign west, and park when the road surface deteriorates. From there, a short walk leads into the towering, golden-walled canyon itself. The prime goal is a group of dramatic Barrier Canyon-style **pictographs** (see p.412), on the north side a quarter-mile along. If that's all you have time for, you can easily be back on the interstate within an hour of leaving it.

Alternatively, with a good map, you can make a day of it by hiking the full length of the canyon, which is barely two miles long, then climbing north over a pass and back down again to meet the San Rafael River, which will lead you back to where you left your car. That demanding fifteen-mile loop will take at least seven hours to complete.

WHAT'S IN A NAME? THE GRAND, GREEN, COLORADO RIVER

But for political shenanigans in the 1920s, the **Green River** might rank among the world's most famous rivers. It starts by flowing north to loop around the Wind River Mountains of central Wyoming, then heads south into Utah, briefly ducks into the northwest corner of Colorado, and then crosses Utah to meet the **Colorado River** after a 730-mile journey.

The Green River was first identified by Fray Alonzo de Posada in 1686 as the boundary between the territories of the Ute and the Comanche. Until 1859, when Captain J.N. Mancomb discovered the confluence deep in the heart of the canyonlands, no one knew that it flowed into the Colorado. The **Colorado River** had been named by the Spanish founder of New Mexico, Juan de Oñate, in 1606, while French trappers in what's now Colorado stumbled across what they named the **Grand River** a century later.

The trouble is, at its confluence with the Green River, the Colorado has flowed a mere 430 miles from the Rockies of central Colorado. As geographical convention dictates that the principal course of a river is its longest, the Green River should be regarded as the main course of the Colorado River, and their combined course should bear the same name. Either the Green should become the Colorado, or the Colorado below the confluence should become the Green – in which case the Grand Canyon should arguably be called the Green Canyon, which doesn't bear thinking about.

The news that the "Colorado River" did not originate in Colorado, as had always been assumed, mortified Colorado's legislators. In the 1920s, they simply defied convention and renamed the Grand the Colorado, which fortunately dovetailed with a vote in conservative Utah against changing the name of the Green River.

Heart of Sinbad Road

The 24-mile **Heart of Sinbad Road** runs from the end of Temple Mountain Road – the spur road off Hwy-24 that leads to Goblin Valley (see p.402) – up to exit 131 off I-70, 33 miles west of Green River. Unpaved, but usually good enough for ordinary vehicles, it provides access to many remote and fascinating areas of the San Rafael Swell. There's no room here to describe them all; pick up a brochure in Green River and choose for yourself.

Green River

Hwy-24 joins I-70 44 miles north of Hanksville, just as the interstate completes a dramatic descent from the uplands of the San Rafael Swell to slope gently east through a landscape of soaring buttes. Within a few miles, a ribbon of green vegetation becomes visible ahead, cutting through the desert at the bottom of a long broad valley – the line of the **Green River**. To the north stand the forbidding **Uintah Mountains**, while to the south the stream burrows into a labyrinth of twisting canyons, so this is the best place to ford the river for hundreds of miles.

7

The town of **GREEN RIVER** has long straddled crucial cross-country routes. For east–west travellers, it remains the major way station between Colorado and Utah, while river-runners from John Wesley Powell onwards have launched themselves south from here towards the Colorado. Slightly more sedate, every Memorial Day, hundreds of boats set out on weekend-long convoy trips that cruise down to the Colorado confluence and then chug back upriver to Moab.

While Green River is a welcome oasis, however – fertile enough to be the "melon-growing capital of east Utah" – it still amounts to little more than a strip of motels, gas stations and fast-food outlets. Given a sensible reluctance to erect permanent structures too close to the river, there's a gap where you might expect downtown to be; most of the built-up strip lies to the west.

John Wesley Powell River History Museum

1765 E Main St • April–Oct Mon–Sat 9am–7pm, Sun noon–5pm; Nov–March Tues–Sat 9am–5pm • $6 • ☎ 435 564 3427, ⊛ jwprhm.com

The thoughtfully laid-out **John Wesley Powell River History Museum**, on the east bank of the river in the heart of Green River, recounts the epic journeys of the Canyonlands region's first true explorer, whose second voyage started here on May 22, 1871. Powell made that second trip partly because he lost the notes from his first, so this time around he ensured his every movement was fully recorded, in photos that now make marvellously evocative viewing. A multimedia show and several rooms of exhibits cover later developments in river navigation, ranging from steamers – none managed more than a handful of voyages – up to the army-surplus rubber inflatables that triggered the postwar boom in whitewater rafting. Glance out of the panoramic windows, and you'll see that the river here is not green at all, but a dark muddy brown.

Sego Canyon

4 miles north along Hwy-74 from I-50 exit 187 at Thompson, a total of 30 miles east of Green River • Free • ☎ 435 259 2100, ⊛ blm.gov

A truly extraordinary and unusually accessible array of **petroglyphs** adorn the walls of **Sego Canyon**, a BLM-run site located ten miles northeast of the point where I-50 meets the road to Moab, US-191. A short walk here leads you past rock art dating from three different eras – going back in time, Historic Ute, Fremont and Archaic. It's the last of those, estimated at two thousand years old, that are the most remarkable, depicting spectral wraith-like figures similar to those on display in Horseshoe Canyon (see p.412). Drive another half a mile beyond the final panel to reach the ghost town of **Sego**, a sandy abandoned mining settlement that's scattered with derelict buildings and the rusted hulks of bygone cars.

ARRIVAL AND DEPARTURE

By train Amtrak's *California Zephyr* calls at the train station at 250 S Broadway daily, heading east towards Denver at 7.59am and west towards Salt Lake City at 5.58pm.

By bus Greyhound buses between Denver and points west stop twice daily at the *Knights Inn*, 1015 E Main St (☎ 435 564 3421).

INFORMATION AND TOURS

Visitor centre In the Powell museum, 1765 E Main St (April–Oct Mon–Sat 9am–7pm, Sun noon–5pm; Nov–March Tues–Sat 9am–5pm; ☎ 435 564 3427, ⊕ greenriverutah.com).

Boat trips Companies running rafting trips from Green River include Holiday River Expeditions (☎ 435 564 3273 or ☎ 800 624 6323, ⊕ bikeraft.com).

ACCOMMODATION

Although Green River is not much of a destination in its own right, it holds around five hundred **motel** rooms. They tend to fill by early evening in summer, partly with the overspill from Moab and partly with long-distance interstate travellers.

Green River State Park Just south of Main Street ☎ 435 564 3633, reservations ☎ 800 322 3770, ⊕ utahstateparks .reserveamerica.com. This attractive waterfront camp-ground, on the river's west bank south of Main Street, offers the best camping in town. It stays open year-round, and also offers one rental cabin. Tents **$21**, RVs **$30**, cabin **$60**

Holiday Inn Express 1845 E Main St ☎ 435 564 4439 or ☎ 800 465 4329, ⊕ ihg.com. Crisp, clean chain motel, next to the museum and visitor centre, with an indoor pool and guest laundry. **$155**

River Terrace Inn 1740 E Main St ☎ 435 564 3401, ☎ 877 564 3401, ⊕ river-terrace.com. High-quality motel, often filled by tour groups, with a pool, river views and adjacent restaurant. **$131**

EATING

Green River Coffee Co 25 E Main St ☎ 435 564 3411, ⊕ grcoffeeco.com. Lively coffee-bar-cum-antique store, just south of the main drag a mile or so west of the river. Breakfast specials and lunchtime sandwiches alike cost $6–8. Mon–Thurs 7am–2pm, Fri–Sun 7am–5pm.

Tamarisk Restaurant 1710 E Main St ☎ 435 564 8109, ⊕ tamariskrestaurant.com. Brisk, busy restaurant, overlooking the river opposite the museum. The menu is wide-ranging and cheap, with full dinners costing $10–16, but the salad bar is atrocious. Daily 7am–10pm.

Canyonlands National Park

Canyonlands National Park is divided into four sections: the Island In The Sky district (see p.407), Horseshoe Canyon (see p.411), the Maze district (see p.413) and the Needles district (see p.413) • $25 per vehicle, $15 for motorcyclists, $10 cyclists and pedestrians, valid for 7 days • ☎ 435 719 2313, ⊕ nps.gov/cany

CANYONLANDS NATIONAL PARK, the largest and most magnificent of Utah's national parks, is as hard to define as it is to map. Its closest equivalent, the Grand Canyon, is simply an almighty crack in an otherwise relatively flat plain; the Canyonlands area is a bewildering tangle of canyons, plateaus, fissures and faults, scattered with buttes and monoliths, pierced by arches and caverns, and penetrated only by a paltry handful of dead-end roads.

The 527 square miles of the park are just the core of a much larger wilderness that stretches to the horizon in every direction. To nineteenth-century explorers, this was the epitome of useless desolation; only since uranium prospectors blazed crude trails across the trackless wastes in the 1950s has it become at all widely known. Even after Canyonlands park was created in 1964, it took a couple of decades before tourists arrived in appreciable numbers.

Canyonlands focuses upon the Y-shaped confluence of the Green and Colorado rivers, buried deep in the desert forty miles southwest of Moab. There's only one spot from which you can see the rivers meet, however, and that's a five-mile hike from the nearest road. With no way to get down to the rivers, let alone cross them, the park therefore splits into three major sections. The **Needles**, east of the Colorado, is a red-rock wonderland of sandstone pinnacles and hidden meadows that's a favourite with hardy hikers and 4WD enthusiasts, while the **Maze**, west of both the Colorado and the Green,

BACKCOUNTRY PERMITS IN CANYONLANDS

Only limited numbers of visitors are allowed to spend a night or more in the **backcountry** of Canyonlands National Park, and all such groups are required to have permits. **Backpacking permits**, covering a maximum party of seven persons in the Needles and Island In The Sky districts, or five persons in the Maze, cost $30. Permits for **four-wheel-drive** or **mountain biking** expeditions that involve backcountry camping, issued for groups of up to three vehicles with a total of fifteen people in the Island In The Sky, ten in the Needles, or nine in the Maze, are $30. **Day-use** permits, costing $10, are also required for bikes and 4WD vehicles that enter Horse or Lavender canyons in the Needles district.

Though not compulsory, **reservations** are essential for popular activities such as overnight backpacking in the Needles district or expeditions on the White Rim in the Island In The Sky, especially in spring and fall. They can be made up to four months in advance, either online at ⓦcanypermits.nps.gov, or at visitor centres in the region, including the NPS Reservations Office (2282 S West Resource Blvd, Moab; Mon–Fri 8am–noon; ☎435 259 4351). Permits must be picked up in person – with every member of the group present – from the appropriate park visitor centre, at least one hour before it closes.

7

is a virtually inaccessible labyrinth of tortuous, waterless canyons that presents a stiff challenge even to expert climbers and backcountry hikers. In the wedge of the "Y" between the two, the high, dry mesa of the **Island In The Sky** commands astonishing views across the whole park and beyond, seen from overlooks that can easily be toured by car. Getting from any one of these sections to the others involves a drive of at least a hundred miles. The Needles and the Island In The Sky are reached via long approach roads that leave US-191 north and south of Moab respectively; the Maze is an endless jolting ride on dirt tracks from either Hwy-24 or the town of Green River.

Just for good measure, a fourth subsection of the park, **Horseshoe Canyon** in the west, was added in 1971 to preserve the Southwest's finest collection of ancient **rock art**.

The **rivers** themselves count as Canyonlands' final major component. A **rafting** expedition from Moab (see p.427), is the best way to experience the eerie stillness of the deep canyons, at once exhilarating and supremely restful. However, since there's no way out before Lake Powell, you'll need to set aside several days, and several hundred dollars – and be prepared to face the intense whitewater rapids of **Cataract Canyon**, just beyond the confluence.

With no lodging and little camping in the park, you'll probably need to make repeated visits on successive days, and as there's no loop road to whisk you through it, it takes a full day to have even a cursory look at a single segment. If you're among the many visitors who find the conditions too gruelling to spend much time out of your car – summer temperatures regularly exceed 100°F, and most trails have no water and little shade – then the Island In The Sky is the most immediately rewarding option. If you fancy a long day-hike, on the other hand, you'd do better to set off into the Needles.

Island In The Sky

It's not obvious from most maps, but like the Colorado River confluence over which it looms, the mesa known as the **ISLAND IN THE SKY** is itself shaped like a "Y". After a steady climb of around 25 miles, **Hwy-313**, which heads southwest from US-191 eight miles north of Moab, enters the park across the slender **Neck** that forms the right-hand fork of the Y. It then branches to the northwest, to run as far as the crater of ̶ ̶ Dome, and to the south, where it ends at the overwhelming **Grand View Poin**

Most Island In The Sky visitors simply drive from one overlook to the ne also walk one or two of the short, easy trails that cross its thin capping of K sandstone, to gaze over the brink of the sheer Wingate cliffs that hold it up.

7

Dead Horse Point State Park (8 miles) and Moab (33 miles)

Labyrinth

Taylor Canyon

Taylor Canyon

Shafer Canyon

Gooseneck Trail

Visitor Centre ℹ️

The Neck

SHAFER TRAIL ROAD

Potash Road

Labyrinth

Upheaval Canyon

Above Spring Trail

Hardscrabble Bottom

Upheaval Dome

Neck Spring Trail

Lathrop Trail

Potato Bottom

Musselman Arch

ACCOMMODATION
Willow Flat Campground 1

White Trail

Aztec Butte

Washer Woman Arch

Airport Tower

Mesa Arch

WHITE RIM ROAD

Candlestick Tower

1

Mesa Arch Trail

Candlestick

Green River Overlook

Green River

Lathrop Canyon

WHITE RIM ROAD

N

Gooseberry Trail

Gooseberry

Murphy Trail

White Rim Overlook

Murphy Hogback

Grand View Trail

CANYONLANDS NATIONAL PARK ISLAND IN THE SKY

Grand View Point Overlook

Monument Basin

Colorado River

Junction Butte

0   5
miles

possible, however – either in a sturdy 4WD vehicle, or by some very strenuous hiking – to make your way down to the pale plateau of the **White Rim**, prominent a thousand feet below.

By the middle of each day, the entire landscape takes on a hazy pallor; for the best **photographs**, you'd ideally be at the national park overlooks early in the morning, and the overlooks of the nearby **Dead Horse Point State Park** at sunset.

Dead Horse Point State Park

Drive 10 miles north from Moab on US-191, 20 miles southwest on Hwy-313, then 7 miles southeast to the point itself • $10 per vehicle, National Parks passes not valid • ☎ 435 259 2614, 🌐 stateparks.utah.gov/parks/dead-horse

Just north of the boundary of Canyonlands National Park, a turning to the east leads in four miles to the smaller but equally breathtaking **Dead Horse Point State Park**. This miniature version of the Island In The Sky stands at the tip of a narrow mesa, poised two thousand feet above a stupendous "gooseneck" loop in the Colorado, which here is much more visible, receding into the distance, than from the national park. Off to the east, the turquoise ponds of Moab's potash plant (see p.426) make a garish contrast with the red rocks, while the Anticline Overlook (see p.429) stands guard above the far side of Meander Canyon. A mile or so of easy paved trails lead to alternative overlooks, and there's plenty of picnic space scattered about.

The visitor centre

3 miles before Dead Horse Point overlook • Daily 9am–5pm • ☎ 435 259 2614

Dead Horse Point's **visitor centre** is located three miles short of the main overlook. In summer, a trailer outside sells coffee and snacks, while inside you'll find a **Desert** ...um of human and natural history. Displays here explain the park's name:

nineteenth-century cowboys used the mesa as a corral, herding wild horses behind the piñon fence that blocked its ninety-foot neck. One band of horses was too scared to cross the gap even when the gate was left open, and perished of thirst. For that matter, Dead Horse Point remains a death trap for unwary pet **dogs**; the current record is three drop-offs in a month.

ACCOMMODATION   DEAD HORSE POINT STATE PARK

Kayenta Campground Dead Horse Point State Park ☎ 435 259 2614, reservations ☎ 800 322 3770, ⓦ utahstateparks.reserveamerica.com. The park campground makes an excellent alternative if there's no room in Canyonlands, with good restrooms but no showers. Closer to the point itself, they've recently added three yurts, each of which sleeps up to six in bunk beds, again with modern restrooms nearby. Tents $\overline{\underline{\$30}}$, yurts $\overline{\underline{\$99}}$

Island In The Sky visitor centre
Drive 10 miles north from Moab on US-191, then 22 miles southwest on Hwy-313 • Daily: March–Oct 8am–6pm; Nov & Dec 9am–4pm; closed Jan & Feb • ☎ 435 259 4712, ⓦ go.nps.gov/isky

Seven miles south of the turn-off to Dead Horse Point, and a mile or so in from the entrance to Canyonlands National Park, the **Island In The Sky visitor centre** stands to the right of the highway. Rangers can provide details on road and trail conditions as well as campsite availability; simply cross the road to get your first sweeping views over the canyonlands.

7

Mesa Arch Trail
Trailhead: 4 miles beyond visitor centre • 0.5 miles round-trip; 30min

The best short hike in the Island In The Sky, the **Mesa Arch Trail**, starts from a small parking lot just before the fork in the road. It's more of a walkway than a trail really, cemented for some of its length and running across bare slickrock elsewhere, equipped with occasional stairways. During a half-mile loop around the mesa-top hillocks, it runs to the very rim of the abyss, where long, shallow **Mesa Arch** frames an extraordinary view of the La Sal Mountains, 35 miles northeast. Admiring Washer Woman Arch and Monster Tower, closer at hand, it would be easy to stumble right through the gap – there's no barrier.

THE GEOLOGY OF CANYONLANDS

In a land with so little water, the sheer *effort* that went into creating the splendour of **Canyonlands** is almost impossible to conceive. As you look out from the park's highest point, atop the Island In The Sky, the cliffs drop away a thousand feet, with the rivers a thousand feet below that. For a hundred miles south, successive plateaus, benches and tablelands diminish into the distance, studded with the occasional butte. And yet twelve million years ago, this entire landscape was one vast plain, level with where you're standing. Bit by bit, at the rate of two inches every thousand years, the topsoil has crumbled to silt and been carried away by the rivers. Most was deposited at the edge of the Pacific, but now it's gradually filling up Lake Powell instead.

Canyonlands was not literally carved by the rivers, however. Both the Green and the Colorado began life as gentle streams. In the last twelve million years, as the Colorado Plateau has pushed up, they have remained in their original courses, ever more deeply entrenched into the earth. Meanwhile, ice produced in a ceaseless cycle of freezes and thaws has chiselled away at the rocks that surround them, tumbling boulders into the water to be swept away.

Canyonlands is unique in that it rests on a mile-thick bed of **salt**, deposited on the bottom of an ancient sea three hundred million years ago. That salt was covered by subsequent layers of sediment, themselves interspersed with further deposits of salt. Under the pressure of thousands of feet of harder rock, the salt layers are squeezed like toothpaste until they flow far underground, then bubble up toward the surface. As they do so, they push up fins and spurs of rock that crack and split to create phenomena such as the Needles, or they may hit ground water and dissolve, leaving gaping caverns behind.

Grand View Point Overlook

Grand View Point Overlook, at the southern end of the road, is the Island In The Sky's definitive vantage point. An agoraphobe's nightmare, it commands a hundred-mile prospect of layer upon layer of naked sandstone, here stacked thousands of feet high, there fractured into bottomless canyons.

The most conspicuous feature is the plateau formed by the **White Rim** layer, a thousand feet below, whose faint smattering of grass is crisscrossed by abandoned mining trails and ends at the White Rim itself. That peters out in the mass of white-capped red-rock pillars known as **Monument Basin**, amid which the **Totem Pole** may look the size of a pencil but is actually 305ft tall. Neither river can be seen; the Colorado River is tucked out of sight another thousand feet down, while the equivalent canyon of the Green River is hidden by the twin buttes to the west. Everything is mirrored by an identical chaos on the far side, however, rising towards the snow-capped peaks of the **Abajo Mountains**, forty miles south.

Grand View Trail

Trailhead: Grand View Point Overlook • 2 miles round-trip; 1hr

The **Grand View Trail**, which sets off across a lovely level shelf just below and to the right of Grand View Point Overlook, enables you to contemplate the whole jigsaw puzzle from countless additional angles. Every now and then, you may spot the silhouette of the Needles, far to the south. Keep going beyond the end of the shelf, and you'll eventually reach the very tip of the promontory, where you can clamber atop various rocky eminences for wonderful views to the north as well.

Green River Overlook

A couple of hundred yards north of the fork in the park road, a paved 1.2-mile spur road leads to a parking lot a few short steps away from the **Green River Overlook**. The expanse of the White Rim that spreads below – clearer and flatter than at Grand View Point – is pierced by the green-trimmed meandering course of the river itself, as it flows through placid **Stillwater Canyon**. At this very spot, in the 1965 biblical epic *The Greatest Story Ever Told*, Max von Sydow (aka Jesus) delivered the Sermon on the Mount to an audience of Moab Rotarians bedecked in false beards and tea towels.

Upheaval Dome

The park road ends five miles north of the fork, at the geological oddity of **Upheaval Dome**. This jagged 1500ft-deep crater is a highlight of air tours (see p.427), but from close up, at the end of the steep ten-minute climb from the parking lot, it's a disappointment. Elaborate theories that explained the prongs of pale stone bursting from its darkest depths as the product of undulating subterranean salt have recently been abandoned in favour of the simpler notion of a sixty-million-year-old **meteor strike**.

Over the Edge: the White Rim Road

The reason the Island In The Sky is accessible at all, and that crude dirt tracks strike off into the wilderness everywhere you look, is that this region was a prime target for freelance **uranium prospectors** in the 1950s (see p.422). They knew that uranium is often found in the grey-green rocks of the **Chinle formation**, which here forms the talus slopes at the bottom of the Wingate-sandstone cliffs, not far above the White Rim.

The rough-and-ready hundred-mile **White Rim Road**, scraped by would-be miners at the base of the cliffs, is now most often explored on three- or four-day **4WD expeditions**, with overnight stops at primitive campgrounds en route by permit only (see p.406). Only the hair-raising **Shafer Trail Road**, which drops just south of the visitor centre, connects the mesa-top with the White Rim; otherwise drivers join the White Rim Road by means of the **Potash Road** from Moab (see p.426), or along **Mineral Bottom Road**, which runs west from Hwy-313 a couple of miles north of the Dead Horse Point turn-off. None of these routes should be attempted in ordinary vehicles.

Hikers can, however, clamber between the Island In The Sky and the White Rim along various trails. All are too demanding for a round-trip day-hike down to the White Rim – let alone to either river – to be a good idea. Register with the Park Service before you set off on a multi-day trip. Options include the **Lathrop Trail**, an utterly exhausting nine-mile route all the way to the Colorado, passing close to abandoned but potentially toxic uranium mines; the **Upheaval Canyon Trail**, which drops down to the Green River from the far side of Upheaval Dome; and the **Shafer Trail Road** itself.

ACCOMMODATION	ISLAND IN THE SKY

Willow Flat Campground Green River Overlook ☎ 435 259 4712, ⓦ go.nps.gov/isky. The Island In The Sky's only developed campground, just back from the overlook, has twelve basic sites, with vault toilets but no water. Available first-come, first-served only, it's usually full in spring and fall. **$15**

Horseshoe Canyon

Remote **Horseshoe Canyon**, a detached chunk of Canyonlands National Park located northwest of its main body but 42 miles by dirt road southeast of Green River, is home to the most extraordinary **rock art** in North America. No one now knows the meaning of the mysterious, haunting figures that line the sandstone walls of the **Great Gallery**. Although to the modern eye they suggest an astonishing sophistication, they are among the **oldest** such images to survive.

The San Rafael Desert: the road to Horseshoe Canyon and the Maze

Unless the weather has been dreadful – check at the Green River visitor centre (see p.406) – ordinary vehicles should have no problem driving to Horseshoe Canyon. Of the two possible approach routes, the one that starts from **Green River** is, for anyone who wants to sleep in a motel the night before, more convenient than the one from Hwy-24 detailed below, but it's marginally more likely to be impassable. Assuming it's clear, follow signs for the airport from the town centre until you cross the railroad tracks. Once the surface has turned to gravel, fork left at a BLM sign pointing toward the San Rafael River.

After an initial flat section, the road from Green River pushes through painted-desert badlands formed by the fossil-rich Morrison Formation, then winds down to a glorious panorama of Monument Valley-style buttes. It crosses the **San Rafael River** on a rickety wooden bridge after nineteen miles, then climbs again to offer views that stretch west to the Henry Mountains and east to the La Sals.

Just over forty miles south of Green River, beyond **Antelope Valley** – home to one of Utah's few surviving herds of pronghorn antelope – an easily missed spur road branches off east. The **Horseshoe Canyon trailhead** is at its far end, at the edge of the plateau two miles along.

As the road veers west, a junction 5.5 miles beyond the Horseshoe Canyon turn-off marks the start of the 21-mile drive south to **Hans Flat Ranger Station**, the main point of access for the Maze (see p.413). Keep going west, though, and a total of 32 miles from Horseshoe Canyon – in optimum conditions, around an hour's driving – you'll finally meet **Hwy-24**, just south of Goblin Valley (see p.402). This last stretch crosses Sweetwater Reef before dropping into the **San Rafael Desert**, where it insinuates itself between two impressive buttes known as Little Flat Top and Big Flat Top.

If you're heading east from Capitol Reef, it's much quicker to reverse the route described above; just be sure you have enough gas.

Horseshoe Canyon Trail

Trailhead: 42 miles by dirt road southeast of Green River • 7 miles round-trip, 5hr, elevation change 750ft • Ranger-led guided hikes Sat 9am in spring and fall • ☎ 435 259 2652, ⓦ nps.gov/cany

Even if you're not a rock-art enthusiast, the **Horseshoe Canyon Trail** down to the Great Gallery – there's no road access – ranks among the most beautiful hikes in Utah. With

THE ROCK ART OF HORSESHOE CANYON

At the time it was first studied, Horseshoe Canyon was called **Barrier Canyon**, and that name still defines the style of **rock art** for which it's famous. Such art is characterized by anthropomorphic figures, roughly life-sized but weirdly elongated, and often lacking both arms and legs. Those that have eyes have large round ones, or simply empty sockets, and many seem draped in stylized robes; for most visitors to this lonely desert backwater, the cumulative effect is to suggest **ghosts** or spirits from another, different time.

While spear points found in Horseshoe Canyon date back twelve thousand years, archeologists believe the pictographs were produced by people of the **Archaic** culture, which flourished between 7500 BC and 500 AD. At the start of that period, the climate was much wetter, and the canyon held lakes, ponds and plentiful game. When conditions dried out, it was briefly abandoned, but then reoccupied.

Life was now far more difficult, and **shamanistic rituals** attempted to ensure successful hunting. These involved the creation first of clay statuettes, from 5000 BC onwards, and later of figurines made from split willow-twigs. Many represent what seem to be deities or shamans as well as animals, and the Great Gallery pictographs are thought to depict those same entities.

As for **technique**, the Great Gallery is very literally rock art. To produce the paint, different coloured rocks were ground up, dissolved in water, and bonded with saliva produced by chewing seeds. The red is hematite, heavy with rust; the white is gypsum or chalk; even the blue comes from a local stratum. Some figures were produced with brushes, others by blowing or flicking paint at a stencil. Digital manipulation of photos of the images reveals not only faded colours but even different layers, so archeologists can see how specific figures were changed and redrawn over the centuries.

Experts estimate the gallery to be between 1600 and 6000 years old. Certain sites seem to have been rendered inaccessible by rockfalls that occurred a very long time ago indeed. All that's certain is that none dates from later than 400 AD, when the Archaic people acquired the bow and arrow – not shown in any Great Gallery images – and began to transform into the **Fremont** culture. Fremont art, as seen elsewhere in Utah as well as here in Horseshoe Canyon, has its own very distinct style.

either forty miles of dirt road to negotiate south of Green River, or 32 miles southeast from Hwy-24, before you even reach the trailhead, few visitors come this way, so you may well get the gorgeous red-rock canyon, rustling with wildlife, to yourself. It's a long, exposed hike though, so carry all the provisions you might conceivably need, and either start early, or sit out the midday sun down in the canyon.

The route picks its way down from the trailhead, marked by cairns as it crosses patches of deep sand alternating with slickrock. Once you reach the bottom, after perhaps half an hour, follow the sandy wash to your right. Stay initially on its left bank, and within ten minutes you should spot the first rock-art site, the **High Gallery**, above the talus on the canyon's left wall. It's not easy to see detail here, though, so you'll soon be ready to press on.

All the remaining sites lie across the wash on the right wall. The first, the **Horseshoe Shelter**, nestles beneath an overhanging cliff a hundred yards further on. When Harvard archeologists excavated this site in 1930, it held several rooms; all that remains is a vivid band of **pictographs** in the palest stratum of the rock, which was above the roofs of the shelters and is thus now out of reach. The animals, squiggles, and triangular figures – many with strange protuberances on their heads – date from the Fremont era, but the scattering of ghostly footless figures are in the earlier Barrier Canyon style.

Another twenty minutes' walk on, beyond several twists and turns in the canyon walls, climb up into a massive pale sandstone alcove, where a red-and-white band of rock holds another small collection of pictographs.

Eventually, after twenty more minutes, you round the final bend to be confronted by the **Great Gallery**, suddenly apparent beneath a lesser overhang. It's a breathtaking moment. Framed between the cottonwoods, a long row of dark, hollow-eyed, otherworldly entities stands stark against the pale rock. Though the details grow clearer the closer you get, somehow a sense of vast, alien distance remains.

Apart from a couple of well-shaded stone benches, and pit toilets nearby, there are no facilities for visitors.

It was from the Horseshoe Canyon trailhead, incidentally, that **Aron Ralston** set off on the 2003 hike to Blue John Canyon, beyond Horseshoe Canyon, which culminated in his having to cut off his right arm, as immortalized in the film **127 Hours**. Since the movie came out, around twenty people have had to be rescued from Blue John Canyon, which despite its on-screen appearance does *not* contain a lush deep lagoon.

ACCOMMODATION	HORSESHOE CANYON

Horseshoe Canyon Trailhead campsite No camping is permitted in Horseshoe Canyon itself, but there's a basic site with no services beside the parking lot at the Horseshoe Canyon Trail trailhead. Free

The Maze

7

The name of Canyonlands' **Maze** district is no exaggeration. This brainteaser of convoluted canyons and barren desert washes, west of the Green and Colorado rivers, must be the least explored region of the US. If you're determined to get away from it all, the Maze is the place for you; getting back to it all when you've finished is more of a problem.

Somewhere in the heart of the Maze is the legendary **Robbers Roost**, a canyon fastness used as a hideout by nineteenth-century cattle rustlers and bandits like **Butch Cassidy** and his Wild Bunch. They'd escape the long arm of the law by riding the Outlaw Trail up from the Green River near Mineral Bottom; lacking their familiarity with the terrain, pursuing posses had to turn back defeated. No roads entered the region until uranium prospectors bulldozed their way in during the 1950s.

Even today, you'll need a high-clearance 4WD vehicle to get any further than **Hans Flat Ranger Station**, which stands 21 miles south of the road through the San Rafael Desert to Horseshoe Canyon (see p.411). Though technically the ranger station is in Glen Canyon NRA, it's the main source of information for hikers and drivers setting off into the Maze.

The **jeep roads** beyond Hans Flat take another twenty or thirty miles to jostle and switchback into the actual Maze. One route in ends at the **Maze Overlook**, another at **Doll House Butte**, which marks the far end of the **Land of Standing Rocks**, above the west bank of Cataract Canyon and straight across from the Needles.

Having come this far, most backcountry hikers launch themselves into the wilderness for days or weeks at a time. There are few formal trails, but favoured destinations include **Pictograph Canyon**, not far beneath the Maze Overlook, where Barrier Canyon-style pictographs seem to record the moment when the Archaic people first acquired agriculture. However, unless you're extremely self-sufficient, a workhorse when it comes to carrying vast quantities of water, and a fearless, fully equipped rock climber, you're never going to see them.

INFORMATION	THE MAZE

Hans Flat Ranger Station 46 miles east of Hwy-24, 66 miles south of Green River (daily 8am–4.30pm; ☎ 435 259 2652, ⓦ nps.gov/cany.

The Needles

Thanks to its intricate tracery of backcountry trails, which offer the chance to engage with the landscape rather than merely marvel from a distance, **THE NEEDLES** district is Canyonlands National Park's most satisfying segment for hikers, bikers and 4WD drivers. While it has its share of long-range vistas – including the park's only

Confluence Overlook – the Needles is noted primarily for its namesake thickets of candy-striped **sandstone pillars**. Clustered on scrubby rock outcrops, concealing pockets of incongruous grassland, these intriguing formations can be explored on brief forays or multi-day backpacking expeditions.

The **Needles** area is a very long way from civilization, at the far end of the stunning **Hwy-211**, a total of 75 miles from Moab and fifty from Monticello. If you're planning a number of successive day-hikes, it makes sense to camp overnight; reserve a site as soon as you know you're coming (see p.406). Note, incidentally, that the **Needles Overlook** is not in the national park, but in the BLM's Canyon Rims area (see p.428).

Ordinary mortals, as opposed to obsessive canyoneers, should also be warned that even casual **hiking** in the Needles may be the hardest thing you've ever done. Carry a good map and at least four pints of water per person, stick to the trails, and above all be very careful how far you climb. It's much easier to go up than it is to come down, so you run the risk of getting "rim-rocked", or stuck on the rim without a route down.

7 The road to the Needles: Squaw Flats Scenic Byway

The 35-mile **Hwy-211**, also known as the **Squaw Flats Scenic Byway**, heads west of US-191 forty miles south of Moab. You can't miss the turning; it's marked by a colossal butte immediately opposite, which, if you happen to be hungry, may well seem to resemble a giant brioche.

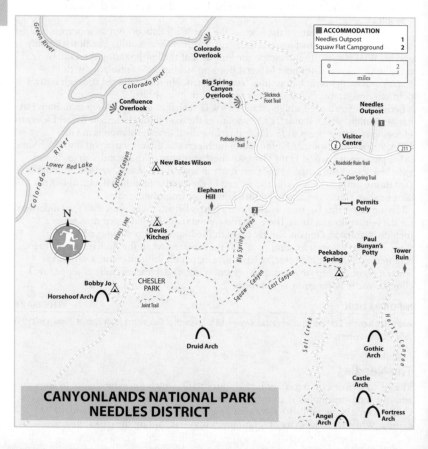

CANYONLANDS NATIONAL PARK NEEDLES DISTRICT

As it winds lazily into the park, between cottonwood-lined **Indian Creek** and canyon walls of rich red sandstone, and overlooked by the twin castellated **Sixshooter Peaks**, the byway seems to carry you back a century, into the unspoiled Wild West. Much of the route lies through open grazing country, making this one of the few spots in the Southwest where you still see genuine **cowboys** riding the range. The Dugout Ranch, halfway along, was established in 1885, and later amalgamated with its neighbours to form the Indian Creek Cattle Company, Utah's largest cattle outfit.

Newspaper Rock

Hwy-211, 12 miles west of US-191 • Daily 24hr • Free

Newspaper Rock Recreation Site, alongside Hwy-211, preserves a panel of black desert varnish that's inscribed, like some prehistoric newspaper, with literally hundreds of **petroglyphs**. For ancient peoples, this made a perfect site to create conspicuous and enduring images, sheltered as it is by a protective rock lintel beneath a hillock at a narrow bend in the valley north of the Abajo Mountains. Besides abstract designs, images include helmeted human figures, buffalo and bighorn sheep, plus lots of six-toed footprints and what look like bear paw prints. Some are probably symbols left by clans who performed particular ceremonies here, or simply passed by. With the obvious exception of recent graffiti, it's hard to say when they were executed, but many are not in fact all that old; nineteenth-century Ute are thought to be responsible for the mounted riders, shown hunting with bows and arrows.

The riverside woods across the road from the rock hold a lovely if basic **campground**, free but waterless. A short way further west, Hwy-211 meets the mountain road from Monticello (see p.430).

Needles Visitor Center

35 miles west on Hwy-211 from US-191, a total of 75 miles from Moab or 49 miles from Monticello • Daily: Early March to Oct 8am–5pm; Nov 9am–4pm; closed Dec to early March • ☎ 435 259 4711, ⓦ go.nps.gov/theneedles

Rangers at the **Needles Visitor Center**, a mile inside the park boundary, can provide up-to-date hiking information. They issue 34 **backpacking permits** per night, each for a group of up to seven people; in high season, if you don't have a reservation (see p.406) the chances are that none will be available. Day-hikers don't need permits.

Three miles beyond the visitor centre, the road forks at the Squaw Flats campground (see p.417). Keep on its main paved section for another four miles to reach the **Big Spring Canyon Overlook**, where you'll confront an array of mushroom-shaped hoodoos, or turn left onto an uneven dirt road and you'll come to **Elephant Hill** in three miles.

Short hikes in the Needles

The Needles' best hiking is unquestionably on its longer trails. If you're pressed for time, however, several shorter routes set off from close to the main park road. A mile south of the visitor centre, the **Cave Spring Trail** is an enjoyable 25-minute hike that begins by leading under a group of overhangs. One holds a remarkably preserved old cowboy camp, another shelters assorted petroglyphs. Two short ladders then climb to the top of a low mesa, where you walk back to your car across the slickrock.

Another two miles west is the half-mile **Pothole Point Trail**, an easy stroll to the top of the roadside ridge. Half a mile on from there, the 2.5-mile, two-hour **Slickrock Trail** is much more challenging. While the trail itself is not technically difficult, if you're on it at all that's probably because you didn't get here early enough to tackle anything longer, so you'll be exposed to the full heat of the midday sun. Its shadeless route nonetheless provides a tremendous orientation to the region, following cairns from one sandstone knoll to the next in a lasso shape, with an initial straight section leading to a longer loop. Four separate spur trails along the way lead to successive overlooks, each with its own long-distance mountain-and-mesa views.

Chesler Park Loop Trail

Trailheads: Elephant Hill or Squaw Flat • From Elephant Hill 11 miles round-trip, 7hr, elevation change 500ft; From Squaw Flat 15 miles round-trip, 10hr, elevation change 500ft

Chesler Park, the high grassy meadow whose stubby sandstone pinnacles gave the Needles its name, makes a great destination for a long day-hike. Simply to reach it requires a six-mile round-trip trek from Elephant Hill, or a ten-mile one from Squaw Flat campground, while looping around the "park" itself adds another five miles.

As you climb across the cairned stretches of slickrock that rise from both Elephant Hill and Squaw Flat, look north for sweeping views to the Island In The Sky, with the White Rim etched beneath it. The two trails meet half an hour up from Elephant Hill, then dip west to cross the wash that runs through **Elephant Canyon** – it may look dry, but there's usually water flowing beneath the sand – before the final ascent to Chesler Park.

For the most part, the **Chesler Park Loop Trail** undulates around the edge of the 600-acre clearing, on the slopes below the red-and-white barber-pole Needles. On the eastern flank, however, it runs straight across the lavender-tinted grassland, while in the far southwestern corner it disappears into an extraordinary mini-canyon whose blackened walls are seldom even three feet apart. This claustrophobic segment, the mile-long **Joint Trail**, is the highlight of the trip. A ledge perched above its eastern end, a 500ft detour off the main trail, provides a superb overview of Chesler Park. Through a gap to the west, the gigantic Doll House Butte (see p.413), across the Colorado, can also be glimpsed. If you have a 4WD vehicle, you can drive up to join the Chesler Park Loop near the Joint Trail, and walk the loop alone as a five-mile hike.

As an alternative to circling Chesler Park, consider following the spur trail that branches south along Elephant Canyon. It takes just over three miles of steady climbing to reach the stunning, sturdy **Druid Arch**, named for its resemblance to the rough-hewn monuments of Stonehenge.

Several more trails connect Chesler Park and Elephant Canyon with Squaw Flat, including routes through **Squaw Canyon** and the upper reaches of **Big Spring Canyon**. Backcountry **camping** is only allowed at specific sites along the jeep road that runs west and north of Chesler Park, of which the closest to the main trails is at Devils Kitchen Camp – and you'd be lucky to get a permit (see p.406).

Confluence Overlook Trail

Trailhead: Big Spring Canyon Overlook • 11 miles round-trip, 7hr, elevation change 20ft

According to writer Edward Abbey, the local business community only agreed to Canyonlands' designation as a national park in 1964 on the understanding that its different parts would be linked by a loop drive, of which the focus would be the **Confluence Overlook**. It was even anticipated that this would be the site of a Junction Dam, which would create an even larger lake than Lake Powell. In the absence of either road or dam, the demanding but utterly magnificent eleven-mile round-trip hike from **Big Spring Canyon Overlook** remains the only way those without 4WD vehicles can reach the spot where the Green River meets the Colorado.

The trail starts with a steep drop into Big Spring Canyon, then laboriously climbs out again. After twenty exhausting minutes you emerge through a natural portal between two huge nodules to be greeted by long-distance views of the red-rock wilderness ahead – and cool shade closer at hand. A short metal ladder brings you out onto a level plateau, but you're soon descending again into **Elephant Canyon**, at this point several miles north of, and considerably broader than, the segment near Chesler Park (see above). Each time you climb back onto the slickrock mesa-top, new views open up, either south to the Needles or north to Junction Butte beneath the Island In The Sky.

Clambering from rock to rock beyond Elephant Canyon, you pass through several lifeless valleys known as **grabens**, from the German for "ditches". These were created

55,000 years ago, when shifting underground salt beds caused landslides. At times, the scrambling is hard going, and you have to haul yourself up onto head-high ledges, but it always stops short of actual rock climbing. Finally, after a half-mile section of jeep road – 4WD drivers can get this far via a nine-mile drive from Elephant Hill – you teeter out to the edge of the plateau and see the confluence for the first time.

A thousand feet below the **Confluence Overlook**, the Green River flows in from the west, and the Colorado from the northeast. They're never the same colour. Sometimes the Green really is a pale green, and the Colorado almost red, tinted with dissolved red sandstone; at other times the Green is more of a yellow, and the Colorado a muddy chocolate. In any case, the two hues remain distinct for the first mile or two after the rivers combine, intermeshing like a zipper as they flow parallel but separate towards fearsome Cataract Canyon.

ACCOMMODATION   **THE NEEDLES**

Needles Outpost Hwy-211 ☎435 896 3968, ⓦneedlesoutpost.com. Reopened by enthusiastic new management in 2015, this privately owned, seasonal grocery store and gas station, up a short spur road just outside the park boundary, has its own small campground, with flush toilets and drinking water. Showers $6 if you're

not staying overnight. Closed Dec to mid-Feb. $15
Squaw Flat Campground Needles District ☎435 259 4711, ⓦgo.nps.gov/theneedles. Space at this first-come, first-served campground, roughly three miles west of the visitor centre, is at an absolute premium in spring and fall. Bathrooms and water year-round. $20

Arches National Park

US-191, 5 miles northwest of central Moab • $25 per vehicle, $15 for motorcyclists, $10 cyclists and pedestrians, valid for 7 days •
☎435 719 2299, ⓦnps.gov/arch

One of the most accessible national parks in the Southwest, just five miles north of Moab, **ARCHES NATIONAL PARK** is arguably the most satisfying to visit within a single day. Approaching 1.5 million visitors a year drive in, explore its twenty miles of paved roads, tick off however many arches they feel they have time for, and drive on to their next destination.

Thanks to *Desert Solitaire*, **Edward Abbey's** lyrical evocation of his spell as a ranger here during the 1950s, Arches has a place in the hearts of environmentalists and wilderness enthusiasts. The irony is that when Abbey was here, there was no road into the body of the park, and the only way to explore it was to blaze your own trails. Now you can cruise round in a couple of hours, and barely step out of your vehicle.

Even so, Arches remains very much worth visiting. The **Colorado River** here is literally peripheral, running unseen along the park's southern boundary. The emphasis instead is on the stark, strangely disjointed **sandstone scenery** of the higher ground to the north. As at Canyonlands, these rocks rest on an unstable layer of salt. Salt Valley, which slopes down across the park toward the Colorado, was formed by the collapse of an underground salt dome. That massive subsidence left high ridges to either side, which cracked along vertical fault lines to create long parallel "fins" of orange-pink Entrada sandstone.

Over the eons, water collects in pores in the fins and scours them into potholes; piece by piece, the stone flakes away, until a hole is worn right through. Estimates of how many such "**arches**" the park holds vary from the eighty or so named on maps to the official count of over two thousand. No one has bothered to define whether a "window" is a type of arch or just another word for one, but it's agreed that an arch or window has to be at least three feet wide. Both are distinct from "bridges", which span running water.

To Abbey, the arches were a "small and inessential" feature of the landscape, and unless you're a real obsessive, the appeal of hunting down arch after arch soon palls. The park's short, straightforward **hiking trails** are enjoyable in their own right, however,

7

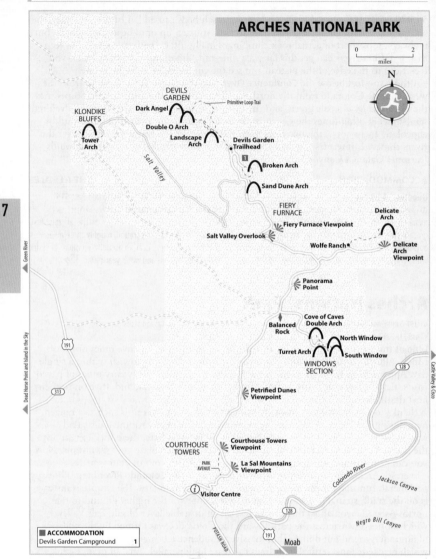

ARCHES NATIONAL PARK

0 ——— 2
miles

N

KLONDIKE
BLUFFS

DEVILS
GARDEN

Dark Angel — Primitive Loop Trail

Double O Arch

Landscape
Arch

Tower
Arch

Salt Valley

Devils Garden
Trailhead

1

Broken Arch

Sand Dune Arch

FIERY
FURNACE

Fiery Furnace Viewpoint

Salt Valley Overlook

Delicate
Arch

Wolfe Ranch

Delicate
Arch
Viewpoint

Panorama
Point

Balanced
Rock

Cove of Caves
Double Arch

North Window

Turret Arch

South Window

WINDOWS
SECTION

Petrified Dunes
Viewpoint

COURTHOUSE
TOWERS

Courthouse Towers
Viewpoint

PARK
AVENUE

La Sal Mountains
Viewpoint

Visitor Centre

Colorado River

Jackson Canyon

128

Negro Bill Canyon

POTASH ROAD

191

Moab

Green River

Dead Horse Point and Island in the Sky

191

313

Castle Valley & Cisco

128

ACCOMMODATION
Devils Garden Campground   1

so you're bound to see a good number of arches along the way. **Delicate Arch** is by far the most impressive, in that it's a free-standing crescent of rock. Most of the rest are just holes, though **Landscape Arch** is such a big one it would be a shame to miss it.

Apart from one solitary cabin, testament to a failed attempt at cattle ranching, very few traces of human occupation remain in this forbidding desert. It became a national monument after the Klondike Bluffs area was found by a wandering prospector in the 1920s, and was enlarged into a national park in 1971.

Most visitors now arrive in **midsummer**, despite blazing temperatures that can reach 110°F. Hiking conditions are much more bearable in spring – when the wildflowers blossom – or fall.

Visitor centre

US-191, 2.4 miles northwest of Colorado River, 5 miles northwest of central Moab • Daily: March & Sept–Nov 8am–4.30pm; April–Aug 7.30am–6pm; Dec–Feb 9am–4pm • Free • ☎ 435 719 2299, ⊛ nps.gov/arch

The fancy **visitor centre** for Arches National Park, alongside the only park entrance, stands at the base of a long, tall escarpment that conceals the bulk of the park from the highway. While it's bursting with the latest technology, its huge model arches are much more show than tell, and there's little information of substance to be found. Rangers do, however, provide hiking advice, and issue free backcountry camping permits. Although you're allowed to camp anywhere that's out of sight of roads, trails and named arches, Arches in fact sees very little overnight backpacking, as most visitors do all the hiking they want within a day.

Immediately beyond the visitor centre, the park road begins its eighteen-mile journey north to Devil's Garden with a steep climb up the cliffs, offering views across to Moab. Note that each **parking lot** along the road is designed to hold a specific number of vehicles, to limit hiker numbers on any one trail. Park illegally, and there's a $25 on-the-spot fine. No vehicles, or bikes, are allowed on the trails.

7

Park Avenue

Trailheads: Park Avenue Viewpoint and Courthouse Towers Viewpoint • 2 miles round-trip; 1hr • Elevation change 320ft

The first parking lot you come to in the park proper, a mile up from the visitor centre, marks the start of **Park Avenue**. Visitors keen to reach the big-name trails and attractions tend to ignore this straightforward one-mile walk, and in truth if you've only time for one hike this isn't the one to choose, but it still makes a very enjoyable, and usually very peaceful, stroll. The best views of the "avenue", named for the "skyscrapers" that top the high ridges to either side of a dry wash, come from the trailhead itself.

The main elevation change on the hike is right at the start, as you drop down to the rocky bed of the wash via a neatly maintained staircase. Once there, you keep going straight ahead, with slickrock and boulders alternating with thick sand underfoot. The long dramatic orange fin to your right peters well before the far end of the trail, which leads to a group of chunky monoliths known as the **Courthouse Towers**. Any arches there may once have been have long since fallen.

Unless you arrange to be met at the northern trailheads, you'll have to walk Park Avenue as a two-mile round-trip. The road in between the two passes the **La Sal Mountains Viewpoint**, which offers the first glimpse of the peaks to the east.

Windows Section

In the heart of the park, almost ten miles up from the visitor centre, the extraordinary, fifty-foot **Balanced Rock** rests precariously on its slanted pedestal. Immediately beyond, a spur road to the right leads in three miles to the **Windows Section**. Several fine arches can be admired from the parking lot at the end, the largest in the park, which is also the starting point for a couple of very popular short trails.

North and South Windows

Trailhead: Windows parking lot • 1 mile round-trip; 30min

The busy loop trail to the North and South Windows ambles gently upwards for a couple of hundred yards towards **North Window**, the only one of the pair visible from the road. Take the steeper spur trail that leads right up to it, gaze through, and you'll appreciate why the word "window" is so appropriate. So far the gaping aperture has framed only blue sky, but now a magnificent desert panorama comes into view.

South Window is just a few yards away, though you have to rejoin the main trail and round one last pinnacle in order to see it properly. You can't climb right up to it, though a rougher and much quieter unpaved trail continues around the back and leads eventually back to the parking lot, adding around half an hour to the total length of the hike. Alternatively, you'll have noticed by now that the lone fin across the main trail is pierced by **Turret Arch**. Wander over there, then look back for a shot of the two windows side by side – a pair of dazzling blue eyes, separated by a bulbous snub nose.

Double Arch

Trailhead: Windows parking lot • 0.5 mile round-trip; 15min

A separate half-mile trail leads from the Windows parking lot to **Double Arch**, where the roof of a wedge-shaped arch has fallen in to create either a skylight, or two distinct arches, depending on your point of view. On the far side, the **Cove of Caves** is packed with incipient future arches, burrowing into the cliffs.

Delicate Arch

7

As befits the state's single most remarkable natural phenomenon, **Delicate Arch** has become a symbol of Utah. Oddly enough, its sturdy bow-legged form is not in fact all that delicate. It was originally called "Landscape Arch", for the view of the La Sal Mountains it so neatly frames, and only swapped names with what is now Landscape Arch (see p.421) due to a mapmaker's mistake.

A side road towards Delicate Arch leaves the park road shortly beyond **Panorama Point**. The arch itself can only be reached via the demanding **Delicate Arch Trail**. If you lack the time or energy for that, you can see it from afar from the **Delicate Arch Viewpoint**, at the end of a level hundred-yard trail that begins a mile further on. For **photographs**, Delicate Arch Viewpoint is best in the early morning, while the Delicate Arch Trail is better in the afternoon.

Delicate Arch Trail

Trailhead: Wolfe Ranch parking lot • 3 miles round-trip; 2–3hr • Elevation change 480ft

The **Delicate Arch Trail** may be just 1.5 miles long, but the round-trip to the arch and back involves a steep climb across bare slickrock that can take the wind out of the hardiest hiker's sails. The trail starts just short of **Wolfe Ranch**, 1.2 miles along the spur road, where Civil War veteran John Wolfe built a cabin in 1906, using cedar and cottonwood logs hauled seven miles from the Colorado. His cattle had by then been denuding the nearby slopes for almost twenty years; when sheep farmers began to graze their animals on this impoverished soil as well, Wolfe gave up and moved back to Ohio.

Beyond the cabin, a footbridge crosses the shallow perennial **Salt Wash**, and the trail begins its determined ascent. Considering that fewer than ten inches of rain fall here each year, the terrain is surprisingly varied, from the scrubby riverbanks, choked with tamarisk, by way of a small-scale piñon-juniper forest, up to the naked rock three-quarters of a mile up. An alcove off to the left, just below the hilltop, cherishes "**hanging gardens**" of rushes and even orchids, fed by a spring that stains the rocks.

It's easy to lose the sparsely cairned trail at the top of the mesa; the trick is to follow a narrow ledge in the rock that leads around the back of a high fin. Suddenly, from a viewing area neatly fenced off by a waist-high natural rock parapet, you're confronted by the full glory of **Delicate Arch**. Standing in superb isolation on the high lip of a canyon, it looks taller than its 45 feet. Quite how much closer you dare to approach depends on your confidence walking across the steeply inclined slickrock. There's no physical reason to stop you from standing right under it; lots of people do.

Delicate Arch is deservedly the most popular place in the park from which to see the **sunset**. Be sure to arrive at the trailhead at least an hour before the sun is due to go down, and longer in busy periods, when parking is at a premium. The sumptuous red glow of the arch deepens right until the final moment, so it's worth staying up there as long as you can – which means you'll be glad of a **flashlight** or torch for the hike back down again.

Fiery Furnace

Guided hikes daily: April to mid-June & Sept 10am & 2pm; mid-June to Aug 9am & 4pm • $16, ages 5–12 $8 • Reserve up to six months in advance on ⓦ recreation.gov

An uninspiring overlook three miles on from the Wolfe Ranch turn-off gives little idea of the labyrinthine complexity of the **Fiery Furnace**. Named not for any exceptional heat but for its golden late-afternoon glow, this warren of high-walled dead-end gullies and parallel fins is so disorientating, and so fragile, that you're strongly advised to enter it on a ranger-led **guided hike**. The hikes are fascinating, but don't involve walking all that far; most of the time is spent standing still, while the ranger explains the rock formations and signs of life along the way. Reserve as far ahead as you can; for spring and fall dates especially, places get snapped up almost as soon as they become available, six months in advance. If you're unlucky, check at the visitor centre as soon as you arrive, to see whether any extra hikes have been added to the schedule.

A limited number of visitors each day are allowed to hike into the Fiery Furnace without a guide. To do so, you have to buy a $6 permit, and watch an introductory safety video, at the visitor centre. No backcountry camping is permitted.

Devil's Garden

Trailhead: Devil's Garden • **Landscape Arch** 1.6 miles round-trip; 1hr • **Double O Arch** 4 miles round-trip; 2–3hr

The park's largest concentration of arches is found in the **Devil's Garden**, beyond the far end of the road eighteen miles up from the visitor centre. The prime target here is the 300ft **Landscape Arch**, reached within a mile by a gravelled, reasonably level trail. This slender span is so frail that hikers are not allowed up to or through the arch itself. A sixty-foot-long slab dropped off it in 1991, and lesser rockfalls happen all the time, such as the one that destroyed nearby **Wall Arch** in 2008. Arch aficionados will probably still be debating whether Landscape Arch or Kolob Arch in Zion National Park (see p.363) is the world's longest arch when it finally disintegrates. Landscape Arch is much harder to photograph than Delicate Arch, especially when the sun is behind it in the afternoon; try to come as early in the day as you can.

If your appetite for high-desert hiking has been whetted, press on beyond Landscape Arch on a trail that immediately becomes far cruder. After another mile – during which one hundred-yard section obliges you to totter along the top of a narrow sandstone fin – you round a corner to see **Double O Arch** on the skyline. At first, only its large upper oval is visible; as you approach, you'll see the much smaller ring beneath it as well. The pallid alkali wastelands that stretch away to the east were once prime uranium territory, and one heavily polluted section is still known as the "**Poison Strip**".

The four-mile round-trip hike to Double O Arch also leads past half a dozen other named arches and assorted minor pinpricks and peepholes. Real gluttons for punishment can turn it into a seven-mile loop, by circling back on the Primitive Loop Trail, but that route is every bit as exhausting as its name implies.

Klondike Bluffs

Trailhead: Klondike Bluffs • **Tower Arch** 2 miles round-trip; 2hr

For hikers keen to escape the crowds, Arches' most readily rewarding destination is the **Klondike Bluffs** area, reached by a narrow but good-condition road that branches west from the main road a mile or so south of Devil's Garden. After seven miles, take the second of two all but adjacent left turns, then park at the end another mile along. The wonderful **Tower Arch Trail** sets off straight up the steep bluff ahead of you. The arch itself, at the far end, is totally stupendous, an enormous graceful arc topped by a giant hoodoo, but the high-desert landscape en route, overlooked by the so-called **Marching Men**, orange monoliths reminiscent of Canyonlands' Needles district, is equally enjoyable.

ACCOMMODATION   ARCHES NATIONAL PARK

Devil's Garden Campground Devil's Garden ⚊ 518 885 3639 or ⚊ 877 444 6777, ⓦ recreation.gov. Rangers at the visitor centre will know whether there's room at Arches' only campground, 18 miles north at the far end of the road. The campground remains open all year; all its 50 sites, which hold up to ten people each, can be, and usually are, reserved between March and October; between November and February, 24 of them are first-come, first-served. No showers. Note that at the time this book went to press, the campground was due to be closed between March and October 2017, during road-building work in the park. **$20**

7 Moab

Boom-and-bust cycles are a familiar theme in Western history, but few communities have experienced such a rollercoaster ride as **MOAB**. Within the last seventy years, it has gone from an insignificant backwater in the 1940s to being celebrated as "The Richest Town in the USA" during the 1950s, before slumping into depression in the 1980s only to re-emerge, almost against its will, as the Southwest's number-one adventure-vacation destination.

CHARLIE STEEN: THE URANIUM KING

In the early 1950s, as the Cold War gathered steam and nuclear power stations seemed to hold infinite promise, the US government offered a $10,000 reward to anyone who discovered a mineable domestic **uranium** deposit – even on public land – and guaranteed to buy whatever it produced for the next ten years.

Freelance prospectors converged on the Colorado Plateau, where uranium had been found and mined as early as 1912. Their war-surplus jeeps piled with provisions, they set off into Utah's uncharted backcountry, waving their Geiger counters at any likely-looking rocks. Most knew which strata offered the best odds, and searched for places along the cliffs and canyon walls where they might be exposed.

Charlie Steen, a geologist from Texas, was mocked for insisting that he could find uranium by **drilling**. Projecting the angle of the canyonlands' crazily tilted slopes deep underground, he'd calculate where the precious mineral might have accumulated atop layers of harder rock. Concentrating on the **Lisbon Valley**, thirty miles southeast of Moab, he staked out countless claims and gave each a Spanish name.

In July 1952, the 31-year-old Steen broke his last drill bit in a 200ft bore on the **Mi Vida** ("my life") claim. Driving back to his trailer home in despair, he pulled into a gas station in Cisco, Utah. The attendant offered to test the final plug of rock on Steen's pick-up; his Geiger counter went straight off the scale.

Following his $60-million strike, Steen opened a processing mill in Moab that became Grand County's largest employer. As the "**Uranium King**", he built himself a hilltop mansion above town and threw a lavish annual party for all its citizens. He'd circle above Moab at night in his own plane, since TV reception was better at that altitude, and was even a celebrity guest on *I Love Lucy*. In quick succession, he was elected to the Utah senate, then resigned after failing to change the state's liquor laws. Selling Mi Vida, he moved to Nevada, only to fritter his entire fortune away, losing $250,000, for example, on a pickle factory.

By the early 1970s, Steen was back in Utah, once more searching the canyon country as a penniless prospector. This time he travelled in disguise under a false name, in order both to avoid media attention and to protect any discoveries he might make. Success eluded him, however, and he eventually conceded defeat and moved to Colorado, where he died in 2006.

Through it all, Moab has never been a large town – its population remains little more than five thousand – and neither is it, in itself, a particularly attractive one. The **setting** is what matters. With two national parks on its doorstep, plus millions more acres of public land, Moab is an ideal base for **outdoors enthusiasts**. The first to turn up were **jeep** drivers, taking advantage of the remote dirt roads cleared by the uranium prospectors. Then the **whitewater rafting** companies moved in, and the town swiftly started to lure in **mountain bikers**, too. These days, Moab is almost literally bursting, all year, with lycra-clad holiday-makers from all over the world.

Main Street, the broad five-mile section of **US-191** that sweeps through the heart of Moab, is lined with gas stations, diners, motels and other businesses. For two blocks north and south of **Center Street**, window-shopping pedestrians stroll the sidewalk and browse the menus. Elsewhere, everybody drives or cycles. Squeezed between Swiss Cheese Ridge to the east and the Moab Rim to the west, the town has little room to expand, but you can still see a few pioneer homes, and the occasional apple orchard, if you venture down the side streets.

Perhaps the main reason Moab has grown so fast is that out-of-state visitors tend to find Utah's other rural communities so irredeemably boring. As soon as Moab emerged from the pack, it became a beacon in the desert, attracting tourists ecstatic to find the only southern Utah town that stays up after dark.

Brief history

Moab stands just south of the Colorado River, at the north end of a long valley created by the collapse of an underground salt dome. A similar valley slopes down to the river on its northern side, making this the best place to cross the Colorado in all Utah. Though Ute Indians passed this way for generations, the site was first recorded by Juan de Rivera in 1765, and a ferry service later helped travellers on the **Old Spanish Trail**. Mormon pioneers named the farming settlement they established here in the 1870s for the biblical wilderness of Moab, at the edge of Zion.

Until Charlie Steen discovered **uranium** in 1952, the biggest thing to hit Moab was when **Butch Cassidy** hijacked the Colorado ferry on his way home from a bank job. The uranium boom lasted well into the 1970s, but as it dwindled, the local political scene turned very sour. Moab was a major focus of the **Sagebrush Rebellion** (see p.378), which pitted mine-owners and Utah businessmen, together with their fearful workforce, against the burgeoning national coalition of **environmentalists** and the federal government. Grand County commissioners repeatedly defied federal legislation by smashing bulldozers into protected wilderness areas, hoping to open them for mineral exploitation.

While they may have won the bitter **Bulldozer Wars** – Ronald Reagan came to power proclaiming that he too was a "Sagebrush Rebel" – Utah's conservatives were no match for the world economy. When the uranium market crashed in 1980, and the bottom also fell out of oil, coal and potash, unemployment in Moab rocketed, and the population dwindled.

The wilderness devotees seized their opportunity. Out of nowhere, Moab became the West's hottest new **tourist** destination, the desert equivalent of chic mountain hideaways like Aspen in Colorado. Sadly, though, almost everyone agrees that things have now gone too far. Most of the old-timers have left, driven out by rising real-estate prices and reluctant to swap mining for minimum-wage motel clerking. Low-impact ecotourism seemed a real possibility when only the select few had heard of Moab, but the canyonlands have taken as hard a battering from the fat-tyre brigade as they did from the mining conglomerates. Just to make matters worse, the price of uranium has started rising again. Amid rumours of another uranium boom in Utah, a handful of mines have already reopened, and nearby Green River is even planning to build a nuclear power station.

MOAB

● EATING	
Desert Bistro	3
Eddie McStiff's	4
Jailhouse Café	1
Peace Tree Juice Café	2
Red Rock Bakery & Net Café	5

■ ACCOMMODATION	
Aarchway Inn	1
Adobe Abode	7
Best Western Greenwell Inn	13
Best Western Plus Canyonlands Inn	12
Castle Valley Inn	2
Gonzo Inn	8
Inca Inn	4
Lazy Lizard International Hostel	10
Pack Creek Ranch	11
Red Cliffs Lodge	3
Sunflower Hill B&B	6

■ CAMPGROUNDS	
Canyonlands	9
Sand Flats Recreation Area	5

Museum of Moab

118 E Center St • Mon–Sat: mid-April to mid-Oct 10am–6pm; mid-Oct to mid-April noon–5pm; • $5 • ☎ 435 259 7985, ⓦ moabmuseum.org

Local history is enjoyably recalled at the **Museum of Moab**, also known as the Dan O'Laurie Museum. Displays start with a mammoth tusk dredged from the Colorado and a replica petroglyph claimed to show the "Moab mastodon". The usual small-town assortment follows, ranging from an Ancestral Puebloan basket to Moab's first telephone switchboard, plus souvenirs from the uranium days.

ARRIVAL AND DEPARTURE

By bus Moab Luxury Coach (☎435 940 4212, ⓦ moabluxurycoach.com) runs shuttle services to Moab from Salt Lake City ($399 one-way per vehicle) and the Amtrak station at Grand Junction, CO ($225 per vehicle).

By air The only scheduled flights to Moab Airport, on US-191 16 miles northwest of town, go to and from Salt Lake City on Fridays and Mondays (Utah Airways, $375 one-way, ⓦ flyutahair.com).

GETTING AROUND AND INFORMATION

Taxis and shuttles Taxis in town, including shuttle services for bikers, rafters and hikers, are operated by Coyote Shuttle (☎435 260 2097, ⓦ coyoteshuttle.com) and Roadrunner Shuttle (☎435 259 9402, ⓦ roadrunnershuttle.com).

Moab Information Center Center and Main (Mid-March

to Oct Mon–Sat 8am–7pm, Sun 9am–6pm; Nov to mid-March Mon & Thurs–Sun 9am–5pm, Tues 1–5pm, Wed 9am–2pm; ☎800 635 6622, ⓦ discovermoab.com). Info on nearby parks and public lands, plus free wi-fi. The website has a calendar of local events and festivals.

ACCOMMODATION

If you've already been in Utah for a while when you reach Moab, its glittering **motel** signs may come as a surprise. On many nights between mid-March and October, all the 1500-plus rooms in the town's thirty-plus motels are taken, so **reservations** are strongly recommended. **Room rates** can drop as low as $50 per night in winter, but you'd be lucky to find anything much below $100 in high season.

7

HOTELS, MOTELS AND HOSTELS

Aarchway Inn 1551 N Hwy-191 ☎435 259 2599 or ☎800 341 9359, ⓦ aarchwayinn.com. Large, well-equipped motel with a nice heated pool and a basketball court, not far from the Colorado River at the north end of town. **$169**

Best Western Greenwell Inn 105 S Main St ☎435 259 6151, ⓦ bestwesternmoab.com. Central, modern hotel that offers spacious good-value rooms with tasteful furnishings and fittings. **$148**

Best Western Plus Canyonlands Inn 16 S Main St ☎435 259 2300 or ☎800 649 5191, ⓦ canyonlandsinn .com. Dependable upscale *Best Western*, across from the visitor centre in walking distance of restaurants, with a fitness centre, large pool and its own bicycle storage and repair room. **$249**

Gonzo Inn 100 W 200 South ☎435 259 2515 or ☎800 791 4044, ⓦ gonzoinn.com. Luxurious if rather self-consciously hipper-than-thou 43-room inn – or "funky place to crash", if you prefer – complete with kitsch-retro furnishings, quirky artworks and an espresso bar. **$174**

★ **Inca Inn** 570 N Main St ☎435 259 7261 or ☎866 462 2466, ⓦ incainn.com. This clean budget motel has been cleverly updated with touches including pueblo motifs and a bicycle weather vane. More importantly, though, it offers decent-sized rooms with very comfortable beds and rather amazing disco-light showers, along with an outdoor pool. **$100**

Lazy Lizard International Hostel 1213 S Hwy-191 ☎435 259 6057, ⓦ lazylizardhostel.com. This laidback independent hostel, tucked away off the highway a mile south of the centre, is really nothing special, but budget

travellers appreciate its six-person dorms, and private rooms and cabins, and it also has a hot tub, kitchen and wi-fi. Dorms **$11**, doubles **$30**, cabins **$35**

B&BS

Adobe Abode 778 W Kane Creek Blvd ☎435 259 7716, ⓦ adobeabodemoab.com. Attractive, low-slung, Pueblo-style home, which despite being a few hundred yards from downtown Moab feels like it's way out in the desert. All its six B&B rooms are comfortable and tastefully furnished, and the breakfasts are superb. **$159**

Sunflower Hill B&B 185 North 300 East ☎435 259 2974 or ☎800 662 2786, ⓦ sunflowerhill.com. Antique-furnished former farmhouse, now a twelve-room B&B, away from the bustle on a dead-end side street. All units are en suite, some are in separate cottages, and they share the gardens, pool and hot tub. **$175**

CAMPING

Canyonlands Campground 555 S Main St ☎435 259 6848 or ☎800 522 6848, ⓦ canyonlandsrv.com. Large, well-shaded, year-round site in the heart of town, catering mainly to RVs but also equipped with tent sites and small bunk-bedded cabins that sleep up to six. Tents **$30**, RVs **$45**, cabins **$85**

Sand Flats Recreation Area 1924 S Roadrunner Hill ☎435 259 2444, ⓦ sandflats.org. Minimally developed BLM campground, intended primarily for mountain bikers, in a spectacular setting near the Slickrock Bike Trail, atop the mesa east of town. **$15**

EATING

Moab offers by far the greatest choice of **restaurants** in southern Utah, and for once most places make a serious effort to cater to **vegetarians**. There's also no problem getting a **drink** – Moab even has two pubs and its own winery. Several bike shops have espresso counters for early-morning customers.

★ Desert Bistro 36 South 100 West ☎ 435 259 0756, ⓦ desertbistro.com. Top-notch dinner-only restaurant, set in a former 1892 home with outdoor seating at both front and back. On the modern Mediterranean-influenced bistro menu, mains like smoked rabbit *agnolotti* or honey-glazed rack of lamb cost up to $60. Tues–Sun 5.30–9.30pm; closed Dec–Feb.

Eddie McStiff's 57 S Main St ☎ 435 259 2337, ⓦ eddiemcstiffs.com. Central pub, where interesting beers include raspberry and blueberry. Menu items range from inexpensive salads, via fancy Southwestern pizzas (with toppings like sundried tomatoes and jalapeño peppers) for around $15, to $20 pasta and steak dinners, but the service can leave a lot to be desired. Daily 11.30am–10.30pm.

Jailhouse Café 101 N Main St ☎ 435 260 9961. Very popular central café, open for breakfast only. Indoor and outdoor seating year-round, and great specials like ginger pancakes and eggs Benedict, for around $12. Mon & Wed–Sun 7am–noon.

Peace Tree Juice Café 20 S Main St ☎ 435 259 0101, ⓦ peacetreecafe.com. Café-restaurant in the centre of town that, besides delicious smoothies and vegetable juices, serves full cooked breakfasts like *huevos rancheros* for $10; good sandwiches and wraps for $9–13; and dinner mains like lasagne or trout for up to $20, plus steaks for $27. All are best enjoyed on the large outdoor patio. Daily 7am–10pm.

Red Rock Bakery & Net Café 74 S Main St ☎ 435 259 5941. Small café-bakery opposite the visitor centre, with good coffee and pastries. Be sure to try their "spin", a swirl of spicy, cheesy bread that's available for breakfast with egg, bacon and avocado. Mon–Sat 7am–4pm, Sun 7am–3pm.

Around Moab

Although most visitors head straight for the national parks, several lesser-known areas in the Moab region are well worth exploring. Both upstream and downstream, minor roads run alongside the **Colorado River**, while the **La Sal Mountains** to the east make a snowy contrast to the aridity of the desert.

Hunter Canyon

Hunter Canyon, which lies 7.5 miles along **Kane Creek Boulevard** from its intersection with US-191 not far south of central Moab, can be explored on a glorious half-day hike that's every bit as good as anything the national parks have to offer. The trail begins at a clearly marked parking lot, three miles after the road cuts away from the east bank of the Colorado to follow a narrow bench just above Kane Creek itself. From there, hikers repeatedly crisscross a small stream that glows with wonderful golden reflections of the stark red-rock cliffs on both sides. After roughly two miles, the going becomes too difficult to continue, thus creating a four-mile round-trip hike that takes up to four hours.

Potash Road

The dead-end **Potash Road**, Hwy-279, which doubles back southwest along the Colorado's west bank from just north of the bridge on US-191, passes several intriguing **rock-art** sites and provides a great close-up view of the river. In this stretch the Colorado is broad and lazy, tinted the same reddish brown as the Navajo sandstone cliffs, often busy with **rock climbers**, that tower above it.

Seven miles along, a group of **petroglyphs** a dozen feet up on the canyon wall to the right were scraped into the dark "desert varnish" by Fremont Indians, between 700 and 1300 AD. They depict animals and anthropomorphic figures, including a chain of linked humans resembling paper dolls. There are more petroglyphs a mile further on, this time higher on the cliffs.

Just beyond the frankly unremarkable **Jug Handle Arch**, seven miles on and seventeen miles from US-191, the valley floor widens. The road officially ends here, at an ugly green plant that produces salt and **potash** (potassium carbonate), accompanied by billowing clouds of white smoke. How much further you choose to drive will probably depend on whether you own the vehicle you're driving. The surface is paved for another 1.3 miles, while 1.7 bumpy miles beyond that you get your first glimpse of the 23 vinyl-lined

ADVENTURE TRAVEL IN MOAB

Moab is filled with companies that specialize in guiding and equipping adventurous travellers. The visitor centre supplies free route maps for bikers and 4WD drivers, plus lists of tour operators and rental outlets, online at ⓦdiscovermoab.com/tour.htm. The National Park Service keeps a similar list at ⓦnps.gov/cany/planyourvisit/guidedtrips.htm.

COLORADO RIVER TRIPS

Virtually everyone who goes **rafting** on the Colorado River does so with one of Moab's river-running operators. Motorized half- and one-day Colorado River trips start at around $50; multi-day expeditions, and day-trip combinations such as jeep-and-raft or horse-and-raft, are also available. **Shorter** trips start northwest of Moab, near Fisher Towers, and arrive near town in the afternoon; many companies give passengers the chance to float quieter stretches in two-person kayaks. While there are enough stretches of small-scale whitewater to whet the appetites of first-timers, a little romance is lost by the fact that the road runs alongside the river for much of the way. **Longer** (2–7 day) trips head through **Cataract Canyon** and other wild Canyonlands spots. **Oar-powered rafts** are slower but much quieter, and less expensive. Expect to pay from around $1150 for a five-day trip, depending on whether you're prepared to lift a finger to help.

Adrift Adventures ☏435 259 8594 or ☏800 874 4483, ⓦadrift.net
Tag-a-Long Expeditions ☏435 259 8946 or ☏800 453 3292, ⓦtagalong.com
Worldwide River Expeditions ☏435 259 7515 or ☏800 231 2769, ⓦworldwideriver.com

MOUNTAIN BIKING

While the Moab area is ideally suited to **mountain biking**, only experienced riders should attempt its most famous route, the **Slickrock Bike Trail**, in the **Sand Flats Recreation Area** ($5 per vehicle, or $2 per person; ⓦsandflats.org). Laid out as a motorbike trail in 1969, this challenging ten-mile loop explores the sandstone knobs east of Moab, skirting the rim of Negro Bill Canyon. Following the white dotted line around this exposed expanse of lithified red dunes, up steep inclines and along narrow ledges, takes at least four hours. Be sure to allow enough daylight, and carry two gallons of water – far more than you can take in bike bottles alone.

To reach the trail, climb Salt Flats Road up from Millcreek Drive, which branches off 400 East Street four blocks south of Center Street. Several Moab companies, including Roadrunner Shuttle (☏435 259 9402, ⓦroadrunnershuttle.com), offer a shuttle service to carry cyclists up to this and other trails. If you're looking for an easier ride, try the red-rock side canyons east and west of Moab, such as **Kane Creek**.

The following Moab **bike shops** offer daily rental and guided tours, including trips into Canyonlands National Park:

Rim Tours ☏435 259 5223 or ☏800 626 7335, ⓦrimtours.com
Poison Spider ☏435 259 7882 or ☏800 635 1792, ⓦpoisonspiderbicycles.com

JEEP TOURS AND RENTALS

Most of the thousands of miles of **jeep trails** around Moab were built by miners and haven't been maintained since; collect a free map and guide at the visitor centre.

Dan Mick's Jeep Tours ☏435 259 4567, ⓦdanmick.com. Half-day jeep tours for $300, full-day for $600.
High Point Hummer & ATV ☏435 259 2972 or ☏877 486 6833, ⓦhighpointhummer.com. Hummer tours from $69 for 2hr in Arches, plus jeep rentals from $175 per day, ATVs from $189.

SCENIC FLIGHTS

Redtail Aviation ☏435 259 7421 or ☏800 842 9251, ⓦredtailaviation.com. Unforgettable flights over the Canyonlands area from Moab Airport, 16 miles northwest of town on US-91, costing from $180 per person for one hour.

evaporation ponds where the potash is prepared. Dyed a lurid bluish-turquoise to speed evaporation, they're a real eyesore, and clearly visible from Dead Horse Point far above (see p.408).

Only **4WD** vehicles can continue past the ponds and the nearby boat-launch ramp, to meet up in due course with the White Rim Road in Canyonlands (see p.410). The mesa-top a few miles further up was where *Thelma and Louise* freeze-framed their way into the final credits.

Castle Valley and the La Sal Mountains

Turning northeast off US-191 just south of the Colorado bridge takes you onto **Hwy-128**, which follows the river's east bank for 35 miles, then crosses to meet **I-70** ten miles further up. In summer, this superbly scenic stretch of river is busy with one-day rafting trips. Roughly twenty miles along, the three-pronged red butte of **Fisher Towers** rises to the right of the road. These were originally "Fissure Towers"; there was no "Fisher".

For an excellent sixty-mile **loop trip** back to Moab – which takes something over two hours to complete in summer, and is usually closed by snow between November and April – turn right, southeast, fifteen miles along the river road, onto Castle Valley Road. **Castle Valley** is a verdant cleft that boasts some quintessential Western scenery, with red sandstone walls and buttes such as the **Priest and Nuns** to the east and high dark hills to the west. At its far southern end, eleven miles along, another right turn sets you climbing up the volcanic 10,000ft **La Sal Mountains**. A handful of narrow squeezes and hairpins later, a vantage point commands views across the Colorado to Arches and Canyonlands. Beyond that, the road runs through the high mountain landscape of the **Manti–La Sal National Forest**, a feast of colour in late fall. A few campgrounds are tucked into the woods, but you won't see another building before the road eventually drops back towards Moab Valley.

It's equally easy to drive this loop in the opposite direction – for morning starts, heading south from Moab enables you to keep the sun behind you for most of the way.

Hole N" The Rock

11037 S US-191, 15 miles south of Moab • Daily 9am–5pm • $6 • ☎ 435 686 2250, ⓦ theholeintherock.com

The peculiarly punctuated **Hole N" The Rock** is a classic piece of 1950s Americana. Having started out with a roadside diner at the foot of a cliff, Albert Christensen and his wife Gladys ended up hollowing an entire home deep into the red sandstone. Albert was a dreadful taxidermist – his unfortunate donkey Henry has to be seen to be believed – and painter – cross-eyed Christs a speciality – but his cool, well-lit house is a masterpiece. He died in 1957, without completing the spiral staircase that was planned to lead 65ft up to a rooftop patio. In the fine tradition of the jewellery that Gladys made from broken beer bottles, the gift store is stocked with home-spun souvenirs.

Don't confuse the Hole N" The Rock with the Hole-in-the-Rock pioneer river crossing near Escalante, incidentally (see p.382).

Canyon Rims Recreation Area

The vast and almost completely empty mesa, west of US-191, that separates Moab from the Needles district of Canyonlands National Park (see p.413), is largely taken up by the BLM-run **Canyon Rims Recreation Area**. Not much recreation goes on up here, although it has the usual 4WD-only roads, a couple of basic year-round campgrounds, and a scattering of hiking trails.

Only consider visiting the two main overlooks if you have a lot of time to spare – it involves a two-and-a-half-hour detour from the highway – or if you're not going to the Needles district, in which case the **Needles Overlook** provides a (relatively) quick overview as dramatic as any in Canyonlands itself.

Needles Overlook

The paved road into Canyon Rims leaves US-191 32 miles south of Moab. Its dreary 22-mile course westwards comes to an abrupt halt at the windswept **Needles Overlook**, where a short railed footpath gives eagle's-eye views across the canyonlands. Specific landmarks are hard to pick out amid the orange sandstone ledges that spread below, but looking south you should spot the twin **Sixshooter Peaks** and Hwy-211 winding alongside Indian Creek towards the Needles district (see p.413). Further west, the Needles themselves poke from the hillocks, while the Colorado loops from the north toward its confluence with the Green River.

Anticline Overlook

Fifteen miles in from US-191, or seven miles short of the Needles Overlook, forking right onto an even, broad gravel road commits you to the 25-minute drive across the tumbleweed-strewn sagebrush desert to the **Anticline Overlook**. You probably won't pass another vehicle before the final parking lot, from which a five-minute walk leads to a high promontory that faces the potash ponds and **Dead Horse Point** across the Colorado.

Some people, disappointed to realize they've driven almost all the way back to Moab, call this the Anti-climax Overlook. As you'll see if you follow the fence around the headland, only **Kane Creek Canyon** – where the creek is a tiny green sliver in the red wasteland – intervenes. You'll almost certainly hear motorbikes scrambling across the slickrock of the Moab Rim on the far side. To the northeast, silhouetted above a brief stretch of the Colorado, there's a remarkable view of the fins of **Arches National Park** – the line of sight passes straight through the South Window.

7

ACCOMMODATION	AROUND MOAB
Castle Valley Inn 424 Amber Lane, Castle Valley ☎ 435 259 6012, �🌐 castlevalleyinn.com. Large, beautifully furnished B&B, set in spacious grounds in magnificent Castle Valley, 20 miles east of town (see p.428). Five en-suite rooms and three separate bungalows. Doubles $115, bungalows $190	p.428). Its cabins and cottages can host from two to twelve guests, with wi-fi but no phones or TVs, plus assorted pools and tubs. Two-night minimum stay. $175
Pack Creek Ranch La Sal Mountain Loop Road ☎ 435 259 5091 or ☎ 800 879 6622, ⍉ packcreekranch.com. Large guest ranch, 20 miles southeast of town, just off the lower reaches of the La Sal Mountain Loop Road (see	**Red Cliffs Lodge** Mile 14, Hwy-128 ☎ 435 259 2002 or ☎ 866 812 2002, ⍉ redcliffslodge.com. Luxury resort occupying a beautifully verdant location beside the Colorado sixteen miles northeast of town. As well as seventy Western-themed suites, it has spacious riverfront cabins, plus the *Cowboy Grill* restaurant, a large pool, stables and even a winery. Suites $240, cabins $340

Southeast Utah

While it may lack big-name national parks, Utah's **southeast corner** is every bit as scenic as the neighbouring regions. The desert here is so unforgiving that only a handful of widely separated settlements cling to life, and large tracts remain entirely without roads.

Culturally as well as geographically, southeast Utah has much in common with the Four Corners. The **Ancestral Puebloans** were here in force, as countless abandoned pueblos testify. They moved off to the south and east around 1250 AD, but even now almost half the population of **San Juan County**, which covers the bulk of the region and is larger than several states, is Native American. A few are Ute, but most are **Navajo**, many of them descended from families who hid here during the 1860s to escape the Long Walk (see p.483).

The first **Mormons** to reach this far-flung corner were the Hole-in-the-Rock pioneers (see p.380), who established **Bluff** in 1880 and went on to found **Blanding** and **Monticello** as well. All those towns make viable bases, but the real attraction, as ever, is the landscape, with hikers heading for **Natural Bridges National Monument**, more ambitious multi-night backpackers for **Grand Gulch**, and drivers rattling across the desert to the unbelievable **Muley Point**, **Goosenecks State Reserve** and the **Valley of the Gods**.

Monticello

The first fifty miles of US-191 south of Moab are so desolate that it comes as a major shock, on climbing some straggling foothills, to find yourself confronted by ploughed green fields. To Mormon pioneers, this terrain resembled Thomas Jefferson's country home in Virginia – hence the name of **MONTICELLO** (pronounced "monti-sello"), six miles further on. Farming has never been all that easy here, however, and the economy has only recently been steadied by tourism.

East of Monticello, US-491 heads off to Colorado through what looks like a stray segment of the Great Plains, complete with grain silos and fields of wheat and beans.

INFORMATION

Visitor centre 232 S Main St (daily except Tues 9am–6pm; ☎435 587 3235 or ☎800 574 4386, ⓦutahscanyoncountry.com). Holds a small museum of frontier life.

ACCOMMODATION AND EATING

Monticello Inn 164 E Center St ☎435 587 2274, ⓦthemonticelloinn.com. Decent, old-fashioned motel, on the east side of town; adequate rooms at reasonable rates. $89

Inn at the Canyons 533 N Main St ☎435 587 2458, ⓦmonticellocanyonlandsinn.com. Monticello's most modern motel, opposite the *Peace Tree* on the brow of the hill at the north end of town, with clean, simple rooms plus an indoor pool and hot tub. $99

Peace Tree Juice Café 518 N Main St ☎435 587 2601. Small café on the north side of town, allied with the larger Moab outlet, which serves wholesome juices plus cooked breakfasts, burgers and wraps, all costing $8–10. Mon & Thurs–Sun 7am–9pm, Tues & Wed 7am–3pm.

Abajo Mountains

The normal route from Monticello to Canyonlands' Needles District, fifty miles northwest, is to take Hwy-211 west from US-191, 22 miles north of town. In summer, however, it's also possible to take a very different approach, through the volcanic **Abajo Mountains**, which rise west of Monticello to over 11,000ft. The straightforward road up, reached by turning left onto Abajo Drive from the west end of 200 South, passes through some lovely quasi-Alpine meadows where you may spot browsing deer. You then veer north and drop down a much rougher track, to meet Hwy-211 near Newspaper Rock (see p.415).

Blanding

BLANDING, twenty miles southwest of Monticello, was established as "Grayson" in 1905, when a new irrigation channel brought water to this site from the Abajo Mountains. In 1915, East Coast millionaire **Thomas Bicknell** offered to give a library to any Utah town that would change its name to his own. Two jumped in; Thurber, near Torrey, became Bicknell, while Grayson took his wife's maiden name, Blanding. Each got a new library, though it's said they didn't get as many books as they'd expected.

Having skirted the Abajos, US-191 runs due west as it enters Blanding, and at the four-way stop in the centre of town, makes a sharp dogleg turn south. That brief pause is as much time as most travellers give Blanding, whose broad avenues seldom display much sign of life.

Edge of the Cedars State Park

660 West 400 North • April–Sept Mon–Sat 9am–5pm, Sun noon–4pm; Oct–March Mon–Sat noon–5pm • $5 • ☎435 678 2238, ⓦstateparks.utah.gov/parks/edge-of-the-cedars

Edge of the Cedars State Park, on the western fringes of Blanding, preserves a pueblo that was occupied between 700 and 1220 AD. In the only excavated section, visitors can climb down a ladder into a musty, haunting *kiva*. Displays in the excellent museum alongside range from the Ancestral Puebloans to the Anglos. In a town that's notorious for illegal pot-hunting by profit-seeking amateurs – or "Moki poachers" – it emphasizes the importance of proper archeology. Some of the Ancestral Puebloan artefacts are truly remarkable, including pots and pendants, stylish wooden plates, and a complete loom dated to 1150 AD.

ARRIVAL AND INFORMATION
BLANDING

Visitor centre 12 N Grayson Parkway (Mon–Sat 8am–7pm, restrooms daily 24hr; ☎ 435 678 3662, ⓦ blandingutah.org). A good little museum containing fascinating material on the local Ute.

ACCOMMODATION AND EATING

Abajo Haven Guest Cabins 5440 N Cedar Edge Lane ☎ 435 979 3126, ⓦ abajohaven.com. Comfortable, wonderfully rural rental cabins, six miles north of Blanding, each with one double and two single beds, and heated by solar power. Barbecue dinners available, at $20/person. **$89**

Homestead Steak House 121 E Center St ☎ 435 678 3456. Friendly small-town diner, serving ribs, burgers, chicken and steaks for lunch and dinner in the throbbing epicentre of downtown Blanding. Daily 11.30am–8.30pm.

★ **Stone Lizard Lodging** 88 W Center St ☎ 435 678 3323, ⓦ stonelizardlodging.com. Nicely spruced up by new owners, this very central budget motel offers surprisingly comfortable rooms and suites of all sizes, at excellent rates. **$75**

West of Blanding

A mile or so south of Blanding, at a junction marked only by a solitary gas station, **Hwy-95** heads west from US-191, to embark on a magnificent 120-mile trans-Utah journey to Hanksville. Until it was completed in 1976 – hence its other name, the **Bicentennial Highway** – east–west travel was effectively barred by the massive monocline of **Comb Ridge**, ten miles west of Blanding. To the Navajo, this thousand-foot wall of red rock, stretching eighty miles from north to south, was the backbone of the earth, as well as one of four "arrowheads" protecting their homeland. To Mormon pioneers, it was a definitive "reef" (see p.386). To the modern highway builders, it was an obstacle they simply had to blast their way through.

No towns interrupt Hwy-95 apart from the speck that is **Hite**, 87 miles along at Lake Powell (see p.400). Several side canyons off Hwy-95 bear traces of an Ancestral Puebloan presence, while the cattle ranchers who tried their hands here a century ago were succeeded by uranium miners in the 1950s.

Butler Wash Ruins

Trailhead: roadside parking lot, 10.5 miles west along Hwy-95 from US-191 • 1 mile round-trip; 30min

Butler Wash Ruins, a stimulating Ancestral Puebloan site located on BLM land, can be reached by a simple ten-minute hike from Hwy-95. The trail heads gently but consistently upwards from the parking lot, crossing bare slickrock for its latter half, to reach an overlook facing a side canyon just short of the crest of Comb Ridge. The ruins are in the topmost of three natural rock alcoves; a long stone ledge to the left leads down to the fertile wash where the inhabitants farmed. The complex includes one Kayenta-style square *kiva* and three Mesa Verde-style round *kivas*. Invisible from the overlook, but close at hand to the right, a waterfall ends at a natural stone bridge.

Comb Ridge

Eleven miles west of its intersection with US-191, immediately beyond Butler Wash, Hwy-95 picks its way down the intense red wall of **Comb Ridge** to a cottonwood-rich valley, watered by **Comb Wash**. Confronted by this ridge on their endless journey east, the Hole-in-the-Rock party decided to head south, which explains why they ended up at Bluff (see p.435). Don't copy them, however; a tempting dirt road does branch south from the highway beside the stream, with a nice little campground a short way along, but it soon succumbs to deep drifts of sand no ordinary vehicle could hope to overcome.

7

Mule Canyon

Atop the plateau seven miles west of Comb Wash, a dirt road signed for Texas Flat leads north from Hwy-95 to two separate trailheads for **Mule Canyon**. The northern sides of each of this shallow canyon's two forks hold several small, well-preserved Ancestral Puebloan **cliff dwellings**. Both forks are around six miles long, but the most interesting ruins are roughly one mile and three miles along the South Fork, so a six-mile day-hike is enough for most visitors. In itself, it's not a difficult walk, but as few hikers pass this way you need to be prepared for all eventualities. Ask for advice at Kane Gulch Ranger Station (see p.433).

A separate paved turn-off, half a mile along from the Texas Flat road, leads in a few yards to **Mule Canyon Ruin**, a partly restored Ancestral Puebloan pueblo dating from 1000 AD. This small site, a bit too near the highway to be very evocative, is similar to Boulder's Anasazi State Park (see p.385). Its most conspicuous features – a round *kiva* now roofed over for preservation, and a two-storey masonry tower – are connected by an underground tunnel, perhaps used for surprise appearances during ceremonies.

Through the Bear's Ears

Before Hwy-95 was constructed, the main road west of Blanding – and the principal access to Natural Bridges (see below) – was a dirt track that climbed across the southern fringes of the Abajo Mountains. In reasonable weather, ordinary vehicles can still follow this attractive route, by turning north from Hwy-95 seven miles from the intersection. The 32-mile detour takes well over an hour.

After a cool, pleasant drive through mountaintop woodlands, the road crosses a razorback ridge above Arch Canyon to descend between two rounded outcrops known as the **Bear's Ears**. This prominent landmark is regarded by the Navajo as the embodiment of a bear, guarding the northern limits of their territory. The road eventually switchbacks down a sheer red cliff to join the approach road into Natural Bridges.

In 2015, a coalition of several Native American tribes, including the Navajo, Ute, Zuni and Hopi, came together to propose the creation of a new **Bear's Ears National Monument**. A unique collaboration between Native American groups and the federal government, such a monument would incorporate the existing Natural Bridges National Monument, and protect a total of 1.9 million acres from further exploitation.

Natural Bridges National Monument

4 miles north of Hwy-95, a total of 44 miles west of Blanding • Daily dawn–dusk • $10 per vehicle, $5 motorcycle, cyclist or pedestrian • ☎ 435 692 1234, ⓦ nps.gov/nabr

Three of the world's largest natural bridges span the streambeds of the small, unspectacular White and Armstrong canyons, which cut through the white sandstone of **Cedar Mesa** southwest of the Abajo Mountains. **NATURAL BRIDGES NATIONAL MONUMENT** was the loneliest of spots when prospector Cass Hite stumbled across it in the 1880s. Still all but inaccessible when it became Utah's first federal park in 1908, it's now easily accessed by a four-mile spur road off Hwy-95.

Originally dubbed Edwin, Augusta, and Caroline, the bridges were given Hopi names when it was realized that much of the rock art on the canyon walls represented Hopi clan symbols. This was one of the many places that the Ancestral Puebloan predecessors of the Hopi passed through during their migrations, departing around 1270 AD after a stay of perhaps six hundred years.

Each bridge can be seen from overlooks along the looping, one-way, nine-mile **Bridge View Drive**. With considerably more effort, you can clamber down into the canyons for closer inspection, and also follow the stream from one to the next for a potential hike of up to nine miles.

Visitor centre

Daily: April 8am–5pm; May–Sept 8am–6pm; Oct–Nov 9am–5pm; Dec–March 9am–4.30pm • ☎ 435 692 1234, ⊗ nps.gov/nabr

Excellent displays in Natural Bridges' **visitor centre** explain how the bridges were formed, and you can pick up free trail guides. It's also the only source of water for the first-come, first-served, 13-site **campground** nearby ($10).

Sipapu Bridge

The first and largest bridge in Natural Bridges National Monument, **Sipapu Bridge**, was named for the "hole" through which the Hopi emerged into this world. Standing at 220ft high by 268ft wide, it is surpassed only by Rainbow Bridge (see p.398). Although the overlook, accessed by a paved 100-yard trail from the roadside, provides a good straight-on view as it thrusts from a tangle of rocks far below, you'll only really appreciate Sipapu's size if you hike down from the trailhead half a mile further along the road. The monument's most difficult trail involves three short ladders, two metal staircases, and a couple of stretches of slickrock with steep drop-offs, and takes around an hour there and back. A ledge halfway down offers the best photos; by the time you're amid the trees directly beneath it, it's too big for most lenses to squeeze it in.

A roadside parking lot just beyond Sipapu marks the start of a half-mile mesa-top trail that leads to a vantage point above **Horsecollar Ruin**. This small Ancestral Puebloan site, tucked into an alcove low on the canyon walls, is not visible from below.

Kachina Bridge

Kachina Bridge is much thicker than Sipapu, being more of a tunnel beneath a broad span of desert-varnish-stained sandstone. Seen from the overlook, it's far less distinct, with rocks rather than sunlight visible through the gap. On the trail down, railings guide you across the slickrock, and there's a crude staircase made from sandstone slabs. The stream at the bottom is lined by splendid cottonwoods, while pictographs near the base of the bridge resemble the *kachinas* of Hopi religion (see p.66).

Owachomo Bridge

Natural bridges are short-lived phenomena. Even the oldest in the monument – **Owachomo Bridge**, two miles beyond Kachina by road – is a mere five thousand years old, and it's unlikely to last much longer. Though 180ft across, it tapers to just nine feet thick. It now stands slightly to one side of the streambed of Armstrong Canyon, reached by an easy half-mile round-trip hike down from the overlook.

The Streambed Trail

Trailhead: Sipapu Bridge • 8.6 miles; 5hr

In addition to the short trails that connect each overlook with the relevant bridge, it's also possible to hike the **Streambed Trail** that connects all three. Meandering along the sandy wash beneath the trees makes a delightful walk, but unless you double back, returning to your starting point involves a long hike across the mesa-top, which is not as flat as you'd imagine and offers very little shade. If you start from Owachomo or Kachina and hike back towards Sipapu, you might meet up with someone who can give you a ride back to your vehicle.

Grand Gulch Primitive Area

Kane Gulch Ranger Station Hwy-261, four miles south of Hwy-95 and 36 miles southwest of Blanding • March to mid-June & Sept–Oct, daily 8am–noon • Day-use permits $2 per day or $5 per week; backpacking permits $8 per night March to mid-June & Sept–Oct; $5 per night mid-June to Aug & Nov–Feb • ☎ 435 587 1500, ⊗ blm.gov/ut

If you share a passion for archeology with the stamina for long-distance hiking, an expedition into the **GRAND GULCH PRIMITIVE AREA**, south of Natural Bridges, can make you feel like a real-life Indiana Jones. Every twist and turn of this deep, dramatic gorge seems to be filled with relics of its thousand-year occupation by the Ancestral Puebloans, who abandoned the canyon six centuries before it was named by the Hole-in-the-Rock pioneers.

Grand Gulch gouges across Cedar Mesa for just over fifty miles, dropping 2700ft to meet the San Juan River. There's no access for vehicles; the only path in starts from **Kane Gulch Ranger Station** on Hwy-261. Typical backpacking expeditions last as long as a week, and you can only camp overnight in the gulch with a permit. In season (March to mid-June & Sept–Oct), day-hikers and overnight backpackers alike must pick up permits at the ranger station on the day they set off, and thus be there before noon; at other times, you can self-register and leave your payment in a special tube.

Hiking in Grand Gulch

The trail into Grand Gulch begins by dropping steadily down Kane Gulch, a side canyon that deepens as it goes, and joins Grand Gulch proper four miles along. **Junction Ruin** here, the largest ruin in the canyon system, makes a popular day-hike destination, though **Turkey Pen Ruin**, at 4.7 miles, and **Stimper Arch** just beyond, are also within round-trip reach. If you're making a longer trip, it's possible to leave Grand Gulch via **Bullet Canyon** to the east – in which case a total hike of 23 miles brings you back to Hwy-261 roughly seven miles south of the ranger station – or **Collins Canyon** to the west further along – a 38-mile hike that ends at a dirt road south of Hwy-276. For either route, you'll need a car shuttle to get back to your vehicle, but that's probably easier to arrange than fixing for someone to meet you by boat on the San Juan, the only way out if you hike right to the end of Grand Gulch. Most visitors find it simpler just to double back at some point en route.

Kane Gulch Ranger Station can also provide details on day-hikes that head **east** from Hwy-261, into remote side canyons on Cedar Mesa. Road conditions are often treacherous, so don't set off without up-to-the-minute advice.

Muley Point

South of Kane Gulch, Hwy-261 crosses Cedar Mesa for its remaining seventeen miles. Before you take the plunge on the **Moki Dugway**, **Muley Point**, exactly five miles west of the top of the Dugway along a red-dirt road, is an absolute must-see. Note that the turn-off is signposted, but the sign is only conspicuous if you're coming from the north, and that the lesser viewpoint 3.9 miles along is *not* Muley Point.

When they finally get around to declaring all of southern Utah to be one vast national park, Muley Point will surely be the centrepiece. Quite simply, these are among the most stupendous views in the world (though they're at their finest in the morning, when the sun is behind you). You're now at the southernmost tip of Cedar Mesa and the eastern extremity of Glen Canyon NRA. Far below, the San Juan River goosenecks its way west, while the Navajo Nation stretches off on the far side. Features on the horizon include Monument Valley in all its glory, the Sleeping Ute in Colorado, Navajo Mountain, and the cliffs above the west shore of Lake Powell.

Moki Dugway

Hwy-261 doesn't stand on ceremony when it needs to get down off Cedar Mesa; it just plummets over the edge. The **MOKI DUGWAY**, which drops 1100ft in little more than two miles, is an exhilarating switchback ride, much of it still on a "washboard" strip of gravel, although it feels a whole lot safer now that most of its many hairpin bends are paved. This ancient trail was originally improved by mining companies during the 1950s; you'll just have to hope you don't meet a truck-load of uranium coming the other way. If you have the nerve, you'll find that the pull-outs for vehicles to pass make great viewpoints, but it's best to do all your sightseeing at the top.

Soon after the pavement resumes at the bottom of the Moki Dugway, another dirt road marks the western end of the **Valley of the Gods** (see p.436).

Goosenecks State Park

3.5 miles southwest of Hwy-261 on Hwy-316, a total of 8 miles west of Mexican Hat • Daily 24hr • Day use $5, camping $10 • ☎ 435 678 3348, ⓦ stateparks.utah.gov

To reach the extraordinary **Goosenecks State Park**, look out for inconspicuous **Hwy-316**, which branches away west from Hwy-261 shortly before it meets US-163. Although the railed viewing area at the overlook stands a thousand feet below Cedar Mesa, the **San Juan River** is still another thousand feet down – and it's an amazing sight, looping between huge pyramidal buttes in a textbook example of what geologists call an "entrenched meander". Its serpentine coils – once meanders on a muddy plain, later fixed in stone by the uplifting of the Colorado Plateau – are so extravagant that it flows six miles while advancing little more than one mile west. Above the distant sliver of riverbank greenery, alternate layers of grey limestone and red sandstone stripe the cliffs, while Monument Valley stands out on the skyline.

7

Bluff

BLUFF, a pretty little riverside settlement whose somewhat humdrum existence belies the extraordinary efforts its founders made to get here, lies 23 miles south of Blanding on US-191. The 230 **Hole-in-the-Rock** pioneers who reached this site on April 6, 1880, had trekked right across the heart of Utah, literally blasting their way through the canyons of the Colorado (see box, p.380).

Once they arrived, they settled down to a life of ranching and agriculture, made difficult by the propensity of the San Juan River to flood. The back streets still hold a dozen or so of their original sturdy homes, making Bluff the region's least spoiled, most authentic town. Its setting is consistently stunning, from the red-rock pinnacles known as the **Navajo Twins**, which mark the mouth of the narrow **Cow Canyon** gorge through which US-191 drops in from the north, to the cottonwoods that line the San Juan River, glinting against the sheer red bluff that rises on the far side. **Ancestral Puebloan** remains abound, including petroglyphs along Hwy-163 to the east, and the unexcavated mound, thought to conceal a buried pueblo, beside the town cemetery on a hillock just north of the centre.

Bluff is very much at the edge of the desert; driving west you soon descend the southern end of **Comb Ridge** (see p.431) into vintage red-rock badlands, with the buttes of Monument Valley silhouetted above the horizon.

TOURS AND ACTIVITIES   BLUFF

Far Out Expeditions Customized hiking tours, ranging from half-day jaunts to archeological sites to extended backpacking expeditions (☎ 435 672 2294, ⓦ farout expeditions.net).

★ **Wild Rivers Expeditions** Bluff is a centre for river-running on the San Juan; rafts put in at Sand Island Recreation Area, 3 miles west. As well as multi-day voyages, Wild Rivers offer fabulous one-day float trips as far as Mexican Hat downstream, with visits to ancient ruins and plentiful wildlife spotting, including eagles ($175, under-13s $133; ☎ 435 672 2244, ⓦ riversandruins.com).

ACCOMMODATION

Bluff may not be the fanciest place in the world, but its **genuine small-town feel** makes it a nicer prospect than any of its neighbours. It's also a handy overnight stop for Hovenweep National Monument, forty miles northeast.

★ **Desert Rose Inn** 701 W Main St ☎ 435 672 2303 or ☎ 888 475 7673, ⓦ desertroseinn.com. Modern timber-built motel at the west end of town, holding thirty attractively designed and well-furnished rooms, plus individual cabins of similar standard, a summer-only bistro restaurant, and a heated indoor pool. **$160**

7

Far Out Guest House 700 East & Mulberry ☎435 672 2294, ⓦfaroutexpeditions.net. This historic home holds two guestrooms, each of which has six beds and can be rented by groups of up to six people at progressively increasing rates. Most visitors are here to take one of Far Out's tours (see p.435). $100

Kokopelli Inn 161 E Main St ☎435 672 2322,

ⓦkokoinn.com. Friendly, quiet roadside motel, adjoining a gas station and grocery with a deli counter. $99

Recapture Lodge PO Box 309, Main St ☎435 672 2281, ⓦrecapturelodge.com. Pleasantly rural wooden motel, reaching back towards the river, with a pool, plus a few rooms in two old pioneer homes. $95

EATING

Comb Ridge Coffee 680 W Main St ☎435 485 5555, ⓦcombridgecoffee.com. Espressos and pastries in a buzzy gallery setting, opposite the *Desert Rose* at the southwest end of town, plus breakfast eggs and pancakes for $8–12, and dinners of locally sourced beef or bison, with burgers and pot pies for $12–14 and steaks for $26. Tues–Sun 7–10am & 5.30–9pm.

★**Cottonwood Steakhouse** 409 W Main St ☎435 672 2282, ⓦcottonwoodsteakhouse.com. Open-air barbecue at the west end of town, with wooden tables arranged around a giant cottonwood. A great place to enjoy

beer, ribs and steaks (priced at up to $28) beneath the stars – though the menu's a bit short if you're not a beef-eater. One corner of the pseudo-Western stockade serves as Fort Crapper. Daily 5.30–9.30pm.

Twin Rocks Cafe 913 E Navajo Twins Drive ☎435 672 2341, ⓦtwinrockscafe.com. Glass-fronted diner, set against the rocks north of town, just west of US-191. Breakfast bagels and muffins, then salads and sandwiches, Navajo frybread "pizzas", and chicken or fajita dinners for $12–18. The adjoining *Trading Post* is well worth exploring. Summer daily 7am–10pm; winter Mon–Sat 8am–9pm.

Valley of the Gods

Dirt road runs between US-163 beside Lime Creek, 9 miles northeast of Mexican Hat, and Hwy-261, 10.6 miles northwest of Mexican Hat • Daily dawn–dusk • Free

Visitors whose appetites have been whetted by Monument Valley can tour similar, smaller-scale monoliths, with no admission fees, in the **Valley of the Gods**. This "garden" of isolated sandstone columns – said by the Navajo to be petrified warriors – holds no fixed hiking trails. Drivers see it all from a winding **seventeen-mile dirt road** that connects US-163, west of Bluff, with Hwy-261 near the foot of the Moki Dugway (see p.434).

It's a rough road, which becomes impassable when wet, but if you don't mind a few bangs as you cross dry stony washes you should be able to make it in a rental car. The east side holds the best "monuments", and the most difficult terrain, but there's something to be said for driving in from the west, which offers great views all the way along.

ACCOMMODATION   VALLEY OF THE GODS

Valley of the Gods B&B Valley of the Gods dirt road, half a mile east of Hwy-261 ☎970 749 1164, ⓦzippitydodah.com/vog. The only building in the valley, squatting in superb isolation, with a superb sunset-view

veranda. All of its four rooms have baths, dinner is served by prior arrangement, and the owners can also fix backcountry tours. No wi-fi. $165

Mexican Hat

MEXICAN HAT, the last stop in southeast Utah before the Navajo reservation begins across the San Juan River (and thus the last place you can get a beer), is an appealingly dusty outpost that has never amounted to a town. Having sprung into being in 1901, following false reports that gold had been discovered nearby, it was kept going by a genuine oil strike in 1908 and the uranium boom of the 1950s. It now makes a convenient base for **Monument Valley**, twenty miles south (see p.55).

Mexican Hat Rock, the sandstone sombrero for which the settlement was named, looks down on the San Juan a mile north. The highway passes a few hundred yards west, but a gravel road permits closer inspection. It's at its best in the afternoon, when the sun strikes the amazing zigzag striations of the grey and white cliffs across the river. This pattern, known as the **Navajo Blanket**, is said to show the skin markings of a giant bullsnake that lives in the river below, and carved out the "goosenecks" to the west (see p.435).

ACCOMMODATION AND EATING   MEXICAN HAT

All Mexican Hat's four **motels**, except the basic but adequate *Canyonlands*, have their own inexpensive restaurants and stores and are substantially the same. There are virtually no other buildings around.

Hat Rock Inn US-163 ☎435 683 2221, �🌐hatrockinn .com. Modern, timber-built motel, 100 yards up from the river, and run by the same family as the nearby *Lodge*. Good-quality rooms, an "infinity pool" overlooking the river, and a Mexican restaurant, the *Hat Rock Café*. Trail rides and jeep tours available. Closed Nov–Feb. $149

★**Mexican Hat Lodge** US-163 ☎435 683 2222, �🌐mexicanhat.net. Mexican Hat's northernmost motel – a former dance hall – has thirteen rooms of differing sizes. Its open-air *Swingin Steak* restaurant (daily 6–9pm) is everything you could wish for from a cowboy steakhouse,

grilling huge perfect steaks over a fire of sweet-smelling wood, at $24 for an 8-oz steak, $39 for an 18-oz. Closed Nov–Jan. $84

San Juan Inn US-163 ☎435 535 2210 or ☎800 447 2022, ⚓sanjuaninn.net. Solid, long-established motel perched fifty feet above the north bank of the San Juan, beside the highway bridge. They also offer "glamping", in en-suite yurts a mile north of town, while the on-site, riverside *Olde Bridge Grill* serves all meals (daily 7am–9pm), ranging from $10 Navajo tacos to $28 steaks, plus cold beers. Doubles or yurts $88

7

Las Vegas

NEW YORK–NEW YORK

Las Vegas

Little emphasis is placed on the gambling clubs and divorce facilities – though they are attractions to many visitors – and much is being done to build up the cultural attractions. No cheap and easily parodied slogans have been adopted to publicize the city, no attempt has been made to introduce pseudo-romantic architectural themes or to give artificial glamour or gaiety. Las Vegas is itself – natural and therefore very appealing to people with a wide variety of interests. WPA Guidebook to Nevada, 1940

Shimmering from the desert haze of Nevada like a latter-day El Dorado, **LAS VEGAS** is the most dynamic, spectacular city on earth. At the start of the twentieth century, it didn't even exist; now it's home to two million people. Boasting eighteen of the world's thirty largest hotels, it's a monument to architectural exuberance, whose flamboyant, no-expense-spared **casinos** lure in well over forty million tourists each year.

While Las Vegas has been stockpiling superlatives since the 1950s, it doesn't rest on its laurels for a moment. Many first-time visitors expect the city to be kitsch, but the casino owners are far too canny to be sentimental about the old days. Yes, there are a few Elvis impersonators around, but what characterizes the city far more is its endless quest for **novelty**. Long before they lose their sparkle, yesterday's showpieces are blasted into rubble, to make way for ever more extravagant replacements. Thirty years ago, when the fashion was for fantasy, Arthurian castles and Egyptian pyramids mushroomed along the legendary Strip; next came a craze for constructing entire replica cities, like New York, Paris, Monte Carlo and Venice; and the current trend is for high-end properties that attempt to straddle the line between screaming ostentation and "elegant" sophistication.

While Las Vegas has cleaned up its act since the early days of Mob domination, there's little truth in the persistent notion that it's become a family destination. Neither is it as consistently **cheap** as it used to be. It's still possible to find good, inexpensive rooms, and at least a few of the all-you-can-eat buffets offer decent value, but the casino owners have long since discovered that high-rollers happy to lose hundreds of dollars per night don't mind paying premium prices to eat at top-quality restaurants, and the newest properties charge room rates closer to $300 than $30 per night.

Although its metropolitan sprawl measures fifteen miles wide by fifteen miles long, few tourists see any more of Las Vegas than the six-mile stretch of **Las Vegas Boulevard** that includes both the **downtown** area, slightly southeast of the intersection of I-15 and US-95, and the **Strip**, home to the major casinos. Your first hours in the city are like entering another world, where the religion is luck, the language is money, and time is measured by revolutions of a roulette wheel. Once you're acclimatized, the whole spectacle can be absolutely exhilarating – assuming you haven't pinned your hopes, and your savings, on the pursuit of a fortune. Even so, while Las Vegas is an unmissable destination, it's also one that palls for most visitors after a couple of (hectic) days.

If you've come solely to gamble, there's not much to say beyond the fact that all the casinos are free and open 24 hours per day, with acres of floor space packed with ways to lose money: **million-dollar slots**, video **poker**, **blackjack**, **craps**, **roulette** wheels and much, much more. The casinos will just love it if you try to play a system; with the odds stacked against you, your best hope of a large win is to bet your entire stake on one single play, and then stop, win or lose.

Brief history

Las Vegas has a shorter history than almost any other city in the world. The only US city founded in the twentieth century to boast over a million inhabitants, it's also the

Getting married in Las Vegas p.444   **All you can eat** p.454

GONDOLA ON THE VENETIAN'S GRAND CANAL

Highlights

❶ Luxor Festooned in Egyptian motifs, stuffed with corpses and even a chunk of the Titanic, this smoked-glass pyramid epitomizes Las Vegas's postmodern pot-pourri. **See p.445**

❷ New York–New York A loving re-creation of the Big Apple in the heart of the Big Cheese. **See p.445**

❸ The Conservatory The seasonally changing, tongue-in-cheek displays of plants, flowers and assorted oddities at Bellagio's Conservatory are guaranteed to serve up a riot of colour. **See p.447**

❹ Grand Canal Flowing through the heart of the Venetian, the irresistibly absurd Grand Canal is populated by stately, opera-singing gondoliers. **See p.448**

❺ SkyJump In the city's craziest thrill ride, you simply jump from the top of the 1000-foot Stratosphere. **See p.450**

❻ Mob Museum Only in Las Vegas would the mayor open a museum that celebrates the city's notorious links with organized crime in every gory detail. **See p.451**

❼ Le Village Buffet Celebrating the varied splendours of French cuisine, the buffet at Paris is perhaps the most imaginative and enjoyable in the city. **See p.454**

❽ Cirque du Soleil With *Love*, *O*, *Mystère* and *KÀ*, plus plenty more besides, the exhilarating Canadian troupe dominates Las Vegas's entertainment scene. **See p.458**

HIGHLIGHTS ARE MARKED ON THE MAP ON P.442

Downtown Las Vegas (2 miles) & ⑥ ▲

LAS VEGAS

- Las Vegas monorail
- Mirage–TI monorail
- CityCenter monorail
- Mandalay Bay–Excalibur monorail

HIGHLIGHTS

1. Luxor
2. New York–New York
3. The Conservatory
4. Grand Canal
5. SkyJump
6. Mob Museum
7. Le Village Buffet
8. Cirque du Soleil

The Stratosphere ⑤

SLS Las Vegas

Palace Station

Circus Circus

Resorts World (under construction)

Westgate Las Vegas

Las Vegas Convention Center

Trump International Hotel

Guardian Angel Cathedral

Encore

Fashion Show

Wynn Las Vegas

TI (Treasure Island)

The Palazzo

The Mirage

Sands Convention Center

The Venetian ④

The Forum

Harrah's

Caesars Palace

The Linq

High Roller

The Flamingo

The Cromwell

Bally's

Paris ⑦

Bellagio ③

Cirque du Soleil ⑧

The Cosmopolitan

Planet Hollywood

Vdara

Aria

CITY CENTER

Crystals

Mandarin Oriental

Monte Carlo

Showcase Mall

New York–New York ②

MGM Grand

Gold Coast

The Rio

The Palms

Excalibur

The Tropicana

Hard Rock Hotel

Luxor ①

Mandalay Bay

Four Seasons

McCarran International Airport

N

0   1
mile

only one that has consistently prioritized the need to attract visitors over the quality of life of its own residents.

The name *Las Vegas* – Spanish for "the meadows" – originally applied to natural springs where from 1829 onwards travellers would halt as they made their way along the Old Spanish Trail. For the rest of the nineteenth century, the Paiute Indians shared the region with Mormon ranchers, and the valley had a population of just thirty in 1900. Things changed in 1905, with the completion of the now-defunct rail link between Salt Lake City and Los Angeles. Las Vegas itself was **founded** on May 15 that year, when the railroads auctioned off lots around what's now Fremont Street.

The growth of gambling

Strange as it may seem, Nevada was the first state to **outlaw** gambling, in 1909. It was made legal once more in 1931, however, and the workers who built the nearby **Hoover Dam** flocked to Las Vegas to bet away their pay packets. Providing cheap electricity and water, the dam amounted to a massive federal subsidy for the infant city. Hotel-casinos such as the daring 65-room **El Rancho** began to appear in the early 1940s, but the Midwest Mafia were the first to appreciate the potential for profit. Mobster **Bugsy Siegel** raised $7 million to open the **Flamingo** in December 1946; early losses soon forced him to close again, and although he swiftly managed to reopen, his erstwhile partners were dissatisfied enough with their returns to have him murdered in LA in June 1947.

By the 1950s, Las Vegas was booming. The military had arrived – mushroom clouds from **A-bomb tests** in the deserts were visible from the city, and visitors would drive out with picnics to get a better view – and so too had big guns like **Frank Sinatra**, who debuted at the *Desert Inn* in 1951, and **Liberace**, paid $50,000 to open the *Riviera* in 1955. As the stars gravitated toward the Vegas honeypot, nightclubs across America went out of business, and the city became the nation's undisputed live-entertainment capital.

Las Vegas reinvented

The beginning of the end for Mob rule came in 1966, after reclusive tycoon **Howard Hughes** sold Trans World Airlines for $500 million and moved into the *Desert Inn*. When the owners tired of his non-gambling ways, he simply bought the hotel, and his clean-cut image encouraged other entrepreneurs to follow suit. **Elvis** arrived a little later, in 1969, starting a triumphant five-year stint as a karate-kicking lounge lizard at the off-Strip *International* (which subsequently became the *Hilton* and is now the *Westgate*).

Endless federal swoops and stings drove the Mob out of sight by the 1980s, in time for Vegas to reinvent itself on a surge of junk-bond megadollars. The success of Steve Wynn's **Mirage** in enticing a new generation of visitors, from 1989 onward, spawned a host of imitators. *Excalibur* and the *MGM Grand* were followed by *Luxor* and *New York–New York* and then, as the millennium approached, by the opulent quartet of **Bellagio**, *Mandalay Bay*, the *Venetian*, and *Paris*. Although the twenty-first century started with shockwaves, when Steve Wynn was forced to sell *Bellagio* and the *Mirage* to the MGM group, and 9/11 triggered a major downturn, Las Vegas bounced back. The **Venetian** has gone from strength to strength as the flagship for all that the city does best; Wynn himself opened his biggest casino yet, **Wynn Las Vegas**; and MGM Resorts saw the colossal **CityCenter** development through to completion in 2009, even as the storm clouds of recession were looming on the horizon. Since then, Las Vegas seems to have weathered that storm as well; visitor numbers have surged once more, hitting record levels, and a new wave of casino construction appears to be imminent.

The Strip

For its razor-edge finesse in harnessing sheer, magnificent excess to the deadly serious business of making money, there's no place like the **LAS VEGAS STRIP**. It's hard to imagine that Las Vegas was once an ordinary city, and Las Vegas Boulevard a dusty thoroughfare scattered with edge-of-town motels. After seven decades of capitalism run riot, with each new casino-hotel setting out to surpass anything its neighbours ever dreamed of, the Strip remains locked into a hyperactive drive for thrills and glamour, forever discarding its latest toy in its frenzy for the next jackpot.

Each casino is a self-contained fantasyland of high camp and genuine excitement, where the action keeps going day and night, and you rapidly lose track of which is which. Until recently, the casinos deliberately made it difficult to find your way back out onto the streets. Now that much of the Strip is owned by just two giant corporations – MGM Resorts and Caesars Entertainment – they're happy to let you stroll from each to the next, and there's plenty of action outdoors as well as in. In summer, though, the scorching heat of day is often too much to take; night is the best time to venture out, when the digital billboards are blazing their brightest.

Mandalay Bay

3950 Las Vegas Blvd S • ☎ 877 632 7700, ⓦ mandalaybay.com • **Shark Reef** Late May to Aug daily 10am–10pm; Sept to late May Mon–Thurs & Sun 10am–8pm, Fri & Sat 10am–10pm • $20, under-13s $14 • ☎ 702 632 4555, ⓦ sharkreef.com

Glowing like beacons as their gilded windows commandeer the sunset, the twin forty-storey sentinels of **Mandalay Bay** soar above the southern limits of the Strip.

GETTING MARRIED IN LAS VEGAS

Second only to making your fortune as a reason to visit Las Vegas is the prospect of **getting married**. Over 100,000 weddings are performed here each year, many so informal that bride and groom simply wind down the window of their car during the ceremony. Though a Vegas wedding has become a byword for tongue-in-cheek chic, however, most marriages are deeply formal affairs, and casinos and independent chapels alike compete to offer elaborate ceremonies with all the trimmings.

Assuming you're at least 18 years old and carrying picture ID, you don't have to be a local resident or take a blood test. Simply turn up at the **Clark County Marriage Licence Bureau**, downtown at 201 E Clark Ave (daily 8am–midnight; ☎ 702 671 0600, ⓦ clarkcountynv.gov), and buy a marriage licence for $60 cash. You can then walk over to the office of the **Commissioner for Civil Marriages**, at 330 S Third St (Mon–Thurs 2–6pm, Fri 9.30am–8.45pm, Sat 12.30–8.45pm, Sun 2–5pm; ☎ 702 671 0577), and pay another $75 cash to have the ceremony itself performed.

Reckon on paying at least $200 for the most basic service in a wedding chapel, which is liable to be as romantic a process as checking in at a hotel, and to take about as long. The full deluxe service ranges up to whatever you can afford.

Note that **same-sex marriages** have been legal in Nevada since 2014.

WEDDING CHAPELS

Graceland Wedding Chapel 619 Las Vegas Blvd S ☎ 702 382 0091, ⓦ gracelandchapel.com. Home of the King – Elvis will act as best man, give the bride away, or serenade you, but unfortunately he can't perform the service. Daily 9am–11pm.
Little Church of the West 4617 Las Vegas Blvd S ☎ 702 739 7971, ⓦ littlechurchlv.com. This fifty-year-old chapel has moved progressively down the Strip to its current site south of *Mandalay Bay*. Among

the quieter places to exchange Vegas vows. Daily 8am–11pm.
Little White Wedding Chapel 1301 Las Vegas Blvd S ☎ 702 382 5943, ⓦ alittlewhitechapel.com. The chapel (indeed, little and white) where Bruce Willis and Demi Moore married each other, and Michael Jordan and Joan Collins married other people. For those in a major hurry, they offer drive-through ceremonies in the "Tunnel of Love". Daily 8am–midnight.

Originally financed through the profits from its neighbours, *Luxor* and *Excalibur*, *Mandalay Bay* is more upmarket than either, kept lively at night by its excellent restaurants, bars, clubs and shows.

During the day, all it has to offer the casual sightseer is the **Shark Reef** aquarium, a long walk back from the Strip. The emphasis here is more on eye-catching monsters than education, with the basic premise that you're exploring a steamy, half-submerged temple complex, encountering yellow crocodiles, Komodo Dragons and (of course) sharks. Despite the substantial price, it's nowhere near the scale of a major aquarium; many visitors scoot through in around twenty minutes.

Luxor

3900 Las Vegas Blvd S • ☎ 702 262 4444, ⓦ luxor.com • **Bodies** and **Titanic** Both daily 10am–10pm • Each $32, over-64s $30, ages 4–12 $24; combined ticket $42 • ☎ 702 262 4400, ⓦ premierexhibitions.com

Guarded by an impassive Sphinx, the 350-foot black-glass pyramid of **Luxor** stands a block north of *Mandalay Bay*. While it remains an astonishing building, it has been stripped of most of its initial ancient Egyptian trappings, and rebranded as the sort of "hip", upscale casino resort that now dominates the Strip. Its upstairs Atrium Level houses two intriguing permanent exhibitions: **Bodies**, an eye-catching but ultimately sobering collection of genuine but "plastinated" human corpses, and **Titanic**, featuring not just artefacts and reconstructions but also the "Little Big Piece" of the doomed liner, complete with portholes, recovered from two miles down in the Atlantic Ocean.

Excalibur

3850 Las Vegas Blvd S • ☎ 702 597 7777, ⓦ excalibur.com

The architect of *Luxor*, Veldon Simpson, had previously designed **Excalibur**, immediately north. A less sophisticated mock-up of a medieval castle, complete with drawbridge, crenellated towers, and a basement stuffed with fairground-style sideshows for the kids, it's usually packed with low-budget tour groups.

MGM Grand

3799 Las Vegas Blvd S • ☎ 877 880 0880, ⓦ mgmgrand.com • **CSI: The Experience** Daily 9am–9pm, last admission 8pm • $28, ages 4–11 $21 • ☎ 702 891 1111, ⓦ csiexhibit.com

Considering that it was built as the world's largest hotel and is still growing, the **MGM Grand** presents a remarkably small frontage to the Strip. Instead its colossal size only becomes apparent once you're inside, perhaps after you've been walking for twenty minutes and are still nowhere near where you want to go. Created by Veldon Simpson, responsible for *Luxor* and *Excalibur*, it's bigger than both combined. Despite its fine array of restaurants and shows, it holds few attractions for sightseers other than the enjoyable, self-paced **CSI: The Experience**, in which participants attempt to solve various murder mysteries by inspecting the crime scene and then undertaking detailed lab work.

New York–New York

3790 Las Vegas Blvd S • ☎ 702 740 6969, ⓦ newyorknewyork.com • **Big Apple Coaster** Mon–Thurs & Sun 11am–11pm, Fri & Sat 10.30am–midnight • $14 first ride, $25 for an all-day pass

The intersection of Las Vegas Boulevard and Tropicana Avenue is said to be the busiest traffic junction in the US. Its northwest corner, diagonally opposite the veteran *Tropicana*, is occupied by an exuberantly meticulous re-creation of the Big Apple, **New York–New York**. This miniature Manhattan – built vertically, like the original, in response to space limitations – boasts a skyline featuring twelve separate skyscrapers and is fronted, of course, by the Statue of Liberty.

8

Unusually, the interior too is carefully realized, with some nice Art Deco flourishes and entertaining nightlife options in its Greenwich Village area. In one respect, it even surpasses New York itself: you can swoop around the whole thing at 65mph, inside and out, in the little yellow cabs of its hair-raising **Big Apple Coaster**.

CityCenter

The enormous **CityCenter** complex was unveiled in 2009 between the *Monte Carlo* and *Bellagio*, as a bold attempt by MGM Resorts to reshape Las Vegas's urban landscape. Its exciting new theme was that there was no theme: CityCenter is supposedly the kind of project that might be built in any city. Focusing on the **Aria** casino, set back from the Strip, and the Strip-front **Crystals** shopping mall, it was intended to mark the moment that Las Vegas stopped thinking in straight lines, and started to create new multi-purpose districts branching away from the Strip. To many people's surprise, CityCenter has prospered, with the *Monte Carlo* in particular upgrading as it has stretched back to meet *Aria*. The 2016 opening of the 20,000-seat **T-Mobile Arena**, between the two, is expected to boost CityCenter's impact even higher.

The most striking aspect of the complex for visitors is its abundant contemporary artworks, and especially **sculpture**. Big names include Claes Oldenburg, represented by the outsized steel-and-fibreglass typewriter eraser beside the *Mandarin Oriental*; Henry Moore, whose abstract *Reclining Connected Forms* (1969–74) fills the "pocket park" between *Aria* and Crystals; and Maya Lin, responsible for the gleaming 84ft Colorado River, cast in reclaimed silver, above *Aria*'s check-in desks.

Aria

3730 Las Vegas Blvd S • ☎ 702 590 7111, ⓦ aria.com

CityCenter's centrepiece, the 4004-room **Aria**, flaunts a modernist aesthetic that makes its plush marble-clad predecessors seem suddenly old and tired. And yet there's only so far you can take minimalism when you also have a casino to run, filled with slot machines, gaming tables and glamorous trappings. If you approach from the Strip, your first impression is of several curving glass skyscrapers; these turn out to form a single structure, fronted by a fountain that spurts multicoloured pulses of water. Once inside, you're plunged into the usual artificially lit gloom that characterizes most Las Vegas casinos.

The Cosmopolitan

3708 Las Vegas Blvd S • ☎ 702 698 7000, ⓦ cosmopolitanlasvegas.com

The glittering **Cosmopolitan** casino, which from the Strip sidewalk appears to be the main entrance to CityCenter, is actually nothing of the sort – it's an entirely separate, independent entity. With irresistible chutzpah, its owners bought up a former parking lot that had somehow escaped MGM's clutches, squeezed a brand-new casino on top of it, and packed it with lively clubs and bars and top-notch restaurants. It's almost the only property on the Strip that still follows the old fly-trap principle – once you're in it, it can be almost impossible to find your way out again.

Bellagio

3600 Las Vegas Blvd S • ☎ 702 693 7111, ⓦ bellagio.com

In 1998, Steve Wynn unveiled **Bellagio** as his attempt to build the best hotel in world history. It is undeniably a breathtaking achievement, striving to be somehow more authentic than the original town on Lake Como. The trouble is that *Bellagio* is not in Italy; it's in Las Vegas, and stuffed full of slot machines. The main hotel block, a stately curve of blue and cream pastels, stands aloof from the Strip behind an eight-acre artificial lake in which hundreds of submerged **fountains** erupt from two to four times each hour after dark in Busby-Berkeley water-ballets, choreographed with booming music and coloured lights. Wynn himself sold the place long ago; it's now owned by MGM, and seamlessly integrated into the CityCenter complex.

Once inside, *Bellagio*'s proudest boasts are the multicoloured Dale Chihuly glass sculpture, officially named *Fiori di Como*, that adorns the ceiling of the lobby area, and the opulent **Conservatory** immediately behind, where a network of flowerbeds beneath a Belle Epoque canopy of copper-framed glass is replanted every few weeks with ornate seasonal displays.

Planet Hollywood

3667 Las Vegas Blvd S • ☎ 866 919 7472, ⓦ planethollywoodresort.com
Planet Hollywood is a remodelled version of the former *Aladdin*, which hit the rocks in 2004. In keeping with the latest generation of casinos, it's all geared towards a young crowd, with a screaming loud decor it calls "Hollywood Hip". The mile-long **Miracle Mile Shops**, wrapped in a figure of eight around the casino and its theatre, is among the Strip's more affordable shopping malls, but short on decent eating options.

Paris

3655 Las Vegas Blvd S • ☎ 877 796 2096, ⓦ parislasvegas.com • **Eiffel Tower** Mon–Fri 9.30am–12.30am, Sat & Sun 9.30am–1am • $11.50 daytime, $16.50 evening
Paris was the 1999 handiwork of the same designers as *New York–New York*. With a half-size **Eiffel Tower** straddling the Arc de Triomphe and the Opera, it's a little compressed, but the attention to detail is a joy. There's also a fine assortment of top-notch French restaurants. Elevators soar through the roof of the casino and up to the summit of the Eiffel Tower – cheekily positioned to enjoy a perfect prospect of *Bellagio* – for stunning views of the city, at their best after dark.

8

Caesars Palace

3570 Las Vegas Blvd S • ☎ 866 227 5938, ⓦ caesarspalace.com
Across Flamingo Road from *Bellagio* – this is the intersection where Tupac Shakur was gunned down in 1996 – is **Caesars Palace**, which still encapsulates Las Vegas at its best, more than fifty years since it opened. Outside, ever more bars and restaurants fill extensive open-air patios, while the interior is a vast labyrinth of slots and green baize, peopled by strutting half-naked Roman centurions and Cleopatra-cropped waitresses, and filled with grand marble staircases that lead nowhere. Above the stores and restaurants of the **Forum**, the blue-domed ceiling dims and glows as it endlessly cycles from dawn to dusk and back again. The mall itself is now three storeys tall, while gloriously kitsch "living statues" inhabit its various fountains.

The Linq and the High Roller

3535 Las Vegas Blvd S • ☎ 800 634 6441, ⓦ thelinq.com • **High Roller** Daily 11.30am–2am • $27 11.30am–6pm , $37 6pm–2am
The stretch of the Strip immediately across from *Caesars Palace* has long been home to a row of veteran casinos that include the **Flamingo** and **Harrah's**. All belong these days to Caesars Entertainment, which has been steadily transforming the area. The showpiece of the development has been the transformation of the Asian-themed *Imperial Palace* casino into the **Linq**. A narrow pedestrian corridor alongside has become the **Linq Promenade**. Lined with relatively interesting shops, bars and restaurants, it leads to the world's largest observation wheel, the 550-ft **High Roller**. Although set too far back to offer sweeping vistas of the Strip itself, this still affords

superb views across the valley as a whole. It takes half an hour for each of its step-on, step-off cabins to complete a full revolution and return you to safety; don't get carried away if you get a cabin to yourselves, they're constantly monitored for misbehaviour.

The Mirage

3400 Las Vegas S • ☎ 702 791 7111, ⓦ mirage.com • **Secret Garden & Dolphin Habitat** Mon–Fri 11am–4pm, Sat & Sun 10am–4pm • $22, ages 4–12 $17 • ☎ 702 791 7188

Night-time crowds jostle for space on the sidewalk outside the glittering **Mirage**, beyond *Caesars*, to watch the **volcano** that erupts every fifteen minutes, spewing water and fire into the lagoon below. Although veteran magicians Siegfried and Roy were finally driven into retirement by Roy's near-fatal accident in 2003, their trademark white tigers can still be seen in the *Mirage*'s spacious **Secret Garden & Dolphin Habitat**. Visitors who are entirely lacking in basic respect for their fellow creatures can pay extra to do yoga, or even "paint", with the dolphins.

TI (Treasure Island)

3300 Las Vegas Blvd S • ☎ 702 894 7111, ⓦ treasureisland.com

The casino known as both **TI** and **Treasure Island** epitomizes the changing face of Las Vegas. When Steve Wynn built it in 1993, using early profits from the *Mirage* next door, the city was in thrall to the notion of becoming a child-friendly destination. Its entire lower facade was sculpted into a pastel-pretty seafront village straight out of *Pirates of the Caribbean*. A few years back, though, *Treasure Island* was sold to raise funds to build CityCenter, and almost all its lovingly crafted fripperies, including the pirate galleon and British frigate that used to do nightly battle in the lagoon outside, were stripped away. It then became an incongruous blue-collar resort, all country honky-tonks and party bars. As this book went to press, however, the wheel appeared to be turning once more; *TI* had announced plans to devote its second and third floors to interactive attractions based on the **Avengers** and **Transformers** franchises. Check to see whether they've opened by the time you read this.

The Venetian and Palazzo

3355 Las Vegas Blvd S • ☎ 702 414 1000, ⓦ venetian.com • **Madame Tussaud's** Mon–Thurs & Sun 10am–9.30pm, Fri & Sat 10am–10.30pm • $30, ages 7–12 $20 • ☎ 866 841 3739, ⓦ mtvegas.com

The facade of the **Venetian** includes loving facsimiles of six major Venice buildings, as well as the Rialto Bridge and the Bridge of Sighs. The main emphasis in the casino itself is on the **Grand Canal Shoppes**, reached via a stairwell topped by vivid frescoes copied from yet more Venice originals. The ludicrous re-creation of the **Grand Canal** at the top, complete with gondolas and singing gondoliers ($21 a ride), is quintessential Las Vegas, and as such utterly irresistible – it's *upstairs*, for God's sake.

When the *Venetian* first opened, it contained two outposts of the Guggenheim Museum. Both have now closed, leaving just a ridiculously expensive branch of **Madame Tussaud's** waxwork museum, where you can have your photo taken with President Obama in a replica Oval Office.

The adjoining **Palazzo** can be entered either via the Grand Canal Shoppes or directly from the Strip. Officially, it's a resort in its own right, but it's remarkably devoid of any identity, and just feels like a big, bland mall.

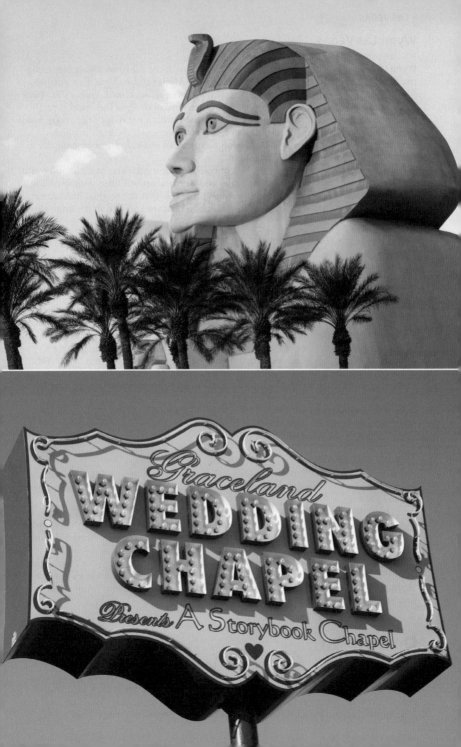

Wynn Las Vegas

3131 Las Vegas Blvd S • ☎ 702 770 7000, ⓦ wynnlasvegas.com

Wynn Las Vegas was built by Steve Wynn on the site of the vanished *Desert Inn*, using the fortune he accrued by building and selling the *Mirage* and *Bellagio*. In a nutshell, it's *Bellagio* re-imagined for a younger, hipper and even richer crowd, with a shift away from European elegance in favour of contemporary Asian design. The resort is partly obscured behind an artificial tree-covered mountain, which turns out once you're inside to be the backdrop for the **Lake of Dreams**, an "environmental theatre" in which ethereal sculpted figures emerge from a large expanse of water, in front of a massive waterfall that continually changes colour.

The interior of *Wynn Las Vegas* is a riot of colour, with spectacular patterns and motifs sprawling all over carpets, mosaics and tiles and a central atrium filled with sparkling trees and dazzling flowers. It has all proved so profitable that the original hotel tower was swiftly joined by a second, taller tower, dubbed **Encore** and clad in the same glossy "Wynn Bronze".

Circus Circus

2880 Las Vegas Blvd S • ☎ 702 734 0410, ⓦ circuscircus.com • **Adventuredome** Mon–Thurs 11am–6pm, Fri & Sat 10am–midnight, Sun 10am–9pm; daily 10am–midnight in school hols • $6–12 individual attractions, $32 all-day wristband, children under 4ft $18 • ☎ 702 794 3939, ⓦ adventuredome.com

A rare constant in the ever-changing world of Las Vegas, **Circus Circus** has remained true to itself for half a century. Back in the 1960s, combining children's entertainment with casino gambling under a single roof was a radical concept. Later on, that idea was embraced as a sure-fire money-spinning formula. When it subsequently became a discredited cliché, *Circus Circus* carried on regardless. Since the recession hit, and the stalwarts along this portion of the Strip were destroyed in order to build replacements that never materialized, pedestrian traffic hereabouts has plummeted, and *Circus Circus* finally seems to be running into the rails.

For kids, though, *Circus Circus* still holds an enjoyable distraction – the indoor **Adventuredome** theme park, sheltered beneath a huge bubble of pink glass.

The Stratosphere

2000 Las Vegas Blvd S • ☎ 702 380 7777, ⓦ stratospherehotel.com • **Tower** Mon–Thurs & Sun 10am–1am, Fri & Sat 10am–2am • **Observation Deck** $20, discounts for guests • **Thrill rides** X-Scream, Big Shot & Insanity $15 each, $36 for an all-day package; SkyJump $120, min age 14

At 1149ft, the **Stratosphere** is the tallest building west of the Mississippi. The outdoor **Observation Deck** just below its summit offers amazing panoramas across the city, while assorted wonderfully demented **thrill rides** can take you even closer to heaven. Insanity and X-Scream dangle riders over the edge, strapped into individual seats and in a precarious gondola respectively; and the terrifying Big Shot is an open-air couch that shunts to the top of an additional 160ft spire, then free-falls down again. As for the **SkyJump** – a "controlled free-fall", more like a zip line than a bungee jump – you simply jump off the top and plummet 855ft.

Downtown

As the Strip has evolved from strength to strength, **downtown** Las Vegas, the city's original core, has been neglected. Long known as "Glitter Gulch", it never really was a "downtown" in the conventional sense, holding few stores or businesses away from its compact row of lower-key casinos. It is, however, forever attempting to recast itself as a genuine rival to the Strip. In the **Fremont Street Experience**, five entire blocks of its central street have been roofed over to form a "Celestial Vault", studded with over twelve million LED nodules to create a screen that's illuminated in dazzling nightly displays (hourly, sunset–midnight; free). The casinos here are on a smaller scale than on the Strip, and much more devoted to the serious business of gambling; the only one that comes even close to matching the Strip giants is the **Golden Nugget**.

Slotzilla

Fremont St • Mon–Thurs & Sun 1pm–1am, Fri & Sat 1pm–2am • Zip line $25, Zoomline $45; weight restrictions apply • ☎ 702 678 5780, Ⓦ vegasexperience.com

Slotzilla is an extraordinary two-tier **zip line** that centres on what's claimed – at 120ft tall – to be the world's biggest slot machine. This huge contraption ejects four riders at a time on each level, who race east–west along the full length of Fremont Street, to land at Main Street. Riders on the upper "Zoomline" level hang prone, enabling them to fly like Superman, and pass through holes cut into the canopy of the Fremont Street Experience.

Mob Museum

300 Stewart Ave • Daily 9am–9pm • $24, ages 11–17 $14 • ☎ 702 229 2734, Ⓦ themobmuseum.org

The most successful of many attempts by former Mayor Oscar Goodman – himself a lawyer who defended Mob-linked figures in court – to bring tourists downtown, the intriguing **Mob Museum** opened in 2012. Filling three storeys of a former courthouse, it explores the ongoing fear and fascination of the underworld figures who once dominated the city, with plenty of gory detail amid its high-minded displays.

8

ARRIVAL AND DEPARTURE

LAS VEGAS

By plane McCarran International Airport is a mile east of the southern end of the Strip, and four miles from downtown. Some hotels run free shuttle buses for guests, while Airline Shuttle (☎ 702 444 1234, Ⓦ bestairlineshuttle .com) runs minibuses to the Strip and downtown costing from around $12/person upwards. Taxi fares from the airport also vary enormously; broadly speaking, expect to pay upwards of $20 to reach casinos at the southern end of the Strip, $30 or more for casinos further north or downtown.

By bus Long-distance Greyhound buses arrive at 200 S Main St downtown (☎ 702 384 9561).

Destinations Flagstaff (2 daily; 5hr 30min), Los Angeles (9 daily; 5–7hr), and Phoenix (2 daily; 8hr 30min).

INFORMATION

Visitor centre 3150 Paradise Rd, east of the Strip – but not worth visiting (Mon–Fri 8am–5pm; ☎ 877 847 4858).
Websites Useful sources of information include the city's official website, Ⓦ lasvegas.com, and sites such as Ⓦ lasvegassun.com, Ⓦ lvrj.com, Ⓦ lasvegasweekly.com and Ⓦ lvol.com.

GETTING AROUND

Traffic is so bad in Las Vegas that if you've just come to explore the Strip, it's not worth renting a car. Be warned, though, that on summer days it's too hot to walk more than a couple of blocks along the Strip.

By bus Both the most useful routes on the RTC network (Ⓦ catride.com) – the Deuce on the Strip (daily 24hr) and the faster Strip & Downtown Express or SDX (daily 9am–midnight) – run the full length of the Strip and connect with downtown. Buy tickets before you board; 2hr pass $6, 24hr pass $8, 3-day pass $20.

By monorail The overpriced and less-than-convenient Las Vegas Monorail runs along the eastern side of the Strip from the *MGM Grand* to *SLS Las Vegas* (Mon–Thurs 7am–2am, Fri–Sun 7am–3am; single trip $5, 1-day pass $12; Ⓦ lvmonorail.com), but doesn't go to the airport or downtown. Separate, free monorail systems also link *Mandalay Bay* with *Excalibur* via *Luxor*, the *Monte Carlo* with *Bellagio* via *CityCenter*, and the *Mirage* with *TI*.

ACCOMMODATION

Although Las Vegas has well over 160,000 motel and hotel rooms, it's best to book accommodation ahead if you're on a tight budget, or arriving on Friday or Saturday; upwards of two hundred thousand people descend on the city every weekend. Even if you stay in the same room for several days, you'll be charged a different rate for each day, depending on the day of the week, and what's going on in town. The only sure-fire way to get a cut-price room is to **visit during the week** rather than on the weekend. Rates rise enormously on Friday or Saturday, by at least $50 extra in a lower-end property, well over $100 in the big-name casinos. On top of that, many hotels won't accept Saturday arrivals. **Room taxes** add an additional thirteen percent downtown, twelve percent elsewhere, while almost every hotel in town adds a so-called **resort fee** of $15–35 per day to all room prices, which generally covers wi-fi access and a few "extras" that you wouldn't normally expect to have to pay for.

THE STRIP

Aria 3730 Las Vegas Blvd S ☎866 359 7757 or ☎702 590 7111, ⊚ arialasvegas.com. The chocolate-brown and gold-toned guest rooms feel subdued and somewhat anonymous by Las Vegas standards, but with their high-end amenities, *Aria* can be a real bargain, especially if you have the time – and weather – to enjoy the superb pool complex. Resort fee $32. Mon–Thurs & Sun $203, Fri & Sat $238

Bellagio 3600 Las Vegas Blvd S ☎888 987 6667 or ☎702 693 7111, ⊚ bellagio.com. Perhaps not quite state-of-the-art any more, but still at the top end of the Vegas spectrum. Plush European furnishings and marble bathrooms now give *Bellagio*'s luxurious rooms a slightly retro feel; some face the fountains at the front, others the superb pool complex. Resort fee $32. Mon–Thurs & Sun $209, Fri & Sat $299

Caesars Palace 3570 Las Vegas Blvd S ☎866 227 5938, ⊚ caesarspalace.com. The older rooms in this epitome of 1960s luxury still burst with pseudo-Roman splendour, while those in the newer towers are more conventionally elegant. Resort fee $29. Mon–Thurs & Sun $205, Fri & Sat $261

Circus Circus 2880 Las Vegas Blvd S ☎800 634 3450 or ☎702 734 0410, ⊚ circuscircus.com. Venerable hotel, popular with budget tour groups. Kids love the theme park and (almost) nonstop circus acts, adults love the low room rates. Rooms in the motel-like Manor section at the back are pretty grim; pay a little more to stay in one of the Towers instead. Resort fee $24. Mon–Thurs & Sun $27, Fri & Sat $99

★**The Cosmopolitan** 3708 Las Vegas Blvd S ☎855 435 0005 or ☎702 698 7575, ⊚ cosmopolitanlasvegas .com. While it's far from cheap, this very central casino is for once on a manageable scale, and offers smart modern rooms in the very thick of things, plus great restaurants and nightlife. No resort fee. Mon–Thurs & Sun $200, Fri & Sat $320

Encore Las Vegas 3121 Las Vegas Blvd S ☎888 320 7125 or ☎702 770 8000, ⊚ encorelasvegas.com. Setting Las Vegas's current standard for high-end luxury, *Encore* ever-so-slightly raised the bar above its older sister *Wynn*. Rooms are plush and colourful, if not quite as red as the public areas downstairs, and the pool (sorry, "Beach Club") is the best in town. Resort fee $29. Mon–Thurs & Sun $229, Fri & Sat $339

★**Excalibur** 3850 Las Vegas Blvd S ☎877 750 5464 or ☎702 597 7777, ⊚ excalibur.com. Some of the 4000 rooms in this garish fake castle are very ordinary, so it's worth paying a few dollars extra to get a renovated one, which are excellent value. Thanks to an endless stream of tour groups and families, the whole place is often uncomfortably crowded. Resort fee $26. Mon–Thurs & Sun $38, Fri & Sat $123

The Flamingo 3555 Las Vegas Blvd S ☎888 902 9929 or ☎702 733 3111, ⊚ flamingolasvegas.com. Bugsy Siegel's oft-renovated *Flamingo* has dropped well below the premier league. The tropical-themed pool complex is great, but the actual rooms vary enormously; some have real flair, but the standard ones can be very shabby indeed. Resort fee $29. Mon–Thurs & Sun $88, Fri & Sat $132

★**Luxor Las Vegas** 3900 Las Vegas Blvd S ☎877 386 4658 or ☎702 262 4000, ⊚ luxor.com. All two thousand rooms in this vast smoked-glass pyramid have tremendous views – and they're much larger than usual. Unlike the extra two thousand rooms in the newer tower next door, however, most have showers, not baths. Resort fee $26. Mon–Thurs & Sun $57, Fri & Sat $156

Mandalay Bay 3950 Las Vegas Blvd S ☎877 632 7800, ⊚ mandalaybay.com. This upscale, young-adult playground is a long way south of the central Strip, but all of its luxurious rooms have both bath and walk-in shower, and there's a spectacular wave pool. Resort fee $30. Daily $235

MGM Grand 3799 Las Vegas Blvd S ☎877 880 0880, ⊚ mgmgrand.com. Waiting for any kind of service, especially check-in, in this behemoth – 5044 rooms and counting – can be horrendous, and now that the rooms have lost their former movie theming, they've become rather anonymous. Resort fee $30. Mon–Thurs & Sun $94, Fri & Sat $191

The Mirage 3400 Las Vegas Blvd S ☎800 374 9000 or ☎702 791 7111, ⊚ mirage.com. The glitzy *Mirage* is not the market leader it once was, and its smallish rooms have even smaller bathrooms. Even so, the public areas remain impressive, the pool complex is nicely laid out, and the entertainment and nightlife options are pretty good too. Resort fee $30. Mon–Thurs & Sun $169, Fri & Sat $250

★**New York–New York** 3790 Las Vegas Blvd S ☎866 815 4365, ⊚ newyorknewyork.com. Sheer attention to detail makes this one of the most exuberantly enjoyable places to stay on the Strip – and it's small enough that you're not always shuffling down endless corridors. The

8

rooms are very nice, if a bit cramped, and filled with Art Deco flourishes. Resort fee $30. Mon–Thurs & Sun $81, Fri & Sat $179

★ **Paris–Las Vegas** 3655 Las Vegas Blvd S ☎877 796 2096 or ☎702 946 7000, ⊛parislasvegas.com. If not the absolute pinnacle of luxury, rooms and services at the flamboyant French-themed *Paris* are still pretty good, and for location, views and ambience it more than holds its own. Resort fee $29. Mon–Thurs & Sun $119, Fri & Sat $195

Planet Hollywood 3667 Las Vegas Blvd S ☎866 919 7472 or ☎702 785 5555, ⊛planethollywoodresort.com. This has some of the nicest mid-rate rooms in town, decked out with movie memorabilia and contemporary furnishings. They're an awful long way from the self-park garage though. Resort fee $29. Mon–Thurs & Sun $90, Fri & Sat $258

The Stratosphere 2000 Las Vegas Blvd S ☎702 380 7777, ⊛stratospherehotel.com. Despite its unfashionable location, the *Stratosphere* has survived thanks to rock-bottom rates and a steady flow of tour groups. Don't expect amazing views – the large, plain rooms aren't in the tower itself – but they're good value, and often have last-minute availability. Resort fee $21. Mon–Thurs & Sun $46, Fri & Sat $155

TI (Treasure Island) 3300 Las Vegas Blvd S ☎800 944 7444 or ☎702 894 7444, ⊛treasureisland.com. Though no longer geared toward families, *TI* remains a fun and convenient place to stay, even if the rooms themselves are relatively small. Resort fee $30. Mon–Thurs & Sun $129, Fri & Sat $140

The Venetian 3355 Las Vegas Blvd S ☎866 659 9643 or ☎702 414 1000, ⊛venetian.com. Even the standard rooms at this upscale Strip giant are split-level suites, with antique-style canopied beds atop raised platforms, plus spacious living rooms, marble bathrooms with walk-in showers, and a mind-blowing array of shops and restaurants at hand. Resort fee $30. Mon–Thurs & Sun $229, Fri & Sat $299

Wynn Las Vegas 3131 Las Vegas Blvd S ☎877 321 9966 or ☎702 770 7000, ⊛wynnlasvegas.com. Since the 1980s, Steve Wynn has repeatedly redefined Las Vegas's highest standard of luxury. The exceptionally large guest rooms boast wonderful beds with fabulous linens, and super-sized tubs in the bathrooms. Resort fee $29. Mon–Thurs & Sun $186, Fri & Sat $339

DOWNTOWN AND OFF THE STRIP

The D 301 E Fremont St ☎800 274 5825 or ☎702 388 2400, ⊛thed.com. One of downtown's best bargains, this offers comfortable renovated rooms and a decent array of bars and restaurants. Resort fee $20. Mon–Thurs & Sun $29, Fri & Sat $99

El Cortez 600 E Fremont St ☎800 634 6703 or ☎702 385 5200, ⊛elcortezhotelcasino.com. Veteran downtown casino, refreshed by a recent face-lift, with cut-price rooms in the main building, and great-value mini-suites in a newer tower. Resort fee $9. Mon–Thurs & Sun $29, Fri & Sat $89

Golden Gate Hotel and Casino 1 E Fremont St ☎800 426 1906 or ☎702 385 1906, ⊛goldengatecasino.com. Downtown's oldest joint dates from 1906, when Las Vegas was just a year old. Now rebranded as a "boutique hotel", it holds a hundred tiny retro-furnished rooms. No resort fee. Mon–Thurs & Sun $24, Fri & Sat $99

Golden Nugget 129 E Fremont St ☎800 634 3454 or ☎702 385 7111, ⊛goldennugget.com. The only downtown casino to make a serious bid for the luxury end of the market is undeniably glittery, with a stunning pool complex and opulent rooms. Resort fee $25. Mon–Thurs & Sun $49, Fri & Sat $124

Hard Rock Hotel 4455 Paradise Rd ☎800 473 7625 or ☎702 693 5000, ⊛hardrockhotel.com. Over a mile east of the Strip, "the world's only rock'n'roll casino" can't match Las Vegas's showcase giants for size or splendour. Instead, it's a relatively intimate and even chic alternative, with above-average rooms, high-class restaurants and fabulous pool. Room rates soar when there's a big-name rock gig. Resort fee $28. Mon–Thurs & Sun $70, Fri & Sat $279

The Plaza 1 Main St ☎888 912 0075 or ☎702 386 2110, ⊛plazahotelcasino.com. Since the management cleverly managed to shoehorn the unused furnishings from the never-opened *Fontainebleau* into the fading *Plaza*, its thousand rooms are looking great, and offer some of downtown's best rates. Resort fee $15. Mon–Thurs & Sun $35, Fri & Sat $99

8

EATING

Las Vegas's restaurant scene ranks among the most varied and vibrant in the US, with each major casino holding as many as ten high-class restaurants. The choice on the Strip is overwhelming, and you'll almost certainly find a good restaurant to suit your tastes and budget in your own hotel. For that reason, the places reviewed here tend toward the higher end of the spectrum; they're the exceptional ones worth making a special effort to reach.

BUFFETS

Bacchanal Buffet Caesars Palace, 3570 Las Vegas Blvd S ☎702 731 7928, ⊛caesarspalace.com. The Strip's newest gourmet buffet – much the best at any Caesars-owned property – features 500 freshly made items daily, from sushi, dim sum and phô soup to fresh oysters and wood-fired pizzas, prepared by chefs at nine separate "show kitchens", each devoted to a different world cuisine.

ALL YOU CAN EAT

In time-honoured Las Vegas fashion, almost every casino offers an **all-you-can-eat buffet**. While standards (and prices) are highest at casinos like *Wynn*, *Bellagio* and *Paris*, most buffets remain locked in the cheaper, more traditional approach; much like a food court in an upmarket mall, you'll get good fast food, but not great cooking. The best of this latter kind are neither on the Strip nor downtown, but in casinos like the *Rio* and the *Stations* chain that depend on locals as well as tourists. By contrast, those at the very largest Strip casinos, like *Excalibur* and the *MGM Grand*, are often poor value.

Prices are the highest in town, though: breakfast costs $31, lunch $38, the weekend champagne brunch $50, and dinner $53 on weekdays, $56 at weekends. Breakfast Mon–Fri 7.30–11am; lunch Mon–Fri 11am–3pm; brunch Sat & Sun 8am–3pm; dinner daily 3–10pm.

Buffet Bellagio Bellagio, 3600 Las Vegas Blvd S ☎ 866 259 7111, ⓦ bellagio.com. Las Vegas's first gourmet buffet set a standard that competitors have since surpassed. While it has cut a few corners, there's still a lot to like, with around 800 items prepared fresh in small quantities. Breakfast costs $21, while lunch (Mon–Fri $25), brunch (Sat & Sun $31; with unlimited champagne $44) and dinner (Mon–Thurs $36, Fri–Sun $41) can include sushi, cold cuts, dim sum, green curry duck, *coq au vin*, roasted salmon and roast lamb with mint sauce, plus fresh-baked focaccia, tasty fruit tarts, and fancy desserts. The large dining area is not especially attractive, but offers spacious seating. Breakfast Mon–Fri 7–11am; lunch Mon–Fri 11am–3pm; brunch Sat & Sun 7am–3pm; dinner daily 3–10pm.

★The Buffet at Wynn Wynn Las Vegas, 3131 Las Vegas Blvd S ☎ 702 770 7000, ⓦ wynnlasvegas.com. *Wynn*'s plush Belle Époque buffet remains the best in town. While each dish is labelled as though on a gourmet menu – marinated snapper with edamame, five distinct ceviches, and so on – it's the sheer variety that makes it exceptional, with buffet staples like Alaskan crab legs and peeled shrimp prepared to perfection (diners grab phenomenal amounts from the bottomless trays) and daily specials like baba ganoush or clams in black bean sauce. It can't quite match a top restaurant, but it's still a definitive Las Vegas experience. On weekdays, breakfast costs $24 and lunch $27; weekend brunch is $35; and dinner is $43, rising to $50 on Fri & Sat. Breakfast Mon–Fri 8am–11pm; lunch Mon–Fri 11am–3.30pm; brunch Sat & Sun 8am–3.30pm; dinner Mon–Thurs & Sun 3.30–10pm, Fri & Sat 3.30–10.30pm.

Golden Nugget Buffet Golden Nugget, 129 E Fremont St ☎ 702 385 7111, ⓦ goldennugget.com/lasvegas. Downtown's best buffet occupies a plain but bright and spacious room on the *Golden Nugget*'s second floor, overlooking the pool complex, and charges relatively down-to-earth prices, with breakfast $13, weekday lunch $15, the weekend brunch $19, and dinner $21 on

weekdays, $27 at weekends, when they offer "seafood and more". The food is wider-ranging than you'll find elsewhere on Fremont Street. Meat mains like roast beef or Chinese orange chicken are relatively ordinary, but more interesting offerings include entire roasted heads of garlic or tasty baked catfish. Breakfast Mon–Fri 7–10.30am; lunch Mon–Fri 10.30am–3.30pm; champagne brunch Sat & Sun 7am–3.30pm; dinner daily 3.30–10pm.

★Le Village Buffet Paris, 3655 Las Vegas Blvd S ☎ 702 946 7000, ⓦ parislasvegas.com. *Paris*'s buffet is unusual in showcasing French dishes only, and does so extremely well. The meat offerings tend to be heavy, from roast chicken fricasseed, as *coq au vin* or with mustard, along with duck à l'orange and a creamy pork and beef cassoulet, but there's plenty of seafood, from scallops, shrimp and crab to Dover sole and rich bouillabaisse. Vegetables such as baby squash and creamed spinach are super-fresh, and there's even a full French cheese board. The setting is a little cramped, squeezed into a very Disney-esque French village, but the food is *magnifique*. Breakfast costs $22 on weekdays, $24 at weekends; weekday lunch is $25; and the weekend champagne brunch and weekday dinner both cost $31; and weekend dinner is $34. Breakfast Mon–Fri 7–11am, Sat & Sun 7–10am; lunch Mon–Fri 11am–3pm; brunch Sat & Sun 10am–3pm; dinner daily 3–10pm.

Wicked Spoon The Cosmopolitan, 3708 Las Vegas Blvd S ☎ 702 698 7000, ⓦ cosmopolitanlasvegas.com. Despite being hidden away at the back of the upper level, the *Cosmopolitan*'s buffet is a big hit with locals and visitors alike, thanks to its extensive array of international cuisines. Each dish is set out on an individual portion-sized plate, so everything looks good, and there's more of the feel of dining in a restaurant. There's no dividing line between breakfast and lunch (both Mon–Fri $27, Sat & Sun $35), while dinner is priced at $38 all week. Mon–Thurs 8am–2pm & 5–9pm, Fri 8am–10pm, Sat 8am–10pm, Sun 8am–9pm.

RESTAURANTS
THE STRIP

★Beijing Noodle No. 9 Caesars Palace, 3570 Las Vegas Blvd S ☎ 877 346 4642, ⓦ caesarspalace.com. Entered via an avenue comprising six large tanks of Japanese goldfish, this casual noodle shop occupies a lovely space, dazzling white, with tracery screens that create the feeling of being in an aquarium. The food, like the Imperial Seafood Dumplings (each of which contains seafood in a hot chicken broth), the salt and pepper shrimp, and the tender beef chow fun with flat noodles, is delicious. With typical mains at $16–23 it's more expensive than you'd pay for noodles elsewhere, but "single" portions are very substantial; one each and you've got a good meal. Daily 11am–10.30pm.

★**Bouchon** Level 10, Venezia Tower, The Venetian, 3355 Las Vegas Blvd S ☎702 414 6200, ⓦbouchonbistro.com. Despite its sky-high reputation and exclusive setting, Thomas Keller's spacious re-creation of a classic French bistro is friendly and (relatively) affordable. Breakfast is a Francophile's dream of croissants, pastries, yogurt and coffee, while brunch is the best value, with sandwiches or quiche for under $20; dinner mains range from $28.50 for sautéed trout to $37 for steak frites. Sitting outside on the huge piazza is a real joy. Mon–Fri 7am–1pm & 5–10pm, Sat & Sun 7am–2pm & 5–10pm.

Estiatorio Milos The Cosmopolitan, 3708 Las Vegas Blvd S ☎702 698 7930, ⓦmilos.ca/restaurants/las-vegas. The $250 lunch menu at this gorgeous Greek seafood restaurant, adorned with replica antiquities, is a real bargain; ideally you'd sit out on their little Strip-view garden terrace. In the evening, it's very much a place for a romantic treat; your pick from an array of succulent Mediterranean fish, freshly arrived from the Athens fish market, will cost well over $50 per person. Mon–Thurs & Sun noon–11pm, Fri & Sat noon–midnight.

Fat Burger 3763 Las Vegas Blvd S ☎702 736 4733, ⓦfatburger.com. There's no more to this gleaming, all-American burger joint, across from the *Cosmopolitan*, than meets the eye. Quite simply, you can walk or drive in from the Strip at any time, and get a perfect burger, fries and shake. Daily 24 hours.

Gordon Ramsay Steak Paris, 3655 Las Vegas Blvd S ☎877 346 4642, ⓦparislasvegas.com. Britain's favourite pottymouth perfectionist has moved into Las Vegas in a big way. This very fancy steakhouse, all but beneath the Eiffel Tower and supposedly designed to resemble the Channel Tunnel, offers prime slabs of beef and veal in all shapes and one size – big. Choose your own from the trolley, and for upwards of $50 it'll soon be slapped down in front of you, cooked to perfection. Even fish'n'chips costs $45. Daily 4.30–10.30pm.

Jean Phillippe Patisserie Bellagio, 3600 Las Vegas Blvd S ☎702 590 7227, ⓦjpchocolates.com. The perfect way to start or finish an indulgent Las Vegas day – spectacle, excess and gluttony: cakes, pastries, pancakes, chocolate and coffee, all served within the warm, swirling embrace of the world's largest chocolate fountain. No reservations. Mon–Thurs 6am–11pm, Fri–Sun 6am–midnight.

Julian Serrano Aria, 3730 Las Vegas Blvd S ☎702 590 8520, ⓦarialasvegas.com. Almost everything in this superbly stylish tapas restaurant comes from Spain, from the glassware to the *pata negra* ham from Extremadura and the olive oil from Jaén. It might sound inexpensive, at $10–16 per plate, but you can quickly eat $100 worth. In general, the more elaborate the dish, the better. The little balls of cocoa butter filled with chilled gazpacho are out of this world, while the avocado cannelone with Scottish salmon and seaweed is exquisite. There are also a few larger mains, including lamb chops at $59 and paellas, designed to share, at $45 and up. Mon–Thurs & Sun 11.30am–1pm, Fri & Sat 11.30am–11.30pm.

Michael Mina Pub 1842 MGM Grand, 3799 Las Vegas Blvd S ☎702 891 3922, ⓦmgmgrand.com. Michael Mina keeps things simple with his take on the gastro pub, serving substantial $18–24 burgers and old-fashioned favourites like fish'n'chips ($28) or succulent St Louis ribs ($23/35), along with $8–12 Happy-Hour "small plates" like brisket sliders or lobster grilled cheese and a couple of dozen draft beers. Mon & Thurs 11.30am–10pm, Fri 11.30am–11pm, Sat 11am–11pm, Sun 10am–10pm.

★**Mon Ami Gabi** Paris, 3655 Las Vegas Blvd S ☎702 944 4224, ⓦmonamigabi.com. The first and the finest casino restaurant to offer open-air seating right on the Strip has the feel of a proper French pavement bistro. At lunch, try the gloriously authentic onion soup ($12), the mussels (seasonal; $14 or $28), or the thin-cut steak frites ($29). Dinner features more expensive steak cuts and fish main courses. Mon–Thurs & Sun 7am–11pm, Fri & Sat 7am–midnight.

Olives Bellagio, 3600 Las Vegas Blvd S ☎702 693 8865, ⓦbellagio.com. *Bellagio*'s best-value gourmet restaurant has a lovely terrace setting, facing the Eiffel Tower across the lake. Even if it is the kind of place that calls a $21 pizza an "individual oven-baked flatbread", and your food will probably be arranged vertically not horizontally, the largely Mediterranean menu is uniformly fresh and superb. It's a great spot for lunch, with $15–22 appetizers like beef carpaccio, pasta dishes like butternut squash tortelli ($19), and specials such as a jumbo lump crab cake sandwich ($27). Dinner mains are pricier, at up to $50. Daily 11am–2.45pm & 5–10.30pm.

Phô TI (Treasure Island), 3300 Las Vegas Blvd S ☎702 894 7111, ⓦtreasureisland.com. If you're looking for a simple, cheap and tasty meal that's a little out of the ordinary, there's no faulting the Strip's only Vietnamese restaurant, which occupies half of the *Coffee Shop* at TI. The speciality here is hearty bowls of *phô* soup, with chicken, beef or vegetable at around $16; rice or vermicelli noodle dishes cost much the same. Mon–Thurs & Sun 11am–11.30pm, Fri & Sat 11am–2.30am.

8

8

★**Scarpetta** Level 3, The Cosmopolitan, 3708 Las Vegas Blvd S ☎702 698 7960, ⦿cosmopolitanlasvegas .com. This wonderful, inventive "new Italian" restaurant enjoys one of Las Vegas's very best views, looking out across the fountains of *Bellagio*. Open for dinner only, until late, just like in Italy, the menu is divided between *primi piatti* such as roasted scallops ($26); pasta, with even the simplest spaghetti sauce at $24; and consistently delicious main courses, like fennel spiced black cod for $35 or trio of Colorado lamb for $50. There's also a $110 tasting menu. Daily 6–11pm.

DOWNTOWN AND OFF THE STRIP

Mr Lucky's Hard Rock Hotel, 4455 Paradise Rd ☎702 693 5592, ⦿hardrockhotel.com. The *Hard Rock*'s 24hr coffee shop is a very stylish joint, and the food is well above average too. As well as all the usual breakfast items, it serves burgers, sandwiches, pizzas and pasta dishes for $12–18, a T-bone steak for $26, and milkshakes or microbrews for $8. Daily 24hr.

★**Oscar's Beef • Booze • Broads** The Plaza, 1 Main St ☎702 386 7227, ⦿oscarslv.com. An absolute only-in-Las-Vegas experience, set in a spherical see-through ball that stares straight down Fremont Street, this dinner-only steakhouse belongs to former mayor Oscar Goodman, husband of current mayor Carolyn Goodman. The food is unimaginative but pretty good, from $27 for roast chicken up to $48 for steak; the booze is exactly what it sounds like; and the "broads" are the hostesses. Mon–Thurs & Sun 5–10pm, Fri & Sat 4.30pm–midnight.

Paymon's Mediterranean Café and Market 4147 S Maryland Parkway at Flamingo ☎702 731 6030, ⦿paymons.com. This simple but highly recommended Middle Eastern restaurant – much easier to reach heading south rather than north on Maryland – is Las Vegas's best vegetarian option. The Cretan murals are attractive, the food tasty and substantial, the service friendly, and there's even a hookah lounge. Salads and pita sandwiches cost $8.50–11, and spinach pie $13.50, while dips such as hummus or the aubergine-based baba ganoush start at $5.50. If you can't make up your mind, try the mountainous best-of-everything combination plate for just $15. Daily 11am–1am.

★**Ping Pang Pong** Gold Coast, 4000 W Flamingo Rd ☎702 367 7111, ⦿goldcoastcasino.com. Las Vegas's best Chinese restaurant is in the closest casino to the city's small local Chinatown, a mile west of *TI*. Packed with Chinese customers around the clock, it has a great selection of inexpensive dim sum on the lunchtime trolleys – try the $11 soft-shell crab, wrapped in rice paper – and a full menu of rice, noodle and meat mains, few of which cost over $15. Daily 10am–3pm & 5pm–3am.

Triple George Grill 201 N Third St ☎702 384 2761, ⦿triplegeorgegrill.com. Its speakeasy decor, mixing exposed brickwork with wood panelling, might not be genuine, but this downtown steakhouse is a real-life hangout for local politicos and lawyers. A "George", incidentally, is in local parlance a big tipper and all-round good guy – the opposite of a "stiff". Come early for lunch, and watch them wheeling and dealing in the back room over $9 Caesar salads, $14 chicken fettuccini or $19 steaks. Mon–Fri 11am–10pm, Sat 4–10pm.

DRINKING AND NIGHTLIFE

As the perfect fuel to turn a dithering gawker into a die-hard gambler, alcohol is very easy to come by in Las Vegas. If you want a drink in a casino, there's no need to look for a bar; instead, a tray-toting waitress will come and find you. All the casinos have actual **bars** as well, but they're just a small part of the picture. The old-fashioned **Las Vegas lounge** has returned in force, whether knowingly retro-styled for 20-something rockers, glammed up as an "ultra-lounge," or lovingly re-created for older visitors looking to recapture the decadent flavour of the Rat Pack era. Las Vegas is also an international **clubbing** capital; all the major casinos have opened their own clubs, often with spectacular results.

BARS AND LOUNGES

Chandelier The Cosmopolitan, 3708 Las Vegas Blvd S ☎702 698 7979, ⦿cosmopolitanlasvegas.com. Festooned in the dangling tentacles of a colossal chandelier, this three-level bar is the epicentre of the glamorous *Cosmopolitan*. Kick-start your night with a cocktail, or spend the whole evening in its enclosed DJ section. Casino level open 24hr, other levels hours vary.

Chicago Brewing Co Four Queens, 202 E Fremont St ☎702 924 5222, ⦿fourqueens.com. Downtown's liveliest bar has something of the feel of a pub, especially once you've sampled a massive 60-oz flagon of beer ($14), brewed on site. Mon–Fri 11.30am–1.30am, Sat & Sun 10am–1.30am.

Gilley's Saloon TI, 3300 Las Vegas Blvd S ☎702 894 7111, ⦿gilleyslasvegas.com. This raucous, earthy, no-nonsense country and rodeo saloon typifies the new *TI*. Bikini-clad "Gilley Girls" ride mechanical bulls, and there's a free line-dancing lesson most nights at 7pm. Afterwards, you can drink two-for-one rum cocktails until 10pm, or dance to honky-tonk bands until way past midnight. Mon–Thurs & Sun 11am–2am, Fri & Sat 11am–4am. Cover from $10 after 10pm.

Minus5 Ice Lounge Mandalay Bay, 3930 Las Vegas Blvd S ☎702 740 5800, ⦿minus5experience.com. There's nothing tricksy about the name here; it's minus 5, and it's an ice lounge. What's an ice lounge? It's a lounge where everything – the seats, the bar, the walls and even the glasses – is made of ice. Customers are kitted out in Eskimo-style parkas and furry hoods, the better to savour frozen margaritas and the like. You can look around for $19, but you only get to drink if you buy a two-cocktail package for $39. Mon–Thurs & Sun 11am–2am, Fri & Sat 11am–3am.

Nine Fine Irishmen New York–New York, 3790 Las Vegas Blvd S ☎ 866 815 4365, ⓦ ninefineirishmen.com. The affinity between New York and all things Irish finds expression in this wood-panelled pub, shipped from Ireland and featuring Irish musicians, singers and dancers nightly. Daily 11am–11pm. Cover $5 Wed & Thurs, $10 Fri & Sat.

Parasol Up, Parasol Down Wynn Las Vegas, 3131 Las Vegas Blvd S ☎ 702 770 7000. Matching pair of see-and-be-seen bars, decked out in *Wynn*'s signature psychedelic palette and facing the Lake of Dreams; *Up* is at the top of the central staircase, while *Down*, at the bottom, offers additional outdoor seating that's very much in demand. Mon–Thurs & Sun 11am–4am, Fri & Sat 11am–5am.

CLUBS AND MUSIC VENUES

Encore Beach Club Encore, 3121 Las Vegas Blvd S ☎ 702 521 4005, ⓦ encorebeachclub.com. Las Vegas's premier "dayclub" even before Prince Harry's 2012 escapade made it world-famous, this extraordinarily lavish labyrinth of pools, bars and patios makes the perfect venue for a no-expense-spared lost weekend or two. March–Oct Fri noon–7pm Sat & Sun 11am–7pm. Cover $25–75.

House of Blues Mandalay Bay, 3950 Las Vegas Blvd S ☎ 702 632 7600, ⓦ hob.com. The voodoo-tinged, folk-art-decorated *House of Blues* has a definite but not exclusive emphasis towards blues, R&B, and the like, though weeknights tend to see DJs rather than bands. Typical prices range from around $35 for B-list names and from $170 for the regular "intimate evenings" with Carlos Santana. Mon–Thurs & Sun 8am–11pm, Fri & Sat 8am–midnight.

The Joint Hard Rock Hotel, 4455 Paradise Rd ☎ 702 693 5222, ⓦ thejointlasvegas.com. The venue of choice

for big-name touring rock acts is now capable of holding 4000-plus audiences. Tickets to see the Rolling Stones here cost $505 and $1005, but more typically admission for performers such as the Scorpions ranges $50–150. See website for schedule and prices.

★**Marquee** The Cosmopolitan, 3708 Las Vegas Blvd S ☎ 702 333 9000, ⓦ marqueelasvegas.com. This indoor-outdoor club, artfully put together by the clubbing masterminds of the TAO group, features top DJs day and night, but also holds lower-key bars and lounges. Expect to pay heavily to enjoy its full amenities. Nightclub Mon & Thurs–Sat 10pm–4am; Dayclub daily 10am–7pm; cover varies $25–100.

Piranha 4633 Paradise Rd ☎ 702 791 0100, ⓦ piranhavegas.com. Extravagant gay club in the so-called "Fruit Loop", the focus of Las Vegas's off-Strip gay scene. Beyond either a flaming waterfall or a wrap-around piranha-filled aquarium, you'll find the frenetic dance floor, with a plush bar alongside and an exclusive VIP section, featuring private "skyboxes", upstairs. There's also a fabulous outdoor patio, with individual fireplaces. Daily 10pm–5am. Cover varies, typically $20.

Omnia Caesars Palace, 3570 Las Vegas Blvd S ☎ 702 785 6200, ⓦ omnianightclub.com. Unveiled in 2015 as the successor to the massively popular *Pure*, this hot-ticket club boasts a huge open-air Strip-view terrace. Ordinary mortals can expect a long wait before being admitted, and to pay astonishing prices for drinks ($28 for a beer), but for a once-in-a-lifetime full-on Las Vegas experience, with the world's biggest-name DJs, it can't be beat. Tues & Thurs–Sun 10.30pm–4am. Cover $20–50.

Tao The Venetian, 3355 Las Vegas Blvd S ☎ 702 388 8588, ⓦ taolasvegas.com. The decor at *Tao* is extremely opulent, and very Asian-influenced, with lots of glowing golden Buddhas, and it attracts very big names indeed. The rooftop, poolside *Tao Beach* opens in summer only. Nightclub Thurs–Sat 10pm–5am; Tao Beach 11am–sunset. Cover $20–50; weekend wristband $100.

ENTERTAINMENT

Live entertainment remains a crucial component of the Las Vegas package, and it's nothing like as kitsch as first-time visitors might imagine. One by one, the cheesy, feathers-and-tassels revues have gone – the last, the much-lamented *Jubilee*, finally closed down in 2015 – to be replaced by postmodern shows by the likes of the now-ubiquitous Cirque du Soleil and the Blue Man Group. More generally, individual performers, like comedians, magicians and singer-impressionists, tend to have been supplanted by ensemble pieces such as Broadway shows. There's still a place for the old-fashioned **headliner**, though – Celine Dion paved the way for a new generation in the 4000-seat Colosseum at *Caesars Palace*, and she's been followed by the likes of Elton John, Rod Stewart, Mariah Carey, and, at *Planet Hollywood*, Britney Spears. Tix4tonight sells **discounted show tickets** from a dozen Strip locations (☎ 877 849 4868, ⓦ tix4tonight.com).

Absinthe Caesars Palace, 3570 Las Vegas Blvd S ☎ 800 745 3000, ⓦ absinthevegas.com. Staged in the round, in a marquee on Caesars' outdoor Roman Plaza, this no-holds-barred circus-tinged burlesque show has taken Las Vegas

by storm. Conceived as a crude and abrasive counterpoint to Cirque du Soleil, and eschewing PC in all its forms, it's more of a drunken night out than a traditional show, and for all its "alternative" stance, it still charges Cirque-level prices. Wed–Sun 8pm & 10pm; $99–139.

★**The Beatles Love** The Mirage, 3400 Las Vegas Blvd S ☎702 792 7777, ⓦcirquedusoleil.com. In which the Cirque du Soleil do their stuff to a remixed Beatles soundtrack. Sometimes intimate, sometimes exuberantly all-embracing, it's a beautifully judged and profoundly moving show. Nostalgic and visionary, it celebrates the Beatles' achievement while avoiding anything too literal – the actors don't play specific Beatles, for example. The costumes, lighting and staging are all magnificent, and some set-pieces astonishing. When all's said and done, it's a dance show, but if that might normally put you off, don't let it – it's an irresistible evening. Mon & Thurs–Sun 7pm & 9.30pm; $86–196.

★**Big Elvis** Harrah's, 3475 Las Vegas Blvd S ☎702 369 5000, ⓦharrahslasvegas.com. No Las Vegas trip would be complete without an audience with the King. The lounge at *Harrah's* is always packed for the undeniably sizeable Pete Vallee's good-natured, full-throated, sweat'n'sequins Elvis tribute show. Mon, Tues & Thurs & Fri 2–6pm. Free.

Blue Man Group Luxor, 3900 Las Vegas Blvd S ☎800 557 7428, ⓦblueman.com. Blue Man Group have become long-term fixtures on the Strip, where so many other shows – shows with stars, plots and even words – have failed within months. How? By the synchronized munching of breakfast cereal; by performing live endoscopies on audience members; by catching marshmallows in their mouths. Their deadpan humour is complemented by exhilarating music, including lots of meaty drumming, and some truly stunning special effects. Daily 7pm & 9.30pm; $69–125.

Human Nature The Venetian, 3355 Las Vegas Blvd S ☎702 414 9000, ⓦhumannaturelive.com. As soon as this vocal quartet bounds on stage, they acknowledge that four fresh-faced, clean-cut, and, above all, white Australians singing the music of black America makes a pretty odd fit. And then, quite simply, they blow your socks off, with good old-fashioned panache and hard work, plus the aid of a hot six-piece band. From fierce stompers to sweet a cappella numbers, it's much more than pastiche, and the audience laps it up. Tues–Sat 7pm; $66–121.

Jersey Boys Paris, 3655 Las Vegas Blvd S ☎702 777 7776, ⓦjerseyboysvegas.com. While Broadway shows are normally truncated to suit restless Las Vegas audiences, this hugely enjoyable romp lasts the full 2hr 10min – there's simply so much material to cover, in what's a genuine emotional narrative rather than simply a vehicle for the songs of Frankie Valli and the Four Seasons. Expect quick-fire repartee, lightning-fast staging and, above all, irresistible music. Tues–Sun 7pm; $49–176.

★**KÀ** MGM Grand, 3799 Las Vegas Blvd S ☎702 531 3826, ⓦka.com. With so many superb Cirque du Soleil productions running in Las Vegas, it's all too easy to overlook KÀ. In fact, it's an absolute must-see, boasting a quite extraordinary set; the stage floor not only rises, but can swivel and pivot in every direction. One moment it's a steep cliff face, to which the performers cling for dear life; the next, they simply fall, mid-battle, into the abyss below. KÀ is much more plot-driven than other Cirque shows, allowing more scope for darkness and emotional impact in its truly breathtaking set pieces. Mon–Wed, Sat & Sun 7pm & 9.30pm; $75–196.

Mac King Harrah's, 3475 Las Vegas Blvd S ☎702 693 6143, ⓦmackingshow.com. This afternoon magic show is one of Las Vegas's best entertainment bargains. Mac King's an endearing innocent in a plaid suit who specializes in good old close-up magic, using ropes, cards, torn-up $20 bills and the like. His corny patter leaves plenty of room for good-natured improvised gags. Tues–Sat 1pm & 3pm; $35.

★**Mystère** TI, 3300 Las Vegas Blvd S ☎702 894 7722, ⓦcirquedusoleil.com. Cirque du Soleil's original Las Vegas show is such a visual feast that it barely matters whether you see its dreamscape symbolism as profound and meaningful or laboured and empty. Seen at first as being too "way-out" for Las Vegas, its success redefined the city's approach to entertainment. Above all, it's a showcase of fabulous circus skills, with tumblers, acrobats, trapeze artists, pole climbers, clowns, and strong men, but no animals apart from fantastic costumed apparitions. Mon–Wed, Sat & Sun 7pm & 9.30pm; $75–136.

★**O** Bellagio, 3600 Las Vegas Blvd S ☎702 693 8866, ⓦcirquedusoleil.com. In this Cirque du Soleil triumph, any part of the stage at any time may be submerged to any depth. From the synchronized swimmers onwards, performers display their magnificent skills to maximum advantage. Highlights include a colossal trapeze frame draped like a pirate ship and crewed by fearless acrobats and divers, and footmen flying through the air in swirls of velvet drapery. Wed–Sun 7pm & 9.30pm; $107–180.

Terry Fator The Mirage, 3400 Las Vegas Blvd S ☎702 792 7777, ⓦmirage.com. If you saw Terry Fator win *America's Got Talent*, you'll know why this amazing ventriloquist-impressionist so quickly became a Las Vegas headliner. The man is quite extraordinary; while manipulating animal puppets, he delivers note-perfect imitations of anyone from Marvin Gaye and Roy Orbison to Gary Numan and Lady Gaga – without moving his lips. Even if his humour is hardly cutting-edge, it is at least funny. Mon–Thurs 7.30pm; $65–163.

Around Las Vegas

Spend more than a day or two in Las Vegas and you'll soon be gasping for a blast of sunlight and fresh air away from the casinos. To reach anywhere interesting, you have to cross an expanse of empty desert, but exhilarating day-trip destinations do exist, including **Red Rock Canyon** and the **Hoover Dam**. A much more distant day outing is the **Grand Canyon**, or more precisely, the so-called Grand Canyon West (see p.328).

Red Rock Canyon

17 miles west of the Strip • **Visitor Centre** Daily 8am–4.30pm • ☎ 702 515 5350, ⓦ redrockcanyonlv.org • **Scenic Drive** Daily: March 7am–7pm; April–Sept 6am–8pm; Oct 6am–7pm; Nov–Feb 6am–5pm • $7 per vehicle

For a taste of Southwestern canyon scenery, head west along Charleston Boulevard to **Red Rock Canyon National Conservation Area**, a cactus-strewn desert basin that's surrounded by stark red cliffs and pierced repeatedly by narrow canyons. The **Scenic Drive**, a thirteen-mile loop road, provides access to the cool, slender **Ice Box Canyon** (a 2.5-mile round-trip hike), and the three-mile **Pine Creek Trail**, which follows a flower-lined creek beyond a ruined homesite towards a towering, red-capped monolith.

Lake Mead

30 miles southeast of the Strip • **Visitor centre** US-93, 4 miles northeast of Boulder City • Daily 9am–4.30pm • ☎ 702 293 8990, ⓦ nps .gov/lake

Many Las Vegas visitors make the pilgrimage to **LAKE MEAD**, the vast reservoir that straddles the border between Nevada and Arizona, behind the Hoover Dam. As with the similarly incongruous Lake Powell (see p.393) it makes a bizarre spectacle – the blue waters a vivid counterpoint to the surrounding desert – but it can get excruciatingly crowded. The best views along its five-hundred-mile shoreline come from the Nevada side; call in at the **visitor centre** to enjoy a sweeping prospect of the whole thing.

8

Hoover Dam

30 miles southeast of the Strip • ☎ 702 494 2517, ⓦ usbr.gov/lc/hooverdam • **Parking** Daily: April–Sept 8am–6.15pm; Oct–March 8am–5.15pm • **Visitor Center** Daily: April–Sept 9am–6pm; Oct–March 9am–5pm • $10 • **Powerplant Tour** April–Sept 9.25am– 4.55pm; Oct–March 9.25am–3.55pm • $15, seniors & ages 4–16 $12 • **Dam Tour** April–Sept Mon–Thurs 9.30am–4pm, Fri & Sat 9.30am–4.30pm; Oct–March daily 9.30am–3.45pm • $30, no reductions, min age 8

Beyond Boulder City, across the rocky ridges of the Black Mountains, US-93 reaches the **Hoover Dam** itself. Completed in 1935, and designed to block the Colorado River and provide low-cost electricity for the cities of the Southwest, it's among the tallest dams ever built (760ft high), and is made of enough concrete to build a two-lane highway from the West Coast to New York. Three levels of visit are possible. You can simply explore the **Visitor Center** on the Nevada side of the river; take the half-hour **Powerplant Tour**, in which you ride an elevator to the base of the dam; or join the hour-long **Dam Tour**, which involves an additional mile or so of walking in the damp dark tunnels deep inside the dam.

NAVAJO WOMAN IN CANYON DE CHELLY,
EARLY TWENTIETH CENTURY

Contexts

History

What is now the Southwest USA has been home to Native Americans for about twelve thousand years. Around four hundred years ago, a small group of Hispanic colonists claimed the region for Spain as New Mexico, while two centuries later it passed briefly into the hands of the newly independent nation of Mexico, before being taken over by the United States.

Throughout that long history, the Southwest has been either controlled, or at least heavily influenced, by distant powers. Its best-known ancient inhabitants, the Ancestral Puebloans and the Hohokam, drew their cultural inspiration from Mexico; the settlers of Santa Fe looked to Mexico City and Madrid for financial and spiritual support; and even today the region owes much to federal funding from Washington.

What makes the Southwest so fascinating is that so many of the different peoples who have migrated into the region are still there, and still interacting with each other. In the words of an anthropologist from Zuni Pueblo, "the Anasazi are alive and well and living in the Rio Grande Valley". The Navajo, relative latecomers, form the majority population in the Four Corners; Santa Fe is still a visibly Hispanic, Catholic city; Utah remains over sixty percent Mormon; and Phoenix and Las Vegas typify the Anglo impact.

The Paleo Indians

No trace of human beings in the Americas has been dated any earlier than 15,000 BC. Around that time, the true pioneers of North America, nomadic hunter-gatherers from Siberia, first reached Alaska. Thanks to the last ice age, when sea levels were three hundred feet lower than the modern Bering Strait, a "**land-bridge**" – actually a vast plain, measuring six hundred miles north to south – connected Eurasia to America.

Separated by impenetrable glacier fields from Canada, Alaska was then effectively part of Asia rather than North America. Much like an air lock, the region "opened" in different directions at different times. Thus migrants reaching it from the west, oblivious to the fact they were leaving Asia, found their way blocked to the east. Several generations might pass, and the connection back to Asia be severed, before an eastward passage appeared. This migration was almost certainly spurred by the pursuit of large mammal species, especially the mammoth, that were already extinct throughout almost all of Eurasia. Imagine therefore the glee of the so-called **Paleo Indians** when they finally encountered America's own indigenous "megafauna", such as mammoths, mastodons, giant ground sloths and long-horned bison, all of which had evolved without fear of human predation.

The original group of human settlers may have been very small. It's been calculated that a band of a hundred individuals, advancing eight miles deeper into the virgin continent each year, with an annual population growth of 1.1 percent, could have filled North and South America with ten million people within a thousand years.

15,000 BC	11,000 BC	10,000–8000 BC
First nomadic peoples from Asia reach Alaska	Almost all North America's large mammals, from mammoths to horses, become extinct, possibly due to over-hunting	Clovis culture present in New Mexico

Between 10,000 BC and 8000 BC, the Southwest was dominated by the so-called **Clovis** culture, whose distinctive flaked-stone spear points were first identified at Clovis, New Mexico. Living in small groups, constantly on the move, Clovis hunters pursued their prey across large distances. Their weapons have been found poking from the ribs of mammoths, and they seem to have been such successful killers that they drove the indigenous fauna – which included horses – to extinction.

The Archaic culture

As the large animals died out, early Southwesterners adapted to become **hunter-gatherers**. Learning where and when particular plants ripened, the people of the **Archaic** or **Desert culture** would migrate seasonally within limited areas, such as between canyons and nearby hillsides. Hunting for small mammals such as rabbit and deer remained important. Clay statuettes and split-twig figurines, found in remote locations in the Grand Canyon and elsewhere and depicting deities as well as animals, show that shamanistic rituals evolved. The most remarkable manifestation of Archaic culture was the mysterious rock art of the **Great Gallery** in Canyonlands National Park (see p.412); these people also constructed giant earthworks in the deserts of southwest Arizona. Few traces of their actual homes survive, however; it's thought they lived in caves wherever possible.

The arrival of **agriculture** from Mexico played a crucial role in ending the Archaic era. **Corn** – as tiny fingers of maize, much smaller than today's strains – may have been cultivated in the highlands of southern Mexico as early as 5000 BC. Knowledge of how to grow it then spread northwards from group to group, accompanied by the prayers and rituals necessary to ensure a good harvest, and may have reached southern New Mexico around 1500 BC. Like hunter-gatherers the world over, notoriously reluctant to give up a lifestyle that offers food in return for comparatively little effort, Southwesterners at first simply used a low level of farming – more like gardening – to supplement their traditional diet. Communities only made the transition to intensive agriculture once population levels increased.

The Basketmakers

Southwestern peoples embarked on the large-scale cultivation of crops – corn, together with a more recent arrival, **squash** – from around 100 BC onwards. The first such society was named **Basketmaker II** by early archeologists, who assumed that more primitive "Basketmaker I" sites waited to be found; they never were. The Basketmakers lived in extended family groups, in shallow **pithouses** – rectangular pits two to six feet deep, with earth-covered roofs that rose above ground level. By now they had also domesticated **dogs**, for hunting, and **turkeys**, for feathers rather than food. They hunted using *atlatls*, spear-throwing devices similar to the gadgets used by modern dog owners to throw balls for their pets. Cooking entailed dropping hot rocks into waterproof yucca-leaf baskets lined with pitch.

Pottery too spread from Mexico, during the first few centuries AD. All pots were made by women, hand-coiling successive strips of rolled clay one atop the next, then smoothing them together. The use of fragile ceramic vessels presupposes a sedentary

4000 BC onwards	**1500 BC**	**100 BC**
Archaic artists create Great Gallery in Canyonlands	Agriculture reaches the Southwest from Mexico	The first Basketmakers start to live in pithouses, growing corn and squash

society, but one with great benefits: **beans** are much easier to boil in a pot than a basket, so the Southwest acquired its third great staple food, and basketmaking declined.

Around 500 AD, the so-called **Basketmaker III** culture emerged. As well as corn, squash and beans, they grew another Mexican import, **cotton** – originally cultivated mainly for its oil-rich edible seeds – and used **bows and arrows**. Sizeable **villages** started to appear. Later called **pueblos** by the Spanish, each village soon focused around a single extra-large pithouse, probably set aside for public or ritual use. Such buildings are recognizable as the first **kivas** – the ceremonial underground chambers that remain at the heart of Pueblo religion. Each *kiva* was entered from above, via an opening that also served as a smokehole. A bench ran around its circumference, and niches were set into the walls, perhaps to hold ritual objects. A small depression in the floor in front of the central firepit, known as the **sipapu**, symbolized the hole through which human beings emerged onto this earth.

The Ancestral Puebloans

By 700 AD, much of the Southwest was populated by the forerunners of modern Pueblo Indians. Archeologists and Pueblo Indians alike now call these people "**Ancestral Puebloans**" instead of the previously common term "**Anasazi**". The Hopi especially object to that name, which comes from a Navajo word meaning "enemy ancestors", preferring to use either their own word for "ancestors", **Hisatsinom**, or the more generally applicable "Ancestral Puebloans".

Between 700 AD and 1300 AD, Ancestral Puebloan civilization spread beyond the **Four Corners** to cover most of what's now northern Arizona and New Mexico, as well as southern Utah and Colorado, and parts of southern Nevada. Besides the initial increase in the size and sophistication of villages came a crucial change. Individuals stopped living in pithouses, and instead built surface structures of mud plastered onto a brushwood framework – a style known as wattle-and-daub. However, they continued to dig large subterranean *kivas* for communal or ceremonial use. Many such *kivas* could now also be accessed via concealed tunnels, thus enabling costumed priests or dancers to make surprise appearances during rituals.

The Ancestral Puebloans were the first North Americans to use looms to **weave** cotton. In addition to cotton clothes, they made blankets and even socks from yucca leaves interwoven with turkey feathers, and wore yucca sandals. For a time, they flattened and broadened their skulls by binding infants' heads against cradleboards. Women averaged around five feet in height, men a few inches more, and **life expectancy** was thirty or less, although perhaps one in ten reached the age of fifty. Adults were plagued by arthritis and loss of teeth, which were worn away by grit, the result of grinding corn between a hand tool or *mano* and a flat slab known as a *metate*, both made from sandstone. They also had some **medical** expertise, using cottonwood bark, which contains the main ingredient of aspirin, as a painkiller, and piñon sap as an all-purpose antiseptic.

By the time the Ancestral Puebloans reached their cultural peak in the Four Corners, during the eleventh century, three main subgroups had emerged, centred on Chaco Canyon in what's now northwest New Mexico, Mesa Verde in southwest Colorado, and the Kayenta region of northeast Arizona.

350 AD	500	700–900
Hohokam civilization constructs canals and ball courts in Phoenix Basin	Pottery and cotton become established, and the first pueblos appear	The Hohokam establish their largest settlement, Snaketown

The **Chacoans** seem to have been the most sophisticated of all, as witnessed not only by the architectural complexity of the multistorey pueblos of Chaco Canyon (see p.92), but by the fact that the canyon was so unsuited for large-scale occupation that they must have survived by extracting tribute from surrounding regions. Their wealth demonstrates that by 1050 AD the Southwest was crisscrossed by extensive **trading routes**. In the absence of pack animals, most trade was in lightweight ritual or ornamental objects. In exchange for **turquoise**, which passed from group to group all the way down to the Aztecs, the Ancestral Puebloans received silver and copper goods from Mexico, seashells from the Pacific, and the most prized ceremonial treasures of all – live **macaws**.

During the first half of the twelfth century, the decline of Chaco was mirrored by a general decline in the Ancestral Puebloan population. Following a period of instability and mass migrations, however, Ancestral Puebloan civilization had a majestic final flourish in the Four Corners during the thirteenth century. Major **towns** were constructed, including eight large pueblo complexes in Colorado's Montezuma Valley that held over a thousand people each. The nearby "**cliff dwellings**", squeezed into alcoves on the canyon walls of **Mesa Verde** National Park (see p.74) were home to a smaller, probably peripheral group; though compellingly beautiful to modern eyes, they represent a relatively minor aspect of Ancestral Puebloan life.

The disappearance of the Ancestral Puebloans

The "**disappearance**" of the Ancestral Puebloans from the entire Four Corners region between 1275 and 1300 AD is still often presented as a great mystery. Modern Pueblo peoples are so self-evidently their descendants, however, that it's clear the Ancestral Puebloans migrated away rather than simply dying out. *Why* they did so is harder to explain. Traditional accounts say that a sustained **drought** forced them to leave, but such droughts were not uncommon, and the region remained capable of producing enough food.

It seems more likely that the drought coincided with a period of cultural upheaval and violent conflict. Recent proof of cannibalism has shattered notions of Ancestral Puebloan society as being utterly peaceful, and isolated groups appear to have banded together in larger settlements for mutual defence.

The influence of the blood-drenched civilizations of ancient Mexico was also at its height. Centring on supernatural entities that, at this formative stage, closely paralleled the warring deities of the Aztecs, the **kachina** religion spread rapidly across the Southwest; some archeologists argue, somewhat controversially, that it was introduced by cannibalistic warrior refugees from the south. In any case, over time, religious emphasis shifted away from blood and sacrifice towards ceremonies designed to bring rain, and thus corn. The drought of the late thirteenth century may have been the first crucial test of, or judgement upon, those rainmaking powers; charismatic religious leaders may perhaps have persuaded their followers that the failure of the harvest was a signal to move on.

The Ancestral Puebloans had also severely depleted their **environment**, stripping the landscape around their settlements bare; the pueblos of Chaco Canyon, for example, used over 200,000 large wooden beams. It may be no coincidence that the Four

---

This Contexts section also includes separate histories of the **Hopi** (see p.478), and of the **Navajo** and **Apache** (see p.482).

1050	1100	1250–1300
Ancestral Puebloan culture reaches its peak at Chaco Canyon in the Four Corners	The Mimbres people of southern New Mexico produce exquisite ceramics	The ancestors of today's Navajo and Apache migrate into the Southwest

Corners remained all but deserted until the arrival of the Navajo during the sixteenth century; it may have taken that long to recover from overexploitation.

The Hohokam

While the Basketmakers and Ancestral Puebloans held sway to the north, the deserts of southern Arizona and northern Mexico were home to the equally sophisticated **Hohokam** civilization. This region was not then so barren as it appears today – much of it was covered with grass until it was overgrazed by Spanish cattle – and the Hohokam were primarily **farmers**. They lived in what the Spanish later called **rancherías** – sprawling farming communities, where each homestead consisted of a framework of timber, brush-coated with mud. Thousands of such villages were scattered across the desert, interspersed with larger "towns" that were probably ceremonial and trading centres rather than residential districts. The population was most heavily concentrated in the **Phoenix Basin**, where inhabitants compensated for the lack of rainfall by digging over three hundred miles of irrigation **canals**. Constructed without the use of metal tools, and requiring constant maintenance, these enabled the Hohokam to reap two separate harvests each year, with corn, beans and squash as their staple crops.

Whether the Hohokam arrived from central Mexico around 300 BC, as some archeologists believe, or simply evolved from indigenous desert peoples, they were clearly heavily influenced by Mexican culture. Each major town had at least one Mexican-style **ball court**, where a ritual game was played with a rubber ball, and a raised-earth **platform mound** used for religious ceremonies. Like the Ancestral Puebloans, with whom they had little direct contact, the Hohokam traded commodities like cotton and salt for ritual items from the south, such as copper bells, onyx, parrots and macaws.

During the eleventh century, the Hohokam trading complex known as **Snaketown**, at the confluence of the Gila and Salt rivers, rivalled Chaco as the Southwest's largest settlement. Though Snaketown subsequently declined, the Phoenix Basin became one of the most densely populated areas in North America, holding perhaps eighty thousand inhabitants in the thirteenth century. However, the Hohokam **disappeared** at much the same time as the Ancestral Puebloans, around 1350 AD. The very word "Hohokam" means "all used up" in the language of the later **O'odham** people of southern Arizona. So extensively did they drain every drop of sustenance from the land that their descendants were reduced to an impoverished subsistence lifestyle. In addition, by the end of the seventeenth century the arrival of European **diseases** such as smallpox, measles and typhus reduced the population of the Phoenix Basin to fewer than five thousand.

While no modern Native American group claims direct descent from the Hohokam, certain cultural traits endure. The *ranchería* style of dwelling persisted until recently among tribes like the Yavapai, Havasupai and O'odham. Those peoples' individualistic system of belief – lacking *kachinas* or *kivas*, and depending on shamans rather than priests – also matches what little is known about Hohokam religion.

The Mogollon

Archeologists distinguish a third significant group among the pre-Columbian peoples of the Southwest – the **Mogollon**. Contemporaneous with the Ancestral Puebloans and

1275	1300	1350
The three "Hopi Mesas" in northern Arizona are home to 35 villages, including Oraibi, the oldest	Shortly after constructing the cliff dwellings of Mesa Verde, the Ancestral Puebloans leave the Four Corners	Hohokam people disappear from southern Arizona

the Hohokam, and sharing elements of both cultures, the Mogollon occupied what's now west-central New Mexico and east-central Arizona. The Mogollon people lived on the cool plateau above the **Mogollon Rim**, a 200-mile long escarpment that marks the southern limit of the Colorado Plateau, farming the upland meadows and hunting in the mountains.

Being so close to Mexico, the Mogollon heartland, which focused on the valleys of the **Gila** and **Mimbres** rivers, was probably the first area of the Southwest to acquire agriculture and pottery. The Mogollon only stopped building pithouses around the eleventh century, and the few pueblos they constructed, such as the one now preserved as Gila Cliff Dwellings (see p.200), were on a small scale. In one respect, however, Mogollon culture was unsurpassed – the extraordinary **pottery** produced by the **Classic Mimbres** people (see p.200).

Much like the Four Corners, the entire Mogollon region became **depopulated** during the fourteenth century. As the Mogollon peoples had probably introduced the *kachina* religion to the Southwest, their descendants presumably helped to create modern Pueblo culture. Specific Mogollon-descended pueblos may well have been the hardest hit by the arrival of both the Spaniards and the Apache, however, and if their inhabitants survived at all, they probably fled north as refugees.

The Pueblo world and the Spanish invasion

Although the Ancestral Puebloan era ended with their departure from the Four Corners, their immediate descendants created the Southwest's largest pre-Hispanic communities of all. The city of **Casas Grandes**, which flourished between 1300 and 1400 AD in what's now northern Mexico, consisted of over two thousand rooms and served as a major macaw-breeding centre.

However, the most enduring legacy of the Ancestral Puebloans was the emergence of **Pueblo** communities throughout what had previously been under-populated areas of northern New Mexico. Most Mesa Verdeans migrated to the northern reaches of the **Rio Grande** Valley, where they founded **Taos Pueblo** among others; their language, known as Tanoan, evolved into today's Tiwa and Tewa languages. The Chacoans, on the other hand, who spoke the language that became Keresan, moved further south to establish pueblos like Cochiti and Kewa, as well as **Acoma** and **Zuni** to the west.

By the time the Spanish arrived, the Southwest may have held a hundred separate pueblos, with a total population approaching one hundred thousand. New forms of social organization had emerged, and individual pueblos consisted of alliances of either **clans** – each with its own religious or military responsibilities – or **moieties** – societies in which half the pueblo might belong to a *kiva* associated with winter ceremonies, and the other half to one connected with summer. However, pueblos did not have chiefs or leaders in the European sense, and neither was there any tradition of alliances between pueblos. That lack of political unity seriously weakened their ability to resist the Spanish invaders, who turned their attention northwards after completing the conquest of Mexico.

The coming of the Spaniards

The first Spanish expedition to reach what's now the US, led by **Ponce de León**, sailed up the Atlantic coast in 1513 and named **Florida**. The next Spanish voyage, in 1528,

1521	1528	1539
Hernán Cortés and his conquistadors seize control of the Aztec capital of Tenochtitlán	A Spanish expedition is shipwrecked in Florida; Cabeza de Vaca and three survivors, including Esteban, a black African, take eight years to walk to Mexico City	Esteban, now serving as the advance party for Fray Marcos de Niza's expedition from Mexico, is killed at Zuni

ended in shipwreck, but a junior officer, **Alvar Núñez Cabeza de Vaca**, survived. Together with three shipmates, he spent eight years on an extraordinary trans-continental odyssey. Living with various Native American groups – initially held as slaves, later revered as seers – they made their way across Texas, following the Pecos River and the Rio Grande. While they never reached modern New Mexico or Arizona, they heard descriptions in the Rio Grande pueblo of the Jumano tribe of larger pueblos that lay further north, and they were given emeralds in northern Mexico that had been purchased with parrot feathers from a people who lived to the north.

The first entrada: Esteban and Fray Marcos de Niza

After Cabeza de Vaca's sensational arrival in Mexico City in 1536, the Viceroy of New Spain resolved to investigate his tales of golden cities deep in the desert. After all, it was still less than twenty years since the Spanish had conquered the inconceivably wealthy Aztecs. One of Cabeza de Vaca's companions, a black African ex-slave from Morocco called **Esteban de Dorantes**, volunteered to map the route for a new expedition led by the Franciscan friar **Fray Marcos de Niza**. He set off in 1539, following a long-established native trading route north across the Rio San Pedro into what's now Arizona.

A giant of a man, dressed like a shaman in jewellery and feathers and accompanied by two colossal greyhounds, he amazed the native peoples he encountered, and soon acquired a large entourage. Having arranged to send a signal back to Fray Marcos if he discovered anything to rival the marvels of Mexico, he duly did so as he approached the pueblo of **Zuni**. A major trading centre, Zuni nonetheless simply consisted of adobe houses clustered into small villages. Esteban's demands for tribute appearing incompatible with his claims to be a medicine man, the Zuni punished his sacrilegious behaviour by killing him, cutting him into strips, and distributing his flesh among their neighbours.

On news of Esteban's death, Fray Marcos fled back to Mexico. Although he had probably not even reached Arizona, he announced "this land … is the greatest and best of all that have been discovered". Calling the six Zuni villages the **Seven Cities of Cíbola**, he identified them with the Seven Cities of Antillia, legendary Christian communities long sought by Spanish explorers.

The Coronado Expedition

On February 22, 1540, a second Spanish expedition, led by **Francisco Vásquez de Coronado**, set off into the Southwest from Compostela in northern Mexico. More than three hundred Spanish soldiers, along with hundreds of Indian "allies" and servants and several thousand horses and cattle, marched through Arizona to reach Zuni on July 7. In front of the town of Hawikku, the Zuni drew a line of sacred cornmeal along the ground, and forbade the Spaniards to cross. During the pitched **battle** that ensued – the first ever fought between Europeans and Native Americans – Coronado himself was knocked unconscious, but Spanish weapons prevailed. When the town was taken, its storehouses revealed not gold, but something by now equally precious – food.

Within two weeks, news of the fall of Zuni spread throughout the Southwest. Coronado made his headquarters in the conquered pueblo and dispatched exploratory parties in all directions. One such, under Pedro de Tovar, forced the "warlike" Hopi pueblos to surrender (see p.479) and reached as far as the **Grand Canyon**; another, commanded by Melchor Diáz, crossed the Colorado further south, and thus penetrated

1540–42	1598	1610
Coronado Expedition reaches the Grand Canyon and devastates many New Mexican pueblos before losing its way on the Great Plains and returning to Mexico empty-handed	Don Juan de Oñate establishes the colony of New Mexico	Founding of Santa Fe

modern **California**. A detachment led by Hernando de Alvarado headed east to the pueblos of the Rio Grande.

Meanwhile, emissaries from the Pueblo world were travelling to Zuni. Peaceful overtures from two men known to the Spaniards as **Cacique** ("Governor") and **Bigotes** ("Whiskers") persuaded Coronado to move his expedition east. Camping for the winter beside the Rio Grande, in a region they called **Tigüex**, they commandeered an entire pueblo for a base. Relations soon degenerated into full-scale war, and in a bloody succession of sieges and massacres, all the Tigüex pueblos were destroyed.

Coronado remained convinced that gold lay somewhere to be found. In the spring of 1541, he decamped northeast to prosperous **Cicuyé** (see p.118), where Pueblo peoples traded with nomads from the Plains. In what may well have been a deliberate plot, Cacique and Bigotes introduced him to "**the Turk**", a Pawnee captive, who knew of a city far to the east, **Quivira**, that was rich in gold. Details of the story suggest the Turk was familiar with the culture of the Mississippi Indians; the leaders of Cicuyé probably hoped he'd lead the Spaniards into oblivion on the endless Plains.

In the event, the expedition wandered for three fruitless months across what they called "the domain of the cows", in honour of its vast buffalo herds. From the Llano Estacado or "Staked Plains" of **Texas**, where they drove wooden stakes into the ground to avoid losing their way, they veered northeast into **Kansas**. They did indeed reach a land known as Quivira, but its inhabitants were nomadic, gold-free buffalo-hunters. At that point, Coronado lost patience; the Turk was garrotted and the Spaniards returned to the Rio Grande.

Remarkably, at their furthest east Coronado's party may have come within a hundred miles of Hernando de Soto's even more rapacious military expedition, which having marched up from Florida was then exploring west of the Mississippi. Legend has it that one unfortunate Indian band fleeing Coronado's advance blundered into the de Soto group.

After another beleaguered winter in Tigüex, the Coronado expedition embarked on the long journey back to Mexico, leaving behind a handful of (swiftly martyred) missionaries and many of their Mexican-Indian allies.

The colony of New Mexico

During the fifty years after Coronado's departure, unauthorized Spanish adventurers made occasional forays into the Southwest. Not until 1598, however, was **Don Juan de Oñate** granted royal permission to establish a permanent **colony**. His expedition, consisting of 130 families and two hundred single men, crossed the Rio Grande near modern El Paso on May 1 and took possession of the land as **New Mexico**. Broadly speaking, the colony's as-yet-unspecified boundaries extended from the Colorado River in the west to the Pecos River in the east; as well as what's now New Mexico, it included all of Arizona, plus parts of Utah, Colorado, Nevada and California. The name "Mexico" then referred only to Mexico City itself, so "New Mexico" was named in the hope that it would match the riches of the Aztecs.

Each pueblo that Oñate's party reached as they travelled north had been hurriedly deserted by its inhabitants, fearful of being captured as slaves. Eventually, at the confluence of the Rio Grande and the Chama River near modern Española, the settlers took over the pueblo of Ohkey Owingeh, renamed it San Juan, and made it their

1626	1640	1680
First Spanish mention of "de Nabajú", the people who became the Navajo and the Apache	Thanks to horses, newly acquired from the Spaniards, the Navajo are by now regularly raiding Pueblo settlements	New Mexico's Native American population join forces to drive out the Spaniards in the Pueblo Revolt

capital. Like Coronado before him, Oñate despatched soldiers in every direction in search of gold; and like Coronado he soon found himself at war. After a group commanded by Oñate's nephew was all but wiped out, he launched a full-scale artillery onslaught on Acoma Pueblo. Over eight hundred Acomans were killed, and eighty male prisoners had their feet chopped off in the pueblos of the Rio Grande.

By the time Oñate returned to his capital, most of the colonists had given up and returned to Mexico. Oñate himself was recalled to Mexico City in disgrace once Franciscan missionaries reported his cruelty. Meanwhile, however, Captain Pérez de Villagrá had trumpeted his "achievements" in an epic poem, *Historia de Nueva México*. Villagrá's insistence that New Mexico could become the greatest kingdom in the Spanish empire was sufficiently believed for Madrid to launch another attempt at colonization. **Don Pedro de Peralta** was therefore sent to New Mexico to found a new capital, and the city of **Santa Fe** was duly laid out in 1610.

New Mexico in the seventeenth century
New Mexico's first Spanish colonists dreamed of emulating their predecessors in Mexico, who had accumulated land and wealth in prodigious quantities. However, it soon became clear that New Mexico was the end of the road, with no access to the ocean and no rich neighbours either to trade with or plunder. Santa Fe never grew into a mighty city, but remained a remote military outpost of crude adobe buildings. Enterprising colonists therefore dispersed up and down the Rio Grande Valley, appropriating Pueblo farmlands – and often enslaving Pueblo peoples – to create **ranches** to raise sheep and corn and grow peaches, plums and cherries. **Wheat** was the most significant new crop. Unlike corn, beans and squash, which must be grown in spring and summer, wheat can be planted in December for harvest in June.

At the same time, **Franciscan missionaries** set out to convert the Pueblo Indians to Catholicism. One or two friars would attach themselves to a pueblo, recruit Indian labour to build adobe mission churches, and set about persuading the Pueblos that their *kachina* cults and corn ceremonies were wicked. The Spanish civil and religious authorities found themselves at perpetual loggerheads. While deploring violence against the Pueblos, the church demanded the eradication of their beliefs; the military governors preferred not to antagonize the Indians unnecessarily, but felt their authority ultimately rested on the sword.

Quite apart from any specific actions, the very presence of the Spaniards utterly disrupted the region. Settled communities like the Rio Grande villages were especially vulnerable to **epidemic diseases** such as smallpox, measles and typhus, unknown before the arrival of the Europeans. By 1640, the Pueblo population had dropped from a hundred thousand to around thirty thousand, and more than half of all pueblos had been abandoned. Existing patterns of **trade** were shattered, and the Rio Grande Valley became a prime target for raiders who coveted Spanish arms and, above all, **horses**. Tribes such as the Navajo and the Apache turned from wandering nomads into fearsome mounted warriors, and all too often the Pueblo peoples bore the brunt of their attacks.

The Pueblo Revolt

In 1675, aware that traditional Pueblo beliefs still endured beneath a veneer of Catholicism, the Spanish arrested 47 Pueblo religious leaders. Three were condemned as "witch doctors"

1696	1693–1750	1720
Don Diego de Vargas completes the Reconquest of New Mexico	Living alongside Pueblo refugees in the remote Pueblitos of Dinétah, the Navajo acquire Pueblo skills such as weaving and sheep farming	A joint force of French and Pawnee defeats a Spanish-Pueblo incursion into Nebraska

and hanged at Santa Fe; the rest were publicly horsewhipped. One of these, a man called **Po'pay** from Ohkey Owingeh, made his way to Taos Pueblo and turned a *kiva* into the centre of a campaign of resistance. A date was set for a concerted uprising against the Spanish, and knotted strings were sent out to all the pueblos, with the instruction to untie one knot each night until the last signalled the arrival of the great day. Somehow, the plot was betrayed, so the **Pueblo Revolt** began a day early, on August 9, 1680.

For the first and only time in their history, the Pueblos of the northern Rio Grande, plus their cousins in Acoma, Zuni and the Hopi mesas, combined in unison; they were even joined by the Navajo and the Apache. Their anger fell especially upon the missionaries; 21 out of New Mexico's 33 priests were murdered, as were 375 men, women and children out of a total of 2350 Spanish colonists.

After a ten-day **siege of Santa Fe**, the governor, the garrison and one thousand citizens were allowed to retreat south. They were joined en route by the Christianized majority from Isleta Pueblo – the only modern pueblo not to join the attack – and all the Pueblo peoples who lived south of Albuquerque. For the next thirteen years, the refugees remained together at what's now Ciudad Juarez, across the Rio Grande from El Paso.

Back in Santa Fe, the doors and windows of the Palace of the Governors had been sealed and the building turned into a multistorey pueblo. Po'pay was nominally in control, but the concept of a central political administration was alien to the Pueblos, and the alliance soon fragmented.

Reconquest

In 1692, the Spanish crown appointed a new governor of New Mexico, **Don Diego de Vargas**. His exploratory expedition encountered no opposition when it returned to Santa Fe that September. He set off again with a party of colonists the following year; this time they had to fight before they could re-enter the city, in December 1693. The return of the Spanish triggered mass migrations throughout the region. Modern Navajo culture originated from the intermingling of the ancestral Navajo with Pueblo refugees during this period. Further minor insurrections followed, but the **Reconquest** was completed by 1696.

The eighteenth century

Although Hispanic settlers continued to dominate New Mexico for 150 years after the Pueblo Revolt, this was always a peripheral part of the Spanish empire. Cut off by vast tracts of empty desert, the colonists were obliged to be self-sufficient, and found themselves thrown into alliance with the Pueblo peoples to resist the threat of Ute and Comanche attack. In some ways, the Spaniards and the Pueblos had much in common; the New Mexican landscape was similar to that of Andalucia in Spain, as indeed were its adobe hamlets or pueblos. The Pueblos had long been subsistence farmers who traded for rare luxuries with far-off civilizations to the south, and the Hispanic ranchers slotted into the same pattern. Although there was little intermarriage, Pueblo communities acquired sizeable populations of *genízaros*, the bastard offspring of captured Plains Indians and their Spanish masters.

When the **French** established their own colony to the east, **Louisiana**, early in the eighteenth century, the Spanish responded by setting up missions among the Indians of what now became a separate province of New Spain, **Texas**. As the French and Spanish

1776	1821	1830
Spanish colonists establish Tucson; Father Garcés visits the Havasupai Indians; and fathers Domínguez and Escalante explore Utah	Mexico achieves independence, with New Mexico as part of its territory	Joseph Smith establishes the Mormon Church in upstate New York

zones of influence expanded, there were armed clashes; thus a combined force of Spaniards and Pueblos was defeated by a French–Pawnee alliance near North Platte, Nebraska, in 1720.

In general, the French coexisted more amicably with Native Americans than did the Spanish. Predominantly traders, eager to acquire beaver and other furs, they were less interested in converting Indians to Christianity. Unlike the Spanish, they were also prepared to supply Indians with **guns**. As a result, the Comanche, Ute and Apache, equipped with European firearms, consistently raided along the Rio Grande at harvest time, seizing crops and livestock, while the Hispanic villagers, inadequately supplied from Mexico, could only offer minimal resistance with their bows and arrows. The colonists financed the occasional retaliatory expedition by selling Indian captives to work as slaves in the silver mines of Mexico, thereby incurring ever greater Indian hostility.

Louisiana ultimately proved no more profitable to France than was New Mexico to Spain, so Louis XV of France simply gave it to Spain in 1762. The Mississippi River now formed the Spanish frontier in North America. Determined to resist encroachment by the infant United States, King Carlos III placed the entire region under direct control from Spain in 1776. However, too few Hispanic settlers moved in to make any difference, and in 1802, as the Spanish empire weakened, he handed Louisiana back to Napoleon. Carlos's hope that the French would serve as a buffer against the Yankees was misplaced; Napoleon sold his American territories to the US the next year, in the **Louisiana Purchase**.

At the end of the eighteenth century, Santa Fe was home to around two thousand Hispanic citizens, while the Pueblo population had dwindled to perhaps nine thousand, in a mere nineteen pueblos.

The settlement of Arizona

Before the Pueblo Revolt, the Spanish presence in New Mexico was confined to the valley of the Rio Grande and the scattered pueblos to the west. Under the names of **Pimería Alta** and **Papaguería**, what's now southern Arizona was left to peoples the Spaniards called the **Pima** and the **Papago**, known today as the **O'odham**.

Around 1700, however, **Jesuit** missionaries conceived the notion of erecting a chain of missions from New Spain to California, and built churches in a couple of O'odham villages. Hispanic ranchers and prospectors also drifted in. In 1736, a Yaqui Indian created a silver-mining camp, a few miles southwest of modern Nogales, called **Arizonac**. The name came either from the O'odham *ali shonak*, meaning "small springs", or from the Basque language of Spain, in which *arritza onac* means "valuable rocky places", and *aritz onac* means "good oaks".

After an O'odham rebellion killed several Jesuits, the Spanish installed a military *presidio* (fort) at **Tubac** in 1752, which was relocated forty miles north to San Agustín de **Tucson** in 1776. Another Indian revolt in 1781, in which 150 settlers were wiped out during Mass at **Yuma**, dashed Spanish hopes of establishing a permanent trail to California this far south, and Tucson, like Santa Fe, came to be seen as an insignificant dead-end town. In 1804, when around a thousand Spanish colonists lived in the vicinity, its commander reported, "we have no gold, silver, lead, tin, quicksilver, copper mines, or marble quarries … the only public work here that is truly worthy of this report is the church at **San Xavier del Bac**" (see p.232).

1847	1854	1864
Mormon settlers found Salt Lake City; then, following the Mexican War, the US acquires Texas, California and New Mexico north of the Gila River	The $10 million Gadsden Purchase buys southern Arizona for the US	The Navajo are rounded up and sent on the Long Walk to the Bosque Redondo reservation in New Mexico, from which they return in 1868

The end of the Hispanic era

Even as New Mexico declined in importance to its Spanish rulers, it was coming into increasing contact with the rest of North America. In the closing years of the eighteenth century, permanent trails were established across the north of the region, both west to California – in the form of the **Old Spanish Trail**, painstakingly mapped across Utah by Franciscan friars **Domínguez** and **Escalante** in 1776 – and east to St Louis, along the **Santa Fe Trail** blazed by French explorer Pedro Vial in 1792. After the Louisiana Purchase, official US expeditions also crossed the Plains, including **Lewis and Clark**'s trek to the Northwest in 1804 and **Lt Zebulon Pike**'s incursion into New Mexico in 1807.

Within a few years, the Spanish grip on the New World finally loosened; Mexico became an independent nation following a **revolution** in 1821. Although the governors of both New Mexico and California swiftly transferred allegiance to Mexico City, neither saw any advantage in their new status as Mexican territories. As the flow of resources from the south – including the handouts that were keeping the Apache relatively docile – dwindled, the effect on the New Mexican economy was crippling.

For the authorities in Santa Fe, the only answer seemed to be to increase trade with the US. Traffic along the Santa Fe Trail swiftly turned New Mexico into an entrepôt through which American goods were shipped south into Mexico. No Americans were permitted to live in New Mexico, but freebooting Anglos made their way across the Plains to seek their fortunes in the West. Fur-trapping "**mountain men**" such as **Bill Williams** and **Kit Carson** made extended forays along the region's rivers in pursuit of beavers (nicknamed "hairy banknotes"). **Taos** became renowned for its annual **Rendezvous**, at which Anglo, Hispanic and Native American traders gathered far from the authority of any government.

Meanwhile, enough Yankee newcomers had flocked into **Texas** to outnumber its loyal Mexican subjects. In 1836, after Texas fought to gain independence from Mexico and then voted for annexation by the US, the president of Mexico attempted to hold onto New Mexico by closing down the Santa Fe Trail. It was too late. The doctrine that it was the United States' "**Manifest Destiny**" to extend across the whole continent led the US government first to try to **buy** New Mexico and California, and then, when negotiations failed, to declare **war** on Mexico in 1846. American economic might was neatly illustrated when the US Army of the West took Santa Fe without a fight, in August 1846; the Mexican governor was simply paid $50,000 to leave, along with his garrison.

Territorial days: New Mexico and Arizona

Under the **Treaty of Guadalupe-Hidalgo**, signed in September 1847 after US soldiers had captured Mexico City, the United States paid $18.25 million to take formal possession of New Mexico, Texas and California. New Mexico, which consisted of all of modern New Mexico and Arizona that lies north of the Gila River, plus areas of Nevada and Utah, was generally regarded as an arid, worthless wasteland; California was seen as the real prize.

Ironically, only the discovery of **gold** in California in 1847 gave New Mexico any great value to the US – as a route west. Surveyors mapping possible courses for a southern transcontinental railroad soon realized that the best routes lay on the Mexican side of the border. The Mexican government accepted the least extensive of five

1869	1880	July 14, 1881
An expedition led by John Wesley Powell explores the canyons of the Green and Colorado rivers for the first time	New Mexico governor Lew Wallace publishes the novel Ben Hur	Sheriff Pat Garrett kills Billy the Kid in Fort Sumner, New Mexico

suggested land deals, and in June 1854, the $10 million **Gadsden Purchase** gave the US what's now southern Arizona, including Tucson, Tubac and Tumacácori.

Another 25 years passed before the railroad reached the Southwest, but prospectors trekking to and from California soon began to investigate the region more thoroughly. After gold was found near the confluence of the Gila and Colorado rivers, **miners** fanned out across central Arizona, and reports of rich silver and copper lodes lured ever more migrants in.

Feeling little in common with the Hispanic farming communities of the Rio Grande, the new arrivals argued that the territory was too large to govern as a single unit and should be split in two. Many came originally from the South, and seized upon the start of the **Civil War** in 1861 to declare the formation of the Confederate Territory of **Arizona**, consisting of all the Gadsden Purchase lands. Its capital was Mesilla, in what's now New Mexico. The Confederate cause in the Southwest was short-lived: a Confederate army was turned back by Union forces outside Santa Fe in March 1862. The federal government recognized the existence of Arizona in 1863, but to avoid giving it a built-in Confederate majority drew a north–south boundary rather than an east–west one, and thereby delineated the two modern states.

The Indian wars

In the early years of the Civil War, US Army outposts throughout the Southwest were abandoned when the troops were sent east. That spurred a new era of raiding by the **Apache** and **Navajo**, and the Anglo and Hispanic settlements of southern Arizona in particular became depopulated. By late 1861, only two significant non-native settlements survived in Arizona; two hundred citizens remained in Tucson, while a band of miners held out at Patagonia.

However, the army soon returned in greater strength than ever, resolved to eradicate the Indian "menace" once and for all. Brigadier General James Carleton and Kit Carson drove the **Navajo** into exile in New Mexico in 1864 – they were soon back in Arizona, but never again posed a military threat – while a long cycle of treaties, betrayals and guerrilla campaigns wore down **Apache** resistance by 1886.

Towards statehood

The increasing subjugation of the region's Native American population opened the way for an influx of Anglo settlers. During the 1860s, ancient Hohokam canals in the Salt River Valley were reopened to irrigate the new city of **Phoenix**, which swiftly became the capital of Arizona. Mining camps in the mountains, such as **Silver City** in New Mexico and **Tombstone** and **Jerome** in Arizona, turned into fully fledged towns, while massive cattle ranches spread across the open desert.

At first, the Anglo newcomers were almost exclusively male and married into Hispanic families. Spanish remained the lingua franca, Catholicism the dominant religion, and silver Mexican pesos the common currency. With the coming of the **railroad**, however, around 1880, things began to change, and north–south links were replaced by commerce oriented to east and west. The Southwestern economy became increasingly **extractive**, digging up minerals and depleting natural resources for shipment to distant cities. Where Native Americans and Hispanics had farmed for self-sufficiency, the Anglos sought profit. During the 1880s, huge herds of sheep and

October 26, 1881	1886	1896
Wyatt Earp and "Doc" Holliday emerge victorious in a shoot-out at OK Corral, in Tombstone, Arizona	Geronimo is tricked into surrendering in southern Arizona, thus ending Apache resistance to the US Army	The Mormon church having renounced polygamy, Utah becomes a state

cattle were introduced to marginal grasslands that swiftly proved incapable of supporting them.

Towards the end of the nineteenth century, tensions pitted the large-scale mining and cattle-raising concerns, backed by wealthy eastern corporations and the federal government, against individual prospectors and cowboys. Such conflicts swiftly became so acute, and so recurrent, that some historians speak of a **Western Civil War of Incorporation**. Many iconic Wild West incidents, like the **Gunfight at the OK Corral** in Tombstone, Arizona and the **Lincoln County War** in New Mexico, stemmed more from behind-the-scenes political manoeuvring than from the whims of trigger-happy outlaws.

Besides luring cowboys, miners and other adventurers to the Southwest, the railroads also created new industries. Communities like Flagstaff and Williams sprang up to exploit the vast ponderosa forests of northern Arizona, while the increased accessibility of the Grand Canyon, publicized by the voyages of John Wesley Powell (see p.403), meant that the first **tourists** began to arrive.

Meanwhile, in New Mexico, Hispanic villagers looked on helplessly as their lands were parcelled out to newly arrived Anglo ranchers. New Mexicans had traditionally owned small plots for individual use, with grazing lands shared in common, but American courts refused to recognize communal land rights.

To a considerable degree, it was anti-Hispanic Anglo racism that delayed **statehood** for both Arizona and New Mexico. For many years, Republicans in Washington clung to the idea that they should be reunited and admitted as a single state, in the hope that Arizona's larger Anglo population would help to "temper" the Hispanic majority in New Mexico. Arizonans overwhelmingly defeated that proposal in a referendum in 1906 (which passed in New Mexico), and both were finally admitted in 1912 – **New Mexico** in January as the **47th state**, **Arizona** in February as the **48th**, the last of what are now known as the "**Lower 48**".

Utah in the nineteenth century

Until the nineteenth century, the history of what's now the state of **Utah** forms a minor adjunct to that of the Southwest as a whole. Its main Ancestral Puebloan groups, the Virgin and the more nomadic Fremont peoples, abandoned southern Utah around the same time their Four Corners brethren moved away. By the time Spanish explorers began to pass through, searching for a route to California, it was the domain of Ute and Paiute Indians. Twelve to thirty thousand were present in 1850; most had traditionally been farmers, but they had recently acquired horses and were starting to raid travellers on the newly created **Old Spanish Trail**, which linked Santa Fe to Los Angeles.

The reports of men like the fur trapper **Jedediah Smith**, who named the Virgin River, and **John C. Frémont**, who mapped much of southwest Utah in the early 1840s, attracted the region's first permanent white settlers. By far the most important of these were the massed ranks of the Church of Jesus Christ of Latter-day Saints, known to the outside world as the **Mormons**.

The coming of the Mormons

Although it was widely assumed that the Mormon Church would disintegrate after the death of Joseph Smith – and one of his sons decamped to Missouri with his own

1905	1908	1912	1935
The city of Las Vegas is founded, following the arrival of the railroad	President Theodore Roosevelt creates Grand Canyon National Monument, which becomes a National Park in 1919	Arizona and New Mexico achieve statehood	The Hoover Dam blocks the Colorado River near Las Vegas

JOSEPH SMITH AND THE MORMON CHURCH

The founder of the Mormon church, **Joseph Smith**, was born to a family of itinerant farmers in Sharon, Vermont, on December 23, 1805. Smith was a farmhand in Palmyra, New York, when he had his first vision of the **Angel Moroni** in 1823. On his third annual visit, Moroni led him to a set of golden plates hidden in a nearby hillside. Only Smith ever saw them; concealed behind a curtain, he translated them from the "reformed Egyptian" with the aid of two mysterious devices (the Urim and the Thummim), and thus dictated the **Book of Mormon**. Described by Mark Twain as "chloroform in print", this revealed that two Israelite families fled Jerusalem around 600 BC, and sailed east from the Red Sea to the "Promised Land", led by a man named Lehi. His sons later quarrelled; Nephi remained loyal and was rewarded by a visit from the risen Christ, while Laman and Lemuel led the dissident, cursed **Lamanites**, the ancestors of the Native Americans. After a thousand years of conflict, the Lamanites finally defeated the Nephites in a great battle at the hill of Cumorah. The one Nephite survivor – Moroni, son of Mormon – buried the plates close by.

Smith proclaimed his new church on April 6, 1830. He was not unique among frontier prophets in attracting thousands of followers. Rooted in the economic uncertainty of his own life, his vision of an ordered, communalistic society struck a deep chord with his peers. To their **"Gentile"** neighbours, on the other hand, leadership by divine revelation smacked of Catholicism, and the Mormons were suspected of owing loyalty to their church not their country. Their most controversial trait was **polygamy**, or "celestial marriage". Smith denied this to outsiders, pointing to a passage in the Book of Mormon that called polygamy "abominable". In private, however, he declared his disciples to have a sacred duty to marry and produce children, thereby freeing disembodied spirits from limbo by giving them bodily form. Preaching that the dead could be baptized by proxy, he argued that Mormon marriage was different to the "until death do us part" Christian sacrament. Church elders had a duty to establish polygamous, patriarchal families that would endure into the afterlife. Smith also became a Mason, and many of his church's rituals were inspired by Masonic practices.

In the face of constant harassment, Smith moved his family to Kirtland, **Ohio** – where they built their first temple – and then on to **Missouri** in 1838. After bloody clashes between slave-holding Gentiles and the Mormon militia, the Sons of Dan, he was captured and sentenced to death, then allowed to escape by sympathetic guards. The Mormons were next given sanctuary by the governor of **Illinois**, who saw them as hard-working potential citizens, and their new settlement of **Nauvoo** swiftly became the largest city in that state, with a population of 25,000.

In 1844, when Joseph Smith announced that he was running for president, the Latter-day Saints were being attacked not only by their neighbours but also from within. When a group of anti-polygamy dissenters attempted to establish a rival church in Nauvoo and set up their own newspaper, Smith ordered that its presses be destroyed. Together with his brother Hyrum, Smith was arrested and imprisoned in nearby Carthage. A "blackface" mob attacked the jail, and both men were **shot**.

monogamous splinter group – his successor, **Brigham Young**, held the flock together. Promising the governor of Illinois in 1845 that the Mormons would abandon Nauvoo, Young set about organizing a mass **westward migration**. In the winter of 1846, ten thousand Saints camped near modern Omaha, Nebraska, while Young scouted ahead. Descending the western flank of the Rockies, he declared "This is the place", and in 1847 his followers founded **Salt Lake City**.

1938	1945	1947
John Ford films *Stagecoach* in Monument Valley	Developed in secrecy at Los Alamos, the first atomic bomb is exploded at the Trinity Site in central New Mexico	After crash-landing near Roswell, New Mexico, "alien invaders" begin to seize control of earth

At that time, the all but empty wilderness claimed by the Mormons as **Deseret** (a Mormon word meaning "honeybee", to denote industry), or the **Great Basin Kingdom**, still belonged to Mexico. As well as what's now Utah, its putative boundaries included almost all of modern Nevada, most of Arizona and southern California, and sizeable chunks of four other present-day states. Mormon dreams of establishing an independent theocracy, outside the United States, were dashed within a year, however, when the US government **annexed** the entire region and the **Gold Rush** wagon trains began to roll west. The Saints therefore petitioned Congress for Deseret to be granted statehood. Suspicious of its religious underpinnings, Congress instead recognized a smaller area as the **Territory of Utah** in 1850, and appointed Brigham Young as its first governor.

Embarking on a vast communal effort to irrigate the desert, the Mormons were joined over the next decade by converts recruited throughout America and Europe, to reach a total by 1860 of over fifty thousand. Fifteen thousand arrived from England alone, of whom three thousand literally walked across America, pushing their belongings in handcarts ahead of them.

During the 1850s, and especially once Young, who felt no further need for diplomacy, had publicly acknowledged the existence of polygamy in 1852, the federal government came to see the Mormons as a significant threat to the Union. The newly formed Republican party railed against slavery and polygamy in equal measure, as "twin relics of barbarism". Congress decided to appoint a new non-Mormon governor of Utah, and sent him west with a detachment of 2500 soldiers, representing one-sixth of the US Army. Salt Lake City was temporarily abandoned, but thanks to the secession of the Confederacy, the anticipated **Mormon War** never quite happened.

When the **Civil War** in the East cut off supplies of commodities such as cotton, Brigham Young redoubled his commitment to making the Mormons **self-sufficient**. Pioneer parties created "missions" throughout the Southwest, but while many such farming communities still survive – including **Cedar City** and **St George** in southern Utah – they did little to diminish Utah's economic interdependence with the rest of the US. The advent of the railroads and the arrival in Utah of ever-increasing numbers of non-Mormons – especially miners – exacerbated the situation.

As the Mormons set out to "tame" the wilderness, the **Ute** fought back. After the **Black Hawk War**, waged between 1865 and 1867, the Ute were confined to reservations in the territory that by now bore their name, and the Mormons spread throughout southern Utah. The "**Hole in the Rock**" party (see p.380), for example, trekked across the central deserts in the winter of 1879–80 to establish **Bluff** in the east. Little now survives from simultaneous Mormon attempts to settle in **northern Arizona**, apart from a few tiny settlements along the **Arizona Strip**.

Meanwhile the federal authorities renewed their attacks on polygamy. When the Supreme Court subjected polygamists to disenfranchisement and the confiscation of their property in 1878, Utah retaliated by giving women the vote, so Mormon women could consolidate the church's hold on state power. The **Edmonds-Tucker Act** of 1887 hit back, dissolving the church and confiscating its assets, and once more disenfranchising women.

Brigham Young had died in 1877, and new Mormon leaders sensed they'd do better to drop polygamy on their own terms before they were forced to do so. Polygamy was therefore formally renounced in 1890, clearing the way for Utah to become a **state** in **1896**.

1963	1967	1996
Stopping the flow of the Colorado River into the Grand Canyon, the Glen Canyon Dam creates Lake Powell	Elvis Presley films *Stay Away Joe* in Sedona, Arizona	President Clinton creates Grand Staircase–Escalante National Monument, in southern Utah

The modern Southwest

Arizona, New Mexico and Utah spent most of their first century of statehood battling to secure ever greater quantities of **water**. In the early years, the main objective was to prevent California from grabbing the lion's share of the flow of the Colorado River. Later on, cities like Phoenix fought for federal funds to build grandiose water-diversion schemes. Since the completion of the **Central Arizona Project** in 1991, John Wesley Powell's nineteenth-century prediction that "All the waters of all the arid lands will eventually be taken from their natural channels" has all but come true.

While New Mexico at the start of the twentieth century remained a cluster of farming towns along the Rio Grande Valley, Arizona was prospering on the large-scale exploitation of its mineral wealth. **World War I** saw copper prices leap, and in alliance with state politicians mine owners easily quashed labour disputes. Arizona employers could also take cynical advantage of the vast pool of potential workers just across the border to the south. After the Wall Street Crash of 1929, for example – by which time the state was responsible for half of all US copper production – over five hundred thousand Mexican labourers, now surplus to requirements, were deported.

Though the **Depression** hit hard across the Southwest, the region also benefitted from a massive injection of federal cash, in the form of make-work public projects such as dam- and road-building. **World War II** not only renewed demand for copper and other metals but kick-started **urbanization** throughout the Southwest. Partly to make them less vulnerable to attack, defence installations were relocated away from the coasts, presenting **Albuquerque** and **Phoenix** in particular with their first major industrial plants, as well as greatly increased numbers of consumers. A former school in **Los Alamos**, New Mexico, was transformed into the laboratory that developed the atomic bomb – hence, some say, the alien crash-landing at **Roswell** in 1947.

After the war, the defence and other industries stayed on, and the ensuing period of mass migration to the Southwest resulted in an extraordinary population boom. Arizona and New Mexico were home to around five hundred thousand people each in 1940; Arizona's population is now approaching seven million, with half that number in the metropolitan Phoenix area alone; while New Mexico holds over two million. Even more striking is the fact that whereas Arizona was 84 percent rural at the start of the twentieth century, around 90 percent of the population were city-dwellers by the end. **Las Vegas**, Nevada, did not even exist until 1905; it now boasts two million inhabitants.

Meanwhile, **southern Utah** has remained sparsely inhabited. Attempts at large-scale ranching in the late 1800s resulted in destructive overgrazing, and the region relied on subsistence farming until the discovery of **uranium** in 1952 (see p.422) triggered a **mining bonanza** that sent prospectors scurrying into every nook and cranny of the wilderness. Local Mormon businessmen of southern Utah lobbied hard for mine and dam projects in the face of growing environmental opposition. Calling themselves the "**Sagebrush Rebels**", they attracted support from then-president Ronald Reagan, but were ultimately defeated as much by the realities of world commodity markets as by the "tree-huggers" they despised. Since the collapse of mining in the early 1980s, **tourism** has finally been appreciated as a major industry, and towns like **Moab** have developed facilities for travellers smitten by the lure of the desert.

2011	2013	2015
Spaceport America completed in southern New Mexico. US congresswoman Gabrielle Giffords survives assassination attempt in Tucson	Hit TV series *Breaking Bad* brings Albuquerque international attention	Ongoing drought shrinks Lake Powell, while Lake Mead drops to lowest-ever level

The Hopi

Nowhere in the Southwest is the continuity between the present and the pre-Hispanic past more apparent than on the three Hopi mesas, on the southern edge of Arizona's Black Mesa (p.66). The Hopi have lived here for at least one thousand years, preserving their culture despite repeated incursions from outsiders.

The origin of the Hopi

According to Hopi mythology, this, the **Fourth World**, is inhabited by the righteous people who escaped the destruction of the Third World by climbing a reed through the dome of the sky. They emerged in the depths of the Grand Canyon, through a hole beside the Little Colorado River known as the *sipapu*. There they were greeted by the terrifying but kindly disposed deity **Maasaw**, who explained the rules of life in this world and despatched them on migratory journeys to the four points of the compass. Their wanderings ended with a return to the **Sacred Circle** and the establishment of the villages on what are now the **Hopi mesas**.

Both myth and history depict the Hopi as a peripatetic people who became ever more sedentary as they learned agriculture and pottery. Archeologists and Hopi alike recognize their cultural continuity with the ancient peoples of the Southwest. There's no doubt that the earliest occupants of the Hopi mesas migrated from nearby Kayenta Anasazi and Sinagua settlements, but whether they had previously wandered into central America, where the language and beliefs of the **Aztecs** show clear parallels to the Hopi, remains unproven.

Though the Hopi mesas were probably inhabited by around 700 AD, what the Hopi call the "**gathering of the clans**" peaked between 1100 and 1300 AD, and thus coincided with the Ancestral Puebloans' abandonment of the Four Corners region. One by one, small groups of refugees arrived at the mesas and petitioned for land and the right to settle. Each was required to demonstrate what it had to offer, with the crucial factor being the ceremonial power to produce **rain**. Once allowed to stay, each group – most were no more than individual families – was regarded as a separate **clan**.

The Bear clan, said to have come from Mesa Verde, was the first to arrive, and thus retains precedence to this day. It established Maseeba as the Second Mesa's "mother village" at the foot of the mesa, which changed its name to **Shungopavi** when it relocated to the mesa-top several centuries later. Similarly, **Walpi** on First Mesa, when founded by the Snake clan from Hovenweep, stood several hundred yards below its present, highly defensible mesa-top site. **Oraibi**, the "mother village" of Third Mesa, is generally regarded as the oldest Hopi village because it has occupied the same spot since its foundation; beams have been dated to 1260 AD, but some dwellings may be a century or more older.

By 1275 AD, the three mesas held 35 villages. The Fire, Water and Coyote clans had come from the cliff dwellings of Keet Seel and Betatakin, now in Navajo National Monument; the Flute clan from Canyon de Chelly; the Rabbit clan from the south, perhaps Casas Grandes in Mexico; and others had streamed in from Chaco Canyon and the Sinagua sites of Wupatki and Walnut Canyon. While each village remained autonomous, this disparate community forged a common culture, adopting its own variation of the **kachina** religion as it spread throughout the Southwest (see p.66).

The coming of the Spaniards

Hopi prophecies have long predicted the return of *Pahaana*, the "True White Brother" separated from the Hopi at an early stage of their migrations. Assuming that he finds the Hopi living in purity and righteousness, he will help solve any problems they face and lead them into the Fifth World.

If the Hopi saw *Pahaana* in the first **Spanish explorers** to reach the mesas, their illusions were soon shattered. Exactly what happened when a detachment of Coronado's expedition, led by Lieutenant Pedro de Tovar, arrived in 1540, is uncertain. Alerted by the Zuni, the Hopi greeted the party in the fields, signalling them not to cross a line of sacred cornmeal sprinkled on the earth. According to the official Spanish report, a Franciscan friar, exasperated by the rigmarole, commented, "To tell the truth, I do not know why we came here" – and that was enough to trigger a Spanish onslaught. By the next sentence of the account, however, the two sides are at peace, and Hopi guides went on to lead a group of Spaniards to the Grand Canyon.

During that and subsequent sixteenth-century Spanish incursions, the Hopi took care to make their lands – which the Spanish called **Tusayan** – appear valueless. As a result, the Spanish never bothered to leave either a garrison or any settlers. Franciscan **missionaries** did, however, return in 1629 to build churches in Awatovi, Shungopavi and Oraibi. The one at Awatovi was on a similar scale to the mission that still survives at Acoma, and its construction required a similar amount of forced Indian labour; others involved filling in and "rededicating" existing *kivas*. The missionaries also introduced sheep and cattle, making the Hopi the first people to raise livestock in Arizona.

The Hopi were enthusiastic participants in the **Pueblo Revolt** of 1680, sacking the churches and killing four priests. Fearing a Spanish return, they welcomed Tewa-speaking Pueblo refugees from the Rio Grande, who founded the First Mesa village of Hano. By now, the **Navajo** – said by the Hopi to bash in their captives' skulls with a rock, and thus called *Tasavuh* or "head pounders" – had entered the picture. They too joined the Pueblo Revolt, but they were also starting to crowd the Hopi away from their summer farming and grazing lands, and to raid for animals. During this unsettled period, the villages of Walpi, Shungopavi and Mishongnovi moved to fortified positions on the mesa-tops.

After the Spanish reconquered New Mexico, those Hopi who still regarded themselves as Christians gathered in **Awatovi**. When the other Hopi villages realized that the people of Awatovi were willing to invite the missionaries back, they determined to eradicate the Christian menace once and for all. At the end of 1700, the men of Awatovi were betrayed by their headman, who called a predawn meeting in the *kiva*. Warriors from all the other villages pulled up the ladder, rained arrows down on the trapped men, and then set light to the *kiva*; surviving women and children were shared out as booty.

That brutal act probably spared the Hopi both internal dissent and missionary interference for the rest of the Spanish and Mexican era. The mesas were, however, increasingly beleaguered by mounted Navajo and Ute war parties and slave raiders from the south.

The Hopi under the United States

By the time the Southwest was acquired by the United States, during the 1840s, the Hopi were desperate for protection from the marauding Navajo. Hopi scouts eagerly participated in General Carleton's 1864 round-up which forced the Navajo on the Long Walk to Bosque Redondo (see p.483).

Within a few years, the Navajo were back, reasserting control over their former territory and raiding to replenish their herds. Called to define who "owned" what land, the US government was inadequate to the task. The very concept of a "tribe" was a federal invention; neither Navajo nor Hopi recognized any authority above clan or village level. Moreover, the idea of a reservation only worked if one group or other had exclusive use of an area. Only villages and fields counted as the "possession" of land;

hunting grounds were regarded as unoccupied. Because the San Francisco Peaks are sacred to, and used by, both the Navajo and the Hopi, they belong to neither.

Until the 1920s, the Hopi were generally known by a name coined by the people of Acoma: Moki or Moqui. Because that sounded too much like a Hopic word meaning "to have died", they then changed to Hopi, which means "well-behaved". The **Moqui Indian Reservation**, established in 1882 as a rectangle measuring 70 by 55 miles, did not even include all the Hopi villages. The hundred Hopi at Moenkopi were excluded, while three hundred Navajo lived within the boundaries. As was standard, the decree creating the reservation states that it was intended not only for the Hopi but for "such other Indians as the Secretary of the Interior shall settle thereon". The resultant disputes have simmered ever since.

Outsiders now appeared on the mesas in ever-increasing numbers. Mormon and Mennonite **missionaries** came and went, and **anthropologists** stuck their oars in; Jesse Walter Fewkes called the Hopi "the most primitive aborigines of the United States" in 1891. **Tourists** too came by bus and railroad, with two-thousand-plus turning up for the annual Snake Dances. Century-old images of Hopi ceremonies make it clear why **photography** was soon barred altogether; crowds and cumbersome equipment made it all but impossible to move. Above all, the federal agents of the **Bureau of Indian Affairs** caused the most grief, ordering haircuts for all Hopi men, for whom long hair is a sign of initiation, and kidnapping Hopi children to attend distant boarding schools, from 1887 onwards. Nineteen elders who protested against compulsory Christian education were imprisoned on Alcatraz in 1894.

The modern era

At the start of the twentieth century, the Hopi were divided between what outsiders perceived as the **"Friendlies"**, who if not well disposed towards the federal government at least felt that resistance was futile, and the **"Hostiles"**, who sought to defend and preserve the old ways. Their differences in fact stemmed largely from tensions between clans, and a breakdown in the allocation of resources and land. The split became explicit at **Oraibi**, where the two factions declared themselves unable to coexist any longer. On September 8, 1906, each lined up behind its leader, with each man's hands on the shoulders of the next, for a "pushing contest". Literally pushed out, the "Hostiles" established their own village of **Hotevilla** nearby.

The dispute at Oraibi politicized the role of each village's ceremonial priest, known as the **kikmongwi**. When the Hopi were obliged to adopt a Tribal Constitution in 1936, the *kikmongwis* were automatically appointed as governors of their village. Part of their function was to endorse members elected to the new **Hopi Tribal Council**. Ever since then, however, many *kikmongwis* have refused to recognize the authority of the tribal council and aligned themselves instead with the **Traditionalists**, the heirs of the "Hostiles".

Paradoxically, the Traditionalists, who regard themselves as the guardians of all that is truly Hopi, have raised awareness of the Hopi throughout the world. Rather than waiting for their saviour *Pahaana* to appear, they have embarked on a search for him. The movement started immediately after World War II, when certain Hopi elders announced that following the use of the atomic bomb it was time to reveal teachings and prophecies that were supposed to remain secret until "a gourd of ashes fell from the sky". Since 1948, the Traditionalists have written to every US president, and addressed the United Nations, with a message stressing Hopi sovereignty and religious integrity and the importance of respecting the environment. Among their successes was the recognition of Hopi religion as a "peace religion", which excluded Hopi from military service.

In practical terms, the Traditionalist movement has been a focus for opposition to **mineral leasing**. After the Hopi Constitution's definition of the role of the tribal council as being to *prevent* leasing was illegally overruled by the Secretary of the Interior in 1961, strip mining by the Peabody Company devastated much of Black Mesa (see p.55).

Almost all the income the leases earned during the 1960s was invested in an unsuccessful bra factory near Winslow. In the 1980s, the leases were renegotiated on much more favourable terms, including environmental stipulations, and mining became more acceptable to many Hopi. However, Traditionalists resistant to becoming dependent on external agencies continued to strive through the courts to have the mines closed down, and although they didn't succeed, Black Mesa Mine did indeed cease operations in 2006.

Meanwhile, the **Navajo–Hopi land dispute** has raged on. By 1958, the Navajo living on Hopi lands outnumbered the Hopi by more than two to one, and the Navajo reservation had completely surrounded the Hopi mesas. Much of the impetus to resolve the problem came from the federal authorities and the mineral companies, who could not start mining until definite title to the land was established. Public sympathies, and court rulings, swayed back and forth for decades. A **Joint Use Area** was established in 1958, to be shared equally between the Hopi and the Navajo, but it soon became evident that 98 percent of it was being used by the Navajo alone. In the 1970s, therefore, separate Hopi and Navajo **Partitioned Lands** were defined, stipulating that Hopi living on the Navajo side of the line relocate, and vice versa. More Navajo than Hopi were affected, and the plight of the **Big Mountain** Navajo in particular, who were given five years to move in 1981, made them a national *cause célèbre*.

The **Navajo–Hopi Land Dispute Settlement Act**, authored by John McCain, was signed by President Clinton in 1996. It allowed Navajo residents of Hopi land to sign 75-year leases, after which ownership will revert to the Hopi. Since then, low-level tensions have simmered on. Many of those most immediately impacted feel that the underlying issues have not truly been resolved, and dissident Navajo argue that the problem has simply been postponed for another generation.

The Navajo and the Apache

Thanks largely to their fierce resistance against the US Army in the nineteenth century, the Navajo and the Apache are the best-known Native American peoples in the Southwest. Now largely concentrated in Arizona, both also occupy parts of New Mexico, and the Navajo Nation extends into southern Utah as well. Both are also relative newcomers, having moved into their current territories around the time that the Spaniards arrived, and with just as devastating an impact.

Although the Navajo and the Apache are now distinct peoples, their languages are, with patience, mutually comprehensible. Their paths only diverged within the last five hundred years. Both are descended from **Athabascan** peoples, whose Asian ancestors crossed into Alaska seven or eight thousand years ago, long after the New World's first migrants. Other Athabascans remained in the north, becoming the **Dene** peoples of Alaska and northwest Canada, and the **Na** of the northwest US, who included the Haid and Tlingit. At some point, however, the ancestral Navajo and Apache migrated south, hauling their possessions on dog sleds as they pursued bison down the eastern flanks of the Rockies.

Estimates of when they first arrived in the Southwest – somewhere on the edge of the Plains, east of the Rio Grande – range between 575 and 1525 AD, with the most likely date being 1250 to 1300 AD. Like nomads the world over, they traded the fruits of their hunting and gathering, especially buffalo hides, for the agricultural produce of more settled communities like the Rio Grande pueblos. Chroniclers travelling with Coronado in 1540 drew no distinction between the Navajo and the Apache, referring to both as *Querecho*. However, by the time the Spanish returned at the end of the century, the Navajo, who called themselves the *Diné*, had separated from the Apache, or *Ndee*.

The Navajo

It used to be thought that it was the arrival of the warlike Navajo in the Four Corners that forced the Ancestral Puebloans to leave at the end of the thirteenth century (see p.464). In fact, however, the Navajo only moved west to occupy the now-empty San Juan Basin after the Ancestral Puebloans had gone. Some even suggest that when the Ancestral Puebloans headed east to establish pueblos along the Rio Grande, they displaced the ancestors of today's Navajo from their riverside homes.

During the late sixteenth century, a region centred on Largo Canyon, east of modern Farmington – still the core of Navajo territory – became known as the **Dinétah**, meaning "Among the People". The *Diné* defined their new realm as lying between four **sacred mountains**: *Sis Naajini*, or Blanca Peak, away to the east in Colorado; *Dibé Nitsaa* (Hesperus Peak), further north in Colorado, near modern Durango; *Tsoodzil* (Mount Taylor), further south in New Mexico; and *Dook'o'oosliid* (the San Francisco Peaks) near what is now Flagstaff, Arizona. Legends grew up detailing how First Man and First Woman lived near **Huerfano Mountain**. They found a baby on **Gobernador Knob** whom they named Changing Woman, who in turn gave birth to the Navajo Twins, Monster Slayer and Child Born for Water.

The Lords of the World

By the 1580s, the Navajo were impinging upon the pueblos of Acoma, Zuni and Hopi. Their expansion was given a huge boost when a permanent Spanish presence enabled them to acquire **horses**. From 1606 onwards, the Navajo embarked on a cycle of raiding Hispanic and Pueblo settlements along the Rio Grande, seizing livestock, new crops and metal goods. In the Tewa language, spoken in many pueblos, *apache* means "strangers" or "enemies", and *nabajú* means "big planted fields". The first Spanish mention of the "**Apaches de Nabajú**" appeared in 1626, and the name was soon truncated to "Navajo".

The Navajo and Pueblo peoples were not always at war, however. Some Navajo joined the 1680 **Pueblo Revolt**, and when the Spanish reconquered the region a dozen years later, many Pueblo peoples escaped their revenge by retreating to live with the Navajo. Modern Navajo culture, a hybrid of Athabascan and Pueblo elements, was forged in the remote "**Pueblitos of Dinétah**", in Largo and Gobernador canyons (see p.90).

By the eighteenth century, the Navajo had acquired such Pueblo skills as pottery and weaving, as well as Pueblo-influenced social and religious structures. Obtaining horses vastly increased their mobility, while their large flocks of **sheep** enabled them to live well on what had previously been marginal lands. They therefore expanded westwards to cover a much greater area, occupying most of northeast Arizona and encircling the Hopi.

To contemporary Spaniards, the Navajo were **Los Dueños del Mundo**, the "Lords of the World" – feared horsemen with a solid economic base in their own lands who still plundered the pueblos at will. For most of the eighteenth century, however, the Navajo and the Hispanic settlers of New Mexico were nominally at peace, united in resisting incursions by the **Ute** and **Comanche** from the north. Then the Navajo realized that the Spanish were tacitly encouraging Ute and Comanche raiders, and buying their Navajo captives as slaves. After 1786, when the Spanish signed a formal treaty with the Comanche, they were at constant war with the Navajo.

With conversion to Christianity as an excuse, Navajo women and children were shipped into slavery in Mexico; the Navajo replenished their numbers by carrying off Pueblo villagers. Certain mission settlements had to be abandoned in the face of Navajo attacks. By and large, the Navajo heartlands remained impregnable, although **Lieutenant Narbona**'s party of 1805 penetrated the Canyon de Chelly and massacred over a hundred Navajo (see p.60).

War with the United States

Mexican independence in 1821 did nothing to diminish the conflict, and the Navajo and the Hispanic settlers of New Mexico were still at loggerheads when the US Army took control of the Southwest in 1846. To Navajo amazement, the American invaders expected them to make peace with their old enemies, on the basis that the New Mexicans were now themselves Americans.

A major factor in the American failure to sign and keep treaties with the Navajo was the fact that the Navajo did not have "chiefs", let alone a single paramount chief. No Navajo could speak for much more than his immediate family, or felt bound by a pact signed by another. Even so, the Navajo remained broadly at peace with the Americans until a widely respected elder – who, confusingly, had taken the name **Narbona** – was murdered and scalped by US soldiers, under a flag of truce, in 1849. For the next fifteen years, Narbona's son-in-law, **Manuelito**, fought a running war with the US cavalry.

In 1863, **General James Carleton** resolved that the Navajo should be removed from their lands altogether, partly so that they might "become an agricultural people and cease to be nomads" and partly to allow New Mexicans to expand beyond the Rio Grande Valley. A scorched-earth campaign led by veteran scout **Kit Carson** culminated in 1864 with the destruction of the *hogans*, fields and peach orchards of Canyon de Chelly. As the starving Navajo surrendered, they were sent to "Fair Carletonia", the **Bosque Redondo reservation** at Fort Sumner in eastern New Mexico (see p.179).

Nine thousand Navajo made the **Long Walk** of 370 miles to Bosque Redondo, where three thousand of them died. The reservation was utterly unsuitable for agriculture; far from being self-supporting, it became a burden on the federal government. Carleton was dismissed, and in 1868, after four years, twelve Navajo leaders – including

NAVAJO CLANS

The **basis of Navajo society** and family life is the **clan** system. Each Navajo child is born "to" its mother's clan, and "for" its father's clan. Navajo identify themselves to each other by the clans of their parents; no one is supposed to marry a member of either their mother's or father's clan. Traditionally, all clan members were responsible for each other's crimes or debts.

Originally, there were just four clans, each descended from one of the four pairs of men and women created in the west by Changing Woman. New clans arise when a woman from another tribe or place marries into the Navajo, however, so now there are more like sixty. While certain clan names identify the descendants of Zuni, Mescalero, Mexican, Ute and Jemez newcomers, most hark back to specific locations on the reservation, mythical incidents, or other attributes – the Turning Mountain Clan, Salt Clan, the People That Have Fits Clan, the Rock-Extends-into-Water Clan and so on.

Barboncito, who pleaded "I hope to God you will not ask me to go to any other country except my own" – signed a treaty that allowed them to return home.

The Navajo Nation

The 1868 treaty (or "Old Paper") formed the basis of the Navajo Indian Reservation – or **Navajo Nation** – as it endures to this day. The original reservation of 1868 was, however, just a small rectangle of northeast Arizona and northwest New Mexico, which included Canyon de Chelly and Shiprock but not Window Rock. Here the survivors of Fort Sumner rejoined those Navajo who had evaded capture in the backcountry; some had hidden near **Navajo Mountain**, and now regarded it too as a sacred peak.

During the twentieth century, the Navajo **population** grew at a phenomenal rate, from twenty thousand in 1900 to well over three hundred thousand today. Similarly, the reservation expanded from six thousand to 27,000 square miles. A formal Navajo **government** was only established in 1923, when the major oil companies needed someone to sign leases so that they could exploit the reservation's newly discovered oil reserves. The **chapter** system of local administration was set up soon afterwards, and Window Rock became tribal headquarters in 1927.

In 1933, insisting that over-grazing was washing silt into the Colorado and threatening the new Hoover Dam, the federal authorities killed off a million sheep and goats and reduced the total Navajo herd to half a million animals. That traumatic **stock reduction** had the effect of forcing a change away from pastoralism towards wage labour.

Since World War II, the Navajo Nation has continued to modernize, acquiring its first paved road in 1947 and the first college ever built on an Indian reservation, Tsaile's Navajo Community College, in 1969. While many families still manage to live a traditional Navajo lifestyle, the exploitation of **mineral** resources has brought the greatest change. Mines and generating stations have appeared across the region, often just outside the reservation but still dependent on Indian labour. Many projects have been deeply controversial. The **Four Corners power plant** near Farmington has been described as the single worst source of pollution in the US – the three oldest of its five generating units finally shut down in 2012 – while the Peabody Company's strip-mining of **Black Mesa** to feed the **Navajo Generating Station** at Page is widely regarded as an environmental tragedy. In 1979, **Church Rock**, northeast of Gallup, was the scene of the worst contamination in US nuclear history, when a dam burst at the United Nuclear Corporation mill and released almost a hundred million gallons of radioactive water and a thousand tons of radioactive mud.

In 1975, Tribal Chairman **Peter MacDonald** (subsequently jailed for corruption) helped set up the Council of Energy Resource Tribes, which he described as a "domestic OPEC". While the mineral leases of the 1950s and 1960s paid pitifully low returns, more lucrative agreements have now strengthened the Navajo economy. Navajo opposition to the principle of mineral exploitation has also grown however, as its long-term effects become apparent. Many feel that the long-running **Navajo–Hopi land dispute** (see p.481) has been manipulated by federal politicians and mineral companies for their own ends.

The Apache

Around 1600 AD, as the Navajo began to incorporate Pueblo elements and become an entirely distinct people, the **Apache** fragmented into several separate groups. The **Western** Apache occupied the mountains of central Arizona; the **Jicarilla**, regions of northwest New Mexico between the Chama Valley and the Four Corners; and the **Lipan** moved east onto the plains of west Texas. At the same time, in southern New Mexico, the **Mescalero** started to range east of the Rio Grande, while the **Chiricahua** spread west as far as what's now southern Arizona.

These groups were not the "tribes" that outsiders like to imagine. Apache lived in nomadic, clan-based societies of between thirty and two hundred people, each with its own "chief". A chief's primary responsibility was to ensure his band got enough food; his authority collapsed in the event of failure. Most groups raised a few seasonal crops, but supported themselves above all by **raiding**, against not only settled Pueblo communities, but also the Navajo, and even each other.

The coming of the Spaniards gave the Apache **horses** for the first time. At first, they stole them solely to eat, but once they learned to ride they swiftly adapted to a calendar of raiding the Rio Grande villages at harvest time, while allowing them to continue unmolested for the rest of the year. It was beneath Apache dignity to breed their own horses, let alone sheep like the Navajo; they simply stole livestock as they needed it.

The colonists of New Mexico, who throughout Spanish and Mexican rule remained confined to a fragile ribbon of riverside land, called the vast Apache-dominated territories that surrounded them **Apachería**. Since the Apache never united to engage in formal warfare – no Apache war party in history exceeded two hundred warriors – it was impossible to take concerted action against them. In the first half of the eighteenth century, the Apache were nonetheless forced to consolidate into smaller and more mountainous areas, as even more aggressive mounted **Comanche** warriors swept in across the Plains with ever-increasing regularity.

Later in the eighteenth century, the Spaniards managed to pacify the Apache by establishing *presidios* or forts that supplied them with food, alcohol and even guns (adequate for hunting but not war). When Mexico became independent, however, in 1821, the new administration could no longer afford such subsidies. Instead it placed a bounty of $100 on each Apache scalp – male or female, young or old – brought into the *presidios*.

The Apache Wars

To the US government, which took over New Mexico in the 1840s, the Apache way of life was anathema. As a group of Mescalero Apache acknowledged to a US Army quartermaster in 1850, "We must steal from somebody … if you will not permit us to rob the Mexicans, we must steal from you or fight you". In total, the Southwest held between six and eight thousand Apache. By far the strongest resistance came from a group of just over a thousand, the **Chiricahua**, led by a chief known as **Cochise**, or "Oak".

Conflict between the US Army and the Apache flared into war in 1861, when Cochise agreed to meet Lt George Bascom in southeast Arizona, and found himself falsely accused of kidnapping a child. Although Cochise managed to escape into the Dragoon Mountains, his brother and two nephews were hanged. Cochise then rampaged across Arizona, killing miners, prospectors, stagecoach passengers and soldiers. As Anglos packed up and fled the territory, he imagined he had driven them out forever. Little did he realize that his campaign had coincided with the start of the Civil War, so all US forces had been withdrawn east.

Within a year, the Union army was back, led by General James Carleton. His Apache policy, directed at first against the Mescalero rather than the Chiricahua, was simple: "All Indian men of that tribe are to be killed whenever and wherever you can find them". During the winter of 1862–63, the Mescaleros were rounded onto the **Bosque Redondo** reservation in eastern New Mexico, where they were soon joined by the Navajo.

In 1862, Cochise's group had linked up with another Chiricahua band, the **Warm Springs** Apache of New Mexico, under the veteran **Mangas Coloradas**. The treacherous murder of Mangas Coloradas the following year, after US soldiers invited him to peace negotiations at Pinos Altos, hardened Chiricahua resolve. Over the next ten years, the US Army spent $38 million on campaigns that killed a total of a hundred Apache; the Apache meanwhile accounted for over a thousand Americans.

During this period, the name of **Geronimo** became widely feared. He was born around 1823 into the Bedonkohe subgroup of the Chiricahua Apache, near New Mexico's Gila Cliff Dwellings. Named Goyahkla, "One Who Yawns", he reached adulthood without seeing a white American. After his mother, wife and three children were killed by Mexican soldiers at Janos in northern Mexico, in 1851, he sought revenge in repeated raids on Mexico. Somehow, the Mexican battle cry to St Jerome, "Geronimo", became the name he used for the rest of his life. Although he became a respected healer and medicine man, he was never, strictly speaking, a "chief".

In the **Camp Grant Massacre** of 1871, a Tucson-based alliance of Tohono O'odham Indians, Hispanics and Anglos massacred 144 Apache – of whom no more than eight were men – supposedly under the protection of the US Army in Aravaipa Canyon, Arizona. A public outcry back East led President Grant to adopt a new policy towards the Apache, under which the **White Mountain** and **San Carlos** reservations were established in 1872.

Any Apache who failed to present themselves at the reservations were deemed renegades. **General George Crook**, ordered to hunt them down, adopted the scorched-earth strategy of "total war", developed during the Civil War. Employing White Mountain Apache scouts, he "overhauled" the Tonto Basin during the winter of 1872–73, killing five hundred Apache.

Following an uneasy truce, the Chiricahua were granted their own reservation, a fifty-mile square centred on what's now Chiricahua National Monument. Within three years, however, renewed cross-border raiding after the 1874 death of Cochise caused the reservation to be disbanded. The Chiricahua were moved onto the San Carlos reservation.

In 1877, another Chiricahua leader, **Victorio**, assembled a five-hundred-strong band of Apache from the many different groups who hated life at San Carlos. A lengthy guerrilla campaign across New Mexico and West Texas resulted in a thousand more Anglo deaths before the Chiricahua were driven into Mexico and killed in Chihuahua in October 1880. The few survivors were sold into slavery.

Geronimo, who had not joined Victorio, now became the focus for dissident Apache. During the 1880s, he repeatedly burst out of the reservation and onto the warpath, each time with a dwindling band of followers. The first time was in 1881, when he passed within a few miles of Tombstone and was pursued by Wyatt Earp and his brothers. In 1883, General Crook tracked him down in the Sierra Madre in northern Mexico, and was briefly captured by the Apache before Geronimo chose instead to surrender to him.

Geronimo fled the reservation again in 1885 and surrendered to Crook once more in Mexico in 1886, on the understanding that he'd be exiled to the eastern United States for not more than two years. Before Crook could get him back to San Carlos, Geronimo got drunk and escaped yet again. Crook resigned his command, to be replaced by **General Nelson Miles**.

The Chiricahua's final five-month guerrilla campaign, in the summer of 1886, pitted 37 Apache, of whom eighteen were warriors, against five thousand soldiers, a quarter of the entire US Army. General Miles eventually managed to contact Geronimo in Mexico, and falsely told him that all the Chiricahua who remained on the reservation had been shipped to **Florida**. In despair, Geronimo **surrendered** for the fourth and final time in Skeleton Canyon, Arizona on September 3, 1886. The general's lie now became the truth. Geronimo and five hundred Chiricahua – along with the Apache scouts who had fought alongside the US Army – were indeed sent to Florida. Men and women were segregated in separate camps. In time, the Chiricahua were reunited on reservations in first Alabama, and then Oklahoma, but Geronimo never returned to the Southwest. Among many public appearances in his later years, he rode at the head of Teddy Roosevelt's inaugural procession in 1905; he died in 1909.

In 1913, the 261 surviving Chiricahua were allowed to choose between remaining in Oklahoma or joining the Mescalero Apache in New Mexico; around two-thirds made the trip. It's thought that the army never did round up perhaps ten Chiricahua, who stayed hidden in Mexico; free Apache were reported still to be fighting in the Sierra Madre as late as the 1930s.

The Apache today

Around twenty thousand Apache now live in the Southwest. Their largest two reservations are in Arizona: the **Fort Apache** reservation (see p.261), which has the third-highest population of all Native American reservations in the US, and the neighbouring **San Carlos** reservation (see p.220). The **Jicarilla** still live in northwest New Mexico, concentrated around Dulce (see p.159).

Visitors are most likely to come into contact with the **Mescalero Apache**, who share their modern lands with the descendants of the last Chiricahua in the mountains of southeast New Mexico, stretching between Cloudcroft and Ruidoso. Although they call themselves the Shis-Inday, or "People of the Mountain Forest", as nomads they originally roamed far beyond the mountains, hunting buffalo out on the plain and gathering food in the desert. They derived their staple diet from the mescal plant; hence the name they were given by the Spanish. Among recent ventures that have brought them a rare degree of economic security are the thriving Ski Apache **ski resort** (see p.183), which the tribe bought for $1.5 million in 1962 and which features the luxurious *Inn of the Mountain Gods* hotel/casino.

Books

The following books proved useful, interesting or entertaining during the research for this guide.

HISTORY AND ARCHEOLOGY

Donald A. Barclay, James H. Maguire and Peter Wild (eds) *Into the Wilderness Dream*. Gripping collection of Western exploration narratives written between 1500 and 1800. Thanks to numerous little-known gems, this is the best of many such anthologies.

★**Pedro de Castañeda** *The Journey of Coronado*. The eyewitness journals of a Spaniard who accompanied Coronado into the Southwest in 1540, and an invaluable historic document.

Richard Flint *No Settlement, No Conquest*. A satisfying and accessible overview of current knowledge about Coronado's epochal expedition, from an author who's written and edited several more academic volumes.

Jack D. Forbes *Apache, Navajo, and Spaniard*. An unsettling but thoroughly documented account of seventeenth-century frontier conflicts, which challenges much received wisdom by suggesting, for example, that the Ancestral Puebloans violently displaced the Navajo along the Rio Grande.

Pat Garrett *The Authentic Life of Billy, the Kid*. "I have known the Kid personally since and during the continuance of what was known as the Lincoln County War, up to the moment of his death, of which I was the unfortunate instrument" – irresistible Western history, straight from the horse's mouth.

Robert Goodwin *Crossing The Continent*. A valiant and always stimulating attempt to chronicle the life of Esteban, the black African ex-slave who in 1539 became the first explorer ever to penetrate the Southwest.

Paul Horgan *Great River: The Rio Grande in North American History*. Horgan's monumental study of New Mexican history makes weighty reading; his more accessible *The Centuries of Santa Fe* is a lightly fictionalized set of biographies drawn from different periods of history.

John D. Lee *Mormonism Unveiled*. In this, "Life and Confession", John Lee, of Lees Ferry fame, doesn't quite tell all he knows – like where he buried the gold – but there's a lot of eye-opening material in here.

Stephen Plog *Ancient Peoples of the Southwest*. Much the best single-volume history of the pre-Hispanic Southwest, packed with diagrams and colour photographs.

Carroll L. Riley *The Kachina and the Cross*. A history of the early relations between Pueblo peoples and Hispanic colonists, highlighting how they grudgingly came to share the land of New Mexico. The same author's *Rio del Norte* traces the story of the upper Rio Grande Valley from prehistoric times to the Pueblo Revolt, while his *Becoming Aztlan* explores links between the ancient Southwest and Mexico.

Joe S. Sando and Herman Agoyo (eds) *Po'pay: Leader of the First American Revolution*. A remarkable collection of essays by Pueblo Indians on the history of the Pueblo Revolt and its charismatic leader.

Thomas E. Sheridan *Arizona – A History*. Stimulating reassessment of 11,000 years of Arizona history.

Alex Shoumatoff *Legends of the American Desert*. Anecdotal and entertaining first-person survey of several centuries of Southwestern history.

Hampton Sides *Blood And Thunder*. Hugely readable retelling of the exploits of Kit Carson and his role in the campaigns against the Navajo.

Marta Weigle (ed) *Telling New Mexico*. This fascinating anthology holds more than fifty essays on different aspects of New Mexico's history, from the geological past to the hippy impact on Taos.

★**Richard White** *It's Your Misfortune and None of My Own*. Dense, authoritative and all-embracing history of the American West, which debunks romanticization of the rugged pioneer by stressing the role of the federal government.

NATIVE AMERICANS

★*Between Sacred Mountains*. Superb overview of Navajo history, culture and politics, written by Navajo teachers and parents as a sourcebook for Navajo students.

Nancy Yaw Davis *The Zuni Enigma*. An intriguing if ultimately unconvincing elaboration of the author's theory that a wandering group of Japanese pilgrims joined the Zuni tribe during the thirteenth century.

Angie Debo *Geronimo*. Gripping full-length biography of the Apache medicine man who led the last Native American uprising against the US Army.

Paula Richardson Fleming and Judith Lynn Luskey *The Shadow Catchers*. A history of nineteenth-century photographers of Native Americans, with some stunning images of the Hopi and Navajo.

Robert H. Keller and Michael F. Turek *American Indians and National Parks*. What happens when the federal park system appropriates land from its former indigenous inhabitants; Mesa Verde, Rainbow Bridge and the Grand Canyon are among examples considered in detail.

Raymond Friday Locke *The Book of the Navajo*. Comprehensive history of the Navajo, from their mythic origins to the present day.

Robert S. McPherson *Sacred Land Sacred View*. Intriguing anthropological account of how the Navajo perceive the Four Corners region.

★**David Roberts** *Once They Moved Like The Wind*. Excellent, fast-moving history of the Apache.

Polly Schaafsma (ed) *Kachinas in the Pueblo World*. Well-illustrated survey of the *kachina* cult in the Southwest (see p.66).

Lucinda Delaney Schroeder *Plunder of the Ancients*. A remarkable if somewhat depressing saga of the modern black market in Native American artefacts, told by the federal agent in charge of investigating a particularly egregious conspiracy.

Tom Steinbach, Sr. *Mimbres Classic Mysteries*. A rather beautiful collection of the enigmatic but compelling designs created by Mimbres ceramicists. Brief essays attempt to set each motif in context.

Stephen Trimble *The People*. Superb introduction to all the Native American groups of the Southwest, bringing the history up to the late twentieth century – though, sadly, no further – via contemporary interviews.

Frank Waters *The Book of the Hopi*. As authoritative an account of Hopi religion as it's possible to find, though it's said that Waters' informants were not themselves initiated into all the secrets of the *kiva*.

TRAVEL

Edward Dolnick *Down The Great Unknown*. Deft retelling of the saga of John Wesley Powell's first Grand Canyon voyage that takes great pains to make it all intelligible to modern readers, with the analogies flowing thick and fast.

Colin Fletcher *The Man Who Walked Through Time*. Enjoyable account by the first man to hike the full length of the Grand Canyon.

Susan Shelby Magoffin *Down the Santa Fe Trail and into Mexico*. Absorbing first-person account by a trader's wife who reached Santa Fe in August 1846 in time to witness the Yankee takeover of New Mexico.

John Wesley Powell *The Exploration of the Colorado River and Its Canyons*. Powell adjusted the details of his first epic journey down the Colorado – see p.403 – for public consumption, but his journals still make exhilarating reading.

Douglas Preston *Cities of Gold*. Long but very readable account of a horseback journey in the steps of Coronado, which throws a lot of light on history both ancient and modern.

David Roberts *In Search of the Old Ones*. An engaging chronicle of one man's obsession with Southwestern archeology.

★**Mark Twain** *Roughing It*. This rollicking account of Twain's peregrinations across the nineteenth-century West may well be the greatest story ever told, though only his account of the Mormons is of much relevance here.

Ted J. Warner (ed) *The Domínguez-Escalante Journal*. The extraordinary diary of the two Franciscan friars who crossed Utah in 1776 in search of a new route to California, and came back via the Grand Canyon.

THE CONTEMPORARY SOUTHWEST

Christina Brinkley *Winner Takes All*. The inside story of how billionaires Steve Wynn and Kirk Kerkorian battled to shape twenty-first-century Las Vegas.

Alan Hess *Viva Las Vegas*. A beautifully illustrated survey of Las Vegas's architectural history, throwing fascinating sidelights on the development of the city.

Shawn Levy *Rat Pack Confidential*. Enjoyable hymn to the "last great showbiz party", when Las Vegas prostrated itself at the feet of Frank Sinatra and the boys.

Scott Norris (ed) *Discovered Country*. Essays on the impact of tourism on the Southwest, with some interesting material on the repackaging of Native American culture for Anglo consumption.

Hal K. Rothman *Devil's Bargains: Tourism in the Twentieth-Century American West*. Thought-provoking assessment of how tourism has shaped the modern West, which overturns many a cosy historical myth about places such as Santa Fe and Las Vegas.

Jim Stiles *Brave New World*. An idiosyncratic Moab writer lays out how tourism, though supposedly environmentally aware, has served southeast Utah no better than did mining and ranching.

Hunter S. Thompson *Fear and Loathing in Las Vegas*. Classic account of a drug-crazed journalist's lost weekend in early-1970s Vegas; what's really striking is how much further over the top Las Vegas has gone since then.

Chris Wilson *The Myth of Santa Fe*. Eye-opening and very detailed account of how the Santa Fe known to tourists today is largely a twentieth-century concoction.

ENVIRONMENT AND NATURAL HISTORY

Edward Abbey *Desert Solitaire*. Abbey's classic evocation of his year as a ranger at Arches National Park was the first of his many volumes championing the wildernesses of the Southwest.

Philip L. Fradkin *A River No More*. The story of the Colorado River, from John Wesley Powell to the water-management issues of today.

Michael P. Ghiglieri and Thomas M. Myers *Over The Edge: Death in Grand Canyon*. In their bid to account for the demise of every single person known to have died within the Grand Canyon, the authors transcend the merely morbid to throw fascinating light on every aspect of the canyon's history, and provide masses of useful advice on how to avoid becoming another fatality. The morbid stuff's good, too.

Russell Martin *A Story That Stands Like A Dam*. Meticulously chronicled indictment of the West's last great dam, which inundated Glen Canyon in the 1960s.

Lisa Michaels *Grand Ambition*. Gripping, novelistic reconstruction of a true-life romantic mystery; just what did happen to honeymooners Glen and Bessie Hyde in the winter of 1928, when they tried to row down the Grand Canyon?

Barbara J. Morehouse *A Place Called Grand Canyon*. Fascinating academic analysis of how the Grand Canyon has been defined and exploited.

John A. Murray *Cinema Southwest*. A critical, well-illustrated overview of the long history of movies filmed in the Southwest, with plenty of location information.

Marc Reisner *Cadillac Desert*. The damning saga of the twentieth-century damming of the West.

★**David Roberts** *Finding Everett Ruess*. The poignant story of Everett Ruess, a young adventurer who disappeared somewhere in southern Utah in 1934, aged just twenty. His lyrical diaries and letters have earned him acclaim as a sort of proto-environmentalist, while Roberts' investigation of his death makes for a gripping real-life mystery.

★**Jeremy Schmidt** *Grand Canyon National Park – A Natural History Guide*. A superb single-volume account of the Grand Canyon's environment, ecology and geological origins.

Bette L. Stanton *Where God Put The West*. Photo-packed history of moviemaking in Monument Valley and Moab.

FICTION

Edward Abbey *The Monkey Wrench Gang*. Classic wishful thinking from the wilderness advocate, this fast-paced novel centres on plans by environmental saboteurs to destroy the Glen Canyon dam.

★**Willa Cather** *Death Comes for the Archbishop*. Not as sensational as the title implies, but a magnificent evocation of the landscapes and cultures of nineteenth-century New Mexico. Cather's *The Professor's House* features an extended account of the discovery of Ancestral Puebloan remains on a remote New Mexican mesa.

Zane Grey *Riders of the Purple Sage*. Gloriously purple prose, first published in 1912, from the doyen of Western writers.

Tony Hillerman *A Thief of Time, The Dark Wind* and several others. The late Tony Hillerman wrote around a dozen entertaining, intricately plotted detective novels set on and around the Navajo Nation, all packed with fascinating detail about Navajo, Hopi and Zuni culture and beliefs.

★**Barbara Kingsolver** *Pigs in Heaven*. A magnificent evocation of tensions and realities in the contemporary Southwest, by a Tucson-based writer who ranks among America's finest prose stylists.

Laila Lalami *The Moor's Account*. This first-person narrative of the extraordinary odyssey of Esteban, the black African who became the first outsider to penetrate the Pueblo world, was shortlisted for the Booker Prize in 2015. Sadly, though, he remains a one-dimensional character.

Cormac McCarthy *Blood Meridian*. A disturbing portrayal of the West in all its bloody reality – the scenes at Yuma Crossing are horrendous – if a tad macho for some tastes.

N. Scott Momaday *House Made of Dawn Time*. Pulitzer Prize-winning novel, written by a Kiowa Indian, about the spiritual crisis of a young Pueblo Indian.

John Nichols *The Milagro Beanfield War*. Thanks to the Robert Redford movie, this entertaining saga of a water-rights rebellion by dispossessed Hispanic villagers in northern New Mexico is the best known of Nichols' *New Mexico* trilogy (the others are *The Magic Journey* and *The Nirvana Blues*).

★**Michael Ondaatje** *The Collected Works of Billy the Kid*. Slim volume that combines poetry with contemporary accounts to create an evocative picture of New Mexico's most famous tearaway.

Simon J. Ortiz *Men on the Moon*. Evocative contemporary short stories by an Acoma Indian poet.

Leslie Marmon Silko *Almanac of the Dead*. Epic novel, by a Laguna Pueblo Indian, of a Native American mother searching for her lost child on the fringes of the Tucson underworld; look out also for Silko's *Ceremony*.

Glossary

adobe Construction material, consisting of bricks of mud, sand and grass or straw; by extension, a building itself (see p.107).

Anasazi Term formerly used for the ancient people of the Four Corners region, now superseded by Ancestral Puebloan (see p.463).

anticline Geological term for a dome or ridge shoved upwards by subterranean bulging.

arroyo Flat, often dry desert streambed.

atlatl Spear-throwing device – a sort of detachable, lever-like handle that gave extra power and accuracy – used by ancient Native Americans.

backcountry Term used particularly in national parks to signify wilderness areas that cannot be reached by road (as opposed, occasionally, to frontcountry).

bulto or **santo bulto** Carved wooden statue of a saint, characteristic of Hispanic New Mexico.

butte A flat-topped outcrop of rock that's taller than it is wide, usually formed by the erosion of a larger mesa.

casita Cottage, now applied mainly to individual guest accommodation in upmarket B&Bs.

cuesta Long sloping mesa terminated by an abrupt bluff.

desert varnish A natural veneer, caused by leaching minerals, that accretes on exposed rock faces and makes an ideal surface on which to etch petroglyphs.

genízaros In colonial New Mexico, the mixed-race offspring of captured Plains Indians and their Spanish masters.

graben Narrow valleys created by the erosion of underground salt beds, from the German for "ditches".

Grand Staircase Topographical feature stretching from the Grand Canyon to Bryce Canyon (see p.337).

Great House Archeological term for a defensively oriented, multistorey ancient pueblo with hundreds of rooms, as seen at Chaco Canyon (see p.92).

Great Kiva Archeological term for a *kiva* that was used by an entire community rather than an individual clan or family.

heishi Necklace of threaded disks, usually cut from seashells, as made originally by Ancestral Puebloans and now by Kewa Pueblo.

Hisatsinom The name used by the Hopi for their Ancestral Puebloan forebears.

hogan Navajo dwelling (see p.62).

Hohokam Ancient people of southern Arizona (see p.465).

hoodoo Natural sandstone formation in which a boulder is left balanced on a slender pillar, as at Bryce Canyon.

kachina (also spelled *katsina*) "Spirit messengers", central to the religions of the Hopi and other Pueblo Indians (see p.66).

kiva Chamber used for religious ceremonies by Pueblo Indians, usually located underground.

latilla Light pole used in the roof construction of adobe buildings.

LDS Abbreviation to denote the Latter-day Saints, or Mormons.

mano Hand-held stone traditionally used to grind and crush seeds.

mesa From the Spanish for "table"; a large, broad flat-topped outcrop of rock.

metate Stone slab or trough, used with a *mano* for grinding seeds.

Mimbres Ancient people of southern New Mexico, renowned for their pottery (see p.200).

Moki or **Moqui** A name formerly applied to the Hopi people of northern Arizona.

monocline An abrupt irregularity in the usual stratification of rocks, often resulting in a dramatic cliff.

Penitentes Catholic sect in nineteenth-century New Mexico (see p.144).

petroglyph Ancient rock-art image carved or pecked into stone.

pictograph Ancient rock-art image painted onto stone.

presidio Spanish term for a fortress built during the colonial period.

Pueblo Spanish word meaning "village"; applied to ancient Native American dwellings and also to modern Indian communities and peoples.

reef Word applied by early Anglo settlers to such vast natural barriers to their progress across the desert (usually created by monoclines) as Utah's Capitol Reef (see p.386).

reredos Painted altarpiece, as seen in Hispanic churches at Chimayó (see p.145) and elsewhere.

retablo A kind of Hispanic religious folk art, painted on tin or wood.

ristra Garland of chile peppers, sold as souvenirs in New Mexico.

santo In Hispanic folk art, an image or holy object.

Sinagua Ancient people of central Arizona.

sipapu In Pueblo religion, the hole through which humans reached this earth.

slickrock Pioneer term for smooth, undulating stretches of sandstone, as a rule only slick after rain.

syncline The opposite of an anticline, a syncline is a rock formation created by an underground collapse.

talus Fallen rock debris which accumulates to form slopes at the bases of cliffs and canyon walls.

viga A broad beam of ponderosa or fir, as used by the Ancestral Puebloans in roof construction, and prominent in adobe architecture today.

Small print and index

Rough Guide credits

Editor: Rachel Mills
Layout: Jessica Subramanian
Cartography: Swati Handoo, Katie Bennett
Picture editor: Phoebe Lowndes
Proofreader: Susanne Hillen
Managing editor: Keith Drew
Assistant editor: Divya Grace Mathew

Production: Jimmy Lao
Cover photo research: Sarah Stewart-Richardson
Photographer: Greg Ward
Editorial assistant: Freya Godfrey
Senior DTP coordinator: Dan May
Programme manager: Gareth Lowe
Publishing director: Georgina Dee

Publishing information

This seventh edition published October 2016 by
Rough Guides Ltd,
80 Strand, London WC2R 0RL
11, Community Centre, Panchsheel Park,
New Delhi 110017, India
Distributed by Penguin Random House
Penguin Books Ltd, 80 Strand, London WC2R 0RL
Penguin Group (USA), 345 Hudson Street, NY 10014, USA
Penguin Group (Australia), 250 Camberwell Road,
Camberwell, Victoria 3124, Australia
Penguin Group (NZ), 67 Apollo Drive, Mairangi Bay,
Auckland 1310, New Zealand
Penguin Group (South Africa), Block D, Rosebank Office
Park, 181 Jan Smuts Avenue, Parktown North, Gauteng,
South Africa 2193
Rough Guides is represented in Canada by DK Canada, 320
Front Street West, Suite 1400, Toronto, Ontario M5V 3B6
Printed in Singapore
© Greg Ward, 2016
Maps © Rough Guides

504pp includes index
A catalogue record for this book is available from the
British Library
ISBN: 978-0-24124-585-9
The publishers and authors have done their best to
ensure the accuracy and currency of all the information
in **The Rough Guide to Southwest USA**, however,
they can accept no responsibility for any loss, injury, or
inconvenience sustained by any traveller as a result of
information or advice contained in the guide.
1 3 5 7 9 8 6 4 2

MIX
Paper from
responsible sources
FSC
www.fsc.org FSC™ C018179

Help us update

We've gone to a lot of effort to ensure that the seventh
edition of **The Rough Guide to Southwest USA** is
accurate and up-to-date. However, things change – places
get "discovered", opening hours are notoriously fickle,
restaurants and rooms raise prices or lower standards. If
you feel we've got it wrong or left something out, we'd like
to know, and if you can remember the address, the price,
the hours, the phone number, so much the better.

Please send your comments with the subject line
"**Rough Guide Southwest USA Update**" to ✉mail
@uk.roughguides.com. We'll credit all contributions
and send a copy of the next edition (or any other
Rough Guide if you prefer) for the very best emails.
Find more travel information and plan your trip on
🌐roughguides.com.

ABOUT THE AUTHOR

Greg Ward has been writing about the Southwest for more than twenty years. As well as being exclusively responsible for all six previous editions of this book, he has also written separate Rough Guides to Las Vegas and the Grand Canyon. He's also the sole author of many other Rough Guides, including those to Hawaii, Brittany & Normandy, Blues CDs, US History and the *Titanic*, and the joint author of others including Provence, Spain, Barcelona and Belize; has edited many more; and has written books on travel and music for several other publishers. For more information, visit ⊛gregward.info.

Acknowledgements

Greg Ward: Thanks a million, once again, to my wonderful wife Sam Cook, for a spectacular road trip and so much more, and to Rachel Mills, my editor at Rough Guides, for her understanding and meticulous work. Thanks too to everyone who helped me along the way, and in particular Allan Affeldt, John G. Feins, Jenelle Jacks, Nancy Johnson, Anne Klein, Doug MacKenzie, Audrey Nadia John O'Hara, Grant Peck, Kimberlee Schear, Gordon Watkins, Siera Whitten, Jon at Monument Valley and Paco in Taos. And many thanks to those readers who have written in with updates and recommendations, including Val Burnett, Richard Crighton, Rob Purvis, Adam Renak, and Mike and Anne Roche.

Photo credits

All other images © Rough Guides
(Key: t-top; c-centre; b-bottom; l-left; r-right)

1 SuperStock: Mauritius / Walter Bibikow / Courtesy of MGM Resorts International
2 Alamy Stock Photo: lucky-photographer
4 Alamy Stock Photo: Radius Images
5 Getty Images: Sapna Reddy Photography
9 Corbis: JAI / Alan Copson (br); All Canada Photos / Chris Cheadle (tl); Blaine Harrington III (bl).
Getty Images: Harald Sund (tr)
10 4Corners: Udo Bernhart
11 Corbis: Dave G. Houser (b); George H.H. Huey (t). **Getty Images**: John P Kelly (c)
12 Corbis: Nativestock Pictures / Marilyn Angel Wynn
13 Getty Images: Yuko Smith photography
14 Corbis: F1 Online / A. Geh
15 Getty Images: Danita Delimont (t); Rozanne Hakala (b). **Courtesy of La Fonda on the Plaza** (c)
16 Alamy Stock Photo: Kumar Sriskandan (cl). **Corbis**: Doug Meek (cr); Nik Wheeler (t, b)
17 Alamy Stock Photo: David Cobb (t). **Corbis**: Minden Pictures / Konrad Wothe (c); Robert Harding World Imagery / Neale Clark (b)
18 Corbis: Hemis / John Frumm (t). **Getty Images**: Robert Alexander (b). **Courtesy of Daniel Lutzick, La Posada Hotel** (c)
19 Alamy Stock Photo: M L Pearson (tl). **Corbis**: Blaine Harrington III (b). **Getty Images**: Sam Diephuis (tr)
20 Corbis: Robert Wagenhoffer (t)
21 Corbis: SuperStock / Keith Kapple (b); Visuals Unlimited / Mark Skalny (cl). **Getty Images**: John Wang (t); Markos Berndt (cr)
22 Courtesy of Cirque du Soleil: Mystère image by Matt Beard © Cirque du Soleil (b). **Getty Images**: Danita Delimont (t)
23 AWL Images: Aurora Photos (br). **Corbis**: Patrick J. Endres (tl); Aurora Photos / Whit Richardson (bl). **Getty Images**: Gary Koutsoubis (tr)
24 Getty Images: Bob Stefko
26 Corbis: SuperStock
44–45 Getty Images: Sapna Reddy Photography
47 Corbis: George H.H. Huey

65 Alamy Stock Photo: Enrique R. Aguirre Aves (t). **Corbis**: George H.H. Huey (br). **Getty Images**: Robyn Beck / AFP (bl)
87 Getty Images: Larry Gerbrandt (b)
102–103 Corbis: Myles McGuinness / Aurora Open
105 Corbis: ZUMA Press / Arnold Drapkin
125 Corbis: ZUMA Press / Arnold Drapkin (br); Blaine Harrington III (bl)
157 Corbis: Jay Syverson (b); Eye Ubiquitous / Paul Seheult (t)
164–165 Corbis: Science Faction / G. Brad Lewis
167 Getty Images: Robin Wilson Photography
189 Alamy Stock Photo: Danita Delimont (t). **Corbis**: Tom Bean (bl). **Getty Images**: Nativestock.com / Marilyn Angel Wynn (br)
202–203 Corbis: Richard Cummins
205 Getty Images: Hisham Ibrahim
217 Alamy Stock Photo: robertharding (b). **Getty Images**: Walter Bibikow (t)
237 Corbis: Robert Harding World Imagery / James Hager (t); David Kadlubowski (bl)
252–253 Getty Images: Marco Brivio
255 Alamy Stock Photo: Greg Vaughn
281 Corbis: David Kadlubowski (b); Ocean (t)
294–295 Getty Images: Don Smith
297 Corbis: Minden Pictures / Tim Fitzharris
315 Getty Images: Matt Dil
340–341 Getty Images: J. Martin Paige III
343 Getty Images: Keiji Iwai
373 Getty Images: Ropelato Photography (b); EarthScapes (t)
401 Alamy Stock Photo: imageBROKER (b)
460 Corbis: Milton Snow

Front cover & spine: *Bryce Canyon National Park, Utah* **AWL Images**: Mark Sykes
Back cover: *Las Vegas Skyline* **Alamy Stock Photo**: John Kellerman (t). *Saguaro National Park, Arizona* **Alamy Stock Photo**: George H.H. Huey (bl). *U.S. Route 66 road sign* **AWL Images**: Stefano Politi Markovina (br)

Index

Maps are marked in grey

Map symbols

The symbols below are used on maps throughout the book

International boundary	P Parking	⊠–⊠ Gate
State/province boundary	✉ Post office	Mountain range
Chapter division boundary	ⓘ Tourist office	▲ Mountain peak
Motorway	✚ Hospital/clinic	Cave
Road	General point of interest	Undeveloped campground
Unpaved road	Museum	Gorge/canyon/cliffs
4 wheel drive	Ruins	Waterfall
Railway	Lodge	Spring
Cable car	Ranger station	Arch
International airport	■ Pueblo	Rapids
Domestic airport	Bridge	Butte

Viewpoint/overlook	
Ski area	
Golf course	
Observatory	
/ǀ\ Crater	
Hoodoo	
Building	
Church (town)	
⊞ Christian Cemetery	
Park/monument	
Indian reservation	

Listings key

■ Accommodation	
● Eating	
■ Drinking and Nightlife	
● Shopping	

DEC - - 2016